Between Republic and Empire:
Interpretations of Augustus
and His Principate

Between Republic and Empire

Interpretations of Augustus and His Principate

edited by
Kurt A. Raaflaub and Mark Toher

with contributions by
G. W. Bowersock, W. Eder, H. Galsterer, E. S. Gruen,
B. A. Kellum, J. Linderski, T. J. Luce, C. Meier, W. Mierse,
S. G. Nugent, S. E. Ostrow, J. Pollini, M. C. J. Putnam,
K. A. Raaflaub and L. J. Samons II, M. Reinhold
and P. M. Swan, H. P. Stahl, M. Toher,
G. Williams, Z. Yavetz

UNIVERSITY OF CALIFORNIA PRESS
Berkeley   •   *Los Angeles*   •   *London*

University of California Press
Berkeley and Los Angeles, California

University of California Press, Ltd.
London, England

First Paperback Printing 1993

Library of Congress Cataloging-in-Publication Data

Between republic and empire: interpretations of Augustus and his principate / edited by
    Kurt A. Raaflaub and Mark Toher ; with contributions by G. W. Bowersock
    ... [et al.].

        p.   cm.
    Includes index.
    ISBN 0-520-08447-0
    1. Augustus, Emperor of Rome, 63 B.C.–14 A.D. 2. Rome—History—
Augustus, 30 B.C.–14 A.D. 3. Roman emperors—Biography.
I. Raaflaub, Kurt A. II. Toher, Mark. III. Bowersock, G. W. (Glen
Warren), 1936-
DG279.B43 1990
937'.07'0924—dc 19
[B]   89-4788
                                                              CIP

Printed in the United States of America
1   2   3   4   5   6   7   8   9

Contents

Editors' Preface   xi

1. H. GALSTERER (Technische Universität, Aachen)
   A Man, a Book, and a Method: Sir Ronald Syme's
   Roman Revolution after Fifty Years   1

2. Z. YAVETZ (University of Tel Aviv and Queens
   College, New York)
   The Personality of Augustus: Reflections on Syme's
   Roman Revolution   21

3. J. LINDERSKI (University of North Carolina,
   Chapel Hill)
   Mommsen and Syme: Law and Power in the
   Principate of Augustus   42

4. C. MEIER (Universität München)
   C. Caesar Divi filius and the Formation of
   the Alternative in Rome   54

5. W. Eder (Freie Universität, West Berlin)

   Augustus and the Power of Tradition:
   The Augustan Principate as Binding Link
   between Republic and Empire   71

6. T. J. Luce (Princeton University)

   Livy, Augustus, and the Forum Augustum   123

7. M. Toher (Union College)

   Augustus and the Evolution of
   Roman Historiography   139

8. M. Reinhold (Boston University) and
   P. M. Swan (University of Saskatchewan)

   Cassius Dio's Assessment of Augustus   155

9. H. P. Stahl (University of Pittsburgh)

   The Death of Turnus: Augustan Vergil and
   the Political Rival   174

10. M. C. J. Putnam (Brown University)

    Horace *Carm.* 2.9: Augustus and the
    Ambiguities of Encomium   212

11. S. G. Nugent (Brown University)

    Tristia 2: Ovid and Augustus   239

12. G. Williams (Yale University)

    Did Maecenas "Fall from Favor"? Augustan
    Literary Patronage   258

13. B. A. Kellum (Smith College)

    The City Adorned: Programmatic Display at
    the *Aedes Concordiae Augustae*   276

14. W. Mierse (University of Vermont)

    Augustan Building Programs in the
    Western Provinces   308

15. J. Pollini (University of Southern California)

    Man or God: Divine Assimilation and Imitation
    in the Late Republic and Early Principate   334

16. S. E. Ostrow (College of the Holy Cross)
   The *Augustales* in the Augustan Scheme   364

17. G. W. Bowersock (Institute for Advanced
   Study, Princeton)
   The Pontificate of Augustus   380

18. E. S. Gruen (University of California, Berkeley)
   The Imperial Policy of Augustus   395

19. K. A. Raaflaub and L. J. Samons II (Brown
   University)
   Opposition to Augustus   417

   Index of Subjects   455
   Index of Persons and Places   465
   Index of Scholars   472
   Index of Sources   475

Editors' Preface

"At the beginning kings ruled the city of Rome." Brutus established the free Republic; its working was interrupted in emergencies and times of civil strife by dictatorships and other forms of autocratic rule. Pompey's and Crassus' predominance was overturned by Caesar, that of Antony and Lepidus by Augustus. "He found the whole state exhausted by civic dissensions and took it under his *imperium,* using the name of *princeps*" (*urbem Romam a principio reges habuere* . . . *[Augustus] cuncta* . . . *nomine principis sub imperium accepit*). So Tacitus at the beginning of his *Annals* (1.1). The cycle, that is, was closed; Rome once again was ruled by a monarchy.

Augustus, Tacitus continues, seduced the army with gifts, the people with cheap grain, everybody with the sweetness of peace. Gradually, he took over the functions of the senate, the magistrates, even the law. Nobody resisted; the fiercest spirits had been eliminated in wars and proscriptions, the other nobles tamed by the prospect of wealth, honor, and security in direct reciprocity to servile subordination. And to the provinces the new order guaranteed an end of the suffering caused by fighting potentates and corrupt magistrates (1.2).

This, in a nutshell, is Tacitus' conception of the nature and success of

Augustus' principate. "Probably nothing more malicious has ever been
written than the description of the last years of Augustus and the survey
of his achievements in the opening of the *Annals*," said the great Eduard
Meyer in 1903 in an address to the Association of German Historians,
and he continued:

> It is particularly perfidious that Tacitus replaces the funeral oration con-
> tained in his sources with a report of the *sermones de Augusto* (1.9f. [the
> debate about Augustus supposedly waged in Rome after his death]) which,
> while appearing to be quite objective, in fact creates and intends to create the
> impression that the worst and most absurd accusations represented histori-
> cal truth.[1]

Perfidious or not, in those *sermones* Tacitus in fact sharply and lucidly
defined the two positions between which the "debate about Augustus"
has been waged ever since.

Almost by necessity, those who judge the first *princeps* favorably distinguish between Octavian, the avenger, proscriber, military adventurer,
and civil war general, and Augustus, the *princeps* and creator of the *res
publica restituta*, benevolent leader of Rome, Italy, and the reunited empire, bringer of peace, reformer, and organizer. For this concept, a break
and new beginning in the years 30–27 is almost indispensable. The
achievements and blessings of the principate are perceived as more than
mere atonement for the brutal shortcomings and crimes of the civil war
period. Velleius Paterculus, often maligned as "court historian" and
spineless flatterer but the only contemporary among the extant historians, is the first to endorse this view, with much support from the poets.

By contrast, the opposing, negative view of the Augustan principate
is "unitarian": there was no break, no new beginning, no transformation. Octavian and Augustus were the same, logical and consequent
from beginning to end, ruthlessly pursuing but one end: power. Character and goals did not change, whatever the methods and façades chosen to disguise the realities.

Admittedly, these are the two extreme positions, but there is no doubt
that Tacitus preferred the latter. Under his influence and praise of the
libera res publica this is the *sermo* that prevailed, with few exceptions,
until the middle of the nineteenth century. Montesquieu's verdict on the
rusé tyran (the cunning tyrant) was echoed in Gibbon's "subtle tyrant,"[2]

1. E. Meyer, "Kaiser Augustus," *HZ* 91 (1903) 385–431 (= id., *Kleine Schriften*², vol.
1 [Halle 1924] 423–74); editors' translation.
2. Cf. W. Schmitthenner, ed., *Augustus,* Wege der Forschung 128 (Darmstadt 1969)
VIIIf.

and resounded again, more than 150 years after Gibbon, in Sir Ronald Syme's *Roman Revolution,* for which Tacitus served as one of the crown witnesses.

Theodor Mommsen, *il grande Teodoro,* as he was sometimes called in Italy,[3] in his *Staatsrecht* defined the principate as a magistracy and the Augustan order as a "dyarchy"[4] in which power and responsibilities were fairly evenly divided and a large amount of cooperation was realized between senate and *princeps.* The republican element thus was emphasized, and scholarship, particularly in Germany, with its predilection for the history of law, was set on a predominantly legalistic track. Mommsen himself slightly modified his views in later publications, and reaction against these views was strong already among his contemporaries.[5] Still it took two generations to dismantle the dyarchic model, which was fully accepted by, among others, Victor Gardthausen and Eduard Meyer. Its last remains were buried, together with the predominance of the legalistic approach, by Syme's *Roman Revolution.*[6]

The first truly comprehensive biography of Augustus and analysis of his time was published almost one hundred years ago, between 1891 and 1904, by Victor Gardthausen.[7] On its level of detailed discussion and thorough documentation it has, so far, found no successor. The great figures of the period, Augustus' forerunners, contemporaries, and successors, have all received their comprehensive biographical tribute in recent decades; Augustus has not. Certainly there have been many biographical sketches,[8] and a few years ago the results of previous scholarship and the state of our knowledge were summed up in a learned and useful book by Dietmar Kienast.[9] But there is no comprehensive, penetrating, modern analysis of Augustus, the man, his work, and his time.[10]

This gap in scholarship, instructive in itself, has several explanations, among them the sheer mass of scholarship published annually on dozens of hotly debated questions, the problems caused by the very difficult

---

3. E. Kornemann, *Augustus: Der Mann und sein Werk (im Lichte der deutschen Forschung),* Breslauer histor. Forsch. 4 (Breslau 1937) 1.

4. T. Mommsen, *Römisches Staatsrecht³,* vol. 2. (Leipzig 1888).

5. T. Mommsen, *Abriss des römischen Staatsrechts* (Leipzig 1893) 340–45; J. Kromayer, *Die rechtliche Begründung des Principats* (Marburg 1888).

6. But see now J. Linderski in his contribution to the present volume.

7. V. Gardthausen, *Augustus und seine Zeit,* 2 vols. in 6 parts (Leipzig 1891–1904; bibliography added 1917; reprint with new bibliography, Aalen 1964).

8. One of the best by A. H. M. Jones, *Augustus* (London 1970).

9. D. Kienast, *Augustus: Prinzeps und Monarch* (Darmstadt 1982).

10. *Pace* M. A. Levi, *Augusto e il suo tempo* (Milan 1986), which represents a revised and rethought combination of two earlier books: *Ottaviano capoparte* (Florence 1933) and *Il tempo di Augusto* (Florence 1951).

source situation, and the constant flow of new evidence, mostly epigraphical and archaeological, from excavations all over the empire. The
sculptures of the *sebasteion* and inscriptions of the theater in Aphrodisias in Asia Minor and the giant *solarium* (sundial) of Augustus on the
Campus Martius in Rome are only two spectacular recent examples of
the latter.[11] Furthermore, whoever attempts a new comprehensive treatment of Augustus and his time must come to terms with Syme's *Roman
Revolution*. Although beginning with the year 60 (and thus neither with
the year of Augustus' birth nor with that of his entry into politics) and
emphatically disclaiming to be a biography of Augustus or a study of
his career and principate,[12] Syme's book is nevertheless all that and
more: it contains many elements of a biography of the individual named
Caesar Augustus and, collectively, of the Roman upper class in his lifetime, and "it is also a general interpretation of the Augustan principate."[13] In view of all these obstacles the most enterprising scholar
might well be deterred by the formidable task of writing a new "Gardthausen."

Gardthausen himself had been fairly critical of Augustus. Eduard
Meyer in turn strongly defended the positive, "Republican" view.[14] The
pendulum kept swinging for a while: as late as 1933 Meyer's assessment
was endorsed vigorously by Mason Hammond.[15] But in the 1930s,
when the bimillennium of Augustus' birth was approaching and being
celebrated with lavish exhibitions and congresses and sensational excavations (of the Forum of Augustus, his mausoleum, and the Ara Pacis,
among others), the pendulum swung far beyond the limits of sound
scholarly debate: Augustus became the idealized figurehead and patron
of another *novus status,* Mussolini's new Roman Empire.[16]

It was against such uncritical glorification of Augustus and under the
impression both of the seemingly unstoppable success of the Continen-

11. *Sebasteion:* K. T. Erim, *Aphrodisias: City of Venus Aphrodite* (London 1986). Inscriptions: J. Reynolds, *Aphrodisias and Rome: Documents from the Excavation of the
Theatre at Aphrodisias,* JRS Mon. 1 (1982). *Solarium Augusti:* E. Buchner, *Die Sonnenuhr
des Augustus* (Mainz 1982).

12. R. Syme, *The Roman Revolution* (Oxford 1939) vii.

13. A. Momigliano, *JRS* 30 (1940) 77 (review of Syme's *Roman Revolution*), reprinted
in id., *Secondo contributo alla storia degli studi classici e del mondo antico* (Rome 1960)
410.

14. Cf. H. E. Stier, "Augustusfriede und römische Klassik," *ANRW* 2.2 (1975) 3f.

15. M. Hammond, *The Augustan Principate in Theory and Practice during the Julio-
Claudian Period* (Cambridge, Mass. 1933).

16. Cf. K. Hönn, *Augustus im Wandel zweier Jahrtausende* (Leipzig 1938) 46; K.
Christ, "Zur Beurteilung der Politik des Augustus," *GWU* 19 (1968) 336f.; A. Momigliano, *Terzo contributo alla storia degli studi classici e del mondo antico* (Rome 1966) 732.

tal dictators and of the publication of the new constitution of the Soviet Union that Ronald Syme wrote his first major book.[17] *The Roman Revolution* was immediately hailed as the best book on Roman history since Mommsen, Rostovtzeff or Eduard Meyer:[18] "a work of art unmatched among major historical works, and one which would still be read as such even if the day were to come when our knowledge of Roman history has been transformed by new evidence, or when we have found wholly new means of interpreting it."[19] The achievement was most impressive indeed, the glory well deserved. With his subsequent books[20] and a host of articles collected in several volumes,[21] Syme went on to become the "Emperor of Roman History,"[22] that title, too, well deserved. On the occasion of the publication of the first two volumes of the *Roman Papers* in 1979 and of Syme's eightieth birthday in 1983, his achievement was acknowledged and discussed by several scholars.[23]

Despite the high acclaim it immediately won among those who had the opportunity to read it, "*The Roman Revolution* had to wait a long time for widespread recognition. The Second World War effectively kept the book from entering the mainstream of historical scholarship, and it was not until the early 1950's that Syme's impact began to be felt. But the impact, when it finally came, was tremendous."[24] For its healthy reaction to the traditional and often abused benevolent assessment of Augustus, for its intellectual honesty, for its methodology, immense prosopographical knowledge, and total control of sources and facts, for its sensitivity toward literature, and for its brilliant "Tacitean" style the book proved and remained irresistible.[25] For fifty years now it has been

17. Cf. G. Alföldy, *Sir Ronald Syme, "Die römische Revolution" und die deutsche Althistorie*, SBHeid 1983, no. 1, 21; F. Millar, "Style Abides," *JRS* 71 (1981) 146; Momigliano (supra n. 16) 730.

18. G. Bowersock, "The Emperor of Roman History," *The New York Review of Books*, 6 March 1980, 8.

19. Millar (supra n. 17) 146; cf. D. R. Shackleton Bailey, "The Roman Nobility in the Second Civil War," *CQ* n. s. 10 (1960) 266, n. 3: "No desert island would be desirable without that dazzling, venerable, wise, and sometimes exasperating classic, *The Roman Revolution*"; both quoted by Alföldy (supra n. 17) 5.

20. *Tacitus*, 2 vols. (Oxford 1958); *Sallust* (Berkeley and Los Angeles 1964); *Ammianus Marcellinus and the Historia Augusta* (Oxford 1968); *Emperors and Biography: Studies in the Historia Augusta* (Oxford 1971); *The Historia Augusta: A Call for Clarity* (Bonn 1971); *History in Ovid* (Oxford 1978); *The Augustan Aristocracy* (Oxford 1986).

21. *Ten Studies in Tacitus* (Oxford 1970); *Danubian Papers* (Bucharest 1971); *Roman Papers*, vols. 1 and 2 (Oxford 1979), vol. 3 (1984), vol. 4 (1987), vol. 5 (1988).

22. Bowersock (supra n. 18).

23. Alföldy, Millar, Bowersock (supra nn. 17 and 18).

24. Bowersock (supra n. 18).

25. Cf. Momigliano's comment on the book's "intrinsic value" (1940: supra n. 13) 75 (= 1960 [supra n. 13] 407): "the enormous, unpedantic store of information; the per-

the standard work on the transition from republic to principate, on the dramatic changes in the aristocracy of that period—and on Augustus.

Certainly, *The Roman Revolution* has its faults and weaknesses too; they have been pointed out in reviews and occasional critical essays.[26] In many ways it is, as it wants to be,[27] a disturbing book. Not only is it deliberately critical of Augustus, it attempts "to record the story of the Roman Revolution and its sequel, the Principate of Caesar Augustus, in a fashion that has now become unconventional, from the Republican and Antonian side."[28] Thus it accepts the position taken by Sallust, the elusive Pollio, and Tacitus and the social and political point of view of the "doomed nobility" with its limitations and prejudices. It focuses on the organization of power, the composition of factions and "parties," and thus on Augustus, the *Machtpolitiker*. It therefore does not treat equally extensively all areas of Augustus' activity. Yet it still passes judgment, implicitly and explicitly, on Augustus the *princeps* and his achievement. Indeed, political success does not have to be praised or idealized. But Syme's claim that Augustus' "ability and greatness will all the more sharply be revealed by unfriendly presentation"[29] remains largely unfulfilled—unless the ability to reach and maintain power serves as the main criterion for greatness. Tacitus, some will feel, is no reliable guide to the Augustan principate, and the *libertas* that, according to Syme (and Tacitus), was slaughtered at Pharsalus, Philippi, and Actium and received its definitive funeral in A.D. 14 meant little or nothing to the overwhelming majority of Augustus' contemporaries.

Every scholar is entitled to his own method and bias. The issue is not to return to a "favorable" or "benevolent" assessment of Augustus, but rather to arrive at a balanced view. One would expect that a book with such a pointed thesis, conscious and admitted bias, and, in essential ways, limited approach to the analysis and reconstruction of history should have become, despite its numerous merits and outstanding qualities, the focus of intensive scholarly debate. This did happen in some specific areas—concerning Syme's concept of faction and "party" (in

---

sonal method of combining particulars just at the point at which a general construction is possible; the gusto in describing men and situations; and, above all, the vigorous power of working out from a trite subject a new image full of life and revealing a consciousness of values more profound than the simple acceptance of life itself."

26. Cf. esp. A. Momigliano, *JRS* 30 (1940) 75–80 (= id. 1960 [supra n. 13] 407–16); A. F. Giles, *CR* 54 (1940) 38–41; and H. Galsterer's contribution to the present volume. Stier (supra n. 14) 3–54 overstates his case.

27. Syme (supra n. 12) viii; cf. Giles (supra n. 26) 39.

28. Syme (supra n. 12) 6f.

29. Ibid., 7.

connection with the possibilities and limitations of prosopography), for example, and his use of the term *revolution*.[30] Otherwise, attempts to enter a direct, serious, and productive *Auseinandersetzung* with Syme's assessments and particularly his view of the nature and achievement of Augustus' principate have been rare and, at least in one recent case, hampered by emotion and polemics.[31] Why this is so cannot be discussed here; suffice it to state the case: Syme's achievement is unquestionably monumental, but his Augustus and the principate created by Augustus remain in need of reassessment.

Yet such reassessment has been going on, on a small scale, ever since *The Roman Revolution* was published. As Zvi Yavetz points out, many of the gaps left open by Syme have been filled.[32] Alternative interpretations have been offered—by Christian Meier, for example, on the crisis of the Republic, on the achievement and failure of Julius Caesar, and on Augustus' rise and success.[33] And in the scholarly contributions of a great number of specialists in various disciplines who keep analyzing and reanalyzing old and new evidence the reassessment is being carried on every day. To give just a few examples:[34] what can be known about Pollio's history has been thoroughly discussed by B. Haller, and, thanks to A. J. Woodman, we now understand better the nature of Velleius Paterculus' work; nor have the other historians been neglected.[35] Augustus' relationship to the people of Rome and their ways of expressing their sentiments have been explored by Z. Yavetz, R. Gilbert, H. Kloft, and T. Bollinger; the "taming" of the civil war armies and the soldiers'

30. For a brief discussion, see Bowersock (supra n. 18) 8–10; Alföldy (supra n. 17) 8ff.; and Galsterer in the present volume.

31. Stier (supra n. 14) 3–54.

32. Z. Yavetz, in the opening section of his contribution to this volume, with examples in his notes; cf. K. Galinsky, "Recent Trends in the Interpretation of the Augustan Age," *The Augustan Age* 5 (1986) 22–36; see also the titles listed in the following notes.

33. C. Meier, *Res publica amissa* (Wiesbaden 1966; 2nd ed., Frankfurt 1980); id., *Caesar* (Berlin 1982); id., "Augustus: Die Begründung der Monarchie als Wiederherstellung der Republik," in id., *Die Ohnmacht des allmächtigen Dictators Caesar: Drei biographische Skizzen* (Frankfurt 1980) 223–87; cf. Meier's contribution to the present volume.

34. For recent bibliographies, see B. Haller, "Augustus und seine Politik: Ausgewählte Bibliographie," *ANRW* 2.2 (1975) 55–74; Kienast (supra n. 9) 431–52.

35. B. Haller, *C. Asinius Pollio als Politiker und zeitkritischer Historiker: Ein Beitrag zur Geschichte des Übergangs von der Republik zum Prinzipat in Rom, 60–30 v.Chr.* (Diss. Münster 1967); A. J. Woodman, *Velleius Paterculus: The Tiberian Narrative: 2.94–131*, Cambr. Class. Texts and Comm. 19 (Cambridge 1977). Much useful work has been done on Cassius Dio: F. Millar, *A Study of Cassius Dio* (Oxford 1964); B. Manuwald, *Cassius Dio und Augustus: Philologische Untersuchungen zu den Büchern 45–46 des dionischen Geschichtswerkes*, Palingenesia 14 (Wiesbaden 1979); M. Reinhold, *From Republic to Principate: An Historical Commentary on Cassius Dio's Roman History Books 49–52 (36–29 B.C.)*, Amer. Philol. Assoc. Mon. Ser. 34 (Atlanta 1988).

role in the new system are the subject of recent studies by B. Campbell
and K. Raaflaub, while F. Vittinghoff and L. Keppie have discussed the
wide range of civil and military colonization under Augustus.[36] Augustus' policy toward the Greek East was analyzed by G. W. Bowersock,
that toward the Parthians by K. Ziegler, and his German policy by C.
Wells.[37] The role of the senate as a whole and of various segments of the
senatorial and equestrian elite in Augustus' scheme was examined by P.
Sattler, P. A. Brunt, T. P. Wiseman, and others; the role of the *princeps*
in jurisdiction by J. Bleicken and A. H. M. Jones, that of the *consilium
principis* by J. Crook, while R. Szramkiewicz systematically assembled
all available information about Augustus' provincial governors.[38] E. S.
Ramage and various commentators have devoted much attention to the
purpose, date, and content of the *Res Gestae*, C. Habicht and S. R. F.
Price to the beginnings of the cult of the emperor, and J. Béranger and
A. Wallace-Hadrill to various aspects of the "imperial ideology."[39] Finally, E. Simon and P. Zanker have written not only many individual

36. Z. Yavetz, *Plebs and Princeps* (Oxford 1969; reprint, New Brunswick, N.J. 1988);
R. Gilbert, *Die Beziehungen zwischen Princeps und stadtrömischer Plebs im frühen Principat* (Bochum 1976); H. Kloft, *Liberalitas Principis* (Cologne 1970); T. Bollinger, *Theatralis licentia: Die Publikumsdemonstrationen an den öffentlichen Spielen im Rom der
früheren Kaiserzeit und ihre Bedeutung im politischen Leben* (Winterthur 1969); cf. also
P. Veyne, *Le pain et le cirque* (Paris 1976); J. B. Campbell, *The Emperor and the Roman
Army, 31 B.C.–A.D. 235* (Oxford 1984); K. Raaflaub, "Die Militärreformen des Augustus und die politische Problematik des frühen Prinzipats," in G. Binder, ed., *Saeculum
Augustum*, vol. 1, Wege der Forschung vol. 266 (Darmstadt 1987) 246–307; F. Vitting-
hoff, *Römische Kolonisation und Bürgerrechtspolitik unter Caesar und Augustus*, Abh-
Mainz 1951, no. 14 (Wiesbaden 1952); L. Keppie, *Colonisation and Veteran Settlement in
Italy, 47–14 B.C.* (London 1983).
37. G. W. Bowersock, *Augustus and the Greek World* (Oxford 1965); K. Ziegler, *Die
Beziehungen zwischen Rom und dem Partherreich* (Wiesbaden 1964); C. M. Wells, *The
German Policy of Augustus: An Examination of the Archaeological Evidence* (Oxford
1972); cf. also S. L. Dyson, *The Creation of the Roman Frontier* (Princeton 1985).
38. P. Sattler, *Augustus und der Senat: Untersuchungen zur römischen Innenpolitik
zwischen 30 und 17 v.Chr.* (Göttingen 1960); P. A. Brunt, "The Role of the Senate in the
Augustan Regime," *CQ* n. s. 34 (1984) 423–44; T. P. Wiseman, *New Men in the Roman
Senate, 139 B.C.–14 A.D.* (Oxford 1971); H. H. Pistor, *Prinzeps und Patriziat in der Zeit
von Augustus bis Commodus* (Freiburg 1965); G. Pfister, *Die Erneuerung der römischen
iuventus durch Augustus* (Regensburg 1976); J. Bleicken, *Senatsgericht und Kaisergericht*
(Göttingen 1962); A. H. M. Jones, *The Criminal Courts of the Roman Republic and Principate* (Oxford 1972); J. Crook, *Consilium Principis* (Cambridge 1955); R. Szramkiewicz,
*Les gouverneurs de province à l'époque augustéenne: Contribution à l'histoire administra-
tive et sociale du principat*, 2 vols. (Paris 1976).
39. E. S. Ramage, *The Nature and Purpose of Augustus' "Res Gestae,"* Historia Einzelschr. 54 (Stuttgart 1987) (with literature); C. Habicht, "Die augusteische Zeit und das
erste Jahrhundert nach Christi Geburt," in O. Reverdin, ed., *Le culte des souverains dans
l'empire romain*, Entretiens sur l'ant. class. 19 (Vandoeuvres and Geneva 1973) 39–99;
S. R. F. Price, *Rituals and Power: The Roman Imperial Cult in Asia Minor* (Cambridge
1984); cf. also A. Wlosok, ed., *Römischer Kaiserkult*, Wege der Forschung 372 (Darmstadt 1978); J. Béranger, *Recherches sur l'aspect idéologique du principat* (Basel 1953);

studies but also major comprehensive works on the art and archaeology of the Augustan monuments in Rome.[40]

Thus work has been progressing on many fronts, carried on by a great number of scholars in many countries. Reflecting the complexities and contradictions in the personality, the life and achievement, and the period of Augustus, there is as yet no single direction, no united development, in Augustan scholarship.[41] Efforts to produce comprehensive summaries of the results of research in major areas (such as those by E. Simon and P. Zanker) are rare. Despite the impressive list of recent works mentioned above (which could be continued almost *ad libitum*), it still is true that, in Syme's own words, "there is work to be done."[42] In fact, it might be said, the time for a comprehensive reassessment has not yet come, because among other reasons so many individual problems still await thorough treatment and better understanding.

In the master's spirit the papers united in this volume discuss both *Einzelfragen* and more general interpretations in various areas of Augustan studies. They provide modern and penetrating analyses of important issues on the present horizon of Augustan scholarship. By achieving a better understanding of parts of the Augustan question, they are intended to advance our understanding of the whole, thereby contributing their share to the ongoing reassessment, or rather multiple reassessments, of Augustus and his principate.

Most of the papers were presented in earlier versions at a series of colloquia held at Brown University in the spring of 1987. These were organized in conjunction with an interdisciplinary graduate seminar that analyzed the Augustan principate from the perspectives of historiography, poetry, art, religion, and politics. These approaches, representing five major categories of evidence and problems intensely dis-

---

id., *Principatus* (Geneva 1973); A. Wallace-Hadrill, "The Emperor and His Virtues," *Historia* 30 (1981) 298–323; id., "The Golden Age and Sin in Augustan Ideology," *P & P 95* (1982) 19–36; id., "Image and Authority in the Coinage of Augustus," *JRS* 76 (1986) 66–87.

40. P. Zanker, *Forum Romanum: die Neugestaltung durch Augustus* (Tübingen 1972); id., *Forum Augustum: das Bildprogramm* (Tübingen 1968); id., *The Power of Images in the Age of Augustus* (Ann Arbor 1988 = *Augustus und die Macht der Bilder* [Munich 1987, transl. A. Shapiro]); E. Simon, *Augustus: Kunst und Leben in Rom um die Zeitenwende* (Munich 1986); see also, for example, P. Gros, *Aurea templa: Recherches sur l'architecture religieuse de Rome à l'époque d'Auguste* (Rome 1976).

41. Cf. Galinsky (supra n. 32) 33, who emphasizes that it is not the scholar's main task to straighten out such contradictions: "They are, in fact, essential for the dynamic tensions which kept the age of Augustus from becoming self-satisfied and stagnating."

42. Syme, *Roman Papers* 2:711.

cussed in the field of Augustan studies, largely determined the selection
of the participants in the colloquia. Thus the selection of topics covered
in this volume is to some extent fortuitous. At the same time it is programmatic, because it gives expression to the firm belief that no valid
reassessment of Augustus' principate is possible without comprehensively taking into account all categories of evidence and all aspects of
life, administration, and politics. The format, content, and sources of
the *elogia* chosen for the statues of famous *triumphatores* in the *forum
Augusti,* the ambiguities in a Horatian *encomium* to the *princeps* and
those in Ovid's longest poem from exile, the programmatic display of
rare pieces in the *aedes Concordiae Augustae* dedicated at the very end
of Augustus' life and the significance of pictures and symbols chosen for
his coins, the emergence and function of the new college of *Augustales*
and the social and religious role thus attributed to freedmen, and the
contradictions between the martial self-representation and the pragmatic foreign policy of the new regime—all these topics and the others
discussed in this volume represent important contributions to a comprehensive and balanced assessment of a complex man, system, and period.[43]

◆ ◆ ◆ ◆ ◆

The abbreviations of periodicals in the footnotes follow those suggested
by the *American Journal of Archaeology (AJA)* or, in cases not listed
there, the *Année philologique.* Standard works are referred to as the
AJA directs. Classical works and authors are abbreviated in accordance
with the *Oxford Classical Dictionary.*

Finally, we wish to thank the Departments of Classics, History and
Religious Studies, the Center for Old World Archaeology and Art, the
Program in Art History and the Ancient Studies Program as well as the
Lectureship Fund at Brown University for their generous support of

---

43. For other recent collected volumes that in many ways are complementary to this
one, see F. Millar and E. Segal, eds., *Caesar Augustus: Seven Aspects* (Oxford 1984); T.
Woodman and D. West, eds., *Poetry and Politics in the Age of Augustus* (Cambridge
1984); *Klio* 67.1 (1985), containing the papers of a conference held in Jena in 1982 on
"Die Kultur der Augusteischen Zeit"; R. Winkes, ed., *The Age of Augustus: Conference
Held at Brown University, Providence, R.I., 1982,* Archaeologia Transatlantica 5 (Louvain-la-Neuve and Providence 1986); G. Binder, ed., *Saeculum Augustum,* vol. 1, *Herrschaft und Gesellschaft* (Darmstadt 1987), vol. 2, *Religion und Literatur* (1988), vol. 3,
Kunst und Bildersprache (forthcoming). Although belonging to the "Wege der Forschung"
series, all three *Saeculum Augustum* volumes contain some contributions specifically written for the occasion.

the colloquia at which most of the papers in this volume were first read; Gregory Bucher, James Kennelly, Jonathan Robbins and, particularly, Ruthann Whitten for their invaluable assistance in preparing this volume; the anonymous referees who read the entire work or individual contributions; Marian Shotwell who painstakingly copy-edited the typescript; and Richard Holway, Mary Lamprech and other staff members of the Press whose enthusiastic and patient support was crucial for the success of this project.

◆   ◆   ◆   ◆   ◆

It was our intention, enthusiastically shared by all contributors but as yet unknown to the honoree, to dedicate this volume to Sir Ronald himself on the occasion of the fiftieth anniversary of *The Roman Revolution*. On 4 September 1989, however, he passed away, only three days before that anniversary. Sadly and respectfully, we now offer this volume as a dedication to the memory of an extraordinary scholar.

—September, 1989

A Man, a Book, and a Method:
Sir Ronald Syme's *Roman Revolution*
After Fifty Years

If history is to be seen, as it still often is today, essentially as the deeds of
great men, the question naturally arises, What makes a particular individual "great"? What is it that elevates one man so far above his contemporaries?[1] To answer this question fully, a comparison of the great
individual with his less-exalted coevals is necessary, for only an understanding of the achievements and expectations, the beliefs and ambitions, of these less-known "normal people" permits one to define the
great man's peculiar attributes. In the case of the Romans the problem
raised is even more urgent: What made certain persons rise so far above
their peers that they achieved a "quantum leap" from "greater than" to
simply "great"? No period of Roman history lends itself quite so well
to such a personality-centered treatment as the fall of the Republic and
the establishment of the Augustan monarchy. It was an age replete with
great figures, from Marius and Sulla to Caesar, Augustus, and even

---

1. This paper was first given as a lecture in 1979. Dormant for many years, it was
"rediscovered" by friends and largely rewritten for the present occasion. I should like to
thank K. Raaflaub and J. Kennelly very much for improving the English translation and
the editors for useful suggestions.

Cleopatra. Many aspired to imitating Alexander in word, image, and deed, and one of these great individuals quite programmatically assumed Alexander's title in his name: Pompeius Magnus.[2]

This paper, however, is not primarily about those great people but rather about a book centered upon arguably the greatest of them and about a method. Sir Ronald Syme's epochal study of Augustus' establishment of the principate, *The Roman Revolution,* is one of the few classics produced by an ancient historian in this century and has been recognized as such for a long time.[3] Prosopography, the methodology so closely associated with both the book and its author, is one of the few methods in the field of ancient history that is related to methods used in the social sciences and has been the subject of serious scholarly debate. If it seems unfair to subject a book to review after fifty years, it may be replied that a classic work is a classic precisely because of its lasting value and its ability to offer at least partial answers to questions that the author could not originally foresee.

On 7 September 1939, one week after the outbreak of World War II, Oxford University Press published the book of a scholar from New Zealand who had previously worked primarily in the field of Roman military history. The book was *The Roman Revolution*; the scholar, Ronald Syme. The timing was not auspicious. The war naturally precluded a wide dissemination of the book on the Continent; any impression it might have made there is not visible until the 1950s.[4] More importantly, even for the less discerning of his contemporaries, Syme's somber portrayal of the slow metamorphosis of Octavian, the gambler and terrorist, into the most exalted father of the fatherland, *Augustus pater pa-*

2. For the background, cf. E. Rawson, "Caesar's Heritage: Hellenistic Kings and Their Roman Equals," *JRS* 65 (1975) 148–59; for the archaeological evidence, P. Zanker, *Augustus und die Macht der Bilder* (Munich 1987).

3. See the important review by A. Momigliano, *JRS* 30 (1940) 75–80 (= id., *Secondo contributo alla storia degli studi classici e del mondo antico* [Rome 1960] 407–16), and Momigliano's introduction to the Italian translation of Syme's *Roman Revolution* (Turin 1962) ix–xv (= id., *Terzo contributo alla storia degli studi classici e del mondo antico* [Rome 1966] 729–37). See also G. Alföldy, *Sir Ronald Syme, "Die römische Revolution" und die deutsche Althistorie,* SB Heid 1983, no. 1; and the reviews of Syme's *Roman Papers,* vols. 1 and 2 (Oxford 1979) by G. Alföldy in *AJAH* 4 (1979 [1981]) 167–85 and by G. Bowersock in *The New York Review of Books,* 6 March 1980, 8–13. *The Roman Revolution* is the focus of most contributions to F. Millar and E. Segal, eds., *Caesar Augustus: Seven Aspects* (Oxford 1984), the "non-Festschrift" marking Syme's eightieth birthday.

4. With the exception of Momigliano's detailed discussion mentioned in the previous note, there appeared, to my knowledge, only short reviews, for example, on the Continent, A. Piganiol, *REL* 18 (1940) 221–24; P. Lambrechts, *AntCl* 11 (1942) 147–51.

triae, invoked comparisons with the dictatorships of Mussolini and Franco, Hitler and Stalin.[5] The book decidedly, if not overtly, took a position in the battles waged at Oxford during the Spanish civil war and up through 1939 about the proper policy to adopt toward the Continental dictators. Thus, inasmuch as the outbreak of war preceded the book's publication, the implicit warning it contained fell flat to some extent.[6]

What was new in *The Roman Revolution?* It may be useful at this point to look back at the explanations current in the 1930s (and even now considered valid by many) of the establishment of the principate. On the one side there was the juridical interpretation, receiving its inspiration from Mommsen's *Staatsrecht* and represented in contemporary England principally by H. Last.[7] This school focused on the explanation of the constitutional prerogatives of the *princeps* and tried to trace them back to republican precedents. Perhaps the most influential work written from this angle was Eduard Meyer's *Caesars Monarchie und das Principat des Pompeius,* published in 1918. Meyer argued that Caesar had aimed at a divine kingship ("Gottkönigtum"), while Pompey's goal was rather, following Cicero's ideals, a *principatus* based on *auctoritas.* In this way Pompey became a direct ancestor of the Augustan principate.

Meyer's successor in the Berlin chair of ancient history, Wilhelm Weber, took a different approach. He emphasized the ideology and the "Geistesgeschichte" of the period. His Augustus, referred to as "Führer" in more than linguistic affinity to the ruling party, sometimes seems to disappear in a dense fog of imperial mysticism—which is in part also due to Weber's pathetic and emotional language, which was influenced by Stefan George.[8] On the other hand, the third school of interpretation was more political and sociological. Following in the wake of landmark studies by Matthias Gelzer and Friedrich Münzer on

5. The *Mostra Augustea* of 1937, staged with much ado by Fascist Italy to mark the bimillenary of Augustus' birth, had the effect of appropriating the Roman *princeps* completely for modern Italian aspirations.

6. Cf. Momigliano (1966: supra n. 3) 730.

7. Last was Syme's predecessor in the Camden Chair at Oxford. A history of Augustus as seen by the successive Camden Professors Last, Syme, Brunt, and Millar might be instructive.

8. W. Weber, *Princeps,* vol. 1, *Studien zur Geschichte des Augustus* (Stuttgart 1936); cf. W. Kunkel's remarks in *Kleine Schriften* (Weimar 1974) 588; and the review by W. Kolbe in *GGA* 1939, 152–69. Kolbe (153) comments on the *communis opinio* of previous reviewers preferring the book of von Premerstein (mentioned infra in the text) to that of Weber.

the structure of the republican nobility,[9] Anton von Premerstein's post-humously published *Vom Werden und Wesen des Prinzipats* (1937) examined the methods employed by Octavian in founding and leading his "party." Premerstein, too, was clearly influenced by contemporary politics in his view of the principate's establishment.

Syme, for his part, in typically Anglo-Saxon fashion, seems to have disliked the plethora of abstract nouns endemic to Continental, and particularly German, scholarship.[10] In addition, he possessed a skepticism, not unusual among intellectuals of the time, toward politics and the specious pronouncements of the politicians who were held responsible for both the outbreak of war in 1914 and the disastrous policies pursued against the rise of Fascism in the 1930s; programs and slogans often were suspected of hiding selfish aims. Consequently, Syme eschewed the old methods of interpretation. Instead of starting with constitutions and ideologies he looked to the politicians themselves, and not exclusively to the top echelon. He took into account all of the senators and the most important of the *equites,* at least to the extent that something could be known about their careers and affiliations, with the goal of reconstructing and understanding Augustan politics; lists of office-holders were employed as the key to determining a particular political group's influence and changing fortunes.[11]

The same methodology had been used—obviously unknown to Syme—with immediate success some ten years earlier by a Jewish immigrant from Lemberg, Ludwig Bernstein Namierowsky, the later Sir Lewis Namier, in his book *The Structure of Politics at the Accession of George III* (1929). Namier explained that it was not so much political differences between the "parties" of Whigs and Tories that determined

---

9. M. Gelzer, *Die Nobilität der römischen Republik* (Leipzig and Berlin 1912) (= id., *The Roman Nobility,* trans. R. Seager [Oxford 1969]); F. Münzer, *Römische Adelspar-teien und Adelsfamilien* (Stuttgart 1920; reprint, Darmstadt 1963). Augustus as seen through the eyes of German scholars from the mid-nineteenth to the mid-twentieth century is the subject of the study of I. Stahlmann, *Imperator Caesar Augustus: Studien zur Geschichte des Principatsverständnisses in der deutschen Altertumswissenschaft* (Darmstadt 1988), with 108–84 on the time of the Weimar Republic.

10. "To free Roman history from the domination of a faction of abstract nouns": F. Millar, dedication to Syme, *JRS* 63 (1973) XI. Syme himself generously comments about man, the world, and how humans, especially politicians, behave in this or that situation. But he is very reticent concerning his own person. Alföldy (1983: supra n. 3) as well as Momigliano (1966: supra n. 3) emphasize Syme's distaste for public self-reflection. Some further information is to be found in his preface to the recent Italian translation of *Colonial Elites* (Milan 1989).

11. One wonders whether Syme had read Proust, in whose works the same interest in families and groups found its literary expression.

politics in mid-eighteenth-century England, but rather matrimonial alliances and agreements between family groups. Namier's method, which was to obtain a kind of collective biography through the classification of groups of persons and their common characteristics, spread rapidly to the fields of medieval and modern history. Indeed, it was not farfetched to speak of a "Namierization" of history.[12] From the archbishops of Trier to the officer corps of the second French Empire, from the canons of Laon to students from Brabant, no group has been neglected. And with the proliferation of computers the pace of such research was accelerated.[13]

Already by this time the term *prosopography* had come to designate this type of historical research in the field of ancient history. When Mommsen applied it in 1897, in the preface to the first edition of the *Prosopographia Imperii Romani,* he still felt obliged to excuse himself for its use.[14] However, prosopography had its forerunners even in antiquity, although less so in Athens where most offices were allotted and hence not necessarily indicative of a man's status. Moreover, the Greek system of names made the reconstruction of family relationships more difficult than in Rome.[15] Nevertheless, industrious antiquarians produced catalogues of the persons mentioned in comedies, lists of famous courtesans, and so on. In Rome, however, descent was of great political importance: renowned ancestors aided an individual's chances of electoral success; the *imagines* of illustrious ancestors were to be seen in the reception rooms of the nobility, together with a brief account of each man's *cursus honorum;* and it was the *res gestae* of the deceased in conjunction with a recapitulation of his descent that formed the main part of a funeral oration. It is small wonder, then, that a type of prosopographic research was practiced in Rome, as is illustrated, for instance,

12. T. Rabb, *Enterprise and Empire: Merchant and Gentry Investment in the Expansion of England, 1575–1630* (Cambridge, Mass. 1967) 8–9.

13. Cf. J.-P. Genet, "Die kollektive Biographie von Mikropopulationen," in F. Irsigler, ed., *Quantitative Methoden in der Wirtschafts- und Sozialgeschichte der Frühneuzeit* (Stuttgart 1978) 69–100. In fact, many French and American dissertations were produced by "Namier, Inc.," as it was called by L. Stone, "Prosopography," *Daedalus* 100 (1971) 51 (= F. Gilbert and S. R. Graubart, eds., *Historical Studies Today* [New York 1972] 112).

14. Neither W. Drumann nor P. Groebe used the word in the prefaces to their curious *Geschichte Roms in seinem Übergang von der republikanischen zur monarchischen Verfassung . . . nach Geschlechtern und mit genealogischen Tabellen,* whose second edition (by P. Groebe) began to appear in 1899.

15. On the possibility of Roman-style prosopography with Greek material, cf. J. K. Davies, "La storia di Atene e il metodo di Münzer," *RivStorIt* 80 (1968) 209–21; contra: D. H. Kelly, "Lysias XII 72," *Historia* 28 (1979) 98–101.

by the histories of the Junii, Fabii, Marcelli, and other *gentes,* commissioned by these families from Pomponius Atticus. At least for historians, it seems, they provided good reading.[16]

Despite its long history and widespread use, prosopography itself does not seem to have been explicitly defined as a methodology. Pauly-Wissowa's *Real-Encyclopädie* does not even contain the lemma. One of the most popular introductions to ancient history, that of Bengtson, tells us only—and quite rightly—that without inscriptions there can be no prosopography.[17] The *Grand Larousse* of 1963 refers to it as an ancillary discipline of both ancient history and epigraphy, devoted to the investigation of the family lineage and the *cursus* of great men. G. Alföldy's excellent introduction to Roman social history is silent on the topic, although the author himself is a leading prosopographer. Finally, as an indication of the general failure to define the methodology, of the three articles on prosopography in *Aufstieg und Niedergang,* those written by prosopographers themselves do not touch upon method; in fact, only the nonpractitioner seems marginally interested in the problem.[18]

Perhaps this lack of interest in method is due to the rather irrational tension that sometimes seems to exist between those who practice prosopography and those who do not.[19] Indeed, "prosopographer" is not always meant as a compliment, while, for their part, those engaged in the art have the tendency to interpret any inquiry into their methodology as a sign of disparagement and ill will.[20] A discussion of the proper fields of application for prosopography at the FIEC congress in 1969 came to nothing.[21] In Syme's opinion,

16. Thus Nep. *Att.* 18.1–4: *quibus libris nihil potest esse dulcius;* cf. Syme, *Roman Papers,* vol. 1 (Oxford 1979) 339: "Families in their rise and duration are a theme that cannot fail to charm and detain."

17. H. Bengtson, *Introduction to Ancient History,* trans. R. I. Frank and F. D. Gilliard (Berkeley and Los Angeles 1970).

18. *Le Grand Larousse* 8 (Paris 1963) 845; G. Alföldy, *The Social History of Rome,* trans. D. Braund and F. Pollock (Totowa, N. J. 1985); H.-G. Pflaum, "Les progrès des recherches prosopographiques concernant l'époque du Haut-Empire durant le dernier quart de siècle (1945–1970)," *ANRW* 2.1 (1974) 113–35; A. J. Graham, "The Limitations of Prosopography in Roman Imperial History," ibid., 136–57; W. Eck, "Beförderungskriterien innerhalb der senatorischen Laufbahn, dargestellt an der Zeit von 69 bis 138 n. Chr.," ibid., 158–228.

19. A comparable tension exists in medieval and modern history between those who work extensively with statistics and those who do not.

20. Cf. the remarks of A. Guarino, *La coerenza di Publio Mucio* (Naples 1981) 14.

21. Cf. W. den Boer, "Die prosopographische Methode in der modernen Historiographie der Kaiserzeit," *Mnemosyne* 22 (1969) 268–80; C. Nicolet, "Prosopographie et histoire sociale: Rome et l'Italie à l'époque républicaine," *Annales ESC* 25 (1970) 1209–28. To my knowledge, the provocative article by T. F. Carney, "Prosopography: Payoffs and Pitfalls," *Phoenix* 27 (1973) 156–79, did not elicit the expected reaction.

the science (or rather the art) of prosopography has been much in fashion in recent age, being adduced to reinforce historical studies in the most diverse of periods. Some deprecate. For various reasons. Among them (one surmises) distaste for erudition on a narrow front, to the neglect of broad aspects and "the higher things." Which may cheerfully be conceded. One uses what one has, and there is work to be done.[22]

However, there seems no need for a defensive mood. The written sources for social life in antiquity, as is well known, are anecdotal in the worst possible way; mostly we are informed about prominent and strange things, that is, the exceptions.[23] Thus we have notice (based on Roman census statistics or lists of curiosities) of persons who lived to an exceptionally old age, or of women who gave birth to extraordinary numbers of children; but, obviously, it is impossible from these notices to arrive at conclusions about average age or fertility rates. While in modern times we know as a fact that only 44 percent of the German people voted for Hitler in March of 1933, and can use this fact to refute Göring's claim that Hitler was supported by the overwhelming majority of Germans, we have no similar ability to disprove statistically Augustus' assertion that he was supported by a *consensus universorum* in his struggle against Antonius, however skeptical we might be of his boast.[24]

Given these circumstances, we can profit from inscriptions. In Rome the standing of each man, his *dignitas,* was dependent upon the *honor* he had acquired through the holding of magistracies. Unlike the situation prevalent in Greece, where honorary inscriptions explain in rather general terms that the person to be honored had deserved well of his king, city, or political group, Roman honorary, funerary, and even dedicatory inscriptions frequently enumerate all magistracies, priesthoods, and functions a particular man had ever held.[25] The material for "multiple career-line analysis," as it is called by modern sociologists, thus is at hand. Work along these lines began even prior to the nineteenth century and continues today under the impetus of newly discovered inscriptions that add precision to our knowledge or cause new doubts. We now

22. R. Syme, "People in Pliny," *JRS* 58 (1968) 145 (= id., *Roman Papers,* vol. 2 [1979] 711).

23. To use such information may be dangerous, as was shown by R. Saller, "Anecdotes as Historical Evidence for the Principate," *GaR* 27 (1980) 69–83.

24. Cf. J. C. Fest, *Hitler* (Berlin 1973) 550; for opposition to the *consensus universorum,* cf. G.-C. Susini, "Gratia coniurandi (Suet. *Aug.* 17, 2): a proposito del papiro di Gallo da Qasr Ibrim," in E. Bresciani, G. Geraci et al., eds., *Scritti in onore di O. Montevecchi* (Bologna 1981) 393–400.

25. These inscriptions were read attentively: in a letter to Atticus (6.1.17) Cicero comments disparagingly upon Metellus Scipio's committing historical errors when composing the inscriptions for a family monument on the Capitolium.

have at our disposal chronological lists, *fasti*, of magistrates, priests, and governors of provinces, of *equites* in the emperor's service, and of senators coming from the eastern parts of the empire, sometimes with all the data known about a given person.[26]

However, prosopography can be no better than the material on which it is based. Due particularly to the nature of epigraphical evidence, our knowledge is not evenly distributed. Since there is every reason to believe that the preserved inscriptions are representative of the total that once existed and since most honorary inscriptions deal with members of the upper classes, Roman prosopography necessarily is elite prosopography.[27] Of course, one could assemble lists of all known soldiers or artisans, but the result would scarcely be worth the effort. The prosopography of the masses, such as that done by Le Roy Ladurie on nineteenth-century French recruits, is quite simply impossible for antiquity.[28]

Nevertheless, prosopographical research has provided numerous important insights into the administrative structure of the Roman Empire, indicating the patterns of career advancement and considerations on which to determine the relative importance of positions in the imperial administration.[29] The knowledge and experience gained by such work aids the specialist in filling out gaps in mutilated inscriptions and reconstructing entire careers on the basis of scarce and scattered hints.[30]

A difficult, but not impossible, task is to add temporal dimensions to the careers thus reconstructed. After all, a simple entry such as PR COS in an inscription does not reveal whether the individual in question became consul two or twenty years after being praetor. More importantly, statistics for average careers do nothing toward explaining the individual case. If a man was appointed governor of Syria or Lower Germany,

26. Cf. the conspectus of literature given by H.-G. Pflaum (supra n. 18) and by G. Alföldy (supra n. 18) 191, n. 129. For the eastern senators, cf. H. Halfmann, *Die Senatoren aus dem östlichen Teil des Imperium Romanum bis zum Ende des 2.Jhdts.n.Chr.* (Göttingen 1979).

27. Cf. Eck (supra n. 18).

28. M. Demonet, P. Dumont, E. Le Roy Ladurie, "Anthropologie du conscrit: une cartographie cantonale (1819–1930)," *Annales ESC* 31 (1976) 700–60.

29. "To muster the principal allies of a ruler, to inspect their quality and performance": R. Syme, "Paullus the Censor," *Athenaeum* 65 (1987) 7.

30. Such experience can be usefully applied to other fields as well. E. Birley, a prosopographer himself, was employed in World War II by the British Secret Service to reconstruct careers of German officers and to infer impending strategic moves from sudden changes in the assignment of such officers; cf. Birley, *Überlegungen zur Geschichte des römischen Heeres: Vortrag anlässlich der Promotion zum Doctor honoris causa an der Universität Heidelberg am 12. Mai 1986* (Heidelberg 1987) 2. On the other hand, it seems to be one of the myths in our profession that Sir Ronald himself was working in this field of modern prosopography.

was it because of his own ability, because no one else was available, or because he had paid enough money to the emperor's valet?[31] Quinctilius Varus' ill-fated promotion to the German command is a good example. Was he sent there because of his connection through Agrippa to the Julian family or because Augustus anticipated a peaceful administrative assignment suited to Varus' proven talents? Was he incompetent, or did he simply succumb to bad luck?[32] These are questions that cannot be answered by inscriptions. Similarly in the case of promotions in equestrian careers inscriptional evidence can show only those rational criteria that were almost exclusively emphasized in the epoch-making work of Hans-Georg Pflaum, but fails to reveal other factors such as patronage that have been recognized more recently as possibly equally crucial for individual careers.[33] Or, to give a further example, there was a tendency, discernable already since Augustus, to exclude more and more the most prestigious group of senators, the patricians, from the military commands in the most important imperial provinces. Did the emperors consider it too dangerous to give such commands to patricians, or did the patricians themselves show little interest in these often bothersome assignments because, for instance, the honor to be gained in such positions could not add much to the prestige they already possessed by birth? The sources we have do not give us the information needed to answer such questions. Moreover, we have grown more skeptical about the rational nature of man, and we are far removed today from such optimism as prevailed in the nineteenth century, when Macauley wrote that "when we see the actions of a man we know with certainty what he thinks his interest to be." [34]

There are many aspects of the lives of senators about which we are still woefully uninformed. Property provides a good example. The minimal census for a senator was one million sesterces; if it is correct that on the average one could expect about sixty thousand sesterces of inter-

---

31. Trusted servants might be important enough to die suddenly a few days after their master; cf. the *lictor proximus* of Trajan in *ILS* 1792, and the comments of H. Dessau, "Die Vorgänge bei der Thronbesteigung Hadrians," *Beiträge zur Alten Geschichte und Geographie: Festschrift H. Kiepert* (Berlin 1898) 85–91; and Graham (supra n. 18) 139, n. 10. Cf. also Dio 75 (74).6.1. on Pescennius Niger: he was neither too good nor too bad, so Commodus made him governor of Syria.

32. On Varus, cf. now R. Syme, *The Augustan Aristocracy* (Oxford 1986) chap. 23. On methods of appointment to provincial posts under Augustus in general, cf. R. Szramkiewicz, *Les gouverneurs de province à l'époque augustéenne: Contribution à l'histoire administrative et sociale du principat,* 2 vols. (Paris 1976).

33. Cf. R. P. Saller, "Promotion and Patronage in Equestrian Careers," *JRS* 70 (1980) 44–63. Some thoughts on the shortcomings of prosopographical explanation were expressed already in 1940 by Momigliano (supra n. 3) 77–78.

34. Quoted by C. B. Namier, *Personalities and Power* (London 1955) 1.

est annually on that sum, it was not a very large total, given the costliness of a senator's life-style. Gavius Apicius, bon vivant, gourmet, and author of a well-known cookbook, probably knew what he was doing when he committed suicide after his fortune fell to a mere ten million sesterces. We know of some of the top fortunes, but we can only guess to what extent the average senator was drawn to the emperor's service not only by the promise of influence, power, and an increase in social standing, but also because he depended upon salaries to be obtained by such employment.[35]

What has been said thus far is relevant primarily to the prosopography of the principate, when inscriptions are our main source for the composition and careers of the governing class. But inscriptions were put up in large numbers only from the time of Augustus.[36] By contrast, the prosopography of the Roman Republic depends upon even more tenuous evidence: the lists of the annual magistrates and an occasional hint in the historical works about marriage alliances and political agreements among members of the aristocracy. While imperial prosopography thus is principally concerned with the investigation of officials and their careers, republican prosopography considers the politician and his political connections. Whereas, for example, we are ignorant of any magistracy held by one of the most important figures of the late Republic, Marcus Crassus the triumvir, before his proconsulship in Spain in 72/71 B.C., we are well informed about every position held by much less powerful senators, such as Iulius Severus and Lollius Urbicus in the second century A.D.—although admittedly we have no idea of their political aims and convictions.

Ever since Münzer one of the most important tasks in republican prosopography has been the search for well-defined parties or *factiones*. The starting point was the assumption—which, incidentally, guided Namier's analyses as well—that the political attitudes of a given person usually were not founded on strong convictions but on ties of family and friendship, and thus should be surmisable from that person's choice of *adfines* and *amici*. Thus, if a Fabius had married an Aemilia and was consul together with a Sempronius Gracchus, this should indicate an alliance among the Fabii, Aemilii, and Sempronii. Moreover, if, two generations later, a Fabius and a Sempronius Gracchus were once again colleagues, this would indicate that such an alliance had continued

35. Some information on these issues can be found in R. J. A. Talbert, *The Senate of Imperial Rome* (Princeton 1984) chap. 2.
36. Which was due in part to the recent availability of high quality marble from Luni.

through all this time. Such rather mechanical interpretation (admittedly a bit overstated here) of data provided mostly by the lists of officeholders (*fasti*) made little allowance for the personal feelings and preferences of the individuals concerned. It has lost much of its appeal due to recent studies of the structure of politics in republican Rome conducted in the tradition of Matthias Gelzer by Christian Meier and several of his pupils. They have shown that through the end of the republic there were no enduring political groups; the vertical and horizontal links that are indicated by the terms *clientela* and *amicitia* were much too complex and contradictory to admit of the long-term political alliances that had been envisaged under the "factional theory." [37] The dangers inherent in any undifferentiated application of this theory are well illustrated by the example of Julius Caesar. In every one of his magistracies, he was the colleague of Marcus Calpurnius Bibulus, and his wife was a Calpurnia. According to theory, then, the Julii and Calpurnii should have been in close political alliance throughout the seventies and sixties of the first century B.C. Instead, as is well known, nothing was as enduring as the bitter antagonism between the two men. Indeed, the model seems to have worked best for the illumination of those periods where not too many annoying details are known.[38] Another, slightly later, example concerns the *fasti consulares* of Augustus' last decade. All the consuls are known, although in most cases they are to us nothing but names. Even so, no fewer than five attempts at prosopographical elucidation of these lists were made through 1971, endeavoring to assign the names to different court factions and interpreting them as indicators of the growing or decreasing influence of such factions. One theory went so far as to refer to two of these "parties" by the names of Agrippa and Maecenas, both of whom were by then long dead[39]—which is to show that long-term alliances are still considered plausible by some scholars.

Syme's *Roman Revolution* is located at the crossroads of republican

37. C. Meier, *Res publica amissa* (Wiesbaden 1966; reprint ed. with an important new introduction, Frankfurt 1980); R. Rilinger, *Der Einfluss des Wahlleiters bei den römischen Konsulwahlen von 366 bis 50 v.Chr.* (Munich 1976) 8 with n. 35; K. Raaflaub, *Dignitatis contentio: Studien zur Motivation und politischen Taktik im Bürgerkrieg zwischen Caesar und Pompeius* (Munich 1974).

38. Which is decidedly not the case in the late Republic. Two books, simultaneously written, arrived at absolutely opposite conclusions about Crassus the triumvir, his political attitudes, and the political groups (*factiones*) he relied upon: B. A. Marshall, *Crassus: A Political Biography* (Amsterdam 1976), and A. M. Ward, *Marcus Crassus and the Late Roman Republic* (Columbia, Mo. 1977).

39. Cf. A. Ferrill, "Prosopography and the Last Years of Augustus," *Historia* 20 (1971) 718–31, who reviews older theories, including Syme's (*The Roman Revolution* [Oxford 1939] 434–39).

and imperial prosopography with their specific sources and methods. "When histories fail, profit accrues from the study of senators and their careers, of kinship and alliances": thus did Syme restate his subject of 1939 in a later work.[40] The combination of both methods, the literary and the prosopographic, is necessary. Thus Syme's second great book, *Tacitus* (1958), deals with the first century A.C., the period of Roman history that is best represented by both epigraphical and literary evidence. But, on the other side, Syme never ventured to penetrate farther back into the Republic than the period analyzed in his *Sallust* (1964).

Taking all this into account, what did Syme understand under "Roman Revolution"? We need not concern ourselves with the fact that his use of the word *revolution* is entirely pragmatic—which elicited from Continental, and particularly from German, scholars much discussion as to whether the word had been accurately employed.[41] Whether there was a Roman revolution, and if so, when and how it took place: these were popular questions when each and every thing from sex to fashion had its revolution; they need not detain us here. What Syme had in mind when he used the word is shown by his synonymous phrase "transformation of state and society between 60 B.C. and A.D. 14."[42] Here "revolution" clearly means the change in the composition of the ruling oligarchy and, less overtly, a change in the way politics were conducted by the members of this new oligarchy. "Ever alert for the contrast of name and substance,"[43] Syme dissolved the so-called parties of *optimates* and *populares* into groups of politicians fighting with one another for positions of power: men solely interested in their own welfare. Syme also attempted to dispense with the differences, much emphasized by earlier

40. *The Crisis of 2 B.C.,* SB Münch 1974, no. 7, 6 (= *Roman Papers,* vol. 3 [Oxford 1984] 914).

41. Cf. H. J. Gehrke, "La rivoluzione romana: le angolazioni più recenti," *Labeo* 26 (1980) 191–98. On "revolution" as a concept in antiquity, cf. C. Meier, " 'Revolution' in der Antike," in O. Brunner et al., eds., *Historisches Lexikon zur politisch-sozialen Sprache in Deutschland, Geschichtliche Grundbegriffe:* vol. 5 (Stuttgart 1984) 656–70. From the Marxist point of view, of course, the loose use of *revolution* had to be condemned; cf., for example, B. Zuchold, "Die sogenannte römische Revolution und Alfred Heuss," *Klio* 62 (1980) 583–91.

42. Syme (supra n. 39) viii. Syme's starting point is 60 B.C., the last "free" year of the Republic. In this he followed Asinius Pollio ("a pessimistic Republican and a honest man, hating pomp and pretence" 166), but the date does not become more logical by repetition, as was stated early on by Momigliano (1940: supra n. 3) 78. Better to begin, like Sallust, with the death of Sulla, who for the last time tried to restore pre-Gracchan conditions in public life by eliminating the factors that caused the rise of the great military leaders. The abandonment of the "Sullan system" between 79 and 60 B.C. and Pompey's great commands are highly important prerequisites of Syme's "Roman Revolution."

43. So Syme (supra n. 39) 324 on Tacitus.

writers, between the programs pursued by Octavian and Antonius. In this battle of changing alliances there remained in the end, after decades of civil war and proscriptions, murder and suicides, one heir to power and to the riches of the empire: the future Augustus. The aristocracy that had ruled Rome previously nearly bled to death in these "years of tribulation" [44] and was revived only by a transfusion of new blood from among the *equites* and the flower of the Italian municipal aristocracies. Socially and economically these men did not differ greatly from the old nobility, but as *novi homines* they carried with them a different mentality and motivation. We shall return to this point later.

When reading *The Roman Revolution,* one immediately gains the impression that history is made within a narrow oligarchy and that the common run of people need not be taken into account: "In all ages, whatever the form and name of government . . . an oligarchy lurks behind the façade." [45] This view fits well with the prevalent notion that under the empire the masses were interested exclusively in "bread and circuses," having been excluded from politics since the time of Caesar. However, it is worthwhile to take a closer look at the famous lines in Juvenal where he speaks of *panem et circenses* and to read them in their context (10.56–113, esp. 77–81). This passage concerns Seianus, who in A.D. 31 reconvened the *comitia centuriata* after a hiatus of seventeen years in order to have himself elected consul. This was done, of all places, on the Aventine, that is, in the section of the city with the strongest popular and plebeian traditions. [46] Even under Tiberius apparently the Roman electorate was not wholly unpolitical nor a totally reliable tool in the hands of the ruler. The same may be surmised from the reform of the *comitia* in A.D. 5, when the old *centuria praerogativa* (the *centuria* chosen by lot from the first class to vote first and set the trend for the others) was abolished and superseded by ten new voting units composed of senators and *equites,* from which, moreover, the two urban tribes, Esquilina and Suburana, were explicitly excluded. [47] The only

44. Syme (supra n. 32) 9.

45. Syme (supra n. 39) 7. This openly elitist view of history accounts for some of the doubts expressed in the seventies about *The Roman Revolution* and prosopography in general. Not uncharacteristically, such reactions have decreased markedly in the eighties.

46. *ILS* 6044; and M. Pani, *Comitia e senato: Sulla trasformazione della procedura elettorale a Roma nell'età di Tiberio* (Bari 1974) 114. In "Seianus on the Aventine," *Hermes* 84 (1956) 257–66 (= *Roman Papers*, vol. 1 [1979] 305–14), Syme himself duly underlined the importance of the inscription, but there is more to it than Seianus "parading his ambitions" (p. 266 and 314, respectively).

47. The discussion about the *Lex Valeria Cornelia*, known from the *tabula Hebana*, was revived recently after the publication of the *tabula Siarensis;* cf. the *Acta* of the collo-

plausible explanation of this change is that the old system using the *praerogativa* had not worked as smoothly and reliably as Augustus had hoped for; the people had not been so liable to manipulation as one might think.[48]

In 23 B.C. Augustus accepted the *tribunicia potestas*,[49] and we are reminded repeatedly, not least by Augustus himself in his *Res Gestae,* that the populace of Rome was one of his primary concerns. Indeed he boasts of the tremendous sums he spent to feed and entertain the masses and, in modern words, to improve their quality of life.[50] But there is another side to such novel use of the *tribunicia potestas.* The invisible but very noticeable presence of the *princeps* among the tribunes of the *plebs* represented, at long last, the complete integration of the tribunate into the organization of the state. No protest from the plebeians was now possible through traditional channels. Instead of relying on their tribunes,[51] the populace was now compelled to use more informal methods of protest: choruses in the theatre, at the circus, and in like places. For their part, the masses must have quickly understood the meaning of Phaedrus' line in the fable of the ass: *in principatu commutando saepius nil praeter domini nomen mutant pauperes* (1.1.1–2). Thus there may indeed have been political reasons to strip the people of their voting privileges.

Besides underestimating the urban population of Rome, Syme in his *Roman Revolution* also underrated the role of the army—which he had before and has since elucidated himself in a series of important articles.[52] In a brilliant paper of 1958 on the evolution of the emperor's

---

quium held at Seville in 1986: J. Arce and J. González, eds., *Estudios sobre la Tabula Siarensis,* Anejos de Archivo Español de Arqueología 9 (Madrid 1988).

48. The actual background of this "reform" unfortunately is unknown; it has been connected with Tiberius' return to power or to the mysterious conspiracy of Cornelius Cinna. For discussion, see D. Kienast, *Augustus: Prinzeps und Monarch* (Darmstadt 1982) 136.

49. Some of the tribunician rights he had assumed already in the thirties; cf. Kienast (supra n. 48) 88–91.

50. *RG* 15–24 with the other sources cited in the commentary of P. A. Brunt and J. M. Moore, *Res Gestae divi Augusti* (Oxford 1967) 57–66. The stress laid by Augustus on his gifts to the *plebs urbana* convinced many scholars from Mommsen to Syme (supra n. 39) 523, n. 4 that the *plebs* was the principal addressee of the *Res Gestae;* contra: Z. Yavetz, "The *Res Gestae* and Augustus' Public Image," in Millar and Segal (supra n. 3) 1–36.

51. Thus it is not by chance that M. Egnatius Rufus in 19 B.C. staged his alleged coup by exploiting the popularity he had gained as an aedile (for sources and literature, see the contribution to this volume by K. A. Raaflaub and L. J. Samons).

52. They are mostly collected in Syme's *Danubian Papers* (Bucharest 1971); cf. on this subject now J. B. Campbell, *The Emperor and the Roman Army, 31 B.C.–A.D. 235* (Oxford 1984), with the review by P. Le Roux, *REL* 63 (1985) 42–49.

nomenclature, he showed that the prominence afforded the title *imperator* ("generalissimo") as the *princeps'* new *praenomen* must be explained as a bow to the army, the most solid pillar of the new regime.[53] As in politics, so too in the military sphere the previous era of equilibrium and a loyalty divided among several *imperatores* was replaced by the unquestioned primacy of one individual. After 27 B.C. the army was stationed almost exclusively in the so-called imperial provinces, a fact as much in the interest of the soldiery as of the *princeps;* for the soldiers had not yet forgotten that in the final analysis it was their general who had to guarantee both their pay in the present and their settlement in the future, with his own funds if need be. In the new dispensation of the principate, this could only be the emperor.[54]

Syme also neglected, perhaps deliberately, the entire sphere of "creation of beliefs" or "ideology." [55] This causes surprise because of the important part their mastery of public opinion had played in the success of dictators such as Hitler and Mussolini. The emperor's full name after 27 B.C. was *Imperator Caesar divi filius Augustus,* while other Romans were simply called, for example, *Marcus Tullius Marci filius Cicero.*[56] Thus in his titulature—which had almost supplanted the personal name—Augustus was represented as son of a new god and as such "holy" and venerable himself. Even assuming the upper classes at Rome, enlightened skeptics (like Syme himself), did not take it seriously, there must have been a target group for this type of propaganda: presumably the mass of citizens and noncitizens throughout the empire. Unconcerned with the details of constitutional law and ignoring the differences between the *princeps'* direct rule in his own provinces, his indirect control over those administered by the senate, and his position as *princeps senatus* in Italy, these people looked to the emperor to solve their manifold problems and to secure for them law and order.[57] The

53. "Imperator Caesar: A Study in Nomenclature," *Historia* 7 (1958) 172–88 (= *Roman Papers,* vol. 1[1979] 361–77).

54. This aspect was discussed by P. A. Brunt, especially in "The Army and the Land in the Roman Revolution," *JRS* 52 (1962) 69–86; and recently by K. Raaflaub, "Die Militärreformen des Augustus und die politische Problematik des frühen Prinzipats," in G. Binder, ed., *Saeculum Augustum,* vol. 1 (Darmstadt 1987) 246–307.

55. The chapters "Political Catchwords" and "The Organization of Opinion" in Syme's *Roman Revolution* were complemented later on by, among others, *A Roman Post-Mortem: An Inquest on the Fall of the Roman Republic,* Todd Memorial Lecture 3 (1950) (= *Roman Papers,* vol. 1 [1979] 205–17). There are some very disparaging remarks on that field of study in Syme (supra n. 32) 441.

56. The magic of name and the equation new name = new man evidently were put to work in 27 B.C.

57. Cf. F. Millar, *The Emperor in the Roman World* (London 1977).

parable in Mark 12.17 on the emperor's picture on the *denarius* is a poignant illustration of the unity of empire and emperor in the view of the provincials. We are told repeatedly that Augustus was frequently offered nearly divine honors in the provinces already during his lifetime, particularly in the East.[58] This was a sign of deeply felt gratitude toward the man who had put an end to the ravages of civil war and had begun to remedy the worst abuses of provincial maladministration. Having thus been raised far above all other senators, Augustus was in a uniquely favorable position to realize all his plans: it was hard to quibble with a god about constitutional trifles.[59]

Furthermore, Syme, astonishingly, seems only marginally interested in the most revolutionary development of all: the profound changes wrought in the Roman senatorial elite itself, that is, the very class that occupies center stage in *The Roman Revolution*. For centuries politics had been the occupation of *all* senators, and the crisis of the Republic was largely caused by the powerful generals' determination and ability to flout senatorial consensus. As Ramsey MacMullen has pointed out, the "professional ethic" and political mentality of the senators were centered around achievement in the public arena and service to the *res publica*. In this fashion they acquired recognition (*honor*) and political influence (*auctoritas*) from their peers.[60] Under the principate a compromise was reached; for while the senatorial aristocracy was assured a role in the governance of the empire and a share of the traditional magistracies and thus a certain amount of *honor, auctoritas* was now the exclusive possession of the *princeps*.[61] Syme rightly noted that the victory of Augustus was also the victory of the nonpolitical classes of Italy,[62] but he offered no explanation of this phenomenon. Besides considering the state of general exhaustion after two decades of almost uninterrupted civil war, one must take into account the fact that even after

58. Cf. now S. R. F. Price, *Rituals and Power: The Roman Imperial Cult in Asia Minor* (Cambridge 1984) esp. 54–62.

59. The pictorial program of the Temple of Mars Ultor (finished evidently in some haste in 2 B.C. when Augustus became *pater patriae*) without any scruples places the emperor among the *divi* Aeneas, Romulus, and Caesar; cf. V. Kockel, "Augustusforum und Mars-Ultor-Tempel," in *Kaiser Augustus und die verlorene Republik*, Exhibition Catalogue (Berlin 1988) 157. It is interesting to note that in chapter 30, "The Organization of Opinion," of *The Roman Revolution* with one irrelevant exception Syme omits to cite archaeological sources.

60. R. Macmullen, "Roman Elite Motivation: Three Questions," *P&P* 88 (1980) 3–16.

61. But cf. now P. A. Brunt, "The Role of the Senate in the Augustan Regime," *CQ* n. s. 34 (1984) 423–44.

62. Syme (supra n. 39) 513.

the Italians were given Roman citizenship following the Social War they were still not fully integrated into the political structure of the *res publica*. The old nobility and the *plebs urbana* continued to monopolize the traditional political conflicts between *libertas* and *dignitas*.[63] The indispensable prerequisite of a leading political role was the control over large *clientelae*. Despite their exalted status in their hometowns these municipal grandees remained the clients of the ancient Roman nobility rather than becoming *patroni* themselves. Even if through ties of marriage and *hospitia* certain of these men moved into the inner circle of Roman politics, they yet remained *homines novi* and *parvi senatores*.[64] When, by the *consensus universorum* mentioned above, Augustus created for himself a *patrocinium* and *clientela* superior to every other, the municipal aristocracy and those who became senators under his aegis had little difficulty in accepting his predominance, which, moreover, appeared under the disguise of *auctoritas*. In this they differed from the old nobility, the Fabii, Cornelii, Aemilii, and their like, who could bear only with great difficulty their new status as inferiors.

Tacitus' somber view of the nature of the principate has sometimes been taken as representative of the senate at large or at least of its leading members. After all, it is reasoned, if a *novus homo* of probably Gallic extraction[65] was so imbued with republican ideals, this must have been a widespread phenomenon. However, we should not ignore the testimony of Velleius Paterculus, a new senator from Campania,[66] who wrote his history under Tiberius. His genuine enthusiasm for the new order usually is dismissed as naive flattery. But he had experienced the last years of Augustus and may well be a better witness than Tacitus for the spirit of the time and the thoughts of the new aristocracy. Indeed, that men like Velleius were able to gain high government offices may explain in part why Augustus succeeded where Caesar failed and why

63. C. Nicolet, *The World of the Citizen in Republican Rome,* trans. P. S. Falla (Berkeley and Los Angeles 1980) esp. chap. 7, "*Comitia*: The Citizen and Politics"; id., "Augustus, Government, and the Propertied Classes," in Millar and Segal (supra n. 3) 89–128.

64. T. P. Wiseman, *New Men in the Roman Senate, 139 B.C.–A.D. 14* (Oxford 1971) esp. chap. 6, "*Homo novus parvusque senator.*" But F. Millar, "Cornelius Nepos, 'Atticus' and the Roman Revolution," *GaR* 35 (1988) 46–47, draws attention to the fact that a considerable number of *homines novi* belonged to the same social stratum as their *generosi condiscipuli.*

65. Syme, *Tacitus,* vol. 2 (Oxford 1958) 611–24.

66. At least in his mother's line, Velleius descended from Campanian aristocracy, the famous Magii of Capua and Aeclanum; cf. recently (with earlier literature) C. Kuntze, *Zur Darstellung des Kaisers Tiberius und seiner Zeit bei Velleius Paterculus* (Frankfurt 1985) 11 and 254–59.

thereafter the *res publica libera* never was a real alternative to even the worst of emperors.[67]

To Syme, the "Roman Revolution" meant the transformation of the ruling class of Rome. Insofar as this entailed the prosopographical study of the rise of new families and the concomitant eclipse of the old, Syme has elucidated the process in *The Roman Revolution, The Augustan Aristocracy* (1986), and numerous important articles published in between. But whoever thought to find in the long-awaited *Augustan Aristocracy* a synthesis of the innumerable single facets of this story or an account of the makeup of the new Augustan senate was disappointed (and did not really know Sir Ronald). Thus a comprehensive study of the Italian upper classes, comprising not only senators and *equites* but also their cousins in the *municipia* and *coloniae*, remains to be written.[68] These men, who had survived the upheavals and confiscations initiated by Sulla, Caesar, and Octavian, or had profited from them, were wary of future confiscations and proscriptions to be expected from a victory of Antonius. They were instrumental in the formation of the *consensus universorum* of all Italy; the revolutionaries of yesterday had become staunch supporters of the status quo.

Important aspects of the changing identity and mentality of the aristocracy are hardly touched upon in *The Roman Revolution*. For example, the importance of politics as the exclusive purpose and content of life decreased—which made it easier to decline a seat in the senate even when offered one by the *princeps*. The barrier between insiders and outsiders was lowered—which soon caused the social category of *homo novus* to disappear because few could now boast of a long series of *nobiles* among their ancestors. Attitudes toward the provincials, money, and morals, to name only a few issues, changed rapidly. Santo Mazzarino once spoke of a "bourgeois revolution" in Rome:[69] just as the "Biedermeier" style on the Continent or the Victorian way of life in England followed the French Revolution only after a considerable hiatus, so in Rome the late republican life-style continued to be observed

67. As was made abundantly clear to daydreaming senators in A.D. 41; cf. Jos., *AJ* 19.162–273, and A. Momigliano, *Claudius: The Emperor and His Achievement*, trans. W. Hogorth (Cambridge 1961; New York 1962) 20–22.

68. There are two useful recent collections of papers that deal with this subject: M. Cébeillac-Gervasoni, ed., *Les "bourgeoisies" municipales italiennes au IIe et Ier siècle av. J.-C.* (Paris and Naples 1983); S. Panciera, ed., *Epigrafia e ordine senatorio* (Rome 1984); cf. now also S. Demougin, *L'ordre équestre sous les Julio-Claudiens*, Coll. École Franç. de Rome 108 (Rome 1988).

69. S. Mazzarino, *L'impero romano* I (Bari 1976) 211–38, speaking of the time of the apostle Paul.

by the members (both male and female) of the foremost senatorial families through the reign of the Julio-Claudians. Clodia's and Servilia's
heiresses are to be found, both in political ambition and immoral conduct, among the two Julias, Messalina and Agrippina.[70] Only when the
last heirs of the old republican nobility, together with large parts of the
new aristocracy of the early principate, had been destroyed and had
gone down with the first dynasty itself, did a new age of aristocratic
respectability dawn, ushered in by the Flavians, who themselves originated in a small Italian town.[71]

One of the main assumptions of Syme's work is the unity of state and
society at Rome. Due to his sources and the prosopographical method,
but also to the profound political and social beliefs he formed in the
thirties, his interests focus on descent, careers, offices, and marriages of
the members of the senatorial aristocracy. Thus his remained, in a re-
strictive sense, the prosopography of one social class. He refused to aim
at broader generalizations, at combining all the single observations on
individuals and groups into a social history of the entire senatorial aristocracy with its changing identity and self-understanding. This is all the
more remarkable since Syme was completely at home in the literature,
both poetic and historical, of the Augustan Age.[72] Thus Syme would
have been perfectly capable of producing one of those "histoires de
mentalité" or "sensibilité collective" that are fashionable these days and
run the gamut from the heretics of Montaillou to the poor of Byzan-
tium.[73] If he chose not to follow this road, the reason might well be
found in a typically English reluctance to pursue questions that are not
explicitly dealt with and thus "legitimized" by our ancient sources.[74]
Maybe, like his second successor in the Camden Chair, he decided, to
the exclusion of modern concepts such as "mentalité", "not merely to

70. Cf. now R. Syme, "Princesses and Others in Tacitus," *GaR* 38 (1981) 40–51 (= id.,
Roman Papers, vol. 3 [1984] 1364–75).

71. Cf. the remarks of Tacitus (*Ann.* 3.55) on a similar development in an entirely
different field, that of hospitality. For the connection between the change of political system and the replacement of the leading class, see now K. Raaflaub, "Grundzüge, Ziele und
Ideen der Opposition gegen die Kaiser im 1. Jh. n. Chr.: Versuch einer Standortbestimmung," in O. Reverdin and B. Grange, eds., *Opposition et résistances à l'empire d'Auguste
à Trajan,* Entretiens sur l'ant. class. 33 (Vandoeuvres and Geneva 1987) 37–45.

72. This will be evident from even a brief look at his *History in Ovid* (Oxford 1978).

73. E. Le Roy Ladurie, *Montaillou: Village occitan de 1294–1324* (Paris 1975); E.
Patlagean, *Pauvreté économique et pauvreté sociale à Byzance, IVe à VIIe siècle* (Paris
1977).

74. This was demonstrated impressively some years ago at a colloquium in London
where English and German ancient historians met to examine, by discussing late republican and early imperial Roman history, the question of whether the proverbial "typically
German" or "typically English" ways of thinking, arguing, and writing really exist.

attend to the penumbras of attitudes and expectations expressed in those ancient sources which provide our evidence, but, so far as is possible, to base our conceptions solely on those attitudes and expectations."[75]

The preceding remarks are not intended to imitate those bad reviews that tell the author what kind of book he should have written.[76] We all know, and I want to restate it most emphatically, that *The Roman Revolution* is one of the most important (and stylistically most agreeable) books in ancient history written in this century. Nothing could prove this more impressively than the fact that fifty years after its publication classicists and historians feel obliged to pay homage to this work and its eminent author, the "Emperor of Roman History."[77]

75. Millar (supra n. 57) xi.

76. There are many subjects not dealt with in the book, and their enumeration was started already in 1940 by Momigliano (supra n. 3): foreign policy, religion and belief, the lower classes, the economy, and many more. But—to recall once more what was said before—Syme simply did not want to write the comprehensive monograph on Augustus, the new "Gardthausen" now long overdue.

77. Bowersock (supra n. 3) 8.

The Personality of Augustus:
Reflections on Syme's *Roman Revolution*

Reassessments in ancient history very often move in cycles. Two examples will suffice. The study of the population in ancient Rome and Italy started with Julius Beloch's *Bevölkerung,* went through different stages, but relapsed eventually to (roughly) Beloch's basic views expressed in P. A. Brunt's *Italian Manpower.* Nobody claims that Brunt and Beloch reached identical conclusions, but it is plausible to assert that by reassessing Tenney Frank, who reassessed Beloch, Brunt came closer to the latter.[1] The investigation of the *Scriptores Historiae Augustae* went through a similar process: from Dessau's fundamental article in 1894 through Momigliano's memorable paper to Syme's book vindicating Dessau.[2] Has Syme provided us with the definitive answer? Nobody knows. History is an argument without an end, and historical re-

---

1. J. Beloch, *Die Bevölkerung der griechisch-römischen Welt* (Leipzig 1886); T. Frank, *An Economic Survey of Ancient Rome,* 6 vols. (Baltimore 1933–1939); P. A. Brunt, *Italian Manpower* (Oxford 1971).
2. H. Dessau, "Die Überlieferung der SHA," *Hermes* 29 (1894) 393ff.; A. Momigliano, "An Unsolved Problem of Historical Forgery: The Scriptores Historiae Augustae," *JWarb* 17 (1954) 22–46 (=id., *Secondo contributo alla storia degli studi classici e del mondo antico* [Rome 1960] 105ff.); R. Syme, *Ammianus Marcellinus and the Historia Augusta* (Oxford 1968).

visionism is not only inevitable but also inescapable. This is especially true when major events or personalities are involved. The various reassessments of Demosthenes, Cicero, and Julius Caesar are cases in point, and it is only appropriate to look again at *The Roman Revolution,* fifty years after its publication.

This paper will consist of three major parts. In the first part I shall deal with the problem of reassessment in history in general. In the second part I shall take up the problem in connection with Syme's *Roman Revolution* with special emphasis on Augustus' personality. The third part will concentrate on Augustus' personality as reflected in his *dicta* and *apophthegmata.*

I

Let me submit first that scholarly reassessments are legitimate only if new evidence that invalidates the old is discovered, if a new method of research is applied, and/or if a new outlook emerges. The new outlook may be the result of a longer and different perspective or (as some scholars prefer to put it) by a new *Zeitgeist.* I intend to argue that as far as *The Roman Revolution* is concerned, none of these conditions are relevant or applicable.

Firstly, new inscriptions, which could not have been known to Syme in 1939 and which have recently been analyzed by Fergus Millar, have not only not destroyed Syme's basic view of the principate, but have actually confirmed it.[3] Secondly, I can discern no change in the attitude of scholars to dictatorships and political catchwords from 1939 to our own day. To give one example, a pamphlet written in early 1945 encouraged people to fight

> for the freedom of the individual
> for the freedom of religion and conscience
> for the abolition of slave labour
> for property of possessions
> for social justice
> for the right to advancement and education
> without regard to origin.[4]

3. F. Millar, "State and Subject: The Impact of Monarchy," in F. Millar and E. Segal, eds., *Caesar Augustus: Seven Aspects* (Oxford 1984) 37–60.
4. Quoted in A. Clark, *Barbarossa: The Russian-German Conflict, 1941–45* (New York 1965) 367.

The fact that this pamphlet is signed by none other than Dr. Joseph Goebbels still leaves us bewildered. It is therefore hard to believe that anyone would challenge Syme's exquisite chapter entitled "Political Catchwords," in which he taught us to take with a grain of salt phrases like *rem publicam in libertatem vindicavi* in which Eduard Meyer and Guglielmo Ferrero so piously believed.[5]

Secondly, in vain have distinguished scholars like H. Last and A. H. M. Jones deplored the "sad divorce" between Roman history and Roman law that occurred, according to them, in Syme's writings. More and more are subscribing to Syme's view that the conflict between Caesar and Pompey was a "Machtfrage" rather than a "Rechtsfrage"[6] and that passages like *bonum publicum simulantes pro sua quisque potentia certabant* should not be overlooked.[7] From this point of view, *Zeitgeist* is no different in 1989 than it was in 1939.

Thirdly, no one yet has seriously challenged Syme's method of inquiry. The study of ancient history has benefited a great deal from the adoption of methods used in closely related disciplines. Niebuhr brought in philology, Mommsen law, and Rostovtzeff archaeology. Why then reject the social sciences, which became so fashionable and attractive to the younger generation in the second half of our century? Has not M. I. Finley enriched his scholarship by learning from Max Weber, and Christian Meier by studying Carl Schmitt? From this point of view Syme might appear, *prima facie*, as positivistic and old-fashioned. It is true that Syme speaks occasionally with disdain of sociological jargon and politological models applied to ancient history. I think that he would agree with Trilling, who spoke with contempt of a language of non-thought, full of repetitive slogans, easy to memorize and made for indoctrination. Indeed in an article published in the seventies, Syme advised younger scholars not to waste time on meaningless generalizations, reminded them that history dealt first and foremost with people, and urged them to work hard, because in the field of history in particular there was still a lot of work to be done.[8]

5. R. Syme, *The Roman Revolution* (Oxford 1939) 149. See, however, G. Ferrero, *Grösse und Niedergang Roms,* vol. 4 (1909) 259; E. Meyer, *Kleine Schriften*[2] (Halle 1924) 425–74.

6. Syme (supra n. 5) 48.

7. Sall. *Cat.* 38.3.

8. R. Syme, *The Crisis of 2 B.C.,* SBMünch 1974, no. 7, 3–34, esp. 32–34 (=id., *Roman Papers,* vol. 3 [Oxford 1984] 912–36, esp. 935f.); cf. id., "People in Pliny," *JRS* 58 (1968) 145 (=id., *Roman Papers,* vol. 2 [Oxford 1979] 711).

On the other hand, it is also true that *The Roman Revolution* is a sociological analysis par excellence. It is not prosopography for the sake of prosopography, nor is it a Who's Who of Roman nonentities. Rather, it is a means of getting to the bottom of the most important social phenomenon in ancient Rome, patronage.

Syme refused to consider the *princeps* as just another republican magistrate, did not analyze *auctoritas* (like von Premerstein) in legal terms, and did not believe that the real power was concentrated in the hands of the senate and the Roman people. But by analyzing carefully Augustus' following rather than his ideology he reached the conclusion that the "Roman Revolution" expressed itself in the victory of the "nonpolitical classes" of Rome and of the Italian municipalities.[9] The modernity of this kind of analysis has not been seriously contested, and—with few exceptions—the book has been highly praised and considered a classic since the early forties.

In the Soviet Union, however, the term "Roman Revolution" was rejected because in the days of Augustus the slave system continued to prevail and the means of production remained in the possession of the old slaveowners. This attitude may change, and Syme's "Roman Revolution" might even be "rehabilitated." On 2 August 1986, Mikhail Gorbachev equated the word "restructuring" (*perestroika*) with the word "revolution" without intending to shift the ownership of the means of production from one class to another. Moreover, on 28 January 1987, he declared that the Soviet leadership had in mind a "truly revolutionary and comprehensive transformation in society."[10] If so, why reject the term "Roman Revolution"?

In conclusion, neither new evidence nor new perspectives nor new methods of research warrant a significant reassessment. At least, not yet.

II

This does not mean, however, that *The Roman Revolution* is a flawless work, and indeed some deficiencies were pointed out in a review that became a classic itself. Syme was criticized for not having paid enough attention to the provinces (especially the Greek East), for having ne-

9. Syme (supra n. 5) 501.

10. *Pravda*, 2 August 1986; 28 January 1987. Consider also the interesting statement of Yegor K. Ligachew: "The process of restructuring that is now unfolding is revolutionary in nature, both in scale and in content" (*Pravda*, 7 November 1986). I am indebted to Theodore Draper for the references.

glected the role of the lower classes, and for having emphasized marriages and divorces of people more than their ideas.[11] My feeling is that Syme never intended to produce a Le Roy Ladurie kind of "histoire totalisante" and deliberately refrained from dealing with problems that he considered not organically linked with his thesis. Meanwhile these gaps have been conveniently filled by other scholars.[12] However, as far as my understanding goes, their books only complemented *The Roman Revolution* and never intended to shake its conceptual foundations (to the extent that Syme demolished Mommsen's "dyarchy" or Eduard Meyer's "oriental monarchy" of Julius Caesar). This paper is no exception. It offers a corrective in the form of an enlarged footnote and deals with an issue left incomplete in *The Roman Revolution*, namely, the personality of Augustus.

By interpreting Livy's *nec vitia nostra nec remedia pati possumus* Christian Meier coined his famous phrase "Krise ohne Alternative." Antonio Gramsci would have agreed with him, since he too diagnosed as a crisis any situation in which the old was dying and the new not yet born. According to Meier, in 44 B.C. there was no social group that could take upon itself the responsibility of accomplishing the necessary political change. This social group developed slowly and gradually, and only after its formation and growth could Augustus succeed where Caesar failed. Meier would probably go along with Syme's "non-political classes," and for both the personality of Augustus would remain of secondary importance only. This is precisely where I would like to start my remarks, which are more of a clarifying than of a dissenting character.

After World War II, historians felt uneasy when dealing with important personalities. However, the individual leader was not completely banished from center stage, although most preferred to make him represent an idea, a social class, or an economic interest. This time the debate was not mainly between Marxists and anti-Marxists. Other controversies were at work, and two of them may be mentioned briefly. At first psychohistory seemed to have won the day. How else should one explain the great dictators in World War II or the charismatic leaders of the third world? But psychohistory soon went out of fashion, and only a few great books—like Erik M. Erikson's *Young Man Luther* (1958)—made an impact. After Freud, historians were aware that an individual's

11. A. Momigliano, *JRS* 30 (1940) 75–80 (= id. [1960: supra n. 2] 407–16).
12. E.g., C. Wirszubski, *Libertas as a Political Idea in the Late Republic and Early Principate* (Cambridge 1950); G. Bowersock, *Augustus and the Greek World* (Oxford 1965); Z. Yavetz, *Plebs and Princeps* (Oxford 1969; reprint New Brunswick 1988).

personality was indeed shaped in the first few years of his life although it continued its evolution in successive crises through adolescence to maturity. But since trustworthy evidence for those early periods in the lives of their heroes was rarely available, the issue could not be pursued.

Traditional historians could not admit in their midst a study that derived its facts from psychoanalysis, and they expressed strong reservations when even a scholar like Erikson suggested accepting half legend as half history. Psychohistorians considered themselves first of all clinicians, and as such they found nothing wrong in recognizing a major trend even where the facts were not all available. Erikson's proviso that a suspect and doubtful episode should be accepted as history only when it did not contradict other well-established facts was unfortunately disregarded by many psychohistorians; therefore the general scepticism toward the method prevails. Other traditional historians, aware of their incompetence in psychology, accepted Namier's warning not to let loose the unqualified practitioner, not even on the dead, and agreed with him that a mere smattering of psychology was likely to result in superficial, hasty judgments framed in nauseating jargon.

The revival of the worship of the anti-hero, especially after the Vietnam War, was another cause for the decline of the great man. But Vietnam and the aversion to dictatorships after World War II alone cannot explain the renewed decline of the hero in history. Marcel Proust's and James Joyce's influence on anti-hero worship should not be underestimated. *À la recherche du temps perdu* and *Ulysses* destroyed the individual heroism in imaginative creation just as Fernand Braudel's *The Mediterranean and the Mediterranean World in the Age of Philip II* dismissed narrative as superficial, and individuals as not important in history. Lack of concern for the striking of a moral balance became common in history books, and the exercise of individual free will ceased to be the supremely interesting feature of human behavior. Economic determinism and historical materialism had little to do with these trends; nevertheless the description of the individual suffered yet another setback in history books. The individual in history (and in films) looked better, more human, and more trustworthy when he was depicted as flying like a beetle rather than like an eagle.

My proposal is to return to the old and salutary compromise and to leave the problem of deciding in what situation the character of the leader could significantly affect the historical trends to the historians. I firmly believe that the establishment of the principate was one of those situations and that, therefore, the personality of the *princeps* is of prime importance.

A careful reading of *The Roman Revolution* should leave us convinced of Augustus' ability and greatness. Syme, however, having written the book in a period in which "dark conceptions of power and politics prevailed," decided to emphasize Augustus' greatness all the more sharply by "an unfriendly presentation." It was in the early thirties that Werner Schurr depicted Augustus as the "Führer" who redeemed Rome from "einer hundertjährigen Epoche der Zuchtlosigkeit und des Verfalls," and that Wilhelm Weber detected in Augustus not only "indogermanische Urkraft" but also "heilige Wut und Glaube an das beste Blut." [13]

As opposed to some of his epigones, who paraded their wit by humiliating others, Syme never disgraced a fellow scholar, wrong or frenzied as he may appear to have been. Alluding to Weber, Schurr, and perhaps others of their kind, he stressed only that it was "not necessary to praise political success or to idealize men who win wealth and honour through Civil War." He chose the Tacitean "vivid, solemn and suitably ambiguous" style, with the result that many of his humorous understatements (sometimes mixed with innuendoes) were misunderstood, especially when read in translation. Some scholars like Stier complained bitterly that in Syme's writings "schrumpft die Gestalt des Octavian";[14] others like Hammond were shocked by Syme's cynical remarks on the character of Augustus and defended fervently the sincerity of the first *princeps*.[15] Syme never took these objections seriously and cheerfully suggested abandoning such topics altogether and leaving them to moralists and casuists. This is precisely what happened. Many historians disregarded the personality of Augustus and contented themselves with depicting his character as puzzling, elusive, baffling, and inscrutable, like the sphinx engraved upon his signet ring.[16] In the back of their minds they assumed that the understanding of his personality did not matter very much. Instead they concentrated their efforts on analyzing society, institutions, and the economy.

In my own writings I have never underestimated the importance of

---

13. W. Schurr, *Augustus* (Lübeck 1934) 5; W. Weber, *Princeps,* vol. 1 (Stuttgart 1936) 99–100, 240.

14. H. E. Stier, "Augustusfriede und römische Klassik," *ANRW* 2.2 (1975) 3–54.

15. M. Hammond, "The Sincerity of Augustus," *HSCP* 69 (1965) 152.

16. Suet. *Aug.* 50.

social and economic factors,[17] but I have never been able to go along
with Syme's blurring of all personal characteristics of Pompey and Caesar, Antonius and Octavian. In his opinion there was no great difference
between Pompey and Caesar. "Had Pompey conquered in battle, he
would have been killed at the foot of his own statue, by honorable
men," [18] conjectures Syme, who in all other respects refrains rigidly from
speculation and prefers to depend on facts rather than on alleged intentions. Nor does he see a profound difference between Antonius and Octavian, even though a slight sympathy for Antonius on his part is discernible. His view is basically in keeping with the Ciceronian *dominatio
ab utroque quaesita est*[19] or the Tacitean *occultior non melior*,[20] and this
is where I disagree. My contention has always been that even if this were
true, the *existimatio* of Pompey and Caesar, Antonius and Octavian,
was completely different, and even if public opinion had been manipulated, what counted ultimately was the projection of their image rather
than their real character. Plutarch was right in explaining that when the
Romans realized that there was no other choice but an autocracy, they
preferred to take the bitter medicine from the hand of the most delicate
of doctors.[21]

In this paper I intend to show that only a man who could project the
image of a "delicate doctor" could guarantee the victory of the nonpolitical classes—of all those who were yearning to put an end to the
civil war. I admit that to assert that Augustus was the only man capable
of achieving this task is merely to state the outcome and make it seem
inevitable, and I also know that history written without an exploration
of lost and defeated alternatives is neither a full account of the past nor
a real explanation of what happened. No wonder that Eduard Meyer,
attempting to vindicate the "Principate of Pompey" wrote that "dem
Besiegten gerecht zu werden, ist eine der schwierigsten Aufgaben, die
dem Historiker gestellt sind." [22] Modern historians are still grappling
with the fate of a Trotsky or a Bukharin. It would therefore be a praise-
worthy attempt to put Antonius' personality into a more balanced perspective.[23] The sources, however, are hopelessly distorted, and on the
basis of the evidence one would have to agree with Syme that the truth

17. E.g., Yavetz (supra n. 12).
18. Syme (supra n. 5) 51.
19. Cic. *Att.* 8.11.
20. Tac. *Hist.* 2.38.
21. Plut. *Caes.* 28.5 (with reference to Pompey).
22. E. Meyer, *Caesars Monarchie und das Principat des Pompeius*[3] (Stuttgart 1922) 1.
23. See recently, J. Griffin, "Propertius and Antony," *JRS* 67 (1977) 17–26.

has been doubly buried: in erotic romance as well as in political mythology. Of the facts there is and was no authentic record.[24]

One example, picked at random, will prove the point. During the night of 15–16 March 44 B.C. Lepidus succeeded in safeguarding his firm control over the army. According to a contemporary source it seems that a bold military coup would have left no opening for the conspirators.[25] But nothing of this kind occurred, mainly because among the Caesarians themselves there was no consensus. Lepidus and Balbus recommended immediate action. Antonius, on the other hand, suggested a compromise with the conspirators and was supported by Hirtius. The question arises, why was Antonius more moderate? Nobody knows the true answer, and one guess is as plausible as another. Let me suggest four different conjectures:

1. On 15 March 44 B.C. Antonius was more afraid of Lepidus than of Brutus and Cassius. Lepidus was already in command of the army, and Antonius, who had not yet organized his following, did not trust him. He preferred, therefore, a deal with the conspirators.

2. Compromise suited Antonius' character better than anything else. He had no political convictions, and his activities were never guided by moral principles. He was basically a *bon viveur,* and all he was striving to do was to save his own skin and his consulate.

3. On the contrary, Antonius was no playboy, but rather a sagacious politician who planned his steps carefully and prudently. A compromise with Brutus and Cassius was supposed to be only a tactical move. His final aim was to destroy them, but he had first to drive them out of Italy without making them too suspicious. Meanwhile he intended to put his hand on an important proconsular province from which he could control Rome without difficulty. In order to achieve this goal, he had to appear moderate, law-abiding, and loyal to the authority of the senate. A compromise with the conspirators served as a temporary goal but was by no means his final aim.

4. The whole story should be dismissed because there is no truth in it: Augustan propaganda crept into Nicolaus' narrative and was obviously intended to create an anti-Caesarian image of Antonius. For future generations, as for public consumption in the present, only Augustus had to appear as *pius* to Caesar's memory. Antonius had to be

24. Syme (supra n. 5) 271.
25. Nic. Dam. frag. 27 (106).

portrayed as a disloyal adjutant who had betrayed his master and benefactor less than twenty-four hours after the latter's death. No historian,
therefore, should take seriously a story based on vicious propaganda
and malicious gossip.

Antonius lost, and *Vae victis!* By and large we are left with an image
of a man who whenever faced with a problem first of all did nothing;
afterwards did something, but too little; later, a little bit more, but not
enough; then he did quite a lot, but hastily; and eventually he did everything, but too late. No wonder that he became an easy prey to Augustus,
and thus we are left with the victor.

III

The personality of Augustus, however, has never sparked the imagination of writers or historians. From Suetonius' biography, we get the picture of a man who, on the surface at least, cuts a rather dull figure. He
acquired his influence over the army by having been adopted by Julius
Caesar and not through any particular courage or daring of his own. He
made his way into the aristocracy through a felicitous match. All in all,
he was a modest man, worked hard all his life, and made do with only
seven hours of sleep a night. He ate little, nourished for the most part
by simple foods—black bread, small fish, meat, cheese, and fruit,
mainly dates and grapes. He observed moderation too in his consumption of wine. He dressed without ostentation, and his homes were relatively unpretentious. Besides his palace on the Palatine, he possessed
only three villas (in Lanuvium, Tibur, and Capri). Cicero had eight!

He was traditional and conservative, preferring to see his children
dead than see them live in moral disgrace.[26] He admired the young Cato,
who claimed that only someone who adhered to the status quo and opposed innovations was a good man and a good citizen, and like the old
Cato he believed that the commonwealth of Rome rested on ancient
customs and men of virtue.[27] He was a ruler who made efforts to bring
ancient dress back to Rome, who revived obsolete priesthoods, and who
spared no pains to make family life and the raising of children the focal
point of Roman life.

Some would stop here and stress that it was his conservatism that

---

26. *Dicta* 41 Malcovati (infra n. 29; henceforth Malcovati) = Suet. *Aug.* 65.2.
27. Malcovati 62 = Macrob. *Sat.* 2.4.18.

helped him win the day. Augustus' innovations were accepted because his attachment to traditional behavior and values was public knowledge, and because he refrained from offending old sensibilities.[28] All in all, his biography is not particularly breathtaking, and his character not particularly complex. He was impulsive and cruel in his youth; sensible, forgiving, and accommodating at the height of his power; and suspicious in old age. However, there is more than that in our sources, and yet another approach is open to us: "As people express themselves—so they are" ("Wie Menschen sich ausdrücken, so sind sie"), wrote Karl Marx and Friedrich Engels in their essay "German Ideology." Even if this view is only partially correct, we can learn a good deal about Augustus from the things he said, from the statements he made, and especially from his slips of tongue, some spontaneous, some carefully planned and prepared in advance. It is surprising that psychologists have not paid more attention to the considerable material so diligently gathered in Malcovati's volume, which contains not only Augustus' *dicta* and *apophthegmata*,[29] but also his personal letters, his orders to various governors, and even fragments of the poems he wrote in his leisure time, especially when he was sitting in his bath. Maybe Augustus struck psychologists as too normal, and they put their efforts into analyzing the more complex and disturbed personalities of Tiberius, Caligula, and Nero. But I believe that Augustus is no less fascinating.

It should be said from the outset that of course Augustus' *dicta* must be taken with a grain of salt. Only rarely do we find a word-for-word quotation of what he actually said. For the most part, we have paraphrases by people who heard his remarks, sometimes directly, sometimes through rumor. It is also difficult to establish the chronology of his statements with any certainty or to know whether they were attributed to him during his lifetime or after he died. But since I am not psychoanalyzing Augustus, I shall discuss only those statements that are backed by Augustus' actions and surviving letters, for it is clear that certain statements were attributed to him by chance on the principle *se non e vero e ben trovato*.

For our purposes, however, it does not matter whether Augustus ac-

28. Centuries later Kemal Ataturk was successful because he did not speak of a Christian calendar, but of an international one; not of the Swiss civil code, which he adopted in 1926, but of the Turkish one; not of the Latin alphabet, which supplanted the Arabic one, but of the Turkish alphabet; and the new dress, which forbade the turban and the fez, was depicted as the "civilized dress, and not as the European dress." See Dankwart A. Rustow, "Ataturk as Founder of State," *Daedalus* 97 (Summer 1968) 793–828.

29. E. Malcovati, *Imperatoris Caesaris Augusti operum fragmenta*[5] (Turin 1969).

tually said certain things, whether propagandists spread intentional rumors of one sort or another, or whether the public attributed to him
certain assertions because they believed that he was capable of making
them—just as it does not matter whether Louis XIV really said, "L'état,
c'est moi." What matters is that these words were attributed to Louis
XIV and not to Louis XVI. It is with Augustus' public image that we are
concerned. From this point of view, his *dicta* and *apophthegmata* are of
primary importance. They reveal very interesting character traits,
which, in my opinion, are undoubtedly his. Dr. Johnson's remark that
anecdotes are essentially secret history is relevant here.

The young Octavian, who entered the political arena in 44 B.C.,
when he was only nineteen years old, was not content simply to bask in
the inherited glory of his adopted father. From the very first, he made it
clear that he knew where he was going. From the very beginning, his
decisiveness was accompanied by tact, modesty, and deliberation, but
he was always resolute. Upon his arrival in Rome in the spring of 44, he
immediately noticed the fact that Antonius failed to show him the
proper respect and did not come out to receive him. The people in his
entourage felt deeply insulted, but the naive and (supposedly) politically
inexperienced young man calmed them down and said that he would
visit Antonius first, as it was proper for a young man to visit an older
man or for a private individual to visit a consul (Antonius was consul in
44). The young man took it upon himself to pay respects to the senate;
but along with that, he vowed to avenge the murder of Julius Caesar,
come what may, and affirmed that he would rather die than give up his
self-respect. He even quoted the passage from Homer in which Achilles
tells his mother, Thetis, of his desire to avenge the death of his friend
Patroclus.[30] But Julius Caesar was more than a comrade in arms; he was
Octavian's adoptive father, who had been criminally murdered in the
senate. Thus Octavian undertook to act with all the more determination. In order to attain his goal, he made alliances and broke them,
made friends and afterwards sacrificed them without batting an eyelid;
if betrayal served his end, he did not hesitate to betray. He did not trust
anyone, but people also distrusted him. When he learned that Cicero
said of him, "That young man should be lauded, glorified, and eliminated,"[31] Augustus remarked spontaneously that he was in no hurry to
get to the next world. Cicero was known for his poisonous wit, and even

30. Malcovati 47 = App. *BC* iv.3.13. Cf. Hom. *Il.* 18.98.
31. Malcovati 1 = Cic. *Fam.* 11.20.1 (my translation).

if he never said that, it was easy enough to believe that he did. The truth was that Cicero distrusted Octavian, but respected his determination, energy, and talent for organization, and wrote as much in his letters.[32]

Octavian pursued his goals methodically and ruthlessly. After Philippi, he ordered that Brutus' head be cut off and placed at the foot of Julius Caesar's statue. Along similar lines, he refused to permit the burial of one of his enemies. "The birds of prey will take care of that," [33] he said. The cruelty of the young Octavian during the years when he was struggling for power was well known, and he wrote his autobiography in order to perpetuate that image. Thus it is no wonder that during the Perusine War it was said that when one of his enemies was pleading with him and begging him to spare his life, he replied, "He must die." [34] This character trait never changed. He acted on reason and never allowed his emotions to sway him. Only after the battle of Actium did he try to create the image of a softhearted and merciful ruler who would rather mete out light punishments than heavy ones, and rather pardon than punish. But he always boasted of his tenacity and of the immense influence that he had on old people even when he was still young. Once when he was trying to quiet a group of noisy and rebellious young people, he addressed them with the following words: "Listen, young men, to an old man; old men listened to him when he was young." [35] He very much admired the old Athenodoros, who taught him to recite the twenty-four letters of the alphabet before saying anything in anger. Augustus learned from him the principle that silence generates wisdom.[36]

Augustus did not always succeed in acting on this principle, and on more than one occasion was sorry that he did not restrain his anger. He needlessly burst out in the senate when his daughter Julia's shameful conduct was publicly discussed, and was sorry afterwards that he had not kept quiet about it. He claimed that if Agrippa or Maecenas had been alive, they would not have permitted him to act so hastily.[37]

In upper-class Rome, traditional *gravitas* was very much admired and respected. Every kind of quick or impulsive behavior was held to be superficial and frivolous (*levitas*). For this reason, Augustus was not im-

32. E.g., Cic. *Att.* 16.8.1, 9.1, 11.6.
33. Malcovati 27 = Suet. *Aug.* 13.1.
34. Malcovati 28 = Suet. *Aug.* 15; cf. App. *BC* iv.4.8; Sen. *Clem.* 1.10.4.
35. Malcovati 21 = Plut. *Apophth. Aug.* 12.
36. Malcovati 17 = Plut. *Apophth. Aug.* 7. One is reminded of Calvin Coolidge: "The things I never say never get me into trouble" and "I do not recall any candidate for president that ever injured himself very much by not talking."
37. Malcovati 7 = Sen. *Ben.* 6.32.1.

pressed by the quick responses of talented people, such as the brilliant lawyers Vinicius and Haterius. He was opposed to all hasty measures and was amazed that Alexander of Macedon showed no respect for the dull routine of daily management.[38] As opposed to Marinetti's "Velocizzare l'Italia," *Festina lente* was Augustus' motto.[39] He preferred cautious commanders to bold ones[40] and assumed that only that is done quickly enough which is done thoroughly enough. Anyone who is familiar with Augustus' cautious foreign policy can well believe that Augustus compared people who pursued rapid conquests at great risk to a fisherman who fished with a golden hook attached to his fishing rod: if he lost the hook, no catch would be big enough to compensate him.[41]

The more secure Augustus felt, the more tolerant he became of his enemies and opponents, especially those who were no longer alive and could not endanger his position. He praised Cicero to his grandchildren[42] and did not object to the erection of a statue of Brutus in Mediolanum.[43] Gradually but consistently he distanced himself from the memory of Julius Caesar. Virgil could put the major part of the blame for the outbreak of the civil war on Caesar without worry, and Livy did not have to summon up a great deal of courage when he showered praises on Pompey in his writings.[44]

But Augustus did not proceed with great severity against living opponents either, as long as they contented themselves with verbal criticism and refrained from action. In a letter to Tiberius he wrote:

> My dear Tiberius, do not be carried away by the ardor of youth in this matter, or take it too much to heart that anyone speak evil of me. We must be content—if we can stop anyone from doing evil to us.[45]

Tacitus defined the situation succinctly but inexactly: "Deeds were challenged; words went unpunished." [46] Seneca was more precise when he said that although critics of the regime were not punished, the administration did not make their lives easy. Augustus' tolerance had clear boundaries: open critics were under continuous surveillance and thus neutralized; anonymous detractors were mercilessly persecuted. Asinius

38. Malcovati 18 = Plut. *Apophth. Aug.* 8.
39. Malcovati 32 = Suet. *Aug.* 25.4; Gell. *NA* 10.11.5.
40. Quoting Eur. *Phoen.* 559.
41. Malcovati 32 = Suet. *Aug.* 25.4.
42. Malcovati 23 = Plut. *Cic.* 49.3.
43. Malcovati 24 = Plut. *Comp. Dion. et Brut.* 5.2.
44. Malcovati 26. Cf. Tac. *Ann.* 4.34.3.
45. Suet. *Aug.* 51.2 = Malcovati, *Epist.* 8. Cf. Sen. *Ira* 3.23.4, *Ben.* 3.27; Suet. *Aug.* 54.
46. Tac. *Ann.* 1.72.

Pollio was quite accurate in remarking that "it is not easy to write against a man who has all the means of punishment at his disposal" (*non est enim facile in eum scribere, qui potest proscribere*).[47] In public, Augustus pretended that he would never dream of undermining freedom of speech. Asinius Pollio knew that Augustus was not happy with the fact that one of his critics, Timagenes, took shelter in his (Pollio's) house, and he asked Augustus for an explicit order to throw him out. Augustus refused and said, "Do you expect that kind of order from me?"[48]

It has long been recognized that autocratic leadership should be exercised by stealth, and that the ability to conceal his activities is a major asset to a dictator. Indeed, the tendency to dissimulate was a prominent feature of Augustus' personality, and it marked his entire reign. Throughout, the *princeps* studiously avoided committing himself unequivocally on various subjects, and always preferred ambiguous formulations to clear ones. Once someone asked him whether in his opinion Theodotos (procurator of Sicily) was bald or a thief, and he answered, "Yes!"[49] He believed that *eloquentia* was the skill of hiding (*abscondere*) one's eloquence rather than its public demonstration.[50] And indeed this was the policy that guided him throughout his life: to acquire as much power as possible but not to display it. Basically Augustus saw no harm in putting up a front. Shortly before he died, he asked for a mirror and ordered that his hair be combed and his sagging jaws straightened out; he allowed his family and friends to approach, asked them whether he played his part in the play of life well, and closed in Greek: "If I acted well, applaud me and send me off with unanimous praise."[51]

There is no need to accept Tacitus' view that equivocation is no more than reprehensible hypocrisy. Not all dissembling is reprehensible. Men do not appeal to standards no one observes, and hypocrisy serves no purpose where values are not to be found so (Brunt). It has not yet been proven that equivocation accompanied by tact is worse than bluntness, sincere and truthful as it may be. The ambiguity in Bismarck's agreements ensured peace in Europe between 1870 and 1907. The blunt and

47. Macrob. *Sat.* 2.4.21.
48. Malcovati 5 = Sen. *Ira* 3.23.4.
49. Malcovati 16.
50. Malcovati 4.
51. Malcovati 44 = Suet. *Aug.* 99.1. See O. Hirschfeld, "Augustus und sein Mimus vitae," *WS* 5 (1883) 116–19; U. von Wilamowitz = Möllendorff, "Res Gestae Divi Augusti," *Hermes* 21 (1886) 623–27.

hurtful frankness of Wilhelm II was one of the causes of World War I. Should one in fact accuse Augustus of hypocrisy because he was satisfied with the title of *princeps* and firmly refused titles such as dictator, king, and god, even though it was clear to everyone that he was the one and only absolute ruler?

Little can be learned from Augustus' sayings about the judicial and philosophical foundations of the principate, but a great deal can be learned from them about his political behavior. Augustus used to soften his actions with a good joke and to sweeten the pill for his victims with his sense of humor. Without making a psychological analysis of humor, the ancients well understood the purpose of a ruler's humor. In discussing Vespasian, Suetonius explained:

> He particularly resorted to witticisms, . . . seeking to diminish their odium by some jocose saying, and to turn them into a jest.[52]

Modern sociologists agree that jokes usually aim to puncture a pose, a lie, or a reputation.

In fact, Augustus' sense of humor was very successful and popular with the masses—for three reasons. First, it was known that the *princeps* could take a joke against himself, provided it hit the mark but was not too nasty. Second, it was known that he could laugh at himself. Third, his jokes were meant to show off his own wit rather than to hurt others, and most of the time enabled him to get out of a sticky situation gracefully, without doing very much harm to anyone.

A few examples bring home the point. Once Augustus told a Roman knight that it wasn't nice to eat and drink during a play. "When I want to have my fill," commented Augustus, "I go home." "But your seat is reserved," answered the knight, "and you don't have to worry that someone will take it."[53] On another occasion he met a man who looked almost exactly like himself and might have been mistaken for his twin brother. "Tell me," Augustus asked (apparently unaffected by the laughter of the people around him), "has your mother ever been to Rome?" "My mother has never visited Rome," the man answered, "but my father came here frequently."[54]

Augustus tried his hand at poetry and wrote *fescenni* for fun, and even a tragedy called *Ajax*. But he did not take his play seriously and threw it out. Since he did most of his writing in the bath, he said that his

52. Suet. *Vesp.* 23.
53. Malcovati 9 = Quint. *Inst.* 6.3.63.
54. Macrob. *Sat.* 2.4.19.

Ajax "fell on the sponge." [55] His ability to laugh at himself enabled him to laugh harder at others. Roman humor was for the most part crude and vulgar, and it was quite acceptable to joke about parts of the body and at the expense of the handicapped. Augustus added nothing new here. He brought with him from his hometown in Italy conservatism, superstition, and an uncouth sense of humor that sometimes shocked the Roman aristocracy, just as the jokes of Truman, Johnson, and Krushchev were thorns in the sides of their more cultivated contemporaries. Augustus readily made fun of hunchbacks, of men who suffered from gout, and of women with white hair and bald spots. But over the years, he became more cultivated and civilized. He studied and read, he became familiar with literature and Greek philosophy, and even though he did not display his erudition, he knew how to use just the right quotations from Homer and Euripides, Ennius and Virgil, in a way that commanded respect. Thanks to his extensive contacts with writers, poets, and artists, his taste became more refined and he forbade jokes that were not in good taste. He developed an impressive feeling for language, and he was particularly fond of puns and wordplay. It makes sense, therefore, that his joke that it was easier to survive as Herod's pig than as Herod's son was said in Greek and not in Latin.[56] He enjoyed teasing his friends with good humor and without any maliciousness. He also joked about things that annoyed but did not overly disturb him. For example, he once ordered a purple garment, and when the merchant brought it, Augustus remarked that the color was too dark. "Hold it up higher and look at it from below," the merchant suggested, "and the color won't seem so dark." Augustus answered, "Do I have to stroll on the roof of my house so that the citizens of Rome can say I am properly dressed?" [57] Sometimes he joked instead of admonishing, and it is clear that he made his point and achieved his purpose without hurt or insult. Once he was informed that a date tree was growing on the altar that had been built in his honor in Tarraco. "This is incontestable proof," commented Augustus, "of how often you make sacrifices on the altar." [58] Another time he dined with Rhoemetalces, the king of Thrace, who had betrayed Antony and joined his camp. While he was drinking to his heart's content, the king let his tongue run and made a few reproachful comments about his new ally. Augustus turned to one of the

---

55. Suet. *Aug.* 85.2; Macrob. *Sat.* 2.4.1.
56. Malcovati 56 = Macrob. *Sat.* 2.4.10, 2.4.11; Gell. *NA* 10.24.1.
57. Malcovati 58 = Macrob. *Sat.* 2.4.14.
58. Malcovati 12 = Quint. *Inst.* 6.3.77.

other kings present and remarked in a loud voice, "I like treachery, but I don't praise traitors."[59]

Augustus also used humor against people who tried to take advantage of his liking for jokes in order to extract undeserved favors from him. Once Pacuvius Taurus approached him and asked him for a present, backing up his request with the argument that there were rumors circulating that the gift had already been given and now Augustus had no choice but to make them good. Augustus told him, "Don't you believe in rumors!"[60] Another time he was approached by an officer who had committed an offense and was dismissed from the army. The officer asked Augustus, "How will I explain this to my father?" and Augustus replied, "Tell him you got sick of me and that you don't like me anymore."[61] Another officer who had been fired asked him for additional salary so that he could tell everyone that he quit of his own free will. "Tell everyone that you received the salary," Augustus told him, "and I won't deny it."[62]

Nor is the famous Vedius Pollio story to be interpreted as a sign of malicious behavior. Vedius Pollio, who was famous for his wealth and notorious for his cruelty, once entertained Augustus at his home. It so happened that one of his slaves, while serving the guests, broke a crystal goblet. Pollio immediately ordered that the slave be thrown to his lampreys, which had been trained to eat men. The slave fell on his knees before Augustus and supplicated. Augustus tried at first to persuade Pollio to pardon the slave, but Pollio paid no heed to him. Then Augustus requested that the rest of the drinking vessels of the like sort be brought, and when they were brought ordered them to be broken. Only then did Pollio pardon his slave, for he could not punish him for what the emperor also had done.[63] Augustus was Pollio's *princeps,* not his master. He could suggest and advise, not command. The "hint" was costly, but it was part of the game.

IV

It is time for some conclusions. I have dealt elsewhere at some length with the self-representation of Augustus in his autobiography and in his

---

59. Malcovati 15 = Plut. *Apophth. Aug.* 2.
60. Malcovati 50 = Macrob. *Sat.* 2.4.4.
61. Malcovati 10 = Quint. *Inst.* 6.3.64
62. Malcovati 51 = Macrob. *Sat.* 2.4.5.
63. Dio 54.23.2–3.

Res Gestae,[64] and there is no need to repeat the essentials here. Let me just reiterate that in his self-representation, Augustus underscored mainly his *humanitas,* which should be interpreted as it is by the younger Pliny as the gift of endearing oneself to the lowly while at the same time winning the affection of the eminent.[65] When Cicero used the phrase *nisi multis condimentis humanitatis mitigaretur,* he intended to submit that when one must swallow a bitter pill, it is better to have it coated with the honey of kindness.[66] It is not difficult to show that this was precisely the method of Augustus in his contacts with various social groups. His tact served him well in his dealings with the upper classes. When he recommended his sons for positions, he would add, supposedly out of modesty, "if they are deserving,"[67] even though he was certain that his recommendations would be accepted without objection. His patience made it easy for him to attend long and boring meetings of the senate and listen to silly and incompetent speeches,[68] which would have driven mad a man of Julius Caesar's type. Only a tactful man like Augustus could succeed in putting the senators in charge of the traffic lights of the empire—with the assurance that green lights would be turned on whenever his carriage was about to go through.

He got what he wanted from writers and poets, without giving explicit orders.[69] His behavior toward the common people won them over, for, in contrast to Julius Caesar, Augustus loved the games, admitted it openly, and acted accordingly. He never dictated letters during a circus performance,[70] because he kept in mind the most important principle of Roman political behavior: *Idem est quod datur, sed interest quomodo detur.*[71] He hated people who made unreasonable requests of him; therefore he did not pander to the masses in a cheap way and never gave in to extortion. He did only what he promised to do, no less and no more.[72] This was a remarkable achievement, which demanded the utmost tact, flexibility, patience, and moderation—four qualities that were conspicuous by their absence in Julius Caesar's political behav-

64. Z. Yavetz, "The *Res Gestae* and Augustus' Public Image," in Millar and Segal (supra n. 3) 1–36.
65. Pliny *Ep.* 9.5.
66. Cic. *Qfr.* 1.1.21.
67. Malcovati 38 = Suet. *Aug.* 56.2.
68. Suet. *Aug.* 54.
69. See J. Griffin, "Augustus and the Poets: 'Caesar qui cogere posset,' " in Millar and Segal (supra n. 3) 189–218; see also G. Williams' contribution to this volume.
70. For fuller details see Yavetz (supra n. 12) 83–102, esp. 100.
71. Sen. *Ben.* 2.6.1; cf. 1.11.1, 2.1.1.
72. Malcovati 36 = Suet. *Aug.* 42.1.

ior.[73] I dare say that Julius Caesar tried to rape Rome and therefore failed. Augustus seduced Rome and therefore succeeded. This is the only meaning of *dulcedine otii cunctos pellexit*.[74]

Most *dicta* and *apophthegmata* quoted in this paper shed light on the four qualities mentioned above and clearly indicate that the name of the game in the Augustan principate was moderation, or to use the words of Horace, the most Augustan of poets, *est modus in rebus*.[75] The poet believed that there must be something between extravagant wealth and miserable poverty, just as there was a golden mean between respectable matrons and street whores, between castration and adultery, between one who smells like a scent box and one who stinks like a goat.[76] I cannot agree with "topos hunters" who dismiss Horace's *aurea mediocritas* as just an empty motif decorating the writings of many an author, from Diogenes Laertius to Lucretius, from Maimonides to Nietzsche,[77] and having nothing to do with real life. I am convinced that the golden mean enabled Horace to adapt to a sane eclecticism, formulated in his famous *nullius addictus iurare in verba magistri*,[78] to be at home with imaginative Greeks and rational Romans alike,[79] to criticize the regime under which he lived without severing his intimate relationship with the head of state,[80] and to praise Augustus by artfully disguising his admiration for him. Just as Horace's modest villa in Sabinum, with a garden, a spring, a little wood (*nihil amplius oro*),[81] was the sane compromise between wasteful extravagance and petty miserliness, so was the principate for Augustus the *aurea mediocritas* between a dictatorship à la Caesar or à la Sulla and a *libertas* à la Cicero or à la Brutus.

There is one more point to be made. It is not easy to translate into Latin a phrase like "He behaved tactfully." *Lepide et verecunde,* I would suggest, conveys it best. The Latin phrase comes from the following

73. Z. Yavetz, *Julius Caesar and His Public Image* (London 1983).
74. Tac. *Ann.* 1.2.
75. Hor. *Sat.* 1.1.106.
76. Hor. *Sat.* 2.2.53–69, 1.2.28–30 etc.; cf. esp. *Epist.* 1.18.9.
77. Believers in Nietzsche's "extremism" would be surprised to read

> Bleib nicht auf ebenem Feld,
> Steig nicht zu hoch hinaus,
> Am schönsten sieht die Welt
> Von halber Höhe aus.
>   ("Weltklugheit"
>   in *Fröhliche Wissenschaft*)

78. Hor. *Epist.* 1.1.14
79. Hor. *Ars* 323.
80. Hor. *Sat.* 2.1.60ff. (like Lucilius).
81. Hor. *Sat.* 2.6.1–4.

story by Gellius. Aristotle refused to nominate his successor unequivocally since both Theophrastus from Lesbos and Eudemus from Rhodes were excellent. Eventually he found a way out. He asked for a good foreign wine either from Rhodes or from Lesbos. He tasted the Rhodian first and said, "This is a truly sound and pleasant wine (*firmum vinum et iucundum*). Then he tasted the Lesbian wine and said, "Both are very good indeed, but the Lesbian is sweeter." No one doubted that he intended to make clear that Theophrastus was his choice, but Gellius adds that he conveyed his message *lepide et verecunde;*[82] and this was Augustus' style.

Augustus worked hard to achieve his goal, and one should not underestimate the fact that he managed to witness the birth of the granddaughter of his granddaughter and to die of old age in his own bed. (By contrast, Caesar and Pompey, Brutus and Cassius, Antonius and Cicero, Caligula and Nero, all met violent deaths.) This in itself is no mean achievement, and I do not think that Syme would have disagreed with my thesis regarding the importance of Augustus' moderation.[83] Therefore, this paper should not be considered a reassessment of Syme's Augustus; it represents rather a shift in emphasis. I do not think that one should apologize for underscoring Augustus' greatness. An unfriendly presentation misses the point and might be misunderstood. By tactful and patient hard work Augustus succeeded in shaping a new *form* of government, while a great deal of the *content* was left to the personalities of the rulers to come. It is impossible, therefore, to speak in general terms of the early principate by treating mainly law, institutions, economy, and society without paying adequate attention to the personalities of the various *principes*. It is precisely in this area that Augustus' greatness is to be sought, but this was at the same time the source of the weakness of his legacy.[84]

82. Gell. *NA* 13.5.
83. R. Syme, *The Augustan Aristocracy* (Oxford 1986) 439–54.
84. I would like to express my thanks to my friend K. Raaflaub, who read the manuscript of this paper, discussed it with me, and made very valuable suggestions.

Mommsen and Syme:
Law and Power in the Principate
of Augustus

Two scholars and two works of genius have defined for all time the battleground for our understanding of Rome and Augustus: Theodor Mommsen and Ronald Syme, *Römisches Staatsrecht* and *The Roman Revolution.* "Men and dynasties pass, but style abides," [1] and these two works are as dissimilar in style as they are in content. Are they also mutually exclusive, one wrong and the other right? Is there a middle ground between them, or do Mommsen and Syme perhaps illuminate two different aspects of the same phenomenon? Depending upon the method and the instrument of observation light comes out as a corpuscle or as a wave. But the new physics did not simply prove Newton wrong; it also showed that the world reveals itself to observers in guises that mechanistic physics was not capable of conjuring up or understanding. Depending upon whether we look through the prism of prosopography or the prism of law we arrive at one of two appearances of the principate, the vision of Syme or the vision of Mommsen, neither true or false in itself, and neither complete. It is otiose to ask what the

---

1. R. Syme, *Tacitus,* vol. 2 (Oxford 1958) 624.

principate was; in doing so we continue the tradition of Aristotle and the Scholastics, the pernicious preoccupation with definitions and the "essence" of things. It was the liberation from that tradition that gave us the achievements of modern science: we do not define things but ask how they behave.[2] Nature does not answer inane questions, nor does history. But neither scientist nor scholar lives in a void; the world in which we live impinges upon us, suggests questions, and colors perceptions.

"The menace of despotic power hung over Rome like a heavy cloud";[3] it also hung over the world of Syme. *The Roman Revolution* was published in the fatal year of 1939, in the month of September. Although conceived in tranquil Oxford, it was born amid the rising tide of Fascist charismatic dictatorships in Europe; and the scholarly environment was one of adulation of Augustus, which oozed from the sugar-coated commentaries on the Augustan poets, and from new and disquieting arrivals, books like *Princeps* by Wilhelm Weber (Stuttgart 1936), a murky harangue (stuffed with antiquarian footnotes) on the greatness of Augustus, his *Mut, Wut,* and *Kraft.* In 1937–38 the world beheld the extravagant celebrations of the *bimillenario augusteo,* of the old *impero* and the new.[4] Syme's book was a Tacitean reaction to his times,[5] and to cheerful credulity.

Weber's *Princeps* duly appears in Syme's bibliography, but when we arrive at the letter *M,* of all Mommsen's works we find only three listed: one volume of his *Gesammelte Schriften,* the edition of the *Res Gestae Divi Augusti,* and two volumes of his *Römische Forschungen.* The two *Meisterwerke, Römisches Staatsrecht* and *Römisches Strafrecht* are

2. Cf. K. Popper, *The Open Society and Its Enemies* (London, 1945), vol. 1, chap. 3, sect. 6; vol. 2, chap. 11, sect. 2 (= 5th ed., rev. [Princeton 1966] 1: 31–34; 2: 9–26); id., *Conjectures and Refutations* (London and New York 1962) 20–21, 103.

3. R. Syme, *The Roman Revolution* (Oxford 1939) 8.

4. "A memorable and alarming anniversary looms heavily upon us. The poet of the Italian nation was paid his due honours seven years ago, and now all Italy will conspire to acclaim the Princeps who was also Dux," so wrote R. Syme in a review published in *CR* 51 (1937) 194. On the celebrations of the *bimillenario augusteo* and on Mussolini's identification with Augustus, see the informative article (although written from a Marxist perspective) by M. Cagnetta, "Il mito di Augusto e la 'rivoluzione' fascista," *QS* 2 (1976) 139–81.

5. Cf. esp. A. Momigliano, *Terzo contributo alla storia degli studi classici e del mondo antico* (Rome 1966) 729–32 (originally published as the introduction to the Italian translation of *The Roman Revolution* [Turin 1962]); F. Millar, *JRS* 71 (1981) 146 (review of Syme's *Roman Papers,* vols. 1–2); W. Schmitthenner, "Caesar Augustus—Erfolg in der Geschichte," *Saeculum* 36 (1985) 286–91.

missing. No accident here. In his preface Syme professes his debt to five scholars:[6] to the "prosopographical studies of Münzer, Groag and Stein"[7] and in particular to Münzer's "supreme example and guidance";[8] further he acknowledges that his "opinions about the oath of allegiance of 32 B.C. and about the position of the Princeps as a party-leader naturally owe much" to Anton von Premerstein's "illuminating work" (*Vom Werden und Wesen des Prinzipats* [Munich 1937]);[9] finally, gracious mention is made of W. W. Tarn's "writings about Antonius and Cleopatra"—the only author writing in English so honored. Among the German, Swiss, and Austrian *lumina* Mommsen's name is again missing; but even more striking is the absence of Matthias Gelzer.

This fact did not escape the keen eye of Géza Alföldy. In *Sir Ronald Syme, "Die römische Revolution" und die deutsche Althistorie*,[10] Alföldy presents an excellent panorama of Syme's "reception" in Ger-

6. Syme (supra n. 3) VIII.

7. On Münzer (1868–1942, in a concentration camp), see now A. Kneppe and J. Wiesehöffer, *Friedrich Münzer: ein Althistoriker zwischen Kaiserreich und Nationalsozialismus* (Bonn 1983). Edmund Groag (1873–1945) and Arthur Stein (1871–1950) were, *inter alia*, the editors of the second edition of the *Prosopographia Imperii Romani* (1933–1952, vols. 1–4, fasc. 2), but to render *suum cuique* one should not forget that the impulse to elaborate the prosopography of the Roman Empire came from Theodor Mommsen (see his *praemonitum* to the first edition of vol. 1 of the *Prosopographia* [Berlin 1897]).

8. This guidance will have presumably emanated above all from Münzer's numerous prosopographical contributions to *RE* rather than from his *Römische Adelsparteien und Adelsfamilien* (Stuttgart 1920; reprint Darmstadt 1963)—a grand work but one in which there are already present the germs of the sickness that rendered hollow so many prosopographical constructs of the epigones, showing a tendency to infer the behavior of individuals from the behavior of groups. Such inferences have only statistical validity, not factual (cf. C. Nicolet, "Prosopographie et histoire sociale: Rome et l'Italie à l'époque républicaine," *Annales ESC* 25 [1970] 1209–28, esp. 1226; J. Linderski, *CP* 72 [1977] 55–56). On Münzer and Syme, see Millar (supra n. 5) 146 (he evaluates the *Adelsparteien* much more positively); Alföldy (infra n. 10) 18. Alföldy gives an engrossing assessment of Syme's prosopographical method in his review of Syme's *Roman Papers*, vols. 1–2, in *AJAH* 4 (1979 [1981]) 167–85.

9. AbhMünch N.F. no. 15 (1937). After the death of von Premerstein (1869–1935) the work was edited by Hans Volkmann. For an evaluation of von Premerstein's scholarly career, see K. Christ, *Römische Geschichte und Wissenschaftsgeschichte*, vol. 3 (Darmstadt 1983) 115–27.

10. SBHeid 1983, no. 1. Cf. Inez Stahlmann, *Imperator Caesar Augustus: Studien zur Geschichte des Principatsverständnisses in der deutschen Altertumswissenschaft* (Darmstadt 1988). For the enduring fascination with the Roman revolution and *The Roman Revolution*, both in the West and in the East, see the collection *La Rivoluzione Romana: Inchiesta tra gli antichisti*, Biblioteca di Labeo 6 (Naples 1982). On the concept of revolution in Mommsen (and Syme), see also A. Heuss, "Der Untergang der römischen Republik und das Problem der Revolution," *HZ* 182 (1956) 1–28; id., "Theodor Mommsen und die revolutionäre Struktur des römischen Kaisertums," *ANRW* 2.1 (1974) 77–90; E. Tornow, *Der Revolutionsbegriff und die späte römische Republik—eine Studie zur deutschen Geschichtsschreibung im 19. und 20. Jh.* (Frankfurt 1978) 9–34; J. F. McGlew, "Revolution and Freedom in Theodor Mommsen's *Römische Geschichte*," *Phoenix* 40 (1986 [1987]) 424–45.

many. Gelzer's monograph *Die Nobilität der römischen Republik* (Leipzig and Berlin 1912) has rightly been described as "a turning-point" in the study of Roman republican politics.[11] Whence this lack of acknowledgment? The acknowledgment comes, but it comes not in the preface but in a footnote. This is not as surprising as it might seem. Gelzer's express aim was to overcome Mommsen's legacy of a legal (or legalistic) approach to Roman society, but (as Alföldy points out) in contrast to the works of Münzer, *Die Nobilität* is not a prosopographical, but rather a structural, investigation of Roman oligarchy.[12] Syme explicitly accepts Gelzer's definition of the term *nobilis,* and writes, "Gelzer's lucid explanation of the character of Roman society and Roman politics, namely a nexus of personal obligations, is here followed closely." [13] Still, *The Roman Revolution* would have been possible without Gelzer; without Münzer, however, "it could hardly have existed." [14]

The implicit condemnation of *Staatsrecht* spells out the program: a plea for narrative history. Many years later, in a splendid essay, entitled "Three English Historians," Syme made plain that his sympathies lay "with the narrative historians Gibbon and Macauley, not with the saints and thinkers who are eager to use history for our amendment or punishment." [15] This is what Syme may think he wrote but it is not what he did, for *The Roman Revolution* is no more a work composed *sine ira et studio* (Tac. *Ann.* 1.1.6) than are the *Annals* of Tacitus or the *Decline and Fall* of Gibbon. To appreciate the winner,[16] it was written from the graves of the vanquished: it certainly "amended" both the writing of history and the history of Augustus. It punished credulity and moralistic obfuscation, rewarded clear thought and scepticism. This was achieved not by the impartial assemblage of facts but by selection and comment. The standard modern book on Caesar is Matthias Gelzer's renowned monograph.[17] Syme offers unqualified and instructive praise: "The au-

11. R. T. Ridley, "The Genesis of a Turning-Point: Gelzer's *Nobilität," Historia* 35 (1986) 474–502. Cf. also C. Simon, "Gelzer's *Nobilität der römischen Republik* als 'Wendepunkt,'" *Historia* 37 (1988) 222–40; and the contributions of J. Bleicken, C. Meier, and H. Strasburger in J. Bleicken, ed., *Matthias Gelzer und die römische Geschichte,* Frankfurter Althistorische Studien 9 (Kallmünz 1977).

12. Alföldy (supra n. 10) 14.

13. Syme (supra n. 3) 10, n. 3.

14. Ibid., VIII.

15. "Three English Historians: Gibbon, Macauley, Toynbee," *The Emory University Quarterly* 18 (1962) 140. On Gibbon and Syme, cf. G. Bowersock, "The Emperor of Roman History," *The New York Review of Books,* 6 March 1980, 10.

16. For a composite picture of Syme's Augustus, see Alföldy (supra n. 10) 21–22.

17. *Caesar, der Politiker und Staatsmann,* originally published in Stuttgart and Berlin in 1921. The last edition, the sixth, appeared in Wiesbaden in 1960 (trans. P. Needham [Oxford 1968]).

thor is not arguing a thesis; and remembering that history is narrative, not research, disputation, and the passing of judgments, he lets facts speak for themselves." [18] But "facts" never speak for themselves; it is the historian who weaves happenings into history.[19]

Eadem magistratuum vocabula (Tac. *Ann.* 1.3.7); "Names persist everywhere while substance changes." [20] In procedures and institutions the new Tacitus shows as little interest as the old. It is "the real and ultimate power" that "needs to be discovered." [21]

People, not institutions, are the natural subject of narrative history, and, for Syme, not all people but (almost solely) the governing class. Slaves and other lower classes may be boring indeed (unless they cause trouble),[22] but the soldiers? In the civil wars they were a ubiquitous and decisive fact of life—and death; in *The Roman Revolution,* however, they take a back seat to even those nobles who barely escaped their swords. We are offered no analysis of military institutions or of the *milites* as a social group—a surprising omission in a work devoted to the discovery of "the real and ultimate power" behind the veil of the principate.[23]

Syme's attitude toward institutions is perhaps best illustrated in his chapters 26 and 27, "The Government" and "The Cabinet" (the latter in its modernistic outlook reminiscent of the young Mommsen's linguistic innovations in his *Roman History*). Syme refers to the government and the cabinet as "they," not "it." He does not talk of the senate and its organization or of the *consilium principis,* but of the men who ruled and administered the empire, of the *principes* of the dying Republic, of Agrippa, Maecenas, and Livia (no less a man than they), of Marcellus, of Livia's sons, Drusus and Tiberius, and of that splendid and evanescent constellation of generals and administrators who helped Augustus to become a success in history, in all a procession of some forty names or so. Syme talks of men who led the armies of conquest and governed the provinces (whether in the name of the *princeps* or the senate) or who

18. *JRS* 32 (1944) 92 (= *Roman Papers,* vol. 1 [Oxford 1979] 149). Syme reviewed the enlarged and thoroughly revised second edition of 1941.
19. For a critique of the "positivist" understanding of "facts," see J. Linderski, "*Si vis pacem, para bellum:* Concepts of Defensive Imperialism," *PAAR* 29 (1984) 140–41.
20. Syme (supra n. 3) 406.
21. Ibid.
22. See the delightful pronouncement of Syme quoted by Alföldy (supra n. 10) 17.
23. Cf. now H. Botermann, *Die Soldaten und die römische Politik in der Zeit von Caesars Tod bis zur Begründung des zweiten Triumvirats* (Munich 1968); K. Raaflaub, "Die Militärreformen des Augustus und die politische Problematik des frühen Prinzipats," in G. Binder, ed., *Saeculum Augustum,* vol. 1 (Darmstadt 1987) 246–307.

supervised the treasury and took care of the aqueducts. He does not talk of the duties of provincial governors, of the voting arrangements in the senate, or of the *aerarium* or the *cura aquarum.*

In the Republic it is the consulars who are "the government"; in the new state of Augustus, "the Princeps, the members of his family and his personal adherents." The description of the working of the "Cabinet" ends thus quite appropriately on the theme of "a crisis . . . at the very core of the party," the scheme of Augustus to promote his adoptive grandsons, and Tiberius' morose retirement to Rhodes. That is not to say that after 6 B.C. the government ceased to function. Far from it. The "New State" endured, as it had after the death of Agrippa, for "it was well equipped with the ministers of the government," except that "the enemies of Tiberius . . . now had their turn" in "the syndicate of government." "The Succession" now becomes the prevailing aspect of the *arcanum imperii,* and it is to this murderous subject that Syme directs his pen. *Primum facinus novi imperii* (Tac. *Ann.* 1.6), the execution of Agrippa Postumus at the accession of Tiberius, prompts the author to a remark that may stand as an emblem of his perception of the political and the legal: "The arbitrary removal of a rival was no less essential to the Principate than the public conferment of legal and constitutional power." [24]

At the very outset of *The Roman Revolution* a phrase catches the eye: Augustus' "constitutional reign as acknowledged head of the Roman State." Augustus' title was, however, "specious"; the revival of republican institutions "convenient"; but "all that made no difference to the source and facts of power." To the source perhaps; but if it made no difference to the facts of power, why did Augustus promote the myth? At the same time, " 'the Restoration of the Republic' was not merely a solemn comedy, staged by a hypocrite." There is discrepancy here, and uneasiness. The letter of the law did not matter: "The Princeps stood pre-eminent . . . and not to be defined." [25] The same chapter and verse is repeated again and again, and rightly so, for there were, and are, students of the past who from willful blindness or good nature remove all unpleasantness from history and lose sight of that new, permanent, and overwhelming alien body, the *dux,* the *princeps,* the *imperator.*[26]

24. Syme (supra n. 3) 387, 414, 413, 401, 425, 439.
25. Ibid., 1, 2, 3.
26. Cf. ibid., 324, n.5 and the names of the scholars mentioned there; and see now, for example, H. Castritius, *Der römische Prinzipat als Republik* (Husum 1982), who maintains: "[Es] erweist sich als nötig der von Augustus restituierten römischen Republik eine juristische und politische Wirklichkeit—und dies für einen längeren Zeitraum—zuzuer-

When a contemporary ancient historian professes to be writing history, it is likely that what he really is engaged in is prosopography. This is in keeping with "Syme's law," according to which "in all ages, whatever the form and name of government, be it monarchy, republic or democracy, an oligarchy lurks behind the façade."[27] But the strange peculiarity of an authoritarian regime is that there is also a despot, cruel or benign. To find him one need not look behind the façade: he lurks everywhere.

The story of the young adventurer seizing power with the help of his acolytes and the army, and maintaining it through repression and intimidation, is banal enough; however, the story of the same adventurer creating in a great empire a new and enduring form of government is a theme of world history; for "power" cannot be separated from the form in which it is ensconced. Searching after a tangible "substance,"[28] we often forget that forms too are real and can be brushed aside only with great peril to the actors (they risk their lives, as Caesar the dictator can testify), and to the historians (they risk being drowned in "facts" and rhetoric).

An oracular pronouncement by Christian Meier in his Delphic *Res Publica Amissa* captures exquisitely the reality of the formal transition from the Republic to the principate: the crisis of the Republic was a crisis without a solution ("Krise ohne Alternative"), and as a result "die bestehende Ordnung [wurde] allmählich vernichtet, ohne dass sie verneint worden wäre" ("The existing order was destroyed without being negated"). No power existed that was able either to defend the whole of the old system or to create an entirely new one.[29] The "collective monarchy of the nobles" was abolished,[30] but the husk of the Republic endured, and it endured because it mattered: the shadow of the past provided legitimacy for the victor in the Roman Revolution, and for that reason the elusive form of the principate was also its substance.

---

kennen" (21). Castritius concludes that Cicero's declaration (*Leg. agr.* 2.17) that *omnes potestates, imperia, curationes ab universo populo Romano proficisci convenit* "galt . . . kaum weniger für die sog. Prinzipatszeit" (111).

27. Syme (supra n. 3) 7.

28. Ibid., VII: "The composition of the oligarchy of the government . . . emerges . . . as the binding link between the Republic and the Principate: it is something real and tangible, whatever may be the name or theory of the constitution."

29. C. Meier, *Res Publica Amissa* (Wiesbaden 1966) 201–5, and L, LIV, LVII in the new introduction to the reprint edition (Frankfurt 1980).

30. To borrow the phrase from Andreas Alföldi, *Caesariana* (Bonn 1984) 316 (= id., Review of *Die Vergottung Caesars*, by H. Gesche [Kallmünz 1968], *Phoenix* 24 [1970] 166).

It is reported that the notorious constitution of the Soviet Union of 1936, "the Stalin Constitution," as it was called in adulation, made a profound impression on Syme as a supreme sham.[31] To the citizens it guaranteed all sorts of civil liberties, and to the constituent republics the right to free and unconditional secession from the union. In the eyes of the West, and in plain fact, Stalin was a dictator, but the form of his constitutional rule as the acknowledged head of the Soviet state continued to baffle observers no less than the "constitutional reign" of Caesar Augustus. Like the Caesars, Stalin was the master of death; but to live and rule he had to remain a comrade within the party, as his Roman counterparts had to remain the *principes* within the *res publica*.

In his review of *The Roman Revolution* Arnaldo Momigliano remarks concisely and cogently that Syme considers "spiritual interests of the people . . . much less than their marriages." And he continues: "But if L. Caesar, cos. 64 B.C., wrote a book *de auspiciis,* Ap. Claudius Pulcher, cos. 54 B.C., a work on augural discipline . . . and if C. Scribonius Curio gave the name to the *logistoricus* of Varro *de deorum cultu* . . . , then the way to the religious policy of Augustus is clearer."[32] And as *religio* and *res publica* were in Rome intertwined, a consideration of the juristic and antiquarian preoccupations of the defeated, but not annihilated, republican aristocracy might have thrown light on the constitutional sensitivities of the principate. It will not do simply to discard Appius Claudius Pulcher as "superstitious" or Varro as "the old scholar" who "lacked style, intensity, a guiding idea,"[33] memorable as these phrases may be, and unjust; Varro was possessed of a quick wit and a robust sense of humor, and Appius Claudius was the guiding light for Cicero the augur.[34]

Men (and princes) sought enlightenment from the astrologers and believed in "the inexorable stars";[35] politically the *quattuor amplissima sacerdotia* were more important, and we should not treat the priests solely as quarries for the prosopographical hunt.[36] They were the ex-

31. Millar (supra n. 5) 146.

32. *JRS* 30 (1940) 76 (= *Secondo contributo alla storia degli studi classici e del mondo antico* [Rome 1960] 409).

33. Syme (supra n. 3) 45, 247.

34. Cf. J. Linderski, "Cicero and Roman Divination," *PP* 37 (1982 [1983]) 31–32; id., "The *Libri Reconditi,*" *HSCP* 89 (1985) 226–27.

35. Syme (supra n. 3) 9, 418.

36. Characteristically enough, in two recent books on the *fratres Arvales,* John Scheid's *Les Frères Arvales* (Paris 1975) and Ronald Syme's *Some Arval Brethren* (Oxford 1980), there are hundreds of names and (again to quote Momigliano) "marriages," but only scant word about doctrine and ritual.

pounders of a doctrine. And both Caesar the dictator and Augustus the *princeps* paid a great deal of attention to priestly doctrines.[37]

If *The Roman Revolution* is "a modern version of the book on Augustus that Tacitus failed to write,"[38] should we say that Mommsen's *Staatsrecht* is the modern version of a lost republican treatise *De magistratibus?*[39]

First of all we have to dispel the persistent and noxious myth that the Romans were not interested in public or "constitutional" law. They were; and if all the writings in this field had survived, they would have filled many Oxford or Teubner volumes.[40] But Sempronius Tuditanus, Valerius Messala, or Varro would feel much more at home in the *Römische Alterthümer* of Ludwig Lange (1825–85) than in Mommsen's *Staatsrecht*.[41] To judge from the extant fragments, Roman writings on sacral and public law were explanatory and antiquarian; and Lange was the last true antiquarian, and a resolute critic of Mommsen. Indeed, Mommsen's *Staatsrecht* was directed against this antiquarianism. It was an offspring of the *Pandektistik,* and it brilliantly applied the *begriffslogische Methode,* triumphant in civil law, to the description of the Roman state and its public law. As Mommsen put it himself, in the preface to the first edition of the first volume (p. ix); his was "die begrifflich geschlossene und auf consequent durchgeführten Grundgedanken wie auf festen Pfeilern ruhende Darlegung" ("the conceptually complete presentation, resting, as if on firm pillars, on notions that are basic and are consequently carried out").[42] The guiding notions of the *Staatsrecht*

37. Cf. J. Linderski, "The Augural Law," *ANRW* 2.16.3 (1986) 2181–84.

38. "Es ist die neuzeitliche Version des Buches über Augustus, das Tacitus nie geschrieben hat": A. Momigliano in his review of Syme's *Tacitus, Gnomon* 33 (1961) 55 (= id. [supra n. 5] 740).

39. I give here a synopsis of the editions of Mommsen's *Römisches Staatsrecht,* all published in Leipzig: vol. 1 (1871), 1² (1876), 1³ (1877); vol. 2, parts 1 and 2 (1874–1875), 2² (1877), 2³ (1887); vol. 3, parts 1 and 2 (1887–1888).

40. See the fragments of various "constitutional" writers in the collections of F. P. Bremer, *Iurisprudentiae Antehadrianae quae supersunt,* vols. 1 and 2, parts 1–2 (Leipzig 1896–1901); and H. Funaioli, *Grammaticae Romanae Fragmenta* (Leipzig 1907); and for Varro, B. Riposati, *Varro: De vita populi Romani fragmenta* (Milan 1939); and B. Cardauns, *M. Terentius Varro: Antiquitates Rerum Divinarum,* 2 vols. (Wiesbaden 1976). For a summary discussion of this literature, see E. Rawson, *Intellectual Life in the Late Roman Republic* (Baltimore 1985) esp. 201–14, 233–49, 298–316.

41. The editions of Lange's work: vol. 1³ (Berlin 1876; 1st ed., 1856); vol. 2³ (1879; 1st ed., 1862); vol. 3² (1876; 1st ed., 1871). For Lange's critique of Mommsen, see his review of vol. 1 of the *Staatsrecht,* in his *Kleine Schriften,* vol. 2 (Göttingen 1887) 154–65 (originally published in 1872). Against Mommsen's "dogmatisch-juristische Formulierung des römischen Staatsrechts" Lange upholds the validity of "historisch-antiquarische Forschung" (155). Even a cursory comparison of *Römische Alterthümer* and *Römisches Staatsrecht* demonstrates the enormous conceptual difference between these works—and the greatness of Mommsen's achievement.

42. Mommsen (supra n. 39) 1¹:IX.

were not (as Jochen Bleicken reminds us)[43] simply excogitated by
Mommsen, but derived directly from Roman sources. The pivots of the
Staatsrecht, the concepts of *magistratus* and *privatus*, of *imperium* and
auspicium, of *potestas* and *coercitio*, are all Roman notions familiar to
every reader of Latin literature.

But legal notions are often a poor guide to history, and nowhere is
this more glaringly obvious than in Mommsen's treatment of the institution of the principate. The second volume of the *Staatsrecht* treats of
"die einzelnen Magistraturen" ("the individual magistracies"). It begins
with the kingdom and ends with the principate. That *princeps qua princeps* was a magistrate is dubious,[44] but a special fury of criticism today
greets Mommsen's theory of dyarchy, the co-rule of the princeps and the
senate.[45] This criticism is based on a grievous misunderstanding. The
accusers depict Mommsen as oblivious to the historical and social realities of the empire, a picture neither likely nor reasonable. Where the
source of power lay Mommsen was well aware, but he was not writing
of the *arcana imperii*.[46] The "formal and official theory of the Principate
as the government of the Senate and the People" was for him "hollow"—as hollow as the presentation of the senatorial government in the
Republic as the "Selbstregierung der freien Bürgerschaft" ("the self-
government of the free citizenry").[47] An essential feature of a republican
magistracy was the strict delimitation of its sphere of competence; in
the principate the notion of magisterial competence is so broad that it
comes close to license: "der Competenzbegriff . . . ist in dem Principat
so weit ausgedehnt, dass diese Schranken factisch der Schrankenlosig-
keit nahe kommen."[48] It is only at this point, after all these caveats, that
Mommsen formulates his idea of dyarchy. From the point of view of
public law—*staatsrechtlich*—the principate cannot be described as
monarchy; hence "the description as dyarchy . . . will express more cor-

---

43. J. Bleicken, *Lex Publica: Gesetz und Recht in der römischen Republik* (Berlin
1975) 16–51, esp. 23–24, 36–38, 41, 49. For a recent appraisal and critique of the *Staatsrecht*, see also Y. Thomas, *Mommsen et l' "Isolierung" du Droit (Rome, l'Allemagne et
l'État)*, published separately (Paris 1982) and as the introduction to the reprint of the
French translation of the *Staatsrecht*. Thomas' study will be read with profit in conjunction with the remarks of G. Crifò, review of Thomas' *Mommsen, SDHI* 52 (1986) 485–
91; and E. Gabba, review of Thomas' *Mommsen, Athenaeum* 64 (1986) 245–47.

44. Mommsen himself admits ([supra n. 39] 2^3: 749, n. 2) that he does not know of
any source in which the emperor is described as *magistratus*.

45. Cf., for instance, Z. Yavetz, "The *Res Gestae* and Augustus' Public Image," in F.
Millar and E. Segal, eds., *Caesar Augustus: Seven Aspects* (Oxford 1984) 24.

46. Mommsen (supra n. 39) 2^3 VII.

47. Ibid., 747.

48. Ibid., 747–48.

rectly the essence of this remarkable institution."[49] The essence, *das Wesen*, of which Mommsen writes is—in contraposition to von Premerstein and Syme—not the historical and social essence of the principate but solely legal. The principate was a social institution of which Mommsen intended to give, and gave, a legal description.[50] Or as Wolfgang Kunkel expressed it, Mommsen largely excluded from his discussion the political and social aspects not because he failed to see them or was not interested in them ("das Gegenteil beweist jede Seite seiner Römischen Geschichte," "each page of his *Roman History* proves the opposite"), but because he wished to present the Roman state "as a pure legal system" ("als reine Rechtsordnung").[51]

"Das reale" is buried in a footnote.[52] Commenting on the claim of Augustus in the *Res Gestae* (6.12) *in consulatu sexto et septimo . . . rem publicam ex mea potestate in senat[us populique Romani a]rbitrium transtuli*, Mommsen writes that this testimony and other contemporary texts are "decisive for the formal interpretation of the act," and he adds that among the contemporaries only the Greek Strabo gives "the real interpretation." And Strabo (13.3.25 = p. 840) stresses that Augustus, far from restoring the Republic, remained *kyrios* of war and peace for life. Mommsen expressed the same thought even more clearly in his commentary on the *Res Gestae: Vides aetatis Augustae auctores Romanos plane ut facit ipse Augustus rem ita narrare, quasi vere tum rem publicam reddiderit; solus Strabo . . . liberius sic enuntiat non rerum speciem, sed ipsam rem.*[53] Mommsen was well aware that the *Staatsrecht* dealt with the *species rerum*, but unlike many recent interpreters he also knew that no *res* exists *sine specie*.

If Mommsen had ever written a fourth volume of his *Römische Geschichte*,[54] he probably would have preempted Syme—not in his proso-

---

49. Ibid., 748: "Die Bezeichnung als Dyarchie, das heisst als eine zwischen dem Senat einer- und dem Princeps als dem Vertrauensmann der Gemeinde andrerseits ein für allemal getheilte Herrschaft, würde das Wesen dieser merkwürdigen Institution zutreffender ausdrücken."

50. Alan Watson's definition comes to mind: "A legal institution is a social institution looked at from the legal point of view" (*The Evolution of Law* [Baltimore 1985] 111).

51. W. Kunkel, "Theodor Mommsen als Jurist," *Chiron* 14 (1984) 371.

52. Mommsen (supra n. 39) 2³: 746, n. 2.

53. T. Mommsen, *Res Gestae Divi Augusti*² (Berlin 1883) 146.

54. The third volume ends with the battle of Thapsus. Why Mommsen failed to produce the history of the empire has been the subject of much speculation; see Demandt (infra n. 55) 497–506 (a full catalogue of various opinions); G. Bowersock, "Gibbon's Historical Imagination," *The American Scholar* 57 (1988) 46–47. For the history of the composition of the *Römische Geschichte* and for its evaluation and appreciation, see L. Wickert, *Theodor Mommsen*, vol. 3 (Frankfurt 1969) 399–422, 618–75, and vol. 4

pographical analyses, but as a Tacitean judgment of Augustus. His university lectures on the empire are fairly well documented, and in these lectures he spoke with the voice and style of *Römische Geschichte,* not that of the *Staatsrecht.* He shares with Syme an admiration for Gibbon and Tacitus, and Asinius Pollio; he shares with Syme the conviction that in the empire "die Geschichte in dem Kabinett liegt," and, like Syme, he detests Augustus but appreciates his achievement.[55]

In July 1858, in his *Antrittsrede* as a member of the Berlin Academy, Mommsen forcefully pleaded for "die Verschmelzung von Geschichte und Jurisprudenz" as "die erste Bedingung organischer Behandlung der römischen Dinge" ("the amalgamation of history and jurisprudence" as "the first premise for an organic treatment of Roman matters").[56] This is still our goal; for the *Staatsrecht,* in its grand fallacy that it is possible to describe and understand a social organism by studying only its formal law, has (against the wish of its creator) largely eliminated history,[57] and *The Roman Revolution,* in its contempt for fiction, is oblivious to the fact that fictions abide too.

The reconciliation of Mommsen and Syme, of law and power, is a Vergilian and Augustan theme, ambiguous like the principate itself:

Remo cum fratre Quirinus . . . / iura dabunt.[58]

(1980) 332–48; and the introduction of K. Christ to the new edition of Mommsen's *Römische Geschichte,* vol. 8 (Munich 1976) 7–66 (= Christ [supra n. 9] 26–73).

55. Cf. V. Ehrenberg, "Theodor Mommsens Kolleg über römische Kaisergeschichte," *Heidelberger Jahrbb.* 4 (1960) 94–107 (= K. F. Stroheker and A. J. Graham, eds., *Polis und Imperium: Beiträge zur Alten Geschichte* [Zurich and Stuttgart 1965] 613–30, esp. 618–21); and, above all, A. Demandt, "Die Hensel-Nachschriften zu Mommsens Kaiserzeit-Vorlesung," *Gymnasium* 93 (1986) 497–519, esp. 512–15. On the striking similarities between Mommsen's and Syme's art of writing and understanding history, see Alföldy (supra n. 10) 33–40.

56. T. Mommsen, *Reden und Aufsätze*[2] (Berlin 1905) 36.

57. But it is important to remember that in his *Abriss des römischen Staatsrechts* (Leipzig 1893), before proceeding to a systematic presentation, Mommsen devoted the whole first book to a historical outline of constitutional developments. Cf. Gabba (supra n. 43) 246. Crifò (supra n. 43) 487, rightly observes that "Lo stesso Mommsen . . . la cui intera attività era rivolta al superamento della frattura [tra 'storia' e 'diritto'] paradossalmente . . . aveva contribuito con la sua 'scientificizzazione' dell'esperienza pubblicistica romana a costruire un sistema di diritto pubblico che con la storia sembrava aver poco a che fare."

58. Verg. *Aen.* 1.292–93.

C. Caesar Divi filius and the Formation of the Alternative in Rome

I

After the middle of the second century B.C. Rome found itself in a difficult crisis.[1] As we realize today, its causes lay in a disintegration of Roman society, in an irreparable erosion of the basis of the Roman constitution, and in the impossibility of solving the manifold problems of the Republic in such a way that new and more dangerous ones did not grow out of the solution itself. This crisis was brought to a head by the rise of particularly powerful individuals such as, ultimately, Pompeius and Caesar, Marcus Antonius and Octavianus Augustus. The senate feared the power of these men and fought bitterly against them. In these conflicts, which eventually developed into civil wars, the Republic was crushed.

Yet, although the Roman constitution and some of the basic pre-

1. This paper was delivered as a lecture at several American universities. Some of the ideas presented here are discussed in more detail in C. Meier, *Res publica amissa: Eine Studie zur Verfassung und Geschichte der späten römischen Republik* (Wiesbaden 1966; 2d ed. with new preface, Frankfurt 1980); id., *Die Ohnmacht des allmächtigen Dictators Caesar: Drei biographische Skizzen* (Frankfurt 1980); id., *Caesar* (Berlin 1982).

requisites for its functioning increasingly failed to meet the political needs of the Republic or broke down completely, at least until the time of Caesar (and probably even later) the legitimacy of the existing constitution was not questioned. That it did not function well in many ways was well known, but no one knew of anything better with which to replace it. At most, parts of the order were disputed, usually those of secondary importance. On the whole, there was no alternative; that is, there existed no social and political force that could have insisted effectively upon introducing major constitutional changes.

In particular, the senate remained the unchallenged, central, and authoritative agent of government, responsible for the whole of the Republic. However fiercely and continually it was attacked, however many defeats it suffered, well into the fifties (and, in slightly weakened form, long thereafter) there apparently remained a fundamental and widespread conviction that the senate's regime, and only the senate's regime, was legitimate and correct. Such a discrepancy between continuing confirmation and acceptance of the old order on the one hand and its weakness and manifold failures on the other presents a difficult (and, for many today, hardly comprehensible) problem. How was it possible not only that the causes of the crisis were not recognized, but that the solution, if any was envisaged at all, was sought in restoring the traditional constitution rather than in changing it? Why could the crisis not be formulated in terms of political antitheses, and why could the critical points not be made the objects of conscious, direct discussion and then alteration?

My thesis is that this was a crisis without an alternative. That means power and interests were distributed and arranged in such a way that no force could be built up that was sufficiently strong and consistently directed toward overcoming the crisis. There were defenders of the old Republic, but no (or, at any rate, very few) advocates of a new order. Thus there could not be a struggle about the future form of the Republic. Instead, changes (which, in fact, led to the continuation and increasing seriousness of the crisis) for the most part resulted from side effects of political actions and were often initiated by the senate itself in its effort to defend the Republic. To put it differently, although the Romans at that time generally wanted to preserve the Republic, they—and in particular the senators, as advocates of the old constitution—through the unintended effects of their actions, themselves contributed to the dissolution of their Republic. Indeed, it was a remarkable kind of crisis, in which the affected society as a whole was incapable of making its own organization (in its critical points) the object of political dispute and action.

It is difficult to figure out when and to what degree things changed after the outbreak of the civil war of 49 B.C. Even if one believes, however, that Caesar grasped the scope and nature of the Roman crisis and sought ways to overcome it within the framework of the traditional institutions, one cannot deny that he was unsuccessful; he clearly was unable to institute a new legitimate constitution in Rome. Furthermore, there is no indication that any attempt he may have made to implement such a plan would have met with the understanding of Roman society (or even of his own followers). Apparently Caesar never even mentioned publicly what he had in mind—if indeed he had a clear idea of a future constitution at all.

By contrast it is clear that his adopted son, C. Caesar Divi filius, later Augustus, through direct political action and political discussions or confrontations with the senate succeeded in realizing a profound alteration of the Roman constitution (in the broadest sense of the word), by which the crisis of Rome was resolved. There can be no doubt that he created a new order that took root broadly across all of Roman society. Thus after a crisis of about one hundred years based on social and political power a manifest alternative to the traditional order was shaped in the form of the principate of Augustus. It is the purpose of this paper to analyze the origins and development of this alternative in the last phase of the crisis of the Roman Republic at the time of Caesar Divi filius. I shall first describe briefly the nature of the "crisis without an alternative" during the late Republic, then outline the helplessness of Julius Caesar when faced with this crisis, and lastly discuss the evolution of the conditions that were necessary for the establishment of a new constitution under Augustus.

My discussion concentrates on Roman society, not on the great politicians. It refers less to the plans and actions of these politicians than to their concerns, objectives, and potentialities, and to the conditions that influenced their actions. More specifically, personal factors will mostly be ignored. For example, not much attention will be paid to the assumption (generally accepted today) that Augustus had learned from his father's fate and, further, that he was of a completely different character: not such a brilliant, impatient, and active personality but rather, it seems, a patient, moderate man of extraordinary political tact. The significance of these factors is not to be denied, but in the present discussion I am interested in other issues. Simply put, the focus of my question is whether the conditions of action for the Divi filius were not such that the solution that he found resulted more or less directly from, or was imposed upon him by, these conditions. To exaggerate somewhat, Was Augustus' work perhaps determined by the whole power structure existing at that time rather than a personal achievement of the first *princeps*? Whether or not this was the case remains to be seen, but I consider this a fruitful question that at the same time clearly defines the starting point of my discussion.

II

The lack of an alternative in the late Republic was most conspicuous in the fact that the traditional constitution, although obviously malfunctioning badly, was generally considered the only acceptable one. Rome had conquered the world with this constitution, which had proved only too good and effective. It is important to remember here that the old aristocratic structures had been confirmed and solidified by their dissemination throughout the worldwide empire. So the *Gemeindestaat* took root across the *Weltreich*. The more one lived with the traditional institutions, the more one became accustomed to them.

All in all, these institutions were also still sufficient to satisfy the interests of large parts of Roman society, provided that unlimited funds were available from, and continually supplied by, the empire. Thus a situation developed that can be characterized by the following formula: satisfaction for all those who were, even potentially, powerful, and powerlessness for the potentially dissatisfied. In these circumstances, no fundamental misgivings concerning the existing situation could arise; in particular, those who suffered were too weak to join together and effectively promote an alternative.

Furthermore, for centuries without interruption there had existed unquestioned certainty about what was to be considered the true constitution. All opposition had occurred within a framework that equally pertained to political and social matters. Thus the political and social constitutions were never separated (as they were, for example, in Greek city-states or are in modern states). Thus, naturally, there were no institutions in and by which dissatisfaction about the customary order regularly could be expressed, whether politically or, at the very least, intellectually. At the same time (and consequently) the senate was generally recognized as the ruling power in the Republic, and the entire range of politics was left in its hands; that is to say, both politics and political thought remained the domain of a small elite, the Roman nobility. Others took an active part only if, and as long as, specific (and primarily apolitical) interests forced them into politics; their involvement usually lasted only for a limited time. The senate was thus regarded as authoritative in politics, and this conviction was deeply rooted.

In these circumstances, the numerically very large and potentially influential second class of Roman society, the *equites*, could not easily develop or uphold an alternative to the existing order. The *equites* remained bound to the senate as long as the latter—at least in extreme cases—held decisive power in Rome and was the guarantor of law and order. Even when the senate's power declined, however, no thought about a basic alteration of the existing order seems to have arisen or met with approval among the *equites*. In 56 B.C., Cicero stated that the pursuit of *otium* and *dignitas* no longer amounted to the same thing—that is, that concern for the constitution and concern for law and order were no longer concentrated in the same place (in the senate), but that some preferred one and others the other. Even so, there was no question of whether the *equites* might form a stable foundation for the struggle for monarchy. Their constitutional ideas remained closely tied to those of the senate.

Finally, we have to take into account that ancient societies could scarcely conceive of the political order as a mere instrument. Political order was what they were, not what they had. Their expectations concerning structural change were very constrained; the only improvement ancient societies could anticipate was the increase of political participation by individual classes. But in the late Republic the main problem was just the opposite: how to achieve the reduction of political participation in favor of a monarchical regime. And for a long time there was no cause that might justify such a loss of influence—or even of societal identity—on the part of the ruling class.

Thus all political aspirations remained focused within the framework of what was customary, although the unintended side effects of politics contributed to a gradual weakening of this framework. The most important factor in this weakening process was the dispute between the senate and the powerful dynasts, particularly Pompeius and Caesar. As it turned out, the difficult external problems of the Republic (for example, the wars against the Cimbri and Teutones, Mithridates, or the pirates) could only be solved effectively by exceptional individuals who expected certain returns for their achievements, such as distribution of farmland to their veterans. As a result, these individuals became exceedingly powerful. Although, with the possible exception of Caesar, they had nothing against the rule of the senate, the senate had something against them—understandably, since the senate's leadership and responsibility for the Republic fundamentally depended upon equality within the oligarchy or at least its influential groups. Such equality was threatened when individuals became too powerful. Moreover, after the first bitter experiences the norms that were accepted as valid within the senate became so narrow that eventually only mediocrity was cultivated and respected. The more the Republic depended on the great individuals, the more they were resisted. The more they were resisted, the more they had to strive to win further power, and the more dangerous they became. In this struggle the institutions were worn down, and, paradoxically, Pompeius and Caesar were actually compelled to become increasingly powerful, chiefly by the actions of those who tried to uphold the authority of the senate. Hence, against the desire of all participants (except, possibly, Caesar), the unintended consequences of their actions combined to cause and accelerate the process that resulted in the destruction of the Republic. Not until 52 was the senate prepared to cooperate with Pompeius, and then it did so mostly because it desperately needed his support against Caesar.

The way to monarchy was paved, then, by the rise of powerful dynasts, but such a development was not yet reflected in the distribution of interests and the aims typically pursued in the late Republic. We are able to discern, on the individual level, new patterns of forming power (particularly through military *clientelae*), new capacities and standards of achievement, and new forms of behavior, such as were later typical of Augustus; but in Roman society at large we can find no point of departure for a would-be monarch to combine his own interests with those of influential groups, no cause that, in the long run, would justify his claim to power as objectively necessary on behalf of the state or society as a whole; for there was neither a state nor a society other than the traditional *res publica*. Roman society necessarily implied republican forms of government.

The problem of how to develop a new form of legitimacy should not be underrated. After all, on the solution of this problem depended the rise of new political landmarks, new orientations for the politicians, new expectations toward them. But any new political order could be persuasive and stable only if it was based on a political alternative (in the sense described above). Straight and immediate constitutional reform would have been possible only if there had been a cause on behalf of which an ambitious politician could have formed an alliance with large groups. In the absence of such a cause, the best the exceptional individuals could hope for were commissions for limited tasks. The only legitimation they had for their claim to power was their personal capacity for achievement.

III

Pompeius and Caesar embodied this dilemma of the powerful individual in very different ways. All along, it remained Pompeius' aim not to break with the senate and the *boni*, the well-to-do; rather, he wanted to gain their approval. His own interests often brought him into conflict with, and for some years into continuous opposition to, the senate, and experience made him distrustful; thus he could not afford to become dependent on the senate. Nevertheless, all in all he anxiously avoided doing more than necessary against the senate. Where possible, he observed the traditional norms. The unique nature of the crisis without an alternative therefore caused him to pursue fluctuating and feeble politics that failed to convince, and to maintain a friendly face toward the senate even while engaging in hostile actions; for often those who opposed him were the very people on whom he depended.

Caesar, on the other hand, broke with the senate and the constitution in the year 59. He had to do so if he wanted to succeed in passing his laws. However, whether or not he got along well with the senate does not appear to have made much difference to him; by then he had already distanced himself from the ruling oligarchy in Rome. In his isolation he took the Roman aristocracy's ideal of achievement (or *dignitas*) very seriously, even absolutely; thus he no longer respected the limits set for personal ambition by the aristocratic society. First in Gaul and then in the control of Rome and its whole empire, Caesar wanted to show the high-ranking and often incompetent *principes* what one man could achieve. Since there was no cause and no alternative to which he could bind himself, his legitimation could only be his own person—which forced him to prove his greatness everywhere.

When he started the civil war in 49, he did so for the sake of his *dignitas*, his very personal claim to leadership and authority, which was based on his achievements. He had not intended this war; he had tried through diplomatic means to avoid it; but when he was certain that war was inevitable, he invaded Italy with his well-trained and absolutely loyal army. Many senators were with him or joined him, although the senate as a whole was against him. In the course of the civil war, he defeated Pompeius and the senate. Having set out to ward off personal injury, he ended up holding power over the whole Roman empire. All power was his; although he was forced to make some concessions to his followers, for all practical purposes he now could rule alone.

The colossal standards of performance that he had set for himself in his lonely self-assertion against Roman society now took effect; he lapsed into restless action. For the most part, he devoted himself to organizational and administrative tasks; correspondingly he gave orders, commanded and decreed what was to happen. Most importantly, he failed to consult with the senate or even his friends. Thus he occupied a lonely control tower. The senate granted Caesar the appropriate powers of authority and tried at the same time to acknowledge his victories with ever greater honors. Finally, some divine honors and the status of *dictator perpetuo* were bestowed upon Caesar. In sum, whatever the cause of this enthusiastic heaping of honors on one man, it clearly demonstrated the vast distance that now separated Caesar and Roman society. The senate could reach Caesar only by ever increasing the height of the pedestal on which he stood. There could be no question of cooperation with the senate or of the establishment of a new monarchical legitimacy.

What Caesar thought about the future order of Rome is unknown. He lived the part of a monarch but did not declare this to be his intention. When it was obvious that he intended to remain a monarch for life, the well-known conspiracy arose, of which he became the victim. Caesar's assassination on the Ides of March in 44 B.C., however, only documented his failure. In fact, he realized himself that he had not mastered—and did not know how to master—the task of reconstituting and reintegrating the commonwealth (*constituere rem publicam*). It is hard to find a different explanation for his decision to evade this task by engaging in a war against the Parthians. Perhaps he thought he could present himself more convincingly through new and unprecedented military achievements. Perhaps, however, the war against the Parthians was simply an escape.

Caesar's real difficulty arose from the fact that there existed no support for a new constitution. If the *equites* were in favor of Caesar's monarchy—for which there is no evidence—Caesar still could not gain sufficient support in the senate. The senators might support him in one way or another, but they could not be convinced to support a monarchy. That Caesar, as it seems, did not even try to convince them is hardly surprising; he generally found it too troublesome even to ask the senators for their advice. In fact, it became more and more difficult for the senators to make contact with Caesar. He lived in anything but close contact with the leading persons in Rome; even his own followers often had no part in his decisions and hence in the government of Rome and its empire. The breathtaking abundance and grandeur of the honors he received were an indication, result, and cause of his increasing isolation. Without the senate, however, a legitimate order could hardly be built up in Rome at that time.

Even if—as Caesar seems to have seen it—membership in the senate and tenure in magistracies had been chiefly a matter of honor and not of influence, the great tradition of the house necessarily also entitled many honored members of Caesar's own party to a certain claim to power; they rightly demanded to be respected and to be heard. At least the more important among Caesar's supporters, whom he honored with patrician status, magistracies, or a senate seat, were no longer only, and probably no longer chiefly, Caesar's followers. They apparently had no other conception of the senate than the traditional one. If the honor they had received was deduced from the traditional *senatus auctoritas,* how much could that honor be worth if the senate's *auctoritas* was missing? If they had fought to win a position within the *res publica,* what had they gained if the institutions did not work and, whatever was to happen, depended on Caesar?

So Caesar's greatness as the conqueror of Gaul and as a civil-war leader, which had fascinated them and which they had followed, could not be translated into convincing statesmanship. The extraordinary will for achievement, which had become his way of life in Gaul, made him great, effective, and at the same time powerless when faced with the task of building up a stable order (of whatever kind) in contact with the decisive authorities in Rome. In short, he had a great deal of power within the circumstances but very little power over the circumstances. That there was no alternative and no cause thus meant for a man of his stature both power and powerlessness—once he had removed himself so far from Roman society. Otherwise he would have had to accept the advice of two of his loyal followers "to hold on with arms to the principate that he had sought with arms" (*ut principatum armis quaesitum armis teneret,* Vell. Pat. 2.57.1). This, however, he could not do, since, "as he often said, he would rather die than be feared" (*dictitans mori se quam timeri malle,* Vell. Pat. 2.57.1).

IV

We do not know to what extent Caesar, in the long run, encouraged or discouraged the thought of a monarchy or of the need for monarchy in Rome. What he certainly did was to leave a heritage: his large following among the veterans, the memory of Divus Julius—and the obligation to avenge his death. It is one of the great ironies of history that the eighteen-year-old great-nephew whom Caesar, having no children of his own, had adopted according to an aristocratic tradition was willing to accept this doubtful heritage, and that he had what it took to pursue the thorny path on which he then found himself—all the way to the point at which the principate was established.

What is particularly interesting about this piece of history (as has already been said) was the evolution of the structural preconditions for the monarchy, that is, the alternative to the Republic. In this context it must be mentioned that the period of renewed civil war after Caesar's assassination, with its widespread suffering and stress, probably caused such an increase in the yearning for peace, security, and safety of property that a potential monarch could exploit it to his advantage and gain a following—if, that is, he could credibly present himself as the only person capable of realizing peace. To that extent exhaustion was a basis of sorts for the development of an alternative; it was a premium for anyone who aimed at building up a monarchy after the victory. After all, "assurance of each and every citizen's property rights" (*certa cuique rerum suarum possessio*, Vell. Pat. 2.89.4), to cite one example, was an effective catchword.

A further advantage for the young Caesar was that he had been able to learn from the fate of his father. Yet it seems to me that it was really another factor that was decisive for his success. This was the special mixture of power and weakness by which the Divi filius was—without knowing it—enabled to take advantage of all opportunities in order to prepare, step by step, the building of an alternative.

Caesar's legacy, the obligation to avenge his father on the murderers, and, moreover, the unscrupulous way in which he handled the proscriptions put the Divi filius in a bad light compared with his rival, Caesar's old general, Marcus Antonius. Octavian's harshness and cruelty repelled, while Antonius was distinguished by his generosity and reserve. Furthermore, to the young man had fallen the least rewarding position in the division of functions in the triumvirate: the government of Italy and the distribution of land to vast numbers of veterans—which was only possible if land was first expropriated on a grand scale. Admittedly, an advantage was connected with this unpleasant duty: Caesar won and consolidated the following of the veterans. Moreover, as ruler of Italy, he had the best recruits at his disposal. On the other hand, he made himself even more unpopular among influential circles of society in which, by contrast, Marcus Antonius was held in high esteem.

From the weakness that resulted from his position, however, the Divi filius derived a great advantage: he was forced to prepare as comprehensively as possible the critical armed conflict against his rival Antonius, not only on the military, but particularly on the political, level. He was isolated, and he had to compensate somehow for his disadvantages. One way in which he tried to do so, as early as 36, was to pledge that he would renounce his extraordinary powers and return the Republic to the senate and people—if Antonius did the same. Thus in his distress he wooed the senate and the well-to-do who supported the old Republic. This spectacular declaration seems to have been in line with his other policies, for Caesar needed the senate. The only flaw was that he found little trust and certainly could not supplant his rival Antonius in the favor of the senate.

Then, in fact, Antonius himself came to Octavian's aid; for being in a stronger position and better regarded, he was at the same time less concerned and more magnanimous. This was precisely what made him attractive to the senate. But most importantly, for whatever reason, Antonius was extremely devoted to Queen Cleopatra. This caused him enormous difficulties, for it provided his opponents with an opportunity to slander him as a traitor of Rome. Antonius' friends in Rome realized that and warned him, but without success. Eventually, some of them admitted defeat and defected to Caesar. The particulars are not important here. In any case, Caesar managed to present himself as the defender of Italy's cause. In towns all over the country he arranged for an oath to be sworn that somehow entailed the demand that he become the leader against Cleopatra. The people of *tota Italia* wanted to defend themselves under Caesar's leadership against the danger threatening from the East. The same oath was sworn by the towns of the western provinces.

Thus a totally new situation emerged: the Divi filius had a strong cause by means of which he could identify himself with Roman society. Where earlier—in the cases of Sulla and Pompeius—a civil-war leader could at best take the field for the cause of the nobility or the senate, it was now possible to mobilize the interests of all Roman and Italian society against persons who seemed to be the champions of eastern despotism. This scheme did not go off entirely smoothly and was by no means always convincing, but Caesar and his helpers were able to start up a process of building consent that later became increasingly suggestive. Many will have been glad for the opportunity to subscribe to a cause that justified their decision to follow Caesar—which was, of course, advisable anyway if one lived in his sphere of influence.

War was solemnly declared against the Egyptian queen, not against Antonius. As a precaution, Caesar took a large number of senators with him on his campaign. For all their sworn loyalty, it did not seem advisable to leave them behind in the center of Italy in the back of the army. Apparently, the greatest caution was imperative.

Perhaps it goes too far to assume that Caesar Divi filius needed to rely on the senate, but, according to all we know, it is certain that he was in a far weaker position in relation to Antonius than his father had once been in relation to Pompeius and his successors: not necessarily from a military point of view but with regard to the senate. This was very important, for the senators obviously had learned a great deal since 49. They had often been put to the test, had become resourceful, were much sought after, and had gathered new experience and new power in the armies of the civil wars and in the many endeavors to mobilize forces. Such senators were dangerous; they could not be left behind in Italy. They could possibly, although not necessarily, represent a powerful influence that could carry great weight. Such influence was no longer based on *clientela* but rather on the esteem that the senate could potentially enjoy in spite of, and even because of, the civil war and the general longing for peace. This indeed could have tipped the balance. Unlike his father, Divi filius could not simply break out of his isolation. There was no Rubicon behind which he could prepare the war, nor did he have to cross a Rubicon in order to defend his political existence. Precisely for this reason, Caesar had to be friendly to the senators and cooperate with them. He had to bind them to himself—which also meant that he had to commit himself to them.

In this weakness, however, lay Caesar's chance after the war. He was not so easily tempted into simply raising himself above the senate and society. Of course, he could have done so with the support of his army, but it would have entailed breaking solemn promises, using terror, and reigning "with loaded guns." If Caesar was clever at all, this could not seem advisable to him.

In fact, his strength lay precisely in the obligations that made him dependent upon the senate and society; for the cause that he had adopted made it possible for him to represent the entire commonwealth: Rome and Italy as the war leader, peace and security as the victor in the last battle, and lastly the old Republic by keeping his promises and returning the management of the *res publica* to the senate and the people. It paid to identify with the cause of Rome if he did so in the sense in which it was seen at the time—in the sense of the traditional order. Thus Caesar's political course was charted; what he lost in political scope for the moment, he gained in strength in the long run.

Once he decided to "play the civil game," Augustus was bound by the existing power structure. By choosing this course, incidentally, he did what Roman politicians had always preferred to do: if possible at all, they aligned their policy with the senate and the *boni,* the "good ones." Only Divus Julius had scorned this course or, perhaps, been incapable of pursuing it. The rules of the civil game prescribed that it was only the senate that could, more or less voluntarily, give Augustus what he needed. Clearly, once the senators joined the game, they could not deny him all his demands. Moreover, he had tied many senators to himself. Some had belonged to his party for a long time; others joined it after his victories. After all, Augustus was in a position to offer many honors and advantages, and he needed many senators for a great variety of military and administrative tasks. In addition, unlike his father, he took care that such service was attractive to the senators and that his supporters were not alienated from, or repelled by, him; rather, he kept in constant touch with them. Thus Augustus and the senate had a great deal to offer each other and depended on each other, and by necessity a certain balance had to develop between them.

Above all, Augustus' position was determined by the fact that he was able to outdo the senate in one crucial respect; for the decisive question that emerged was, Who best represents the interests of the *res publica,* Augustus or the senate? There were at least two strong reasons to answer this question in Augustus' favor.

First, Augustus had saved Rome and restored the Republic. Thus he deserved those special honors and powers that were bestowed upon him by the senate. The restoration of the Republic and the special position of the man who had restored it corresponded to each other. At the same time, this new association necessarily contributed to loosening the traditional one, between the cause of the Republic and that of the senate.

Second, there occurred a shift in the central issues of Roman politics, or rather in the evaluation of those central issues. In the late Republic the senate's policy had been concentrated upon the defense of the Republic. In view of this absolute priority, important military and administrative achievements of exceptional individuals like Pompeius or Caesar could not adequately be acknowledged as beneficial in the long run; for all that mattered in the short run was the immediate threat to oligarchic equality that was inherent in such individual achievements. With Augustus' victory, however, this situation changed. On the one hand, during the period of civil wars so many military and administrative problems had accumulated that they could not be neglected any longer. On the other hand, there was no need to defend the Republic against the man who had restored it. Thus the Roman commonwealth became more and more a *curandum* rather than a *defendendum:* care and administrative responsibility replaced defense and survival as political priorities. As far as the capacity to take care of the innumerable *curanda* was concerned, Augustus was clearly and decisively superior to the senate.

Reasonably enough, Augustus at first took over only external duties, the defense of the border provinces. This offered two advantages: it further increased his credit, and it helped the Romans realize, whenever unrest arose in the capital, that the saving hand of the *princeps* was indispensable in the domestic sphere as well. It became more and more obvious that Rome could not do without him. In—probably difficult— disputes with the senate, new agreements and compromises were reached. In such repeated give-and-take, however, Augustus always took a little more than he gave. Thus gradually, step by step, monarchy was established.

Such a monarchy had a firm foundation in the legions. Augustus had a strong party of his followers in the senate. And the *equites* "repaid by confidence in the government" the guarantees they received from it.[2] As F. Adcock said with regard to the coins bearing the emperor's portrait, the more they had the emperor in their pockets, the more the emperor had them in his.[3] But in all this, a decisive prerequisite for the stability

2. R. Syme, *The Roman Revolution* (Oxford 1939) 351.
3. F. E. Adcock, *Roman Political Ideas and Practice* (Ann Arbor 1959) 103.

of the new government was that it was established on behalf of the Republic: from this it gained its legitimacy.

V

To sum up, Augustus' restoration of the Republic was not simply the result of his—often presumed—conservative attitude or of his genuine desire to reform Rome while retaining as much of the republican constitution as possible. Whatever his attitude may have been—nobody knows for sure—the Republic confronted him not only with opinions, beliefs, and traditions, and not only with the expectations raised by his own promises, but with concrete interests, which he himself considered significant—even and especially within the framework of the civil game he had decided to play. Given this framework, the position of the *res publica* was particularly strong in its relation to Augustus himself. But since he knew that, he had, in fact, crucial control over the champions of the *res publica*. Because he had set limits to his power, within these limits his power was all the more firmly established. One special form of power to which Augustus liked to refer was *auctoritas*, based on voluntary and unquestioned recognition of his achievement and merit. In this form in particular, power within the circumstances now really converged with power over the circumstances.

Consequently, Augustus accepted few honors—even fewer extraordinary ones—and only the necessary minimum of formal powers—these too in the form of a commission and for a limited time. He wanted to be no more than the first citizen. Certainly this claim was to some extent hypocritical, for Rome by that time *was* a monarchy! Most Romans and especially most senators were fully aware of that, and some poets or flatterers even welcomed it. But there is a great difference between really being a monarch and conceding or even pretending to be one. By pretending to be something he was not in reality, Augustus succeeded in reconciling the new reality of the monarchy with the old one of the Republic. Obviously it was only possible to create an alternative to what was traditional in Rome by thoroughly supporting that very tradition. The *princeps* too had to deduce his power from the *res publica* and the concerns of society, because the particular structure of Roman society made it impossible for the *princeps* to find sufficient new support (among the *equites,* for example) outside of and against the established power and authority of the senate. Thus it was not only wise but necessary for Augustus—imposed upon him by the rules of his own game—

to win over the established powers in the state. He had no choice but to style himself the defender of the old system and to fight for the *causa senatus*—if necessary even against the senators.

Therefore it was the power structure itself that suggested to Augustus the solution he was looking for. Much of it simply resulted from his decision to play the civil game. That decision was the crucial precondition that enabled him to succeed where his father had failed. But this decision and all the skills Augustus demonstrated in playing his game should not be taken for granted. They were not self-evident but born out of extraordinary intelligence, patience, delicacy, a strong sense of power, shrewdness, cunning, and many other characteristics. Among these, Augustus' art of performing deserves special attention.

Indeed, in order to succeed the *princeps* had to be able to play a specific role and to do so with much self-denial: he had always to appear less than he really was. I was once asked whom Augustus would and could fool. My answer is that he could not, of course, conceal his power from those who knew something about politics. But he could make it less perceptible and mitigate its effects—which must have been very comforting in day-to-day business. He did not only fake constitutional behavior. Certainly it makes a great difference whether one wants to appear as the first citizen or present oneself as the emperor.

Accordingly, a good *princeps* had to be a good actor: *qualis artifex.* Augustus knew that. In commenting that Augustus changed color like a chameleon, Sir Ronald Syme refers precisely to his taking on a new role. At the end of his life, Augustus asked his friends to applaud if he had played his part well (Suet. *Aug.* 99.1). This phrase was by no means meant only as a metaphor (as the prudery of nineteenth-century philology would have it). By contrast, Tiberius was not a good actor and was, as a result, beset by great difficulties throughout his reign. Nero, a young man and thoroughly overtaxed, finally took the theatrics so seriously that he literally performed on stage. Thus the principate was formed in dialectic interaction with the development of a role and of role expectations.

The position of *princeps* was extremely delicate, but that was less the consequence of Augustus' special creation than of the peculiar structure of Roman society. It resulted from the fact that even in the fundamentally changed conditions after the civil wars any alternative to the existing system had to be linked to the tradition, which was republican through and through.

Consequently, Augustus could only defeat the Republic thoroughly and definitively by restoring it. Jean Béranger pointed to this paradox: "*res publica amissa*—la République persiste; *res publica restituta*—la monarchie du principat l'a évincée."[4] In other words, the alternative could be realized only if a monarch succeeded in insinuating himself into the role of the foremost defender of the Republic. Then, finally, the turning point in the history of Roman legitimacy was reached.

To put it more generally, it was very typical of the particularly political culture of antiquity that a truly political (i.e., republican) ideal was needed, not only a politicized apolitical one (such as the mere upholding of law and order or of favorable conditions for the pursuit of economic ends). Law and order, the guarantee of property, some sort of aesthetical propaganda, and so on might provide strong piers, but the bridge to the principate had to be built with the very elements of, and thus on behalf of, the traditional Republic. Afterwards, the monarch had to be successful enough and his regime had to last long enough to enable the alternative to take root and the new order to become a matter of course.

Whether Augustus fully grasped the complexity of this problem we do not know. But his initial weakness suggested to him the course he followed, and he was clever enough to recognize and exploit his opportunities. And that was all he had to do in order to establish the monarchy in Rome.

4. J. Béranger, Review of *Res publica amissa* by C. Meier, *REL* 45 (1967) 594.

Augustus and the Power of Tradition:
The Augustan Principate as Binding Link between Republic and Empire

To speak of Augustus means to speak of power: of power overtly exercised, of power disguised, of power relinquished; of the relationship between power and authority; of the delegation of power among collaborators and among public bodies such as the senate, the colleges of magistrates, and the assembly. It also means to speak of the power of destiny, which made the heaven-sent young man[1] Octavian the executor of a curative scheme that set up in place of the decaying republican system the blessings of a peaceful monarchy mandated by history.[2]

Augustus made it no simple matter to identify clearly "the real and ultimate power" on which his position in the *res publica* rested.[3] This difficulty is connected, first, with his personality, his specific role in Roman history and the long period of almost seventy years in which he determined that history, alone or in company of others. Then, too, it is a result of the particular historical conditions of his times, in which the standards of political conduct seemed to have been lost. And finally it

1. Cic. *Phil.* 5.16.43: *divinus adulescens.*
2. See, for example, H. E. Stier, "Augustusfriede und römische Klassik," *ANRW* 2.2 (1975) 35.
3. R. Syme, *The Roman Revolution* (Oxford 1939) 406.

springs from the fascination which this period—signifying both a decline and a climax—held for later generations of historians, who tried
time and again to reduce its contradictions to a single, unified account.

I. The Power of Images and the Power of Tradition:
   Introduction and Thesis

The first difficulties appear in the mere attempt to delimit the *saeculum
Augustum*. In antiquity some had considered designating the year of
Octavius' birth, 63 B.C., as the beginning of the new age.[4] It would be
rash to see flattery as the sole motive for this; it is much more likely to
be a certain "republican" perplexity at how to come to terms with this
individual—whose success people would rather have ascribed to god-
given talent than to his position in the politics of the state. It is easier to
accept Octavian's adoption in the year 44 B.C. as the point at which he
began to exercise a long and continually growing influence over politics.[5] Yet this extended period shows no unifying characteristics. After
the victory over Cleopatra and Antonius, Augustus himself did all he
could to sink his "Octavian phase" in oblivion.[6] The *Res Gestae* shows
almost a complete blank between Philippi and Actium:[7] none of his fellow triumvirs are mentioned, the victory over Sextus Pompeius is rather
intimated than reported,[8] and, understandably, the proscriptions are
passed over. Naturally enough, it is just this phase that has provided his
critics with the most material.[9]

Today it is a matter of course to set a dividing line between the old
and the new, between the Republic and the principate or monarchy, with
Actium in 31 B.C. or with the restoration of the *res publica* in 27 B.C.
For Augustus' contemporaries, however, this division was apparently
not so natural. Rather, it seems, it was not until after his death (and
perhaps, too, as an effect of the publication of his *Res Gestae*) that these
particular years were considered a decisive turning point.[10] The writers

4. Suet. *Aug.* 100.3; cf. Verg. *Ecl.* 4.
5. On the will and the adoption, see W. Schmitthenner, *Oktavian und das Testament
Caesars*[2] (Munich 1973) esp. 32–64.
6. F. M. Ahl, "The Rider and the Horse: Politics and Power in Roman Poetry from
Horace to Statius," *ANRW* 2.32.2. (1984) 46: "Octavian simply vanished."
7. A. Heuss, "Zeitgeschichte als Ideologie: Komposition und Gedankenführung der
Res gestae divi Augusti," in E. Lefèvre, ed., *Monumentum Chiloniense, Festschrift für
Erich Burck* (Amsterdam 1975) 89.
8. *RG* 25: *mare pacavi a praedonibus.*
9. See Tac. *Ann.* 1.10.
10. The earliest sources are Strab. 6.4.2 (288C) and Sen. *Clem.* 1.4.3; *Ben.* 2.20.2.

and historians of the time of Augustus were no more disposed to see a
fresh start at this point than was Augustus himself: he did not begin the
consecutive enumeration of the years of his administration until the year
23 B.C., when he was vested with the tribunician *potestas;*[11] nor did he
believe his exertions on behalf of the *res publica* had found a worthy
conclusion until 2 B.C., the year of his elevation to *pater patriae*—an
event he deliberately placed at the end of the *Res Gestae.*[12] It seems that
it was not until the peaceful and smooth transfer of power to Tiberius—
who could not, like Augustus, convincingly presume upon an *auctoritas* that had accrued to him as a savior in time of need—that people's
eyes were opened to the existence, behind the façade of the Grey Eminence, of a new system of government not linked with a particular
person.[13]

THE IMAGE OF POWER AND THE POWER OF IMAGES

It was only in retrospect that the principate of Augustus acquired a formal structure that set it in contrast to the republican era. Of course no
agreement surfaced for some time about the meaning Augustus held as
the founder of a new political system. For Velleius, Augustus was a republican *princeps* for the very reason that the historian could not or
would not discern any unrepublican qualities in Tiberius.[14] By contrast,
Suetonius—although he spoke of a *novus status* of the *res publica* under
Augustus[15]—began his series of the biographies of the Caesars with Julius. For Plutarch, too, Augustus is the second monarch.[16] Oddly
enough, even Tacitus, who leaves no doubt about his critical attitude
toward Augustus, makes no unequivocal statement on this issue. Is Augustus the last in the long series of republican strongmen who have oppressed the Republic with their *dominationes* since the time of Cinna,
or has a new condition arisen since Actium, because of the concentration of all *potentia ad unum?*[17] Does he see a distinction between *domi-*

11. *RG* 4, and cf. 6.
12. Ibid., 35.
13. On Livy, see J. Deininger, "Livius und der Prinzipat," *Klio* 67 (1985) 265–72.
According to Deininger (270), "deutet alles darauf hin, daß Livius den Prinzipat gerade
nicht als eine 'neue' politische Ordnung im Sinne eines Systemwandels erfaßt hat."
14. Vell. Pat. 2.89.1–4.
15. Suet. *Aug.* 28.
16. J. Geiger, "Das Bild Caesars in der römischen Kaiserzeit," *Historia* 24 (1975)
444ff.
17. Tac. *Ann.* 1.1.1; *Hist.* 1.1.1 respectively.

natio and the *imperium* that Augustus exercises *nomine principis?*[18] Not
until Cassius Dio do we come across a clear tripartite schema: after the
(republican) phase of *demokratia* (up to Philippi: Books 3–47), follows
a *dynasteia* (up to 29 or 27 B.C.: Books 48–52), and finally the *monarchia* (Books 51–80).[19]

These or similar divisions of Roman history, deduced *ex post facto*,
had their imprint on every later discussion of the principate. They express themselves in the form of an unintentional ambiguity in the recent
comprehensive observations of Paul Zanker on another component of
power—the power of images. "As we look back on the *saeculum augustum*, it was certainly a decisive turning point . . . With the establishment
of one-man rule, however, there began in every cultural sphere a comprehensive move toward standardisation . . ."[20] Zanker refers to a retrospect on his own presentation. At the same time, however, his findings
are based upon a retrospective on a period that because of its transitory
nature should not be unequivocally aligned with either a republican or
monarchical "reality." Therefore the basic issues confronting modern
scholars are, as they have always been, questions about how this "binding link between the Republic and the Empire"[21] should be put into
proper perspective. Was Augustus the last *princeps* in a long series of
republican *principes* or was he the first *princeps* of a new era?

Analysis of the principate is made doubly difficult because it is bound
up inseparably with one's estimate of the *princeps* himself. Even in antiquity divergent explanations were advanced concerning the foundations of his power and his authority. Vergil and Horace stress the salvation of the state from the troubles of the civil war and the role of the
princeps as a prince of peace.[22] This accomplishment, bordering as it
did on the superhuman, must have evoked the natural gratitude of those
saved. Tacitus saw the origin of the power of Augustus and of the eerie
silence that met it in the ruthlessness of the *princeps,* the corruption and

18. Tac. *Ann.* 1.1.1; this conflict is visible even in the so-called "Totengericht" (*Ann.*
1.9.3) in spite of the predominantly negative tone. Both the advocates of praise and those
of blame are called *prudentes.*

19. On Dio's classification, see B. Manuwald, *Cassius Dio und Augustus: Philologische
Untersuchungen zu den Büchern 45–46 des dionischen Geschichtswerkes,* Palingenesia
14 (Wiesbaden 1979) 77–100; D. Fechner, *Untersuchungen zu Cassius Dios Sicht der
römischen Republik* (Hildesheim 1986) 8–11. Cremutius Cordus also has the Republic
end with the deaths of Cassius and Brutus (Tac. *Ann.* 4.34.1).

20. P. Zanker, *The Power of Images in the Age of Augustus* (Ann Arbor 1988 = *Augustus und die Macht der Bilder* [Munich 1987, trans. A. Shapiro]) 323.

21. Syme (supra n. 3) VII.

22. See, for example, Verg. G. 1.498ff. and Hor. *Carm.* 1.2.41ff. For the notion of a
prince of peace, see A. von Premerstein, *Vom Werden und Wesen des Prinzipats* (Munich
1937) 117ff.

lethargy of the senate, and the general enervation of a people who either were unacquainted with the alternative—the freedom of the Republic—or had experienced only its negative side.[23] Cassius Dio referred to the supreme control Augustus had over the military and the devotion of a bodyguard suborned with double pay.[24]

In his *Res Gestae* Augustus himself gave a clear indication of the basis of his *auctoritas,* even if that indication is complicated somewhat by his obvious intentions in writing the work: his authority derived from his care for the *res publica,* which he had freed from its foes and ultimately returned into the hands of the people and the senate in accordance with his mission.[25] His *auctoritas*—his influence and his prestige—rests, he says, not on oppressive might (*potestas*),[26] but on his oft-proven military and political expertise. The consensus of the people and the inhabitants of the empire have created him their leader, and the resolutions of the senate and the people have granted him a place of honor in the *res publica.*[27] He has always taken pains to act in accordance with the laws of the *res publica,*[28] and voluntarily abolished measures dating from the time of the triumvirate that deviated from them.[29] As for the rest, he has given pardon to all who asked for it.[30] He has declined the dictatorship on several occasions and thereby made clear that he aspires to no arbitrary power.[31] The senate and the people have elevated him to the status of first citizen,[32] but he is also the first servant of the *res publica,* whose domestic splendor he has increased still more and whose external power he has extended and strengthened following the example set by the *summi viri* of the Republic.

Because the estimate of his personality ran the gamut from lyric adoration by the poets through the "objective" self-assessment of the individual himself to strict condemnation, even the very abundance of ma-

23. Tac. *Ann.* 1.2f.; cf. Dio 56.44.3f.
24. Dio 53.12.3, 11.5.
25. *RG* 1: *rem publicam a dominatione factionis oppressam in libertatem vindicavi.* 34: *rem publicam ex mea potestate in senatus populique Romani arbitrium transtuli.*
26. Cf. the virtues on the *clupeus virtutis* (ibid., 34): *clupeus aureus in curia Iulia positus, quem mihi senatum populumque Romanum dare virtutis clementiaeque et iustitiae et pietatis causa testatum est per eius clupei inscriptionem. post id tempus auctoritate omnibus praestiti, potestatis autem nihilo amplius habui quam ceteri, qui mihi quoque in magistratu conlegae fuerunt.*
27. Ibid., 25: *tota Italia sponte sua* [*in verba mea iuravit*] *et me belli . . . ducem depoposcit.* Cf. 34 and 9.
28. Ibid., 2: *iudiciis legitimis.*
29. On the amnesty legislation of 33 B.C., see Dio 49.43.5.
30. *RG* 3: *omnibus veniam petentibus civibus peperci;* cf. Dio 51.2.4 and Vell. Pat. 2.86.2.
31. *RG* 5.
32. Ibid., 34 and 35.

terials available to historical research did not make it possible to reach any certain understanding of Augustus. Every generation of scholars was at liberty to link the portrait of Augustus with the perception of the use or abuse of power determined by its own times and in each case to sketch the portrait anew.[33] Furthermore, the history of the varying scholarly reception of Augustus shows that the limits set by the sources—which in any event allowed great latitude—were in no way respected. National pride in the achievements of the monarchs of the nineteenth century and national Führermania in the twentieth century tempted advocates and opponents of modern forms of the concentration of power to use the example of Augustus to demonstrate the advantages and dangers of that power. Ecstatic praise and harsh censure stood side by side.

Of these two reactions, that of uncritical and effusive veneration reached its sorry climax in the era of the new "leaders" in Fascist Europe: *il Duce* Mussolini used the bimillennium in 1937 of the birth of the *dux* Augustus to surround himself and his nation with a colossal *Mostra Augustea* in the great tradition of the *imperium Romanum*,[34] and the "Führer" north of the Alps did not hesitate to celebrate Augustus as well.

At this time a book emerged in Oxford that was neither able nor willing to ignore the *Zeitgeist*—or rather the *Zeit-ungeist*—on the Continent. Its dedicated author admitted that the book "has not been composed in tranquillity; and it ought to be held back for several years and rewritten," for "its imperfections are patent and flagrant." "But the

33. For a summary of the scholarship, see the bibliographies in D. Kienast, *Augustus: Prinzeps und Monarch* (Darmstadt 1982) 431–52; G. Binder, ed., *Saeculum Augustum*, vol. 1, Wege der Forschung vol. 266 (Darmstadt 1987) 389–403 (compiled by W. Kierdorf); E. S. Ramage, *The Nature and Purpose of Augustus' "Res Gestae,"* Historia Einzelschr. 54 (Stuttgart 1987) 117–57 (who registers his differences with the research on the *Res Gestae*); as well as the Editors' Preface and the contributions of J. Linderski and H. Galsterer in this volume.

34. The archaeologist Giglioli concluded his opening speech on 23 September 1937 (year XV of the new calendar), which was addressed to the "*civis romanus*" Mussolini, with the words of *il Duce*, which also shone forth over the entrance to the exhibition: "Italiani, fate che le glorie del passato siano superato dalle glorie dell' avvenire!" (Catalogue of the *Mostra Augustea della Romanità*, Rome 1937, VIII). The "Führer" at the northern end of the Rome-Berlin political axis, undaunted by the German campaigns undertaken by the man celebrated, also found it convenient to glorify Augustus. He too was arming for battle against impending danger from the decadent East—not, of course, against the *fatale monstrum* Cleopatra (Hor. *Carm.* 1.37.21), but against a party chief who had just adorned himself with a new "republican" constitution (see the Editors' Preface at n. 17 and H. Galsterer's contribution to this volume at n. 5). The Roman exhibition of 1937 cast long shadows. Even at the beginning of the eighties, the "force of tradition" prevented a large-scale exhibition in Rome. The event did find another place for itself in 1988—ironically enough, in Berlin, the other end of the old axis; cf. the Exhibition Catalogue, *Kaiser Augustus und die verlorene Republik* (Berlin 1988).

theme," he added, "I firmly believe, is of some importance."[35] Nothing could delay Ronald Syme's *Roman Revolution* any longer; his political message, which was cleverly enveloped in superb scholarly method, went over the heads of most politicians—and over the heads of many colleagues, who thought that the book was urgently in need of substantial corrections by "serious" scholarship.[36] Nevertheless, the book, which appeared in 1939, together with A. von Premerstein's work *Vom Wesen und Werden des Prinzipats*[37] (published two years earlier), represented a clear turning point in research on the principate. The research of the nineteenth and early twentieth centuries had focused on the effort of categorizing the constitutional arrangement of this strange and unique system, which clothed itself in the outward forms of a republic and yet included the all-overshadowing authority of a ruler. With his attempt to define the principate according to constitutional criteria as a dyarchy, Mommsen had cut, rather than loosened, the Gordian knot. His impressive edifice presented challengers time after time with the problem of having to defend their prorepublican or promonarchical tendencies against arguments from the arsenal of Mommsen's powerful *Staatsrecht*.[38]

With the work of von Premerstein and Syme, a new and dynamic element entered the picture alongside the static view of the principate, which was in danger of being mired in the discussion of constitutional law. Both authors were searching for the societal bases of power and looking to these for an explanation of the lasting success of the principate. Von Premerstein's portrait of a *princeps* as *patronus* of innumerable *clientes* in Italy and in the provinces provided a plausible explanation for Augustus' uncontested position as well as for the dynastic continuity of the early principate. Syme honed still more the notion of party leader developed in von Premerstein's analysis and, masterfully utilizing the prosopographical method, presented Augustus as a cool power politician at the head of a loyal and power-hungry clique of upstarts. The *princeps*, together with this new revolutionary leadership-elite—both parties driven by their association as accomplices and their interest in keeping the power they had won with the sword—succeeded in securing lasting power.

---

35. Syme (supra n. 3) IX (all three quotations).
36. So Stier (supra n. 2) 6; cf. 7: "vorwissenschaftliche Kategorien."
37. Von Premerstein (supra n. 22).
38. A concise and accurate summary of the discussion can be found in W. Kunkel, "Über das Wesen des augusteischen Prinzipats," *Gymnasium* 68 (1961) 360ff.; D. Timpe, *Untersuchungen zur Kontinuität des frühen Prinzipats*, Historia Einzelschr. 5 (Wiesbaden 1962) 1ff. See also Linderski's contribution to the present volume.

Even these interpretations, although recognized for their ground-breaking and accurate observations, have found no unanimous approval. One of the gaps that was criticized in Syme's portrayal, namely, the neglected aspect of the role of the army, has since been closed—partly by Syme himself, who later became interested in the problem, and partly by others who, following less cautiously where Mommsen once trod, have interpreted the principate as a military monarchy or even as a military dictatorship.[39] Yet neither the form nor the content of the principate permits us to find the *arcanum imperii* in military power, even if no one will deny its importance. True, the power of the *princeps* rested in large part on the legions in the provinces and on the numerous veterans in the colonies and *municipia;* yet he had a military monopoly only between Actium and January 27 B.C., when he gave up his plenary power. Before that he had had to share the command of the Roman army with the consuls, with his colleagues in the triumvirate, and finally with Antonius; afterwards, the senate controlled, at least initially, about eight legions in the not insignificant provinces it administered. Even the later rearrangements in favor of the *princeps* do not alter the fact that the senate formally vested the *princeps* with command at regular five- or ten-year intervals. One is tempted to see this as a mere formality; yet it remains striking that Augustus always made an effort to be present in Rome when the renewal was due. At no point did he have to think about using his legions for anything other than the expansion of the Roman Empire. For their part, Augustus' veterans showed no inclination to leave their settlements and go to Rome, in sharp contrast to the veterans of the late Republic, who strongly resisted being settled.[40] To have turned about three hundred thousand battle-hardened old blades into farmers again—and into farmers who remained farmers—is an achievement of Augustus all too little noticed, one that is surely to be valued more highly than raising an army of five hundred thousand.[41]

39. So, for example, N. A. Maschkin, *Zwischen Republik und Kaiserreich: Ursprung und sozialer Charakter des augusteischen Prinzipats* (German trans. of Russian, Leipzig 1954; first published, Moscow and Leningrad 1949); H. Schneider, *Die Entstehung der römischen Militärdiktatur: Krise und Niedergang einer antiken Republik* (Cologne 1977). For Syme, see Galsterer's contribution to this volume, at nn. 52–54.

40. On the veterans of the late Republic, see H. Aigner, *Die Soldaten als Machtfaktor in der ausgehenden römischen Republik* (Innsbruck 1974) 42 and 148f. According to Sallust (*Cat.* 16.4) there were many veterans in Catiline's army who had served under Sulla. According to Appian (*BCiv.* 3.2.7) there was the promise that they would be allowed to leave their farms again before twenty years had elapsed—an important concession made by Caesar's assassins to the soldiers. By contrast, the unrest in the army of Octavian (Dio 51.4) arose because of the delay in the settlement.

41. On the number, see *RG* 4. On Augustus' settlement policy, see L. Keppie, *Colonisation and Veteran Settlement in Italy, 47–14 B.C.* (London 1983) 101–33.

Attempts were also made either to classify the principate as a constitutional type sui generis, that is, to define it according to modern political-science criteria as a "constitutional monocracy," or to describe it as a democracy or to proclaim the "principate" a "republic." [42] But these all represent a reversion to the legalistic discussion about constitutional categories. It seems as if a simple *horror vacui* requires placing an unmistakable label on the "binding link" between the Republic and the empire of the Caesars, so that "eine juristische und politische Wirklichkeit" [43] can at last be conferred upon it.

Those who wished to set the label of monarchy on Augustus' rule found an ally in archaeology. Paul Zanker means to close a further gap in Syme's work with the discovery of the power of images, or so it seems; for, as he says, "Unfortunately, his fascinating chapter on 'The Organization of Opinion' takes no account of the role of art and architecture." [44] For Zanker the goal is "to examine the complex interrelationship of the establishment of monarchy, the transformation of society, and the creation of a whole new method of visual communication." [45] Through the power of images, whose enthusiastic reception was "routed in a general feeling of approval for the new regime" by the citizenry, who "responded to him with all manner of honors, whether as individuals or through their various organizations and chosen representatives," [46] he was able to establish a new mythology and ritual of power for himself that "transcended the realities of everyday life." [47]

There is no question that for Zanker this reality is a monarchy in which a great ruler ruled over an empire; for in the power struggles between Caesar and Pompeius, between Octavian and Antonius, the old Republic supposedly perished, and with it the "dissolving effects of the images." The new positive pictorial language of a monarchy took the place of the old power of images, making no attempt to disguise the monarchy, because the tendency to treat Augustus as a monarch came naturally, and everyone was well prepared to do so. [48]

It seems as if the premise determines the outcome here. The archae-

42. K. Loewenstein, "Die konstitutionelle Monokratie des Augustus," *Zeitschrift für Politik* 8 (1961) 197ff. (= W. Schmitthenner, ed., *Augustus* [Darmstadt 1969] 531ff.); A. Guarino, *La democrazia a Roma* (Naples 1979); H. Castritius, *Der römische Prinzipat als Republik* (Husum 1982).

43. Castritius (supra n. 42) 21.

44. Zanker (supra n. 20) V.

45. Ibid., 3.

46. Ibid., 100.

47. Ibid., 4.

48. Ibid., V, 2, 98, 100, 93 (in the order of the paraphrases).

ologists will continue to debate details in the work such as the identification of the so-called master of the bath, the types of classicizing portraits found in the late Republic, and the interpretation of devotional
images.[49] All the historian can do, however, is either to greet the book
with a cheery *quod erat demonstrandum,* if he agrees with the author's
premises; or to express his regret that in the midst of such admirable
perspicacity and scientific precision an opportunity was missed to examine not only the peculiarity of, but also—and with equal thorough-
ness—the traditions behind, the great wealth of material dealt with in
the book. Of course, the connection with the republican tradition did
not escape Zanker's notice; for he speaks of the personal modesty exercised by the *princeps;* of his *pietas,* so much like that of olden times; in
a word, of his "Republican style."[50] He also recognizes the necessity
that existed of bringing out "equally their ancient traditions and their
relevance to the present,"[51] and he detects a continuity in the "pyrami-
dal stratification of Roman society."[52] But his fixation on monarchy as
the form of the state prevents his sound observations on the power of
tradition from bearing fruit.[53] He knows the means to free himself from
the confines of his premises, namely to acknowledge that there is in fact
"a typical compromise between Hellenistic/Late Republican traditions
and the values of the new Rome"[54] or to take seriously that the "chief
characteristics of the Augustan pictorial vocabulary are its broad spectrum of associations and the general applicability of the individual symbols, but also a corresponding lack of specificity in any particular
case."[55] But he does not go on to use these latter characteristics as the
starting point for a refinement of his observations that gives more credit
to the self-assertiveness of the citizens of Rome.[56] In this way the deter-

49. Zanker (supra n. 20) 5 identifies, for instance, the statue of the so-called master of
the baths with a Roman general—a much contested identification; J. D. Breckenridge,
"Roman Imperial Portraiture from Augustus to Gallienus," *ANRW* 2.12.2 (1981) 485,
sees classical, Polyclitan, features in portraits from as early as the mid-first century B.C.; as
for "devotional images," see Zanker (supra n. 20) 175.
50. Zanker (supra n. 20) 77.
51. Ibid., 110, cf. 126–29.
52. Ibid., 151; cf. however, 149, where Zanker attributes to the clever conduct of the
princeps the "consolidation of the new[!] social order."
53. See Zanker (supra n. 20) 192: "The new state and Augustus' dominant role in it
required a legitimacy drawn from the past."
54. Ibid., 249 (the allusion is to the statue type with nude upper body and drapery
around the hips).
55. Ibid., 177 (on the representation of the *aurea aetas*); cf. also T. Hölscher, *Victoria
Romana* (Mainz 1967) 136ff.; id., "Die Geschichtsauffassung in der römischen Repräsen-
tationskunst," *JdJ* 95 (1980) 265–321, at 280f.
56. See, for instance, Zanker (supra n. 20) 141: ". . . the people really did feel as if they
owned these great works"; and 164: "the sight of the white *togati* . . . must have been a
proud one."

minative feature becomes a break between Republic and Empire that can neither be verified by historical research nor established with such conclusiveness in the development of these representational images. What is more, the identity created by these images threatens to become one with no basis at all, one that no longer stands even on the ruins of the Republic. It becomes rather the product of a way of thinking that has not only resigned itself to the loss of the old Republic, but takes part quite readily in the formulation and propagation of a program that centers around the emperor as the champion of his political friends.

Although this basic thesis approximates Syme's proposed model, or at least is indebted to it, it still remains questionable whether Zanker has pierced to the heart of the matter. In contrast to Zanker, Syme did not especially emphasize Actium as a turning point; instead he began his analysis with the year 60 B.C. Above all, however, Syme, like Mommsen and Tacitus, shied away from assigning to that constitutional twilight zone, the *saeculum Augustum,* any of the labels traditionally used to describe government, including monarchy, although they all fully appreciated the authoritarian aspect of that regime.[57] Both Cassius Dio and most of those analyzing the *optimus status* in our times were less cautious on this point and, by choosing between the labels of republic and monarchy, overlooked the genuinely transitory nature of this phase. Those who, like Zanker, have opted for the monarchy label, will naturally see an Emperor peering out from behind every pictorial representation—or perhaps, with Syme again, they will see the oligarchy that, as he put it, "in all ages, whatever the name and form of government . . . lurks behind the façade"[58]; but from both these perspectives, the force of the republican tradition is reduced to insignificance. The argument is close to becoming a vicious circle.

Even as penetrating an observer as Christian Meier has not escaped this pitfall.[59] For him too, it is beyond question that the principate was

<hr>

57. In Tacitus (*Ann.* 1.1) the circle from the *reges* to the *princeps* does not close (see the beginning of the Editors' Preface), insofar as the conceptual difference continues to exist. Mommsen uses the notion of "Dyarchie" to describe the constitutional systems (on deviations from it, see Linderski's contribution to this volume, at nn. 34–39). Syme (supra n. 3) handles the idea of monarchy with great caution in characterizing the "binding link between the Republic and the Empire" (VII); cf. 516: "To be sure, the state was organized under a principate—no dictatorship or monarchy."

58. Syme (supra n. 3) 7. But Syme sees the republican aspect of this oligarchy clearly when he adds that "Roman history, Republican or Imperial, is the history of the governing class."

59. See C. Meier, "Augustus: Die Begründung der Monarchie als Wiederherstellung der Republik," in id., *Die Ohnmacht des allmächtigen Dictators Caesar: Drei biographische Skizzen* (Frankfurt 1980) 225–87; see also Meier's contribution to the present volume.

a monarchy and that Augustus wished to be a monarch, even though he played the role of the First Citizen so well.[60] Of course Meier does recognize that there is in the "äußeren [scil. republican] Gewand . . . zweifellos ein Stück Wirklichkeit," but it was consonant with the "Charakter dieser Monarchie" not only to be "was sie 'im Grunde' war, sondern auch was sie zu sein intendierte."[61] This oracular ambiguity achieves a happily monarchic resolution: Augustus could, "indem er soweit wie möglich anknüpfte an republikanische Traditionen, seine Monarchie am ehesten, am festesten und am praktischsten begründen."[62] Would it not also be worth asking if Augustus was so credible as a republican figure because he had used his power to bring to a successful settlement that period of trial, decades in duration, in which other strongmen since Sulla's time had attempted to heal the Republic? And certainly it did not harm his credibility that the settlement he effected lay within the republican tradition, which needed no advocacy from him, and was indeed more than mere drapery.

It seems more than a *lapsus calami* when Meier translates with downright carelessness the single source document that he considers worthy of a word-for-word rendering, in order to stress the elements in Augustus' "Programm" that were novel and directed toward the future, namely *Res Gestae* 8.[63] Augustus at that point does not speak of having reintroduced "viele in unserer Zeit in Vergessenheit geratene Beispiele der Väter"—not of *exempla exoleta,* but of *exempla exolescentia,* of still-existing examples that were in danger of disappearing.[64] The words of Augustus, which were indubitably chosen with care, cannot be fitted so smoothly into the program of the great innovator that Meier has outlined. It is the link with the past, above all, that is expressed here, not merely a restoration and further development.[65] In spite of their partially novel character, the new laws and his own *exempla* are set in the long series of republican efforts to shore up collapsing *mores.*[66] At the very least, the choice of words should give cause for thought.

60. Meier (1980: supra n. 59) 226, 242–43, 273.
61. Ibid., 273.
62. Ibid., 247.
63. Ibid., 281.
64. *RG* 8: *legibus novis me auctore latis multa exempla maiorum exolescentia iam ex nostro saeculo reduxi et ipse multarum rerum exempla imitanda posteris tradidi.* Heuss (supra n. 7) 8 has called attention to this important distinction.
65. Meier (supra n. 59) 281.
66. See also H. Bellen, "Novus status—Novae leges," in Binder (supra n. 33) 308–48, esp. 322–28.

THE "REALITY" OF A TIME OF CHANGE:
THE NEW PATRIOTISM

Cause for thought can be found also in considering what is manifestly
one of the greatest difficulties in the analysis of the principate of Augustus: the political structure of the Republic simply cannot be outlined
with clarity. If an agreement exists that the constitution of the Republic
"nur ein System traditioneller Begriffe und Leitsätze [war], die keines-
wegs immer mit der politischen Realität Schritt gehalten haben," [67] so
much the more carefully should one deal with the definition of "realities" in the principate. The range of the changes made—and the range
of the political conditions of the *res publica* that could still be considered as republican in nature by contemporary leaders and those they
led—can then hardly be conceived of broadly enough. For the very reason that the nature of the *res publica Romana* was determined by inter-
personal relationships, it rested "weitgehend auf Machtverhältnissen
statt auf Rechtsverhältnissen." [68] Because of this segmentation of power
among various personalities, the republican constitution could be
adapted to changing realities over the course of centuries and demonstrated an immense flexibility. Even the identification of the *res publica*
with the laws, which was stressed in the first century B.C., essentially did
not alter such flexibility at all. In fact, such an identification made it
considerably easier to subsume even substantial political changes into
the republican tradition, as long as they rested on purely formal legal
models and concepts.[69] The proud insistence upon legal concept, visible
in *Res Gestae* 34, when Augustus maintains that he has never possessed
more power (*potestas*) than his colleagues in office, has its basis—late
republican indeed, but solid nonetheless—in the legal rhetoric and the
juridical science of the Republic;[70] and thus it was understandable and
acceptable to his contemporaries.

The inquiry into the true nature of the principate is, then, no longer
a question of the transition from one form of government to another.
Instead, another problem has come to the fore: that of the creeping,
barely discernible transition into a system in which a genuine republican
principle—the formation of a social and political power based on per-

67. W. Kunkel, *Untersuchungen zur Entwicklung des römischen Kriminalverfahrens
in vorsullanischer Zeit* (Munich 1962) 76.
68. H. Buchheim, "Wie der Staat existiert," *Der Staat* 27 (1988) 13.
69. J. Bleicken, *Lex Publica* (Berlin and New York 1975) 403–39.
70. U. Wesel, *Rhetorische Statuslehre und Gesetzesauslegung der römischen Juristen*
(Cologne 1967); R. A. Bauman, *Lawyers in Roman Traditional Politics* (Munich 1985).

sonal relationships and dependencies—was carried to extremes. Therefore new questions arise: Were Augustus and his contemporaries aware
of the "qualitative leap" implied in this development? Was it truly so
simple to discern whether the citizens of Rome were the subjects of a
Caesar or the fellow citizens of a *princeps?*

In order to head off any ready misunderstanding, let it be said that
the answers to these questions shall neither deny the power of images
nor stylize Augustus into a heaven-sent savior or make the principate
into a republic. They shall, however, make Syme's felicitous depiction of
the principate as the "binding link" a starting point for a serious review
of the power of the linkages of tradition. Without any doubt, the power
of images—of monuments, statues, and memorials—is well fitted to illustrate what exists, to make visible the ideologies behind the reality,
and to amplify sentiments as well as faint identities. All the same it
seems problematic to ascribe to these images and symbols the power to
create new identities. Even in the case of pictorial programs with an
ideological basis that have long years to work an effect upon the be-
holder, the axiom still holds: "One only sees what one knows." Therefore the effectiveness of the program in creating new identities is dependent upon the degree of familiarity in the conveyed content of the
message. Particularly a statement in a new guise, which works to cultivate a taste through its aesthetic form and stimulates emulation, must,
in order to become politically effective, emphasize references to what is
customary, that is, to the past itself. Recollection of previously assimilated material is well known to promote successful new learning.

Would it not then be advisable, in the matter of interpreting these
images, to see in the setting of the Augustan epoch formed by these images not the fair semblance of a monarchy that commits to oblivion the
Republic of the past, but rather the fair semblance of a Republic that is
self-confident enough in its new raiment to tolerate one who is "exalted" in its midst? As far as the effect of images on the consciousness is
concerned, these alternatives do not differ; however, in appraising the
purpose of the images and the reason for their undeniable effectiveness,
the distinction between the alternatives is significant: the purpose of
these images was not to create a monarchy, but to improve a republic.
They did not possess power in and of themselves; rather, they drew on
the power of tradition for their effectiveness. Their purpose, above all—
and here the alternatives unite—was to distract from the reality, to lull
the onlooker. In an aesthetically attractive and architecturally impressive setting, the question of the political organization of power becomes

secondary as long as this power does not encroach upon the realm of private life, the most important primary needs of human life are met, and the contradiction between the claims of the ideal and the claims of politics as they are actually conducted does not provoke further opposition and resistance.

The traces of resistance against the *princeps* are relatively feeble—which does not, of course, prove that he was considered either a good-natured man or a republican.[71] Octavian's role in the proscriptions and his betrayal of Cicero, the cruel slaughter of citizens and senators at Perugia, the breach of the pact with Sextus Pompeius, his perfidious behavior to Lepidus, his vengefulness and ruthlessness, cannot be omitted from the record. These things render him an unsympathetic figure, but not an entirely unrepublican one. But also not to be omitted is the astonishing fact that a much-feared warlord, who had come, sword in hand, into the possession of total power in the state (*potitus rerum omnium*),[72] and made no attempt to conceal this fact, was able almost instantaneously to dispense with martial threats—directing the silver statues that commemorated his own career to be melted down,[73] sending the greater part of his soldiery home, and becoming a beloved prince of peace. He even succeeded in making the military activities at the fringes of the *imperium Romanum* the focal point of public attention and in surrounding them with the aura of an activity that would secure eternal peace. War and peace became an indivisible unity.[74]

No less astonishing than his success with the sword was his ability to maintain his position through more than forty years of peace and to live almost unmolested in the midst of countrymen whom he had allegedly robbed of their republican freedom. For who it was who had the last word on every question could hardly be concealed; his affable demeanor permitted no doubt about the effective power of the Father of the Country; scarcely a member of the senate or a magistrate will have failed to take into consideration consciously or unconsciously whatever he presumed to be the will of the *princeps* in any given matter. How is it—so

71. See the contribution of K. A. Raaflaub and L. J. Samons in this volume (on resistance).

72. *RG* 34.

73. Zanker (supra n. 20) 86 speaks of "proud victory monuments." In his discussion Zanker overlooks the fact that only silver statues are in question. Where were the statues made of other materials? On this and on the use of silver, see T. Pekáry, "Statuae meae . . . argenteae steterunt in urbe XXC circiter, quas ipse sustuli," in Lefèvre (supra n. 7) 96–108.

74. On the significance of the wars for domestic politics, see E. S. Gruen's contribution to the present volume.

the basic question goes—that all this was tolerated, that the Romans made no attempt to defend themselves against such crippling authority? Is it not possible that this authority was not really perceived as crippling, because the Romans had learned already in republican times to hearken continually to strict authority figures such as the *pater familias,* the magistrates with *imperium,* the *principes senatus?* Or, to put it differently: Must Augustus' contemporaries have recognized the "necessary and salutary fraud" of the principate,[75] if fraud it really was? Did not the *princeps* operate rather in such a way that all classes of the populace, without having to charge themselves with blatant self-deception, could come to the conviction that Augustus acted largely within the traditional political system? Perhaps he did not exactly act *as* a republican, but he certainly acted *like* a republican—or at least not like an all-oppressive monarch.

In retrospect (and precisely because it is in retrospect) it may seem that this view has arisen out of mere wishful thinking. Nevertheless, as is shown by the programmatic series of statues of the *summi viri* in the Forum Augustum and the long column of republican portraits at his funeral procession, Augustus was concerned to the very end of his life to place himself in the tradition of the Republic. This intent is nowhere clearer than in the composition of the *Res Gestae.* He featured most prominently in the text those sentences in which he boasts of having rescued the freedom of the *res publica* and of having reestablished the *res publica* itself.[76] Set at the commencement and the close, like declarations of his program, they frame his deeds, his honors, and his financial and military achievements. Such clear and pointed declarations would have been useless, out of place, even laughable, on the grave of a "monarch" if the sense of identity of the Romans had already detached itself from the traditions and values of the Republic and been transformed, through the effect of images upon their spirit, to an acceptance of a monarchical system.[77]

The last lines of the *Res Gestae* furnish, indeed, a decisive indication of how Augustus wished his place in the state to be understood and why it was so easy for his contemporaries to believe in the *res publica: senatus et equester ordo populusque Romanus universus appellavit me pa-*

75. *RE* 22 (1954) 2070, s.v. princeps (U. Wickert); cf. Syme (supra n. 3) 516: "necessary and salutary fraud."

76. See supra n. 25.

77. On the date of the *Res Gestae* (A.D. 14), see E. S. Ramage, "The Date of Augustus' Res Gestae," *Chiron* 18 (1988) 71–82.

trem patriae.[78] He deliberately deviates from the usual formula *senatus populusque Romanus* by listing the *equester ordo* next to the senate and characterizing the *populus Romanus* as *universus*. To them all he bequeathed, as a *pater,* not only a *res publica restituta* but even a *patria,* a fatherland. His pride in this achievement shows in his placement, explained above, of these lines at the end of the *Res Gestae* and in the naming of the dignified places at which this decision of the *universi* was to be publicized.[79]

From this point of view, the *princeps'* role in the *res publica* appears less important than the meaning of the fatherland itself. Augustus wished to create a *mythos* of the state more than a *mythos* of a ruler, inasmuch as he had fashioned out of a republic of oligarchs a republic for all Romans and had thereby put it within reach of all to feel themselves primarily as masters of the world. His greatest political achievement consists in having promoted the development of a patriotism that combined the legacy of the Republic and his own accomplishment in preserving that legacy. The Republic lived on, because Augustus had summoned once more to the consciousness of the Romans the responsibility that was traditional to them and befit them alone, namely, the responsibility of ruling over the earth: *Tu regere imperio populos Romane memento.*[80] In this the achievements of past generations were recognized as important preconditions of the existing situation, and the responsibility his contemporaries held in common was specified. This statement was directed primarily at the senatorial ruling class, particularly those members of it who were in positions of military command and were directly concerned with attaining dominion over the earth. It was, however, directed also at the *equites,* who administered the fruits of this dominion, and it was directed also at the people. Because the attainment of this patriotic purpose was linked inseparably with the role and person of Augustus, who cultivated his connection with the people, broad segments of the populace were afforded the possibility of identifying with the *res publica* and its values through the person of the *princeps* himself. Thus personal pride in the fatherland, in particular a feeling of "we-ness," was encouraged, which permitted each Roman to find his own place as a *civis Romanus* and as part of the history of the Roman state.

78. *RG* 35.
79. Ibid.: *idque in vestibulo aedium mearum inscribendum et in curia Iulia et in foro Aug. sub quadrigis, quae mihi ex s.c. positae sunt,* [scil. *senatus et al.*] *censuit.*
80. Verg. *Aen.* 6.851.

This new patriotism—new at least in its intensity—was a crucial factor in the stabilization and recognition of the *novus status* as the *optimus status* of a *res publica*. This thesis will gain credibility if it can be established that the development of the principate and its inner structure did not (to say the least) run counter to republican ideas of political conduct. In the following sections of this paper, therefore, the events of the individual phases of this development shall be reconsidered by focusing primarily on visible references to republican traditions and on the conduct of Octavian/Augustus himself.

II.   The Power of Tradition in the Formation of the Principate

With certain qualifications, the time from the death of Caesar to the commencement of Tiberius' administration can be divided roughly into five phases. (For the sake of clarity, these phases have been defined more strictly than is historically appropriate.)

The first phase, from 44 to the end of 33 B.C., includes the entrance of the young Octavian into politics, the time of the triumvirate, and its gradual disintegration, as well as the beginning of the propaganda war between Octavian and the *neos Dionysos,* Antonius.

The second phase stretches from 32 until the end of 28 B.C. Here the tensions between Octavian and Antonius exploded in the battle of Actium on 2 September 31 B.C. After the occupation of Egypt and the death of the enemy of the state, Octavian confronts the difficult task of finding a new role in the *res publica.*

The third phase, from 27 to 23 B.C., represents, in its constitutional aspect, the most important segment of the development of the principate. It begins with the restoration of full authority to the senate by Augustus and a preliminary organization of government and administration of the empire, including the future position of Augustus; it ends with the correction of these arrangements.

The fourth phase extends from 22 until 2 B.C. It has no unifying features. Worthy of note are the first years, up to 19 B.C., in which Augustus takes care of important but hitherto neglected matters relating to the provision and security of the city. During the same period unrest occurs in Rome, which in the absence of Augustus assumes dangerous proportions. With the festival of the new *saeculum* in 17 B.C., Augustus declares the arrival of a new epoch in Roman history. His nomination as *pontifex maximus* in 12 B.C. signifies a high point in a long series of priestly offices,[81] and his elevation to *pater patriae* in 2 B.C. represents the last of the official honors that the senate and the people of Rome bestow upon him.

The fifth phase, up to his death in A.D. 14, sees the *princeps,* his position secure, engaged in transferring this position to a successor. After several failed attempts, which had already been undertaken during the previous fourth phase, his stepson Tiberius is finally built up into "coruler" and thereby acknowledged as his designated successor. Although this last phase is of least importance for the structural development of the principate of Augustus, it attains a special significance as the period of preparation for the continuation of the principate—the form of government in which the administration of the empire is to endure.

FROM *VINDEX LIBERTATIS* TO DEFENDER OF ROME

From the perspective of an adherent of the old Republic the beginning of the first phase was not exactly promising. Octavian, now nineteen years old, had returned to Italy after the murder of Caesar and learned of his adoption.[82] On his own resolve, he gathered an army [83] and vowed at a *contio* in mid-November 44 B.C. to rescue the state from the tyranny of Antonius, who was, after all, a loyal follower of Caesar. This vow was, indeed, connected with an emphatic expression of "his hopes of rising to his father's honors." [84]

It was a blunt proposal—and it was self-contradictory. How exactly was a second Caesar supposed to save the Republic? Too blunt, these words—they show Octavian's lack of political experience and can only be understood in the context of the uncertain situation in which Octavian had found himself since his adoption had become known. If he accepted the will, he had to enter politics, in order to fulfill and execute the testamentary trust; if he rejected it, he nevertheless remained in public opinion and in the thinking of Caesar's veterans the principal heir, as provided for by the adoption, and therefore a potentially dangerous rival of Antonius.[85] As for Antonius, he had lost no time in getting rid of

81. *RG* 10. On the preeminent role of that priesthood, see G. W. Bowersock's contribution to the present volume.

82. On the situation after Caesar's death, see A. Alföldi, *Oktavian's Aufstieg zur Macht* (Bonn 1976) 25–29.

83. *RG* 1: *annos undeviginti natus exercitum privato consilio et privata impensa comparavi.*

84. Cic. *Att.* 16.15.3.

85. Alföldi (supra n. 82) 23f.: "Entscheidend war für Caesars Soldaten und für die . . . hauptstädtischen Massen die Willensäußerung des 'gottgewordenen Julius' für die Aner-

an alleged son of Marius who surfaced after Caesar's death.[86] Octavian
had good reasons to fear the same, the more so since Antonius probably
thought from the very beginning what he later said openly—that Octavian owed everything to his name.[87] Octavian himself was very much
aware of the political risk represented by the sons of powerful fathers;
after the conquest of Alexandria he did not hesitate to order the execution of the son of Antonius and his own "adoptive half-brother" from
the union between Caesar and Cleopatra. If Octavian wished to survive
in this situation, there remained for him essentially only one option: to
make clear his claim to a political position in the res publica. Only thus
could he assure himself of the loyalty of Caesar's veterans in his private
army and at the same time hope to find influential helpers among the
opponents of Antonius.

Octavian did not stand alone when he made his attempt to gain both
power and the favor of the people,[88] but he lacked the support of trustworthy republican leaders. Thus he was concerned from the start to ask
Cicero's advice about the use of his army that had been recruited *privato
consilio*.[89] It would doubtless be premature to draw from this the conclusion that Octavian felt himself particularly obligated to the Republic.
All the same it afforded Cicero the opportunity to point out to this
young and (seemingly) tractable man that it was definitely possible to
satisfy the claims of an outstanding individual within the traditional,
flexible limits of the republican constitution. Cicero called for a public
acknowledgment of Octavian's private decisions.[90] He proposed to have
bestowed upon Octavian the *imperium* of a *propraetor,* to have him received into the senate and afforded exemption from the age limitations
on candidacy for office.[91] Cicero believed he could even give his own
word for the young man's good conduct as a republican.[92] In this, admittedly, Cicero doubtless overestimated his influence over Octavian. In
a brilliant analysis of the role of Cicero in the rise of Octavian, H. Bellen
has shown the delusory nature of Cicero's conviction that the career of
the *adulescens* was all his doing. At all stages of the development, it was

---

kennung der Sohnschaft seines Großneffen"; Schmitthenner (supra n. 5) 111 as well sees
the political significance of the will more clearly in his second edition.
    86. Cic. *Phil.* 1.2.5; Livy *Epit.* 116; App. *BCiv.* 3.2–3; Val. Max. 9.15.1.
    87. Cic. *Phil.* 13.11.24–25.
    88. Alföldi (supra n. 82) 31–54 (Balbus and Oppius).
    89. Cic. *Att.* 14.11.2; cf. 9.3, 10.3; 16.14.1. See also Alföldi (supra n. 82) 48–52.
    90. Cic. *Phil.* 3.2.5 (*cui quidem hodierno die, patres conscripti, . . . tribuenda est auc-
toritas, ut rem publicam . . . possit defendere*); cf. 3.3.7.
    91. Cic. *Phil.* 5.16.45ff. On the legal questions, see Bauman (supra n. 70) 61f.
    92. Cic. *Phil.* 5.18.51.

the actual military might behind Octavian that hastened events.[93] Even Octavian, however, could not ignore the fact that it was before all else the *imperium propraetore,* defended by Cicero with historical precedents, that served him as the springboard for his entire later career: it bound the soldiers to him and won him, first, acclamation as *imperator,* then a triumph, and finally (with the help of the soldiers who had grown more and more attached to him) the consulate; and with this he gained, for the first time, a position that Antonius had to recognize by incorporating him into the triumvirate.

This in no way implies an intention to see in Cicero the spiritual preparer of the principate.[94] It is Cicero's abiding achievement, however, to have bound Octavian into the spiritual and political tradition of the Republic by means of his counsel and his actions. With his praise of Octavian's leadership qualities, his courage, his strength of purpose, his *virtus* and his *auctoritas,* he ranked him *expressis verbis* with such great men of the Republic as Scipio Africanus, T. Flaminius, and Pompeius, who as youthful heroes had accomplished great deeds on behalf of the *res publica.*[95] Is it far-fetched to see in this ranking an inspiration for the gallery of *summi viri* later exhibited in the Forum Augustum, or to think that such focus on youthfulness suggested to Augustus the possibility of emphasizing eternal youth in his portraiture?[96] Bellen concludes his examination with these words: "Ohne Cicero hätte dieser so wichtigen Phase seines Lebens der Katalysator gefehlt, der in ihm jene Reaktion auslöste, die ihn an die *res publica* band. Überspitzt kann man sagen: Es war Ciceros Werk, daß Oktavian am 13.Januar 27 v.Chr. die *res publica* aus seiner Machtbefugnis in die Verfügungsgewalt von Senat und Volk zurückgab."[97] These experiences, won out of the close collaboration with Cicero and bound up with Octavian's bad conscience at having betrayed to the proscriptions a man who had assisted him, may have led the later Augustus to see himself as the *gubernator* of the *res publica* whom Cicero had hoped for, and who, after fulfilling his duty as savior of the *res publica,* had to step back again into the ranks of his peers.[98]

There will be manifold evidence in the following pages that Octavian

93. H. Bellen, "Cicero und der Aufstieg Oktavians," *Gymnasium* 92 (1986) 161ff.

94. On this, see M. Schäfer, "Cicero und der Prinzipat des Augustus," *Gymnasium* 64 (1957) 310–20; H. Cambeis, "Das monarchische Element und die Funktion der Magistrate in Ciceros Verfassungsentwurf," *Gymnasium* 91 (1984) 237–60, esp. 259.

95. Cic. *Phil.* 5.8.23, 19.53, 17.48.

96. Zanker (supra n. 20) 36: "Octavian's youth was exploited masterfully."

97. Bellen (supra n. 93) 189.

98. On *rector* and *gubernator rei publicae* in Cicero, see Cic. *Rep.* 5.3.5, 5.4.6, 5.6.8; 6.1.1. Further, cf. 2.29.51; 5.7.9; 6.8.8; Cambeis (supra n. 94) 241ff., 258. Schäfer (supra

had a masterful grasp of the art of the possible; but it will also become
clear that he frequently did not take the possibilities of power to their
limits. Already during the period of the triumvirate he showed some
sensitivity concerning republican ideas—a sensitivity that became still
stronger after the victory over Antonius.[99] Considering the well-known
ruthlessness of Octavian, the possibility suggests itself that this was a
clever tactic to throw a veil over his own actions. By the same token, on
the other hand, the distinctive traces of his relationship to the tradition
of the Republic can be detected in this sensitivity; they are so difficult to
discover only because—naturally enough—they could not be revealed
clearly under the exceptional conditions that prevailed during the period of the triumvirate, and because after he had obtained total power
they could be denounced all too easily as mere attempts to palliate the
actual situation.

Octavian did not insist any longer on his avowed purpose of attaining the honors that his adoptive father had, after his "Cicero experience"; or at least not in the flagrant form of a dictatorship. His position
among the triumvirs in any event offered him hardly any opportunity to
pursue ends of that type. The purpose of the pact that was struck at the
end of October 43 B.C., among Antonius (who had been Caesar's fellow
soldier), Lepidus (the governor of Spain and Gallia Narbonensis), and
Octavian, was rather to collaborate in putting an end to the civil wars
and to reorganize the commonwealth.[100] Octavian was patently the
least among the greatest—men who had assigned themselves the paradoxical duty of restoring the *res publica* on behalf of the *res publica* and
yet at their own discretion. In contrast to the completely private agreement among Pompeius, Caesar, and Crassus in the so-called first triumvirate of 60 B.C., the pact of Bononia provided for a ratification in the
Roman *comitia*—which was secured by a *Lex Titia* on 27 November
43 B.C.[101]

The procedure thus remained within the framework of republican
usage; even the substance of the powers assumed could, as Klaus Bringmann has recently emphasized, be based on the model of the extraordinary military commands of the late Republic—although with one cru-

n. 94) 321 finds ideas of Cicero's "bis in die Formulierungen hinein" in the works of
Augustus and the Augustans.

99. Linderski (see at nn. 32–34 of his contribution to this volume) emphasizes in conjunction with the religious policy "the constitutional sensitivities of the principate."

100. On the pact of Bononia, see V. Fadinger, *Die Begründung des Prinzipats* (Berlin
1969) 31–47.

101. On the *Lex Titia,* see Fadinger (supra n. 100) 48–56.

cial innovation: the extension of proconsular power to the domain of *domi*.[102] By this means, of course, martial law was brought into the city, and the bounds of the constitution were broken, even if "[sich] formal ... die Routine der Regierungstätigkeit in den gewohnten Bahnen des Zusammenspiels der Organe der res publica [vollzog]."[103] Bringmann, contradicting Mommsen's definition of the formal powers of the triumvirs, in accordance with his own close examination of the sources, determines that nothing indicates that the office of the triumvirs "die Verfassung außer Kraft gesetzt hätte oder gar zu dem Zweck eingesetzt worden wäre, die Verfassung umzugestalten. Eine Rechtsprechungsbefugnis besaßen sie ebensowenig wie ein Gesetzgebungs- und Beamtenernennungsrecht."[104] In this Bringmann does of course run the risk not, like Mommsen, of misunderstanding "den politisch bedingten Rechtsbruch als Ausdruck einer Rechtsidee,"[105] but of confusing the substance of the triumvirs' authority with its procedural enforcement.

The problem is that the *comitia*, on the one hand, had no ability, as a body provided for in the constitution, to confer authority that lay outside the constitution; and on the other hand, the crisis of the state (*necessitudo rei publicae*) could very well make decisions necessary that brought with them a substantial self-limitation or even a partial abolition of the powers of the decreeing body. In this respect the function of the senate and the people no less than the substance of the *potestas* of the triumvirs remained within the long, though not actually glorious, tradition of the Republic. The state had rescued itself from earlier *necessitudines* by similar means: with the *senatus consultum ultimum*, which as the "ultimate" or "final" decree of the senate gave the consuls a temporary monopoly of executive powers; with a dictatorship of Sulla's type, which reduced senate and *comitia* to rubber stamps for his solitary decrees; with the extraordinary *imperia* of Pompeius and his consulate *sine collega*, which in their substance and consequences were as effective as they were unusual. What marked each of these measures as republican was the time limit and/or the definition of the duties that were to be fulfilled. The triumvirs avoided evoking the memory of the *dictator perpetuo*, Caesar, by limiting their term to five years[106] and by describing

---

102. K. Bringmann, "Das Zweite Triumvirat: Bemerkungen zu Mommsens Lehre von der außerordentlichen konstituierenden Gewalt," in P. Kneissl and V. Losemann, eds., *Alte Geschichte und Wissenschaftsgeschichte, Festschrift für K. Christ* (Darmstadt 1988) 22–38, esp. 32ff.
103. Ibid., 36.
104. Ibid.
105. Ibid., 38.
106. Livy *Per.* 120: *per quinquennium*.

their mission as the restoration of the Republic (*rei publicae constituendae*).[107] It was also certain, however, that after the fulfillment of this mission the *potestas* of the triumvirs could not serve as the foundation for personal predominance in a republic, however it was constituted.

The precedence of the will of the triumvirs over the powers of the *comitia* is demonstrated by the fact that the persecution of opponents in the proscriptions began even before the *Lex Titia* was passed.[108] It can also be seen in the nomination of those persons whom the triumvirs wished to see as consuls of the subsequent years[109] as well as in the *praenomen imperatoris,* which Octavian bore as a component of his name from 38 B.C., if not from 40 B.C.[110] The Imperator Caesar began to insist upon the military *and* dynastic foundations of his position within the triumvirate and the *res publica.*

The characteristics of an emergency authority, especially the hallmarks of a private agreement external to the state, grew still more pronounced when the triumvirs continued to hold their powers beyond the scheduled termination of the triumvirate at the end of 38 B.C. and finally renewed it by themselves in the spring of 37 B.C., in the pact of Tarentum.[111] It was now obvious who defined the public state of emergency. This manifest fact could hardly be altered by the belated and retroactive authorization by the *comitia* for the extension of the *potestates* of the triumvirs, urged through only by Octavian and ignored by Antonius. Yet, despite Octavian's emphasis on the military and dynastic components of his power, his decision to seek such authorization did bring to light a new political sensitivity. The triumvir with the least political experience began to think of his political future, which he probably already conceived of in republican terms. Thus in 36 B.C. he protected himself against persecution by the *sacrosanctitas* of the tribunate of the plebs,[112] and he proclaimed the end of the civil wars after the victory over Sextus Pompeius, by which he relieved Italy of supply difficulties

107. *RG* 1.1; Livy. *Per.* 120.
108. Fadinger (supra n. 100) 41, 82.
109. Ibid., 36.
110. Syme (supra n. 3) 113, n. 1.
111. On the pact of Tarentum, see Fadinger (supra n. 100) 84–98.
112. *RG* 10; Dio 49.15.5. Meier (supra n. 59), who identifies an important "Realitätsveränderung in Rom" (252) in the year 36, appears (perhaps following Sattler [infra n. 143]) to underestimate the awarding of *sacrosanctitas:* "relative Bescheidenheit der Ehrung" (253). Its significance lies in its legal substantiation by the leading lawyer of his time, Trebatius Testa, and thus in the phasing out of a genuinely republican office through republican means. See also Bauman (supra n. 70) 132f.

and himself of unrest among the city populace.[113] Nor did he retract his professed intention to restore the Republic in company with Antonius when Antonius showed no interest.[114]

Octavian could not keep his promises, however, for the tensions among the triumvirs were increasing noticeably. In 36 B.C. "a strange delusion" [115] on Lepidus' part—who hoped to exploit to his own advantage the victory over Sextus Pompeius—furnished a pretext for eliminating Lepidus completely from the triumvirate, by means of a *lex de imperio abrogando* initiated by Octavian.[116] The formalities were observed also by allowing Lepidus, who lived far from Rome, to continue in the office of *pontifex maximus*.[117] At the same time Octavian began to distance himself cautiously but perceptibly from Antonius, who continued to live in the East, for the most part with Cleopatra. The building of a temple to Apollo on the Palatine, begun in 36 B.C., might be interpreted as a political countermove to the Dionysian affectations of Antonius (now married to Cleopatra, although not divorced from Octavia) rather than as a genealogical reference to the Julian clan.[118] In 34 B.C., the *neos Dionysos* of the East made it considerably easier for the ruler of the West to present himself as the defender of Roman values: the splendiferous triumph of Antonius over Artavasdes of Armenia took place in Alexandria far from the Roman Capitolium and in an alien mode;[119] the children of Cleopatra—of a woman with whom any valid *conubium* was precluded by Roman law—were recognized by Antonius as legitimate; in Augustus' eyes, the gifts of land to Cleopatra robbed the Roman people of a part of the national territory of the Republic. Still more disturbing to Octavian must have been the fact that Antonius thereby gained a rich and powerful ally for what now seemed the unavoidable confrontation between the triumvirs. And particularly irritating, because unequivocally directed against his own person, was the recognition by Antonius of the son of Caesar and Cleopatra as the legitimate successor of Divus Julius. In Caesarion's veins flowed the blood

113. App. *BCiv.* 5.13.128, 130, 132.
114. Ibid., 5.13.132; see Fadinger (supra n. 100) 178.
115. Syme (supra n. 3) 232.
116. Livy *Per.* 129; Dio 49.12.4.
117. *RG* 10; Dio 49.15.3.
118. So, for example, O. Immisch, "Zum antiken Herrscherbild," in *Aus Roms Zeitenwende,* Das Erbe der Alten 20 (Leipzig 1931) 29ff.; and Zanker (supra n. 20) 44ff. (although on 44 again with strong partiality for the genealogical connection).
119. Dio 49.39.3ff.; 49.41.1–4; Plut. *Ant.* 54.3–5. On the political significance, see Fadinger (supra n. 100) 150ff.

of the man to whose name Octavian supposedly owed everything, while Octavian himself could only point to the last line (*in ima cera*)[120] of Caesar's will.

At the beginning of 33 B.C. Octavian found himself, overall, in a rather promising situation: The fresh splendor of his successfully concluded war in Illyria[121] contrasted favorably with Antonius' lack of success against the Parthians and the unearned triumph against Artavasdes. Yet that was not enough to make up for the end of the second term of the triumvirate, which loomed at the close of the year. "Then the trial would come."[122] Antonius continued to enjoy strong support in the senate; generals continued to triumph who stood closer to Antonius than to Octavian, and they ornamented the city with building projects that underscored the good republican and traditional style of Antonius' party: Pollio restored the *atrium Libertatis* and furnished it with the first public library; Sosius dedicated a temple—to Apollo, of all gods—with the booty of the war of 34 B.C.; Ahenobarbus even repaired the Temple of Neptune, who had been the patron of Sextus Pompeius.[123]

Octavian now had to prove himself the best of the Romans. He began to expand his attacks into several areas, but he coordinated them so adroitly, with the help of his friends of many years, Maecenas and Agrippa, that no suspicion of a massive attempt on his part to influence public opinion could arise. Maecenas and his circle of poets had long since relieved Octavian of the thankless task of self-praise, and still kept up the good work.[124] Agrippa too concentrated his efforts, in the decisive year 33, on demonstrating that the circle around Octavian was especially concerned about the well-being of the people of Rome: the former consul accepted with the aedileship the task of repairing all the aqueducts, of building a new one, and of staging sumptuous games, at which he most generously distributed donations and *congiaria*—all this out of his own private means.[125] Octavian could concentrate on the literary feud that he began to wage against Antonius.[126]

The result of these united efforts was an increasing, self-incurred obligation on the part of Octavian's circle to act as protectors of the Ro-

120. Suet. *Jul.* 83.2.
121. See Gruen (at n. 22 of his contribution to this volume); W. Schmitthenner, "Oktavians militärische Unternehmungen in den Jahren 35–33 v. Chr.," *Historia* 7 (1958) 189–236.
122. Syme (supra n. 3) 241.
123. A synopsis is found in Syme (supra n. 3) 241 and Zanker (supra n. 20) 65–71.
124. On the poetic propaganda, see Syme (supra n. 3) 459–75.
125. Hor. *Sat.* 2.3.182–86; Pliny *HN* 36.24.121; Frontin. *Aq.*1.9; Dio 49.43.1–4.
126. Fadinger (supra n. 100) 180–94.

man values and traditions. What could still have been thought of, since about 36 B.C., as propaganda, had gained independent life now and become a program that, by its mere existence, achieved a reality of its own and thus no longer admitted—and admits—of any distinction between seeming and being. Octavian and his adherents, as rescuers of tradition and the Republic, could no longer turn back. If they wished to remain credible, they had no choice but to internalize and intensify these roles. So armed, they could only wait to see how they would pass over the reef of the expiration of the triumviral *potestas*. Much depended upon the behavior of Antonius and his followers in Rome.

FROM *DUX PARTIUM* TO *PRINCEPS* AUGUSTUS

In spite of all these preparations, at the commencement of the second phase in early 32 B.C. Octavian's situation was uncertain. One thing alone was clear: there was no question of a second extension of the office of the triumvirs. Cooperation along the lines of the pact of Tarentum was also impossible. Since the outbreak of the propaganda war between them, Antonius and Octavian had no interests in common. Moreover, Antonius' offer to lay down his triumviral powers, made to the senate and people of Rome at the end of 34 B.C., blocked all rapprochement.[127] Octavian seems never to have considered any one-sided, formal extension through the *comitia*, because of the legal objections that could be raised, or at least because of political considerations. How could he, a single individual, have himself confirmed in an office with the complete authority of three, without risking that the removal of collegial intercession would awaken the worst memories of dictatorship? For the time being, a one-sided surrender of all the powers connected with the office of triumvir was not possible either. True, the purpose of the *Lex Titia* could be considered at least partially fulfilled with the declaration of the end of the civil war following the defeat of Sextus Pompeius, but the essential goal—namely, the organization of the *res publica* as the common responsibility of the triumvirs—seemed at the moment unattainable. Antonius clung to his triumviral *potestas* in the East, as his coins show.[128] Thus for Octavian, a return to private life following the precedent set by Sulla was unthinkable. He would have made himself a helpless target of his numerous and powerful enemies.

For these reasons it was necessary for him to find a way that allowed

---

127. Dio 49.41.4–6; cf. Suet. *Aug.* 28.1.
128. Fadinger (supra n. 100) 265f. with the relevant data.

him to continue the authority of the office of a *triumvir rei publicae constituendae,* without actually holding the office, in order to avoid giving the impression that, as a *privatus,* he was operating with a huge army. What Octavian needed was a commission for himself and his army, somewhat comparable to that which Pompeius had been given by the *Lex Gabinia* and the *Lex Manilia,* and which would not lead to a renewal of the civil war, since he had already taken credit for ending it. It cannot be decided whether what followed fulfilled a farsighted plan or ensued from the developing circumstances. Some of the activities of Agrippa in the previous year suggest that some kind of plebiscite was under consideration, and that perhaps also options were studied to shape Augustus' commission after the pattern provided by the promagistracy—that is, a *prorogatio imperii* and thereby a formal separation of the office and the power of the office—which was rooted in a long and thoroughly republican tradition. But too much remained unsettled for any certain plans to be made.

The year 32 B.C. began with the attack of the new consul, Sosius, on Octavian in the senate.[129] As it happened, Sosius made the mistake of not fully representing the case for Antonius on the latter's terms, but instead conspicuously avoided reading aloud a letter of Antonius, although he praised him in effusive terms. This gave Octavian the opportunity, in a later session of the senate, of demanding the reading of the letter, with whose contents he apparently was familiar. Sosius declined once again, because he thought the contents—which had to do with Antonius' request to the senate to ratify his dispositions in the East—would not make a positive contribution to Antonius' public image. Octavian seized the chance to cast stinging reproaches upon Antonius and Cleopatra and to portray himself in the most favorable terms. He was able to persuade the majority of the senators, who had grown suspicious, that Cleopatra's hunger for power and Antonius' unsteady character represented a danger for Rome; thus it was more vital than ever to continue the authority of one of the triumvirs beyond the expiration of the term, in order to protect the West from the impending peril out of the East. He even offered to submit incriminating written evidence in a later session of the senate, in order to prove the correctness of his assessment of the situation.

This, of course, only happened months later. The consuls of 32 B.C., Sosius and Ahenobarbus, left Rome in haste together with about three hundred Senators and betook themselves to Antonius at Ephesus with

---

129. On this and the following, see Fadinger (supra n. 100) 195–213.

the evidence.[130] But even there some took objection to Antonius' conduct, observing the role played by Cleopatra.[131] Two of the most closely trusted of Antonius' associates, Munatius Plancus and Marcus Titius, departed Antonius' camp with several others and were received with open arms by Octavian in Rome.[132] From them he learned how he could obtain the evidence he had promised; it was contained in the will of Antonius deposited with the Vestals. Much indignation arose over the unheard-of breach of law and trust of which Octavian had to make himself guilty in order to gain possession of the will; but it was eclipsed when the senate—which had by now been emptied of all followers of Antonius anyway—heard the details, which until now had been mere rumors; Roman territories were to be given away, Cleopatra's children were to become Antonius' legitimate heirs, and Antonius was to be buried at Alexandria. Thus Octavian's accusations were proved sound and it appeared perfectly believable that the army assembled at Ephesus was being mobilized not against the Parthians, but against the West.[133]

The political implications of the will and its damaging contents led, in the middle of 32 B.C., to a *consensus universorum:* a unanimous decision of the majority of the Roman people—or, to put it more precisely, of the majority of the classes and groups out of which Roman society was composed.[134] Implicit in this *consensus* was the tacit recognition of the continuation of the *potestas* of a triumvir who no longer openly held the office of triumvir—the separation of the office and its powers was carried over even to an extraordinary office. From this point Octavian was able to continue in the authority of a triumvir without formal approval, even if only on the dubious legal ground of an informal approval by the *universi,* a concept with no constitutional meaning. It is tempting to think of the *consensus omnium bonorum* that Cicero emphasizes, wishing it to be the foundation of the politics of the Republic, but Cicero was certainly not thinking of it in connection with an extraordinary office.[135]

The question still remains, Why, in his search for a new position within the *res publica* that would at least secure legitimacy for his ex-

---

130. Dio 50.2.6f.; Suet. *Aug.* 17.2. On the question of the coup d'état, see the discussion of Fadinger (supra n. 100) 214–22.

131. Plut. *Ant.* 56ff.

132. Dio 50.3.1.

133. Fadinger (supra n. 100) 223–44.

134. On the *consensus universorum* and its consequences for Octavian's plans, see Fadinger (supra n. 100) 272ff.

135. Cic. *Har. resp.* 3.5, 11.22; *Sest.* 16.38 (*senatus, equester ordo, cuncta Italia, omnes boni*). Cf. H. Strasburger, *Concordia ordinum: Eine Untersuchung zur Politik Ciceros* (Frankfurt 1931; reprint, Amsterdam 1956) 59–70.

traordinary powers, did Octavian expose himself to the imponderables of the chance that put the last will and testament of his opponent into his hand? Why did he not, as did Antonius, simply continue his triumviral power, supported by the swords of his soldiers, who had extorted the consulate for him in 43 B.C.? Was his political sensitivity, his respect for the usages of traditional politics, perhaps not a mere mask—did it perhaps originate in the insight won from Cicero, that in the long run one could establish oneself in a republic only by acting in a republican fashion? The state of our knowledge allows no answer to this question, and probably none is necessary. In what other way should Octavian have dealt with this situation—he who had for years increasingly portrayed himself as the protector of Roman tradition[136]—if he would not bring the entire edifice tumbling down, whether constructed on principle or stratagem? He had imprisoned himself in his own program, it seems.

On the basis of the *consensus universorum* the further decrees against Cleopatra and Antonius ensued without difficulty: Antonius was stripped of the authority of a triumvir, without, however, being declared an enemy of the state;[137] the declaration of war was directed against Cleopatra.[138] The new war was not going to be a civil war.

With these decrees Octavian became the sole possessor of all power in the state—*potitus rerum omnium.* Because Antonius was not prepared to recognize these decrees—in fact, refused to abandon the enemy of the state, even now that she was threatened with war—he branded himself guilty of high treason.

Octavian must have been conscious from the very beginning of the precarious legality of his power especially in regard to the conflict with Antonius. Therefore he did not content himself with the *consensus universorum* and with the military might that was at his disposal; instead he sought to broaden his basis in the society. Immediately after the declaration of war against Cleopatra, the *hostis,* he bound the entire populace of Rome and Italy to himself by means of a military oath of allegiance.[139] The promise of *fides* and armed support against the *inimicus*—thus against Antonius, the domestic enemy—made the oath

136. The construction of the mausoleum for Octavian was also started at this time; see K. Kraft, "Der Sinn des Mausoleums des Augustus," *Historia* 16 (1967) 189–206. Zanker (supra n. 20) 72–77 appears to me to downplay somewhat the reference to ancient Roman tradition.

137. Dio 50.4.3, 26.3; differently, Suet. *Aug.* 17.2.

138. Dio 50.4.4; Plut. *Ant.* 60.1.

139. *RG* 25; on the oath, see Fadinger (supra n. 100) 284; J. Linderski, "Rome, Aphrodisias and the *Res Gestae:* The *Genera Militiae* and the Status of Octavian," *JRS* 74 (1984) 74–80.

into a party oath and Octavian into a private *dux partium,* into a party leader.[140] The oath, in which private obligations and public interest were inextricably intertwined, obtained for Octavian a *clientela* without number in all levels of Roman society, and with this *clientela* an enormous potential for influencing politics without violating the formal rules of the interplay between institutions. Of particular significance was the large number of senators, who became his military followers.[141] The course seemed open toward an institutionally intact republic. It only remained to be seen how the Republic could take upon itself a *patronus* with unrivalled *auctoritas;* but this question would be settled only when, after Antonius was dispensed with, the time had come to integrate into the *res publica* a *dux* without precedent. Would the Republic remain a *res publica* or would it become the *res privata* of Octavian?

After the victory over Cleopatra and Antonius at Actium on 2 September 31 B.C. and the conquest of Egypt on 1 August 30 B.C., Octavian had risen to the position of the "national commander in chief," with a monopoly on military power; and he had, furthermore, been elevated from *dux partium* to *princeps civitatis* by means of the oath of allegiance sworn by the provinces of the East. In his *fides* and his following were included essentially all Roman citizens and subjects in the *imperium Romanum.* To be sure, as the *patronus* of an empire that spanned the world, he still faced a mission of the greatest difficulty. For with the end of the civil wars the crisis which had created the state of emergency had come to an end. Consequently the powers that had been warranted by the state of emergency became superfluous, even void. If Octavian wished to continue on his course in a credible manner, he had to dispose of these powers and find a place in a properly constituted *res publica;* and furthermore this position had to be both incontestable and not oppressive to the state.

The interval between the triumphal reception prepared for the victor by the citizens of Rome (in mid-29 B.C.)[142] and the official resignation of his all-encompassing power on 13 January 27 B.C.[143] was utilized by Octavian to convince his fellow citizens not only that he deserved to be the first citizen, but that he was prepared to play this role in a *res publica*

---

140. Syme (supra n. 3) 294–312; Fadinger (supra n. 100) 278f., 284.

141. *RG* 25: *qui sub signis meis tum militaverint, fuerunt senatores plures quam DCC, in iis, qui vel antea vel postea consules facti sunt ad eum diem, quo scripta sunt haec, LXXXIII, sacerdotes circiter CLXX.*

142. Vell. Pat. 2.89.1f.

143. On this period, see P. Sattler, *Augustus und der Senat: Untersuchungen zur römischen Innenpolitik zwischen 30 und 17 v. Chr.* (Göttingen 1960) 24–57.

that was not a republic in name alone. In other words, his attempt to marshal around him the forces of the *res publica* by means of the *consensus universorum* and the oath of allegiance was now followed by his efforts to reintegrate his own person into the machinery of republican normality.

It was also in the year 29 B.C., immediately after his return from the East, that Octavian had the Temple of Janus shut.[144] He made a solemn promise of a future policy of peace and bolstered it by discharging many soldiers and reassigning the province of Asia to the senate. In the same year he paid out 400 sesterces each to about 250,000 citizens and 1,000 sesterces each to 120,000 veterans in the colonies.[145] Simultaneously, or shortly beforehand, he spent about 700 million sesterces for the purchase of land for his soldiers, thereby disassociating himself demonstratively from the detested practice of confiscation.[146] Also in this and the following year are to be dated the account for the restoration work on a total of eighty-two temples, which had been in progress for some time, and the costs for the great games on the occasion of the victory celebrations.[147] A rough estimation puts this sum at about 80 million sesterces. This total expenditure of about 1,000 million sesterces demonstrates either his concern for the people of Rome, the sincerity of his "policy of disarmament," and his respect for the ancient gods of Rome, or—seen through the eyes of the critic—his willingness to purchase his recognition as first citizen and benefactor. It is hardly an accident that Cassius Dio sets the famous debate between Agrippa and Maecenas, on the question of republic versus monarchy, in this period of ostentatious liberality, thereby signifying his preference for monarchy as the future form of the state.[148]

In the following year, 28 B.C., Octavian decisively advanced the reconstituting of the Republic.[149] Little by little he dissociated himself from his past, removing the brilliant testaments of his "Octavian phase" by having eighty silver statues melted down; even the name itself disap-

144. *RG* 13; Dio 51.20.4–5.
145. *RG* 15.
146. Ibid., 16.
147. Ibid., 19, 20, 22, 23. Zanker (supra n. 20) 108–9 sees the fact that many of the old temples were repaired rather than completely rebuilt as an indication that there had been a dramatic decline in the value of those divinities and temples. One can just as well attribute this to the well-known traditionalism of the Romans with regard to religious questions.
148. Dio 52.2–40 and 41.1. See also Fechner (supra n. 19) 71–86.
149. Vell. Pat. 2.89 puts this as early as 29 B.C.; see also H. Volkmann, *Zur Rechtsprechung im Prinzipat des Augustus* (Munich 1935) 12.

peared. In the *Res Gestae* he sets the restitution of the *res publica* at the beginning of his sixth consulate. He made no more use of his full powers; instead he executed all his official duties as consul with his colleague Agrippa at his side, who now once again bore twelve *fasces,* as did Augustus.[150] Agrippa was also his colleague in the office of censor,[151] which was intended to prepare the citizenry and the senate for their duties in the *res publica:* The census showed the immense number of over four million citizens[152] and put an end to the uncertainty among new citizens and adherents of his opponents that had arisen in the confusion of the civil wars. Thus the citizenry was constituted anew.

A preliminary *lectio senatus* reduced the senate, which had swollen to about one thousand members in the time of Caesar, by about two hundred members.[153] The two later *lectiones senatus* make this first *lectio* look extremely adroit, for Octavian decreased the number of senators by careful stages and returned the senate to its "republican" dimensions.[154] By so doing he avoided any powerful opposition to the *lectiones,* extracted the elements that were unworthy and of little significance, and enhanced not only the prestige of the senate, now permanently reduced in size, but also the readiness of the remaining or newly added members to see their participation in the formation and administration of the *res publica* as an honorable and meaningful responsibility.[155] Thus the senate too in 28 B.C. was reconstituted and given increased importance.

Finally, at the close of the year Octavian put an end to the uncertainty and confusion over the validity of illegal, questionable, or contested acts and measures from the time of his triumvirate by means of an edict that explicitly declared invalid all acts of his that were in contravention to the constitution.[156] Thus a clear line was drawn; the laws of the Republic once again represented the standard of political conduct.[157] When Cassius Dio explicitly comments, in discussing Octavian's abdication of his sixth consulate, that as consul Octavian had abided by the laws,[158]

---

150. Dio 53.1.1.
151. Ibid., 52.42.1; see also Sattler (supra n. 143) 31–34.
152. *RG* 8.
153. Ibid.
154. Dio 54.13–14.
155. Dio 52.42.1; Suet. *Aug.* 35.1: *indignissimi . . . quos orcivos vulgus vocabat.*
156. Dio 53.2.5; Tac. *Ann.* 3.28.2.
157. On the part taken by Aulus Cascellius against triumviral acts even in the period of the triumvirate, see Volkmann (supra n. 149) 13 and Bauman (supra n. 70) 117–23.
158. Dio 53.1.1: "oath in the manner of the fathers"; for the interpretation, see Sattler (supra n. 143) 34.

he discloses another essential feature of the relationship of the *princeps* to the *res publica*—a continuation of an attitude characteristic of the late Republic, which one can term legalistic, and which demonstrates the tendency to let the validity and effectiveness of statutory laws serve as the standard by which the stability and the republican quality of the constitution may be measured. Thereby, the emphasis on the legality of one's actions becomes an argument proving republican conduct; the constitution becomes the sum total of statutory standards. Thus the abolition of illegal acts by Octavian and his emphasis on the legality of his actions easily could be interpreted by his contemporaries as a return to a conduct that was in accordance with the Republic.[159] This was the principle on which the final restitution of the *res publica* was soon to be expected. In the solemn session of the senate on 13 January 27 B.C., at the beginning of the seventh consulate of Octavian, the capstone was set upon a reorganization prepared with great care over many years. At the same time a new phase began, in which the design had to be tested in real life.

PRINCE OR *PRINCEPS?*
THE PRINCIPATE AS EXPERIMENT

According to the *Res Gestae,* in the famous session of the senate mentioned above Octavian resigned the last remains of his triumviral *potestas,* declared the *res publica* reestablished in accordance with the decree promulgated in the *Lex Titia* of 43 B.C., and returned control over the Republic to the people and the senate.[160] It was now primarily the responsibility of the senate to reformulate the relationship between the *res publica* and the man who had formerly possessed total power. To slight

159. The extent to which the Romans both complied with the rules and tried to do justice to extraordinary situations is demonstrated in the election of the younger Scipio to the consulship of 147 (App. *Pun.* 112). Because he had not yet reached the prescribed age, the senate suggested to the tribunes that they repeal the *lex annalis* and introduce it again in the next year. Similarly, there was a move to reintroduce once again at the end of the year the laws from Caesar's consulate in 59 in order to avoid any obstruction by means of *obnuntiatio* and *intercessio* (Cic. *Prov. cons.* 19.46). On this, see A. E. Astin, *Scipio Aemilianus* (Oxford 1967) 61–69; C. Meier, *Res publica amissa* (Wiesbaden 1966; 2nd ed., Frankfurt 1980) 126, n. 143.

160. *RG* 34: *in consulatu sexto et septimo, postquam bella civilia extinxeram per consensum universorum potitus rerum omnium, rem publicam ex mea potestate in senatus populique Romani arbitrium transtuli. quo pro merito meo senatus consulto Augustus appellatus sum et laureis postes aedium mearum vestiti publice coronaque civica super ianuam meam fixa est et clupeus aureus in curia Iulia positus, quem mihi senatus populumque Romanum dare virtutis clementiaeque et iustitiae et pietatis causa testatum est per eius clupei inscriptionem.*

this responsibility as a mere formality would not do justice to the contemporary attitude toward law and the constitution. In the late Republic, formalities had developed into criteria for the way reality should be
viewed. So in this case there was certainly no "business as usual," but
neither was there "unusual business" when the senate, as it had in its
republican days, made decisions about honors, assignment of provinces,
and special powers.[161]

It would be foolish to attempt to play down the differences between
the old Republic and the new. They arose from, among other causes, the
necessity of dealing with the son of a *divus* as fellow citizen. The emphasis on the importance of formalities concerns the mere fact that the senate was issuing decrees rather than the content of those decrees. And yet
even in the contents distinct degrees of innovation were apparent. The
bestowal of the *corona civica* in gratitude for the rescue of citizens from
death existed in the tradition of the Republic. The inscription on the
clupeus virtutis, which mentioned *virtus, pietas,* and *clementia,* was
firmly oriented toward traditional values. Admittedly a new element
was introduced with the mention of *iustitia,* which had not been part of
the canon of virtues before.[162] But even this element had its roots in the
new legal thinking that emerged in the late Republic. The fact that the
golden shield was bestowed at all and that it was hung up in the Curia
Julia—these, like the laurels on the doorposts of Augustus' private
house, are novel features. Unique also is the bestowal of the title Augustus, which moved his person, through its connection with *augurium,*
into the company of Romulus, the founder of the city, and elevated him
beyond mortal limits.[163]

With the assignment of the provinces the senate returned to the
earthly sphere of its duties.[164] The final settlement of 27 B.C. bears the
earmarks of a practical distribution, approximately equal in terms of
square area, in which the division of troops produced no military monopoly for Augustus; and yet it fell in with the *princeps'* declared purpose of securing the peace, since the restless provinces with most troops
were allotted to him. A senator thinking in republican terms could live
comfortably with this adjustment, since Augustus promised to give his
provinces back to the senate once they were pacified. Empowered by the

161. On the activity of the senate in the Augustan Age, see Brunt (infra n. 198). W. K.
Lacey, "Octavian in the Senate, January 27 B.C.," *JRS* 64 (1974) 176–84, emphasizes the
"normality" of the proceedings.
162. C. J. Classen, "Virtutes Romanorum," *Gymnasium* 95 (1988) 289–302, at 301.
163. Dio 53.16.7–8; cf. Ov. *Fast.* 1.607ff.
164. On the distribution of the provinces, see Sattler (supra n. 143) 44–46.

Lex Gabinia, Pompey had been entitled to encroach far more on the provinces bordering on the Mediterranean—which at that time meant almost all the existing provinces.

The senate administered its pacified provinces as had the Republic, by pro-magistrates of consular or praetorian rank. Sulla had instituted this principle long ago. Senatorial legates were assigned to these pro-magistrates as assistants in jurisdiction. In its essential features this too was an instrument that the senate itself had developed early in the second century B.C. in the interest of smooth provincial administration.[165] Among the senatorial provinces were such important regions as Africa, a breadbasket for the supply of Rome and Italy, and Illyria and Macedonia, which lay in strategically favored positions near Italy and, like Africa, were provided with several legions.

The *provincia* of Augustus comprised Gaul, Spain, and Syria. These were not only counted among the restive provinces, but their situation on the border—besides requiring larger numbers of legions—also permitted Augustus to conduct an expansive policy and to portray himself continually both as a conqueror and as a defender of the *orbis Romanus.* This in turn means that the military should not primarily be seen as a decisive factor in the maintenance of power in the principate of Augustus. Military success rather became a means by which achievement on behalf of the *res publica* could be visibly demonstrated and the person responsible for such achievement could be awarded special *dignitas.* This was a way of thinking that was not alien to republican perceptions. The same applies to the method of administering the provinces of Augustus: the legates with consular or praetorian rank—whom he personally selected just as he appointed the legates of the legions—had their model in the legates with whose help Pompey and Caesar had their provinces administered during their attendance at Rome.

What does seem unique and highly unusual is the constitutional basis for Augustus' command over his provinces. This command was first assigned to him in 27 B.C. for a period of ten years. Scholars have differed as to whether any special authority was conferred upon him with this command. The traditional division between the *imperium domi* and the *imperium militiae,* defined purely in geographical terms and more sharply delineated by Sulla, has persuaded scholars to see the basis for the power of the *princeps* in the provinces in an *imperium proconsulare.* This *imperium* was supposedly conferred on him by the people and the

---

165. B. Schleußner, *Die Legaten der römischen Republik* (Munich 1978).

senate with a temporal limitation and greatly broadened territorial extension. Lucullus and Pompey may perhaps be seen as offering precedents in the Republic for such an *imperium proconsulare*. Augustus, however, continued to be consul at the same time, year after year. Thus in his provincial administration there emerges a constitutional abomination: a *consul pro consule*. This conjunction would have been unique. It bears no parallel even in the consulate of Pompey in 52 B.C., as Ridley has established in his exacting examination of the supposed accumulation of Pompey's commands in the fifties.[166] It is more appropriate, therefore, to see with Badian the authority of the *princeps* to control the legions in his provinces as contained in his *imperium consulare*.[167] Thus at least an accumulation of commands, so offensive to republican notions, would have been avoided. An *imperium proconsulare* was only necessary when Augustus gave up the consulate—and we can actually observe this structural alteration taking place in 23 B.C.

The comprehensive settlement of this year drew the consequences from the experience gained in the reconstituted Republic since 27 B.C. The fact that Augustus continually held the consulship had not only proved a flaw that contradicted the principle of annuity insisted upon during the Republic, it had shown itself to be an actual hindrance. Because of the paramount authority of this consul, uncertainty and unrest arose in the senate in his absence, preventing any independent functioning of that body. Augustus, who had, since the end of 27 B.C., stayed first in Gaul and then in Spain, perceived these problems and applied himself after his return in 24 to renovating the structure of the *res publica*. Here again careful planning is apparent. Money played a role again, as it had during Agrippa's aedileship in 33 B.C. and in the years before the resignation of the triumviral office in 27 B.C. Once again 400 sesterces was paid out to each of about 250,000 citizens, followed by extensive grain distributions in the following year, 23 B.C.[168]

Of course it was even more important to have the *nobiles* on his side. Among the potential aspirants to the consulate, Augustus' continuing occupation of one of the two positions had led to irritation, and it had produced a congestion of candidates.[169] It was vital to free this position in order to cooperate with the upper class, which was striving for equal

166. R. T. Ridley, "Pompey's Commands in the 50's: How Cumulative?" *RhM* 126 (1983) 136–48.
167. So E. Badian, "The Young Betti and the Practice of History," in G. Crifò, ed., *Costituzione romana e crisi della repubblica* (Perugia 1986) 79ff.
168. *RG* 15.
169. Cf. Dio 53.32.3f.

opportunity in holding offices. Augustus combined this gesture with yet another testimony to his respect for the tradition of the *res publica:* as a first step, in a cleverly scripted scenario, a convinced republican was to be elected Augustus' colleague in office for 23 B.C. In the following year Augustus would withdraw completely from the consulate. Nothing suggests that, with the reshuffling of 23 B.C., Augustus was reacting to a crisis or a conspiracy.[170] On the contrary, the very republican Augustus had wished for, Piso, who must have been in on the plan, was chosen consul for 23 B.C.[171] Thus the consul Augustus, with the consul Piso at his side, presented himself as a champion of the old Republic. But then the plan miscarried: for Augustus fell ill, and his very life hung in the balance.

And yet even when he seemed to be on his deathbed Augustus proved himself a republican: he entrusted the official documents to his fellow consul Piso and his seal ring to Agrippa,[172] who as *homo novus* had always manifested a close connection with the Republic. On the other hand, Marcellus, who was expected by many to be the designated successor of the *princeps,* came away empty-handed.[173] As Badian rightly stresses, Augustus could in no way better demonstrate that he shared the opinions and concerns of the *nobiles.*[174] This attitude of Augustus cannot be interpreted as a mere farce. It seems that Augustus wished to go down in the annals of history as the savior of the Republic. This wish is most apparent on those occasions when as "propaganda" it was of little use to his political future—namely, when he seemed to be on his deathbed in 23 B.C., and after his death, with the publication of his *Res Gestae.* Should we not then at least take under consideration the possibility that in his full political life as well he did not use the tradition of the Republic as a veil for monarchy, but instead considered this tradition valuable and worth reviving, because he had found himself a way, within the pale of the Republic, to guarantee the recognition of his special achievement for the *res publica?*

A glance over his activities after his unexpected recovery does not contradict this view. On 1 July 23 B.C., he resigned from the consulate,

170. E. Badian, "'Crisis Theories' and the Beginning of the Principate," in G. Wirth, ed., *Romanitas-Christianitas: Untersuchungen zur Geschichte und Literatur der römischen Kaiserzeit, Joh. Straub zum 70. Geburtstag gewidmet* (Berlin and New York 1982) 18–41, offers convincing criticism of the widely popular crisis theories.

171. Tac. *Ann.* 2.43.2; Dio 53.30.1.

172. Dio 53.20.2; cf. Suet. *Aug.* 28.1.

173. Dio 53.30.2. In 24 B.C. Marcellus, the eighteen-year-old nephew of Augustus, had obtained the right to run for the offices early and sit among the praetorians in the senate: Dio 53.28.3.

174. Badian (supra n. 170) 34.

to reassume it again only twice for short periods (in 5 and 2 B.C.).[175] His command over the legions in the provinces, which was now no longer covered by his consular office, was secured by bestowing upon him an *imperium proconsulare* styled *maius*. Augustus took this temporally limited *imperium* seriously; he made an effort to counteract any notion that his periodic renewals were automatic by being present in Rome for that very purpose at the proper time. He even seems to have prepared for the renewal of 13 B.C. by means of a large donation to his discharged soldiers.[176]

A second basis of support for his position as *princeps* was provided after 23 B.C. by the *tribunicia potestas*.[177] Long before, elements of the authority of the tribune had been vested in him: in 36 B.C. the *sacrosanctitas*, a form of sacral protection, and the *ius subsellii*, as well as the *ius auxilii* in 30 B.C., the venerated right of protection possessed by the tribunes of the plebs—which also implied a protective obligation, and therefore approached in essence the meaning of the *corona civica*, also previously received by Augustus. Now the *ius cum plebe agendi*, the last element of tribunician authority, was bestowed upon him too. Part of the powers of the consulate he had resigned were thereby reassumed, inasmuch as Augustus through the *tribunicia potestas* also gained a legislative function. His authority was still further augmented by the *ius cum senatu agendi* likewise vested in him.

The *tribunicia potestas* eventually proved the centerpiece of the principate. It offered Augustus and his successors in the principate a complete basis for the leadership of the state, and it was not subject to the intercession of the tribunes in office at any given time, because it comprised not the office proper, but rather only the power of the office. All the same this *potestas* remained, in spite of its close relation to the old Republic, an odd instrument of power, which greatly contradicted the practices of the traditional *res publica*. The separation of the tribunician power from the office was without precedent. Moreover, even this power without office appeared strange in the hands of a patrician; for even though the division of the *populus Romanus* into plebeians and patricians had long been meaningless politically, it was a truism of the Republic that the tribunician power was only vested in plebeians.[178] Besides, the practice of serving multiple terms of this office in unbroken

175. Dio 53.32.4. His successor was Sestius, a former partisan of Brutus'.
176. *RG* 16.
177. Ibid., 10; Tac. *Ann.* 1.9.2; Dio 53.32.6.
178. Cicero's notorious opponent, Publius Clodius Pulcher of the patrician clan of the Claudii, had to become a plebeian in order to be able to be elected *tribunus plebis* for 58 (Cic. *Dom.* 29.77, *Sest.* 7.16).

succession had been considered tantamount to *adfectatio regni;* it had aroused furious resistance and contributed considerably to an escalation of violence in the late Republic.[179] Augustus, however, bore this *potestas* in his title from 22 B.C. on and used it to reckon his "years of service." Of course, Augustus could quite properly point to the fact that technically speaking he did not actually hold the office; but all the same, the power of the office had been the reason why in republican times its extension was considered so problematic.[180]

On the other hand, there were factors that could reduce the appearance of anything extraordinary in this situation. For one thing, there was the gradual nature of the transference of the tribunician *potestas,* which occurred in stages separated by long intervals, and its yearly renewal, which was in keeping with republican principles. For another, the office of tribune had never enjoyed any special repute in the eyes of the *nobiles.* It did not belong to the necessary stages of the *cursus honorum;* it had never found a firm definition in the form of a *provincia*—of any particular sphere of duty—and it may well have been considered by many as superfluous. Thus, it may have become obvious only to later observers, such as Tacitus, that behind the use of the *tribunicia potestas* stood more than a gesture aiming at popularity. Among the broad masses of the populace the question was, of course, not phrased as a problem of constitutional law. In their eyes the paramount issue was the extent to which Augustus actually realized what they had always expected from the tribunes of the plebs—that is, the improvement of their quality of life. If by taking over the *tribunicia potestas* he also obligated himself to consider the protection and prosperity of the plebs his permanent responsibility—so much the better.

In one respect, the end of 23 B.C. saw Augustus in the same position in which he had begun the year 44 B.C.: as a *privatus* without office, backed by a huge army. In another respect he was in the same situation in which Sulla had been in 79 B.C.: in a *res publica restituta* whose political mechanisms were once again in working order and in which no effectual political opposition existed or could come into existence. Would the return to private life follow? Even to ask the question is to suggest a negative answer. He was only a *privatus* because he filled no

179. For the senate's reaction to T. Gracchus' attempt to have himself elected *tribunus plebis* for a second time, see E. Badian, "Tiberius Gracchus and the Beginning of the Roman Revolution," *ANRW* 1.1 (1972) 668–731, at 721–26.
180. Tac. *Ann.* 3.56.1 speaks of the *tribunicia potestas* as the *summi fastigii vocabulum.*

office in the Republic; through his *imperium proconsulare* and his *tribunicia potestas*, however, he was so deeply integrated into the administration of the empire that the new *res publica* could not operate efficiently without him. On the other hand, the fact that Augustus exercised his duties without actually holding an office permitted the thought or hope that, if necessary, the state could get by without the *princeps*. For this reason the next phase acquires a particular significance, especially in its early years.

FROM *RES PUBLICA* TO *PATRIA*

The years after 22 B.C. raised doubts as to whether Augustus had not gone one step too far with his decision to resign the consulate—namely too far back to the Republic.[181] The institutions that made up the *res publica* were apparently not capable of ending the turmoil, which evoked memories of the difficult years of the Republic. A famine in 22 B.C. caused the plebs to demand that Augustus should become *dictator* in order to guarantee supplies. Augustus refused, however, as soon as he detected the latent opposition of the senate.[182] As long as there were other means that had a precedent in the tradition of the Republic, it was better to have recourse to them;[183] so at least Augustus seems to have thought. Therefore he undertook the *cura annonae* on the strength of his *imperium proconsulare*,[184] perhaps following the precedent set by Pompey; and he brought the crisis to a surprisingly prompt conclusion. In the next year Augustus left Rome to go to the East. During election time the city was shaken by unrest and by demagogic intrigues; even Agrippa, who had been sent back to the capital, could not put an end to the agitation.[185] Augustus quite openly hesitated to give his attention to restoring the peace, although he was requested to do so.[186] One suspects that he wanted it to be quite clear particularly to the *nobiles,* in whose interests he had withdrawn from the consulate, that he was necessary to an orderly working of the *res publica.*[187] Perhaps he thought this lesson was worth risking his credibility with the people as the reliable guarantor of peace and tranquillity.

---

181. For the particulars of the years 22–19 B.C., see Sattler (supra n. 143) 72–86.
182. *RG* 5 (the refusal of the permanent consulship that was offered him is also mentioned here); Dio 54.1.3.
183. *RG* 6: *nullum magistratum contra morem maiorum recepi.*
184. Ibid., 5.
185. Dio 54.6.1, 6.5–6.
186. Ibid., 54.6.2f.
187. Sattler (supra n. 143) 82–84.

There is much to indicate that Augustus willingly suffered these disturbances to take place, and perhaps even that he expected that they would. It is striking that in the period of his absence an abundance of republican practices revived in Rome. These can only have had his support and approval. Even before his departure Augustus refused the invitation to assume the censorship and provided for the election of two censors.[188] With his permission the proconsul Atratinus celebrated a triumph in the year 21 B.C., as did the proconsul Balbus in 19. Both were governors of a senatorial province, Africa. The opportunities for grandiose forms of self-exhibition among the *nobiles* seemed to have returned. At the same time Augustus restored two provinces to the senate, thereby fulfilling a promise that had probably been little believed in 27 B.C.[189]

Yet the bad times of the Republic came back along with the good. The two censors were soon locked in an argument.[190] The electioneering intrigues of a certain Egnatius Rufus in 19 B.C. violated the sequence of offices customary in the old Republic. As an aedile in the year 21 B.C., Egnatius had won an excellent reputation as the organizer of a fire-fighting squad—which was no small merit in a Rome still built of wood. Buoyed up by his popularity, he was elected praetor immediately following his aedileship.[191] This in itself was against the rules. But now he attempted to attain the consulate, again without observing the minimum interval of time. The consul in charge accordingly refused to admit Egnatius' candidacy.[192] He thereby set off violent unrest among the people of the city, who felt themselves strong, as in the old days, and justified in rewarding their champion. The more levelheaded may not have been exactly enthusiastic at this palpable proof that the Republic was still hearty. No one wanted to have the Republic of a Saturninus or a Clodius back again.

For this reason Augustus could count on some understanding when, returning in the spring of 19 B.C. with the bright trappings of the Roman battle standards of Crassus he had "wrenched" from the Parthians, he restored order with an iron hand. Egnatius, with several others, was accused of taking part in a conspiracy and executed—whether justifia-

188. Dio 54.2.1.
189. Dio 54.4.1.
190. Vell. Pat. 2.95.3; cf. Dio 54.2.2.
191. Vell. Pat. 2.91.3; cf. Dio 53.24.4ff.
192. Vell. Pat. 2.92.2–4.

bly or not remains obscure.[193] The settlement of 23 B.C., concerning the position of the *princeps* in the *res publica,* was augmented by a lifelong *imperium consulare,* which enabled Augustus to carry the *fasces* and to take his seat between the current consuls on the *sella curulis,* as the third colleague, so to speak, in the authority of the office, but not in the office itself.[194]

The following period, between 18 B.C. and the death of the *princeps,* appears "eigentümlich starr und monumental," [195] as if the development of monarchy had already been accomplished. Nevertheless, the appearance is deceptive. The only process that had been concluded was the difficult one of finding a compromise between the claims of the *princeps* for recognition of his unique role in the *res publica* and of his actions on its behalf, and the demands of tradition, which made it necessary to observe at least a formal continuity in the makeup of the *res publica.* The development of a new public consciousness had by no means been concluded—a consciousness that focused on the solidarity of the Roman people and rendered insignificant the perturbing questions about the legal role of the *princeps* among them. And another phase of Augustus' life had hardly begun—a phase that would become the most important for later assessments of his intentions and the constitutional "reality" of his principate: the arrangement of the succession.

The impression of "Starrheit"—fixity—arises from the fact that the constitutional "incorporation" of the *princeps* into the essentially republican forms of the *res publica* after 18 B.C. received no further important alterations. The phase seems "monumental" because under the protection of this structure a patriotism developed that was furthered by means of monumental images but compatible with the tradition of the Republic. To the superficial observer it may have seemed, after Augustus' withdrawal from all the offices, not only as if the Republic had been rescued after the period of the civil war, but even that it had been freed from a few ugly innovations of the late Republic.

Certainly the all-overshadowing authority of the *princeps* curtailed the authority of the magistrates. On the other hand, none of the old offices was actually abolished. Even the censorship, badly neglected by

---

193. Ibid., 2.91.3f. For other sources and literature, see the contribution to this volume by Raaflaub and Samons.

194. Dio 54.10.5. In addition to this there was a *censoria potestas* for five years: Dio 54.10.5. Cf. *RG* 8.

195. Kienast (supra n. 33) 100.

the late Republic, had survived and, because of Augustus' refusal to accept the *cura morum et legum*,[196] was hardly devalued. Moreover, the individual magistracies had not been reduced in prestige by vastly increasing their number, although the need for more administrative personnel in the empire could easily have suggested a multiplication of offices.[197] Furthermore, the employment of members of the *ordo equester* by Augustus may have been perceived as an indication of his respect for the senatorial officeholders, not as a privatization of politics and contempt for the magistrates. For by filling new functions in the imperial administration with *equites,* Augustus preserved the exclusive nature of the senatorial offices and the high social standing of those who had traditionally served as functionaries—a standing based precisely upon their small numbers. In all provinces the important offices remained in the hands of the senatorial holders of an *imperium;* for many senators unprecedented careers opened up. The offices in the city continued to serve as they always had as the first step toward the most important posts in the provinces. The suffect consulates enlarged the chances of many without infringing upon the standing of any individual. By contrast, the tribunate of the plebs probably suffered most, standing, after 23 B.C., entirely in the shadow of the *tribunicia potestas* of Augustus. This loss may have affected the senate and the *nobiles* little; the people for their part saw their protection in Augustus; and as far as the institution of the tribunate and its prestige was concerned, the time of the powerless tribunate, between Sulla and the year 70 B.C., had been its absolute nadir.

If one considers the role of individual senators in the imperial administration, the loss of political influence that the senate had to endure as an authoritative body appears less significant. In contrast to the partly disdainful attitude that Caesar had shown toward the senate, Augustus respected the senate and its function.[198] This had already become appar-

196. *RG* 6.
197. Only the number of praetors seems to have risen, by about two positions in 23 B.C. (Vell. Pat. 2.89.3), and temporarily up to 16 positions in A.D. 11 (Dio 56.25.4).
198. On the conflict between Caesar and the senate as early as his consulate of 59 B.C., see Meier (supra n. 159) 284 with n. 106. On Caesar's waning respect for the senate in his last years, cf. Suet. *Jul.* 78. On the new senators whom Caesar promoted into that august body, see Suet. *Jul.* 76.3, 80.2 and Dio 42.51.5; 43.47.3. On Augustus, see the survey of the senatorial nominations in the *Res Gestae* in H. Braunert, "Die Gesellschaft des römischen Reiches im Urteil des Augustus," in Lefèvre (supra n. 7) 18–20 and analysis on 31–36. P. Brunt, "The Role of the Senate in the Augustan Regime," *CQ* n.s. 34 (1984) 423–44, concludes from a careful examination of the sources that "there was then no part of the public policy and administration under Augustus and Tiberius in which the Senate did not remain in appearance the great council of the state" (442).

ent by 37 B.C., when he had asked the senate to authorize retroactively the renewal of the triumvirate; it became patent at the beginning of 32 B.C., when he tried by force of argument and by promising to present supporting evidence to convince the senate of the necessity to continue the triumviral *potestas;* and such sensitivity for the self-esteem of the senators is visible also behind the discussions about the organization of the future *res publica* in the year 27 B.C. With each purging of the senate and each reduction of the number of senators, the senate gained in value and exclusivity. The second *lectio senatus* of 18 B.C. attests his respect for the senate as well as his intention of trimming it down to three hundred members, its traditional size under the Republic.[199] Why this number if the senate had been degraded to a mere honorary body, and why should the senators put up a resistance if this body no longer counted for anything?[200] Augustus gave up the attempt because of that very resistance and in the end reduced the senate to six hundred, the number in Sulla's times. A third purging of the senate, reported by Dio but of uncertain date, seems more likely to have been a revision, for many of those disqualified later returned to the senate by means of holding offices.[201]

Although it is undeniable that the senate no longer played the role it had before Sulla, two things make it difficult to maintain that the individual senator felt himself forced out of the center of the action. One was the well-known effort of the *princeps* to maintain a good relationship with the senators, and the other was the fact that mere proximity to Augustus doubtless tended to raise the status of the senate. Furthermore, the senate even received a formal increase of its powers that had been long desired and even demanded by Cicero:[202] decrees of the senate gained the force of law. Finally, under Augustus the senate began to assume jurisdictional competence in criminal cases concerning its own members, which must have contributed to a consolidation of the *ordo senatorius.*

The development of senatorial jurisdiction necessarily brought with it changes in the jurisdiction of the *comitia.* In the same way, the right of the *princeps* to recommend or make binding nominations of candidates for offices signified a reduction of the electional freedom possessed

---

199. Dio 54.14.1.
200. According to Suet. *Aug.* 35.1 and Dio 54.12.3, Augustus wore armor under his toga during this period and made use of a bodyguard when he went to the senate.
201. Sattler (supra n. 143) 99.
202. Cic. *Leg.* 3.3.10: *eius* [scil. *senatus*] *decreta rata sunto.*

by the people's assembly—which, however, had already been reduced in republican times to a mere choice between preselected candidates, since the official in charge of the election possessed the right to make nominations, and the *nobiles* worked out their agreements beforehand. The sovereignty of the people's assembly had been a chimera anyway, even at the height of the Republic, since it lacked the right of initiative, was limited by the obligations imposed by *clientela* and depended upon the summons of a magistrate. Thus the changes taking place under Augustus were not that significant, and they were balanced in part by the fact that the people found new opportunities to voice their opinion in the theater and continued to play a role in legislation.[203]

Even the justifiable objection that the *princeps* held an entirely unrepublican position can be countered by the assertion, already repeatedly stressed, that apart from the separation of the tribunician *potestas* from the office itself each element of the *princeps'* authority and the design of the principate is rooted in republican parallels or analogies. There was no need to invent anything new here. Moreover, the *princeps* carefully avoided raising the suspicion that he was after a dictatorship along the lines of the Caesarean model. The bitter propaganda war against Antonius forbade him to aim at a monarchy of Hellenistic type. He quickly dropped his preference for the provocative honorary name Romulus and showed himself personally indulgent and affable.[204] Thus he made it easier for his contemporaries to see him rather as a *princeps* among *principes* than as a ruler among his subjects. Moreover, the accumulation by an individual of the *imperia* of the consuls and proconsuls and the *potestas* of the tribunes of the plebs had the salutary effect of rendering these magisterial powers, which had been so potent and dangerous in the late Republic, incapable of being turned against one another, since they were now balanced and united in a single person.

By 19 or 18 B.C., Augustus had reached his goal. His place in the state was secured, his importance in Roman politics had been demonstrated. The foundations of the Republic thereby had not been destroyed, as everyone could see. And yet Augustus was to live another thirty years in this republic. What was there left to do? His generals and armies provided a continual confirmation of his achievements on behalf of the *res publica,* but could that be all there was? These questions call attention

203. Dio. 53.21.3; cf. Suet. *Aug.* 40.2 and Dio 53.21.6.
204. Suet. *Aug.* 7.2; Dio 53.16.7. On the republican tradition of Romulus' name, see Sattler (supra n. 143) 51. Suet. *Aug.* 53.1 (on the ban on the form of address *dominus*) and 54; Dio 56.43.1–3; cf. 55.4.3. See also Z. Yavetz's contribution to this volume.

to the fact that it is questionable methodology to base conclusions about the political intentions of Octavian or Augustus before this period on the images deriving from the period that followed. The images may be worthy of a monarch, but they were primarily designed to reflect the dignity of Rome and the greatness it had achieved over the centuries. Certainly the beginning of a new epoch was supposed to be stressed in the celebration of the *saeculum* in 17 B.C. What was novel, however, was not the adornment of a monarch who had grown self-confident, but the glorification of Rome and the Romans, the advancement of pride in Roman citizenship and patriotism, the emphasis upon the consciousness that the *gens Romula* was something extraordinary, because its *custos* was someone extraordinary and yet at the same time one of them.[205] This sense of being Roman was what distinguished Augustus' fellow citizens from the Alexandrian seamen who called out to Augustus at Puteoli that it was thanks to him alone that they lived, thanks to him alone that they sailed the sea, thanks to him alone that they enjoyed freedom and prosperity.[206] The citizens of Rome, in the tradition that had arisen with the origin of the empire, were able to partake of the feeling that they were the source of the freedom and prosperity of the provinces.

It was indeed not at all difficult to be grateful to the man who had established the *pax Augusta,* which secured peace and prosperity—and not difficult to forget the cost that had been paid for that peace, chiefly by others. Octavian/Augustus had purposefully staked huge sums of money to reach his political goals. He carefully accounts for more than 2,000 million sesterces in his *Res Gestae;* so important did his expenditure on behalf of the people seem to him. He showed himself generous and concerned in other ways as well. Thus from time to time he accepted the responsibility (*cura*) for the grain supply and gradually took upon himself the responsibility for the public welfare. He concerned himself personally or through official assistants (or occasionally through regular magistrates such as the aediles) about water supply, road building, protection against floods of the Tiber, fire protection, and in general the need for order in the city. Augustus became the greatest single benefactor, and would not allow himself to be eclipsed by anyone. He who had rescued his country from the crisis of the civil wars now became the caring benefactor in matters that the senate had always

205. Hor. *Carm.* 4.5.1f.: *Divis orte bonis, optime Romulae custos gentis.*
206. Suet. *Aug.* 98.2.

treated with reprehensible neglect. Of course it was not enough only to play the role of a *patronus* who took seriously his economic obligations to his *clientes*. Beneficence in grand style may create a sense of obligation and gratitude in the recipients and bring confidence and prestige to the giver, but it also leads to the dependency of those who receive it, and for that reason is not fitted to awakening self-confidence and pride. Augustus' relationship to the *gens Romula* was to become closer and more personal: he wanted to become *pater* in a Roman *patria*.

This is precisely the "image" that is sketched out in the *Res Gestae*. H. Braunert has pointed out, by analyzing Ciceronian word usage, that the identification of *res publica* and *patria* is established as early as the first sentence of the *Res Gestae*. Each in its turn is identical with Rome.[207] Thereby the word *potestas* in the penultimate chapter is relieved of its constitutional meaning, and the word *auctoritas* is connected with the *patria potestas* of the *pater patriae* in the last chapter. The circle is closed.[208]

Augustus certainly did not neglect the advancement of the Roman nation's sense of self-esteem. A few lines from Suetonius' life of Augustus show his purpose in a nutshell:

> Believing it, moreover, to be of the greatest importance to keep the people pure and uncorrupted by any taint of foreign or servile blood, he only rarely conferred Roman citizenship, and set a limit on manumission. . . . He also eagerly desired to bring back the ancient style and fashion of dress; and once when he saw in an assembly of the people a group of men dressed in dark cloaks, he cried out indignantly, "Look at them—'the Romans, masters of the world, the people of the toga'!" He charged the aediles not to let anyone appear in the Forum or its vicinity from that time forward who had not first put aside his cloak and donned a toga.[209]

Behind all this stands an effort to create inward unity—one might almost say uniformity—and, in outward terms, to establish clear boundaries against non-Romans,[210] and the wish to create a Roman self-confidence and self-assertiveness. Each and every Roman could identify with the mission of being "masters of the world," even if he left its actual execution to the *princeps*—after all, the people and the senate had vested in him the powers necessary to realize this mission.

His striving to have as many citizens as possible participate in the life

207. Braunert (supra n. 198) 39ff.
208. Cf. Heuss (supra n. 7) 95.
209. Suet. *Aug.* 40.3–5; cf. 44. The quote is from Verg. *Aen.* 1.282.
210. Egyptian cults were removed from the city centers: Dio 53.2.4; 54.6.6.

of the state represents a common characteristic of Augustus' religious policy, his building program and his support of the arts. None of these areas can be neatly separated from the others. Augustus was everywhere visible, but nowhere did he impose himself. His activities in the venerable priestly *sodalitates,* woken to life once more, show him alongside the descendants of the most important families of Rome. The Ara Pacis shows him with his family, but also with priests of the state, in a set of images referring in every respect to Rome and Italy. His house on the Palatine remained modest, although a *princeps* and a *pontifex maximus* lived there. The Temple of Apollo annexed to it was an indication of the rationality and rigor of the Roman nation, which had made Rome great, and counteracted the irrationality of the East, quite properly subjected by the Romans. Mars dominated the Forum Augustum, as the national god of the Romans;[211] in the sculptural program, the ancestors of the *princeps* were counter-balanced by the *summi viri,* the ancestors of the Romans. A third connecting element was Augustus himself, who as *pater patriae* represented less the incarnation of an abstract idea of the state than the idea of a Roman world in which each visitor could find his own independent place—for the interpretation of what was seen was left up to the viewer. T. Hölscher has shown, in his work on the *pax Romana,* how pictorial programs, toward the end of the Republic, yield fewer and fewer correspondences with concrete historical events.[212] Such timeless representation of values, inasmuch as it approaches the abstract, provides a broad spectrum of possible meanings, which can be associated with personal experiences and longings.

Among these longings, the longing after a monarchy may have influenced the interpretation least of all, especially since the person of the *princeps* was overshadowed, not only in pictorial representation but also in literature, by the emphasis given to "Roman-ness" ("Römertum") and the Roman nation—a notion that has been disengaged from any political setting and thereby also from any glorification of power.[213] The object of this pride was Rome. The "feeling" of being a Roman was all the more certain to determine the interpretation of images since the viewer could also have a part in these gleaming structures in a thoroughly concrete fashion: namely as councillor, judge, priest, senator, or

211. J. A. Croon, "Die Ideologie des Marskultes unter dem Prinzipat und ihre Vorgeschichte," *ANRW* 2.17.1 (1981) 246–75, esp. 258f.: "abgesehen von der Verbindung Mars-Venus . . . nur nationalrömische Aspekte vorhanden" (259).
212. Hölscher (supra n. 55).
213. On the nonpolitical literature, see D. Little, "Politics in Augustan Poetry," *ANRW* 2.30.1 (1982) 254–370.

even as a visitor to the theater[214] or as an artisan who participated in the construction. No one was excluded from the bright beauty of the buildings and their ornamentation. Even in abandoned corners of the city one stumbled upon evidence of Augustan art in the *lararia,* after Augustus had refurbished many of the 265 shrines of the *lares compitales* at his own cost. Certainly the reorganization of the *ludi compitales* and of the *vici* of the city was intended primarily as a means to control the *collegia* that presented no few political dangers, but the connection of the cult of the *lares* with the *genius Augusti* gave the *vicomagistri* a new, elevated role in society.[215] Even the new citizen, the freedman, had here, as in the priesthood of the *Augustales,* the opportunity for an intense identification with the *res publica Romana.*[216] Was it, in a setting that enhanced such feelings, still worth seeking for the "ruler" if everyone came from the same stock and had the same *pater?*

THE HEIR SEEKS AN HEIR

For Augustus himself the search for a successor became gradually more pressing. He knew how difficult it would be in a republic to pass down a position of power that had been won by an individual. His republican program was opposed in principle to any bequeathal of his practical dominance of the field of politics. True, he himself had inherited his name too, but from a man who had paid little or no attention to the *res publica* in the process of laying down the foundations of his power. Augustus, on the other hand, as the savior of the Republic, had taken pains to ensure that he did not elevate his position in the *res publica* above the constitution and thus make it inheritable. To a certain extent, of course, *auctoritas* within a family could be passed on even in the old Republic, since the social position of the *nobiles* rested, on the one hand, on the prestige of the family, on its *clientes* and on its property, which were all inheritable, and on the other, on their own political contribution to the *res publica.* But for Augustus, unlike, for example, the late Republican Metelli, it was not simply a matter of making the consulate into a family affair. For him the problem consisted of transferring to a successor a position that was both extraordinary and tailored precisely for his per-

214. On the orders in the theater, see E. Rawson, "*Discrimina ordinum:* The *Lex Iulia Theatralis,*" *BSR* 55 (1987) 83–113.
215. See also *RE* 8A (1958) 2480–83, s.v. Vici magister (J. Bleicken).
216. See R. Duthoy, "Les Augustales," *ANRW* 2.16.2 (1986) 1254–1309, and S. Ostrow's contribution to the present volume.

son; nor could his successor claim, as could Augustus, that he had restored the *res publica.*

Augustus acted in republican fashion, insofar as he sought his successor within his family; and yet, too, he trod a new course, however cautiously, insofar as he distinguished the designated person with special
honors and responsibilities but had these bestowed by the senate, the
people, and the *equites.* To put it bluntly, he tried to obtain for his heir
a repetition of the *consensus universorum* that had marked him as the
sole possessor of power. Basically his *auctoritas* provided the justification for the institutional bodies and social classes or groups involved to
follow his wishes and to commit themselves gradually to his successor.
At least it would have been hard for them to deny recognition after the
death of Augustus to a person whom they had frequently acknowledged
in their decrees to be worthy of especial honor and recognition. Seen in
these terms, the *res publica* chose the next *princeps* itself.

The pattern began to show from about 24 B.C. on.[217] Marcellus and
Tiberius were supposed to be permitted to run for office five years before
the usual time. Marcellus died in the next year; Tiberius was awarded
the rank of praetor early, as a twenty-three year old in 19 B.C., and in
13 B.C. he was elected consul as a twenty-nine year old. In 6 B.C. he held
the *tribunicia potestas,* although it was limited to five years. There
ended for the time being the advancement of Tiberius, for Augustus
openly preferred two other members of his family, namely his grandsons
from the marriage of his daughter Julia with his proven assistant,
Agrippa. Gaius (born 20 B.C.) and Lucius (born 17 B.C.) were adopted
by him in 17 B.C. and marked out as his successors.[218] In 5 B.C. Gaius
was designated by the people and the senate for the office of consul for
the year 1 B.C.; the same was decreed for Lucius in 2 B.C. Furthermore
the senate added that *ex eo die, quo deducti sunt in forum*—in other
words, as soon as they were presented as adults to the people—Gaius
and Lucius should be permitted to take part in the administrative ses-
sions of the senate. The Roman *equites* honored the two princes with
the dignity of *principes iuventutis.* These were clear signs of consensus.
The people of the city and the veterans were given significant sums of
money in the time-tested fashion.[219] The planned military probation of

217. For the particulars, see Syme (supra n. 3) 415–39.
218. On what follows, see *RG* 14.
219. Expenditures for 5 B.C.: 60 sesterces for 320,000 recipients; for 2 B.C.: 60 sesterces for 200,000 recipients (both in *RG* 15). In addition, numerous games were given in
the name of his sons and grandsons (*RG* 22).

the two princes ended soon, however, for Gaius died of a wound received in a campaign against the Armenians (A.D. 4). This blow was all the harder for Augustus because Lucius, who had been supposed to earn his military spurs in Spain, had died in Massilia already in A.D. 2.

Now Augustus had to bring the long-forgotten Tiberius back into consideration as a successor. In A.D. 4 he adopted him too and had him invested once again with the *tribunicia potestas*. In A.D. 13, by a decree of the people, Tiberius received the same authority for administering the provinces and leading the army as Augustus had. As co-regent he conducted the census together with Augustus in A.D. 14. Shortly after the death of Augustus on 17 August A.D. 14, the consuls, the senate, the *equites,* and the people swore to Tiberius Caesar the same oath of allegiance that they had also sworn in 32 B.C. to the Imperator Caesar.[220] The Republic had a new *dux* and *princeps.*

Or did the principate instead have a new emperor? It was not the intention of this essay to decide this question; possibly it cannot be decided at all. It is not the state that makes its society, but the society that constructs a state for itself. The minds that made an image for themselves of their state and its *optimus status* in the time of Augustus are not our minds. This is not a relapse upon a crude historicism, but merely the understanding that scholarly truth is no dogma; it is largely determined by each historian's times. Ronald Syme's view of the principate as government by a clique was in its time superior to all others. If it should no longer be so today, that is due to the half century that has transpired since, not to the principate itself. However, with his description of the Augustan principate as the "binding link" between the Republic and Empire, Syme has given us a clear indication of an important criterion that makes possible a new understanding of the politics of Augustus: the power of tradition.

220. Tac. *Ann.* 1.7 (on the beginning of Tiberius' rule: *consules primi in verba Tiberii Caesaris iuravere . . . mox senatus milesque et populus*).

Livy, Augustus,
and the Forum Augustum

Augustus' forum, dedicated in 2 B.C.,[1] expresses forcibly how the emperor wanted his countrymen to view the sweep of Roman history and his place in it. Although the Temple of Mars Ultor had been vowed on the field of Philippi in 42 B.C. (Suet. *Aug.* 29.2; *RG* 2), forty years passed before it was dedicated. The press of judicial and other business caused the forum to be used before the temple was finished (Suet. *Aug.* 29.1); how long the plans for the forum as a whole had been maturing is not known. It may be that some features had been settled well before 2 B.C., perhaps including the selection of heroes in the Roman "Hall of Fame," whose statues, along with their *elogia,* were placed in the two porticoes and exedrae on either side of the temple.[2] In any event, it is

1. More probably on 12 May of that year (Ov. *Fast.* 5.550–52) than 1 August (Dio 54.5.3): C. J. Simpson, "The Date of the Dedication of the Temple of Mars Ultor," *JRS* 67 (1977) 91–94. I wish to thank E. J. Champlin and B. W. Frier for their comments on an earlier draft of this paper.

2. The forty-year delay has not been satisfactorily accounted for. That the plans were drawn up in the twenties B.C. does not seem likely to me: T. Frank, "Augustus, Vergil, and the Augustan Elogia," *AJP* 59 (1938) 91–94; and H. T. Rowell, "The Forum and Funeral *Imagines* of Augustus," *MAAR* 17 (1940) 131–43. Nor does Vergil's influence seem probable: H. T. Rowell, "Vergil and the Forum of Augustus," *AJP* 62 (1941) 261–76; contra: A. Degrassi, "Virgilio e il Foro di Augusto," *Epigraphica* 7 (1945) 88–103. See also J. C.

clear that Livy's history of Rome was well under way when plans for the forum were drawn up, whether we assign an early or late date to them. The first book was completed between 27 and 25 B.C.; very likely the whole of the first pentad was finished by then.[3] Evidence for dating other portions of the history is lacking, save that the publication of the last twenty-two books was delayed until after Augustus' death in A.D. 14.[4] If we conservatively postulate an even rate of production for Books 6–142 between 25 B.C. and A.D. 14, the average of roughly three and a half books a year would suggest that by, say, 5 B.C. Livy had reached at least Book 75, which answers to the period of the Social War (89 B.C.). In short, Livy's account of much of republican history had probably appeared by 2 B.C.; certainly the books that survive to us had long been known.

It is a commonplace that Livy's achievement "swept the field." His work almost immediately found itself touching on some urgent concerns of the emperor (4.20.5–11), acquaintance with Augustus and the imperial family developed (Tac. *Ann.* 4.34.3; Suet. *Claud.* 41.1), and Livy acquired wide and lasting fame (Pliny *Ep.* 2.3.8; Pliny *HN* 1 *praef.* 16). The Forum Augustum and the *Ab urbe condita* were thus the two most famous monuments to republican history in the Augustan Age, and their creators knew one another. One might therefore expect to see some relationship between their conceptions of the Roman past, whether by influence or reaction. This study will investigate the topic by looking first at their overall conception of Roman history and second at the choice of men made for the Hall of Fame, together with the information contained in their *elogia*, comparing especially those *elogia* of men who also appear in the surviving portions of Livy's history.

Anderson, Jr., *The Historical Topography of the Imperial Fora*, Coll. Latomus 182 (Brussels 1984) 65–100; M. C. J. Putnam, *Artifices of Eternity: Horace's Fourth Book of Odes* (Ithaca, N.Y. 1986) 327–39. Final selections for the Hall of Fame were made no earlier than 9 B.C., when the elder Drusus died; his *elogium* survives: A. Degrassi, *Inscriptiones Italicae* 13.3 (Rome 1937) D 9. A statue in triumphal garb of Cn. Sentius Saturninus in the forum honored the consul of A.D. 41, not the consul of 19 B.C., as is sometimes claimed (whose praenomen in any case was Gaius): A. R. Birley, *The Fasti of Roman Britain* (Oxford 1981) 360–61.

3. The emperor has the title Augustus, voted on 16 January 27 B.C. (1.19.3), but in the same passage the emperor's second closing of the Temple of Janus in 25 B.C. is not mentioned. Cf. T. J. Luce, "The Dating of Livy's First Decade," *TAPA* 96 (1965) 209–40.

4. The superscription to Book 121 reads *qui editus post excessum Augusti dicitur.* I am not convinced by L. Canfora's objection to accepting the superscription: "Su Augusto e gli ultimi libri liviani," *Belfagor* 24 (1969) 41–43. It meets, however, with J. Deininger's recent approval: "Livius und der Prinzipat," *Klio* 67 (1985) 269, n.46.

I

The forum as a whole was based on a unitary conception of which the Hall of Fame was only a part.[5] On the architrave of the temple, which dominated the central space, Augustus' name was emblazoned in large letters (Ov. *Fast.* 5.567–68). The middle of the pediment was occupied by the bearded statue of Mars Ultor, surrounded by Venus, Fortuna, Romulus, the personified Palatine Hill, Roma, and Father Tiber. The cella within held the statues of Mars Ultor, Venus, and the deified Julius, Augustus' adoptive father.[6] The forum contained a large statue of Augustus in triumphal dress driving a quadriga, on the base of which was inscribed PATER PATRIAE (*RG* 35), a title that had been voted earlier in the same year. In the middle of each exedra was a niche of double size. The one on the north contained a statue of Aeneas carrying Anchises on his shoulders, surrounded by statues of Aeneas' Julian descendants. In the central niche on the south Romulus was shown carrying off the *spolia opima;* around him were statues of great men of the Republic, their deeds inscribed on plaques affixed below.[7]

These are the chief features of the Augustan forum, although the whole was considerably more complex than the sketch given here since the site was a repository of mementos and artistic works of all sorts and of diverse decoration.[8] Among the mementos were the standards Crassus and Antony had lost to the Parthians, which Augustus had recovered (by diplomacy) in 20 B.C. (*RG* 29; Dio 54.8.3).

Thus the Forum Augustum was an amalgam of personal and public elements, with pronounced emphasis on the personal. Augustus determined that the fulfillment of his vow at Philippi must be his alone. Accordingly, he purchased privately the land on which the forum was to

5. I follow the reconstruction of P. Zanker, *Forum Augustum: das Bildprogramm* (Tübingen 1968). See also id., *The Power of Images in the Age of Augustus* (= *Augustus und die Macht der Bilder* [Munich 1987, transl. A. Shapiro]), esp. 210–15.

6. So E. Strong in *CAH* X, 578, and Zanker (supra n. 5) 20, who does not believe that Julius Caesar also appeared in the Hall of Fame. This supposition receives support from Dio (56.34.2–3), who reports that Caesar's image was not carried in Augustus' funeral procession among the *imagines* of his ancestors on the ground of Caesar's divinity.

7. Ov. *Fast.* 5.563–66:
>Hinc videt Aenean oneratum pondere caro
>   et tot Iuliae nobilitatis avos,
>hinc videt Iliadem umeris ducis arma ferentem
>   claraque dispositis acta subesse viris.

8. Cf. Pliny *HN* 35.27, 93–94; see Zanker (supra n. 5) 7–14, 23–24; Putnam (supra n. 2) 332–35.

be placed and would not dispossess those unwilling to sell by having the area declared public land and the project a public undertaking. His purchases produced a more constricted area than he would have liked: clearly one or more landowners were unwilling to sell.[9] The forum in its final form put great emphasis on his person: the great dedicatory inscription on the temple's architrave, images of his divine ancestors within and without, and his triumphal statue occupying the central space before the temple. Velleius tells us that the names of Spanish and other peoples whom Augustus had conquered were also displayed in the forum (*quarum titulis forum eius praenitet* 2.39.2). Most scholars have supposed that this took the form of an *elogium* on the statue base. This may be doubted: it would compete with the simple PATER PATRIAE on another part of the base and would not have had the prominence that Velleius' word *praenitet* suggests. A more suitable place for the names might be the architraves between the upper and lower rows of columns supporting the porticoes, each of which is over 100 m long. The letters would be large, the names running down the long sides of the open area and leading the eye to Augustus' name on the temple's architrave.

The Hall of Fame was subordinate to and supportive of this grand scheme. Surrounding the statue of Augustus' ancestor Aeneas in the central niche in the north exedra were statues of his Julian ancestors, including the fourteen kings of Alba Longa (fragmentary *elogia* of four have survived: D 2–5),[10] Julius Caesar's father (praetor ca. 92, died in 85: D 7) and another member of the clan, Caesar Strabo (curule aedile in 90, died in 87: D 6). These Caesares illustrate the relatively undistinguished record compiled by the Julii in the course of the Republic. Ovid's description (*Fast.* 5.563–66) might be strictly interpreted to mean that the Julii were on one side of the forum, everyone else on the other. But since there was room for up to 108 niches (D 2), it is doubtful that anywhere near 54 Julii could be mustered to fill one side, even allowing for the Alban kings and for those related by marriage or adoption. *Elogia* for Augustus' son-in-law M. Claudius Marcellus (D 8), who died in 23, and for his stepson Nero Claudius Drusus (D 9), who

9. Suet. *Aug.* 56.2: *forum angustius fecit non ausus extorquere possessoribus proximas domos.* The retaining wall to the rear is irregular, and the temple seems to have been pulled forward, partially occupying what should have been an open space between the two exedrae. Yet see the remarks of Anderson (supra n. 2) 66, 74. E. A. Judge, *On Judging the Merits of Augustus,* Center for Hermeneutical Studies in Hellenistic and Modern Culture, Colloquy 49 (Berkeley 1984) 9–10, well emphasizes the private aspects of the forum, noting (in reference to *RG* 21.1) that "in contrast with his public works, this temple was to open the catalogue of his private endowments." Cf. H. T. Rowell (1940: supra n. 2) 141.

10. Degrassi (1937: supra n. 2) hereafter cited in the text as D.

died in 9, were found in the area of the north exedra.[11] Zanker is probably right in supposing that the statues of some *summi viri* (as they are
called at S.H.A. *Alex. Sev.* 28.6), not related to the Julii, were also on
the north side.[12] The division between relatives and nonrelatives was
also observed at Augustus' funeral, for which the emperor left detailed
instructions (Dio 54.33.1). In the procession three likenesses of Augustus preceded the *imagines* of the Julii, who in turn were followed by an
image of Romulus, which headed up the *imagines* of other Romans (Dio
54.34.2–3).[13] The presence and arrangement of ancestors and of other
great Romans are similar in both the forum and the funeral procession.

Why did Augustus appropriate distinguished nonrelations to grace
both his forum and his funeral? Suetonius (*Aug.* 31.5) tells us that "next
to the immortal gods he honored the memory of those leaders who had
raised the Roman empire from small beginnings to greatness. Accordingly, . . . when setting up statues of men in triumphal dress in the two
porticoes of his forum, he declared in an edict that he had done so in
order that the citizens might measure both himself and succeeding *principes* by the standard set by those men in their lives." Thus the statues
and *elogia* of the forum established a competition by comparison. The
elogia specify the points of comparison in the choice of achievements
that Augustus selected for mention in the case of each honorand. As for
Augustus' own *elogium,* he composed it himself; the *Res Gestae* was to
be displayed before his mausoleum and to be reproduced for display
throughout the Roman world. In a recent article P. Frisch has well argued that the achievements meticulously recorded in the *Res Gestae*
were meant to be measured against the achievements of the men whose
elogia appeared in the forum, and were meant to be found far greater.[14]

In short, the *Res Gestae* is a great comparative document, just as the
Forum Augustum is a great comparative monument, with continuous
emphasis by statement and suggestion on those matters in which Augustus was the first to do this or that or did more than others or had done

11. All Claudii did not stand on the north side, however; the *elogium* for Appius Claudius Caecus (D 12) was found in the area of the south exedra: Degrassi (1937: supra n. 2)
5.

12. So also Putnam (supra n. 2) 331.

13. Agrippa's funeral in 12 B.C. followed the same pattern as that of Augustus (Dio
54.28.5). Drusus' funeral in 9 included images of both Claudii and Julii, although Drusus
had not been adopted into the Julian family (Tac. *Ann.* 3.5.1).

14. "Zu den Elogien des Augustusforums," *ZPE* 39 (1980) 93–98. Pliny *HN* 22.6.13,
quod et statuae eius [Scipio Aemilianus] *in foro suo divus Augustus subscripsit,* if interpreted literally, would mean that Augustus composed the *elogia* himself. This is improbable. But that he supervised them closely is maintained by most recent scholars, notably
Frisch.

so with greater glory and to greater effect. It was not enough for Augustus to claim that he matched or surpassed the achievements of his linear ancestors, which was the ideal of the nobility throughout the Republic. The chief message of the forum and of the *Res Gestae* is that Augustus matched or surpassed the deeds of all great men of Roman history.

Did Livy subscribe to this claim? Several obstacles stand in the way of a clear view. The first is that we do not know how he regarded the principate as a political institution, as J. Deininger has argued in a recent article.[15] The second concerns the degree of friendship and amount of contact that the two men enjoyed; it might have been fairly close and sustained, but it need not be so interpreted. Moreover, when we come to estimate the significance of Livy's references to Augustus (or the lack thereof: the emperor is not mentioned in the preface), one must allow for the independent stance that Livy was obliged to take in reference to powerful contemporaries if he wished to be judged an honest historian.[16] In postponing publication of Books 121–42 (covering the period 43–9 B.C.) until Augustus was dead, Livy may have been prompted by two seemingly contradictory motives at once: that is, he both feared giving offense for plain speaking and feared being charged with flattery and partisan feeling. There is evidence to suggest that Livy was influenced by both factors. On the one hand, his independence from Augustus is attested by the statement that Tacitus places in the mouth of Cremutius Cordus (*Ann.* 4.34.3). Other examples are his discussion of the descent of the Julii from Julus (*quis enim rem tam veterem pro certo adfirmet?* 1.3.1–3); his evenhanded, somewhat sceptical attitude toward Augustus' version of how Cornelius Cossus won the *spolia opima* (4.20.4–11, cf. 32.4); and his wondering out loud whether it would have been better for the world if Julius Caesar had never been born (Sen. *QNat.* 5.12.4). On the other hand, he could easily have avoided mentioning the emperor by name altogether; yet his references to Augustus are markedly complimentary.[17]

Thus Livy was probably influenced by both motives. Yet it is doubtful that he believed Augustus to be the last and greatest in a long line of great men of the Republic. Livy viewed Roman history as the joint achievement of leaders and the led; the *mores* of the people as a whole

15. Deininger (supra n. 4) 265–72.
16. See T. J. Luce, "Ancient Views on the Causes of Bias in Historical Writing" *CP* 84 (1989) 16–31.
17. See 1.19.3, 28.12.12, and *Per.* 59. At 4.20.7 his phrase *Augustum Caesarem, templorum omnium conditorem ac restitutorem* is a strong, even hyperbolic, expression.

is a constant in his history: how the national character developed, matured, and decayed.[18] Naturally, the character of individuals is given great prominence, but even his greatest heroes have flaws; more significant is his belief that Rome was the product of a long line of leaders, not of any single individual (see 9.18.9).

On one point in particular Livy and Augustus were in emphatic agreement: history was the great repository of *exempla* by which one might pattern one's life and against which one might measure the worth of one's own contributions. Livy's remarks in his preface (10) coincide with the emperor's faith in the power of *exempla* in Roman life.

II

Might Livy and his history have suggested to Augustus the choice of certain men as *summi viri*? The large majority needed no Livy to establish their preeminent fame, since most were great *triumphatores*.[19] Furthermore, Augustus' selection was nonpartisan. Marius, a relative by marriage, was there, for example, and his *elogium* survives almost complete. The end of his career is described in this way: *post LXX annum patria per arma civilia expulsus, armis restitutus est. VII cos. factus* ("When he was seventy, he was driven from his country by civil war, and by war he was brought back. He became consul for the seventh time"). Contrast Livy's summation as preserved in *Periocha* 80: *editisque plurimis sceleribus idibus Ianuariis decessit, vir cuius si examinentur cum virtutibus vitia, haud facile sit dictu utrum bello melior an pace perniciosior fuerit. adeo, quam rem publicam armatus servavit, eam primo togatus omni genere fraudis, postremo armis hostiliter evertit* ("Having committed a great many crimes, he died on the Ides of January; if one compares his virtues with his vices, it would be difficult to decide whether he was more serviceable in war or more pernicious in peace—so much so that the country he saved by war he overthrew in peacetime, first by every sort of wrongdoing, and finally in arms like a foreign enemy"). Clearly Livy and Augustus were looking at the same man as an *exemplar* from very different perspectives. On the other hand, Frisch has made out a strong prima facie case for supposing that Pom-

18. See T. J. Luce, *Livy: The Composition of His History* (Princeton 1977) 292–94.
19. Suetonius is wrong to imply that all were in triumphal dress (*Aug.* 31.5); fragments of togate statues have been found, and of those for whom *elogia* survive, neither Appius Claudius Caecus nor L. Albinius celebrated triumphs. On the military functions that were to be performed in the forum, see Dio 55.10.3; Suet. *Aug.* 29.2.

pey was included among the *summi viri*,[20] a nonpartisan gesture of which Livy doubtless would have approved.

There are two unexpected choices among the nineteen known *summi viri*. The first is C. Cornelius Cethegus (D 64). It would be a knowledgeable student of Roman history who could without some searching identify this Cethegus, including, one might imagine, Livy himself, although almost all our knowledge of the man comes from his pages. Cethegus' exploits against the Insubres and Cenomani in northern Italy while consul in 197 are recorded at 32.28–31, the debate over his triumph and that of his colleague at 33.22–23.[21] His was a creditable career, to be sure, but it is difficult to believe that Livy's brief account prompted Augustus to make the selection.

The second is L. Albinius (D 11). Once again, it would be a well-informed student of Roman history who could identify him offhand, for he was the plebeian (Livy 5.40.9) who gave the Vestal virgins a ride to Caere in his wagon as they fled the Gauls during the sack of the city in 390. Livy represents our only literary version of the event, since all later accounts derive from his (Plut. *Cam.* 21; Val. Max. 1.1.10; and Florus 1.7). Here, one might think, is a strong prima facie case for supposing that Livy's narrative suggested to Augustus the choice of Albinius, who had no public career of which we know.[22] But, as will be explained below, it is doubtful if even Albinius was suggested by Livy's history.

Elogia survive in some form for ten men whose careers are covered in the extant books of Livy. What does a comparison reveal about Livy as a possible source of information? In two cases no conclusions can be drawn because next to nothing survives.[23] For the other eight many discrepancies appear, both major and minor.

A. Postumius Regillensis (D 10). The few extant words of the *elo-*

20. Frisch (supra n.14) 97–98. Pompey's image was carried in Augustus' funeral procession (Dio 56.34.2–3), which reproduced the same conception of Roman history that we find in the Forum Augustum. Note too, that Pompey's *elogium* was among those set up at Vesontio in the Antonine age, which appear to have been patterned after those of the Forum Augustum: Degrassi (supra n. 2) 7; *CIL* I², p. 201, no. xxxviii and vol. XIII, 5381.

21. Livy otherwise mentions him briefly: 30.41.4–5, cf. 31.49.7 (proconsul); 31.50.7–10 and 32.7.14 (curule aedile); 34.44.4–5, 35.9.1 (censor in 194).

22. Unless he is to be identified with the military tribune with consular power of 379, whom Livy names as Marcus (6.30.2), Diodorus as Lucius (15.51.1).

23. For L. Cornelius Scipio Asiaticus (D 15) only a fragmentary part of the inscription on the statue base survives, which gives his names and offices. For L. Papirius Cursor (D 62) the fragmentary *elogium* describes the beginning of the clash with his *magister equitum*, Q. Fabius Ambusti f. Maximus, which agrees with Livy's version at 8.30–36. That the forum contained a statue of M. Valerius Corvinus is known from Aulus Gellius *NA* 9.11.10; no *elogium* survives.

gium refer to the presence at the battle of Lake Regillus of the sons of Tarquinius Superbus: [*f*]*iliis et gen*[*tilibus*]. For Livy only one son was present (2.19.10: *filius*), who must be Titus, since the other two sons are already dead (Sextus at 1.60.2 and Arruns at 2.6.9). In the version of Dionysius of Halicarnassus both Sextus and Titus are present at the battle (*Ant. Rom.* 6.4.1ff. and 6.5.4).

M' Valerius Maximus (D 60, 78). The *elogium* records his triumph over the Sabini and Medullini; the latter are absent in Livy's version. Dionysius records that at the start of the year the Medullini conspired with the Sabines (4.2.1, 3), but he does not mention them thereafter. The *elogium* named Valerius as the one who ended the secession of the plebs by bringing them back from the Mons Sacer and reconciling them with the senators. Livy credits Menenius Agrippa with these actions (2.32–33). Dionysius' elaborate account gives Valerius a prominent role in the negotiations, but he too names Agrippa as the one who ended the secession (6.57ff. and 6.96). The *elogium* also says that Valerius persuaded the senate to relieve the plebs of their burden of debt; in Livy he signally fails in his effort, prophesying a bad outcome and resigning the dictatorship (2.31.8–10; the secession then follows). The *elogium* also adds some unique or unusual details: Valerius' augurate, his being *princeps senatus,* and the precise spot in the Circus where the *sella curulis* was placed for him and his descendants.

M. Furius Camillus (D 61). The *elogium* gives Camillus' victories in his third dictatorship in this order: Etruscans, Aequi, Volsci; Livy reverses the order of conquest (6.2.7–4.3). The elogium speaks of Camillus' settling of the revolt of Velitrae, which according to Livy (6.36.1ff.) began in 370 and was still in progress in 367 when Camillus was declared dictator for the fifth time, specifically to deal with a Gallic war. Livy does not record the actual capitulation of Velitrae: we do not hear of it again after 6.42.4. Plutarch (*Cam.* 41.6–42.1) says that Camillus' fifth and final dictatorship saw the defeat of the Gauls, in the course of which he took Velitrae.

L. Albinius (D 11). The *elogium* reads: [*Cum Galli ob*]*siderent Capitolium,* [*virgines Ve*]*stales Caere deduxit;* [*ibi sacra at*]*que ritus sollemnes ne* [*intermitte*]*rentur, curai sibi habuit;* [*urbe recup*]*erata sacra et virgines* [*Romam re*]*vexit* ("When the Gauls were besieging the Capitol, he conducted the Vestal virgins to Caere; there he saw to it that the sacred rites and ceremonies were not interrupted; and when the city was recaptured he brought the sacred objects and the virgins back"). Both that Albinius brought the Vestals back to Rome and that at Caere he saw to it that the sacred rites were not interrupted are not in Livy. The part about the return is trivial, but Albinius' actions at Caere are not. For how could a plebeian have anything to do with sacred rites conducted by patricians? This is the chief reason why Borghesi, Hirschfeld, Schwegler, and others have supposed that the *elogium* must refer not to Albinius but to the unnamed *flamen Quirinalis* in Livy's account (5.40.7).[24] Others, such as Mommsen, find it difficult to believe that an *elogium* in the Forum Augustum would honor a man whose name has not come down to us in any source (yet only the Livian tradition preserves Albinius' name).[25] Moreover, just what might a plebeian do to insure the continuance of the rites? Degrassi suggests, *exempli gratia,* that he might have lent the Vestals the use of his house at Caere. But Albinius was a Roman, not a Caeretan, and it is difficult to believe that an action like the loan of living quarters would be so magnified. The more one ponders the *elogium,* the more problematic it becomes. The information in it cannot possibly come from Livy; it may represent a version radically different from that of Livy.

Appius Claudius Caecus (D 12, 79). The *elogium* preserves the oddities of iterated praetorships and curule aedileships for Caecus, as well as such precise facts as his having been thrice interrex and thrice military tribune. The events of 296 are described in the *elogium* thus: *complura oppida de Samnitibus cepit, Sabinorum et Tuscorum exercitum*

24. B. Borghesi, *Oeuvres complètes,* vol. 3 (Paris 1864) 6–7; O. Hirschfeld, *Kleine Schriften* (Berlin 1913) 815; A. Schwegler, *Römische Geschichte,* vol. 3 (Tübingen 1872) 250, n. 3. Most recently, E. A. Judge (supra n. 9) 11, also opts for the flamen.

25. *CIL* I², p. 285, no. 84. B. A. Kellum, in her response to Judge (supra n. 9) 41, opts for Albinius. One of her reasons is that L. Sestius Quirinalis, suffect consul of 23, is supposed to have taken the cognomen from his mother's side of the family (she was an Albinia: Cic. *Sest.* 6—but see below); in this she follows R. Syme, *CP* 50 (1955) 135, in a review of T. R. S. Broughton's *Magistrates of the Roman Republic,* vols. 1 and 2 (Cleveland 1952); Broughton in vol. 3: *Supplement* (Atlanta 1986) lists the consul as L. Sestius P. f. L. n. Quirinalis Albinianus, the last cognomen derived from ALB on three brick stamps that have Sestius' same (*CIL* 15.1445). Yet it seems odd to select Quirinalis rather than Vestalis as a cognomen to honor the ancestor of Sestius' mother. The *flamen* is not mentioned explicitly as having been given a ride, although in Livy's source(s) the *flamen* clearly accompanied the Vestals and went to Caere (5.40.7–10, 7.20.4). Hence the *flamen* is absent in the accounts derived from Livy. The *elogium* does not mention him. D. R. Shackleton Bailey, *Two Studies in Roman Nomenclature* (State College, Pa. 1976) 6–7, prefers Albanius as the name of Sestius' father-in-law on the basis of the manuscript tradition, although G. V. Sumner in his review, *CP* 73 (1978) 159, opts for Albinius. Even if we follow Sumner and Broughton in preferring Albinius, it does not seem likely to me that the cognomen Quirinalis derives from L. Albinius' exploit during the Gallic sack of Rome. R. M. Ogilvie, *A Commentary on Livy, Books 1–5* (Oxford 1965) 723, identifies the "Lucius" who, according to Aristotle, saved Rome (*apud* Plut. *Cam.* 22.4) with Albinius.

fudit. Livy knows of no Sabini, only Sabelli (10.19.20).[26] Moreover, in his version the proconsul P. Decius Mus is credited with the victories in Samnium (10.17.1–10); in an aside Livy notes three variants in his sources, none of which answers to the version of the *elogium* (10.17.11–12). Finally, in Livy's narrative of events in Etruria, Caecus cuts a poor figure (10.18).

Q. Fabius Maximus Verrucosus (D 14, 80). The *elogium* refers to events of Fabius' fourth and fifth consulships in 215–214 before mentioning that as dictator (in 217) he saved his *magister equitum* M. Minucius (yet at this point Minucius has been elevated to a position of sharing equal power, according to Livy 22.25.10, 22.26.5–7).[27] Minucius' army hails Fabius *pater* (so also Pliny *HN* 22.10), whereas in Livy, Minucius himself does so (22.30; so also Plut. *Fab.* 13.3). Fabius' two terms each as interrex, quaestor, and military tribune are known only from the *elogium*.

C. Cornelius Cethegus (D 64). Only the letters]ET CENOM[are preserved from the first line of the plaque affixed below the statue base and]VCEM EO[from the second line. As noted above, the reference is to Cethegus' victory and triumph as consul over the Insubres and Cenomani in 197. The reference in the second line is doubtless to the Carthaginian leader Hamilcar, who some historical accounts said was captured in the course of the fighting and led in the triumph. Our knowledge of the variant comes from Livy (32.30.11–12, 33.23.5; cf. Zonar. 9.16), but it is not the version Livy reproduces. For him, Hamilcar's death had come in the year 200 (31.21.18).[28]

L. Aemilius Paullus (D 81). The *elogium* supplies details of his career unmentioned in other sources: interrex, quaestor, and thrice military tribune. It also assigns his victories in Liguria to his first consulship in 182 (so also Vell. Pat. 1.9.3; *Vir. Ill.* 56), whereas Livy puts them in 181 when he was proconsul. The *elogium* also says *copias regis [decem*

---

26. *Vir. Ill.* 34 is the only other source to agree with the *elogium* on this point. On the oddity, see M. Sage, "The *Elogia* of the Augustan Forum and the *De Viris Illustribus*," *Historia* 28 (1979) 197.

27. Degrassi (1937 supra n. 2) 6, views this as an attempt to sketch at one stroke the events of Fabius' first four consulships. Sage (supra n. 26) 199, is right to see this as an error, since all other *elogia* give events in chronological order.

28. At *CIL* I², p. 341, Hülsen notes that although only the tops of the letters EO are preserved, enough is left to show that E, not P, is correct (D]VCEM PO[ENORVM would give excellent sense). Yet it is difficult to see how Hülsen's suggestion of EO[RVM could be right: there seems to be no room for POENI, much less CARTHAGINIENSES, to appear earlier, to which EO[RVM could refer (unless in this version Hamilcar is credited as a *dux* of the Insubres or Cenomani!). EO[DEM PROELIO or TEMPORE?

dieb]us quibus Mac[edoniam atti]git deleṿ[it. Yet both Livy (45.41.5) and Diodorus (31.11.1) say it took fifteen days after he entered Macedonia before he defeated Perseus' forces. The *elogium* has too little room to supply [*quindecem dieb]us* and too much for [XV *dieb]us.* Bormann's restoration (*CIL* 11.1829), which Degrassi follows, is probably correct: the *elogium* thus gives a reckoning different from our other sources. Moreover, in the sentence before the one just discussed, the *elogium* reads: *iterum cos. ut cum rege/[Per]se bellum gereret, ap/[. . . f]actus est.* The obvious restoration is *ap[sens f]actus est* (so Bormann; there is not enough room for Mommsen's *a p[opulo]*). Scholars have been reluctant to accept the restoration, because it disagrees with the version of Plutarch (*Aem.* 10); nor is there any mention in Livy of Paullus' absence (44.17–18). Yet Bormann's restoration is likely to be right.

In the information they provide the *elogia* are independent, quirky, and willful. They like to give the exact number of times a man was interrex, military tribune, and *princeps senatus,* and to preserve such oddities as iterated quaestorships, curule aedileships, and praetorships. Yet they do not seem to differentiate between magistracy and promagistracy or take note of lesser offices (e.g., the fact that Aemilius Paullus was *triumvir coloniae deducendae* in 194 [Livy 34.45.3–5]). The *elogia* also have a pronounced antiquarian bent, not only in reference to such early personalities as·the Alban kings, but, for example, in ferreting out the fact that M' Valerius Maximus (D 60, 78) *princeps in senatu semel lectus est* and that the seat at the Circus given him and his descendants was located precisely *ad [sacellum] Murciae* (so also Festus, p. 464L). Most striking, however, are the many disagreements not only with Livy but with all other extant sources concerning the achievements of the *summi viri.*

When *Quellenforschung* was in its heyday, speculation inevitably arose as to the sources of the *elogia.* The claims of such late annalists as Valerius Antias and Licinius Macer and of Atticus' *Imagines* by way of Verrius Flaccus have been advanced.[29] But such guesses were bound to seem feeble, given the vast time span covered by the *elogia* (from the fall of Troy to the death of the elder Drusus) and what must have been a remarkably wide-ranging search for the sometimes arcane and unique

29. *RE* 5.2 (1905) 2447, s.v. Elogium (A. von Premerstein); Degrassi (1937 supra n. 2) 6; and Frisch (supra n. 14) 91 with n. 5 review these efforts. An anonymous referee believes the most likely candidate to be Varro's *Hebdomades,* or *De imaginibus,* compiled in 39 B.C., which featured portraits of seven hundred famous Greeks and Romans from all spheres of endeavor, each picture accompanied by an epigram in verse and a brief *elogium* in prose.

information found in them. Mommsen believed that the sources themselves were authentic and reliable, but that those responsible for using
them were careless and unlearned. Yet, as Degrassi has noted, the number of certain errors that we can detect are few.[30]

We now know of another and more probable candidate as a source,
which was contemporary, lengthy, markedly antiquarian, and covered
events from the fall of Troy down to, one would guess, at least the 120s
B.C. I refer to the eighty volumes of the *annales maximi*, which, as B. W.
Frier has argued in a recent book, were almost certainly an Augustan
compilation.[31] To my mind Frier has convincingly shown that the
eighty-volume edition mentioned by Servius (*ad Aen.* 1.373) cannot be
the same as the jejune *annales pontificum maximorum* that Cicero
spoke of (*De Leg.* 1.5–6), which reported only dates, persons, places,
and deeds in a chronicle devoid of all ornamentation (*De or.* 2.51–53).
Frier argues that all references to this eighty-volume edition derive from
the Augustan antiquarian Verrius Flaccus. The edition contained the
most detailed account of Roman history we know of, beginning with
Aeneas' departure from Troy. Book 4, for example, dealt with individual
Alban kings; around Book 9 the history of the Republic began, since the
story of the statue of Horatius Cocles appeared in Book 11 (which answers to the period covered in Book 2 of Livy). If the *annales maximi*
stopped in the 120s B.C., when the *pontifex maximus* P. Mucius Scaevola ceased to put up the *tabulae dealbatae* (Cic. *De or.* 2.52), then some
seventy books were devoted to a period of republican history that Livy
covered in around sixty. Frier has characterized the nature of the antiquarian information preserved from citations from the early books:
often late republican in formulation, prone to favor odd and trivial variants, intricate and sometimes bogus in combining bits of information
from sources of widely different provenances and credibility.[32]

30. Degrassi (1937 supra n. 2) 6; the only significant error, in his view, is Paulus' defeat
of the Ligurians as consul rather than as proconsul.
31. *Libri Annales Pontificum Maximorum: The Origins of the Annalistic Tradition,*
PAAR 27 (Rome 1979). I have seen no convincing refutation of Frier's main thesis, despite
the reservations and alternate hypotheses of some: e.g., T. J. Cornell, "The Formation of
the Historical Tradition of Early Rome," in I. S. Moxon, J. D. Smart, A. J. Woodman, eds.,
Past Perspectives: Studies in Greek and Roman Historical Writing (Cambridge 1986) 71
with n. 21; R. Drews, "Pontiffs, Prodigies, and the Disappearance of the *Annales Maximi,*" *CP* 83 (1988) 289–99; cf. Ps. Aurelius Victor, *Les origines du peuple Romain,* ed.
J.-C. Richard (Paris 1983) 9–48, esp. 38–48. I would presume that the *tabulae pontificum*
that Cato and Cicero knew were available for "consultation" by researchers such as Varro,
but we do not hear of anyone actually using them or citing information from them.
32. Frier (supra n. 31) 50–67, esp. 55–56 (on the descent of Julus) and 60–66 (on the
statue of Horatius Cocles).

In at least one instance we can perhaps see how the compilers of the *elogia* may have worked with their antiquarian material. The *elogium* of Manius Valerius Maximus (D 60, 78) states that he was augur, which R. M. Ogilvie discounts as an antiquarian reconstruction, believing with Mommsen and others that the guess was based on Livy (3.7.6), who for the year 463 notes the death of the augur Marcus Valerius. Manius, already an old man in 494 (Dion. Hal. *Ant. Rom* 6.39.2), could scarcely have survived another thirty years. Ogilvie concludes that "the identification of the augur with the dictator need be no more than a guess by the author of the Elogium who in an endeavor to fill out a biography gathered and combined material from every source. . . . The testimony of the Elogium can be discounted as an antiquarian reconstruction." [33]

The purpose of the eighty-volume edition "remains mysterious," as Frier concedes.[34] But that its provenance was Augustan seems certain, and Frier has made out a plausible case for supposing that it was compiled shortly after 12 B.C., when Augustus succeeded Lepidus as *pontifex maximus*. The *annales maximi* were so named, Verrius Flaccus claimed in a novel interpretation, not because of their size, but because the *pontifex maximus* compiled them.[35] A flurry of religious activity connected with Augustus' new position quickly followed after 12 B.C., especially in the area of sacred records. Moreover, Augustus had about him specialists who were historical and antiquarian experts: those who had helped earlier to compile the *fasti Capitolini* and *acta triumphalia*, those who gathered the information for the *elogia* (whatever their sources), and those who late in the reign compiled the lists of the major priestly colleges.[36] I believe that Frier's proposed dating makes sense, and would suggest that in the decade after 12 B.C., as the compilation for the eighty-volume *annales maximi* was under way, it provided much or all of the information for the *elogia* as well. Certainly the research for the *annales maximi* must have been wide-ranging; Frier's detailed analysis of the legend of Horatius Cocles' statue shows how complex the reconstruction by the compilers could be, involving aetiological explanations based on "archival notices," arcane religious lore, literary verses, topographical siting, and the like.

The *elogia* thus pursue an independent course in the information they

---

33. Ogilvie (supra n. 25) 407–8. He emends the M. Valerius of Livy's MSS to M' at 2.30.5.
34. Frier (supra n. 31) 196.
35. Paulus (W. M. Lindsay's Teubner edition of 1913, p. 113), summarizing Verrius. See Frier (supra n. 31) 47–48, 195.
36. Frier (supra n. 31) 196–200.

provide about the *summi viri,* disagreeing not only with Livy, but on some points with all other sources that survive to us. The disagreements with Livy, however, are curiously many, especially when we consider that the *elogia* for the most part select for mention the highlights of the careers of famous men: doubly curious, given that most *elogia* are very fragmentary and given how brief the few are that survive complete, or nearly complete; triply so, given the fame that Livy's history enjoyed.

The suspicion arises that on particular points the *elogia* may have deliberately been making correctives or ripostes to Livy's version of events: for example, L. Albinius is credited with providing much more than a ride to Caere for the Vestals. The *elogium* of Appius Claudius Caecus is pointed in its disagreement about Caecus' victories in Samnium. Livy gives full credit for them to Decius Mus, and adds three variants (10.17.11–12): that Fabius Maximus deserved even greater credit than Decius for the victories; that the new consuls, Caecus and Volumnius, shared the glory; and that Volumnius alone earned it. The *elogium* selects the one variant that Livy fails to report: the credit goes to Caecus alone (or primarily). Disagreement is even more marked in the *elogium* of M' Valerius Maximus. At 2.18.5–6 Livy rejects the possibility that Valerius' nephew was chosen dictator in 501, because of a law requiring that dictators be consulars. Yet at 2.30.5, when he reports that the uncle, a nonconsular, was appointed dictator, he takes no notice of his dictum a few pages earlier that would invalidate such an appointment. The *elogium* (D 60, 78) is firm on the matter: *priusquam ullum magistratum gereret dictator dictus est.* And where in Livy, Valerius signally fails in his effort to relieve those oppressed by debt, in the *elogium* he fully succeeds. Finally, in the *elogium* Valerius ends the secession of the plebs, but in Livy, Menenius Agrippa does so.

In conclusion, Livy and Augustus agreed on the exemplary value of history, although for Livy the emphasis was on imitation or avoidance in the conduct of one's personal life and public career, whereas for Augustus it was on the achievements against which he and succeeding *principes* should be measured in the judgment of posterity. But in all else there is little common ground. I do not believe that Livy viewed Augustus as having surpassed the achievements of all *summi viri* of the past or that he thought Roman history reached its acme in Augustus' lifetime (Livy's preface trenchantly rejects any such interpretation, at least up to ca. 25 B.C.).[37] Moreover, it does not appear that Livy's history suggested

---

37. Recently A. J. Woodman, *Rhetoric in Classical Historiography* (London, Sydney, and Portland, Oreg. 1988) 128–40, has argued that Livy, like Horace, developed an admiration for Augustus during the course of the principate.

to Augustus any of the choices of the men whom we know to have been represented in the forum. As for the information set forth in the *elogia*, the numerous and marked differences between Livy and the exiguous fragments show that those men whom Augustus assigned to gather and select the information treated Livy's version of Roman history with calculated indifference. Augustus accepted their suggestions. The friendship between the emperor and the historian may not have been as close or congenial as some have supposed.

At first glance the *elogia* appear harmless enough; it is only on closer inspection that the many disagreements come into view. I have a picture of Livy touring the Hall of Fame on his first go-round with cheerful approval; but when he stopped to inspect the *elogia* at greater leisure, disappointment and annoyance supervened, to be replaced in the end by sharp irritation.

Augustus and the Evolution
of Roman Historiography

The year 31 B.C. is generally taken to have inaugurated a new age in Latin letters and art; it is also generally accepted that history, along with oratory, was a victim of the Augustan era.[1] In the early part of the principate there were the memoirs of those who had participated in the civil wars, and a few may have written the history of the early years of the Augustan principate. However, most avoided the task. Even Livy may have delayed his chronicle of the years down to 9 B.C., and then only to concentrate on foreign affairs. The evidence, fragmentary and vague as it is, indicates that after the generation of participants at Actium contemporaries avoided the task of a history of the new age.

1. The topic of this essay requires a much fuller analysis in a wider context, but a preliminary presentation of its thesis seems appropriate in a volume that attempts a first step in a reassessment of Augustus and his era. E. Badian, Michael Flower, Erich Gruen, John Marincola, Kurt Raaflaub, and Meinolf Vielberg all kindly read this piece, and while no one of them necessarily agrees with its conclusions, it is much better for their advice and comments. It was composed during time filched from a project of a completely different nature pursued at the Center for Hellenic Studies, and I gratefully acknowledge my debt to the Center's director, Professor Zeph Stewart, and to the other Fellows for a happy and profitable year. Special thanks are due to Dr. Ellen Roth, librarian of the Center, who through seemingly limitless resources promptly and cheerfully acquired material necessary for this essay which was outside the subject areas of the Center library.

At the beginning of the *Annals* Tacitus addresses the issue of the effect of the Augustan principate on the composition of Roman history by native authors:

> The successes and disasters of early Rome have been recorded by illustrious writers, and suitable talents were not wanting to record the history of the Augustan era until they were deterred by a rising tide of flattery. (1.1.2)[2]

Modern analyses of the issue are little more than a gloss on the passage of Tacitus: at the beginning of the regime it was in the *princeps'* interest to tolerate "independent and even hostile literature," but in the later part of his rule Augustus resorted to more open and intimidating methods of repressing offensive literature, as the exile of Ovid, the burning of the works of T. Labienus, and the prosecution of Cassius Severus demonstrate. Despite the works of Cremutius Cordus and Asinius Pollio, historiography under Augustus was leading inevitably to Velleius Paterculus.[3] When the obligatory citation of the infamous passage of Dio, 53.19.3–4, concerning the difficulty of writing history after 27 B.C., is appended, an outline of the prevailing view on the issue is essentially complete. Although Tacitus credited the decline under Augustus not to repression but to *adulatio,* the modern mind, with its long experience of totalitarian regimes, has no difficulty in making a correlation

---

2. *Sed veteris populi Romani prospera vel adversa claris scriptoribus memorata sunt; temporibusque Augusti dicendis non defuere decora ingenia, donec gliscente adulatione deterrerentur.* Both F. R. D. Goodyear, *The Annals of Tacitus, Books 1–6* (Cambridge 1972) 96–97, and H. Furneaux, *The Annals of Tacitus* (Oxford 1896) ad loc., think the clause *donec gliscente adulatione deterrerentur* refers to a change of attitude during the lifetime of Augustus, but there can be no certainty about this. The *Historiae* (1.1) open with a statement that is also ambiguous in this respect: "Many historians have treated the earlier period of eight hundred and twenty years from the founding of Rome, and while dealing with the Republic have written with equal eloquence and freedom. But after the battle of Actium, when the interest of peace required that all power should be concentrated in the hands of one man, writers of like ability disappeared" (*postquam bellatum apud Actium atque omnem potentiam ad unum conferri pacis interfuit. magna illa ingenia cessere*). In any case, the change Tacitus refers to definitely occurred during the reign of Tiberius, if not before; cf. infra. n. 6. (All translations of Latin passages in the notes are taken, with some minor modifications, from the Loeb Classical Library.)

3. To outline and quote the argument of the best and most recent commentary on the *Annals:* Goodyear (supra n. 2) 96–97. His comments well summarize the prevailing view. Cf. A. J. Woodman, *Velleius Paterculus: The Tiberian Narrative: 2.94–131,* Cambridge Classical Texts and Comm. 19 (Cambridge 1977) 38, for the restrictions Augustus imposed on "independent history" (although his is much the most sympathetic recent treatment of the evolution of Roman historical writing during the early empire), and A. Momigliano, "The Historians of the Classical World and Their Audiences: Some Suggestions," in id., *Sesto contributo alla storia degli studi classici e del mondo antico* (Rome 1980) 371.

between panegyric history and an increasing difficulty for an "honest writer to tell the truth."[4]

That there was a reluctance on the part of Roman historians to write the history of events after 31 B.C. and therefore a decline in the genre under the first *princeps* is undeniable, based on the extant evidence; that modern analysis of this phenomenon has not been more elaborate is understandable for a number of reasons. The nature and paucity of the evidence discourage the attempt. The specimens of Roman historiography from the period are unsatisfactory: the relevant books of Livy remain only in epitome, and the other authors, with the exception of Velleius Paterculus, are either completely lost or remain only in fragmentary form. Other literary sources for Augustus—the Greek historians and the encomiastic poems in both Latin and Greek—do not encourage belief that the tone of the Latin histories would have been much more independent or objective. Finally, the explanation outlined above seems so obvious as to need no elaborate analysis to support it. The experience of Ovid would seem sufficient evidence to demonstrate that Roman historiography went the way of Roman oratory and for similar reasons.[5]

One cannot doubt that the situation outlined above had become reality in the course of the first century A.C.,[6] and the almost complete disappearance during the Augustan era of Roman histories dealing with events after 31 B.C. would seem to confirm the traditional view that intimidation and suppression of history began under Augustus. But too often scholars have inappropriately retrojected into the age of Augustus a later, less tolerant attitude. This essay will examine the reasons for both the disappearance of contemporary histories of the Augustan principate and what may be seen as a degeneration of traditional Roman historiography during the Augustan era. There is no good reason to think that Augustus employed "state" machinery to suppress or even inhibit independent and critical history, and the reluctance of Roman writers to compose a history of events after the battle of Actium can be seen as a much more subtle and interesting development, a development that was more a factor of the nature and themes of traditional Roman

4. Goodyear (supra n. 2) 97.
5. E. Gabba, "Literature," in M. Crawford, ed., *Sources for Ancient History* (Cambridge 1983) 9–10.
6. The change to serious repression seems to have occurred quite suddenly with the reign of Tiberius; cf. Tac. *Ann.* 4.34–35 and the remarks of A. Momigliano, *Claudius: The Emperor and His Achievement,* trans. W. Hogarth (Cambridge 1961; New York 1962) 4.

historiography than of a supposed modern antithesis between "monarchy" and free enquiry.

It might be stated by way of preface that there is almost no significant evidence that free expression of ideas was seriously curtailed by Augustus.[7] The book burnings toward the end of his principate that claim so much modern attention were most likely a function of legal actions to curb irresponsible and libelous attacks on people. There is not a bit of evidence that Augustus tried to control or restrain historical writing, and the *princeps* himself took pains to avoid even the appearance of intolerance.[8] This restraint failed only in the case of Ovid. The manifold issues and bibliography involved in the poet's exile are beyond the limited scope of this essay, but it is significant that the offense of the *carmen* was its transgression of moral precepts, the one aspect of Augustus' program that failed miserably and the one area in which the normally shrewd and calculating sense of the *princeps* gave way to blind stubbornness. But Ovid's experience cannot contravene the lack of any evidence to demonstrate repression or control of historians or the evidence that Augustus was in all other cases quite tolerant of independent thinking and criticism.

Even had Augustus wished to suppress critical history, it would have been all but impossible to do so. To have effectively suppressed critical history he would have had to engage in what amounts to censorship. But censorship in the modern sense of suppression or elimination of offensive writing by state machinery seems to have been nonexistent throughout much of antiquity. As Moses Finley demonstrated in a characteristically perceptive essay on the topic,[9] repression in Rome was exercised against those *teaching* doctrines (rhetoricians or astrologers, for example) that were perceived as posing a threat of political turbulence or revolution; thus the expulsion of the astrologers in 33 B.C. (Dio 49.43.5) and the destruction of oracular literature in 12 B.C. (Suet. *Aug.* 31.1). As the case of Ovid demonstrates, no attempt was made to root out offensive literature from private hands, even when the author him-

7. Cf. K. A. Raaflaub and L. J. Samons in their contribution to this volume.

8. When he took personal offense, Augustus limited his reaction to the traditional Roman procedure of breaking off *amicitia*, as happened in the incident with the Greek historian Timagenes (Sen. *Ira* 3.23.3ff.); Augustus was present for readings of Cremutius Cordus' critical history (Suet. *Tib.* 61.3; Dio 57.24.3), and his own reaction to written criticism was limited to simple retort (Suet. *Aug.* 51.2–3, 55). Later generations would remember the first principate as a time when men's words did not convict them (Sen. *Ben.* 3.27.1).

9. M. Finley, "Censorship in Classical Antiquity," *Times Literary Supplement*, 29 July 1977, 923–25 (= id., "Censura nell' antichità classica," *Belfagor* 32 [1977] 605–22).

self was removed. The reason for this is obvious: for the most part, written works, especially histories, were not a real threat to even the most tyrannical of Roman emperors. The lengthy histories of Cordus, Pollio, and Livy would not have been accessible outside a limited circle of aristocrats, and such an audience was hardly likely to be seduced or corrupted into opposition or revolution by historiography.[10] Even when Cordus was prosecuted by Tiberius, it is clear that his history, which had been around for years, was the pretext for the prosecution, not the cause (Tac. *Ann.* 4.34ff.). In the end, it would not have been worth the effort of the *princeps* to bother to control the writing of history.

Nevertheless, despite the lack of significant evidence for suppression of independent views, a striking fact that becomes clear even from the fragmentary evidence of the Roman historians who were working after 31 B.C. is how few chose to write a history of contemporary affairs.[11] A number chose to write about the tumultuous events of the previous two decades: Messalla Corvinus was complimentary of the assassins of Caesar in his *commentarii* (Tac. *Ann.* 4.34.4), but there is no evidence that he carried his account beyond the end of the civil wars;[12] Q. Dellius seems to have confined his historical efforts to an account of the Parthian campaign of Antony;[13] Asinius Pollio, who described the death of Cicero, probably avoided an account of events after his own retirement from active affairs, and the battle of Philippi provides a reasonable terminus for his history.[14] It is understandable that this early generation of the principate would concentrate on the momentous events in which they themselves were directly involved,[15] and it is quite possible that both Corvinus and Dellius composed not *historiae* so much as autobio-

10. Wide, popular circulation of histories was out of the question; cf. K. Quinn, "The Poet and His Audience in the Augustan Age," *ANRW* 2.30.1 (1982) 75–180; and R. Starr, "The Circulation of Literary Texts in the Roman World," *CQ* n.s. 37 (1987) 213–23. A complete copy of Livy's history, for instance, would have required 142 rolls of papyri (Quinn [supra] 81), and to own a copy would have been beyond the means (and probably the interest) of all but a restricted circle of friends and acquaintances.

11. R. Syme, "Livy and Augustus," *HSCP* 64 (1959) 64 (= id., *Roman Papers*, vol. 1 [Oxford 1979] 440).

12. There is no reason to think his comments on the guests at Augustus' dinner parties (Suet. *Aug.* 74) should be related to this work.

13. On Dellius, cf. the statement of Corvinus quoted by Sen. *Suas.* 1.7; also Strab. 11.13.3 (p. 523 C) and Plut. *Ant.* 59.

14. Suda, s.v. "Poliōn"; also M. Schanz and C. Hosius, *Geschichte der römischen Literatur*[4], vol. 2 (Munich 1935) 27; and H. Peter, *HRRel* II, lxxxvii.

15. "The rich supply of memoirs of the early imperial age was the work of the protagonists in the civil wars, faced with the need to explain and defend political decisions, changes of position, their entire role in the unfolding of the story of those years" (E. Gabba, "The Historians and Augustus," in F. Millar and E. Segal, eds., *Caesar Augustus: Seven Aspects* [Oxford 1984] 78).

graphical *commentarii*. Neither the extent nor date of composition of M. Agrippa's *De vita sua* is known, but it is not likely to have gone much beyond the end of the civil war, if that far.[16]

This absence of Latin histories of the first principate continues even through the next generations to A.D. 14. Pompeius Trogus wrote a universal history (in Latin, uncharacteristic for that type of history), but he seems to have ended it with the early conquests of Augustus in Spain.[17] Maecenas is not to be credited with a serious work of history on Augustus despite the statement in Horace *Carmina* 2.12.9–12.[18] According to his epitomator, it was only after some delay, and possibly only after the death of the *princeps,* that Livy presented his account of the decades before and after Actium, but this will be discussed below. Livy quoted the *res Romanae* of Clodius Licinus (29.22.10), but there is no evidence that this author dealt with the period of Augustus, and L. Arruntius seems to have followed Livy in concentrating on the early period of Roman history.[19] We know nothing of the nature of Labienus' history apart from the fact that he refused to make public parts of it before his death, and there is no clear terminal date for the work of Cremutius Cordus, although he may have ended his account as early as 27 B.C.[20]

Despite the number of Romans writing history of one form or another between 31 B.C. and A.D. 14, we can only be sure that Livy attempted a significant history of the period after the great victory, and his account, as has long been noted, seems to have focused largely on the foreign military campaigns of Augustus down to 9 B.C. Velleius Paterculus, while devoting almost thirty chapters to the events between 44 and 31 B.C., limits his account of the events after Actium to five chapters

16. The latest datable event from the work was the proposed construction of a *portum* at the Lucrine lake (Serv. *ad Georg.* 2.162) in 37 B.C., mentioned in the second book. Cf. D. Kienast, *Augustus: Prinzeps und Monarch* (Darmstadt 1982) 217.

17. He may have been following the history of Timagenes; cf. J. Pendergast, *The Philosophy of History of Pompeius Trogus* (Diss. Univ. of Illinois 1961) 94 with references. The attempt by O. Seel, *Eine römische Weltgeschichte* (Nürnberg 1972) 172–80, to date Trogus to the era of Tiberius is not persuasive and ought not to affect the issue of the scope of his history. R. Syme, "The Date of Justin and the Discovery of Trogus," *Historia* 37 (1988) 366–67, thinks that Trogus' history was composed in the third decade of the Augustan principate and dealt with events down to 10 B.C.

18. Cf. the comments of R. Nisbet and M. Hubbard, *A Commentary on Horace: Odes, Book II* (Oxford 1978) 193.

19. Syme (1959: supra n. 11) 64 (= id.[1979: supra n. 11] 440).

20. B. Manuwald, *Cassius Dio und Augustus: Philologische Untersuchungen zu den Büchern 45–46 des dionischer Geschichtswerkes,* Palingenesia 14 (Wiesbaden 1979) 254–55, maintains that the *lectio* of the senate referred to by Suetonius (*Aug.* 35), normally dated to 18 B.C., actually refers to a *lectio* of 29 B.C. and that Cordus' history would probably have concluded with the year 27 B.C.; contra: H. Tränkle, "Zu Cremutius Cordus fr. 4 Peter," *MusHelv* 37 (1980) 231–41.

(2.89–93), and they too have a bias toward the Augustan military conquests. After this, Velleius' narrative focuses on the career of Tiberius and returns to Augustus only to mention embarrassing or difficult events of his reign that serve to highlight the achievements of Tiberius. Velleius himself implicitly recognizes the lack of Roman histories under Augustus when he states that only Livy of recent historians is worthy of mention (1.17). It is not until the posthumous *res Romanae* of the elder Seneca and the history of Aufidius Bassus, both probably written in the latter half of the reign of Tiberius, that we have evidence of Roman historians other than Livy attempting accounts of events after the battle of Actium; but by then men had become reconciled to the turn history had taken under Augustus.[21] This anomalous situation cannot be easily dismissed with the explanation that given the stark alternatives of panegyric history or silence, the "independent" minds of the Augustan era chose the latter. There might have been some who chose not to write a history of Augustus due to distaste or fear, but they have left no trace in the extant evidence; and certainly this factor alone cannot satisfactorily explain the near disappearance of contemporary Roman histories. Rather, such disappearance seems to indicate that the Augustan principate posed a problem for those contemplating a history of the period in the traditional Roman sense.

It is extremely hazardous to attempt a discussion of the nature and themes of Roman historiography. Before Tacitus only Livy, Sallust, and Velleius Paterculus provide continuous texts, and only Livy is an example (and a late one at that) of the annalistic school of history, which constituted the bulk of the Roman historiographical tradition throughout the Republic. The other Roman historians have been lost or remain only in a frustratingly fragmentary form. Nevertheless, even from these fragments certain distinctive characteristics of Roman historiography can be identified,[22] and it is these characteristics that, when examined in the context and from the perspective of the Augustan principate, provide the basis for a new explanation for the evolution of historiography under Augustus.

21. Cf. Peter, *HRRel* II, 98, F 1. On the scope and nature of the history of Seneca, cf. L. Sussman, *The Elder Seneca* (Leiden 1978) 137–52; and J. Fairweather, *Seneca the Elder* (Cambridge 1981) 15–17.
22. The fundamental analysis of the evidence for the early Roman historians is E. Badian, "The Early Historians," in T. Dorey, ed., *Latin Historians* (New York 1966) 1–38. Cf. also the very instructive discussion in Woodman (supra n. 3) 30–45, and B. W. Frier, *Libri Annales Pontificum Maximorum: The Origins of the Annalistic Tradition*, PAAR 27 (Rome 1979) 201–24.

The most striking characteristic of Roman historiography was its adherence to the annalistic form, which itself was a form of horography,
or local history. Such history dealt only with events in the community
and those external events that directly impinged on the community.[23] It
is understandable that Roman authors, when faced with the task of explaining the commanding position attained by Rome in the middle of
the second century B.C., adopted the form of local history, a form well
established in Roman tradition by the *annales maximi*.[24] Traditional
Roman historiography, in contradistinction to Greek practice, was
characterized by its focus on the community of Rome as the theme of
history; and consequently Roman history was inward looking, unlike
most of Greek history, which was concerned with events beyond the
confines of one community. This focus on the growth and expansion of
the community of Rome allowed the intrusion of non-Roman peoples
and events only insofar as they impinged on Roman affairs,[25] and this
partly explains the attachment of Latin history to the annalistic framework. Even when sufficient evidence had become available to write
"lively narrative history," the Romans persisted with the awkward, but
traditional, annalistic style.[26]

A second significant characteristic of Roman historiography concerns the writers themselves. While a number of Greek historians were
exiles or long separated from their native cities, Roman history during
the Republic was generally the prerogative of the senatorial class, in
most cases composed by the participants in events or their descendants.
Thus the composition of Roman history could not be divorced from the
senatorial struggle for power and prestige within the community.

23. On Roman historiography as essentially a product of the "minor" tradition of local
history, cf. A. Momigliano, "Tradition and the Classical Historian," in id., *Quinto contributo alla storia degli studi classici e del mondo antico* (Rome 1975) 24–25; on horography in general, cf. F. Jacoby, "Über die Entwicklung der griechischen Historiographie und
den Plan einer neuen Sammlung der griechischen Historikerfragmente," *Klio* 9 (1909)
109–19 (= id., *Abhandlungen zur griechischen Geschichtsschreibung,* ed. H. Bloch [Lei-
den 1956] 30–40); on the connection between horography and the development of Roman historiography, cf. C. W. Fornara, *The Nature of History in Ancient Greece and
Rome* (Berkeley and Los Angeles 1983) 23–28.

24. The earliest works of history at Rome may have emulated standard Greek history
in their form, but by the time of Cassius Hemina, the oldest of the annalists (Pliny *HN*
13.84), the annalistic form was established as the characteristic Roman way of writing
history; cf. Fornara (supra n. 23) 25–27 and Frier (supra n. 22) 223.

25. An exception to this might have been the early books of Cato's *Origines*, which
discussed the early histories of other Italian cities, but the *Origines* were probably not
typical of Roman practice in this regard. Frier (supra n. 22) 218–19 regards Cato's work
as "eccentric."

26. E. Rawson, *Intellectual Life in the Late Roman Republic* (Baltimore 1985) 220; cf.
also Fornara (supra n. 23) 41–42, 53.

Finally, the focus on the community of Rome in the earlier annalistic tradition did not easily allow for characterization of individuals and emphasis of their achievements. Cato's refusal in his work to name conquering generals is probably an extreme example of what must have been a general attitude that resisted allowing the glory of individuals to obscure the traditional theme of the success of the community of Rome against her enemies.[27] It is possible that Coelius Antipater's monograph on the Second Punic War focused on the person of Scipio Maior, but until Sallust there were no genuine examples of this practice.[28] While the careers of Philip and Alexander had a profound effect on Greek historiography and allowed for the development of a type of history that centered on the careers and deeds of great men, individuals and their deeds seem to come into prominence in the work of the Roman historians only after the careers of the Gracchi during the crises of the last century of the Republic.

These characteristics of early Roman historiography arose from the purpose that history served for the Romans. As a Roman general served the community by his victory, so the chronicle of the campaigns by the historian served the community, but as the act of serving the community was a source of *gloria et laus* for the generals, so were the histories that described their campaigns. While the individual was not the proper theme for Roman history, the genre did provide reflected glory for the main figures, and, in a way similar to the spectacle of a Roman funeral, it was expected to inspire the reader to emulation of virtue.[29] History was the forum for the display of aristocratic service in behalf of the community. The reason that republican historiography never lost its traditional focus on Rome was that the purpose of the genre was a function of the aristocratic struggle for honor and status in the community.[30] In

27. On Cato, cf. Nep. *Cato* 3.4 and Pliny *HN* 8.11. On the basis of Livy 10.37.4, Woodman (supra n. 3) 30 thinks that Fabius Pictor might also have engaged in such practice; but the evidence of the passage is not conclusive. Cf. also F. Bömer, "Naevius und Fabius Pictor," *SymbOslo* 29 (1952) 39, n. 4.

28. A. Leeman, *Orationis Ratio*, vol. 1 (Amsterdam 1963) 74–75.

29. T. Wiseman, *Clio's Cosmetics: Three Studies in Greco-Roman Literature* (Leicester 1979) 39–40.

30. "The record of past events was a matter of direct concern to the ruling class, whose position was sustained by it and whose members based their claim to high office on the historic achievements of their ancestors. The historical tradition of the Roman Republic was not an authenticated official record or an objective critical reconstruction; rather, it was an ideological construct, designed to control, to justify and to inspire." So T. Cornell, "The Historical Tradition of Early Rome," in I. Moxon, J. Smart, and A. J. Woodman, eds., *Past Perspectives: Studies in Greek and Roman Historical Writing* (Cambridge 1986) 82, who correctly cites the relevance to Roman historiography of J. H. Plumb's analysis of history as a form of social control in *Death of the Past* (Boston 1970). Cf. also A. J. Wood-

this regard, it should be noted that horography, or local history, was the historical form most susceptible to manipulation in support of contemporary and partisan circumstances.[31]

The domestic crises of the late second century and the first century B.C. had their effect on the simplistic annalistic tradition: it was no longer enough to say what battles occurred under what consuls and who triumphed; recent events had demonstrated the complexity of history and the need for deeper analysis by historians.[32] The careers of Marius, Sulla, and Pompey demonstrated the futility of Cato's belief about the strength of the community vis-à-vis her individual commanders.[33] Rome may have been a greater city than any Greek *polis* because it was built by many generations of men, but recent events had made evident the fact that ambitious dynasts could conquer and control Rome. A generation after Asellio, Cicero could still criticize the annalistic tradition for failure to characterize great men.[34] When the Roman historiographical tradition did focus on the individual, it was not necessarily a positive development, as the works of Sallust show. Indeed, Sallust's idealized depiction of the men that made Rome great illustrates somewhat this tension in Roman historiography. According to Sallust, individuals in archaic Rome did not vie with each other for their personal profit, rather such competition was for the benefit of the *res publica* (*Cat.* 8 and 53).[35] In the traditional Roman view, the proper end of a good citizen was to serve the community, and so it was with history. The career of a good citizen might be a source of *exempla* for the reader, but it was not the purpose or focus of history; for to allow an individual to overshadow the theme of the community was the historiographical

man, *Rhetoric in Classical Historiography* (London 1988) 74, who notes the risk such partisan history presented to the historians of alienating parts of their readership; this risk was a concern of Pliny's (*HN praef.* 20) when he delayed the publication of his history.

31. Fornara (supra n. 23) 21, n. 4.

32. So Sempronius Asellio (Gell. *NA* 5.18.7ff.), writing at the beginning of the first century. On a more pessimistic strain that evolved in Roman historiography after the careers of the Gracchi, cf. Woodman (supra n. 30) 125.

33. Cic. *Rep.* 2.2: "Cato used to say that our constitution was superior to those of other states on account of the fact that almost every one of these other commonwealths had been established by one man, the author of their laws and institutions. . . . On the other hand our own commonwealth was based upon the genius, not of one man, but of many; it was founded, not in one generation, but in a long period of several centuries and many ages of men."

34. Woodman (supra n. 3) 31f. with references.

35. *Ambitio* and *avaritia* overcame proper conduct only in the modern, decadent era (*Cat.* 10), and the crisis of the first century B.C. was the product of the *bonum publicum* sacrificed to private interests (*Jug.* 35). Cato alone of the men of Sallust's time deserved his *gloria*, for he did not seek it (*Cat.* 54).

counterpart of individual competition to the detriment of the community. Of course, in the end the ideal was never anything but an ideal, since much of Roman history was the product of the aristocratic competition for status. But as individual *ambitio* had to be cloaked in the guise of propagation of the *bonum publicum,* so did the theme of history.

This reluctance to focus on individuals in Roman historiography accounts, at least in part, for why Romans of the first century turned to Greeks or Greek prose genres for panegyric history of individuals,[36] or engaged in the less respectable but popular genre of polemical autobiography.[37] Biography, the primary genre for depiction of the individual and his deeds, was admitted by its first Latin practitioner to be a *leve genus* in comparison to history.[38]

The circumstances that forced Roman historians to chronicle the unseemly domestic crises and civil wars of the last century of the Republic also popularized an old Greek notion that internal harmony in a community was a function of external threat. This idea can be traced back to Plato and Aristotle and may have been introduced to Roman historiography by Polybius.[39] With the works of Sallust (if not before) the moral decline of Rome and consequently her domestic troubles were ascribed to the loss of the *metus hostilis* after the final defeat of Carthage in 146.[40] In Roman historiography the idea that internal *concordia* depended on external threat is well illustrated in the early books of Livy, where it becomes the generating force of his anachronistic narrative of the archaic "struggle of the orders" by providing a useful bridge between supposed recurrent internal turmoil and its cessation when interrupted by foreign threat. But, as the story of Rome's history wore on, the traditional theme of the expansion and growth of Rome at the expense of her enemies became a function of nostalgia for the historian

---

36. Theophanes of Mytilene (*FGrHist,* no. 188) compared Pompey to Alexander in his history of Magnus' campaigns in the East. Cicero wrote a work in Greek on his consulship as raw material for a history of it by Posidonius (*Att.* 2.1–2), and his famous request to Lucceius (*Fam.* 5.12) may have been for an account in Greek; cf. D. Shackleton Bailey, *Cicero: Epistulae ad Familiares,* vol. 1 (Cambridge 1977) 318.

37. Cf. Badian (supra n. 22) 23–26; Fornara (supra n. 23) 179–81; and Rawson (supra n. 26) 227f. On the unsatisfactory nature of the genre, cf. Cic. *Fam.* 5.12.8.

38. Nep. *praef.* 1.

39. Cf. F. Walbank, *A Historical Commentary on Polybius,* vol. 1 (Oxford 1957) 697, for references. As Walbank notes, this idea may actually have been a consideration in Roman deliberations on foreign affairs in the second century B.C.

40. This is Sallust's date (*Cat.* 10); other writers seem to have dated the onset of the decline earlier; cf. D. Earl, *The Political Thought of Sallust* (Cambridge 1961) 42–43; on the theme of the *metus hostilis* in Sallust, 47–50.

(Livy *praef.* 5) and provided the backdrop that made later domestic crises unseemly to chronicle (*praef.* 4).

Unlike the Greek tradition as demonstrated in Herodotus, Thucydides, and Polybius, the Roman republican historians never seem to have had critical enquiry and objective analysis as their primary purpose in composing history. The evidence demonstrates the presence of patriotism, *apologia,* and vituperation, but no serious and consistent attempt to divorce historical writing from prevailing circumstances in order to provide a picture of the past undistorted by partisan factors or prejudice.[41] The curiosity about events external to the community and the somewhat more dispassionate analysis of past events that were a function of Greek historiography were expressed in the Roman tradition in the work of the antiquarians.[42]

If the outline given above of the evolution and characteristics of Roman historiography is generally accurate, then one can identify a number of developments in the Augustan principate that must have presented difficult problems for a Roman contemplating a history of the period according to traditional methods and themes.

First, the traditional generating force for composition of history at Rome had been removed. History, which had been an extension of the competition for status and honor in the community, lost much of its significance when *gloria et laus* and *auctoritas* became the monopoly of one figure and his family. To the end of the Republic, history had been the domain of the ruling class,[43] whose individual members established claim to authority by achievement in the political and military spheres. As the Augustan principate progressed the opportunities for significant activity in these areas diminished.[44] It is understandable then that the

41. An important corollary of this (despite modern assumptions) must be that a lost historian who was "independent" of the Augustan view might possibly have provided a corrective in terms of prejudice, but there is no good reason to think he would have been any more truthful in an objective sense than the preserved material. Tacitus (*Hist.* 1.1.2–3) seems to have implicitly recognized this: "But while men quickly turn from a historian who curries favor, they listen with ready ears to calumny and spite; for flattery is subject to the shameful charge of servility, but malignity makes a false show of independence." Although he is speaking of the evolution of Roman historiography during the principate, his statement could well apply to history under the Republic. For a recent discussion of the Romans' attitude to truth in history, cf. Woodman (supra n. 30) 82 f.

42. Rawson (supra n. 26) 218, 233–49; Momigliano (supra n. 23) 25.

43. Despite the fact that there are histories by nonsenators from the first century, the significance of which has been overemphasized; cf. Cornell (supra n. 30) 73–74.

44. "The authors of histories in Latin belonged in general to the senatorial class, which was deprived by the new regime of its earlier role at the head of affairs. It is these historians who identified republican freedom with their own pre-eminent position; it is they who linked playing a part in decision-making with freedom of opinion and the ability to write

early generation of the principate can show a number of historical works by men who had participated in the civil wars and who ended their accounts at or not long after the end of the conflict itself.

Second, the military had become the monopoly of Augustus and his family. The consequences early in the principate of M. Licinius Crassus claiming the *spolia opima* and C. Cornelius Gallus' boastful claims of extension of the empire indicate that military conquest in behalf of the *res publica*—the traditional raw material for *commentarii* and history—could no longer be publicized in the name of the commander. Eventually all significant military commands were entrusted only to members of the family of the *princeps,* and even their victories were usurped in the name of the first member of the family.[45]

Finally, the traditional focus on the community of Rome and only secondarily on individuals in Roman historiography would be difficult to maintain now that the *res publica* and one individual had become coterminous. If there truly was a *res publica restituta,* it existed only through the act of one man, and the old fiction of the community of Rome as a function of the achievements of successive generations of men in her service became impossible to maintain.

The loss of the material and impetus to write history and the peculiar nature of the Augustan regime undermined Roman historiography. It is significant that it was no senator, no man of affairs, but an "academic" historian who took up the challenge of writing an extended account of events after 31 B.C. Livy had no personal stake in writing history and no personal investment in the new regime beyond the welcome peace and prosperity it offered to all engaged in letters.[46] The need to propagate a political position or decorate the deeds of ancestors was absent in his case. Livy had little to gain or lose by his history, unlike some others.[47] Nevertheless, the vague evidence of the epitomator, if it is to be trusted, indicates that Livy may have delayed issuing his last twenty-three books;[48] and in his last nine books, which were devoted to the years

---

history truthfully; these were men, in fact, accustomed to make and to write history. This was the class which was the loser in the civil wars," Gabba (supra n. 15) 79; cf. also id. (supra n. 5) 8–9 on Sallust's prefaces as an extension of his political activity.

45. In the *Res Gestae* only Tiberius is mentioned by name (30.1), and Augustan poetry abounds in conquests of others claimed in the name of the *princeps.* On Crassus and Cornelius Gallus, cf. R. Syme, *The Roman Revolution* (Oxford 1939) 308–10.

46. R. M. Ogilvie, *A Commentary on Livy, Books 1–5* (Oxford 1965) 2.

47. Cf. Horace's warning to Pollio, *Carm.* 2.1.6ff., which probably refers to a reaction from the *princeps* like that in the case of Timagenes.

48. The troublesome reference in the *Periocha* to Book 121, *qui editus post excessum Augusti dicitur* (on which cf. Syme [1959: supra n. 11] 38–39 [= id. (1979: supra n. 11)

after 31 B.C., Livy seems to have avoided domestic political events, concentrating instead on military campaigns and conquests, topics that were characteristic of his books on the early and middle Republic.[49] This focus has often been interpreted as reflecting both a fear of dwelling on possibly embarrassing political crises and accession to pressure to glorify Augustus. However, there is another reason why Livy might have changed his focus in his last books.

In concentrating on Roman conquest Livy was returning to a traditional and probably predominant theme of the early annalistic tradition. The era from the mid-second century B.C. to the battle of Actium might provide material for the prurient reader (*praef.* 4), but from the viewpoint of a historian writing under Augustus it could also be seen as an aberration in Roman history, a time when the *metus hostilis* failed and the Roman community turned on itself in unseemly civil conflict. The new era after 31 B.C. was presented as (and probably believed by many to be) one of peace and conquest, when Rome went back to her proper and traditional role of eliminating external threat while enjoying domestic *concordia*. This popular Augustan theme found its proper counterpart in Livy's last books, with their record of the Roman conquest of foreign enemies. This focus of Livy's Augustan books should not necessarily be understood as due to a lack of other "safe" topics. It is just as likely that Livy was here indulging his desire to return to those topics that were the traditional focus of Roman histories.[50] The attrac-

---

412–13], if true, can only strictly mean that Livy withheld the issuance of these books; he could well have written them before the death of Augustus. A statement of Pliny's (*HN praef.* 16) about Livy indicates that the historian did not originally plan to write the number of books he did, and it may indicate a hiatus in the composition of his history: "And I declare that I am amazed that the famous writer Livy begins one volume of his history of Rome from the foundation of the city with these words: 'I have already achieved enough of fame, and I might have retired to leisure did not my restless mind find its sustenance in work.' " Woodman (supra n. 30) 136–38 now argues that Livy only took up the composition of his last twenty-two books because he believed that the Augustan principate was "the realisation or personification of the ambitions which he personally entertained for the Roman state" (138).

49. Syme (1959: supra n. 11) 66f. (= id. [1979: supra n. 11] 442f.); Woodman (supra n. 3) 38 and Frier (supra n. 22) 203. Livy's work seems mainly to have been the "history of Roman armies, with occasional glimpses of the activities of politicians and legislators at Rome," as P. Walsh, *Livy: His Historical Aims and Methods* (Cambridge 1963) 35, observes.

50. "In the remaining books (134–42) . . . Livy seems to have concentrated on wars against foreign peoples; and since many of his earlier books had dealt with the acquisition of Rome's empire, he was thus able to suggest that history had come full circle and that the Augustan age was challenging the past in glory" (Woodman [supra n. 30] 139). Cf. also Syme (1959: supra n. 11) 66–67 (= id. [1979: supra n. 11] 443), who, however, believes Livy was also avoiding difficult domestic topics.

tion of such material for a historian was acknowledged even by Tacitus, who apologized for the poverty of the material for his work in comparison to what had been available to earlier writers.[51]

If Livy did hesitate to compose the last part of his history, it may have been due to his own sense as a historian of just how hollow such an account had to be.[52] The traditional environment of Roman historiography was long lost. It would be almost another century before Tacitus, a senator but not a significant participant in events, would reconcile in a skillful way the problems that the new age presented for Roman historiography. A century's perspective made clear that *adulatio,* and not suppression, was the real threat to history.[53] This development in Roman historiography becomes clear when one turns to the Greek historical writers who flourished under Augustus.

Nicolaus of Damascus, Dionysius of Halicarnassus, and others, working in genres that had been refined by generations of Hellenistic court writers, were equipped with the literary tradition to compose the record of Rome.[54] To these external observers the Augustan era represented salvation from the most dreaded of all communal ills—*stasis*—and the *concordia* of the years after Actium provided the theme of *homonoia* for the *Roman Antiquities* of Dionysius of Halicarnassus.[55] Even the frightening early career of the young Octavian came into perspective when reported by a man like Nicolaus, who himself had survived the intrigue and treachery at the court of Herod the Great. From his viewpoint Julius Caesar's political inexperience (*apeiros politikēs technēs*) had blinded him to the development of the greatest of all conspiracies; his adopted son, on the other hand, did not make the same

---

51. *Ann.* 4.32.1–2: "I am not unaware that very many of the events I have described, and shall describe, may perhaps seem little things, trifles too slight for record; but no parallel can be drawn between these chronicles of mine and the work of the men who composed the ancient history of the Roman people. Gigantic wars, cities stormed, routed and captive kings, or when they turned by choice to domestic affairs, the feuds of consul and tribune, land-laws and corn-laws, the duel of nobles and commons—such were the themes on which they dwelt, or digressed, at will. Mine is an inglorious labor in a narrow field: for this was an age of peace unbroken or half-heartedly challenged, of tragedy in the capital, of a prince careless to extend the empire."

52. Syme (1959: supra n. 11) 73–76 (=id. [1979: supra n. 11] 450–53) has demonstrated how small an impression Livy's account of events after Actium made on later historians.

53. It is notable that the elder Pliny (*HN praef.* 20) withheld his account of the Flavians because he feared being reproached for *adulatio.*

54. Cf. Gabba (supra n. 15) 61–75.

55. In Dionysius' view, even in the periods of greatest *stasis* during the Republic no irreparable steps were taken: cf. 7.18.1–2, 7.26.4; also C. Schultze, "Dionysius of Halicarnassus and His Audience," in Moxon, Smart, and Woodman (supra n. 30) 131.

mistake and survived to bless not only Rome but the whole world with peace and order.[56] The Greek historians were not troubled by the theme of Rome for their histories. Polybius had set the precedent long before, and, at its best, Greek historiography was essentially a function of non-participants who produced histories in which the events became material for reflection on the human condition.

Roman historiography lacked such a detached and contemplative aspect. A product of the senatorial competition for status, it remained internally focused, with a philosophical framework restricted to a limited set of didactic motifs. When the internal circumstances changed, the traditional impetus to write history was lost, and the traditional themes became meaningless. In a later era Roman historians would hail the Augustan Age as one of rebirth and eclipse of the aberrant events of the previous century.[57] But the generations immediately after Actium lacked the perspective and circumstances for such a revisionist view. The disappearance of Roman histories under Augustus was not the result of suppression. Circumstances had simply made traditional historiography irrelevant.

56. On the naiveté of Caesar, cf. Nicolaus, *FGrHist* 90 F130 (59, 67, 81); on benefits of the Augustan Age, cf. F125.
57. Cf. Sussman (supra n. 21) 148–49.

Cassius Dio's
Assessment of Augustus

Antiquity's last comprehensive and notable assessment of Augustus was composed in the early third century by Cassius Dio, a bicultural Roman senator with long and varied experience in the imperial administration climaxed by a second consulship held with the emperor Severus Alexander in 229. Dio's career, pursued in tempestuous times under Commodus and the Severan emperors, spanned almost as many years as Augustus' unbroken hold on power of fifty-seven years, the last forty-three of which were years of relative stability.[1] Unalterably committed to monarchy, Dio deemed, on the basis of his exploration of the thousand-

---

1. Efforts to specify the dates of composition of Dio's *History* from internal evidence have produced a range of approximate chronologies: e.g., 197–219 (F. Millar, *A Study of Cassius Dio* [Oxford 1964] 28–32, 193–94); 201–223 (Vrind); 212–234 (Letta). T. D. Barnes, who offers fresh arguments for a late date (211–231, at the earliest), has recorded documentation for the major scholarly theories in "The Composition of Cassius Dio's *Roman History*," *Phoenix* 38 (1984) 240–55. With regard to publication, M. M. Eisman, "Dio and Josephus: Parallel Analyses," *Latomus* 36 (1977) 657–68, proposes that passages in the *History* critical of Severan emperors are part of a lightly revised version that was prepared after Dio retired and that saw the light of day only after his death (and that of Severus Alexander in 235). Cf. M. Reinhold, *From Republic to Principate: An Historical Commentary on Cassius Dio's* Roman History Books 49–52 (36–29 B.C.), Amer. Philol. Assoc. Mon. Ser. 34 (Atlanta 1987) 11–12; J. M. Carter in the Penguin *Cassius Dio* (1987) 19.

year history of Rome from its founding to his own time, that the transformation of the Roman Republic into a monarchy was a decisive turning point and that the principate of Augustus was a central and seminal
age. To these fateful years (44 B.C.–A.D. 14) he devoted over a seventh
of his *magnum opus,* Books 45–56. For Dio, not only was Augustus
the founding father of the indispensable monarchy and a paradigm of the
good ruler for the Severan age, but the Augustan system figured as the
normative form of monarchy in its constitutional and social modalities.

As its fuller precursors are lost, Dio's *History* provides our most substantial narrative of the whole period from the emergence of the
eighteen-year-old Octavian on the stage of history in 44 B.C. to his
death, as Augustus, in A.D. 14. "Le plus prodigue en renseignements,
vulnérable aux critiques," Dio's *History* is, despite limitations and
lapses that have been amply documented, fundamental to our knowledge of the period.[2] Its narrative detail is confirmed widely by other
literary sources and by inscriptions. Its synoptic power and perspicuity
can be impressive, thanks to Dio's extensive governmental experience
and to the more than twenty years that he devoted to reading and writing Roman history. Nor is his work lacking in independent (if often
anachronistic) interpretations and judgments.[3]

Whatever Dio's sources for Octavian/Augustus—and we do not
know them with any certainty[4]—he was not led slavishly by them, but
imposed his own persona and ideological perceptions on what he read.
For the period of the triumvirate we find him combining materials of
official origin or orientation, predictably intimating greatness to come,
with material too overtly critical, hostile, or realistic to have been published or freely circulated under Augustus or his successor, Tiberius. In

2. J. Béranger, *Recherches sur l'aspect idéologique du principat* (Basel 1953) 97. Dio
makes good (for example) some part of the loss of the histories of Asinius Pollio, Livy (of
which only the exiguous *Periochae* remain for our period), Cremutius Cordus, and Aufidius Bassus. The publication in the sixteenth century of Dio as recovered from the East
revolutionized knowledge of Augustus. A decade after the *editio princeps* of 1548, Xylan-
der wrote: "The war of Caesar Octavianus against Antony, the Battle of Actium, indeed
the whole principate of Augustus, the Varian disaster, and much else—all this our historian has recorded exquisitely and carefully? [*sic*], matters in which our other sources have
virtually abandoned us" (see H. S. Reimar, *Cassii Dionis Cocceiani Historiae Romanae
Quae Supersunt,* vol. 2 [Hamburg 1750–1752] 1387).

3. See, for example, M. Reinhold, "In Praise of Cassius Dio," *AntCl* 55 (1986) 213–
22; P. M. Swan, "Cassius Dio on Augustus: A Poverty of Annalistic Sources?" *Phoenix* 41
(1987) 272–91.

4. Millar's pioneering study marked a turning away from the nineteenth-century obsession with the sources of Dio's *History* to concentration on his historiographic methods
and thought ([supra n. 1] 34–38, 83–102). However, *Quellengeschichte* has not entirely
lost its vogue: see B. Manuwald's valuable *Cassius Dio und Augustus,* Palingenesia 14
(Wiesbaden 1979), though his purpose is to define Dio's thought. Only once does Dio
specify a source by name, Augustus himself, probably his autobiography (44.35.3).

treating the period after the victory at Actium Dio intrudes, if only occasionally, disparaging material that could not come from any official or loyalist account.[5]

To understand his assessment of Augustus we need first to know the "mind" of Dio, especially how the deepening crisis of the Roman Empire that he sensed in his own lifetime shaped his historical thought. With the reign of Commodus, he writes, Roman history declined ominously from a monarchy of gold, that of Marcus Aurelius, to one of "iron and rust."[6] Born of personal experiences, his concerns did not stop short of fears for the very security of the monarchy, the empire, and the senatorial order, whose interests he saw as inextricably interdependent. Chief among these concerns were (1) a descent to tyrannical and self-aggrandizing emperors, who infringed the traditional *libertas,* status, and property of their subjects and risked the security of the frontiers in military adventurism; (2) enlarged armies corrupted by excessive pay and largesses and by the slackening of military discipline; (3) pervasive economic stresses that threatened the wealth of the elite classes, who were overburdened by their obligations as civic benefactors and guarantors and by the fiscal demands of the imperial state in the form of taxes, arbitrary impositions, and even confiscation; (4) the invasion of the senate and the upper echelons of the imperial service by upstarts, which progressively marginalized the senatorial class in the social and economic life of the state and in the governance of the empire. It was out of concerns such as these that Dio in his *History* proffered political and moral edification to his generation.[7]

Though we lack to this day a thoroughgoing study of the substantive

5. Cf. Millar (supra n. 1) 73–118 on "Political and Historical Views"; Manuwald (supra n. 4) 66–76; J.-M. Roddaz, "De César à Auguste: L'image de la monarchie chez un historien du Siècle des Sévères," *REA* 85 (1983) 73–75.

6. 71.36.4.

7. On Dio and the crisis of his time, see G. Alföldy, "The Crisis of the Third Century as Seen by Contemporaries," *GRBS* 15 (1974) 92–93, 98–109; R. Bering-Staschewski, *Römische Zeitgeschichte bei Cassius Dio* (Bochum 1981) 125–34; L. de Blois, "The Third Century Crisis and the Greek Elite in the Roman Empire," *Historia* 33 (1984) 358–77 with references. Dio's sense of crisis is most securely derived from his own direct statements on contemporary events. Much can also be learned, however, from set speeches in which he addresses his concerns through the dramatis personae. The most important of these is Maecenas' speech in his debate with Agrippa (Book 52), on which see Millar (supra n. 1) 102–18; Manuwald (supra n. 4) 21–25; Bering-Staschewski (supra) 129–34; U. Espinosa Ruiz, *Debate Agrippa-Mecenas en Dion Cassio: Respuesta senatorial a la crisis del Imperio Romano en época severiana* (Madrid 1982); Roddaz (supra n. 5) 75–84 (with critical discussion of Manuwald and Espinosa Ruiz). On other speeches, see M. A. Giua, "Clemenza del sovrano e monarchia illuminata in Cassio Dione 55.14–22," *Athenaeum* 59 (1981) 317–37; and id., "Augusto nel libro 56 della Storia Romana di Cassio Dione," *Athenaeum* 61 (1983) 439–56, esp. 452–56. See also 43.15.2–18.5, a set speech of Julius Caesar in the senate (46 B.C.); cf. Millar (supra n. 1) 80–81.

influences of Thucydides on Dio's historiography, it is clear that in assessing the youthful Octavian of Books 45–51 Dio applied the *Realpolitik* of his Athenian model. He delineates Octavian as ruthlessly ambitious, unscrupulous, and cruel, never faltering in his march to *pan kratos*. We see the artful political tactician moving opportunistically, like an Alcibiades, amid the kaleidoscopic maneuvers and shifting alliances of the civil wars. Octavian is a master of the propaganda blitz, especially in his extraordinary campaign of recrimination and vituperation against Antony and Cleopatra, which was whipped up to a frenzy with every media resource of the times.[8] For Dio the victory of Octavian (with the ensuing transition to monarchy) came about through an elemental struggle for sole power among the dynasts: for by human nature men desire to dominate, resorting to force for self-aggrandizement.[9]

Dio viewed the sharing of supreme power by members of the triumvirate as catastrophic for the Roman people and destructive of their *libertas,* which could only be restored by monarchy: "For it is a difficult thing for three men or even two of equal rank who have gained possession of such great power as the result of war to achieve harmony." [10] The defeat and elimination of Sextus Pompey and the deposition from the triumvirate of Lepidus (36–35 B.C.) served merely to narrow the contest for supremacy to Antony and Octavian. Dio is evenhanded in depicting the extravagant ambitions and ruthless conduct of both, and does not cover up the unscrupulous and deceitful machinations of *Octavian*— even though he judged *Augustus* to be the ideal *princeps* and the institutions he established to be the norm for the principate. Using the Thucydidean approach, Dio treats the dynasts' patriotic claims, such as Antony's promise to restore the Republic, as pretexts disguising their real motive, *cupido dominandi,* thanks to which the Roman state hovered between the paralyzed Republic and a fatally flawed dyarchy.[11] No

8. Ambition: e.g., 45.4.3; 46.34.4, cf. 46.3. On the proscriptions, see 47.3.1–13.4; for executions at Perusia, 48.14.3–5, in Sicily, 49.12.4; on the purging of Octavian's lieutenant Salvidienus Rufus, 48.33.1–3. Tactician: e.g., 45.5–6, 14.1–3; 46.51.5–52.4; 48.29.2–3. Propaganda: Reinhold (supra n. 1) Appendix 7, "The Propaganda War of 32–31 B.C.," 222–23. Manuwald (supra n. 4) 70–74 views as foreign to Dio's generally negative image of Octavian the passage 47.7.1–5, which exonerates him from the main responsibility for the proscriptions. Cf. Giua (1983: supra n. 7) 440, n. 5.

9. Struggle for sole power: 45.11.2; 46.34.4; 47.1.1; 50.1.1–2, 2.2; cf. Manuwald (supra n. 4) 13–15, 75–76, 273. "Human nature": see Reinhold (supra n. 1) Appendix 1 " 'Human Nature' in Dio," 215–17; cf. Millar (supra n. 1) 76.

10. Destructive of *libertas:* 47.39.1–5; cf. 46.32.1; 50.1.2. For the quotation, 48.1.2.

11. Cf. 49.12.1: Octavian held that justice was on his and his army's side (rather than on Lepidus') because he was stronger; a similar sentiment is expressed at 49.36.1. Patriotic claims: 45.12.5; 49.41.6; 50.1.4, 4.4–5, 7.1–2.

other extant source treats the motives and maneuvers of the triumvirs so realistically.[12]

Yet for Dio the *cupido dominandi* of the triumvirs, however selfish, had a felicitous public outcome in the acquisition of supreme power by one man: for in so vast and powerful a state only under monarchy were "true democracy and enduring freedom" possible, the balanced and ordered condition of society in which each estate, secure in person and property, could play the part for which it was fitted. The final victory of Octavian brought *libertas* in this sense for all citizens under a responsible *princeps,* including a significant role for the elite in the decision making and governance of the empire.[13] Dio believed that just as the principles of "true monarchy" had answered the catastrophic troubles of the broken Republic, adherence to the same principles would answer the troubles of his own age.

Thus an ambiguous tension between realism and idealism underlies Dio's assessment of the entire career of Octavian/Augustus. Until the victories at Actium and Alexandria, Octavian is often portrayed as a self-serving and ruthless aspirant to power. With victory, however, comes a sympathetic shift. Disillusioned by experiences of civil strife, social instability, and tyrannical emperors, Dio is more in tune with Augustus than with Octavian the triumvir. With reverence, even nostalgia, he harks back to the Augustan principate as a model.[14] The tension between his images of Octavian and Augustus prompts him, *retrospectively,* to mitigate the early ruthlessness: Augustus' "real disposition" was to be sought in what he did "after he had taken undisputed posses-

12. Manuwald (supra n. 4) 25–26, 66–76. Consistent with the realistic portrait of Octavian in Manuwald's thesis (against that of E. Schwartz in *RE* 3.2 [1899] 1684–1722 [= id., *Griechische Geschichtsschreiber* (Leipzig 1957) 394–450]) that Livy was not Dio's principal source here (251–54).

13. See 47.39.4–5 on the beneficial issue of Philippi in advancing the day of monarchy through defeat of the republican side; 52.14.3–5 (Maecenas' speech) on "true democracy and secure freedom" (*tēn dēmokratian tēn alēthē tēn te eleutherian tēn asphalē*) under good monarchy; 56.43.4, Dio's own statement that Augustus, "by combining monarchy and republic, preserved freedom and established order and security"; 52.19.2–3 on the role of the senators, drawn from the *gennaiotatoi, aristoi,* and *plousiōtatoi* of Italy and the empire, as partners in rule of the good monarch. Cf. Reinhold (supra n. 1) 182–85.

14. See especially Giua (1983: supra n. 7) 449–56, who discovers Dio's true view in texts like Tiberius' funeral oration for Augustus, over which he had the most control as author, rather than in his narrative: "Cassio Dione abbia visto in Augusto la figura emblematica da proporre come punto di riferimento positivo per la monarchia del suo tempo" (449). Negative items in the narrative Giua sees as ambiguous rather than as signaling criticism of Augustus. Cf. Millar (supra n. 1), who finds Dio less approving of Augustus: "The essential thing is Dio's attitude of mixed acceptance and indignation. It is noteworthy that he does not waste much time on praise of Augustus" (102). Cf. Manuwald (supra n. 4) 102.

sion of supreme power." The proscriptions and other such drastic acts were "due to the pressure of circumstances." Done "against his will," they were motivated by a desire "to save the majority." [15] Even as *princeps*, however, Augustus is portrayed by Dio less as a saintly than as an efficient and masterful ruler. If his republican *civilitas* is often on display, so are *monarchic* power, authority, energy, even craft—and (though rarely) error and embarrassment.[16]

Real and ideal also jostle in Dio's treatment of Octavian/Augustus as commander of Roman armies. Nowhere is he depicted as a brilliant military strategist, whether in Sicily, Illyria, the Actian campaign, Egypt, or Spain. Defeats, as at Philippi and Tauromenium, are acknowledged.[17] Intensely troubled over the pampering of the armies under the Severan emperors, Dio does not palliate the young Octavian's bribing of the Macedonian legions in 44 B.C. in order to win them away from Antony. (Nor does he let slip the opportunity of stigmatizing the soldiers as utterly mercenary.) He relishes Octavian's embarrassment when, after the victory at Philippi, he is caught between the veterans demanding Italian land and the protests of those about to be dispossessed: "As if anyone had commanded him to wage war or to make such large promises to the soldiers." [18]

Yet Dio credits Octavian with the wisdom that comes of hard experience,[19] and approves repeatedly his austere control and depoliticization of the armies, both as triumvir and as *princeps*. After the victory over Sextus Pompey in 36 B.C. and the cashiering of Lepidus (Dio tells us), while commanding three armies concentrated in the northeast corner of Sicily, and facing incipient mutiny over "pensions," Octavian magisterially demobilized large numbers of soldiers without yielding to excessive demands. In the aftermath of Actium, when he had incorpo-

15. See 56.44.1–2, from Dio's final assessment of Augustus, where he describes the difference between the civil war leader and the *princeps* as "truly very great"; 56.37.3, the eulogy of Tiberius on Augustus. Cf. also supra n. 8; 53.2.5.

16. Power, authority, energy, craft: e.g., 53.11.5, 12.3, 16.1, 21.5–7, 24.6; 54.1.5, 3.1, 6.3–4, 7.6, 10.1–2, 5, 13.1, 4, 23.2–6, 25.1, 26.8–27.1, 31.4, 33.5, 34.4; 55.10.14–15, 26.4–5, 31.1–4; 56.23.2–4, 27.1–3. Error, embarrassment: 54.3.8, 15.7–8, 16.3–6 (with allusion to youthful peccadilloes), 19.3; 55.6.3, 9.5.

17. 47.45.2 (Philippi; Octavian's illness is adduced in extenuation); 48.47.5–6, 49.4; 49.5.1–5 (Tauromenium).

18. Military indiscipline and the army in Dio's time: J. B. Campbell, *The Emperor and the Roman Army, 31 B.C.–A.D. 235* (Oxford 1984) 192–98, cf. 401–14 (who qualifies Dio's criticism of Septimius Severus and argues that this emperor succeeded in maintaining discipline). Bribery: 45.12.1–13.4. Embarrassment: 48.6.1–8.5 (8.5 for the quotation). Cf. 42.49.1–5, disapproving the notion that an army and the money to pay it are the keys to gaining and maintaining *dynasteia*.

19. 48.8.4: *kai ex autōn tōn ergōn emathen*.

rated under his command the defeated troops and war fleet of Antony, he discharged many, satisfying them with promises alone, since he still lacked adequate funds. Elsewhere Dio instances rigorous military discipline exercised by others, notably Agrippa.[20] Clearly implied is disapproval of mounting insubordination in the military of his own day—which nearly cost him his life.[21] His own reputation as a disciplinarian, earned while he was governor of Upper Pannonia, so alienated the Praetorian Guard in Rome that when he was consul in 229 he escaped their wrath only through the intervention of the emperor, Severus Alexander, who had him complete his term of office in safety outside the city.[22]

Dio's ambivalent estimation of Augustus as a general is balanced by approbation of his choice and handling of his helpers in rule, preeminently Maecenas and Agrippa. Maecenas, though entrusted with exigent state missions (for example, the administration of Rome while Octavian campaigned against Sextus Pompey and Antony), "did not lose his head but lived out his life in the equestrian estate." Agrippa, the ideal *adiutor imperii*, was "the best man of his time," a revealing epithet that implies a *moral* primacy earned by subordinating himself voluntarily (*ethelontēs hēttato*) to the general welfare, resigning all destructive ambition for personal power, and even retreating from his personal preference, voiced in the debate with Maecenas, for a republic over a monarchy.[23]

Dio stresses the fact that far from fearing or envying their eminence Augustus treated his lieutenants with honor, gratitude, and generosity.[24] Pique, perhaps rooted in Dio's own experiences, may be detected here toward emperors who resented, even feared, competent subordinates. To expose such perversity he highlights the military feats of Agrippa and

20. Depoliticization: cf. K. A. Raaflaub, "The Political Significance of Augustus' Military Reforms," *Roman Frontier Studies* 1979 (BAR Intern. Ser. 71.3, 1980) 1005–25, revised and expanded in "Die Militärreformen des Augustus und die politische Problematik des frühen Prinzipats," in G. Binder, ed., *Saeculum Augustum*, vol. 1 (Darmstadt 1987) 246–307. Sicily: 49.13.1–14.2, esp. 13.4; cf. 49.34.3–5; after Actium: 51.3.1–5, cf. 4.1–8; also 49.38.4. Agrippa as disciplinarian: 54.11.3–5. Others: 42.52.1–55.3 (Julius Caesar); 45.13.2–3; 49.27.1 (Antony); 56.13.1–2 (Tiberius).

21. Insubordination: e.g., 73.8.1–4; 73.11.2–12.1; 75.12.3–5; 78.3.4–5; 80.2.2–3, 4.1–2.

22. Dio as disciplinarian: 80.4.2–5.1.

23. For Dio's obituary on Maecenas, see 55.7.1–6; for a frost between Augustus and Maecenas, probably beginning in 22, see Suet. *Aug.* 66.3 with 54.3.5; cf. 54.19.3, 6; 55.7.5 (but see G. Williams's contribution to this volume). On Agrippa see Dio's obituary at 54.29.1–2; cf. 52.41.2; J.-M. Roddaz, *Marcus Agrippa* (Rome 1984) 523–33, cf. 125–26, 209–16.

24. 56.38.2 (Tiberius' eulogy on Augustus); cf. 55.7.4; Bering-Staschewski (supra n. 7) 70–71.

Publius Ventidius, both of whom achieved historic victories that put their imperators, Octavian and Antony respectively, in the shade.[25] He documents extensively the decisive successes of Agrippa in Sicily over Sextus Pompey, in the Actian campaign, in Spain (19 B.C.), and elsewhere, as well as his brilliant benefactions to the people of Rome.[26] This man Augustus rewarded with the highest honors and promoted to son-in-law and associate *princeps*. Publius Ventidius met the opposite at Antony's hands. Dio devotes a long and valuable account to the spectacular exploits of Ventidius, the first Roman to celebrate a triumph over the Parthians (38 B.C.). But in contrast to Agrippa, who was rewarded by Augustus, Ventidius was relieved of his command by Antony immediately after his Parthian victories, just before the debacle of Antony's own campaign against the same enemy.[27] Through this antithetical treatment Dio obliquely censured emperors who failed to use to advantage, or recognize the merits of, competent men like himself. Of Caracalla he writes that "he hated all who excelled in anything." [28]

Dio was no admirer of military adventurists. He saw the expansion by Septimius Severus and Caracalla on the eastern frontier as costly and dangerous, and holds up as exemplary Augustus' "moderation" in foreign policy.[29] But in this judgment of Augustus he appears to be wearing rose-colored glasses. The fact is that the first decades of the Augustan principate saw much imperialistic zeal. Soon after Actium, the suicide of Antony, and the annexation of Egypt, the euphoria of victory spawned impetuous plans for (and public expectation of) fresh conquest—evoking dreams of *imperium sine fine*.[30] The image of Alexander hovered

25. Cf. Reinhold (supra n. 1) 45–46.

26. Sextus Pompey: 48.49–51, 49.1–10; Actian exploits: 50.11.3, 13.5; Spain: 54.11.2–6; benefactions: e.g., 49.42.2–43.4, cf. 54.29 (obituary). Cf. M. Reinhold, *Marcus Agrippa* (Geneva, N.Y. 1933); Roddaz (supra n. 23).

27. On Ventidius, see Dio 48.39–41; 49.19.1–22.1; for his dismissal, 49.21.1, 22.1.

28. 77.11.5. On Septimius Severus' pluming himself on the success of subordinates, see 75.2.3–4.

29. 75.3.2–3: Dio criticizes Severus' expansion into the buffer zone between Rome and Parthia; cf. 75.9.1–5. Cf. A. Birley, *Septimius Severus* (London 1971) 285–86; D. L. Kennedy, "The Frontier Policy of Septimius Severus: New Evidence from Arabia," *Roman Frontier Studies* 1979 (BAR Intern. Ser. 71.3, 1980) 879–87. Dio held Caracalla to be "exceedingly reckless" in his aggression against the Parthians (78.3.1), and he had only scorn for his imitation of Alexander the Great (77.7–8). Cf. Bering-Staschewski (supra n. 7) 124.

30. For the quotation, Virg. *Aen.* 1.279. Cf. A. Momigliano, "*Panegyricus Messallae* and 'Panegyricus Vespasiani,'" *JRS* 40 (1950) 39–41; P. A. Brunt, review of *Die Aussenpolitik des Augustus*, by H. D. Meyer, *JRS* 53 (1963) 170–76; C. M. Wells, *The German Policy of Augustus: An Examination of the Archaeological Evidence* (Oxford 1972) 3–13 with references; M. G. Morgan, "*Imperium sine finibus*: The Romans and World Conquest in the First Century B.C.," in S. M. Burstein and L. A. Okin, eds., *Panhellenica:*

over Rome at the time (it was even on Augustus' seal ring).[31] Dio himself records for the twenties B.C. the plans of Augustus to invade Britain, the campaign of Aelius Gallus into Arabia Felix (Yemen), and the push of C. Petronius into Ethiopia.[32] If the year 20, climaxed by diplomatic arrangements for détente with the Parthian empire, brought a pause in Augustus' military ambitions, in the next decade they flared up again with extensive campaigns on the Alpine, Rhine, and Balkan frontiers in which Augustus' stepsons, Tiberius and Drusus, took the lead.[33] In short Dio's search in Augustan foreign policy for models for his own time did not yield clearly positive results. Since Augustus added more territory to the empire than any Roman before or after, Dio was limited to selective highlighting of the arduous and tragic in frontier campaigns and of instances of restraint.[34] He leaves it on record that Augustus preferred to settle his differences with the British through diplomacy (27 B.C.), that the Arabian adventure (under 24 B.C.) was a costly failure (contra Augustus in the *Res Gestae*), that the successes against the Ethiopians came of Roman retaliation, not aggression (under 22 B.C.), and that the instruments with which a rebellion in the Cimmerian Bosporus was contained (under 14 B.C.) were the army of a *client* state (Pontus) and a *show* of force by Agrippa. Having credited Augustus, while still triumvir, with the conquest of Pannonia and Dalmatia to the Danube (35–33 B.C.), Dio treats the later momentous campaigns in Illyricum (and Tiberius' part in them) as the suppression of revolts (13–9 B.C., A.D. 6–9). He barely notices Tiberius' ambitious (if abortive) invasion of Marcommanic territory beyond the Rhine and Danube rivers in A.D. 6.[35] When

---

Essays on Ancient History and Historiography in Honor of T. S. Brown (Lawrence, Kans. 1980) 143–54; R. Syme, *The Augustan Aristocracy* (Oxford 1986) 64–68.

31. Suet. *Aug.* 50; Pliny *HN* 37.10; H. U. Instinsky, *Die Siegel des Kaisers Augustus* (Baden-Baden 1962) 9–38, 43.

32. Britain: 53.22.5, 25.2; cf. 49.38.2. Arabia Felix: 53.29.3–8; cf. G. W. Bowersock, *Roman Arabia* (Cambridge, Mass. 1984) 46–49, 148–53; S. E. Sidebotham, *Roman Economic Policy in the Erythra Thalassa, 30 B.C.–A.D. 217* (Leiden 1986) 116–30, 177–78. On both the Arabian and the Ethiopian campaigns, cf. the fundamental article of S. Jameson, "Chronology of the Campaigns of Aelius Gallus and C. Petronius," *JRS* 58 (1968) 71–84.

33. Parthia: 54.8.1–3; on the ambitious campaigns of Tiberius and Drusus in Raetia, Germany (as far as the Elbe), Dalmatia, and Pannonia, cf. Wells (supra n. 30) passim.

34. Arduous: 49.35.1–4 (Illyria, 35 B.C.); 53.25.6–7 (Spain, 26–25 B.C.); cf. 54.11.4–5; 56.12.3–5. Tragic: death of Drusus in Germany (55.1.3–5); death of Gaius from a wound inflicted in Armenia (55.10a.6–9); Varian disaster (56.18.1–24.5); cf. 56.16.4 on the high cost in men and money of the war in Illyricum A.D. 6–9.

35. Britain: 53.22.5; cf. Strab. 4.5.3.200. Arabia: 53.29.4, 7; *RG* 26.5; cf. Strab. 16.4.24.782. Ethiopia: 54.5.4–6. Bosporus: 54.24.5–6. Dalmatia and Pannonia: 49.36.1–37.6, 38.2–4, 43.8, cf. 50.24.4 (35–33 B.C.). Marcommani: 55.29.1, 30.1; cf. Vell. Pat. 2.108.1–110.1.

he retrojects to the entire reign the policy of nonexpansion that Augustus recommended to Tiberius in a document deposited with his will, the special pleading is evident: "This principle Augustus had really always followed himself, not only in word but also in deed." [36]

In the Agrippa-Maecenas debate in Book 52, Dio has Maecenas ask, *pothen oun chrēmata?* ("Where's the money coming from for the soldiers and for the other expenses that will necessarily be incurred?").[37] The allusion is to Dio's own age. He was alarmed at what he saw as vast, unproductive expenditures on the military, especially by Septimius Severus and Caracalla, and at the tax increases, capital levies, and confiscations by which they were met;[38] these undercut not only the wealth but also the social and political status of the propertied classes.[39] Dio therefore holds up to approval the new start made by Octavian after Naulochus and Actium in not confiscating land outright to give as retirement bonuses to veterans, but reimbursing the owners,[40] and the later conversion of retirement bonuses from land to cash, a measure that aroused confident hopes in the civilian population "that they would not in the future be robbed of their property."[41] In what may be cautionary *exempla* Dio relates the hostile reactions of the propertied classes to financial exactions after Philippi and before Actium. He also approves Augustus' systematization in 13 B.C. of conditions of military service with statutory periods of enlistment and set levels of pensions for the various ranks. He notes archly the baffled response of the soldiers to this settlement, which left them with cause for neither satisfaction nor protest. Dio registers (though without visible preference) the legionary es-

36. 56.33.5–6; cf. 54.9.1–2. Cf. Carter (supra n. 1) 17; J. Ober, "Tiberius and the Political Testament of Augustus," *Historia* 31 (1982) 306–28, arguing that the *consilium coercendi intra terminos imperii* was an invention of Tiberius.

37. 52.28.1.

38. Septimius Severus: 74.2.2–3 (193 B.C.); 74.8.4–5, 9.4 (confiscations, exactions during the civil wars); 76.16.1–4 (Severus' enormous expenditures matched by efficiency in raising revenues); cf. 76.15.2. See 77.9.1–10.4 for a catalogue of Caracalla's exactions and taxes through which he pampered the soldiers: "He made it his business to strip, despoil, and grind down all the rest of mankind, not least the senators." Cf. 77.3.1–2; 78.36.1–3 with Campbell (supra n. 18) 175–76.

39. On the economic problems of Dio's time, see E. Gabba, "Progetti di riforme economiche e fiscali in uno storico dell'età dei Severi," *Studi in onore di Amintore Fanfani*, vol. 1 (Milano 1962) 39–68; J. Bleicken, "Der politische Standpunkt Dios gegenüber der Monarchie," *Hermes* 90 (1962) 444–67; Espinosa Ruiz (supra n. 7) 352–81. De Blois (supra n. 7) argues that Dio saw the troubles of his own class as causes of decline when they were in fact merely symptoms of more profound currents of change. Cf. Reinhold (supra n. 1) 199–203.

40. 49.14.5; 51.4.5–8; cf. L. Keppie, *Colonisation and Veteran Settlement in Italy, 47– 14 B.C.* (London 1983) 69–82.

41. 54.25.5–6 (13 B.C.); cf. Keppie (supra n. 40) 82–86.

tablishment of Augustus as twenty-three or twenty-five legions, that of his own day as thirty-three. And he relates how Augustus set military finance on a permanent basis with the establishment of the military treasury, supported through contributions of his own and through statutory revenues.[42]

Dio also sought to sound the alarm about wasteful civilian expenditures. He criticizes the extravagance of the building projects of Septimius Severus and Caracalla. But he hits hardest at the cities of his day, which wasted the substance of their elites on ambitious municipal largesse, entertainments, and building projects. He advocates, through the speech of Maecenas, the empirewide elimination of the lifetime civic pensions for victors in athletic festivals, except for the most distinguished, and the abolition of chariot races other than those in the imperial capital;[43] for the weight of financial burdens, whether from imperial or from municipal demands, pressed most urgently on the elites, not least on Dio's own class, now drawn in its majority from the cities of the empire. Provoked by such pressures and sensitive to public waste, he contrasts Augustus' disciplined use of public funds. Tiberius, in his funeral eulogy, is made to say that Augustus "was as careful with public funds as if they were his own."[44] Dio praises Augustus' respect for private property, his frugal life-style, his use of his own funds for civic amenities and largesses, his curbing of the competitive extravagance of senatorial magistrates in producing festivals, and his disapproval of conspicuous consumption by the wealthy.[45]

In Dio's political philosophy monarchy was the only workable system for so immense and complex an empire, with such enormous racial, cultural, and religious pluralism; so that in his view Augustus wisely (if instinctively) aspired to monarchy from the outset of his career. "A republic could never be adapted to such vast interests; the leadership of

42. Reactions of the propertied class: 48.8.1–5; 50.10.3–5. Conditions of military service (for citizens): 54.25.5–6 (13 B.C.); cf. 55.23.1 (A.D. 5). Modest legionary establishment: 55.23.2, cf. 24.1–4. Military finance: 55.25.1–6, esp. 3; cf. 56.40.2; 52.28.1–6.

43. Extravagance: 76.16.3; 77.9.7. On unproductive municipal expenditures under the Severi, cf. 52.30.3–10; T. Pekáry, "Studien zur römischen Währungs- und Finanzgeschichte von 161 bis 235 n. Chr.," *Historia* 8 (1959) 485–88; Gabba (supra n. 39); R. F. Newbold, "Cassius Dio and the Games," *AntCl* 44 (1975) 589–604, noting 592, n. 14; Espinosa Ruiz (supra n. 7) 377–79; Reinhold (supra n. 1) Appendix 17, "The Economic Burden of Athletes' Pensions," 233.

44. 56.40.4.

45. Respect for private property: 53.2.3; 54.25.6. Frugality: 56.41.5 (Tiberius' eulogy on Augustus). Generosity in public causes: 53.2.1, 22.1–2, 31.2–3; 55.25.3. For *congiaria*, see 51.21.3; 53.28.1; 54.29.4; 55.10.1. Curbs on extravagance: limits festival expenses, 54.2.3–4; levels the pleasure palace of Vedius Pollio, 54.23.6.

one man would best preserve them." [46] In presenting Augustus as the quintessential monarch, Dio shows that for all his power Augustus surmounted the temptations of tyranny, not least in his relations with the senatorial order, whose status and quality he maintained. Troubled about the future of this his own class under emperors like Commodus and Caracalla, who subjected senators to terror and bloodbath, [47] Dio found in Augustus an exemplar who adhered to the principle of shared power between *princeps* and senate, as respected partners in governance. Such a partnership, free of coercion and based on recognition by the monarch of a dedicated elite, was in Dio's eyes basic to the rule of the good *princeps*, [48] under whom the senatorial order would be threatened neither from above by tyranny nor from below by the upward movement of equestrians or (worse) the "common man." [49]

In Augustus, Dio profiles the very virtues and style of rule that he found wanting in contemporary "iron and rust" emperors. His exemplar, he wishes it known, respected traditional institutions, adhered to due process, and conformed to the time-honored principles of collegiality and fixed terms of office. [50] He has Tiberius say in his *laudatio funebris* that under Augustus the senate enjoyed freedom of speech and voting. [51] Though undeceived as to Augustus' true intent, Dio records his periodic playing out of the ceremony of *recusatio imperii*, a public display of declining untraditional office, such as the dictatorship unsuccessfully pressed on him in 22 B.C. and the principate itself, which he undertook "unwillingly" in 27. [52] Above all, Dio documents amply the

46. 44.2.1–5; 54.6.1; for the quotation, 56.39.5 (Tiberius' eulogy on Augustus); cf. Tac. *Hist.* 1.16.1.

47. Commodus: 72.4.1–7.3, cf. 20.1–21.2. Caracalla: e.g., 77.4.1–6.1. Severus: cf. 74.2.1–3; 75.8.1–4 with Giua (1983: supra n. 7) 447–49, 455.

48. See Dio-Maecenas in 52.14.3–15.4, 19.1–3, 31.1–4, 32.1–3; cf. 53.8.4–5; Reinhold (supra n. 1) 183–85. On the persistence in the future of concern for the status of the senate in the face of imperial power, cf. C. R. Whittaker in the Loeb Herodian (I.lxxi–lxxxii); H. Bird, "Eutropius: In Defence of the Senate," *Cahiers des études anciennes* 20 (1987) 63–72.

49. In his survey of institutions of the principate in Book 53 Dio fixes the priority of senators over *equites* and the corresponding division of labor between them in public administration. He is at pains to praise Maecenas for being content with the station of *eques* (55.7.4). On the other hand, he cites Sejanus, Plautianus, and Macrinus as paradigms of the unwisdom of giving free reign to equestrian careerists. For Dio-Maecenas on the limits of decency in upward mobility, see 52.25.6–7, cf. 19.1–3. Cf. de Blois (supra n. 7) 364–66.

50. Traditional institutions: e.g., 53.1.1, 21.6–7. Due process: e.g., 53.21.4, 31.1, 33.1–2; 55.34.1. Collegiality, limited terms: 53.1.1, 13.1; 54.12.4–5.

51. 56.40.3; see also 53.21.3; 55.34.1; cf. 54.15.7, 16.3–6; 55.4.3, 7.3; 56.43.1.

52. Dictatorship: 54.1.3–5; principate: 53.3.1–11.5; 55.6.1, 12.3; 56.28.1; cf. 56.39.6. Cf. Béranger (supra n. 2) 137–69 ("Le refus de pouvoir"); A. Wallace-Hadrill, "Civilis Princeps: Between Citizen and King," *JRS* 72 (1982) 36–37; J. H. W. G. Liebe-

legislative, deliberative, and administrative role that Augustus gave to the senatorial order.[53] Augustus was eager to be thought *dēmokratikos,* "unmonarchic."[54] Dio writes in his own person that "Augustus comported himself towards senators as if they were free men."[55] He gives prominence to Augustus' *clementia,* a quality that senators of his own day missed painfully in their rulers, composing on this theme a celebrated dialogue in which Livia persuades Augustus that there is greater security in sparing conspirators than in executing them. He has Tiberius recall (in eulogizing Augustus) how as victor in the civil wars Augustus spared *"most* of his surviving opponents," eschewing the example of Sulla; and how, thanks to his mercy, the deposed triumvir Lepidus "lived so long a time after his defeat and continued throughout to be high priest." With the word "most," however, Dio recalls the greater realism of his *narrative,* which on the subject of *clementia* contains a conspicuous admixture of contrary material that is screened out in the dialogue and eulogy.[56]

As much as he exhibits the integrity of Augustus as monarch, Dio sometimes, and in important contexts, describes him as behaving duplicitously. In orchestrating in the senate the constitutional settlement of 13–16 January 27 B.C.—the foundation of the principate—his Augustus is manipulative and hypocritical, consolidating power while ostensibly resigning or sharing it.[57] The brief notices on the periodic renewals of Augustus' ruling powers echo the original charade.[58] Dio recounts how in seeking revenues for the new military treasury in A.D. 6 Augustus disarmed the senators by consulting them about possible sources,

---

schuetz, "The Settlement of 27 B.C.," in C. Deroux, ed., *Studies in Latin Literature and Roman History,* vol. 4, Coll. Latomus 196 (Brussels 1986) 345–65.

53. The legislative role is illustrated in dozens of enactments recorded by Dio: see P. A. Brunt, "The Role of the Senate in the Augustan Regime," *CQ* n.s. 34 (1984) 423–44; Swan (supra n. 3). On the deliberative role of senators, see, for example, 53.21.3–6, 33.1; 55.34.1. On senatorial posts in provincial government: 53.13.2–15.1; cf. 53.15.2–3 on the limited role of *equites.* For Augustus' defense of senatorial privilege, see 53.25.1 (with Suet. *Aug.* 44.1); cf. 56.40.3. Dio says surprisingly little about the senate's emergent role as a court: 55.34.2; cf. 53.23.6–7; 52.31.3–10.

54. 55.4.2–3; cf. 59.3.1; Wallace-Hadrill (supra n. 52).

55. 53.33.1, *hōs eleutherois sphisi prosephereto.* Contra the Loeb and Penguin translations, *sphisi* refers to senators, not to Romans generally (as the context shows).

56. Dialogue on *clementia* (set in the aftermath of a supposed conspiracy by Cn. Cornelius Cinna, cos. A.D. 5): 55.14.1–22.2; cf. Giua (1981: supra n. 7) 317–37; Millar (supra n. 1) 78–79. Tiberius: 56.38.1–2; Lepidus: 54.15.4–8, 27.2; cf. 49.15.3; *RG* 10.2. Punishments: 47.49.4 (after Philippi); 49.12.4 (after Mylae and Naulochus); 51.2.4–6 (after Actium); 51.15.5–16.1 (after Alexandria).

57. 53.11.1–12.3.

58. 55.6.1, 12.3; 56.28.1

yet imposed his own solution, a 5-percent tax (*vicesima*) on inheritances and bequests;[59] then, seven years later, he silenced senatorial opposition to the same tax by conjuring up delusive fears of worse.[60]

In none of these instances, however, does Dio palpably criticize Augustus for his duplicity. The pretense of the *recusatio imperii* is condoned as a "noble lie," a means to the high end of achieving stability and security under monarchy.[61] And in the manipulations through which the *vicesima* was instituted and then preserved we are shown the master mind of the ruler at work.[62] Dio's classic observations on how with the coming of monarchy access to the truth was fundamentally altered reflect his acquiescence in this new state of affairs:

> But from this time forth most things began to be done secretly and *in camera*, so that anything made public is distrusted, being in any case beyond verification; for it is suspected that everything that is said and done has been accommodated to the wishes of emperors or deputies. As a result, much that never happened is rumored, much that actually happened is never known, and with nearly every event a version gains currency that is different from the way it in fact happened. . . . This is why my own narrative of events after this . . . will all be in accordance with the reports given out, whether really the truth or otherwise.[63]

Dio thus resigns himself to official control of information as a tolerable concomitant of the transformation of the state "to a healthier and more secure condition".[64] His disinclination to contradict official accounts of conspiracies stems from the same resignation.[65]

In his enthusiasm for and idealization of Augustus as a model Dio fails generally to reveal how uneasy a truce subsisted between *princeps* and senate. He often skimps on the details of conspiracies against him, like that of M. Aemilius Lepidus, son of the triumvir, in 30 B.C. and those that followed the review of senate membership in 18 B.C. He gives a fuller account of the plot of Caepio and Murena under 22 B.C., but in defending Augustus' countermeasures as temperate and in the public interest he underrates (without actually suppressing) the extent of

59. 55.25.4–5.
60. 56.28.4–6.
61. 53.11.2, cf. 19.1.
62. 55.25.4, "not because he had no plans of his own"; 56.28.6, "his object was that they should fear even greater losses and so prefer to pay the 5 percent."
63. 53.19.3–6.
64. 53.19.1, *pros te to beltion kai pros to sōtēriōdesteron*.
65. 54.15.1–3.

alienation.[66] He all but ignores the extension, under Augustus, of *maiestas populi Romani* to include *maiestas principis*.[67] On the whole there is a conspicuous dearth of negative or critical detail in the *Augustan* narrative, to be attributed at least in part to filtration by Dio himself.[68]

To sum up, Dio in his *History* is a sort of self-appointed spokesman for his class. He sensed that in his time the principate was undergoing a metamorphosis comparable to the historic transition from republic to principate (but a retrograde one). For him Augustus as *princeps* and the imperial institutions he created offered both the foundational precedents and the normative form of the monarchy. And so he reached back selectively to the Augustan roots of the institutions of the principate in order to legitimize his conception of empire and emperor, to validate the continuity of this norm into his own time, and to mitigate or curb dangerous deviations from the origins. In his treatment of Augustus, Dio offers a classic example of the impulse to return to "the origins" in times of great crisis. Around the 250th anniversary of the promulgation of the "constitution of the principate," Cassius Dio was moved to appeal to the "original intent" of the "founding father."

◆ ◆ ◆ ◆ ◆

In enlisting the first *princeps* as a model for the Severan age, Cassius Dio has complicated (and rendered less profitable) the search in his pages

66. For brief anonymous reports of plots, see 54.15.1, 4, cf. 18.1; 55.4.3. The conspiracy of Lepidus is mentioned only in passing, a dozen years after the event (54.15.4; cf. Suet. *Aug.* 19.1). Caepio and Murena: 54.3.2–8.

67. Dio first refers to charges arising from verbal offenses against the *maiestas* of the *princeps* early in his account of Tiberius (who refused to admit them); yet he seems to assume that many such charges had been brought already before this, presumably under Augustus (57.9.2–3). As extant, he is silent (or at least anonymous: cf. 56.27.1) on the celebrated Augustan trial of Cassius Severus *de famosis libellis*, which Tacitus sees as opening the door to abuses of the *maiestas* law (*Ann.* 1.72.3, 4.21.3); cf. Syme (supra n. 30) 409–12. Although Dio offers, under 26 B.C., a repellent portrait of Valerius Largus, who informed against Cornelius Gallus, formerly prefect of Egypt (53.24.1–3), he says little under Augustus (cf. 55.27.3) that would allow us to anticipate the flourishing of delation under Tiberius. It is true that he registers under 8 B.C. the introduction of the practice of having slaves sold to the state treasury or to the *princeps* to qualify them as witnesses against their masters, this in connection with conspiracy trials: 55.5.4; cf. 57.19.1[b]–2. Tacitus attributes this innovation to Tiberius, *novi iuris repertor* (*Ann.* 2.30.3). Cf. R. A. Bauman, *The Crimen Maiestatis in the Roman Republic and Augustan Principate* (Johannesburg 1967); id., *Impietas in Principem: A Study of Treason Against the Roman Emperor* (Munich 1974); F. R. D. Goodyear, *The Annals of Tacitus*, vol. 2 (Cambridge 1981) 141–50 on *Ann.* 1.72.2–74.6.

68. Some of the main hostile texts, few and clustered, are 54.15.4–8, 16.3–6. On the question of whether Tacitus was the first historian to revise the favorable tradition on Augustus, see the works cited by Giua (1983: supra n. 7) 451.

for the *historical* Augustus and Augustan principate. He makes no secret of his preoccupation with the useful past (as when, in surveying
military forces under Augustus, he names only nineteen of the legions—
those still in service in his own day!). But what only a century of scholarship, spurred especially by Meyer, Gabba, and Millar, could demonstrate is how far that preoccupation silently shaped his account through
its importation of third-century issues and constructs and its displacement or diffraction of authentic Augustan material.[69]

The Severan face of *princeps* and principate has been revealed most
clearly in the set speeches, which are now viewed universally as sources
of Augustanism more than of Augustan history. A long series of studies
has proved, for example, that Maecenas' speech in Book 52 from the
debate with Agrippa on constitutions, despite a dramatic date of
29 B.C., addresses the concerns of Dio's age and class. Giua has shown
that the Augustus of Tiberius' funeral oration in Book 56 is in essence
a paradigm of the enlightened monarch as portrayed by Antonine
philosopher-orators.[70] Even at the level of factual information the
speeches provide the historian of Augustus with little that has not already been reported in the preceding narrative.[71] Dio's monumental account in Book 53 of the foundation of the principate, set in 27 B.C.,
offers its own difficulties.[72] Although it is an indispensable source on

69. Legions: 55.23.2–7. In his ground-breaking work *De Maecenatis Oratione a
Dione Ficta* (Berlin 1891), P. Meyer undertook to identify Severan and fictional elements
in the speech of Maecenas in Book 52. Dio was embittered (he held) by his brush with
death, as consul of 229, at the hands of the Praetorian Guard; he therefore amplified an
originally briefer speech of Maecenas so as to advocate enhancing the monarchic position
of Severus Alexander at the expense of his mother, Mamaea, the praetorian prefecture,
and the senate, on all of whom this emperor was excessively dependent. Cf. E. Gabba,
"Sulla *Storia Romana* di Cassio Dione," *RivStorIt* 67 (1955) 289–333; id. (supra n. 39);
Millar (supra n. 1) 73–118.

70. On the Maecenas-Agrippa debate (Book 52), see the works cited supra in n. 69 and
Reinhold (supra n. 1) 165–209; on Octavian's *recusatio imperii* (53.3–10), see A. V. van
Stekelenburg, *De Redevoeringen bij Cassius Dio* (Delft 1971) 121–29; on the dialogue of
Livia and Augustus on clemency (55.14.1–22.1), see Giua (1981: supra n. 7) 317–32; on
Tiberius' funeral oration for Augustus, see Giua (1983: supra n. 7) 439–56. In light of the
contemporary preoccupations in other speeches, Augustus' oration under A.D. 9 promoting marriage and child rearing may reflect to a greater degree than van Stekelenburg (supra) 142–48 thinks a *current* concern about marriage and birthrate, consistent with Dio's
apprehensions about the upward mobility of the unfit into the elite classes.

71. However, the exhortations of their forces at Actium by Antony and Octavian
(50.16–30) appear to preserve genuine elements of anti-Antonian propaganda. See K.
Scott, "The Political Propaganda of 44–30 B.C.," *MAAR* 11 (1933) 44–45; van Stekelenburg (supra n. 70) 99–106; Reinhold (supra n. 1) 105–12.

72. On this account (53.2.6–22.5), in which Dio constantly "switches directly from
the institutions of Augustus to the permanent features of the Principate," see Millar (supra
n.1) 92–100.

imperial institutions, insofar as it pictures the Augustan principate as a completed and "timeless" model of monarchy, it obscures the historical process by which the system grew and evolved in response to challenges, creating new modalities with pragmatic flexibility.

Nor is there reason for surprise that the Augustus of the *Roman History* appears to have a natural philosophy that matches the author's own, bearing the stamp of the later Plato and Stoicism.[73] Augustus, in a speech urging Roman *caelibes* to marry and propagate, is made by Dio to speak in characteristic Platonic/Stoic terms of "that first and greatest god who fashioned us, dividing the mortal race in two, making one part male, the other female, and implanting in them love and compulsion to mutual intercourse . . . so as to render what is mortal eternal in a sense through the succession of offspring." His Augustus shares with Dio the Stoic view that portents offer "scientific" evidence of the divine operating in history—here we see clearly that Thucydides' rationalist influence on Dio as a model in historiography had limits. Himself the host of dream visitations (for example, of Tyche, encouraging him in his historical labors), Dio assumes without reserve that Augustus too could be visited by god in sleep.[74]

By default, it is on the spare *annalistic* material in Dio's Augustan account that the *historical* quest is most usefully focused. His city annals, which are characteristic of that genre as we know it from Livy and Tacitus' *Annals,* offer heterogeneous sets of discrete reports, which are precise, factually dense, and resistant to tampering, on governmental enactments (especially senate decrees), dynastic events, reviews of the senate, dedications of monuments, festivals, imperial liberalities, deaths of dynastic figures, and the like, registered under the consuls of each year.[75] Brief and jejune when compared with their counterparts in Tacitus, and selected to serve his own purposes and interests, Dio's yearly gazettes of urban affairs nevertheless provide, when brought together, an important and trustworthy quarry in which it is possible to recover some historical strands of the process by which Augustus accumulated

73. On late Platonic and Stoic natural philosophy, cf. F. H. Sandbach, *The Stoics* (London 1975) 69–94; A. A. Long, *Hellenistic Philosophy* (London 1974) 151, 164. To judge from shared diction Dio knew the *Timaeus* and *Laws* of Plato well.

74. Creator god: 56.2.4. Dio and Augustus on the "scientific" validity of portents: 54.29.7–8; 56.24.1–5. Dream visions of Dio: 72.23.2–4; 80.5.3; cf. 78.10.1–2; of Augustus: 54.4.2–4 (Jupiter Capitolinus); cf. 54.35.3–4 (where Dio's scepticism does not extend to the *phenomenon* of dream visions).

75. Swan (supra n. 3).

munia senatus magistratuum legum, elaborated dynastic arrangements
through the public careers of heirs, developed the administration of the
imperial city, and transformed its topography.[76] The generic likeness of
Dio's urban annalistic record for the Augustan years to that in Tacitus'
Annals for the early Tiberian years not only confirms its reliability but
also suggests that Dio drew on an annalist (or annalists) who, like Tacitus, used the *acta senatus,* among other sources.[77] Brunt has offered an
example of what can be won from the unprepossessing annalistic material of Dio's Augustan books in demonstrating that Tiberius' extensive
consultation of the senate as recorded in Tacitus *Annals* 1–3 continued,
rather than departed from, Augustan practice: "In fact Tiberius initiated little. . . . Augustus, on the other hand, was a great innovator, and
the Senate was correspondingly involved in the work of reform."[78]

The *external* annals of Dio most often take the form of concise abstracts, reminiscent of the *Periochae* of Livy.[79] Although Dio's annalistic
arrangement often renders history discontinuous, it preserves the dated
items out of which can be reconstructed, province by province and war
theater by war theater, the only intelligible account we have of how
Augustus and his lieutenants, notably Tiberius, promoted and stabilized
the frontiers of the empire.[80] The case should not of course be overstated. Dio was prepared (we have seen) to accommodate his narrative
of external affairs tendentiously to his conception of a defensive foreign
policy maintained throughout the reign. Moreover, valuable as his abstracts are for frontier history, in his more ambitious productions, as
when he recounts the momentous campaigns of A.D. 9 in Dalmatia and
Germany, rhetoric is served before history. In relating the agony of Varus' legions, he summons rarities of diction, dramatic irony, *peripeteia,*
and pathetic fallacy; he even grafts a "Bosnian" landscape onto Lower
Germany, yet fails to register with any useful precision the starting
point, route, or terminus of Varus' fatal progress.[81]

With few exceptions, material and tone in Dio's Augustan annals,

76. For the quotation, Tac. *Ann.* 1.2.1.
77. Swan (supra n. 3); with a millennium of history to write, Dio will not have been
tempted to work up his account from primary materials.
78. Brunt (supra n. 53) 423–44 (442 for the quotation).
79. There are, of course, exceptions, like the ample account of the Balkan campaigns
of M. Licinius Crassus (51.23.2–27.3). It is characteristic of Dio's external annals (as of
Tacitus') sometimes to treat resumptively under a single year the campaigns of two or
more years.
80. Something of the history of Illyricum can be recovered under Dio's accounts of 35–
33, 13–9, A.D. 6–9; Roman-Parthian relations are treated in a set of discrete but consciously articulated texts.
81. See especially 56.11–16, 18–22.

both urban and external, are unremittingly official and uncritical.[82] In part this is because Dio presents Augustus as a model. But it also reflects the nature and origins of his information, on which Tacitus' *modus operandi* in the *Annals* sheds light. The *ultimate* sources of Augustan *annalistica* were in the main governmental. In the case of urban annals the *acta senatus* and *acta diurna* (the public "gazette") were fundamental. The case of external annals is much less clear, but reports of the *princeps* (or an heir or regent), "published" in the senate and subsuming the achievements of legates, may have been definitive. The annalist(s) used by Dio clearly lacked the genius (or freedom) of a Tacitus with which to subvert an Augustan myth resting on such sources. For his part, Dio had from the very advent of Augustus resigned the attempt to penetrate the public veil of government.[83]

As for the historical personality of the *princeps,* except for official facets, it is not to be discovered in Dio. What subsists in the *History* is an abstract, bloodless umbra, in which we miss human, as distinct from idealized, qualities.[84] The authentic glimpses here and there preserved in other sources are wanting—neither the prudent dynast vacillating, in letters to Livia, over the future of the youthful Claudius nor the fragile septuagenarian, with days to live, sceptically rallying an inerrant court astrologer, is to be found in Dio's *History.*[85]

82. A few brief and intrusive bits of negative testimony subsist, mostly concentrated in a brief span (18–16 B.C.: here, for example, appears Augustus' maltreatment of Lepidus). Cf. supra n. 68.

83. "Published" in the senate: see 54.25.5; 55.10a.9; cf. 54.11.6. Millar (supra n. 1) 91 observes that "there is no trace of any conflict of sources in any of Dio's accounts of military operations under Augustus." Resignation: 53.19.6; 54.15.1–3.

84. The Augustus of the speeches cannot be reconciled with history. In the *recusatio imperii* of 27 B.C., Dio produces by turns a blustering general (53.4.1–2), a sanctimonious martyr (53.5.3), the facile propagandist (53.6.1–7.3), a pretentious benefactor (53.8.1), a patent liar (53.9.4). Absent are marks of the well-attested deference to the senate: cf. Wallace-Hadrill (supra n. 52) 37–38. At 53.6.1 the assertion of meek virtues (*epieikeia, praiotēs, apragmosynē*) rings false; the claim never to have taken an "immoderate or extraordinary honor" was "a bold challenge to his hearers' capacity for forgetting facts and events" (H. T. F. Duckworth, *A Commentary on the Fifty-Third Book of Dio Cassius' Roman History* [Toronto 1916] 37 ad loc.). Note in contrast the fearful Augustus of the Cinna dialogue (55.14.2–3, 15.2, 4–7).

85. Suet. *Claud.* 3.2–4.6 (Claudius); *Aug.* 98.4 (Thrasyllus). A profitable source for the historical Augustus is contemporary poetry: see the sensitive study of J. Griffin, "Augustus and the Poets: 'Caesar qui cogere posset,'" in F. Millar and E. Segal, eds., *Caesar Augustus: Seven Aspects* (Oxford 1984) 189–218.

The Death of Turnus:
Augustan Vergil and the Political Rival[1]

In Vergil's version, Aeneas, ancestor of the Julian family, appears in Italy as a peaceful and peace-seeking newcomer. (Perhaps one should call him a homecomer since his distant forefather Dardanus had supposedly emigrated from here, *Aen.* 7.206f., 240; cf. 3.167.) His journey has been supervised by Fate and by Jupiter (1.261ff.; 8.381). He is sent under orders of Apollo, god of prophecy, specifically to occupy the land between Tiber and Numicus (7.241f.), i.e., territory held by King Latinus' people and by the Rutulians of King Turnus. The ultimate purpose of his arrival, according to divine revelation (7.98–101; cf. 1.286ff.), is the worldwide rule his descendant Augustus[2] will one day peacefully exercise from around here.

Aeneas is not spared the saddening experience of resistance, raised by an increasing faction of the native population. There is, above all,

1. In a more detailed fashion, the paper will be part of a larger study concerning the political aspects of the *Aeneid*. An early overview of the argument was presented on May 27, 1983, at the biannual meeting of the Mommsen-Gesellschaft in Cologne, West Germany. Summaries in Stahl 1981 (infra n. 22), 158f., and Renger 1985 (infra n. 5), 74.

2. On the identity of Caesar (= Augustus) at *Aen.* 1.286ff., see H. P. Stahl, *Propertius: "Love" and "War". Individual and State under Augustus* (Berkeley and Los Angeles, 1985), chap. 5, n. 46 (on p. 340, referring to p. 126).

oracle-defying, sacrilegious Turnus (cf. 7.595) who associates with such telltale characters as King Mezentius, most cruel torturer of his own subjects (8.485ff.) and "despiser of the gods" (*contemptor divum*, 8.7); another close companion of his is Messapus who, on the occasion of a peace treaty, delights in killing a king at the altar in full regalia as, in his words, "a better victim for the great gods" (12.289–96). The Julian ancestor is forced to wage a holy war against the godless opposition.

His greater descendant had to face comparable problems. After the assassination of his adoptive father, C. Julius Caesar (the dictator), Octavian (the later Augustus) joined the second triumvirate and its mandate "to organize the republic," *rei publicae constituendae*. Octavian wished his earthly achievements to be viewed as fulfillment of a divine mission—so much so that he would publicly spread the needed information. On a coin of his,[3] one finds his public task, expressed by the three letters *r(ei) p(ublicae) c(onstitutendae)*, superimposed on the outline of a tripod, i.e., on the symbol of Apollo, god of prophecy, whom he considered his personal tutelary deity.

Octavian, as his *Achievements* inform posterity (*R.G.* 2), had to defeat the men "who butchered my father" (*qui parentem meum trucidaverunt*—the customary label for a dictator's assassins, we remind ourselves, would be "tyrannicides"), "when they raised arms against the republic," *bellum inferentis rei publicae*. True to his perception of his mission as serving the common weal, he calls his opponents a "faction" (*R.G.* 1), not dignifying them by mentioning a name.

To sum up, then: a just cause; executor of a divine mission; administrator of the nation's interests; facing irresponsible, godless, and criminal factionalism—these are features shared by the founder of the Julian race (as depicted by Vergil) and by his descendant (as his case is presented by Augustus himself).

It was the ancestor's task, according to the *Aeneid*, to prepare the road that would, in the distant future (i.e., in Vergil's own time), lead to Emperor Augustus. Now: since the portrait of the forefather was being painted at a time (29–19 B.C.) when the descendant had already completed the conquest of his unholy opposition, one cannot a priori ex-

---

3. M. H. Crawford, *Roman Republican Coinage* (Cambridge, 1974), pl. LXIV, 6 = no. 538.2. This is a *denarius* issued in 37 B.C. by a mint "moving with Octavian," showing a "tripod with cauldron" (vol. I, p. 537). "Octavian's coinage of 37 . . . for the first time introduces Apollo (or rather his tripod) as a type" (vol. II, p. 744). The propaganda value of coins was utilized by Octavian consistently throughout his career. See W. Trillmich, "Münzpropaganda", in *Kaiser Augustus und die verlorene Republik*, Exhibition Catalogue (Berlin, 1988), 492–528.

clude that the epic on the ancestor may, at least in part, be designed to set the record "straight" on the ethics and metaphysics of the descendant's career. I do not want to state here "typological" correspondences between the two characters.[4] Nor do I subscribe to the hypothesis that the poetic ancestor was intended to enlighten the real-life descendant about his obligations as a ruler.[5] A question more to the point appears to be: could any reader in the time of Augustus fail to observe the symphonic pitch in epic and present-day political pronouncements, e.g., the declared desire for peace and the unwelcome burden of having had to wage a holy war against sacrilegious rebels who threatened the community? Is the ancestor's enduring loyalty to his divine mission not superbly helpful in guiding the reader and citizen when he ponders the presumed motivation of the latest Julian, his contemporary ruler (as well as that of his adversaries)?

The interpretation to be proposed here is derived from close literary analysis of the epic itself, especially its long-range composition. A comparison with another author may both briefly introduce my reader to Vergil's method and provide a wider background. For this purpose, I choose the situation at the opening of the war in Italy.

In Livy (1.2.1), we find Turnus betrothed to Lavinia, daughter of King Latinus. Upon Aeneas' arrival in Italy, Latinus withdraws his daughter's hand and reassigns Lavinia to Aeneas. Turnus reacts by waging war against both Latinus and Aeneas. A widespread view in Vergilian scholarship wrongly assumes the same setup for the *Aeneid*. In this case, readers would certainly feel sympathy for Turnus who could, through Books 7–12, be seen as trying to recover what is rightfully his. A close reading (which cannot be detailed here), however, reveals that Vergil was careful to avoid making the Julian ancestor a bride-snatcher.

Above all, Vergil's concept, when compared to Livy's, provides a different, more negative, picture of Turnus. This is achieved by the timing (*tempora*, 7.37) of events. Well before Aeneas arrives in Italy, an oracle

---

4. G. Binder, *Aeneas und Augustus. Interpretationen zum 8. Buch der Aeneis* (Meisenheim am Glan, 1971), 2f.

5. See E. Wistrand, "Aeneas and Augustus in the *Aeneid*," *Eranos* 82 (1984), 198; V. Pöschl, "Virgil und Augustus," *ANRW* II 31.2 (Berlin and New York, 1981), 707–27: "Virgil hat so dem Kaiser und seiner Nation und den folgenden Kaisern Leitbilder gegeben, die ihr Wirken prägen sollten" (713); C. Renger, *Aeneas und Turnus. Analyse einer Feindschaft*. Studien z. Klass. Philologie II (1985), 69: "Der Princeps sollte . . . zum selbstkritischen Vergleich angeregt werden." E. Lefèvre, "Vergil: Propheta retroversus," *Gymnasium* 90 (1983), 17–40: Vergil "dürfte sich Augustus als Republikaner, nicht als Monarchen gewünscht haben und wies ihn deshalb auf Aeneas, der sich selbst überwunden und stets der res Romana unterworfen hatte, zurück" (40).

(the one mentioned earlier, 7.96–101) is made known throughout the cities of Italy (7.104f.): Lavinia is destined not for a native suitor (7.96f.) but for a son-in-law from abroad whose descendants will rule the world, etc. In this way, Turnus' persistence in claiming Lavinia (i.e., the Latin throne) must be viewed, in the first place, as disobedience toward divine orders. His later political and military opposition against Aeneas, upon the Trojans' arrival in Italy, is secondary, both in time and in degree of criminality.

One of the major achievements of Augustan Vergil here can be seen in the way he sets his nuances. Far from being a foreign invader, the Julian ancestor is duly welcomed by pious Latinus as the carrier of a divine mission and as a homecomer; but then Aeneas is ruthlessly attacked by the oracle-defying head of a local faction (the opponent does not represent an Italian consensus).

This clearly spells out the negative role of Turnus. As literary critics, we should not be guided by our own desire for fairness or humanity; nor should we carry greater "complexity" or "sophistication" into the poet's design by introducing outside perspectives, such as Dante's programmatic, all-Italian view (*Div. Comm. Inf.* 1.106–108):

> Di quella umile Italia fia salute
> per cui morì la vergine Camilla,
> Eurialo e Turno e Niso di ferute.

Far from seeing in Turnus a hero dying for Italy, the *Aeneid* presents him as a rebel against the gods. Methodologically speaking, the paper presented here concentrates on and, if possible, limits itself to perspectives that can be demonstrated to flow from the epic's text itself. This, of course, does not mean that historical references to the poet's own time are dismissed.

Though my introduction had to be limited to a few hints, the service Vergil is rendering to his ruler is already becoming clear. By identifying the Aeneadae (i.e., the future Julians) with Fate and the will of the highest god, he is able to do two things. He can, on the one hand, disentangle Augustus from the (often gruesome) incidents of the recent civil war: Octavian (here we also recall the aforementioned coin) did not participate as yet another faction. Rather, he is the latest member of a family whose divine mission the *Aeneid* firmly anchors in a mythical past: the poet functions as ideologue of the ruler. Vergil is also able, on the other hand, to define—and in this he again agrees with the published position of Augustus—the political adversary as a criminal opponent of divine authority (a notion of lasting influence in Occidental history). The present investigation traces Turnus' later career in the epic, up to his death at the hands of Aeneas.

As far as scholarship[6] is concerned, the topic of Turnus' death, being the cope-stone of any overall interpretation, has aroused so much controversy that it would seem to be hybris if I claimed that this paper offers something basically new on the subject. The limitations of the present occasion restrict us to merely glancing at some influential positions. In doing so, we must not forget that reaching an objective understanding is especially difficult in the case of a piece of poetry which coordinates its artistic message with a political tendency. The history of Vergilian scholarship (in this similar to scholarship on Thucydides) repeatedly shows how the individual (even the critical) scholar was tied to political and sociological preconceptions of his own time.

For matters of perspective, it seems best to open the selection by quoting a critical and independently thinking contemporary of Vergil. He does not mind pronouncing publicly his lack of interest in a task like the one that was set to Vergil, viz., to found the glory of Augustus on his Trojan forefathers,

Caesaris in Phrygios condere nomen avos.

This quotation from one of Propertius' elegies (2.1.42) suggests that the epic on Aeneas is to be written for the sake of glorifying Augustus.[7] In other words, the ancestor's story must be told in a way that will enhance the reader's appreciation of the descendant, his contemporary. The line, though perhaps somewhat sarcastic, may help us to characterize the traditional understanding of Vergil as the author of an imperial creed.

Comparable to the view taken by Propertius, though somewhat more respectful, is the traditional modern understanding of the *Aeneid*, as

6. For recent surveys of scholarly literature, see especially K. Galinsky, "Main Currents in Recent Work on the *Aeneid*," in "Vergil's Romanitas and His Adaptation of Greek Heroes," *ANRW* II 31.2 (Berlin and New York, 1981), 985–1010; W. Suerbaum, "Hundert Jahre Vergilforschung: Eine systematische Arbeitsbibliographie mit besonderer Berücksichtigung der Aeneis," ibid., 3–358; also his *Vergils Aeneis. Beiträge zu ihrer Rezeption in Geschichte und Gegenwart* (Bamberg, 1985).

7. See also Tib. Claud. Donatus (ed. H. Georgii, reprint Stuttgart, 1969) 2: Vergil "had to show Aeneas in such a light that he was presented as a founder of the family and forefather worthy of Augustus in whose honor this work was being written." He also, says Donatus, had to present Aeneas "free from *any* guilt" (*vacuum omni culpa*). Another coin may be usefully introduced here (see E. A. Sydenham, *The Coinage of the Roman Republic* [1952], no. 1104 = pl. 28), of about 42 B.C., showing on the obverse "head of Octavian bare; C CAESAR IIIVIR. R.P.C." On the reverse: "Aeneas walking r., bearing Anchises on his shoulder"; etc.

represented by Karl Büchner's article in Pauly-Wissowa[8] or in Erich Burck's outline of 1979 in *Das römische Epos*.[9] The interpretation is based on programmatic passages such as Jove's revelation of Rome's future in Book 1, Anchises' prophecy in Book 6, Vulcan's fate-informed survey of Roman history in Book 8 (all culminating in Augustus), and the conversation of Jupiter and Juno in Book 12.

In view of these key passages, it would indeed appear difficult to claim Vergil for another than the traditional pro-Augustan interpretation. The view is further supported by the fact that the Trojan-Julian ancestor, always obedient to Jupiter and the oracles, is found on the side of Fate, i.e., the inexorable course of history which eventually will lead to the Augustan empire. If one asks about the morality of Aeneas' actions, a first and obvious (though indirect) answer is: his two main adversaries, Queen Dido of Carthage and Italian King Turnus, are allowed to die only after an expression of personal guilt (4.547; 12.931). I am using the term "personal" guilt here because, though expressing awareness of their shortcomings in their own limited spheres, they may not fully realize the extent to which they have sinned against the divine order of the universe.

So the signs point to Aeneas' innocence. Nevertheless, a wide segment of scholarship has taken the opposite position for, by now, more than two decades. The two main roots of this situation are perhaps not too difficult to state briefly. One is that recent literary criticism has increasingly felt free from obligations of basing interpretations on the logical and rhetorical organization which is an essential characteristic of ancient literature. Supposedly suggestive leads, supplied by imagery, verbal echoes, presumed ambiguities, etc., have sometimes been assigned the power of overruling the *Aeneid*'s plot line or train of thought.

The other root, it seems to this interpreter, has been a sort of politically occasioned rescue operation, which has continued to this very day and spread from its origins in the English-speaking world. Already after World War II, but especially during the Vietnam War era, a general dissatisfaction with forms of militarism and imperialism spilled over into the reading of literature. Such dissatisfaction potentially threatened the universal acceptance traditionally enjoyed by the chief poet of the Augustan empire.

---

8. See K. Büchner, *P. Vergilius Maro. Der Dichter der Römer* (Stuttgart, 1961: reprint of Pauly-Wissowa, *R.E.* VIII A [1955] 1021–1486).

9. E. Burck, "Vergils Aeneis," in id., ed., *Das römische Epos* (Darmstadt, 1979), 51–119.

European scholars could, already after World War I, react to the fall of an empire by taking recourse to the idea of the Christian-medieval empire. Also, it was not too difficult, by stepping beyond Vergil's historical situation, to see in him a poet of the human condition *in general*.[10] By assigning man his place in a hierarchically structured (political and) metaphysical universe, Vergil appeared as a writer of *Menschheitsdichtung*. A possible bias or partiality on his part was played down or denied. V. Pöschl, a highly influential post-World War II interpreter, quotes Dehmel: " 'Writing poetry means: to embrace the world lovingly and lift it up to god.' Aeneas' enemies, too, are human beings. Turnus is demonic but not evil" etc.[11] Pöschl was able to see Aeneas' humanity at work even at that point when the hero takes eight young enemies captive in order to sacrifice them alive over the grave of his killed young friend Pallas. This, we read still in the third edition of 1977,[12] is a "bitterness" (*Erbitterung*) in which Aeneas' *compassion (das Mitleiden des Aeneas)* for Pallas finds its climactic expression.

Pöschl's English-speaking counterpart, K. Quinn, paints a different portrait: ". . . it is . . . to Aeneas that Vergil ascribes the urge to kill in its ugliest form."[13] Though Pöschl had given a favorable reappraisal of Turnus, contrasting his "demonic passion" with his "noble nature" (*edle Natur*), his "heroism" with the "hellish deceit" (*dem höllischen Trug*) he appeared subject to, and arriving at a tragic portrait,[14] he could not have gone as far as M. Putnam: "It is Aeneas who loses at the end of Book XII, leaving Turnus victorious in his tragedy."[15]

The (Continental-) European road was not open to Putnam and other, especially American, scholars. What rescued Vergil in their eyes was that, upon close inspection, he seemed to speak with "two voices,"[16] a public and a private one. The latter supposedly undercuts

10. See Büchner 1961 (supra n. 8), 438 and 440; Burck 1979 (supra n. 9), 52: "Aussagen über diese augusteischen und allgemein menschlichen Ziele und Werte"; "Gültiger Ausdruck von Roms Kraft und Grösse und seiner Berufung zur Weltherrschaft . . . Diese Einschätzung kommt ihnen" (i.e., the works of Horace and Vergil) "auch heute noch zu"; 58: the *Aeneid* "ein Abbild der ganzen menschlichen Existenz." Also, V. Pöschl (supra n. 5), 727.
11. V. Pöschl, *Die Dichtkunst Virgils. Bild und Symbol in der Aeneis,* 2d edition (Darmstadt, 1964), 175; 3d edition (Berlin and New York, 1977), 175 (author's translation). See also 1964, 218.
12. Pöschl 1977 (supra n. 11), 139; 1964 (supra n. 11), 195.
13. K. Quinn, *Virgil's Aeneid. A Critical Description* (Ann Arbor, Mich., 1969), 17f.
14. Pöschl 1977 (supra n. 11), 128.
15. M. C. J. Putnam, *The Poetry of the Aeneid* (Cambridge, Mass., 1965), 193; cf. p. 243 of his "The Hesitation of Aeneas," *Atti del Convegno mondiale scientifico di studi su Virgilio,* a cura dell' Acc. Naz. Virgiliana (Mantova, Rome, and Naples, 1981), 233–52.
16. A. Parry, "The Two Voices of Virgil's *Aeneid*," *Arion* 2 (1963), 66–80 (republished in S. Commager, ed., *Virgil: A Collection of Critical Essays* [Englewood Cliffs, N.J.,

the former. Turnus the (innocent) victim is more essential to Vergil than his (merciless) conqueror Aeneas, who loses the claim to humanity because his bloody road to victory reveals the vast suffering caused by Rome's rise up to the Augustan Empire. These scholars, then (Parry, Putnam, Quinn, R. D. Williams, along with W. Clausen[17] and others), have expounded the pessimistic Vergil of the "Harvard School" who is so much more appealing to modern tastes. Most recently, this type of literary criticism has laid claim to "Further Voices in the *Aeneid*." [18]

The rhetorical and political function of the individual's suffering within the plot line is usually not investigated, though there clearly is more innocent bloodletting on the Trojan than on the Italian side. One interpreter (if I understand him correctly) has found a sort of schizophrenic Aeneas, a dual personality: he is both a hero of the twelfth century B.C. (who practices revenge and kills Turnus) and a hero of the Augustan Age or of the poet's own sensibility (whose "humanitarian revulsion from slaughter" would spare Turnus). "These moral ambiguities, therefore, bridge the gap between the field of the narrative and either that of the age of Augustus or that of the human condition as such. They belong to, and are characteristic of, the very technique of composition itself." [19]

For reasons of methodology in literary criticism, a third possibility should not be excluded: the "age of Augustus"—and with it, its chief poet—might turn out to be very much like what *our* time would rather wish to relegate to the twelfth century B.C.—in which case the rescue operation of two decades would have failed. The often invoked "lonely individual" who does not fit the cosmic mold would then have to be located outside the *Aeneid*. Recalling Propertius' firm refusal to make his talent available for praising civil-war victor Octavian in an epic, one

1966]); R. D. Williams, *The Aeneid of Virgil,* ed. with Introduction and Notes. Books 1–6 and 7–12 (Basingstoke and London, 1972, 1973). See vol. I, XXI: "But side by side with his public voice is the private voice, expressing deep concern for the lonely individual who does not fit into these cosmic schemes." R. D. Williams, *The Aeneid* (London, 1987), 56: there is a "tension between optimism and pessimism, between Virgil's public voice extolling the greatness (actual and potential) of Golden Rome and his private voice of sympathy and sorrow," etc.

17. W. Clausen, "An Interpretation of the *Aeneid*," HSCP 68 (1964), 139–47.

18. R. O. A. M. Lyne, *Further Voices in the Aeneid* (Oxford, 1987). See p. 217 with notes 1 and 2 for Lyne's professed affinity with the "pessimistic Harvard School"—a term coined by W. R. Johnson, *Darkness Visible. A Study of Vergil's Aeneid* (Berkeley and Los Angeles, 1979), 11 and 15, as contrasted with "the essentially optimistic European school," 9.

19. G. Williams, *Technique and Ideas in the Aeneid* (New Haven, 1983), 231. See also Renger (supra n. 5), 67: Aeneas "auch ein Berserker," "ein Kämpfer aus mythischer Vorzeit, der nach archaischen Maximen handelt."

might think of naming the elegist, writer of some personal and truly independent poetry, as a prime candidate for the prospective vacancy.[20]

Let us now turn to the text of the *Aeneid* itself. The observing reader has been expecting the death of Turnus ever since Book 7. When the Rutulian king and others, "against the prodigies," "against the fates," and "in perversion of the will of the gods" (7.583f.), urge Latinus to raise war against Aeneas, the old king, full of presentiment, exclaims:

> For you, Turnus, (abominable event!) the bitter death penalty
> will be waiting, and too late you will worship the gods with prayers.
>
> *te, Turne, (nefas!) te triste manebit*
> *supplicium, votisque deos venerabere seris.*
>
> (7.596f.)

Aeneas himself, from his point of view, twice in Book 8 points to the broken treaty: "What penalties will you pay me, Turnus!" *Quas poenas mihi, Turne, dabis!* (8.538). And: "Let them ask for battle and break the treaty!" *poscant acies et foedera rumpant!* (8.540). His words combine the functions of judge (*poenas*) and executioner (*dabis*) in one and the same person. But the thoughtful reader, even if he sees such predictions being fulfilled at the end of Book 12, may object: "I do see the connection on the factual level, but not on the moral; for bold Turnus was hardly himself when he urged to go to war. He had just before been deprived of his senses by the Fury Allecto sent by Juno (7.406–66)."

To such a sceptical reader I would, before explaining the Fury's allegorical character and function, suggest that he join me in tracing three other strands which likewise come together in the final scene of the epic. Limitations of space restrict the presentation. I can be fairly detailed in outlining the first strand; of the second, at least Vergil's perspective in describing Pallas' death is being determined; much evidence supporting the third strand must be excluded here and will have to wait until the publication of the larger study I mentioned earlier.

I

Most clearly visible is the development that leads up to the final battle in front of (and for) the city of the Latins, ended by the duel. The development is introduced by Aeneas' words at the opening of Book 11: "Now our road leads to the king and the Latin walls," *Nunc iter ad*

---

20. See Stahl 1985 (supra n. 2), especially chapters 5–7.

regem nobis murosque Latinos (11.17). However, this road will not be as straight as it is being announced here. And the detours to a considerable degree are due to none other than Rutulian King Turnus. In this context, as on other occasions, the poet contrasts Turnus' behavior with that of his greater counterpart, Aeneas.

In Book 11 the bodies of those who died in the great battle of Book 10 are buried. This necessitates some contact between the two warring sides, and thus "good Aeneas" (*bonus Aeneas*, 106), the victor, is given a chance to emphasize that he would be only too happy to grant peace (*concedere*, 111) also to the living, to avoid the war of the two nations and, instead, by way of a deadly duel, leave the decision to god or to personal valor (*vixet cui vitam deus aut sua dextra dedisset*, 118). On the Latin side, it is not only Drances, the invidious opponent of Turnus, who, together with all those (*omnes*; cf. *uno . . . ore*) accompanying him, turns an attentive ear to Aeneas' suggestions (124ff.; 132). The reader is far from feeling increased sympathy for Turnus when the poet goes on to list further groups within the city (the details are well on target):

> The mothers here, and the poor daughters-in-law, the dear hearts
> of the mourning sisters, and the children, bereft of their (slain) fathers,
> they curse the abominable war and the wedding (plans) of Turnus:
> he himself with his arms, he himself with his sword (they order)
> should bring about the decision—he who demands
> the kingdom of Italy and the highest honors for himself.

> *hic matres miseraeque nurus, hic cara sororum*
> *pectora maerentum puerique parentibus orbi*
> *dirum exsecrantur bellum Turnique hymenaeos:*
> *ipsum armis, ipsumque iubent decernere ferro,*
> *qui regnum Italiae et primos sibi poscat honores.*

(11.215–219)

At an earlier point already (9.133–39) Turnus had been unwilling to see that, when encountering the fate-sent Aeneadae, one has to scale back one's political ambitions, even give up one's most personal desires—in this case, his hopes for receiving the king's daughter as his bride (presumptuously, he already called her his "wife", *coniuge*, 9.138).

Now the reader, emotionally influenced by the sorrows of those bereft victims, is given reason to view Turnus' savage rage as a sort of private war that he is waging at the cost of his people to fulfill his personal goals. Thus at the beginning of Book 11 Turnus can by no means be seen exclusively to represent the interests of the Italians. Rather, he is found to be in considerable isolation. It should be noted how, in this section, the reader's judgement is subliminally influenced by the author. Consciously, we first register the voices of Drances and of his fellow ambassadors; then, later, the pitiful and heart-rending pleas of those who lost their loved ones in Turnus' war.

In between, Vergil inserts a description of the burials on both sides (182–214). In spite of the tears (191) and the unwillingness to part with the dead (201) on the Trojan side, there can be no doubt that the pitiable Latins (*miseri*, 203), who pile up "innumerable" (204) pyres and must burn a "huge pile" of anonymous, not individually honored comrades (207f.), receive more of the writer's sympathy. This may, at first sight, seem to reveal impartiality on the poet's part, to express "Virgil's horror of war, and especially his sympathy for the unnumbered and unhonoured dead." [21] But the authorial description of the sorrows experienced by the *miseri . . . Latini* has a less conspicuous function: it conditions the reader to accept as justified the invective which the *matres miseraeque nurus* etc. utter against Turnus. Far from representing *Vergil's* humanity, the appeal to the reader's sense of compassion serves (while on the surface favoring the Trojans' enemies over the Trojans themselves) to discredit Aeneas' Italian counterpart: Turnus, the feeling reader is supposed to conclude, is selfish at the cost of his people's lives. An important facet of Augustan Vergil's literary (and rhetorical) technique is revealed here.

A new warning for Turnus and his followers is effected when the negative answer of the Greek Prince Diomedes is received in the Latin assembly. Diomedes even advises against fighting Aeneas (11.225ff.). He interprets the losses encountered by the Greeks before Troy and on their way home as punishment for their attack on Troy (*supplicia et scelerum poenas*, 258). Today he rates (and in doing so, he employs quite Julian standards) his own attack on Venus (in the *Iliad*, the lowest step in his continual aggression against gods) as the climax of his own madness (*demens*, 276). From personal experience (*experto*, 283) he describes Aeneas' strength in fighting, even mentions a close combat he had with him (*contulimusque manus*, 283) that is unknown to the *Iliad* (the *Iliad* passage only tells us of Aeneas' inferiority toward Diomedes).[22]

King Latinus does understand the meaning of the message: one must not "wage war against the race of the gods and invincible (!) men," *cum*

---

21. R. D. Williams 1973 (supra n. 16), vol. II, *ad* 11.207–9.
22. For details, see H. P. Stahl, "Aeneas—An Unheroic Hero?" *Arethusa* 14 (1981), 173f.

gente deorum invictisque viris (305f.). When proposing peace, he is supported by Drances (the same one who had transmitted Aeneas' demand for a duel, 220f.): "Turnus, we, all of us, ask you for peace," *pacem te poscimus omnes, Turne* (362f.). By openly implying his hostility toward Turnus (364f.), he guarantees his arguments the credibility they deserve, though his approach ("you source and cause of these sorrows for Latium!" 361) is anything but diplomatic. He suggests that the dowry (i.e., the kingdom) is more important to Turnus than the bride (369ff.).

Perhaps not surprisingly, by this appeal Turnus' inclination to violence is kindled even more: *talibus exarsit dictis violentia Turni* (11.376). If he is standing in the way of the common weal (*si . . . bonis communibus obsto*, 445), then, he says, he will accept the duel. Is he aware that Aeneas' call for him alone (220, 221) as a counterpart fighter represents an echo of his own earlier call (10.442) for Aeneas' young friend Pallas as his own adversary (and his alone)? Probably not. But on the reader's ear this echo (which again appears repeatedly in Book 12) is not lost: "For me alone Aeneas is calling. Let him: that is my desire!" *Solum Aeneas vocat. et vocet oro* (11.442).

It certainly does not recommend Turnus to the reader if he now hopes to refute Drances' blame of defeat by bragging (392ff.) that he has struck to the ground "the whole house" of King Evander. The truth is that senior fighter Turnus had killed (in fact, murdered, as we shall see) Evander's son Pallas, almost a boy still (*puer*), on his first (10.508) day in battle. Similarly, he brags about his valor inside the Trojan camp (11.396ff.)—whereas in truth his "unblessed leadership," to use Drances' words (*auspicium infaustum*, 347), had cost his side the decisive victory. Had Turnus only opened the gates to let his fellow fighters enter the Trojan camp, that (Vergil comments) "would have been the last day for the war and the (Trojan) race," *ultimus ille dies bello gentique fuisset* (9.759).

Turnus' erroneous estimation of his own rank is reflected in the tragic irony of his words (11.438–42): he will courageously face Aeneas, (a) even if he should be better than Achilles (he is, in Vergil's concept), (b) even if he should put on armor like that made by Vulcan (he does); (c) "to you and father-in-law Latinus I have dedicated my life" (Latinus is neither destined nor ready to be his father-in-law. And Turnus himself will fail to keep his solemn promise of *animam hanc . . . devovi*).

Turnus' flaming outburst has kept the assembly from finding the peaceful solution old King Latinus had hoped for. When now the facts (Aeneas is reported to approach) overrun all further chances of deliber-

ating—what is Turnus going to do now? Does he, according to his solemn offer, try to meet Aeneas in single combat when he, full of contempt, leaves the assembly and its talk of peace (460) and dashes out?
No way. In a state of fury (*furens,* 486) he arms himself and is exultant
like a stallion finally (*tandem,* 493) freed from his tether (*qualis . . . liber
equus,* 492f.). To Camilla he leaves the fight against Aeneas' advance
horse. He himself, disregarding her advice that he use the foot soldiers
and protect the walls of Latinus' city (506), moves to the mountains
where Aeneas is with his main troops—but not to ask for a duel, no: he
plans to lay an ambush for Aeneas: "A (tricky) stratagem I prepare in
the hollow path of the forest," etc., *furta paro belli convexo in tramite
silvae,* etc. (11.515f.). Vergil could easily, if this plot line required temporary removal of Turnus from the battlefield, have him slightly
wounded (as he has Aeneas in Book 12). We must assume that a further
characterization is intended if Turnus leaves the battle for a ruse.

In the eyes of the reader, the discrepancy between words and deeds
certainly discredits Turnus. But author Vergil still intensifies the negative
impression. His *parecphrasis* ascribes predicates of human deceit to the
place of the ambush:

> There is a valley of curved course, fit for deceit
> and guile of arms, upon which on both sides the flank
> closes in, black with thick foliage, where the slim path is leading
> and the narrow pass guides, together with the malicious approaches.

> *est curvo anfractu valles, accommoda fraudi*
> *armorumque dolis, quam densis frondibus atrum*
> *urget utrimque latus, tenuis quo semita ducit*
> *angustaeque ferunt fauces aditusque maligni.*
>
> (11.522–25)

As I said, the procedure of characterizing is indirect, but the reader can
hardly avoid drawing conclusions from the quality of the landscape—
fraudi; dolis; maligni; cf. *silvis . . . iniquis,* 531—regarding the character of its user Turnus who is familiar with the area (*nota . . . regione,*
530) when planning his *furta belli* (515).

The negative impression is not wiped out by the fact that Turnus'
insidious intentions (*furta*) are not realized because he is prematurely
called back to the city, which is now endangered. As a matter of fact, it
has been Turnus' absence that has made the city itself vulnerable (cf.
872f.). Camilla's dying words (825f.) repeat her earlier (506) demand
that Turnus protect the city.

Camilla has meanwhile paid for her warfare against the Trojans with "too cruel a death penalty" (to use the compassionate words of divine Opis—in the *Aeneid,* guilt does not foreclose pity): *nimium crudele luisti / supplicium Teucros conata lacessere bello!* (11.841f., cf. 585f.). Opis, we register by the way, a priori thinks along those lines which Diomedes, who learned from his experience, recommends—another confirmation of the author's way of thinking. In the *Aeneid,* atonement (*luisti*) by death penalty (*supplicium*) is the result of hostilities against the Trojans.

The next morning (we are now in Book 12), when Turnus sees the eyes and expectations of the discouraged Latins directed at himself, when he feels that fulfillment of his promises is "now (*nunc*) being demanded" (2), he no longer evades his responsibility. "On his own initiative" (*ultro,* 3), similar to the wounded Punic lion who finally (*demum,* 6) accepts the fight, he announces: "No delay through Turnus," *nulla mora in Turno* (11), and asks King Latinus formally to conclude the treaty for the duel with Aeneas.

In doing so, Turnus describes his opponent in highly contemptuous words (*desertorem Asiae,* 15), even states that "the cowardly Aeneadae," *ignavi Aeneadae* (12), cannot withdraw their offer of a close combat. His public appearance again is as courageous as it was in the assembly of Book 11. Neither the arguments of Latinus (who now regrets the outbreak of the war [Book 7], even condemns it—and himself: *vincla omnia rupi . . . arma impia sumpsi,* 30f., and who adduces compassion for Turnus' old father, 43f.) can calm down the *violentia* (12.45; cf. 9) of Turnus who wants to accept death in exchange for fame (*letumque sinas pro laude pacisci,* 12.49); nor is Queen Amata, threatening to commit suicide, able to change his mind—especially not because Lavinia's presence fans his *amor* (70; Latinus, we recall, had set kingdom before bride, 22 and 24). His manly reply, solemnly (pompously?) mentioning himself in the third person, allows only one of the two enemies to live on: "Turnus does not have the freedom to postpone (his) death," *neque enim Turno mora libera mortis* (74), and so his message to Aeneas is, "With our blood let us end the war: on that field Lavinia the wife shall be found!" *nostro dirimamus sanguine bellum: illo quaeratur coniunx Lavinia campo* (12.79ff.).

In the ensuing scene where Turnus is arming himself (for a dress rehearsal, so to speak, not yet for the final combat—though his vivid imagination makes him use the word *nunc* three times, 95–97), however, we again witness uninhibited Turnus as we know him: he hopes to stretch lifeless Aeneas' body, to tear open his breastplate, and to mar his crimped and perfumed hair in the dust (97ff.). While Turnus is happy (*gaudet*, 82) when seeing his snorting horses, Aeneas, feeling his responsibility and trying to console his saddened son as well as his fearful companions by referring to the course of fate—Aeneas is happy "that the war is being settled by the offer of the treaty," *oblato gaudens componi foedere bellum* (12.109).

A similar sense of obligation is shown by Aeneas at the time of the oath: in case of defeat (which he equates with his own death) Iulus would withdraw with the Trojan forces. In case he himself should be victorious, he would *not* demand unconditional surrender (no *parere*, 189), but he would tie both nations to each other, undefeated, by a permanent treaty—a prospect that will be nullified by the breach of the present treaty, as will Latinus' hope for eternal duration of this peace and treaty (202). Aeneas even would leave Latinus (then his father-in-law, *socer*, 193) his army and his rule, while himself having his own city fortified, to be named after Lavinia, 194f. (He would, of course, inherit, through Lavinia, Latinus' city and throne after the old king's demise.)

The solemn words *inter se firmabant foedera* (212) are followed by Juturna's riot (instigated by Juno): the Rutulians, seeing Turnus' "hollow cheeks" (*tabentesque genas*) and his pallor (*pallor*, 221) at the altar, are—against Aeneas' intention—filled with fear that they will have *dominis parere superbis* (236), and thus they arrive at the impious prayer, *foedusque precantur / infectum*, 12.242f. A deceiving omen effected by Juturna—a swarm of swans chases the eagle and makes him give up his prey—is sufficient for the Rutulian augur Tolumnius to throw the first spear. The underlying attitude apparently is to get out of the treaty situation if only a chance is offered. Quickly, general fighting arises.

To the shameful picture of Latinus, fleeing with his beaten gods *infecto foedere* (285f.), is added the other one showing us how warrior Messapus (on whom Turnus can always count), "eager to destroy the treaty," *avidus confundere foedus* (290), forces poor (*miser*, 292) Etruscan King Aulestes, dressed in full regalia because of the solemn occasion, to retreat so he falls backward on the altar. Messapus, in killing him, derides him as "a better victim for the great gods," *melior magnis data victima divis* (296). Thus, the Roman reader's moral indignation about the broken truce is intensified by his religious indignation about the blasphemy. The opponents of his emperor's forefather are found deficient in basic standards of human conduct.

Inevitably the question arises in the reader's mind: how do the two main characters react to the new development? Almost equally inevitable is the answer: *pius Aeneas* (311), his outstretched arm bared of weapons, his head unhelmeted (perhaps somewhat uncautious, but idealistic-impressive in ranking right over reality), tries to check the situation on his side: "The treaty has already been concluded!" (i.e., it is valid), *ictum iam foedus!* (314). Demanding the duel, he reassures his people ("Give up your fears: it will be for me to make the treaty firm with my hand!" *auferte metus: ego foedera faxo firma manu,* 316f.)—until he is (almost equally unavoidably) hit by an arrow from an unknown hand and forced to leave the field, a victim of his loyalty to the treaty in a counterworld of catch-as-catch-can: the ideal of a Roman hero and ancestor of the Princeps.

The anonymity of Aeneas' assailant gives the poet pause to ponder whether it was "chance or a god," *casusne deusne* (321) that provided glory so great for the Rutulians. In Vergil's concept, the Julian ancestor apparently is sacrosanct, not a target for human arms (except by chance, *casus*). Accordingly, Jupiter will later censure Juno for the inappropriateness of the incident: "Was it suitable that a divine person was hurt by a mortal wound?" *mortalin decuit violari vulnere divum?* (12.797). The boundary that separates the Julian ancestor from everyday humanity must not be blurred in the minds of Vergil's contemporaries.

And Turnus on the other hand? A case of "déjà vu": glowing in sudden hope (*subita spe fervidus,* 325), he—*superbus* (326)—allows himself to be carried away in un-Roman, un-Trojan fashion and causes, like *Mavors* himself (332), a bloodbath, insulting (*insultans*) even the miserably slain enemies (*miserabile caesis*) when the hooves of his horses splash through the blood (339f.). Here Vergil leaves his reader hardly a door open for sympathy toward Aeneas' opponent. Once again, the self-chosen obligation of the duel is shed the moment Turnus can hope to gain from its violation.

On the other side one should expect that Aeneas, quickly healed by Venus' miracle and again taking leave from his son, this time in the words of the suicidal (i.e., death-bound) Sophoclean Ajax (435ff.)—that now Aeneas for his part too feels released from the treaty. That at least seems to be what Turnus and the Rutulians are afraid of when seeing him and his army reappear—a fact that drives cold trembling deep into their bones, *gelidusque per ima cucurrit ossa tremor* (12.447f.). Aeneas, leading his troops to attack, is likened to a terrible storm, causing devastation which "the poor farmers," *miseris . . . agricolis,* have anticipated long beforehand in their hearts, *praescia . . . corda,* 452ff. How else can we understand the comparison with the foreknown storm than that in it the guilty conscience of the "poor" Rutulians finds an expression, their awareness of their king's and their own breach of the treaty, and their illegal rage, as well as their resulting, justified fear? Elsewhere too in the *Aeneid,* one finds compassion expressed—*o miseri,* 7.596, cf. 8.537—for an erring and misguided people bound to face the dire consequences of their—and their leader's—conduct (see also 11.841f.).

Aeneas, however, does not justify the expectations of his enemies. He does not dignify (*dignatur,* 12.464) the fleeing Rutulians (among their dead is also Tolumnius, first offender against the truce) to be killed by his own hand, nor does he deal with those willing to face him. "Alone" Turnus (here again, after 315, is the echo) is the one he is looking for, *solum . . . Turnum vestigat lustrans, solum . . . poscit* (466f.).

To keep his reader from overlooking Aeneas' thinking (and conduct), directed even now at fulfilling the treaty, Vergil uses the rare verb *vestigare* three times. When divine Juturna, unsteady like the flying swallow, takes over as Turnus' charioteer and tries to abduct her brother, Aeneas follows that planless movement, *vestigatque virum et disiecta per agmina magna / voce vocat* (12.482f.). The reader (I am not here thinking of the Homeric or Vergilian scholar of the twentieth century A.D., but rather of the Roman boy or man who, in the new national epic, learns to admire his emperor's ancestor), struck by so much loyalty to a treaty, is frightened when he sees that bold Messapus this time chooses even perplexed Aeneas himself for his target. He hits, it is true, Aeneas' crest only (because Aeneas is able to evade the attack); but finally (*tandem,* 497), overcome by this ambush (*insidiis*) as well as by Turnus' continuous evasive movements, and not without often invoking Jupiter and the altars because of the broken treaty (*multa Iovem et laesi testatus foederis aras,* 496)—finally Aeneas gives the reins to his wrath and kills terribly, without discriminating any longer. The choice of the manner of fighting, duel or battle, is no longer left to him. His admirable patience and self-control were wasted, on this kind of enemy.

Thus, a single commenting word, coming from the mouth of the author himself, is able to confirm to the reader that he is on the right track with his understanding of the text. As the Punic lion Turnus "finally" (*demum,* 12.6) was ready to accept the challenge of the duel (he is not necessarily a coward, no, he only takes the chance of evading whenever it is being offered), so Aeneas "finally"—*tandem*—(and formally: *Io-vem . . . testatus*—by no means is he "overcome" by wrath) abandons the incredible self-discipline that he had imposed upon himself since entering into the treaty. "*Tandem*" in this context means that long ago already he would have had reason to state a breach of the treaty and act accordingly. But it also means that what follows is not a series of senseless killings on Aeneas' part but that he is fulfilling his duty as a fighter in battle for his people: only he is better at it than others.[23]

However—the syncrisis continues—Aeneas would never (as does Turnus, 511f.) cut off the heads of his enemies and attach them to his chariot: together with the different attitude toward the treaty goes a different attitude toward the dead enemy. Even when letting go the reins of his wrath, the Julian ancestor does not match the cruelty of his rival. Modern interpreters have often been dissatisfied with Aeneas' rage on the battlefield. But, when interpreting, we should place Vergil's context and the nuances he sets ahead of our own expectations.

Above all, it must be said that Vergil's guidance for his reader goes beyond the *tandem:* for even in the new turmoil Aeneas does not cease to search for Turnus: *vestigans* (for the third time this verb) *diversa per agmina Turnum* (557). The futility of his search finally leads him, inspired by Venus, to turn against the city of the Latins itself—a new target not initially envisaged by him. But no longer can he envisage the contracted peaceful coexistence of the two states; he is forced to reduce the Latins to subjection now: "if they do not grant to accept the rein and, defeated, to obey," *ni frenum accipere et victi parere fatentur* (12.568). The new twist in the plot is ingeniously designed by Vergil: if submission takes place, then it is unintended by the Trojan side. The assault upon the city—the "cause of the war," *causam belli* (567), "resting quiet without being subject to punishment," *impune quietam* (559)—is understood to be the only way still now to force the Rutulians to observe the treaty (the second broken treaty, after all). Aeneas feels (570f.) he can hardly be expected to wait until it pleases Turnus to show up for the duel!

> This, my citizens, is the source, this is the essence of the godless war!
> Hurry to bring torches and demand the treaty with flames!

23. The words of killing "indiscriminately" (*nullo discrimine*) have a negative ring to them for modern ears. Vergil uses them to contrast Aeneas' new general fighting with his preceding search for Turnus *alone*. His uncurbed wrath (*irarumque omnis effundit habenas*) results (*irae*, 494) from Messapus' perfidious attack on Aeneas the supposed dueler. On the justification of Aeneas' wrath, see now also K. Galinsky, "The Anger of Aeneas," *AJP* 109 (1988), 321–48—especially 329f.

hoc caput, o cives, haec belli summa nefandi!
ferte faces propere foedusque reposcite flammis!
                                                              (12.572f.)

Here we see the ancestor of the Julians as an involuntary attacker,
forced by the perfidy of his enemies to assault the city. Once again, we
watch him proceed not without formally accusing Latinus, and calling
upon the gods as his witnesses that he, following the second breach of a
treaty, is being *forced* to resort to fighting (580–82). Is it at all conceiv-
able that the reader is *not* supposed to ponder the conduct and feel illu-
minated about the motives of Aeneas' greater descendant during the
civil war?

Now that all valuations have been prepared (even if some perhaps
are not yet quite explicit), the action quickly approaches its end. Queen
Amata's suicide (her feelings of guilt are not dissimilar to those of Dido:
"She accuses herself as the cause, crime and source of the misery," *se
causam clamat crimenque caputque malorum*, 12.600) is reported to
Turnus together with the city's call for help. Now he is ready to go without further help from his sister, will no longer (*neque . . . amplius*) show
himself indecorous (*indecorem*, 679; cf. *dedecus*, 641), wishes to feel
free from the reproach of cowardice (648f.). It hurts him to have seen
Murranus, his dearest companion, die right before his eyes, calling his
name. (Murranus had been knocked from his chariot by a rock hurled
from Aeneas' hand, then was run over by his own horses, 529–34).

Here, a surprising confession again places him in an ambiguous light:
"Long already" (*dudum*), ever since the breach of the treaty which she
so skillfully brought about (*cum prima per artem foedera turbasti*), and
since she joined the war (as his charioteer: *teque haec in bella dedisti*,
12.632f.), he has recognized his sister, and now too (*et nunc*), he says,
she does not deceive him. Does that not mean that Turnus personally
has consented to the breach of the treaty *right from the beginning*, and
has willingly and consciously allowed himself to be abducted by his divine sister? The words *prima, dudum* and *neque . . . amplius* (cf. also
646) give us from his own mouth what the *demum* in the simile of the
Punic lion expressed, viz.: Turnus has delayed, again and contrary to his
corrective assurance given to Latinus: *nulla mora in Turno* (12.11).

Immense shame, frenzy, love, sadness, rage, self-conscious virtue
(667f.) now drive him to the city, where he keeps back his fighting companions: "It is more appropriate that I alone / for you atone for the
(broken) treaty and decide with my sword," *me verius unum / pro vobis
foedus luere et decernere ferro* (12.694f.). The word we heard from

Opis' lips before, *luo,* together with those just mentioned earlier, *pudor* and *conscia virtus,* once more give away quite clearly his awareness of his situation as one who has broken his commitment—a hint that is not unimportant for interpreting the final scene. Aeneas, on the other hand, *immediately* stopping all assault on the city in order to return to the idea of the duel, is again, as we saw him earlier (109), all joy (*laetitia exsultans,* 700)—about the renewed prospect, of course, of avoiding genocide by solving the conflict according to the terms of the treaty, i.e., by a duel. Turnus, by emphasizing his personal (*unum*) responsibility, has come round full circle to his offer to Latinus (*solus,* 16). Juturna, of course, had stirred the Latins by arguing they should not offer one single life for them all, strong as they were: *pro cunctis talibus unam / obiectare animam* (229f.). Now they are desperate.

The duel itself, as does not have to be explained in detail here, consists of two phases. In the first (12.697–790) Turnus loses the false sword (it breaks apart), Aeneas his spear (it gets stuck in the stump of a tree). Jupiter's preceding act of weighing the lots of the two opponents points to the fact that the result of the duel (it opens the road that, in distant future, will lead to the rise of Rome) has been destined by fate: the Iliadic elements (e.g., staglike Hector being pursued by houndlike Achilles) have been thoroughly integrated into Vergil's own train of thought. This is poetry claiming Homeric stature—but it aims at a new goal.[24]

Before phase II, a conversation (motivated by Juturna's handing over the genuine sword to Turnus) takes place between Jupiter and Juno (12.791–842). The dialogue helps us to see the duel from the vantage point of the epic future, i.e., the dialogue affords Vergil an opportunity to subsume his own time under the mythical norm: to show that today's conditions do not mean what their surface seems to indicate. The *aition* follows the fairy-tale pattern "and that is the reason why today all ravens are black and not, as would be expected from our story, white." It

---

24. J. Griffin, *Latin Poets and Roman Life* (London, 1985), 195, feels that, e.g., Hector's death in the *Iliad* (Vergil's model) influences our reading of Turnus' death in the *Aeneid:* ". . . our response is coloured by our emotions when we see Achilles kill Hector; . . . Hector is humanly an attractive figure, and his death is tragic. So too we feel that the death of Turnus is tragic." G. Williams 1983 (supra n. 19), 221, convincingly says that, beyond this, the model helps to define the difference, "thus modifying the sympathy." I prefer wherever possible to limit the use of Vergil's models in the interpretation of the *Aeneid* to the function which they are assigned by the Vergilian context. After all, we can neither forget all the guidance and distinctive leads Vergil has given us concerning Turnus' unattractive actions and character, nor should we wish to look for a standard of judgment outside of (and possibly alien to) the work of poetry to direct our "responses."

is owed to Juno's pleading intervention that the Italians today, under (as Vergil's Jupiter says still in Book 1) "Trojan" Augustus (*Troianus . . . Caesar*, 1.286), do not speak Trojan but Latin (nor have become Trojans instead of Latins); that they do not dress in Trojan but in their own inherited way; that, together with Troy, also its name has vanished.[25] The Trojan component of the people is denied dominance by Jupiter probably for two reasons. One is that, after all, Trojan-Julian leadership itself has not been visible in Roman history until fairly recently. The other reason is that in Vergil's time Rome and Italy are supposed to feel reconciled to the rule of the Trojan-Julian House, but not suppressed— reconciled like Juno, protectress of Italian Turnus, to the victory of Aeneas.

The singular piety of the new melting pot population (12.839f., cf. 863f.) should probably be understood as Trojan-Julian heritage. We re- call Aeneas' words about his contribution to the prospective union of the two nations: "I shall give rites and gods," *sacra deosque dabo* (12.192). This has been his mission ever since Hector appeared to him in his dream in the night of Troy's fall (see also 1.6): "Troy entrusts to you its holy objects and its Penates," *sacra suosque tibi commendat Troia penatis* (2.293). Jupiter confirms Aeneas' mission once more by giving "custom and rites of sacrificing" to the new nation, *morem rit- usque sacrorum adiciam* (836f.).

All this helps the reader to a correct political classification of details before he reads about the final phase of the duel (857–952). Additional clarification is given immediately before the final phase when Jove sends down one of the *Dirae*, Furies, who come together with *metus* and *le- tum horrificum* (850f.).[26] Turnus' sudden weakness (cf. *metu, letumque,* 916; also 867 and 868) is, he claims, not founded in personal failure or in fear of Aeneas (who blames him because of the new delay, *mora,* 889): "What frightens me are the gods and especially Jupiter my enemy," *di me terrent et Iuppiter hostis* (12.895). Here finally we may

---

25. Propertius, on the other hand, views Augustan Rome as Troy reborn, *resurgentis . . . Troiae,* 4.1.47; cf. *Troia, cades, et, Troica Roma, resurges,* 4.1.87; Aeneas about La- tium: *illic regna resurgere Troiae, Aen.* 1.206.

26. I do not discuss here the moving scene when Juturna, recognizing the signs of her "poor" (*misero,* 881) brother's imminent death, raises her voice in lament. It is as the sister that she has been trying to help, but as the sister she has never considered the possibility of his being guilty. "Sympathy—yes; innocence—no" is Vergil's formula for Aeneas' ad- versaries. The sisterly voice of compassion gives just enough human acknowledgment to Turnus' (self-forfeited) life to make Italian readers feel, if not reconciled to, so at least integrated in the main course of events. Anyway, we saw, Turnus is fairly isolated and does not represent all Italians.

be prepared to believe him that he now no longer wishes to evade his commitment, even if the deity, in spite of his eagerness, denies him the path of virtue (the boulder he tries to hurl falls short of its goal):[27] *sic Turno, quacumque viam virtute petivit, / successum dea dira negat* (12.913f.). And thus, his feelings are conflicting (*pectore sensus vertuntur varii,* 914f.), and his hesitation between fear of death and desire to attack appears *again*—the third time in our series—increasingly to be giving way to thoughts of flight—especially when we see him looking around for his divine sister (his charioteer) and the chariot that would save him (918).

Turnus' hesitancy (*cunctatur,* 916; *cunctanti,* 919) allows Aeneas to launch the decisive throw of his spear, piercing the thigh of Turnus. Under the echoing screams of his Rutulians Turnus collapses.

And what now? It seems to me that Vergil has extended the instability or lack of consistency that we repeatedly observed in Turnus to its final consequence: on the one hand stretching out his right arm in a gesture of *request (dextramque precantem),* he says on the other hand that he is *not asking for mercy (nec deprecor)* but, in acknowledging his guilt (*equidem merui,* 931), he tells Aeneas to utilize his fortune, i.e., to kill him.

But abruptly (*asyndeton,* 932) he again changes his position and appeals to the soft feelings Aeneas fosters toward deceased Anchises. He adduces his own "pitiful" (*miseri,* 932—a word not usually part of Turnus' vocabulary) old father Daunus, to whom he wishes to be returned—he himself or his lifeless corpse. The latter (i.e., the heroic) alternative he immediately proceeds to exclude again by indicating that the terms of the duel have already been satisfied anyway:

> yours is the victory, and the Ausonians have
> seen the defeated stretching his hands; yours is Lavinia as
> your wife; do not strive to go beyond this in hatred.

> *vicisti et victum tendere palmas*
> *Ausonii videre; tua est Lavinia coniunx,*
> *ulterius ne tende odiis.*

> (12.936ff.)

There can be no doubt at all: Turnus who once gave himself the air of a hero "second to none" (11.441); who dedicated his life to his people

27. This is an agreeable change for Aeneas. In the *Iliad,* the boulder hurled at him (by Diomedes, Book 5) put him out of commission. His divine mother (and Apollo) had to save him by removing him from the battlefield.

and his "father-in-law" (11.438–442); who for his declared bride—denied him by the gods—(and for becoming the prospective successor to the throne) was willing to risk his very existence in single combat (12.80); and who, toward Latinus, was unwilling to listen to the argument of "feeling pity" for the old father (*miserere parentis longaevi*, 43f.)—he now chooses the unheroic alternative of survival, now allegedly for the sake of "pitiful" Daunus, his father. Can it surprise us at all that his soul—in the epic's often misinterpreted last line—is "angry" or "indignant" (*indignata*, 952) when going down to the shades below? We shall return to this matter.

As far as the reader's picture of Turnus is concerned, there is the aggravating circumstance that, in his skillful speech,[28] he rewrites his own earlier concept of the duel: earlier, he wanted to decide the war by bloodshed (which then could hardly be understood as thigh blood: *nostro dirimamus sanguine bellum*, 12.79); to mar "effeminate" Aeneas' perm in the dust (which can hardly point to a living enemy, 12.99f.); intended, with his right arm, to send the "traitor of Asia" "into Tartarus," *dextra sub Tartarum mittam* (14)—as he bragged toward Latinus when he himself urgently asked for a formal duel: *fer sacra, pater, et concipe foedus* (13); above all, he declared himself prepared to accept death in exchange for fame: *letumque sinas pro laude pacisci* (49). No doubt, Vergil here again offers us his well-known Turnus who wants to get out of the consequences of an obligation he has eagerly entered before.

And what about Aeneas? Let me state a priori that Vergil has his attitude, too, presented as being complex, as developing in stages. Our point of departure must be that Aeneas, too, exactly as Turnus, had equated the result of the duel with the death of one of the two opponents. This is implied already in his first suggestion, made to Drances (11.118). This also is the motivation for the twofold good-bye to his son, the second time in the style of death-bound Sophoclean Ajax. The author himself tells us during the fight that now life and blood of Turnus are at stake: *sed Turni de vita et sanguine certant* (12.765). We have to realize that Aeneas, after he successfully threw his spear, has naturally been contemplating the deathblow as his next step. Only in this way do

---

28. "His speech to Aeneas is full of equivocation: it is a cloak of nobility, courage, and piety concealing the reality of Turnus: it is meant to deceive or to seduce Aeneas into error" (R. A. Hornsby, *Patterns of Action in the Aeneid. An Interpretation of Vergil's Epic Similes* [Iowa City, Iowa, 1970], 139). The speech was analyzed with regard to its rhetorical topoi by Renger 1985 (supra n. 5), 90–94; Galinsky 1988 (supra n. 23), 324.

we understand that his behavior *after* Turnus' request represents a
countermovement:

> Aeneas, fierce in his arms, ceased,
> rolling his eyes, and curbed his right arm.
> And gradually the speech had started increasingly to change his
> hesitating mind, (when, all of a sudden, etc.).

> *stetit acer in armis*
> *Aeneas volvens oculos dextramque repressit*
> *et iam iamque magis cunctantem flectere sermo*
> *coeperat, (cum . . .).*

(12.938–941)

Let us, for once, analyze Aeneas' situation under the definition his father
laid down of the Roman's task in history[29]: "to fight down the proud
and pardon them when defeated," *parcere subiectis and debellare super-
bos* (6.853), or under the comparable statement of Augustus: "Foreign
nations that could be pardoned safely I have preferred to preserve rather
than to extinguish," *Externas gentes, quibus tuto ignosci potuit, conser-
vare quam excidere malui* (R.G. 3.2). These conditions apply also to
Turnus: called earlier *superbus* (326), he now is *humilis supplexque*
(930) and confesses his guilt. Consequently, we should not be surprised
that Aeneas, against his original conception (cf. already 11.118), calls
himself back from killing the fallen enemy. We should observe that the
appeal to his own sacred bond which ties him as a son to his father
Anchises (as he himself is tied as a father to his son Iulus), is added as
the highest possible human component to the Augustan principle of
right conduct (as defined by Anchises) toward a defeated enemy. To my
mind, the branch of Vergilian scholarship I mentioned earlier is mistaken in denying Aeneas here the feature of *clementia* (only because it is
in the end overruled and replaced by another priority). A close reading
of the text shows that the development which would lead to mercy has
clearly been set into motion, but then itself is interrupted by a third
movement (as grammatically indicated by the so-called *cum inversum*,
941). The third movement is started by Aeneas' sudden perception that

---

29. This is a critical passage for the so-called Harvard School (supra n. 18). Its members see Aeneas here betraying his father's precept of mercy. See, e.g., Putnam 1981 (supra
n. 15), 243: "His deed could be seen, in fact, as the final *impietas*, since he forgets his
father's final utterance," etc. Suerbaum 1985 (supra n. 6), 142f., endorses measuring
Aeneas by his father's demand for *clementia*, while seeing the ethical judgment on Aeneas
changing: "nicht einseitig als *pius*, sondern faktisch auch als *crudelis*."

Turnus is wearing the belt and the baldric of "the boy" (*pueri*, 943) Pallas.

This does not mean that up to now Aeneas has "forgotten" Pallas. Recently (in terms of the epic's structure, through all of Book 12) his mind has been deeply engaged in (and preoccupied with) fighting on the battlefield and enforcing a contracted duel to end the war. For a long time, he tried to prevent imminent genocide by pursuing Turnus to make him fulfill the terms of the treaty. He now (the duel part fulfilled) is thrown back to the earlier situation which demanded that he deal with the murderer of Pallas. The sight of the baldric, *saevi monimenta doloris* (945), brings back the original pain. But the fact that Aeneas will not allow Pallas' killer to be "snatched away from me," *eripiare mihi* (948), shows that in his mind the death of Turnus, killer of Pallas, had been a fixed matter all along. Only temporarily, because of large-scale communal emergencies and, in the end, by Turnus' diversionary speech, had this aspect been relegated to the background. (Similarly, in Book 2 Aeneas thought of—and fought for—his country first; when this option was exhausted—Venus stopped him—he turned to the task of saving his family.) We shall return later to Aeneas' ranking of issues.

I do not want to argue here with those who consider Aeneas' outbreak of wrath and rage, *ira* and *furiae* (946), a loss of his higher self. I have elsewhere and in preparation of the presently proposed thesis shown that there does exist a *iusta ira* in the *Aeneid* (as there do *furiae iustae, iustae irae, iustus dolor*[30] as well as, without a qualifying adjective, the combination *pudor iraque*, 9.44), and that Vergil's ideal Augustan hero does not have to be a follower of Immanuel Kant to such an extent that dutiful acts are acknowledged only if they have been wrested from a resisting inclination. It is a misunderstanding to deny to Vergil's concept of a hero *passionate* fighting or even hot patriotism (an attitude which Vergil is out to develop in his reader). Aeneas is supposed to be, among other things, *also* an Achilles (and a justified one, for that matter),[31] a Super-Achilles able to defeat the "New Achilles" prophesied by the Sibylla (6.89).

---

30. Stahl 1981 (supra n. 22), 166; see also 171.
31. Most recently, this point has been taken up by Galinsky 1988 (supra n. 23): "The Attic orators . . . make it clear that anger is the essential component in the determination of the penalty." When the judge "is meting out the punishment, he should not do so without *orgé*" (326). "This concept continues in Rome." Since Turnus' guilt is clear, the "question is how to punish. To see Aeneas do so without the emotion of anger would have been repugnant to any ancient audience, except for the Stoics. . . . the final scene is rooted . . . in real life, practice, and custom" (327). "In a situation like that the wise man, as defined by the Academics, Peripatetics, and even Epicureans, must act the way Aeneas

I am also ready to emphasize that, according to convention, Aeneas is obliged to take revenge on Turnus,[32] especially so since Pallas' father had, from the grave of his son (so to speak), imposed on him the sacred duty. Evander solemnly spoke of Aeneas' "right arm . . . which, you see, owes Turnus to father and to son," . . . *dextera . . . tua . . . , Turnum natoque patrique quam debere vides* (11.178f.). Thus it is by all means a holy wrath that makes Aeneas strike the deathblow, and the correspondence of the avenging wound and the original one caused by Turnus is pronounced even in metrical symmetry:

> *quem vulnere Turnus* (943)
> *te hoc vulnere Pallas* (948)

Even more: Aeneas himself feels that what he has to perform is a pious act. His expression "you, dressed in the spoils of my close one," *spoliis indute meorum* (947), displays a similar emotional value as does his self-defense in Book 2 where he invokes "the ashes of Troy and the final flame of my dear ones," *Iliaci cineres et flamma extrema meorum* (2.431), to prove that he has piously fulfilled his duty toward his community.[33] It is not Aeneas who is killing here; no, it is Pallas who performs a *sacrifice* and exacts the just punishment from the criminal blood: *Pallas te hoc vulnere, Pallas / immolat et poenam scelerato ex sanguine sumit* (12.948f.).

II

Now we know what Aeneas feels: on the national or ethnic level, he was able to grant mercy to Turnus, but not in matters of revenge for Pallas. The principal question of course must be, What, according to Vergil's intention, is the reader to think and to feel emotionally when he reads of Aeneas' reaction at the sight of Pallas' belt? Has the reader been prepared for the change from mercy to passionate revenge? Since even those who believe that Vergil condemns Aeneas admit that Aeneas' wrath and Turnus' death have their dramaturgical root in Book 10, I suggest we look there for the common ground that has evaded today's

---

does" (340). For the continuing discomfort which members of the so-called Harvard School feel about the ending of the *Aeneid,* see W. Clausen, *Virgil's Aeneid and the Tradition of Hellenistic Poetry* (Berkeley and Los Angeles, 1987), 100: "Yet most readers find the violence and abruptness of the last scene disturbing." It would certainly be interesting to have a statistically reliable sampling of Vergil's readers, especially among his contemporaries.

32. See Burck 1979 (supra n. 9): 90.
33. See Stahl 1981 (supra n. 22), 167f.

interpreters. Here begins the third of those threads that come together in the *Aeneid*'s final scene, i.e., the second of the strands to be traced here.

From the general scope of fighting in Book 10, two scenes stand out: the death of young Pallas at the hands of Turnus, and the death of Lausus, young son of tyrant Mezentius, at the hands of Aeneas. The fact that the latter event appears to be Vergil's own invention makes us ask: if the death of Pallas that eventually will fall back on the killer Turnus is Vergil's version of the death of Patroclus in Homer that eventually will fall back on the killer Hector, to what purpose has Vergil doubled his own scene of the experienced fighter killing the brave young unexperienced? At the end of a syncrisis of the two young heroes, Vergil points out that both will die equally "at the hands of a greater enemy," *maiore sub hoste* (438). I.e., Vergil extends the comparison of the two young victims, Pallas and Lausus, to the two unequal main characters of the *Aeneid* and their conduct in a situation of manifest superiority. The most striking difference, to say it summarily, is that Aeneas kills when being confronted, but Turnus seeks out his young victim, wishing to attack and to kill him.

In fact, Turnus forbids all other Rutulians to go after Pallas: he alone (emphasized twice in the same line: *solus ego ... soli mihi*, 10.442)[34] reserves for himself the right to kill the prey that is "owed" to him (*mihi ... debetur*, 442f.). Why? Pallas is no match for the *maior hostis*, as Vergil brings out when he describes the Arcadians' fear for their leader (452) and Pallas himself viewing the *corpus ... ingens* (446) of Turnus. Like the superior lion coming down on the strong but doomed bull he has stalked (*specula cum vidit ab alta*, 454), Turnus descends from his chariot on Pallas, who sees his only chance (cf. *fors*, 458) for this fight of unequal powers (cf. *viribus imparibus*, 459) in hitting Turnus before he draws nearer. But his spear only grazes Turnus' huge body (cf. *magno ... corpore*, 478), earning nothing but a bullying taunt (481) from his stronger opponent, when Turnus in return hurls his own spear with fatal success (479–89). It definitely is a distorted understanding when a prominent representative of the anti-imperial interpretation writes: "... however much we pity Pallas, he met his death in fair fight ..."[35]

It is Pallas, on the other hand, who—mistakenly—fosters noble ideas about the situation. He shows an honorable desire to encounter the su-

34. This is echoed, as we saw, in Book 11 (442) and 12 (466; 467; cf. 16).
35. K. Quinn, *Vergil's Aeneid. A Critical Description* (London, 1968), 222; cf. 227: Pallas was "killed in fair fight"; 18: "in fair fight."

perior opponent in single combat, either for the highest Roman (!) form of victory (cf. *spoliis . . . opimis,* 449) or for a glorious death: "My father (scil. Evander) is impartial toward either lot," *sorti pater aequus utrique est* (450). The young man's mind, even in the face of death, is concerned with what his father may think of him. His father, we recall, had sent him out to learn from Aeneas as from a teacher (*magistro,* 8.515) the craft of a warrior. When accepting his enemy in order to achieve, in victory or in defeat, the highest honor of paternal recognition, Pallas proves himself a true student of Aeneas. Aeneas, too, when facing certain death in Juno's sea storm in Book 1, wishes he could rather have died fighting for Troy, like those fellow countrymen who fell "before the eyes of their fathers, below Troy's high walls," *ante ora patrum Troiae sub moenibus altis* (1.95).[36]

Turnus, on his part, when seeking the mismatched fight, likewise thinks of Pallas' father (in fact, his taunt has in turn provoked Pallas' noble statement): "I wished his father himself were here and watched!" *cuperem ipse parens spectator adesset* (443). Worlds apart from Pallas (and from Aeneas in Book 1), Turnus (the lion stalking his victim, a predictable kill) holds his Rutulians back not for an honest duel; rather, in claiming Pallas as his own prey and his alone, he primarily intends to *hurt the father.* Pallas' death is a murder.[37]

Accordingly, Turnus' final message is addressed to Evander: "As he has deserved him (i.e., dead), I am sending Pallas back to him," *qualem meruit, Pallanta remitto* (492). "Not a small price is he going to pay for granting Aeneas hospitality," *haud illi stabunt Aeneia parvo / hospitia* (10.494f.). Experienced warrior Turnus has not granted young Pallas ("Pallas the boy," Vergil calls him when bringing back Aeneas' pain, 12.943) the dignity of taking seriously his courage on his first day

36. For the programmatic misunderstanding of Aeneas' prayer by members of the anti-imperial school (W. Clausen, R. D. Williams), see Stahl 1981 (supra n. 22), 160f.

37. Many interpreters have seen the "action of despoiling Pallas" as "the center of Turnus' offence," as R. O. A. M. Lyne put it in "Vergil and the Politics of War," *CQ* 33 (1983), 193f. See already W. W. Fowler, *The Death of Turnus: Observations on the 12th Book of the Aeneid* (Oxford, 1919), 155. "Turnus' 'offence' turns out to be not so very large at all" (Lyne, 1983, 194). I myself had briefly outlined my interpretation in *Arethusa* 14 (1981) (supra n. 22), 158f. B. Otis, *Virgil: A Study in Civilized Poetry* (Oxford, 1963), 356, came very close to Vergil's ranking of priorities in judging Turnus' offense: "The whole episode is thus designed to exhibit Turnus' *culpa* and character," etc. For the comparison of Turnus to a lion stalking a bull, an example from art may serve as a precedent. In the Metropolitan Museum in New York, there is an Etruscan bronze tripod (identifier: 60.11.11, Fletcher Fund 1960), showing on the vertical rods: Hercules and Athena; the Dioscuri; two satyrs. On the arches, one sees: a panther felling a deer; a lion felling a ram; a lion felling a bull. The predictability of the kill seems to be clear in all three cases, with no exception.

(10.508) of fighting on the battlefield. For to Turnus the unequal fight was nothing but a welcome opportunity to make father Evander pay a price.

Turnus' commercial vocabulary is resumed twice by Vergil in describing what follows. Aeneas refuses the ransom money offered by suppliant warrior Magus (who asks to be saved for his son and his father): "These commercial transactions of war Turnus was the first / to abolish—then already when Pallas was killed," *belli commercia Turnus / sustulit ista prior iam tum Pallante perempto* (10.532f.). Thus Magus' appeal to Anchises and Iulus cannot help him: "Thus feels the spirit of my father Anchises, thus Iulus," *Hoc patris Anchisae manes, hoc sentit Iulus* (534). The poet has created an opportunity for Aeneas to explain that his opponent's conduct has invalidated certain conventions that would allow for occasional exceptions even on the battlefield. It was Turnus who replaced the currency of ransom money with that of blood. And it was Turnus who, by violating the father-son relationship, has invalidated any appeal to Iulus and Anchises. It is, Aeneas feels, as if someone has killed me in order to hurt Anchises, or my son Iulus in order to hurt me. Aeneas now acts as the avenger of this cruelly treated relationship and feels that as such he must be inexorable. Releasing Magus would mean taking Pallas' death lightly. No word of criticism is heard from Vergil's lips here (if compared with his earlier comment on Turnus' conduct, 500–505).

We see two things here: first, that Aeneas has put himself in the place of grieving Evander the father long before (in Book 11) Evander obliges him to take revenge for his son. Secondly, that Turnus, when in the final scene of the *Aeneid* he operates with his aged father Daunus and appeals to Aeneas' feelings for Anchises, is using an argument the sanctity of which he himself has forfeited in the most horrible fashion. Viewed from Book 10, Aeneas' unforgiving reaction at the end of Book 12 appears predetermined and inevitable.

If we want to understand all of this in a context contemporary with Vergil's own time, the closest parallel is probably Augustus who, in his *Res Gestae* (2; cf. 21), ascribes a considerable part of his bloody political career to his pious obligation to take revenge for his (adoptive) father's assassination. C. Julius Caesar's avenger (as he liked to call himself), too, was both relentless and persistent in hunting down the killers of his adoptive father. Publius Turullius and Cassius Parmensis, the two last surviving assassins, were executed in 30 B.C., fourteen years after the deed. The Temple of Mars the Avenger was dedicated in 2 B.C., forty(!)

years after the occasion on which it had been vowed. Revenge was in good political standing in Vergil's time. If a contemporary Roman needed help in fathoming the emotions of a loyal avenger of the father-son relationship, the *Aeneid* could supply him with what he needed.

The circumstance that Turnus grandiloquently (*largior*, 494) returns the body for burial, "whatever the honor of a tomb and whatever the consolation of burying is," should not be misunderstood as a sign of his humanity (or clemency, *Milde,* as Pöschl terms it);[38] the diminutive[39] and derogatory statement, *quisquis honos tumuli, quidquid solamen humandi est* (493), proves that it is a small matter in which Turnus is willing to show magnanimity (if it is magnanimity at all and not cruel irony). For, as the main part and climax of his message, there follow the words about the high price he makes Evander pay. What he releases, is small change, so to speak.

Nevertheless, it will be the visible reminder represented by Pallas' belt that will trigger Turnus' death in Book 12.[40] Therefore we understand the comment which the author adds in his own voice (thus emphasizing the plot line) about Turnus exulting in the spoils: the human mind does not know moderation when uplifted by favorable circumstances (10.501f.). (Pallas, after all, had promised the spoils of his last opponent to god Tiber, 421ff.; Aeneas will dedicate the arms of Mezentius to Mars, 11.5ff., while not despoiling at all the corpse of young Lausus, 10.827).

> For Turnus, there will be a time when he will desire an
> untouched Pallas bought at a high price, and when he will
> hate these spoils and this day.
>
> *Turno tempus erit magno cum optaverit emptum*
> *intactum Pallanta, et cum spolia ista diemque*
> *oderit.*
>
> (10.503–505)

38. Pöschl 1964 (supra n. 11), 195.

39. For the diminutive character of the statement, compare Aeolus about his unenviable kingdom (*quodcumque hoc regni,* 1.78), and R. G. Austin's commentary (Oxford, 1971) ad loc. On the other hand, compare Aeneas' utterance after Lausus' death, *teque parentum manibus et cineri, si qua est ea cura, remitto* (10.827), with Vergil's glorification of Caieta, *si qua est ea gloria,* at 7.4.

40. It may well be that the ugly (cf. *foede,* 10.498), sinful (cf. *nefas,* 497) crime depicted on the baldric is supposed to give the reader a hint on how to judge the death of its owner. Pallas dies in the prime of his youth (on his first day in battle), as defenselessly and maliciously set up as those young men (*iuvenum*) killed by their brides in their wedding night. Taken in this way, the scene on the baldric confirms my interpretation of the narrative: Pallas' death was a murder.

In this comment, Vergil not only constitutes the causal nexus between Turnus' hybris and Turnus' death. Also, we here for the third time (in the order of occurrence, it is the second time) see Turnus' metaphor of the price to be paid, and this time Vergil turns it—less than ten lines have intervened—against Turnus himself. His predicted future desire to undo what he has done, especially when announced through the author's intervention, is to me a clear advance indication of Turnus' unheroic desire to survive at the end of the work, and sufficient confirmation for my interpretation of his unwilling (*indignata,* 12.952) departure from this life.

Aeneas' ensuing refusal to allow any *belli commercia* (10.531ff.), then, is in line with the poet's own phrasing. Turnus has introduced the new currency of blood (494); Vergil points out the long-range consequence (503), Aeneas can no longer accept payment in the old currency (530ff.), for the father-son relationship has been cruelly mocked.

Vergil even goes one step further and, confirming one of the alternatives mentioned by Pallas before (449f.), himself directly invokes dead Pallas: "Oh you, about to return to your father as a cause of grief / and a great honor!" *O dolor atque decus magnum rediture parenti* ... (10.507). This picks up the father-son-topic which thus, like the price metaphor, can be seen to permeate all three passages we have been dealing with. If thus the poet himself, like his hero Aeneas, is revealed as sympathizing with dead son and mourning father, where is his reader expected to stand by now?

The question has two answers, the first of which, concerning Turnus, can be given still within the framework of our present section. Vergil has not left the reader with any option of finding his conduct acceptable once we have discovered his diabolic intentions. Killing a brave but physically inferior young man in order to exact a price of grief from his father is humanly so abhorrent that we can no longer sympathize at all with the killer. Neither can we, at this stage in our investigation, fall back on Quinn's excuse for Turnus' wish that Pallas' father may be present at his son's death by speaking of "a characteristic piece of braggadocio,"[41] bragging. Nor may we believe any longer that Pöschl's thesis[42] about the "guiltlessness of Turnus' guilt" and about Vergil being impartial toward Trojans and Italians has fathomed the bottom of the *Aeneid*'s design: how can the poet intend to be impartial if he denies

41. Quinn 1968 (supra n. 35), 221.
42. Pöschl 1964 (supra n. 11), 172, 173 (in discussing Allecto's influence on Turnus). See supra note 11 and its context.

Turnus the morality of action or of motivation that constitutes the characteristic of a human being in the true sense of the word? In other
words, by denying the Italian leader not only—as he did in the preceding books—self-control, religious humility, true intellectual and leadership qualities, but beyond all this even the gift of a pure heart (he might
at least have granted him the benefit of the doubt), Vergil puts his reader
in the same position as he did when he presented to us the heartrending
lament of a Trojan mother who must observe Turnus' Rutulians carrying on sticks the heads of her son and his friend (9.481–97). He does
not lend his art to an Italian mother in a comparable situation.

Repelled by Turnus' unethical, abominable conduct as depicted in
Book 10, the attentive reader will join Aeneas in the end in opting for
revenge rather than for mercy.

III

This already takes me to the second part of the answer; for not only is
the reader being impregnated with antipathy against cruel Turnus, he is
also—and that by an even longer preparation—preoccupied so as to
feel for Turnus' victim, Aeneas' young friend Pallas, and for Aeneas
himself. Here, we encounter the third of the strands to be investigated
in this paper (it, too, will lead up to the epic's final scene): after Turnus'
conduct before and during the duel in Books 11 and 12, and after Turnus' killing of Pallas in Book 10, we now turn to the relationship of
Aeneas and Pallas, and to the subliminal guidance Vergil provides for
his reader.

Immediately before Pallas' death, we witness a sympathetic conversation on the divine level (a rare honor for a mortal in the *Aeneid*).
Divine Hercules, once (8.188ff.) the savior of Evander's community and
now invoked by Pallas for assistance but unable to help him, sheds tears
over the young mortal's imminent fate. Hercules in turn is consoled by
his father Jove who points to fate's inevitability, to the loss of his own
son Sarpedon before Troy, and to the fact that Turnus' own life will be
coming to its end soon (10.464–72). This is much more affection than
will be granted to Lausus when he will be killed by Aeneas: Lausus'
share of sympathy is limited to the same kind of brief apostrophe that
the poet himself gave to Pallas (10.507–9~791–93).

But it is not only the fact of divine compassion that is striking. Much
more so is the *kind* of compassion. We already saw that Aeneas, when
refusing to accept the ransom offered by Magus (531–34), on his part

invokes the father-son relationship that unites him with both Anchises and Ascanius-Iulus, and that he seems to grant Pallas the place of a son in his feelings. The same is done by Jove when he renews the pain about Sarpedon's death (well known from the *Iliad*) and has to turn his eyes away from the scene: *sic ait, atque oculos Rutulorum reicit arvis* (10.473). Gods cannot bear to witness the deaths of their favorite humans, as Diana (11.593ff.) and Juno (12.151) show in the *Aeneid*, Artemis in Euripides' *Hippolytus* (1437f.; cf. *Alc.* 22).

If Vergil has the divine ruler of the universe overcome by grief for mortal Pallas, we may confidently say that this climax of compassion cannot be surpassed poetically. The reader, seeing his own natural feelings sanctioned by the highest authority, cannot but feel an even deeper abhorrence at Turnus' disregard for the most basic human relationship. The reader here will feel grief for Pallas.

But how does the reader feel about Aeneas? One should not, I think, judge (or even condemn) Aeneas' wrath as it is let loose both on the battlefield and after the duel before taking a look at the *Vorgeschichte* to which the poet adds it as a continuation. What is of interest here for us is that the reader views the death of Pallas through the eyes of Aeneas, the mature man and father who is close to Jove in his attitude, but not from the viewpoint of the suffering young man himself. We thus feel even more the pain (and rage) of Aeneas (which is sanctified by the parallel grief of Jupiter). This effect has been prepared for a long time.

The death scene contains an unmistakable reference to Book 8. Pallas, when praying to Hercules, reminds him of Evander's hospitality (10.460). Now, the same hospitality was granted to Aeneas too—on the day of the Hercules festival. It is not arbitrarily that I move Aeneas and Hercules together in their relationship to Evander and his son Pallas. By accepting young Pallas as his apprentice, Aeneas had entered a relationship similar to the one that is ascribed to Hercules in Pallas' prayer.

But there is a difference and a distinction. The relationship of Pallas and Aeneas is characterized by an emotional attachment of the younger to the older, right from the beginning. This relationship even has a root in the distant past. Evander had, as a youth, met Priam and Anchises, and felt great admiration—much greater, as a matter of fact, for the latter than for the king of Troy (he seems to have had a keen eye for the chosen, 8.161–63). When departing, Anchises gave young Evander a bow, a cloak, and a set of reins. The reins are now in Pallas' possession, kindling (we may assume) his youthful imagination. So, at the arrival of Aeneas at Pallanteum, Evander himself recalls the voice and features of

venerated Anchises (8.155f.), and Pallas is bound to be deeply impressed
by the famous name (8.121). He attaches himself to Aeneas as his father
once did to Anchises (8.124 and 164). His father wishes him to learn
grave Martis opus (516) from Aeneas by watching and admiring him at
an impressionable age (*primis . . . ab annis*, 517). And on their way to
Latium, sailing along the coast, we see Pallas sitting next to and leaning
against Aeneas' left side—like a son (we would say) enjoying his superior father's protection (10.159–62)—interrupting the worrying
thoughts of the mature man by asking about the stars in the dark sky,
about Aeneas' "odyssey" (i.e., he becomes acquainted with some of
what the reader knows from Books 1–6). Pallas himself does not know
that his behavior characterizes his age, but our impression is that of a
bright kid to whose naive curiosity the world and a great man are still
new and exciting, and who is not burdened by his teacher's ever-present
grave worries about the vicissitudes of war (*eventus belli varios*,
10.160).

The reader cannot help being frightened by Pallas' interest in the
world of the grown-up because he has seen this promising young man
depart from home under the cloud of aged Evander's fear: Vergil has
anticipated the effect Pallas' death will have on his father by having the
old king faint at the time of departure, after delivering a farewell speech
the intensity of which borders on that of a funeral oration (8.560–83).
In invoking the gods and especially Jove with "the prayers of a father,"
patrias . . . preces (574), Evander touches the reader's heart with a human tone that will—in the light of paternal Jove's later inability to
help—reveal itself as tragic irony. Since Evander made it clear that his
son is his life, the reader cannot but feel sympathy.

The tragic atmosphere is intensified by the actual departure scene
(8.585–96). There the climax of the poet's description, even over
Aeneas, was given to Pallas (*ipse . . . Pallas*, 587), and in seeing him
compared to Lucifer, most dear to Venus of all the stars, and to Lucifer's
"holy face," *os sacrum* (591), we readers cannot but fear for his life
almost as that of a member of Venus' and Aeneas' family.

If thus Pallas is moved into the center of Aeneas' (and our) emotional
attention, taking on the value of a son in the usual father-son relationship, we must not be surprised that Iulus-Ascanius, Aeneas' real son,
has been kept away from the scene. One may object that in Book 8 Iulus
was left behind to guard the Trojan camp. But that was hardly Vergil's
main motive; for (a) Aeneas does not usually leave him out of his sight
for long (not even a farewell is mentioned), and (b) Iulus' role in defend-

ing the Trojan camp during his father's absence in Book 9 is, corresponding to his young age (cf. *puer,* 9.641; 656), limited. Depending for his survival on his father's return (9.257), he can only participate in the call for help (224–313) and later make a token appearance on the battlefield which is incomparably less weighty than the scenes in Book 9 granted to Nisus and Euryalus or to Turnus.

Iulus, too, however, is granted attention from the divine level. Apollo sees to it that this early "Julian" (cf. 1.288) kills no more than one taunting Rutulian. He then addresses the "boy" as "descendant of gods and ancestor of future gods" (i.e., according to Servius, of C. Julius Caesar and of Augustus), *dis genite et geniture deos* (9.642), as being on his way to the stars (*sic itur ad astra,* 641). This characterization comes from the lips of a competent divine source, indeed. Apollo, after all, is the personal tutelary deity of descendant-god Augustus. Accordingly, Apollo does not fail to slip in a prophetic remark on peace and expansion at the time of Augustus (643ff.).

This clarifies Vergil's dramaturgy for us. While Iulus is removed from his father's immediate attention during Books 8, 9, and 10, his importance as a link in the chain of the Julian descent, i.e., the political *telos* of the *Aeneid,* must not be lost sight of by Vergil's reader.

But the circumspectly created vacuum in Aeneas' affection is temporarily (or up to the end of the epic, if one so wishes) filled by Pallas, and the reader's conception of this relationship is tinged by vivid presentations of the relationships Jove-Hercules, Jove-Sarpedon, Evander-Pallas, Anchises-Aeneas, Aeneas-Iulus.

In observing Vergil's long-range design here, we conclude that the reader is to view Aeneas at the time of Pallas' death like a bereft father, and even more: that the reader himself is by that time prepared to feel with him and to react along with him.

Because of space limitations, we have to exclude a detailed investigation into the terms under which Vergil wishes his reader to view Aeneas' fierce fighting after Pallas' death. Suffice it to say that, against many recent interpretations (mostly of the Two Voices School), a close reading of context and author's interventions results in a positive picture.

Whereas the chain of outward events that leads to Turnus' death in Book 12 is triggered by Turnus' inhuman conduct in Book 10 as we have interpreted it, the other chain, that of *subliminal guidance* given to the reader's emotions and subconscious preoccupations, has begun much earlier, viz. in Book 8 where Vergil's pro-Julian partiality turns out to be much more effective (and efficient) and much more subtle than perceived by those who like to discount it.

Likewise, it should be added here, Aeneas' role as the New Achilles who is bound to avenge the New Patroclus on the New Hector (richly documented in literature, e.g., by Klingner's comments on Book 12)[43] is rooted already in the beginning attachment of Pallas to him in Book 8, i.e., already at a time when the other "New Achilles" predicted by the Sibyl, viz. Turnus, is just beginning to unfold his formidable rage. For understanding the *Aeneid's* design, it is indispensable to see that Turnus is called an Achilles only to the extent that he revives and repeats a past threat to the Trojans, but that he is a priori doomed to fall at the hands of an even greater hero, a new Super-Achilles, so to speak, who is Aeneas. The present-day situation of Vergilian scholarship suggests that we once more point out Vergil's emphasis on Aeneas as a fully developed Homeric fighter, who, in avenging Pallas, himself takes on the role he was denied in the *Iliad:* that of Achilles, greatest of all.[44]

IV

Thus, to summarize in concluding, our investigation has traced three (out of at least four) strands that come together in the final scene of the *Aeneid:*

(1) The breach of the treaty concerning the duel, concluded in Book 12, reaches its ultimate consequence. The development can be seen as starting much earlier if one observes that Vergil includes the promise given by Turnus—but not kept later—at the session of King Latinus' council in Book 11.

In this area of political and international relations, Aeneas would be in a position to exercise *clementia* toward the defeated and now humble enemy.

(2) The murder of Pallas, committed in Book 10, finds its atonement. Here Aeneas is not free but *has* to (and eagerly does) avenge the murder, especially so since father Evander has imposed the task on him as an

---

43. F. Klingner, *Virgil. Bucolica, Georgica, Aeneis* (Zurich and Stuttgart, 1967), 589ff. He outlines how Vergil combines the Menelaus-Paris theme and the Achilles-Hector theme in Book 12. See also Galinsky 1981 (supra n. 6), 998f., who, however, tends to discount political reasons for Vergil's presentation in favor of poetic ones.

44. See Stahl 1981 (supra n. 22), 159–65.

inescapable, sacred duty (we recall the word *immolat*, 12.949): "Your right arm owes Turnus to father and to son, you see," *dextera . . . tua . . . , Turnum natoque patrique quam debere vides* (11.178f.).

In the area of revenge, Turnus has, even with his appeal concerning father Anchises and father Daunus, forfeited all claims to mercy because *he himself* has horribly sinned against the sacrosanct father-son relationship by killing the son in order to cause pain to the father.

(3) And, finally, we the readers have, ever since Book 8, been circumspectly subjected to subliminal guidance up to the point where we share Aeneas' savage pain at the sight of Pallas' baldric, the *saevi monimenta doloris* (12.945). We identify with his feelings because the poet's artful psychagogy has taught us to love Pallas as Aeneas does and to see in him a sort of substitute Iulus.

The best key to a poet's partiality is found in those passages where he tries to influence the subconscious self of his reader.

My conclusion then would be not only that Vergil fully agrees (and wishes to guide his reader to the same position) with Aeneas' act of killing Turnus, but views it as the only morally justified solution to his epic. To which degree he even in this is loyally serving the emperor who felt unfit to show mercy toward the assassins of his adoptive father (as well as toward many others who sided with their cause) is a question well worth pondering.

But first, since I initially pointed out that this paper does not have to say anything basically new on the *Aeneid,* my reader will allow me to mention that the understanding presented here is consistent with one of the earliest interpretations of the final scene known to us. According to the ancient commentator Servius (*ad* 12.940), the final scene serves the glory of Aeneas in two ways. He displays *pietas* (piety) because he thinks of pardoning Turnus, and he shows *pietas* because he observes Evander's bidding and kills Turnus. *Omnis intentio ad Aeneae pertinet gloriam.*

One may view the quotation in connection with Propertius' statement (2.1.42, quoted in our introduction) that the epic is supposed to depict Aeneas in order to enhance (or give a foundation to) the fame of Augustus. Then we encounter a situation in which it would be hard not to understand Aeneas' good motives as a supposedly congenial guide to his descendant's feelings (and Aeneas' mythical opponents as giving us guidance on how to judge the guilt of the historical adversaries Octavian had to face). Ultimately, this must remain speculation. But it goes a long way toward explaining Vergil's circumspect endeavor of making his reader appreciate conduct, feelings, moods, emotions and motives of the Julian founding father even in those harsh situations which, at least on the surface, might to (its and) our time seem to allow more lenient handling or a different decision.

Horace (*Carm.* 1.2.44) says that *Caesaris ultor,* "the avenger of (his adoptive father) Caesar," is the name that Mercury-Octavian allows himself to be called in his human manifestation. It appears that, when placing Augustus' forefather in a comparable (and complementary) context of revenge, Vergil wishes not only to win his reader over to seeing Aeneas' actions as just. Beyond this, he wants to convince us that, in order to protect the sacrosanct community of father and son, one may have to show oneself inexorable to any man or party that inflicts violence on either member of the relationship.

It is hard to picture Augustus as not satisfied when reading the new Roman epic and perceiving the kind of subliminal guidance the New Homer was giving the nation. Over the years, the emperor had, both in person and through Maecenas, shown an intense interest in the work's progress. The poet, at the time of his death, considered his epic unfinished and unpublishable (he planned three more years of polishing). Nevertheless, Augustus personally saw to it that the work *was* published.

He must have felt that his interest was sufficiently rewarded. This, at least, is the way Ovid understood the situation. In addressing Augustus (*Trist.* 2.533), he calls Vergil "the . . . author of *your Aeneid,*" *tuae . . . Aeneidos auctor.*

Horace *Carm.* 2.9:
Augustus and the Ambiguities
of Encomium

My essay examines the figure of Augustus as portrayed in the first three books of Horace's *Odes*. These were published as a collection probably in 23 B.C. and largely written, we may presume, in the preceding half a dozen years. In particular I evaluate the ninth poem of the second book and ask how we are to estimate its final lines, where the addressee, Valgius, is exhorted by the speaker to join him in singing the exploits of the emperor.[1] Since my reading of the poem itself and of the context in which it is placed finds the tone of the concluding reference equivocal, I will first assess the conditionality of other bows to the emperor in the initial collection of odes. Then, after a critique of the poem itself, I will briefly locate it among the odes with which Horace carefully groups it and, placing it in a wider intellectual context, then look closely at Virgil's pervasive influence on the ode as a whole. I will conclude with a survey of Horace's lyric career after 23 and speculate on the reasons for the poet's changed stance toward the emperor.

My essay is a form of metonymy. Its argument rests on the premise

1. I am grateful to Lowell Bowditch for several discussions of *Carm.* 2.9, to Kurt Raaflaub for many helpful suggestions, and to Deborah Boedeker Raaflaub and Matthew Santirocco for valuable criticism of an earlier version of my text.

that the close examination of one poem in an extraordinary grouping of lyrics will help us toward the understanding of that collection as a whole. Because the ode I am considering is concerned, at its moment of climax, with Caesar and, in particular, with the emperor as source of the speaker's inspiration, it is also my assumption that it has bearing on the other odes directly or obliquely devoted to the *princeps*. Finally, while moving centrifugally from the poem as core but still remaining drawn to its magnetism, I am equally convinced that its scrutiny sheds light on what one of Rome's most brilliant minds thought of the principate itself and of its prime mover. In other words we will learn something not only of Horace's genius at work but also of how that imagination reacted to, and recreated, Augustus and his times.

I

There is a recent trend among historians to see the lyric Horace, in a positive vein, urging Caesar on to war and conquest in the West and East.[2] The presumption is that civil strife in Italy is now a thing of the past and that the de facto sole ruler of Rome can now unleash his people's aggressive tendencies elsewhere. Hence, we are told, stems the eagerness of Rome's greatest lyricist for campaigning abroad. I suspect that matters are somewhat different: Horace's moments of apparent

---

2. In particular this is the argument of R. Seager, "*Neu sinas Medos equitare inultos: Horace, the Parthians and Augustan Foreign Policy*," *Athenaeum* 58 (1980) 103–18 passim, who summarizes: "Horace not only consistently urges Augustus to undertake the conquest of Parthia but also allows himself to express a striking degree of impatience and dissatisfaction at Augustus' failure to make the attempt" (1). The same interpretation of Horace's tone, slightly modified, is also proposed by E. S. Gruen, "Augustus and the Ideology of War and Peace," in R. Winkes, ed., *The Age of Augustus*, Archaeologia Transatlantica 5 (Louvain and Providence 1986) 51–72: "The sentiments of the poet are subject to dispute and controversy. One may detect incitement or impatience, reflection of the official line or independent prodding" (57). (Cf. also Gruen on Horace's "lament" that civil war "has deflected Rome from her proper objective: defeat of the Parthians" [64]). Whether "adherent or critic of the regime" (Gruen [supra] 65) Horace is seen as warmongering. My own view, more traditional and more ironic, is that Horace was still truly worried about a recurrence of civil war and remained deeply cynical about Roman militarism. Pursuit of foreign enemies is a far better ambition than self-immolation, but as far as Rome is concerned, Horace never loses sight of their interdependence, however deep his patriotism and strong his concern with the continuity of *virtus*.
    The relationship of Horace's poetic development to the political background of Augustan Rome has been treated in detail most recently by E. Doblhofer, "Horaz und Augustus," *ANRW* 2.31.3 (1981) 1922–86 (with full bibliography in n. 5). It also forms part of the following important recent essays: E. A. Schmidt, "Geschichtlicher Bewusstseinwandel in der horazischen Lyrik," *Klio* 67 (1985) 130–38; E. G. Schmidt, "Der politische, der impolitische und der ganze Horaz," ibid., 139–57 (with bibliography in n. 7).

martial ardor arise from a deeper worry that we can sense directly in his
first hymn to Apollo and Diana (*Carm*. 1. 21.13–16):

> Roused by your plea [Apollo] will repel tear-bringing war, will repel pitiful
> hunger and disease from the people and their *princeps* Caesar and bring
> them upon the Persae and Britanni.

Even in a poem published after Actium, civil strife and its concomitant
horrors remain, if in the poet's imagination alone, a threatening reality.[3]
We are still far from the peaceful world, with foreign enemies cowering
before Rome, which Horace, in the *Carmen saeculare*, will envision as
existing in 17 when he addresses the same divinities (53–56):

> Now on land and sea the Mede fears our powerful hand and Alba's swords,
> now the Scythians seek responses from us, now the Indi, proud until recently.

To tell of the emperor, in the first collection of odes, is not the immediately treacherous undertaking that Pollio is said to pose for himself as
he embarks on a history of the civil wars (the subject of *Carm*. 2.1).
Nevertheless, any mention of Augustus brings with it parallel perplexities and perils, and *Carm*. 2.9 is no exception. In fact, all the odes in
Horace's first three books that are addressed to Augustus or indirectly
have him as a major concern are noteworthy for the provisional quality
of their assessment. *Carm*. 1.2 is a prayer for divine help at a time in
Rome's decadence when "a citizen will hear a sword sharpened with
which the menacing Parthians would better perish." Mercury, "allowing
himself to be deemed avenger of Caesar," will be the savior that Rome
craves, but he soon mutates into the new Caesar himself, whom the
speaker urges not to allow the Medes to ride on unavenged. The poem
wills a change, in Rome and in Augustus, from vengeance extracted because of Julius' murder to requital against the victors of Crassus, from
continued civil violence posed against self to martial intensities exercised against foreign foes.

If *Carm*. 1.2 proposes a reorientation of the objectives of *virtus*, the
next ode in the sequence, *Carm*. 1.12, suggests, with due logic, the necessary limitations of its power. Caesar, for all his terrestrial omnipotence, is subject to Jupiter: "You will reign, with Caesar your subordi-

---

3. A parallel juxtaposition of civil madness with foreign military endeavors occurs in
another ode that mentions Caesar, *Carm*. 1.35 (see infra part V). The speaker's indictment
of present Roman immorality rises in a crescendo of questions. Hope lies only in the concluding prayer to Fortuna (38–40):

> O would that on a pristine anvil you might refashion our blunted sword against the
> Massagetae and the Arabes.

nate." "Second to you he will reign in justice over the broad earth." Such words observe Caesar's potential in two distinct ways. They can be taken as laudatory acknowledgment of his automatic humility before the king of the immortals or as a warning that if he is being readied for initiation into the illustrious company of demigods and heroes charted earlier in the poem, he had better behave with appropriate reticence.

Poetry that advises Rome to reorder the priorities for its *virtus* to exploit or that treads the slim line between encomium and remonstrance is followed smoothly by poetry of conditionality in the "Roman" odes that open Book 3. The last four of this stunning sextet deal in large measure with the four qualities for which Augustus was awarded the *clupeus aureus* in 27: *iustitia, clementia, virtus,* and *pietas.* In the third and fifth, the conditionality is direct. From the former we learn that the man who is "just and firm in his undertaking" remains unshaken by external terror. Through this imperturbability Pollux and Hercules attained heaven, "among whom Augustus at his ease will drink nectar with reddened lips."[4] The latter proposes that Augustus will be considered a Jupiter on earth if the Britons and threatening Parthians are added to the empire, if Crassus is avenged, if, more abstractly, Rome can reenliven the *vera virtus* (29) inherited from the past.

In between these adumbrations of future apotheosis for the emperor we have Horace's longest ode (*Carm.* 3.4), on the need for *consilium* and *temperantia* in exercising power against modern-day versions of the Giants and Titans. Subsequent to these odes is the most pessimistic of the group (*Carm.* 3.6), with the simple apostrophe *Romane,* on the need to restore the shrines of the gods as a first step toward curing the viciousness of the present age. The addressee is a generalized Roman everyman, but the resemblance between line 5 ("you rule because you hold yourself subordinate to the gods") and the direct allusion to Augustus in *Carm.* 1.12.57, quoted above, suggests that even here the emperor is not far from the poet's mind as particular source of disquiet and of hope, open at once to respect and to challenge.

Near the middle of the third book Horace places an ode in which praise of Augustus is more open. Like Hercules, Caesar has come home to wife, family, and a public celebration (*dies festus*) for tumult suppressed. Yet even such an event is not treated with a whole heart by the

---

4. Though the manuscripts at *Carm.* 3.3.12 are almost equally divided between the readings *bibit* and *bibet,* the parallel with *Carm.* 3.5.2 (*habebitur*) makes the case for the latter most convincing.

speaker. His festivity is private. The second half of the ode turns away from Caesar to Neaera and to the potential violence of lovers at play. Nevertheless, we sense a shrewd gesture of concord as the poem comes to an end. Neaera may refuse his wishes: "I would not have stood for this in the heat of youth, when Plancus was consul" (*Carm.* 3.14.27–28). Plancus was consul in 42, when Horace, following the model of his poetic forebear Archilochus, abandoned his shield at Philippi. The oblique reference to the defeat of Brutus and Cassius, and to the youth of the speaker, headstrong in arms as well as in love, may offer an equally oblique sign, from the once republican speaker, of reconciliation with Julius Caesar's heir. His celebration may take a personal turn, but it concludes with a public, though wry, avowal in poetry of an ill-conceived, certainly ill-fated moment of hotheadedness when Horace stood against Octavian some two decades before.

Individually, then, these odes contemplate Augustus' potential for constructive endeavor, if he deflects violence from home to abroad, if he holds himself second to Jupiter, if he proves himself worthy of the *clupeus aureus* by epitomizing its virtues in action. In so doing he would even change the mood of a former renegade republican to one of near acceptance. Nevertheless, in the last two odes of the collection over which Augustus' presence looms contingency takes a more negative turn. *Carm.* 3.24.25–29 importunes a hypothetical reformer of Rome's frenzied impiety:

> O whosoever wishes to do away with unholy slaughter and the madness of citizens, if he seeks to have Father of Cities written under his statues, let him dare to rein in untamed license.

The unnamed restorer of moral quality could be none other than Augustus, though once again there is a potential conflict between Augustus' desire for honors and his worthiness to receive them, between his expectations and the speaker's conditions for their fulfillment. All anonymity is dropped in the subsequent poem, *Carm.* 3.25, where the speaker expands on his Bacchic stimulus to sing, in the future, of Caesar and his incipient divinity. Since no odic eulogy is forthcoming, references to Augustus in Book 3 end on a hesitant note. The first ode challenges Augustus to rein in violence so as then to deserve the permanence of naming by a people on his statues, by a poet in his words. The second in fact names the emperor and proclaims him the inspiration for song but proffers no example of his promised eulogy. Ten years would have to elapse before the publication of such verses. In the context of Book 3, the juxtaposition of *Carm.* 3.24 and 3.25 demonstrates how highly qualified Horace's acceptance of Augustus into his lyric world still remains.

II

I would like now to turn to *Carm.* 2.9 and ask how its portrayal of the emperor can be read in relation to the other Augustus poems of the collection:[5]

> Non semper imbres nubibus hispidos
> manant in agros aut mare Caspium
>   vexant inaequales procellae
>   usque nec Armeniis in oris,
>
> amice Valgi, stat glacies iners
> mensis per omnis aut Aquilonibus
>   querqueta Gargani laborant
>   et foliis viduantur orni:
>
> tu semper urges flexibilibus modis
> Mysten ademptum nec tibi vespero
>   surgente decedunt amores
>   nec rapidum fugiente solem.
>
> at non ter aevo functus amabilem
> ploravit omnis Antilochum senex
>   annos nec inpubem parentes
>   Troilon aut Phrygiae sorores
>
> flevere semper. desine mollium
> tandem querellarum et potius nova
>   cantemus Augusti tropaea
>   Caesaris et rigidum Niphaten,
>
> Medumque flumen gentibus additum
> victis minores volvere vertices
>   intraque praescriptum Gelonos
>   exiguis equitare campis.

5. The main subject of debate in recent scholarship on *Carm.* 2.9 is whether or not the boy Mystes is to be understood as dead or merely "stolen," lost to another lover. This latter view is argued strongly from different angles by K. Quinn, *Latin Explorations: Critical Studies in Roman Literature* (London 1963) 160f. and W. S. Anderson, "The Odes of Horace's Book Two," *CSCA* 1 (1968) 35–61. The question is still open, but the metaphors of the opening stanzas (*viduata* in particular), the analogies in lines 13–17 (Antilochus and Troilus are more than figuratively "dead"), and Horace's use of at least one aspect of a *consolatio*, the *suasio* to the person bereaved, tell against this interpretation.

Not always ooze rains from clouds onto dank fields, nor do deranging winds beset the Caspian sea forever, nor on Armenian bounds, friend Valgius, stands ice, listless, month on month, nor toil Garganus' oak groves against North winds nor are its ash trees widowed of leaves.

With mournful numbers you ever pursue Mystes, grasped away, nor do your loves retreat at the uprush of the Evening Star nor as it flees the onslaught of the sun.

But the old man who outlasted three generations did not grieve year after year for lovely Antilochus, nor did his parents or Trojan sisters forever weep for beardless Troilus.

Leave off at last your limp complaints, and rather let us chant the fresh trophies of Augustus Caesar, and stiff Niphates, and the Medes' river, added to subject peoples, rolling its diminished crests, and the Geloni, galloping within the limits of their scanty fields.

Horace is one of the great poets of liminality in that he is fascinated, always as an apparently detached viewer, by the idea of developmental change within the human psyche. The accompanying moments of crisis are often seen in sexual terms. We find Lycidas (*Carm.* 1.4), for whom all the youth is ardent and soon all the girls will grow warm, or Chloe (*Carm.* 1.23), following her mother when spring says that she is ripe for a man, or, changing to the animal world, a goat (*Carm.* 3.13), ready for love but offered, tomorrow, to the *fons Bandusiae* instead. But there are other subjects as well. We have Iccius, for instance, meant for the philosopher's life of the mind but tending toward a soldier's addiction to greed and, in the potential process, corrupting the natural evolution of a girl, whose future husband is killed, and a boy who becomes a servant with fragrant hair rather than an archer, emasculate rather than manly (*Carm.* 1.29). Change, positive or negative, approved of or censured by the speaker, is regularly visualized as a movement from one intellectual locale to another, defining a spiritual or physical shift.

If progress from one sphere to another is the essence of these poems, there is a concomitant set that adopts centrality, not transition, as its major point of reference. The danger here is not metamorphosis per se but a radical veering from the mean toward an extreme, away from what is usually a moral axis of stability toward bounding limits that threaten disintegration. For a positive example we could take *Carm.* 3.7 where Gyges will remain faithful to Asterie, however deftly Chloe may try to lure him away. For a negative, *Carm.* 1.5, on Pyrrha and her ruinous spell, is a good model. Sailing is in any case a treacherous business, but the voyager embarked on the sea of love can be enticed to his destruction by Pyrrha's brilliance, or escape waterlogged but alive, an overreacher at last barely secure, if favored by divinity.

Carm. 2.9 offers a further illustration of such liminality. The moment of transition comes at lines 17–18 with the speaker's command *desine . . . tandem.*[6] Valgius, we learn from the first three stanzas, has been mourning continuously for his boy love, Mystes. It is time, says the speaker, to follow the paradigm of Nestor and the family of Troilus and renounce mourning that exceeds the bounds of normality. Better to join with him and sing the praises of Augustus, of trophies, a mountain and a river conquered and restrained, a Scythian tribe brought within proper bounds. The problematics of the poem revolve on an interpretation of this intellectual journey from elegy to eulogy, from Mystes lost to Augustus accepted. Are we meant to view Valgius' transition as a natural, advisable bridge leading from a superfluity of emotion to a more composed posture of impersonality and control? Such a mutation would imply release, in the elegist's creative personal life, from the constancy of private, over-indulged suffering into the public world of *Realpolitik*. This alteration would be achieved through the replacement of subjective poetry with objective, which substitutes allegiance to the accomplishments of another for first-person solipsistic exercises in rhetorical limitation and assumes at least partial suppression of the lyric "I" in favor of an omnipresent, omnipotent "you" laying total claim to the poet's imagination. Or, by contrast, if we probe deeper into the poem, is there an element of the unnatural in Augustus' eastern adventures, as Horace summarizes them, that makes such a mutation in Valgius' poetic career appear tainted by its own different form of excessiveness?

Certainly in the initial stanzas the speaker leaves little doubt about Valgius' emotional intemperance. Nature's winter, her soul's dark night, is seasonal. We can do no better than imitate her, as Horace the philosopher teaches so often elsewhere, by practicing "flexibility" in our own lives while at the same time reaffirming an inner strength that easily withstands fortune's fickleness. This malleability of spirit is not at present Valgius' own, but so strong is his continuing passion that the speaker imputes its force to the aspects of nature that should serve as a model for change.[7] Valgius is always mourning (*tu semper*), the third

6. The parallel use of *desine tandem* at *Carm.* 1.23.11 is rightly pointed out by S. Commager, *The Odes of Horace* (New Haven 1962) 242.

7. The personification of nature in the opening stanzas was first discussed by F. Bücheler, "Zur Auslegung der horazischen Oden," *RhM* 37 (1882) 230f., and is documented in

stanza tells us, but in the first two stanzas, however strong the initial negative (*non semper*), nature's rich personification mimics his own intensity, reinforcing, rather than mitigating, his emotionality. This depends, as the metaphors imputed to nature make clear, as much on continuing desire as on mourning for lost love. Catullus is the first Latin poet to use the word *imber* for tears.[8] Its appearance in a detailed analogy for frustrated desire—there the speaker's for Lesbia—affects the present context as well. *Hispidos* and *manant* suggest other perspectives on Valgius' outer, as well as inner, being. Both words recur in the fourth book in poems where the speaker is concerned with his attachment to the boy Ligurinus. The first completes a dream of thwarted love (*Carm.* 4.1.33–34):

> sed cur, heu, Ligurinus, cur
>   manat rara meas lacrima per genas?

But, alas, why, Ligurinus, why does a fitful tear trickle across my cheeks?

The second turns aborted desire into curse, as Ligurinus' youthful charm is replaced by the shaggy beard of ugly manhood (*Carm.* 4.10.4–5):

> nunc et qui color est puniceae flore prior rosae,
>   mutatus, Ligurine, in faciem verterit hispidam,
>   dices "heu," quotiens te speculo videris alterum.

and [when] your complexion, which now surpasses the blossom of a crimson rose, Ligurinus, has turned its altered features into shag, you will cry "Alas," as often as you face in the mirror the other you.

By projecting these usages back onto the initial lines of *Carm.* 2.9, we are made to sense not only the continuity of Valgius' longing for the dead Mystes but also the distinction between their physical appearances, reflecting their difference in age. Mystes, who will soon be paralleled in *inpubem Troilon,* presumably possessed at his death the "unblemished cheeks" (*incolumes genae*) that Ligurinus will soon lose through the poet's curse (*Carm.* 4.10.8). Ligurinus will within himself manifest the change from beardless to shaggy, which in his case means a change from desired to undesirable. No such metamorphosis need occur

---

detail by H. P. Syndikus, *Die Lyrik des Horaz I,* Impulse der Forschung 6 (Darmstadt 1972) 392, and R. G. M. Nisbet and M. Hubbard, *A Commentary on Horace: Odes, Book II* (Oxford 1978) 135f. My reading of the opening lines differs from theirs primarily in giving particular stress to the sexual element in the vocabulary.

8. Catull. 68.56.

in *Carm.* 2.9, where *hispidos* at the start already metaphorically suggests Valgius' unceasing weeping for his adolescent lover.

Nature's sympathetic accompaniment continues to complement Valgius' frustrated eroticism in the lines that follow. Her vexations are a lover's trials (*vexant*), her imbalances (*inaequales*) reflect his gain and now his loss.[9] The "listless ice" (*glacies iners*) that in winter months coats Armenian hills reflects the sexual sterility that here comes from deprivation. The oak trees of Garganus that "labor" stand in for the *labores* that accompany any suffering.[10] These in turn are specified in the ash trees, which are shorn of leaves (*foliis viduantur*). The tension among agitation, listlessness, and further turmoil in Valgius' life is brought about by the very bereavement that nature imitates.

Nature's parallelism with and distinction from Valgius reach a climax in the third stanza. The focus narrows as we turn from the greater expansion of seasonal and monthly time to the concentration of daily existence. From one viewpoint nature and lover are at odds. The Evening Star rises and, at dawn, flees the sun, while Valgius' pursuit of Mystes remains sempiternal. But by reechoing the sound of *urges* in *surgente* the poet implies a sexual resilience to nature, specified in Venus' planet, that even here duplicates the constancy of Valgius' erotic impulse. This erotic tenacity is supported by the military metaphors.[11] The Evening Star may rise, but it also flees the onrush of the sun. In contradistinction, Valgius ever presses in pursuit after Mystes, at least in his mind's eye, nor do his "loves" yield place, in spite of the obvious, warning divergence between external nature's regular fluctuations and the persistence of his own inner cravings.

Since *amores* and the *flebiles modi* of their expression are also the love songs of Valgius and their means of expression in poetry, an ele-

---

9. R. Pichon, *De sermone amatorio* (Paris 1902), s.v., citing Ov. *Am.* 2.19.15, defines as follows: *vexare est inquietum sollicitumque facere amantem.*

10. For the erotic connotations of *labor/laboro,* see P. J. Enk, ed., *Sex. Propertii Elegiarum Liber I (Monobiblos)* (Leiden 1946), on Prop. 1.6.23; R. G. M. Nisbet and M. Hubbard, *A Commentary on Horace: Odes, Book I* (Oxford 1970), on *Carm.* 1.17.19; and, most recently, A. Macours, "Horace, Odes I, 9 et III, 13," *LEC* 26 (1978) 218. The earliest uses are Plaut. *Pseud.* 695 and then Ter. *An.* 719, where the heroine is troubled because her *inamorato* loves someone else.

11. Nisbet and Hubbard (supra n. 7) are too hesitant here: "The word [*urgeo*] may maliciously suggest the solicitations of a lover." Just as *modi* imply sexual schemata and means of attack (see *Carm.* 2.1.2) as well as poetic "measures," so *urges* should be allowed the full force of both its physical and metaphysical implications. For its military sense of "press hard in attack," see *OLD* s.v. 5. In commenting on these lines R. Minadeo, *The Golden Plectrum: Sexual Symbolism in Horace's Odes* (Amsterdam 1982) 140, rightly speaks of Valgius' "unconscious prolongation of his intimacy with Mystes."

ment of parody enters into Horace's exposé. Valgius is both lover and elegiac *persona* at once, passionate participant in experience and imaginer of that experience in verse, where he impersonates himself. Horace would have us understand not only the extravagance of inordinate mourning for lost love but the parallel self-indulgence in committing this immoderation to the *modi* of verse. The lover and his poetry stand firmly amalgamated while Horace amuses himself and his readers by stretching out his own rhetorical display, of analogy piled on analogy, to mirror before Valgius the incontinence not only of his emotionality but also of his poetic self-extension, its formal expression of *amores* in elegiac verse.

The human examples of noneverlasting mourning that follow—Nestor for Antilochus, his parents and sisters for Troilus—serve in several ways to help both reader and addressee turn away from this concentrated fervor. The threefold repetition of *semper* at lines 1, 9, and 17 not only centers on Valgius and his continuing sorrow but forms a chiasmus that helps mollify its intensity. But there is a difference in the speaker's earlier and later argumentation. Both formulations gain their point from allusion to wide reaches of time. *Mensis omnis* and seasonal time are balanced by *omnis annos* and the generational longevity of the unnamed *senex*. But the varying means by which *semper* is negated in its initial and final appearances suggest a careful change of tone between the two occurrences. The force of the immediate juxtaposition of *non* and *semper* at the start is soon subtly modified as the poet suggests, against the speaker's stated purpose, a sympathy between the sufferings of nature and man. By contrast, the wide separation of *non* and *semper* between lines 13 and 17, a separation that demarcates the length of the sentence it strongly qualifies, puts greater emphasis on the enclosing truth of both sempiternity and its negation, as a final evolution of the reader's response is held in abeyance until the climactic conclusion. In between we are taken away from the present to the past, from elegy's heightened moment to epic's grander spread (echoed in the three-generation expanse of Nestor's life), from analogies that suggest an equivalence in nature to man's sexuality to comparisons where love for a beautiful youth is placed only in the context of father's response to child, or sister to brother.

The change from an elegiac to an epic frame of reference and the modification of the erotic component from compulsive physicality to the more selfless response of parental or fraternal affection prepare the way for the poem's climactic transition. Valgius, the speaker exhorts, should renounce his "soft complaints" and join with him in praising the emperor's eastern accomplishments. Augustus, in some eyes a *praesens divus,* replaces a Mystes who is, if we may extrapolate from his name, an initiate into a realm beyond the knowledge of living mortals. Valgius' continuous, perverse death of the soul, in imitation of seasonal nature at her wintriest, yields to the claims of *amicitia,* which redirect inner to outer and enthrall the passionate to the reasonable. Self-sorrow surrenders to the concerns of another. In both personal and generic terms sexuality is both displaced and sublimated. Physical yearning becomes a form of spiritual devotion as elegy's despondency is refashioned in encomium's dispassionate praise.

The poet crafts a careful line from *glacies iners* to *mollium querellarum* to *rigidum Niphaten.*[12] For Valgius to turn from Mystes to Augustus means to renounce the "listless," in the analogies he adopts for his despair, and the "soft," in their technical manner of expression, and to adopt the "stiff" subjects of Augustan *res gestae.* The private sexuality of Valgius and its utterance in poetry had documented an effeminacy of feeling and statement. To embrace the deeds of Augustus for subject matter, the speaker would seem to say, is to (re)gain at once both manhood and sexual drive, to deal with a masculine subject in a "masculine" form, with Augustus encapsulated in the epic eulogy of his deeds.

Sexuality deflected and rearoused implies that a worthy form of continence might at last, along with Augustus, enter into Valgius' personal, which is also to say spiritual, life. A beloved lost (*ademptum*) is supplanted by a river gained (*additum*) as the self's diminishment becomes empire's accretion. Valgius is now urged to tell of Augustus' conquests of others, which take on dimensions that gradually change from vertical to horizontal, from high Niphates to the lessened crests of the Euphrates to the Geloni riding on their narrowed fields. To tell in poetry of the

---

12. The correlation between *mollium* and *rigidum* is discussed by Minadeo (supra n. 11), who correctly links Valgius' putative, newfound manliness with the *virtus* of his poetic subject, Augustus (141). Where he views the ode as positive praise for "the splendor of Augustus' military conquests" (161; cf. 150–51), my interpretation differs substantially from his.

For *iners* and sexual dysfunction, see Catull. 67.26, Hor. *Epod.* 12.17. From Plautus (*Aul.* 422) on, *mollis* and its diminutives *mollicellus* and *molliculus* are stock attributes of sexual lassitude, applied to people (e.g., Catull. 25.1; Hor. *Epod.* 12.16) and to effeminate verse (Catull. 16.4, 8). As Syndikus (supra n. 7) 393 observes, this particular qualification of elegy is exampled as early as Hermesianax. For further instances in Latin see *OLD* s. v. *mollis* 3, 13, and 15. Maecenas' *mollitia,* for example, was remarked upon (Vell. Pat. 2.88.2). The sexual use of *rigidus* is first found in Catullus (56.7). Other citations can be found in J. N. Adams, *The Latin Sexual Vocabulary* (Baltimore 1982) 46 and 103.

Just as the military metaphors of the opening stanzas are literalized at the ode's conclusion, so sexuality is both reaffirmed and sublimated. But the affirmation, made by means of the adjective *rigidum,* transfers the force of eroticism away from the sphere of specific personal analogy to simply a list of individual traits yielded to the might of Rome.

regulation of others, be they mountain, river, or distant tribe, is presumably to mimic this hierarchization in one's own inner life. In putting his eroticism at the service of Augustus by embracing public themes and expanding on Rome's domination of potent nature and uncivilized human, Valgius will exhibit a mastery of his inner self parallel to, and therefore capable of honest spiritual correspondence with, Rome's ascendancy over her external territory. As poet, Valgius will become metaphor for Augustus as well as stand-in for Horace, constructing his version of the *princeps*. His subjective *amores,* sung and presumably written, are replaced by Rome's more palpable *praescripta.*[13]

The change is borne out in the military metaphors. In Valgius' psychic life of elegiac lament there was no withdrawal of his *amores,* which held out against the coming and going of planet and sun. What he will now hypothetically welcome as his theme are the *tropaea* of Augustus, those markers, as etymology reminds us, that commemorate Augustus' staying power through crucial "turning points" in battle, the deflections of the enemy in defeat. One of these the poet proceeds to document, as his wordplay turns from Greek to Latin, in the *minores vertices* of the Euphrates, the "turns" of its waves lessened by Roman might. With his power as a writer now at the service of the "prescripts" of Rome, Valgius' rich duty is to catalogue the acts of turning, adding, conquering, lessening, prescribing, and confining that summarize the brilliance of Augustus' prowess as a man of the sword.

But a certain tautness of manner, which enters Valgius' and the ode's life with Augustus, remains disquieting. The very act of naming the emperor is itself noteworthy. This is the only time in Horace's lyric verse that the emperor is given both his *nomen pro gentilicio* and the *cognomen* awarded him by the senate in January of 27.[14] The combination

13. The first use in Latin poetry of the noun *praescriptum,* and its only appearance before Horace, is in Lucretius' prayer to Calliope (6.92–93):

tu mihi supremae praescripta ad candida calcis
currenti spatium praemonstra.

Do you, as I race toward the white bounds of the final goal, mark the track before me.

If Horace is thinking back to this unique earlier usage, then here too he has literalized what was metaphoric, turning the poet's "race" into the factual bounds imposed on Gelonian riders.

14. The only other occasion on which Horace uses both names is in *Epist.* 2.2, part of an equally formal précis of Horace's momentary involvement in the civil war (47–48):

The tide of civil war swept me inexperienced into weapons incapable of competing with the strength of Augustus Caesar.

projects an intellectual distance absent from even the most Pindaric of the odes addressed to Augustus. The resulting formality casts a shadow on the remainder of the poem. It calls to the reader's attention significant differences in the poet's depiction of Valgius' former and prospective poetic worlds.

The deployment of words, for instance, in the opening stanzas serves as careful mimesis of the elegist's enduring struggles. The large verbal sweep from *non semper* to *semper* to *non . . . semper* imitates Valgius' spiritual enclosure and the reiteration of mourning that complements it. Several smaller sonic rounds support this grand chiasmus. The poem's first overarching phrase and the temporality it represents is itself a small chiasmus, beginning with *non semper* and running forward from subject to verb to object clause and then returning in reverse from object clause to verb to subject before reaching the concluding temporal adverb. The ode next sweeps from *nec Armeniis* to *viduantur orni*. Here temporality is at the center, in the phrase *mensis per omnis,* on either side of which are nine words. Finally, in lines 10–12, the crucial moment, *decedunt amores,* is framed by four words before and after—*nec tibi Vespero surgente . . . nec rapidum fugiente solem*—whose sonic repetitions reinforce the constancy of Valgius' lamentations. A series of intense centers, then, are encased in carefully balanced sequences of word and sound. These structures, in their utterance, simulate Valgius' own morbid encasement in his self-structured fabric of weeping.

The entrance of Augustus brings a different pattern of expression, which works its prejudice only by comparison with the initial stanzas. Hypotaxis gives place to parataxis; the circularity and paradigmatic quality sketching Valgius' reiterated grief mutate into the linear, syntagmatic projection of Roman victories.[15] The spiritual perimeters in which the extraordinary rhetoric of Horace's imagination imprisons Valgius become the literal, governmental bounds imposed by Rome on its conquered subjects. This turn, I think, is what should most disturb a positive reading of the ode's conclusion. The presence of Augustus depoeticizes, despiritualizes, the poem (here, too, we have a form of parody, however disguised). The military metaphors defining Valgius' suffering, even the more objective epic past of Nestor, Antilochus, and Troilus, now become the reality of Augustus' political and military incursions

15. N. E. Collinge, *The Structure of Horace's Odes* (London 1961) 120, distinguishes verses 1–17 from 17–24 by observing that the first "passage does not progress" whereas in the second "we can move from topic to topic and place to place."

into the East. Place-names, which in the early segment of the poem served to strengthen the analogy of Valgius' psychic situation with nature's winter, now reappear in the list of Augustus' increments to empire. The Niphates is to be found *Armeniis in oris*, while the Geloni and their now narrowed plains were adjacent to the *mare Caspium*. Once again the figurative becomes literal as Valgius' inner struggle is replaced by the outline of Rome's external wars, and the poet-elegist, as equivalent to suffering landscape, mutates into the poet-encomiast, singing dispassionately about the same topography now become but part of Augustus' imperial accomplishments.

Horace carefully leaves his reader able to evaluate his protagonist's situation in two ways. On the one hand we see him, at the speaker's urging, prepared to replace untimely, solipsistic mourning—and its persistence in the hermetic, effeminate utterance of elegiac verse—with the companionship of joint song about a Roman hero and his distant doings. The self's corrupt involutions are displaced by outreach toward another's prowess. Lack of self-control, parodied by the speaker in verses that mimic the elegist's own intertwined poetics, becomes stated respect for the management of others. Valgius' unnatural inner torture and its reiterations in poetry are exchanged for the apparently "natural," Augustus' and Rome's imperial ambitions and their telling by Valgius in encomiastic verse.

Yet, from another vantage, Rome's militarism imposes the unnatural on its world. Rivers flow with lessened crests, and barbarian tribes, because of Rome's prescripts, ride within newly confined bounds. In their own way, then, Augustus' delimitations of the ordinary propensities of others, propensities of which Valgius' putative eulogy will tell, are as contrived and twisted, in the doing and in the recounting, as the indiscriminate self-pity with which Valgius now indulges himself. To tell of Augustus, it would seem, can have two distinct effects on Valgius' imaginative life. It can mean the regaining of inner balance and manliness, by dwelling on Rome's power to bring conformation to the outlying reaches of its empire. Yet it can also imply, in Augustus' eastern sallies, a rigid, and therefore perverse, systematization of the instinctual in Rome's enemies, whether animate or inanimate. To sing of them (even though third-person epic description, Augustus' "history" as it were, replaces first-person psychic "biography") is, in its own way, poetically to embrace the unnatural in a more pronounced manner even than an eternal voicing of elegiac sorrow. This is true simply because a committed "I" is supplanted by a presumably aloof reorganizer of the deeds of

others, with the self's passions totally projected elsewhere. Seen negatively thus, the transition in Valgius' life can be defined as merely the
transference of immoderate behavior from himself to Augustus, preserved in poetry that either scrutinizes the self or documents the *res gestae* of others.

III

I would like now to study this duality from two further viewpoints. First
I will briefly place *Carm.* 2.9 in its context, a special one in the initial
collection of Horace's odes. Then I will address the question of the Virgilian influence that permeates the poem. In each case I will be asking
what further we can learn to adjudge the speaker's tone as he contem-
plates Valgius' once and future poetry.

The ninth ode of the second book is the second of four consecutive
lyrics that have in common two salient features. One they share with
their predecessors in the book.[16] They alternate, poem by poem, alcaic
meter with sapphic. The other they claim for themselves as a group.
Each of the four poems is twenty-four lines in length. They form the
only such sequence in Horace's masterpiece. This unique combination
of unity and duality, commonality and alteration, on the level of both
numerics and metrics, forges a strong bond among all four poems. This
bond demands of the reader, here, perhaps, more than in any other sequence save the "Roman" odes, that he criticize a constituent ode not
only of itself but as part of a special sequence in which interassociations
with the neighboring three poems will also play a vital part in eliciting
meaning from any individual segment of the group. By placing *Carm.*
2.9 in its setting we create a friction among poems that forces the independent lyric out of the enclosure of its explicit autotelism, out from the
univocal self-centeredness and monotony of the single voice into an implicit intellectual dialogue, with the drama's evolutionary potential for
displaying, or at least clarifying, what an individual character by itself
alone cannot totally divulge. We find Horace once again varying the two
metaphoric modes of defining existence that I suggested earlier, the
transitional and the pivotal, the logical, inevitable movement from one

16. The position of *Carm.* 2.9 in the wider structure of Book 2 as a whole is sensitively
discussed by M. S. Santirocco, *Unity and Design in Horace's Odes* (Chapel Hill, N.C.
1986) 83–93. He rightly emphasizes (91–93) the close relation of *Carm.* 2.9 with *Carm.*
2.11. Poems 8–9 and 10–11 are seen as pairs in a different set of balances by D. H. Porter,
Horace's Poetic Journey: A Reading of Odes 1–3 (Princeton 1987) 32–34, who also traces
a growth in intensity in Horace's speakers from poem 8 to poem 11 and beyond (123–26).

status to another and a static equilibrium tensed between perilous extremes.

In the sequence from *Carm.* 2.8 to 2.11 the two modes seem at first discrete, following the distinctions set by meter. *Carm.* 2.8, in sapphics and addressed to Barine, sees her as an alluring Pyrrha figure, attacking lovers treacherously but unscathed and undermining the stability of relationships by abducting offspring from their mothers and enticing husbands from wives by her "breeze." [17] Life is a journey that should center steadfastly on the endurance of the institutions of family and marriage. The girl from Barium is bent on seducing her victims away from this core and, as a result, on destroying them. *Carm.* 2.10, once again in sapphics, studies further the idea of a spiritual fulcrum poised to mediate intellectually between imperiling opposites. Licinius is urged toward inner equipoise as life's sojourn, in its fluctuations between misfortune and happiness, war and peace, tugs its voyagers toward deeps and shallows, either of which threaten ruin.

Carm. 2.11, the last of the quartet, in alcaics and therefore parallel metrically to *Carm.* 2.9, seems, again in agreement with its spirit, to assert a proper conversion in the life of Quinctius Hirpinus. He is to exchange worries concerning external dangers to Rome for a celebration of the moment, in which wine, women, and music ameliorate or postpone more oppressive, permanent cares.

The two sapphic poems, then, ponder seduction away from the norm or adherence to the dictates of moderation in spite of beguiling appeals elsewhere. The two alcaics describe moments of metastasis. One addressee is urged to replace the constancy of inner turmoil in his life, which in this case is to say in his writing, with encomium's more impersonal narrative, and the other to exchange his anxieties about life's palpable dangers for a festivity that abstracts its participants from time. But differentiation through meter is counterbalanced by the unity of numerics. This unity, supported by many verbal echoes among the poems, suggests that all four odes be read in terms of each other, that the message of the alcaic odes is subtly applicable to the sapphics, and vice versa. If we look specifically at *Carm.* 2.9, this would be to say that what seems at first to be an exhortation to Valgius toward proper modification of his inner life might equally well be a veiled warning that the result of such change might itself be a form of extremism.

17. Cf. *Carm.* 2.8.21–24 with Catull. 61.51–55 (as Nisbet and Hubbard [supra n. 7] on *Carm.* 2.8.21, citing previous literature).

In other words *Carm.* 2.8 and 2.10, as meditations on "mediocrity" and extremity, encourage us once again to question the tone of the intervening lyric. Are we to see Valgius' metamorphosis from elegist to encomiast as a proper alteration, which foregoes emotional and poetic extremes for the moderation of singing Augustus' praises, or as a veering from one polarity to another, each subject to forms of parody based on exaggeration or vapidity? Is Valgius being creatively urged away from an improper poetic and existential attitude toward a more fulfilling one, or enticed into a different set of intellectual difficulties? Do we perhaps have reason to distrust a speaker advocating the sudden change from elegy's singular, erotic focus toward epic's or eulogy's total sublimation of self in the impersonal, public accomplishment of others? Do we not rather expect Horatian lyric and Horatian eroticism to lie somewhere in between these limits and to comprise an intensely felt poetry that brilliantly accommodates both public and private spheres and whose erotic center, by flexibility of feeling, avoids elegy's egoistic involutions on the one hand, epic's chill detachment on the other?

The paradigmatic characterizations of extremism and of negative metamorphosis that we find in the surrounding poems serve, therefore, to reconfirm a negative reading of Valgius' progress from elegist to encomiast. In the first section of the poem Valgius' psychic world cleaves by analogy to one aspect of nature. His inner weather and its projection in poetry mirror an unnatural constancy of winter. Yet to change one's personal and poetic decorums and affirm the conquests of Augustus is merely to embrace the unnatural in another guise. When Augustus subjects to his might the instincts of river and equestrian tribe, he demands that they forfeit what is as natural to them as sequential seasons are to the year. Mention of restraint in the context of panegyric is itself paradoxical enough to intimate that a touch of satire on the author's part is not out of the question. What it more obviously suggests is that Valgius, in renouncing his own highly emotional limitations on nature, is, through the speaker's persuasion, bent on accepting into his vocabulary of praise unnatural limitations imposed on the qualities of others. He therefore at once forswears his own individuality (however overstated its fervencies) and co-opts into his new imaginative mind-set someone totally distinct from himself bent on thwarting those individualities in others. The self-loss is double. Both poet and poetry have the potential to become depersonalized as do the reaches of the Roman world under Augustus.

In other words, looking back in summary, when a positive, nonerotic union is reached at the poem's conclusion, with two singers potentially joined in voicing the praises of Augustus Caesar, the lyric itself becomes dispassionate in terms both of the literal subjects under contemplation and of the emotional involvements adumbrated in singing of them. Mourning mutates to praise, but praise not for love or lover regained but for the distant definer of the order of others, the hypothetical demarcator of the specialness of those who oppose his regime. There is no emotional self-fulfillment in the "fixing" of external troubles.

IV

A survey of Horace's borrowings from Virgil throughout the poem will offer a final means for interpreting the poem's intellectual course. I am particularly interested in the conclusion, but it is well to note the careful bow at lines 10–12 to *Georgic* 4.464–66:

> ipsa cava solans aegrum testudine amorem
> te, dulcis coniunx, te solo in litore secum
> te veniente die, te decedente canebat.

> He himself, solacing love's sickness on his hollow shell, sang of you to himself on the lonely shore, you, sweet wife, you as day came, you, as it departed.

Horace turns Valgius' lamentation from day to night and reinforces its continuity by pluralizing his loves, but the personification of *amor* and its metonymic use for a sad lover's songs, in conjunction with the balanced participles, only further confirm Virgil's presence.[18] This is perhaps Horace's way of warning Valgius about the limitations of the Orphic voice. Virgil's Orpheus may tame the spirits of the dead, but he is unable to bring Eurydice back to life once she has been initiated into death's mysteries. The same will hold true for Valgius and his Mystes.

The recollection also corroborates a certain unoriginality in the rep-

18. We soon find, in *Georgic* 4, Orpheus compared to a nightingale who "weeps the night through" (*flet noctem* 514). In fact so frequent are the parallels between the description of Orpheus mourning for Eurydice, lost a second time, and Valgius' constant lamentation for Mystes that the continuing presence of Virgil on Horace's mind is hardly questionable. We may note, for instance, that Orpheus weeps *septem . . . totos . . . mensis* (507; cf. *mensis per omnis*) and that Virgil also uses the noun *glacies* and the verb *viduo* in his sketch of the loveless landscape into which Orpheus retreats (the latter usage is noted by Nisbet and Hubbard [supra n. 7] on line 8).

Nisbet and Hubbard (on line 10) also rightly attest the parallel between *Carm.* 2.9.10–12 and Cinna frag. 6 (Morel), with reasons for the connection (135). In so doing they further underscore the derivative nature of both Valgius' emotions and their expression and impute a certain triteness to each, whatever the hyperbole involved.

etitiousness of elegy. Its monotony lacks not only the power to charm but the sparkle of individual imagination as well. This deficiency is all the more apparent in the poem's final stanzas. As commentators point out, mention at lines 19–20 of the Niphates and of Augustus' *tropaea* won in the East after Actium is a clear bow to *Georgic* 3.30–33:

> addam urbes Asiae domitas pulsamque Niphaten
> fidentemque fuga Parthum versisque sagittis;
> et duo rapta manu diverso ex hoste tropaea
> bisque triumphatas utroque ab litore gentis.

> I will add the conquered cities of Asia and Niphates routed and the Parthian trusting in flight with his arrows reversed; and the two trophies torn by hand from separate foes and nations twice triumphed over from either shore.

And the lines that follow resemble in detail Virgil's description of the triple triumph of August 29 B.C. Nisbet and Hubbard properly note the reference to *Aeneid* 8.725–28:

> hic Lelegas Carasque sagittiferosque Gelonos
> finxerat; Euphrates ibat iam mollior undis
> extremique hominum Morini, Rhenusque bicornis,
> indomitique Dahae, et pontem indignatus Araxes.

> Here [Vulcan] had fashioned the Lelegae and Carae and arrow-bearing Geloni. The Euphrates now moved more gently with its waves, and there were the Morini, remotest of mankind, and the double-horned Rhine, and untamed Dahae, and the Araxes resentful of its bridge.

Mention of the Geloni and allusion to the Euphrates are common elements of the poems, and Virgil's listing of the Dahae and the Araxes further orients our attention to Scythia and Armenia.[19] We should add also the common stress on *victae gentes*.[20] Horace interweaves the phrase into his catalogue, while in Virgil it precedes his multiple namings (Aen. 8.722–23):

> . . . incedunt victae longo ordine gentes,
> quam variae linguis, habitu tam vestis et armis.

19. Nisbet and Hubbard (supra n. 7) 137 note the similarities with G. 3.30ff. and *Aen.* 8.725ff. Collinge (supra n. 15), 3 n. 1, poses the "puzzle: which was written first—ii.9.22 or Virg. *Aen.* viii. 726?" In marshalling evidence for a solution we should note that at least as early as the publication of Prop. 2.34 (most probably in 25, certainly after the death of Gallus), it was known that the battle of Actium was among the topics to be covered in Virgil's epic (see 61–62). If Horace's lines were written prior to his knowledge of *Aeneid* 8, it makes their reappearance in such a grand context the more vapid.

20. This is Horace's only use of the phrase and Virgil's only example of the plural (at *Aen.* 11.401–2 he speaks of *viris / gentis bis victae*). Just as Horace's unique lyric use of the title Caesar Augustus is in this ode, so Virgil's are at *Aen.* 6.792 and 8.678.

The conquered races march in long array, as diverse in tongues as in fashion of dress and weapons.

In Horace the several participles (and, in the case of *praescriptum*, a participle used nominally) are in appearance morally bland, reflecting through grammar only Rome's power to turn active into passive. Virgil's design is more directly ambiguous, preceded by mention of Augustus' "proud doorposts" (*superbis / postibus* 721–22) and concluding with the Araxes, whose loss of *dignitas* receives from Virgil the place of climax, in Augustus' triumphal procession and on Vulcan's shield.

It may be debated whether or not Horace intends to have Virgil's questioning of Augustus' and Rome's propriety in the act of victory spill over into his lyric. What is irrefutable is the exactness, and therefore purposiveness, of his borrowings. In this connection it is crucial to note their source. The Virgilian contexts that Horace co-opts into his ode are both segments of *ekphraseis*. The first forms part of an imagined scheme to decorate the doors of a temple with replications in gold and ivory of Augustus' martial achievements in the East and West. The second is, of course, at once the central scene on Vulcan's shield and the culmination of its poetic description, devoted to the battle of Actium and its aftermath. *Ekphrasis,* however, in both these instances proves a brilliant device for nonstatement, the compressed outline of deeds projected by words onto a tangible handiwork that by its very nonverbal "palpability" could be seen as rigidifying poetic statement and serving to excuse further elaboration in words. Art, incorporated in present song, in the first instance anticipates, in the second serves as condensed replacement for, Augustan encomia never intended to be elaborated at greater length.[21]

Horace's mimicry of words that Virgil substituted for encomia to Augustus never to be written insinuates that his speaker's proposal to Valgius of the same topics for song is doubly incapable of implementation. By carefully echoing Virgil at the exact moments where his poet friend delimits his public proclamation of Augustus' grandeur to the encasements of art Horace's speaker deliberately reaffirms the lack of originality in the joint venture that he proposes to Valgius. Paradoxically, it has been both done and not done already, accomplished *in parvo* in the *Georgics* and, it is my suggestion, in the still unpublished *Aeneid*, as the

21. The most recent general treatment of Virgil's use of *ekphrasis* is that of R. F. Thomas, "Virgil's Ecphrastic Centerpieces," *HSCP* 87 (1983) 175–84. I have treated the Daedalus episode that opens *Aeneid* 6 in detail in "Daedalus, Virgil and the End of Art," *AJP* 108 (1987) 173–98.

verbal echoes prove, and yet unachievable in any further expansion. In sum, if Virgil's poetic future (which is Horace's intellectual past) does not contain an epic eulogy of Augustus, whether formulated prospectively in the sculptural program of *Georgic* 3 or in the visionary précis of incipient history encapsulated on Aeneas' shield, then the proposal that Valgius and "Horace" sing the same subjects has even less validity, not to speak of potential, for effectuation. The poetic metamorphosis in Valgius' life would therefore initiate a mutation from one type of imaginative staleness to another, from reveling in the stifling reiterations of elegy to putative borrowing of the hypotheses of encomium already formulated elsewhere. Nothing unique remains in either of these termini, nor does reinvigoration of imagination appear possible in the transition from one to the other.

Looking back in summary at the whole, we can see Valgius' alteration in his spiritual life as a positive moment of metamorphosis, when he crosses the threshold from troubled elegy into dispassionate laudation. Or, by contrast, we can view his poetic development as a progress from one extreme to another. The first of these is the unidimensional limitation of mourning, which is unnatural because it eternally sustains one aspect of man's inner nature that should in fact be as flexible and capable of mutation as the seasonal round. The second takes several forms. In terms of subject matter we learn of stringencies in the external ambition of Rome, as Valgius prepares to celebrate the denaturalizing of river and tribe through limitation of the verticality of water and the horizontality of human space. Secondly, in terms of the unfolding of the poem, the entrance of Augustus depoeticizes, turning figurative into literal, analogy into mere enumeration. Lastly, this (magnificently staged) imaginative falling off is complemented by a demonstrable lack of originality when we place the poem in its Roman intellectual context. To borrow from Virgil as blatantly as Horace here does is to suggest that motivation to sing of Augustus belongs, in its own circumscribed way, to Virgil. Valgius' uninspired Augustan encomium will be based on borrowed words that, in their own different way, will be as lacking in imagination as elegy's repetitiveness and the bottled emotions it imitates.

For a moment Horace seems to play with his reader as his speaker does with Valgius. Should Valgius take the exhortation seriously? Are we to assume the authority of Horace himself behind his speaker's words? In two other odes, one addressed to Agrippa (*Carm.* 1.6), the other to Maecenas (*Carm.* 2.12, not coincidentally subsequent to the quartet of poems that I have been discussing), speakers foist off on others the praising of Caesar.[22] Singing in poetry will be left to Varius, bird of Maeonian song (*Carm.* 1.6.9–12):

> while restraint and the commanding muse of the war-less lyre forbid my defacing the praises of Caesar, and of you [Agrippa], through fault of wit.

Prose treatment is left to Maecenas (*Carm.* 2.12.9–12):

> You, Maecenas, will better toll the battles of Caesar in prose history, and the neck of daunting kings led through the streets.

In each case the strong *recusatio* is at least balanced by the lyricist's apparent assumption that eulogy was Augustus' due, though it must emanate from another source. The problematics of *Carm.* 2.9 are more complex. Public prompting of Valgius to tell of Caesar, the direct opposite of a *recusatio,* contains within itself, as we have seen, reasons why a refusal might have been the more feasible course for the elegist.[23]

Only once, in the poet's boldest reference to Caesar, does an Horatian speaker forthrightly promote a subject the moral perplexities of whose telling the poet disguises in *Carm.* 2.9. *Carm.* 1.37, on the battle of Actium, takes us from the causes of a symposium of celebration to the madness of Cleopatra to Caesar's pursuit—hawk after dove, hunter after hare—to the queen's heroic suicide and final refusal to be conveyed in a Roman's proud triumph, *non humilis mulier.* Not Caesar but Cleopatra rules the poem, a reminder that the individual can still stand up to Rome, and be glorified through a lyric poet's candor.

Virgil, as we have seen, offers not Caesar's grandeur but an example of individual dignity, forced to submit to Rome, at the conclusion of his depiction of the aftermath of Actium on the shield of Aeneas. Roman prescripts would be the subject of Valgius' song too, were he to join Horace's speaker in a *laudatio* of Augustus. But, I have proposed, the acceptance of such a challenge would not only offer merely superficial allegiance to the emperor and his *res gestae* but document as well a failure of inspiration on the poet's part parallel to the loss of uniqueness that Rome's conquests seem to suffer after accepting Augustus' sway.

---

22. We find Horace's own first refusal to sing of *Caesaris invicti res* at *Sat.* 2.1.10–20.

23. P. Murgatroyd, "Horace, Odes II 9," *Mnemosyne* 28 (1975) 71, sees the poem's ending as a parody of the *recusatio* theme, which he presumes would have appeared in Valgius' poetry (on which see Nisbet and Hubbard [supra n. 7] 135ff.): "Therefore, in the recommendation to Valgius to leave love-poetry and join Horace in celebrating contemporary events we see again the use of the poet's own themes turned against himself." My sense is that irony, and the rhetoric of parody that it engenders, is as likely directed here toward the bland literalness of encomiastic verse as toward an elegist's (standard) repudiations of its challenge.

Since the speaker's scheme, as conceived by Horace, is devoid of imagination and since the objects of his putative scrutiny have already yielded their integrity to Rome, the final thrust of this multilayered design appears doubly negative.

V

The conclusion of *Carm.* 2.9, therefore, in announcing a hymn for Caesar that is unlikely to be sung, is itself a type of refusal. As such it fits well with what I consider to be the general thrust of the thirteen references to Augustus in the first collection of odes. However varied their settings, all such allusions in some way qualify any putative or expected glorification of the emperor. Let me employ as a summarizing example the appearance of Caesar in *Carm.* 1.35, the powerful ode to Fortuna whose final stanzas run as follows (29–40):

> serves iturum Caesarem in ultimos
> orbis Britannos et iuvenum recens
>   examen Eois timendum
>   partibus Oceanoque rubro.
>
> heu heu, cicatricum et sceleris pudet
> fratrumque. quid nos dura refugimus
>   aetas? quid intactum nefasto
>   liquimus? unde manum iuventus
>
> metu deorum continuit? quibus
> pepercit aris? o utinam nova
>   incude diffingas retusum in
>   Massagetas Arabasque ferrum.

May you keep safe Caesar about to depart for the farthest Britanni and the fresh band of youths, bringing fear to eastern lands and to the red ocean. Alas, alas, the shame of scars and crime and brothers. From what does our hard age forbear? What does our depravity leave untouched? From what has our youth restrained its hand through awe of heaven? What altars has it spared? O would that on a pristine anvil you might refashion our blunted sword against the Massagetae and the Arabes!

A departure of Caesar (whether real or mooted or imagined) for campaigns in the north and east is the subject of the speaker's prayer to the fickle goddess. But the abrupt juxtaposition of Caesar's military activities with an outcry against civil war gives the reader pause, and forces speculation on what Horace means by this very lack of differentiation. Has the youth (*iuvenum*), now imagined leaving for the East, really changed from the youth (*iuventus*) who have no respect for divine majesty? Can the brothers (and the word *fratrum* receives a place of particular prominence, enjambed and concluding its sentence at the start of the line) who fought each other in civil discord now forego their internecine strife and unite at last against non-Roman enemies? Horace's text offers no response (much less answers that soothe) to my questions any more than it does to its own bitter interrogatives, which mine merely vary. Caesar may be ready to depart, but the poet ends not with any assurance of a Roman world free of internal battling but only with a wish that armor overused to guilty purpose can be reforged for better ends, that a different anvil can be discovered as a resource for the necessities of foreign, not domestic, conflict. Only if Caesar departs, one implication remains, if future becomes present, can Rome succeed in deflecting her military propensities away from herself and toward others. But finally all that remains is prayer.

Horace published this and all the other odes in the first three books with allusion to, or direct apostrophe of, Augustus, it seems most probable, in the year 23. In releasing his masterpiece to a wider public at that time he chose not to suppress any of the poems I have been discussing, whatever the ambiguities that temper their hopes and yearnings for Rome and its leader. The reason, I suggest, is a simple one. I do not believe that either Horace or Virgil, as he wrote the *Aeneid* contemporaneously with his friend's outburst of lyric genius, was assured that civil war was truly a thing of the past or that in fact it might ever be absent from Roman affairs. Virgil's epic, throughout its course and almost to the end, allows its narrator to peer into a Roman future with *impius Furor* forever suppressed. But its final moments show its hero, after having rejected his suppliant opponent's prayer to bring *odium* to an end, kill his enemy, who is for all intents and purposes a civil foe, in a burst of fury and anger. The two intellectual realms, future and present, idealizing and realistic, remain in uneasy solution throughout the poem, but it is the immediacy of private vendetta, not *clementia*, that its final words enliven for us.[24]

Nothing in Horace's references to Augustus and his policies in the first three books of odes can be accepted as a wholehearted endorse-

24. I first argued a negative interpretation of Aeneas' final actions in *The Poetry of the Aeneid* (Cambridge, Mass. 1965; rpt., Ithaca, N.Y. 1988) chap. 4 passim and have since discussed the problematics of the epic's ending from several other viewpoints (see most recently Putnam [supra n. 21]). An opposite approach is taken by Hans-Peter Stahl elsewhere in the present volume (see also his "Aeneas—An 'Unheroic' Hero?" *Arethusa* 14 [1981] 157–77).

ment. But, unlike Virgil, Horace lived long enough to dispense with, or at least seem to forego, his previous dubieties. He does so in the dramatically public gesture of the *Carmen saeculare,* composed for and delivered at one of Augustus' most splendid celebrations, the renewal of the *ludi saeculares* in 17.[25] In its midst Horace can say of Augustus (49–52):

> Whatever the famous offspring of Anchises and Venus entreats from you [gods] with [his sacrifice of] white cattle, let him gain, forward against his foe, gentle once the enemy is humbled.

In his grand reevaluation Horace can imagine not only the absence of ambiguity in his own stand toward Caesar but a direct reversal of Virgil's pessimism. At their meeting in the underworld, Virgil has Anchises tell his son to spare the humbled and wear down the proud (*Aen.* 6.853). Aeneas manages to fulfill the second but not the first, far more demanding segment of this imperative. For Horace, by contrast, Aeneas-Augustus can now be projected openly as a warrior given to timely gentleness, at once both heroic and merciful. And the fourth book of odes, published in 13 or 12, five of whose fifteen poems look to the emperor, confirms this positive reappraisal. The book itself is a grand exemplification of a *revocatio,* with song restoring the emperor to a Rome where peace and moral well-being are considered givens.[26] A fu-

25. We may speculate, looking specifically at the emperor's *vita,* on the reasons that induced the poet's *volte-face* between the years 23 and 17. (D. Kienast, "Die Konstituierung eines neuen Saeculum," *Augustus: Prinzeps und Monarch* [Darmstadt 1982] 92–99, offers a rich survey of the importance for the *princeps* of this span of years.) The earlier year was crucial in Augustus' life. For one thing an illness almost caused his death (Dio 53.30; Suet. *Aug.* 81.1). "Had he died, there might well have been civil war," argues E. Badian in his important discussion of the events of 23 (" 'Crisis Theories' and the Beginning of the Principate," in G. Wirth, ed., *Romanitas-Christianitas: Untersuchungen zur Geschichte und Literatur der römischen Kaiserzeit, Johannes Straub zum 70. Geburtstag gewidmet* [Berlin 1982] 34). But this was also the year in which Augustus, first, abdicated the consulship, which he had held annually from 31, and then in its place received the *tribunicia potestas* and the *proconsulare imperium maius,* the twin legal supports for the remaining, nearly four decades of his principate. To be sure there were in closely subsequent years the conspiracies of Murena (22) and Egnatius (19), but their very occurrence, along with other forms of unrest in 21–19 (Dio 54.6, 10–11), served to make the person and presence of Augustus all the more indispensable. It is no wonder that the senate ordered the dedication of an altar to Fortuna Redux on the day of his return from the East to Rome, 12 October 19 (*RG* 11). Augustus could then point to the return of the standards from Parthia in 20 and anticipate the promulgation of the moral legislation of 18 as evidence for the staying power and effectiveness of both his foreign and domestic policies. Whatever propagandistic purposes might lie behind the celebration of the secular games in 17, there is good reason to postulate that Horace would have accepted them for what they manifestly symbolized, a moment at once of renewal and stability, for Rome and for its emperor.

26. I have discussed this and other aspects of the fourth book in *Artifices of Eternity: Horace's Fourth Book of Odes* (Ithaca, N.Y. 1986) especially chap. 15, on Horace's final ode.

ture without civil war is not now a pious wish, which Apollo and Diana or Fortuna, if they chose, might bestow on Rome, but a corroboration of present circumstances (*Carm.* 4.15.17–24):

> While Caesar shields our world, neither the wildness of citizenry nor main force will exile peace nor will wrath, which hammers out swords and sets sad towns to hating. Neither those who drink the deep Danube, nor the Getae, nor the Seres and treacherous Persae, nor the offspring of the Don's neighboring course will rend Julian mandates.

Ten years after releasing his first collection Horace can imagine into lyric praise a Rome as devoid of the anvils of civil war as it is confident of the extent and security of its foreign domination. The odes published in 23 display neither assurance of the former nor pride in the latter. It took the moment of secular festivity to effectuate the poet's metamorphosis from sceptic to professed believer in the Augustan myth of political stability and moral renewal, whose endurance finds no firmer support than his final odes.

Fifty years ago Sir Ronald Syme, apparently surveying all four books of odes, could speak of how Horace "appeared to surrender to . . . a fervent sympathy with martial and imperial ideals." [27] I would stress the word "appeared" but give it a somewhat different tone, questioning, at least for the odes published in 23, even the semblance of fervency. My reading of the Horace of *Odes* 1–3 sees him suggesting the very fragility of what would be assumed as Augustus' ideals and the contingency of their realization on a series of delicate factors. There is no tangible evidence that Horace joined with Valgius to hymn Augustan trophies, nor could there be. His ode, with great imaginative subtlety, gives us ample reasons why.

27. R. Syme, *The Roman Revolution* (Oxford 1939) 462.

Tristia 2:
Ovid and Augustus

Ovid's relationship to the emperor Augustus and his policies presents
the historian of literature as well as the political historian with a tantalizing problem.[1] The problem claims attention not only because of the
particular personalities involved, but also because a solution might have
wider implications for an understanding, in more general terms, of the
complex relations between poets and political regimes. Ovid's exile appears to be an anomalously punitive measure under a reign otherwise

---

1. M. K. Gamal, "Introduction," *Helios* 12 (1985) 5, in an otherwise excellent exposi-
tion of the ideological agendas that inform contemporary readings of Ovid, makes the
surprising claim that "for a while during the 1970's the political implications of Ovidian
texts were a matter of some importance. Whatever the answer . . . it was an important
question. Now there is little interest in it." True, one might see here the apolitical effect of
the highly formalist analysis associated with various methods of "poststructuralist" or
"deconstructive" criticism. This trend among classicists, however, was not only belated in
its arrival but brief in its duration. In fact, as in other fields of literary study, much recent
work in classics (particularly influenced by the invigorating and successful approaches of
feminist studies) has emphasized the recontextualization of texts, together with the recognition that writing is always, in some sense, a political act. Gamal herself actually provides
an excellent counterexample to the above claim, for she continues: "At the risk of seeming
out of date, I insist that political critique is a crucial element of Ovid's work." In this, she
is neither alone nor out-of-date, as I shall try to indicate in what follows. See also now R.
von Hallberg, ed., *Politics and Poetic Value* (Chicago 1987).

characterized by considerable latitude for dissenting opinions and the authors who expressed them.[2] Why did Augustus find himself unable to brook this one poet—particularly one who seems, on the surface, so determinedly apolitical?

The only evidence we have for answering this question—namely, the poet's own repeated allegation that the cause of his exile lies in *carmen et error*—is notoriously elusive. Two millenia of speculation have brought classicists no closer to a satisfactory interpretation of that *error,* as Thibault's exhaustive catalogue of over one hundred scholarly hypotheses vividly illustrates.[3] Ovid's *error* may lie beyond our ken, but as readers we do have direct access to Ovid's *carmina.* If we seek to understand Augustus' attitudes and policies as they extended to the realm of poetic creation, we must ask what there is in the work of this poet that led the emperor to judge his presence in the city intolerable.

One attractive hypothesis suggests that Ovid's very lack of reformatory zeal, his acquiescence in or even celebration of the status quo, marks him as dissident from the Augustan vision.[4] If Augustus dreams of a morally reconstructed Rome, Ovidian cynicism implicitly deconstructs that dream and the imperial propaganda promoting it. To judge the plausibility of this scenario, the literary critic is compelled, however reluctantly, to wrestle with the question of intentionality. The need to ferret out authorial intention seems a bit paradoxical in the case of a poet often faulted for his very superficiality or lack of depth.[5] But if we read with an eye to Ovid's exile, our reception of his work requires a metamorphosis and seems to demand that we search behind the polished surface of Ovidian verse to discern its deeper motives. Of course, as any reader of the *Metamorphoses* knows, judging a book by its cover is a risky business, since appearance is so often deceptive. The metaphysics of Ovid's epic work warns us that only rarely can interior dispositions be reliably read from external forms. Most often, the interplay between surface and essence is both richer and more deceptive. And so it is with Ovid's poetry and his politics; it is a foolhardy reader who thinks to discern one readily from the other—yet the effort toward that discernment must be made. By adducing his poetry as a major cause of the emperor's displeasure, Ovid mandates this search for clues revealing

2. See the contribution of K. A. Raaflaub and L. J. Samons to this volume.
3. J. C. Thibault, *The Mystery of Ovid's Exile* (Berkeley 1964) 125–29.
4. Cf. G. Williams, *Change and Decline: Roman Literature in the Early Empire* (Berkeley and Los Angeles 1978) 70–83.
5. On the imputation of frivolousness to Ovid, see A. G. Elliott, "Ovid and the Critics: Seneca, Quintilian, and 'Seriousness,' " *Helios* (1985) 9–20.

his attitudes toward Augustus; but what is most clearly revealed by the diversity of scholarly opinion is the elusiveness of the clues.

On the question of Ovid's pro- or anti-Augustanism, scholars have taken virtually every possible position. We might map these positions onto a political spectrum, calling Right the view of Ovid as a conservative propagandist for Augustan policies, Left the picture of Ovid as a liberal-to-radical dissenter from the potentially or actually totalitarian regime of the emperor, and Middle the position that, on the basis of our evidence, we can only return the judgment *non liquet*. The difficulty of reaching a satisfactory decision is well illustrated by the number of scholars who have shifted positions along this spectrum.

Brooks Otis provides a case in point. His *Ovid as an Epic Poet,* an important landmark in the modern appreciation of Ovid, emphasizes the importance—and difficulty—of the "Augustan question," for the second, revised edition of the book was occasioned by Otis's move from "Middle" to "Left" (a complete reversal from his earliest published work on the problem, which had advanced the "Right" orthodoxy).[6] Controversy continued in the 1970s, with readers arguing on both sides of the question as framed: that is, for Ovid as either supportive or subversive of Augustan propaganda in his poetry.[7] In addition to these voices pro and contra, a third school of thought (perhaps inevitably) repudiates these very terms. These scholars claim that such politicization is simply beside the point, that we must read Ovid not as a polemicist on either side, but as a poet with other, perhaps less parochial, items on his literary agenda.[8]

Closely related to this controversy over Ovid's political allegiance is

6. B. Otis, *Ovid as an Epic Poet* (Cambridge 1966; 1970²). See also his "Ovid and the Augustans," *TAPA* 69 (1938) 188–229.

7. See, for example, C. Segal, "Myth and Philosophy in the *Metamorphoses:* Ovid's Augustanism and the Augustan Conclusion to Book XV," *AJP* 90 (1969) 257–92; id., "Ovid's Orpheus and Augustan Ideology," *TAPA* 103 (1972) 473–94; W. R. Johnson, "The Problem of the Counter-Classical Sensibility and Its Critics," *CSCA* 3 (1970) 123–51; A. W. J. Holleman, "Ovid and Politics," *Historia* 20 (1971) 458–66; L. Curran, "Transformation and Anti-Augustanism in Ovid's *Metamorphoses,*" *Arethusa* 5 (1972) 71–92. A series of articles on the question has been written by D. A. Little: "The Non-Augustanism of Ovid's *Metamorphoses,*" *Mnemosyne* 25 (1972) 389–401; "Non-Parody in *Metamorphoses* 15," *Prudentia* 6 (1974) 17–21; "Ovid's Eulogy of Augustus, *Metamorphoses* 15.871–90," *Prudentia* 8 (1976) 19–35; "Politics in Augustan Poetry," *ANRW* 2.30.1 (1982) 254–370.

8. Those who have eschewed the terms "pro-Augustan" and "anti-Augustan" as either too simplistic or as inappropriate to the evaluation of the poet include G. K. Galinsky, *Ovid's Metamorphoses: An Introduction to the Basic Aspects* (Berkeley 1975) 210–17, esp. 215 (this is something of a shift from "Left" to "Middle"; cf. his earlier "The Cipus Episode in Ovid's *Metamorphoses* [15.565–621]," *TAPA* 98 [1967] 181–91), and C. R. Phillips, "Rethinking Augustan Poetry," *Latomus* 42 (1983) 780–818.

a debate in recent scholarship over the even more elusive question of
Ovid's tone. At issue here, broadly speaking, is "sincerity." A number of
literary terms may be invoked in this context: persona, irony, parody,
the reliability of the narrator, and so forth. Whatever the critical discourse chosen, however, the fundamental question confronting the
reader is, To what extent or in what sense does Ovid "mean what he
says" (particularly when he speaks *in propria persona*)? Are we to take
him at face value and in good faith? Or are we being asked to read in
some way subversively?

Clearly, the more focused question of Ovid's political views and the
more pervasive questioning of his fundamental reliability or "sincerity"
are closely intertwined. The difficulty of deciding how we are to constitute ourselves as readers of Ovid has been for about a quarter of a century—and with increasing urgency in the last decade or so—the most
significant problem in Ovidian scholarship. Is Ovid to be read as the
lighthearted entertainer with a risqué streak as earlier generations saw
him? Or does a more sophisticated reading enjoin us to become semiotic
detectives, ever probing under the glossy surface for the subtext dealing
in power, violence, manipulation, cynicism, lost faith? Although these
questions were originally raised in the context of Ovid's *magnum opus,*
the *Metamorphoses,* recent criticism has begun to scrutinize other
works as well in the poet's extensive oeuvre, searching for clues to
Ovid's problematic relation to his emperor—and equally puzzling relation to his reader.[9]

It is not surprising that *Tristia* 2, in which the emperor himself is also
Ovid's expressly intended reader, raises these questions of attitude and
sincerity with a vengeance.[10] Among the nine books of poetry from exile, this one is unique. While each of the other books is a collection of
poetic epistles, *Tristia* 2 alone is an extended poem of almost six hundred lines, in which the poet offers, it seems, an *apologia pro arte sua.*
Even more important, for our purposes, is the identity of the addressee,
for *Tristia* 2, alone among the exile poems, is a direct letter from Ovid

9. See, for example, on the political implications of the *Fasti,* W. R. Johnson, "The
Desolation of the *Fasti,*" *CJ* 74.1 (1978) 7–18; J. C. McKeown, "*Fabula proposito nulla
tegenda meo:* Ovid's *Fasti* and Augustan Politics," in T. Woodman and D. West, eds., *Poetry and Politics in the Age of Augustus* (Cambridge 1984) 169–87; D. M. Porte, "Un
épisode satirique des Fastes et l'exil d'Ovide," *Latomus* 43 (1984) 284–306. For an earlier
view, see K. Allen, "The *Fasti* of Ovid and the Augustan Propaganda," *AJP* 43 (1922)
250–67.

10. For a brief summary of the question, see H. Evans, *Publica Carmina: Ovid's Books
from Exile* (Lincoln, Nebraska 1983) 14–17.

to the emperor Augustus.[11] This letter would seem to offer the perfect laboratory in which to study the much-disputed relations between poet and emperor. The document, however, raises more questions on this front than it resolves, for it remains maddeningly—and apparently impenetrably—opaque.

The ostensible purpose of the letter is to offer a defense of the poet's practice and to request, if not a complete reprieve, at least a commutation of his punishment. If this is indeed its *raison d'être,* however, the poem appears remarkably unsuccessful. The letter Ovid writes seems, as a forensic case, not only unconvincing but self-defeating. The problems readers have seen in Ovid's epistolary appeal are many. We might usefully group them under rubrics taken from Aristotle's *Rhetoric.* In his rhetorical handbook, Aristotle stresses that the successful speaker must concern himself with *to pithanon,* the quality or mode of persuasion (Book 1); *to ēthos,* characterization or psychology (Book 2); and *hē taxis,* arrangement (Book 3). On all of these fronts, Ovid seems to blunder.

Tristia 2 is not well arranged as a unified case; although one can discern a basic rhetorical structure, the poem divides sharply between lines 206 and 207. While the first section can be plausibly analyzed as a rhetorically structured plea for clemency, the second section veers off course; although it purports to be an apology for the *Ars amatoria,* it becomes much more of a literary manifesto than an apologia, eventually arguing that *all* poetry is erotic. At least implicitly, Ovid suggests that the emperor, in censuring his work alone, has been naive, unjust, or both. The epistle's ethical characterization, both of author and of addressee, is unstable. Ovid's own stance fluctuates between abject sycophancy and overconfident self-assertion, while his portrayal of Augustus as a very god on earth and the most clement of individuals is hardly credible, juxtaposed as it is with the cruelty of the situation in which he has placed the poet. Finally, the substance of the letter itself appears ill calculated to persuade its recipient. Even in the midst of beseeching the emperor, Ovid seems to have scattered through the text, like small land mines, double entendres alluding to uncomfortable political situations, Augustan hypocrisies, and even particular imperial weaknesses or indiscretions. Many readers find the poem riddled with such references,

---

11. The only comparable document is Hor. *Epist.* 2.1. Indeed, the two letters share intriguing similarities. While these will not be my focus here, they would undoubtedly repay further study.

which run the gamut from embarrassing innuendo to thinly veiled hostility directed against the very reader whom Ovid needs to placate. Far from undoing the alleged damage of the *Ars,* then, ultimately Ovid seems to have framed more of a codicil than a palinode.

Virtually all readers have been disturbed by the peculiar tone of *Tristia* 2, in which gross flattery of his oppressor—which at the same time borders uncomfortably close on sarcastic attack—is voiced by a poet who is himself, by turns, self-aggrandizing and self-abasing. The inappropriateness of the poem as an apologia is hard to escape. On the same grounds, then, some praise the poet's sense of independence, while others lament his foolhardiness:[12]

> Though ostensibly addressed to Augustus as a plea for leniency, it in fact contains much that is critical and even impudent.[13]

> At this distance our anxiety at the harm he risks doing . . . to his own fortunes is overcome by our delight at seeing the old Ovid re-emerge from the wastes of Dobruja to discomfort his not invulnerable oppressor.[14]

I shall not enumerate here the list of passages that have given readers pause in their attempts to understand the poem as an apologia. A fairly exhaustive list might be compiled by combining the insights of Focardi, Marache, and Wiedemann, though each reader will differ somewhat in the selection of troubling passages. For the most part, they can be grouped into thematic categories. These would include references to Augustus' much-vaunted *clementia,* together with clear indication of his inclemency toward Ovid; references to the danger ever threatening on the edges of the empire, despite the much celebrated *pax Augusta;* and a pervasive inconsistency in the poem's tone between sycophantic adulation (indeed, divinization) of the *princeps* and the poet's alacrity in taking him on directly, and suggesting or even dictating behavior to Augustus.

The peculiarity of Ovid's arguments has led scholars to formulate a number of interpretative positions in their effort to defend his defense— or at least to make sense of it. I shall review the most prominent here to

12. In addition to those scholars specifically treated infra, see G. Boissier, *L'opposition sous les Césars*[2] (Paris 1885) 154–55; N. Voulikh, "La révolte d'Ovide contre Auguste," *EtCl* 36 (1968) 378–82; G. Focardi, "Difesa, preghiera, ironia nel II libro dei *Tristia* di Ovidio," *StIt* 47 (1975) 115–29; R. J. Dickinson, "The *Tristia:* Poetry in Exile," in J. W. Binns, ed., *Ovid* (London 1973) 172; R. Syme, *History in Ovid* (Oxford 1978) 222–25; Little (1982: supra n. 7) 347–49.

13. J. Barsby, *Ovid,* Greece and Rome: New Surveys in the Classics 12 (Oxford 1978) 43.

14. L. P. Wilkinson, *Ovid Surveyed* (Cambridge 1962) 145.

indicate both the range of views held and the fact that none of them provides a fully satisfactory resolution for the paradox of an indefensible defense. Perhaps the key to Ovid's strategy lies in its very indirection. If we examine the construction of Ovid's case, we see that he is determinedly oblique, not only in what he says but in what he chooses not to say. Surely it is odd for a defendant to claim, as Ovid does, that although two charges stand against him, he will only address himself to one (and that, as he indicates elsewhere, the less serious one). I suggest that Ovid's apparent failure to defend the *Ars* adequately, together with his explicit failure to address the *error* at all, may indicate that his *point* here is to speak beside the point—in order to stress that in his confrontation with Augustus appearances (including, perhaps, the charges themselves) are not quite what they seem. Playing on the possible confusion between *ars* as proper noun and common noun, Ovid, I believe, crafted *Tristia* 2 such that *Ars celat artem*.

The History of the Question

An excellent edition of and commentary on *Tristia* 2 was produced in 1924 by S. G. Owen. He points out that the work is organized as a more or less formal rhetorical defense, complete with *exordium, probatio, refutatio.*[15] While seeing the purpose of the poem as a quasi-legal defense, however, Owen already had some misgivings. His chapter "Remarks on Ovid's Argument" begins with the rather diffident observation "Ovid's defense . . . is not entirely convincing." Owen is not discomfitted by irony or defiance in Ovid's approach to Augustus, as are later readers; he simply believes that the case made for the *Ars amatoria* being a morally sound work is not a good one.[16]

In considering the poet's position vis-à-vis Augustus, our concern is less with the forensic quality of Ovid's argument than with the *types* of argument he uses and the *relation* he posits between himself and the emperor. One of the most striking features of that relationship, as it is portrayed here, is the ostensible deification of the emperor. Throughout his exilic works, Ovid consistently identifies Augustus with Jupiter (by

15. This scheme has been generally accepted by later scholars, and particularly developed by Focardi, Ford, and Classen; see Focardi (supra n. 12); B. B. Ford, "Tristia II: Ovid's Opposition to Augustus" (Diss. Rutgers Univ. 1977); J.-M. Classen, "Poeta, Exsul, Vates: A Stylistic and Literary Analysis of Ovid's *Tristia* and *Epistulae ex Ponto*" (Diss. Univ. of Stellenbosch [South Africa] 1986) 260–65.

16. S. G. Owen, *P. Ovidii Nasonis Tristium Liber Secundus* (Oxford 1924; reprint, Amsterdam 1967) 55.

whose *fulmen* the poet has been struck), and this epistle is a prime example of that conceit.[17] Writing shortly after Owen, in 1930, Kenneth Scott takes the poet's stance as straightforward adulation. "Ovid gives us a more detailed picture of emperor worship than any Augustan poet," he concludes, "or perhaps any Roman poet."[18] Yet such reverence is surprising in one so patently irreverent as Ovid. Other readers (among whom I am one) are less willing to accept Ovid's portrait of himself as the faithful servant of a god made manifest on earth, and more prone to believe that the poet has tongue firmly planted in cheek. We might note, for example, that no sooner has Ovid invoked Augustus as a god (*per te praesentem conspicuumque deum* 54) than he addresses this deity directly as a man (*vir maxime* 55).

Despite the prima facie unexpectedness of Ovid's terms of address to the emperor, however, Gordon Williams has argued that to consider the *Tristia* as ironic or even paradoxical in its treatment of Augustus is utterly wrongheaded.[19] He contends that, given our own distaste for the mode, we are unwilling and unable to recognize genuine panegyric when we see it, and we *will* go about turning it on its head. He sees the modern predilection for subversive readings as just that—a modern predilection: "Predictably, scholars have tried to distort Ovid's intention."[20] "The difficulty of accommodating panegyric to various poetic genres runs right through Augustan literature," Williams notes, and (writing, to be sure, not of the *Tristia* but of the *Ars*) he speaks of Ovid's skill in this vein: "The problem that Ovid has solved was not how to make fun of Augustus, but how to accommodate panegyric artistically to the context of his poem without painful disruption."[21] This would be a more comfortable view than the one I shall advance, since reading ironically leaves us with difficult and puzzling questions about Ovid's intention or competence or both. Still, my own view is that *Tristia* 2 is to be read in a way that does leave both us (and Augustus) *un*comfortable. That Ovid's intention with respect to his emperor is neither so clear nor so simple as Williams would have it is indicated well enough by the lack of critical consensus on the question; if generations of readers have been so divided in their reception of the text, can Augustus himself have been so certain?

17. Cf. Owen (supra n. 16) 79–81.
18. K. Scott, "Emperor-Worship in Ovid," *TAPA* 61 (1930) 69.
19. Williams (supra n. 4) 53–101.
20. Ibid., 89.
21. Ibid., 79.

A pioneering study in reading *Tristia 2* as an ambiguous and elusive text was that of R. Marache, "La révolte d'Ovide exilé contre Auguste." [22] Marache's thesis is that Ovid recognized and resented Augustus' attempts to *use* poetry programmatically for reasons of state and moral prescription, that the real problem was Ovid's rebellion against the subservience of poetry to politics. More specifically, he believes Ovid is keenly aware of having been condemned unjustly and that he indicates as much with numerous little digs directed against the emperor in the course of the letter. A number of indications, Marache claims, cause us as readers to feel a sense of revolt and even hostility on Ovid's part.

Marache is less convincing, however, in his explanation of the poet's technique. He vacillates on the question of Ovid's intentionality or even *consciousness* of what he is doing. Thus at times he claims that Ovid is hoist with his own petard or has somehow gotten carried away and taken criticism farther than he intended.[23] It is difficult to know what to make of such claims. Marache sees Ovid as mysteriously at the mercy of impulses beyond his control, such that flattery becomes hyperbolic and thus so insincere as to be self-defeating. We seem to see the critic's own *aporia* in his concluding remark that the poet's only true recourse is . . . silence.[24]

A more coherent view was advanced by Marg.[25] Noting particularly the poet's apparently undiminished self-confidence despite his insistent submissiveness, Marg argues that it is difficult to understand Ovid's stance in *Tristia 2*, *except* under the hypothesis that he is paradoxically, by his very self-deprecatory presentation, calling Augustus to task for his injustice and inclemency. This line of interpretation—that the poem is in some way ironic or sarcastic—has been followed by a number of more recent readers, including, as mentioned above, Focardi, Ford, and Classen.[26]

22. In N. I. Herescu, ed., *Recherches sur Ovide publiées à l'occasion du bimillénaire de la naissance du poète* (Paris 1958) 412–19.

23. This "out-of-control" theory is also advanced by M. W. Avery, "Ovid's *Apologia*," *CJ* 32 (1936): "The poet forgets, for the time being, his avowed purpose in writing, and gives expression simply to his own feelings" (95); "being Ovid, he must continue to display his fatal ingenuity. He does not know when to stop" (98). This last remark clearly betrays its origin, namely Quintilian's judgment of the poet as *nimium amator ingenii sui* (*Inst.* 10.1.88). For an important assessment of the ways in which this ancient criticism still holds sway in Ovidian scholarship, see Elliott (supra n. 5).

24. Marache (supra n. 22) 419.

25. W. Marg, "Zur Behandlung des Augustus in den 'Tristien' Ovids," in M. von Albrecht and E. Zinn, eds., *Ovid*, Wege der Forschung 92 (Darmstadt 1968) 502–12.

26. See also now E. Doblhofer, *Exil und Emigration: zum Erlebnis der Heimatferne in der römischen Literatur* (Darmstadt 1987) 201–8, where he explicitly follows Marg's lead.

According to Marg's rather romantic humanism, the poet is empowered to take up his highly independent and ironic stance by the very autonomy of the poetic endeavor: "So nimmt Ovid die Kraft und das Recht dazu aus der Eigenständigkeit und Unabhängigkeit der Poesie." [27] He sees Ovid as confidently addressing himself to a wider audience, and that a double one—both his former reading public at Rome and posterity: "Dies Publikum ist ein doppeltes: Einmal der Kreis seiner früheren Geselligkeit. . . . Des weiteren ist sein Publikum die Leserschaft von Poesie überhaupt, damals, und künftig die Nachwelt, *posteritas*." [28]

The ironic reading of the *Tristia* in general was applied specifically to the understanding of *Tristia* 2 by Thomas Wiedemann. He examines the political context of the work's composition and shows that a number of references in the poem to Augustus' person or policies are disconcerting for the unflattering light in which they cast the emperor. He concludes that, "reminding those of his admirers who were in a position to put some pressure on Augustus just how weak the emperor's political position had become," Ovid had, with the writing of *Tristia* 2, "decided to circulate a major work setting out to show that it was unreasonable and unjust for Augustus to punish one particular poet on the grounds that his verses were immoral." [29]

It is hard to improve upon Wiedemann's concluding summary of the situation:

> If we are to assume that Ovid's intention was to flatter Augustus in order to obtain a mitigation of his sentence, we must conclude either that the poet was somehow unable to hide his bitterness towards Augustus in a poem intended to be read by him, or that he thought the *princeps* would for some reason not notice the embarrassing references to famine, wars, and unpopular legislation. No doubt any conclusion we may reach on this subject is bound to be subjective, but neither of these solutions seems very convincing. The alternative is that *Tristia* II was not intended for Augustus' eyes at all; it was meant to influence the circle of educated Roman aristocrats to whom Ovid's other poems from Tomi were addressed, and Ovid hoped that they would be the ones who, recognizing the absurdity of Augustus' grounds for exiling Ovid, would do their best to see that he was recalled. [30]

Reopening the Question and the Book

Wiedemann outlines here three logical possibilities:

1. Ovid is an incompetent writer (incapable of dissembling).

27. Marg (supra n. 25) 511.
28. Ibid., 503.
29. T. Wiedemann, "The Political Background to Ovid's *Tristia* II," CQ 25 (1975) 268.
30. Ibid., 271. See also Syme (supra n. 12) 226.

2. Augustus is an incompetent reader (incapable of deciphering).

3. Ovid isn't really writing to Augustus, appearances to the contrary (thus, at least, he remains a capable writer addressing a capable audience).

Of these options, Marg and Wiedemann himself have advanced the last, Marache the first. What of the second possibility? I cannot claim to judge whether the emperor Augustus did indeed possess what a modern critic would call "literary competence." [31] Not only is such a judgment beyond the scope of this paper; it is, I believe, beyond the scope of our evidence. What I do claim is that Ovid *organizes* his letter to the emperor precisely around the question of Augustus' competence as a reader. Understood in this way, the poem is neither an attempt to circumvent the emperor nor a direct political attack on Augustus. Rather, Ovid carefully maneuvers Augustus onto his own field of expertise— the judgment of poetry—and directly confronts him there. Wiedemann argues that Ovid's strategy would discomfit the emperor in light of contemporary political factors (famine, wars, unpopular legislation). This may well be so. But such factors remain external to the argument Ovid chooses to make directly in *Tristia* 2. What Ovid includes specifically within the poem is not politics but poetics.

It is striking that, in his own epistolary encounter with Augustus (*Epist.* 2.1), Horace makes precisely the same gesture. He too offers, unasked, a reading of literary history. Ovid, who has been censured for his erotic verse, forces an erotic reading of the classical canon upon Augustus. Horace, in a more complex strategy, having been requested to write of the emperor, stresses contemporary Rome's perhaps undeserved overestimation of things past (to which, curiously, the reputation of the emperor alone provides a counterexample). Asked to write a page of praise, the poet ends with a wry reminder that pages may become mere wrapping paper for cheap merchandise'—or worse. Can it be mere coincidence that both these poets, in their poetic epistles to Augustus, hasten to instruct the emperor in those things that are Caesar's and those that are not, such as their own poetic gifts?

Since determining the status and power of poetry is precisely what is at stake between author and emperor, references concerning poetry itself are the heart of the matter. This is the ground of contention. Ovid ensures also that in *Tristia* 2 poetry itself becomes the ground on which

31. On the elusive criterion of "literary competence," see J. Culler, *The Pursuit of Signs: Semiotics, Literature, Deconstruction* (Ithaca, N.Y. 1981) 50–53.

the struggle will be played out between himself and Augustus. Of the 578 lines in the poet's ostensible apology, over half are devoted to Ovid's views on poetry and its uses, including an *ars poetica,* in which he insists upon his own revisionist reading of the history of classical literature. Has Augustus shown himself morally fastidious with regard to the erotic inclinations of Ovid's verse? Very well; in a *tour de force* of literary criticism, beginning with Homer and sweeping through both Greek and Latin literature down to his own day, the poet takes it upon himself to instruct his reader. Ovid, as self-appointed literary *praeceptor,* demonstrates to his emperor, with example after example, that *all* poetry is erotically charged—from the *Iliad* itself, "nothing other than the tale of an adultress fought over by husband and lover" (371–72), to "your own *Aeneid,* [Augustus]," in which the best-read bit is Aeneas' bedding of the Tyrian queen (533–36).[32] Thus Ovid gains the upper hand on his addressee by staking out the realm of poetic judgment as the arena for this epistolary encounter and by casting doubt on Augustus' competence in that arena. Neither political legitimacy nor power will be under debate—these the poet apparently concedes to his opponent. Instead, the claim he presses, quid pro quo, is the right to determine poetic legitimacy and power by elaborating a theory of reading and an anatomy of taste.

Further, if Ovid has been censured for the ethics of his writing, in *Tristia* 2 he effectively turns the tables by calling into question the ethics of Augustus' reading and indeed his moral judgment at large.[33] By calling attention to questionable aspects of the emperor's character, Ovid effectively puts Augustus on equal footing with himself—or indeed even exchanges roles with him. In this way, the poet links his own defense (concerning the moral qualities of his aesthetic practice) to the tastes and practices of the emperor. Thus, for example, Ovid points out that Augustus possesses erotic works of art and enjoys, even sponsors, bawdy mimes.[34] Do those aesthetic tastes reflect adversely on his moral

32. Doblhofer (supra n. 26) 205 dubs the section a "Literaturgeschichte *sub specie amoris.*" Cf. Owen (supra n. 16) 59: "The survey in the *Tristia* is of a . . . systematic nature . . . such as is not often found in Latin writers."

33. For a survey of our information on Augustus' taste in the visual and literary arts, see N. Rudd, *Lines of Enquiry: Studies in Latin Poetry* (Cambridge 1976) chap. 1, "Ovid and the Augustan Myth," esp. 2–3.

34. Lines 521–28 refer not only to erotica in general, but specifically to paintings in the possession of Augustus' family. See Owen (supra n. 16) 272–73; Pliny *HN* 35.91. We should note that Ovid, like Horace in his epistle to Augustus, devotes considerable attention to deprecating the vulgarity of the mime, an art form of which Augustus seems to have been especially fond (Suet. *Aug.* 43–45).

comportment in the world? Implicitly, Ovid raises this question and in so doing subtly tranfers the charges against himself to his accuser. Perhaps by way of answer to this uncomfortable question, *Tristia* 2 also provides a number of potentially embarrassing references to Augustus' sexual mores and apparently less-than-august proclivities (such as gaming on boards and in beds).[35] Perhaps such a strategy enables the poet to score a point against the emperor with the claim that despite the raciness of his poetry, his own life has never been cause for scandal (349–52). Arguably, however, the problem is more complex. Ovid's subtlety may turn on itself, leaving us not only to question a naive correspondence between art and life, but also to despair of the very possibility of stabilizing the relation between words and the world, between politics and poetry.

Remedial Reading

It is in *Tristia* 2, of course, that Ovid advances the well-known *carmen et error* explanation of his exile. Insofar as the poem is a defense, its strategy is made explicit (211–12): the *error* will not, cannot, be dealt with, Ovid tells us; all that is possible is to exculpate the *carmen,* apparently the *Ars amatoria.* We shall reconsider Ovid's elusive *error* below; first let us consider the case he advances for his art. As Owen noted, there are many problems with the defense that Ovid offers, including the fact that long stretches of *Tristia* 2 seem to reiterate, rather than to repudiate, the earlier work.[36] Particularly ticklish is the very question of the emperor's having read—or not read—the poem in question. In an

---

35. A particularly striking example appears in lines 161–64: "So may Livia complete her wedded years with you—Livia who, unless for you, was not *digna* for any other husband. For if she had not existed, it would have befitted you to live your life celibate and there would have been no woman to whom you could have been husband." This is a truly unfortunate allusion to Livia and Augustus. Perhaps we need to turn to Suetonius, Dio Cassius, or Tacitus to verify the details of this particular marriage made in heaven. Certainly Ovid's contemporaries would have needed no reference works to remind them of Augustus' divorce from Scribonia or the somewhat unusual details of Augustus' taking Livia from her first husband and the father of her children, Tiberius Claudius Nero. (Recall that the bride, who was given away by her husband, was six months pregnant with his child at the time of the wedding.) As Wiedemann (supra n. 29) 269 remarks: "Need Ovid really have told Augustus that under different circumstances he ought to have remained a bachelor?" Cf. also Suetonius' account of Augustus as a notorious womanizer (*Aug.* 69): "Not even his friends could deny that he often committed adultery, though of course they said, in justification, that he did so for reasons of state, not simple passion—he wanted to discover what his enemies were by getting intimate with their wives or daughters. Mark Antony accused him not only of indecent haste in marrying Livia, but of hauling an ex-consul's wife from her husband's dining room into the bedroom—right before his eyes!"

36. Owen (supra n. 16) 55–62.

extended passage (213–44) Ovid manages to present this fundamental issue in such a way as to make it a no-win proposition for Augustus.[37] There are two alternatives: (1) the poem is too frivolous to have merited Augustus' attention, since he has much weightier responsibilities to discharge, so that if he did read it, he stands condemned of at best silliness, at worst neglect of his duties to the Roman people; and (2) since it would have been a waste of his valuable time, Augustus must not have read the poem, in which case he stands condemned of willful and arbitrary vengeance exacted against the poet without justifiable cause, for he has exiled Ovid on the grounds of a poem he hasn't even read (61–66)!

The poet, however, does not hesitate to take upon himself the direction of the emperor's reading. At crucial points throughout the poem, Ovid addresses himself to the question of Augustus' mode of reading. "Did you read my work?" he asks (37–38, 219–24). "If you would only read correctly, there would be no problem" (211–14, 275–76). "That person who led you to misread is my greatest enemy" (77–80). "Read the sections of my work that I select—as I tell you to" (239–44, 557–64). Thus does Ovid prescribe Augustus' reading and, with the extended revisionist reading of earlier texts, foist his own readings upon Augustus. Again Ovid recommends a specific reading of his own works to Augustus: "Just open my books and you'll see what a role you play there, how I really value you." Look more closely, however, at the way in which Ovid phrases this proposition to Augustus. It has two parts. The first (61–62): "Those very books of mine that are *crimina nostra* are filled with your name." The second (63–66), a specific claim for the *Metamorphoses*: "In that work [Ovid confidently asserts to the emperor] you'll find proclamations of your name, pledges of my feeling." But what *is* that book, as Ovid describes it here? It's a *magnum opus in non credendos corpora versa modos*. We might paraphrase: "a work in strains that are not to be believed." Thus Ovid represents himself as a poet who has publicized his emperor, all right—in works that are either blameworthy (even, perhaps, "criminal") or not to be believed. This communication of the poet to Augustus seems somewhat disingenuous. What do we know of Augustus' communication to the poet?

Ovid does have something to say about Augustus' words to him. Specifically, he alludes to the emperor's edict of relegation as *immite mi-*

---

37. This is a variant on the Ovidian technique of representing the emperor that Doblhofer (supra n. 26) 204–8 calls "Augustus im Widerspruch mit sich selbst."

naxque (135). Clearly, this clashes with the poet's first address to Augustus as *mitissime Caesar* (27). Periodically in the first section of *Tristia* 2 the poet alludes in more or less extended and more or less direct ways to the much-vaunted *clementia* of Augustus (27–52, 125–38, 147). In light of this, it is jarring to characterize the emperor's edict itself as *immite minaxque*. In fact, the entire discussion of Augustus' particular handling of Ovid's case (127–38) is markedly ambivalent. In this passage, Ovid describes the "special" treatment his case was given: without a hearing, without an official decree, in a highly irregular procedure, he was summarily dispatched. The resultant edict, though "harsh and threatening" was "lenient in name" (*attamen in poenae nomine lene fuit* 135–36), since the poet is "relegated," not "exiled." Should it escape our notice, however (did it escape Augustus'?), that a mere fifty lines later, as he pleads for a milder place of banishment, Ovid notes that not a single *exul* has been cast farther from Rome than he (*nec quisquam patria longius exul abest* 188)? What these lines stress is the discrepancy between word (*nomen*) and deed on the emperor's part. A non-ironic reading would emphasize the leniency involved in Augustus' designation of Ovid as *relegatus* rather than *exul*.[38] I'm not so sure. What may be more to the point is simple bad faith. By stressing the disparity between the emperor's proclamation and his action, Ovid is constituting Augustus—like himself—as one whose words cannot necessarily be believed.

The most explicit statement of Ovid's own view on whether one's words are (or are not) trustworthy indicators of one's internal disposition and/or external situation is at lines 353–58. Here the poet's claim is both quite clear and—if correctly understood—quite disturbing. "Believe me," he says, "my literature and my life are miles apart; my poems are racy but my life is right." The issue, of course, is not unique to Ovid—Catullus earlier (Catull. 16) and Martial later (1.4.8) make very similar claims. In the context of Ovid's exilic work, however, the assertion is devastating, for it directly contradicts Ovid's stance throughout the entire corpus of his exilic poetry—namely, that his poetry of exile *is* a direct reflection of his life in exile.[39] More specifically, the assertion undermines the claim to credibility that this apologia itself might have.

38. Focardi (supra n. 12) 117–23 notes the irony. For an overview of the technicalities of Augustus' pronouncement, see R. S. Rogers, "The Emperor's Displeasure and Ovid," *TAPA* 97 (1966) 373–78; see also id., "The Emperor's Displeasure—*amicitiam renuntiare*," *TAPA* 90 (1959) 224–37.
39. Contra: Williams (supra n. 4) 99.

Particularly important here is 358 with its admission that a poet may say many mendacious things simply to charm the ears of the hearer. We are left with a paradox like that of the Cretan liar: if we accept Ovid's claim that his poetry isn't to be believed, then why should we believe this poem?

The Future of the Question

I spoke earlier of Marache's inability to find a satisfactory explanation for Ovid's stance in *Tristia* 2. The problem has bothered many readers:

> Why does Ovid, who may have been everything else, but who certainly was not stupid, commit such a stupid blunder as to defend in the most outspoken, almost offensive manner, a perfectly hopeless case, which had, moreover, already been decided against him?[40]

Why does Ovid write as he does in *Tristia* 2? What is his real purpose? The question is by no means easy to answer. But I would argue that if we are to find an answer, we must shift the terms of the problem—from political to poetic considerations. The tracking of particular pieces of legislation or particular campaigns of Tiberius is not going to bring us any closer to resolving the dilemma of interpreting innuendo, for our problem with the poem is, finally, that—an *interpretative* question more than one of *Realpolitik*.[41] A more satisfactory answer will require us to recognize the politics of reading that, both literally and figuratively, lies at the heart of the poem.

For what Ovid presents to Augustus in the most extensive section of the poem is a willful reinterpretation of classical texts. This section has been called a defensive *ars poetica*. It shifts Ovid's confrontation with Augustus into the poet's own realm. In employing this strategy, Ovid's poem is not conciliatory but adversarial. The major portion of Ovid's letter co-opts Augustus as the passive recipient of a lecture on the history and interpretation of literature. Rather than conceding the emperor's right to pass judgment and to bring the Muses under his sway, Ovid asserts his own right to poetic authority, even over the *princeps*.

Writing of the delicate political relations between the emperor and another of "his poets," Horace, one scholar has noted, "a post-revolution situation . . . [replaces] 'the conflict of interest for power with a competition for discourses for the appropriation of legitimacy,'

40. Avery (supra n. 23) 101.
41. Cf. Galinsky (1975: supra n. 8) 215.

and it is clear that Augustus saw the work of his . . . poets as a powerful weapon in the legitimization of his own regime." [42] The correspondence we have been examining may illustrate how a "post-revolution" poet employed his ingenuity in drafting a poetic letter of protest rather than in being drafted to serve a political regime.

A common scholarly assumption in the attempt to understand Ovid's exile has been that Augustus held a rather broad view of the political, which included the moral climate or taste of Roman society, as a matter liable to legislation and, consequently, an area for potentially political dissent. This assumption draws largely on Ovid's own outraged contention in *Tristia* 2 that he alone among poets has been punished for the possibly damaging effect of his verse on Roman *mores*. Ostensibly defending himself against this charge, Ovid has a field day proving that every author who has ever committed an act of literature has potentially contributed to the delinquency of a *matrona*. His prurient survey of classical poetry, in which he exposes the bawd in every bard, is a tendentious and witty *tour de force*.

We might usefully recall here the theorizing of Harold Bloom, who has reminded us that creative "misprision" is the hallmark of the strong poet. Ovid's misreading is indeed a strength; if the individual pieces of his case are comic, the overall structure is compelling as a *reductio ad absurdum* of the morals charge. Even more damaging to the charge brought against him, however, is the near decade of elapsed time between the supposed offense (if we assume it to be the publication of the *Ars*) and Augustus' retaliation. Ovid's plaint that such a delay between the crime and the punishment is incomprehensible as well as unprecedented has never found a satisfactory answer. Perhaps there is none, because the *Ars* was not really the offense in question but merely a pretext.

Did Augustus really believe that witty poetry on wife swapping represented a serious threat to his regime? Did he worry about it years later? When Ovid takes the stand in his own defense, is he a reliable witness? Or is there another, unspoken cause of contention between *princeps* and poet for which a trumped-up morals charge may serve as a foil?

We may look to our own recent political milieu for verification of the curious fact that a public airing of comparatively clear-cut issues of pop-

---

42. M. A. Bernstein, "O Totiens Servus: Saturnalia and Servitude in Augustan Rome," in von Hallberg (supra n. 1) 46.

ular morality may serve conveniently to mask a deeper silence concerning more complex or disturbing issues of political power and policy. The latter, especially when they are less easily reducible to pro-and-contra formulations, may not be easily introduced into public discourse. It is easier to argue about plant closings or the level of taxation than it is to envision the implications of the global economic system toward which we are moving, easier to engage in charge and counter charge concerning the pollution of beaches than to grapple with the unfathomable fact that we are unraveling the very fabric of our atmosphere. Thus debate over marital fidelity or the extent to which the state may intervene in the area of childbearing, both in our own political discourse and in that of the Augustan Age, may actually take the place of potentially more disruptive scrutiny of the very terms that constitute the public sphere. However volatile such moral questions may be, they can at least be publicly articulated; the very fact that the issue may be hotly joined on either side lends it a kind of inherent order. But how does one even begin to articulate the much more amorphous and darker intimation that the political order itself, as currently constituted, is dysfunctional; that the state, as we have known it, may be dying—or may in fact already be dead, without our having realized its passing? And if one does have such an intimation—if Ovid did—how might it be expressed?

Perhaps we resort to the strategies of containment or displacement in public discourse sketched above not just because they are the easiest ways but because they are the only ways we have to talk to one another in a time of crisis or transition, until a strenuous act of imagination maps the world anew. A strong poet might be capable of providing such a map by a monumental effort, nothing short of creating a new poem of the cosmos, from its origins to his own time. I believe Ovid undertook that imaginative effort in his *Metamorphoses* when he described a world in which individual human agents are helpless before the willful and apparently boundless power of the Olympians, whose affinity to the inhabitants of the Palatine Ovid made every effort to stress:[43]

> hac parte potentes
> caelicolae clarique suos posuere penates.
> hic locus est, quem, si verbis audacia detur,
> haud timeam magni dixisse Palatia caeli.
> (*Met.* 1.173–76)

43. For an earlier suggestion that the *Metamorphoses* may have been the source of Augustus' displeasure (on religious grounds), see E. K. Rand, *Ovid and His Influence* (New York 1928) 92.

This is the spot which, were I allowed to speak boldly, I would not hesitate to call the Palatine district of high heaven.[44]

Going out of his way to point out such analogies between the capricious rapist who appears as father of gods and men in the *Metamorphoses* and the *pater patriae* at Rome was indeed audacious on Ovid's part. Writing such a *carmen*, exposing and exploring the workings of power in a world where nothing is quite what it seems anymore, may finally have been an *error*. If so, it was a work worthy of comparison with Hephaistos' mythical net in the *Odyssey*—powerful enough to trap its victims uncomfortably and inextricably, yet so finely woven as to remain invisible. If Ovid's *error* was indeed the anatomy of the trappings of power in the *Metamorphoses,* we can understand that the act was carried out on so monumental a scale that the *princeps* could no longer tolerate its author's presence at Rome, yet with such subtlety that the real ground of contention between them need not—perhaps could not—be openly expressed. It is more possible to debate openly the fashions of moral conduct than the refashioning of a world, by either an author or an emperor.[45]

44. Ovid, *Metamorphoses,* trans. M. M. Innes (Baltimore 1955).

45. I would like to thank the anonymous readers and, especially, my patient and supportive editor, Kurt Raaflaub, who contributed greatly to the improvement of this paper's successive drafts. I owe special thanks as well to Thomas J. Scherer, whose incisive and imaginative counsel helped me to perceive more clearly the implications of the argument.

Did Maecenas "Fall from Favor"?
Augustan Literary Patronage

It has become a cliché of Augustan historiography that after 23 B.C.
Maecenas fell from favor with Augustus.[1] This thesis was given powerful expression, with several new touches, by Ronald Syme in 1939:[2]

> The way of his life, like the fantastical conceits of his verse, must have been
> highly distasteful to Augustus as to Agrippa.[3] Augustus bore with the vices
> of his minister for the memory of his services and the sake of his counsel. Yet
> the position of Maecenas had been compromised. He could not withstand
> Agrippa. Maecenas made a fatal mistake—he told Terentia of the danger
> that threatened her brother. Augustus could not forgive a breach of confi-
> dence. . . . Maecenas might be dropped, but not Agrippa; and so Agrippa
> prevailed.

1. It should be explained that this paper represents a brief statement of part of a thesis
on literature and ideology in the age of Augustus that I am working out at length in a
book. Consequently, some problems have been given less than adequate treatment here:
see especially nn. 14, 16, and 19.
2. *The Roman Revolution* (Oxford 1939) 342, and repeated in his later books: e.g.,
History in Ovid (Oxford 1979) 114; *The Augustan Aristocracy* (Oxford 1986) 389.
3. Whatever can be discerned about the tastes of Agrippa, those of Augustus elude
investigation, and there is no reason to deny that he enjoyed Maecenas. Nor is it clear how
seriously Maecenas intended his verse, which, in that respect, is a lot more enigmatic than
Cicero's.

258

Here the thesis is linked with the wider hypothesis of a power struggle between Agrippa and Maecenas over the succession to Augustus. This does not withstand scrutiny.[4] But the evidence for any repudiation of Maecenas by Augustus is unreliable, and the whole thesis should be called into question.

Suetonius is the only ancient writer to mention Maecenas' betrayal of the danger threatening his brother-in-law, Murena, in 23 B.C. (*Aug.* 66.3): *desideravit enim nonnumquam, ne de pluribus referam, et M. Agrippae patientiam et Maecenatis taciturnitatem, cum ille ex levi frigoris suspicione et quod Marcellus sibi anteferretur, Mytilenas se relictis omnibus contulisset, hic secretum de comperta Murenae coniuratione uxori Terentiae prodidisset.* "For he [Augustus] often longed—to mention no other cases—for tolerance in Agrippa and a discreet tongue in Maecenas, since the former, on a trivial suspicion of coolness and because Marcellus was being favored over himself, dropped everything and retired to Mytilene, and the latter had betrayed the secret about discovery of Murena's plot to his wife, Terentia." What is offered here—and elsewhere[5]—about Agrippa's withdrawal to Mytilene is clearly wrong: "There is no truth in this fancy—a political suspect is not placed in charge of provinces and armies."[6] Why should any credence then be given to the assertion about Maecenas? There is no good reason; and, furthermore, the context in which Suetonius puts forward these assertions has simply been ignored. Suetonius tells of the fall of Cornelius Gallus (who committed suicide when denounced in 26 B.C.) and of Augustus' complaining "that to himself alone it was not permitted to show anger toward his friends to the extent that he wished." He then goes on: "The rest of his friends, men of the highest rank in each order, flourished to the end of their lives in influence and wealth, even despite giving causes for offense." There now follow the cases of Agrippa and Maecenas; and thus Suetonius can be seen to be actually denying any fall from favor of either Agrippa or Maecenas. In fact, the interpretation placed on Maecenas' telling Terentia about her brother's danger (that Augustus regarded it as a betrayal) should itself be questioned. Murena fled when his sister informed him of his danger[7] and thereby provided

4. See, for example, G. Williams, "Horace, *Odes* 1.12 and the Succession to Augustus," *Hermathena* 118 (1974) 151–54.

5. Vell. Pat. 2.93.2; Suet. *Tib.* 10; and Pliny (*HN* 7.149) even speaks of *pudenda Agrippae ablegatio.*

6. Syme (1939: supra n. 2) 342.

7. For examination of the evidence, see R. G. M. Nisbet and M. Hubbard, *A Commentary on Horace: Odes, Book II* (Oxford 1978) 152–58.

what constituted a very welcome public confession of guilt, and so a
perfect justification for his death when apprehended. Maecenas did not
miscalculate—nor did Augustus. A public trial and deliberate infliction
of a death penalty on a prominent aristocrat could only be deeply embarrassing. Maecenas' action avoided that.

What becomes clear when the sources are examined is that there was
great interest in, but little information on, relations between Augustus
and his closest supporters. In these circumstances, both Agrippa and
Maecenas became subjects of exemplary anecdotes that could be used
again and again to illustrate various contexts. When Tacitus wrote the
obituary of Sallustius Crispus (*Ann.* 3.30), he drew a close parallel with
the career of Maecenas, including the idea of a fall from favor in later
years: *igitur incolumi Maecenate proximus, mox praecipuus . . . aetate*
provecta speciem magis in amicitia principis quam vim tenuit. idque et
Maecenati acciderat, fato potentiae raro sempiternae, an satias capit aut
illos, cum omnia tribuerunt, aut hos, cum iam nihil reliquum est quod
cupiant. "Consequently, as long as Maecenas was alive, he [Sallustius]
took second place, thereafter first . . . , though in his later years he had
the appearance, rather than the reality, of influence in the friendship of
the emperor. And the same fate had befallen Maecenas, either because
real influence is seldom long lasting, or because either the one party
becomes satiated after they have given everything, or the other after
there is nothing left for them to desire." Here the anecdote about Maecenas was convenient because it gave ground for philosophical reflections, which climax in a cleverly cynical *sententia* on the nature of relations with the powerful. Yet, in the previous sentence, Tacitus implicitly
denied any decline in Maecenas' power when he asserted that Sallustius
achieved influence only after Maecenas was gone: he could take first
place with Augustus only after Maecenas' death in 8 B.C.

Tacitus used the combined anecdotes about Agrippa and Maecenas
again when he composed a speech for Seneca to deliver to Nero in A.D.
63, in which Seneca pleaded to be allowed to retire (*Ann.* 14.53.3):
"Your great-grandfather Augustus allowed to Marcus Agrippa a withdrawal to Mytilene, to Maecenas a retirement in the city itself that was
like one abroad." Nero takes the point up in his reply (55.1–3): "My
great-grandfather Augustus permitted Agrippa and Maecenas to enjoy
retirement after their labors, but at an age when his authority could
protect everything of whatever kind that he had given them; and moreover he stripped neither of them of the rewards he had conferred on

them. In the dangers of war they had earned them; for it was in such circumstances that the youth of Augustus was spent." It is clear that here the anecdotes are being used—and misused—as *exempla* after the rhetorical practice of the time. A case is to be made: historical proof is not being offered; the anecdotes are shaped to serve their special purpose in the argument.

There is, on the other hand, much evidence that friendship continued as close as ever between Maecenas and Augustus after 23 B.C. There is the fact that Augustus dedicated his *Memoirs* to Maecenas and Agrippa; but since the publication of the work cannot be dated precisely (though a date subsequent to 23 B.C. seems certain),[8] this cannot be pressed. Then there is a fine anecdote recounted by the elder Seneca that must be dated to about 17 B.C.[9] Porcius Latro, in the course of a declamation delivered before an audience that included Augustus, Agrippa, and Maecenas, among others, touched on the topic of adoption and spoke of someone thereby "being raised up from the dregs and insinuated into the nobility." It happened to be the time when Augustus was actively planning to adopt Gaius and Lucius, the sons of Agrippa by Augustus' daughter Julia. On hearing this line of argument, Maecenas gave Latro a sign to finish his declamation as soon as possible since Caesar was in a hurry. Seneca is here illustrating the enviable freedom of speech of the time by showing how witticisms could be made openly at the expense of prominent men like Agrippa; Maecenas is tactfully acting in the interest of Augustus.

Again, Cassius Dio (54.30.4), under the year 12 B.C., records this: "On one occasion, when a case of adultery was being tried in court, and Appuleius and Maecenas were being vilified, not because they had committed any misconduct themselves, but because they were giving strong support to the defendant, Augustus entered the courtroom and seated himself in the praetor's chair. He did nothing to upset the procedure, but forbade the accuser to insult either his relatives or his friends, and then stood up and left the room." Even if the date of 12 B.C. may be mistrusted (since Cassius Dio is not always reliable in recounting events under a particular year), the trial obviously postdates the *Leges Juliae* of 18 B.C.

Further, Cassius Dio (55.7) gives a lengthy and elaborate account of

8. See Z. Yavetz, "The *Res Gestae* and Augustus' Public Image," in F. Millar and E. Segal, eds., *Caesar Augustus: Seven Aspects* (Oxford 1984) 1–4.
   9. *Controv.* 2.4.12–13.

Augustus' distress at the death of Maecenas in 8 B.C. and recounts examples of the great influence Maecenas had on Augustus. He adds that Maecenas made Augustus his sole heir in his will.

Finally, there is the younger Seneca's assertion (*Ben.* 6.32.4) that Augustus regretted his angry reaction to Julia's adulteries in 2 B.C. and lamented that if only Agrippa and Maecenas had been alive, the tragedy would not have happened. Seneca then sarcastically comments, "We have no reason to think that Agrippa and Maecenas normally told him the truth, and, had they lived, they would have been among those claiming to know nothing." Here one should feel as much doubt about the accuracy of Seneca's cynicism as about the genuineness of Augustus' regret at his own action (he was, after all, to repeat the performance within a decade). What does emerge from the anecdote is the continued importance of both men to Augustus long after their deaths.

The evidence suggesting that Maecenas' relationship with Augustus continued unchanged through 23 B.C. and on to 8 B.C. is far more circumstantial than evidence for a fall from favor. This reexamination and revision have been necessary because in 1968 I fully accepted Syme's analysis of the events of 23 B.C. and went on to fit another series of facts into that perspective.[10] It is a remarkable fact that, whereas until 19 B.C. every work of Horace was dedicated to Maecenas and within each work many individual poems were addressed to him, after the publication of *Epistles* 1 Maecenas is only mentioned once and in the third person (*Odes* 4.11). This oddity needs to be aligned with some other pieces of evidence. First, Horace was commanded by Augustus to compose the *Carmen Saeculare,* the performance of which by a choir was to be an important element in the celebration of *ludi saeculares* in 17 B.C. Second, Suetonius in his *Vita Horati* says: "Augustus so approved his writings and considered them likely to live for all time that he not only commanded him to compose the *Carmen Saeculare,* but also odes on the victory over the Vindelici won by Tiberius and Drusus, and he then got him to add, after a long interval, a fourth to his three books of *Odes.*" Third, Suetonius also says: "After reading certain epistles of his, [Augustus] complained that no mention was made of himself, thus: 'Please understand that I am angry with you because, amid very many compositions of this sort, you do not address yourself to me particularly. Are you afraid that the appearance of being on familiar terms with me will bring down infamy on you with posterity?' And so he extorted the spe-

10. G. Williams, *Tradition and Originality in Roman Poetry* (Oxford 1968) 87–88.

cial composition whose beginning is *cum tot sustineas.*" That is, Augustus had been reading *Epistles* 1 and perhaps knew also of *Epistles* 2.2 and 3 (*Ars poetica*), and requested that such poetry also be addressed to himself. Horace responded with *Epistles* 2.1, and consequently that poem effectively dedicates *Epistles* 2 to Augustus. To these facts about Horace must be added the totally changed nature of Propertius' fourth book of elegies, where Maecenas has disappeared and the poet composes poems that are patriotic and supportive of Augustus' political ideology.

In 1968 I explained this complex of evidence with the hypothesis that after 19 B.C. Augustus dispensed with Maecenas as patron of writers and took over patronage of literature himself, actually requesting—or rather demanding—poems on specific topics.[11] This change, therefore, was to be viewed as a further stage in Maecenas' fall from favor. But since Syme's analysis of the effect of 23 B.C. on relations between Maecenas and Augustus must be abandoned, this hypothesis must also be discarded, in this form, at any rate—greatly to the benefit of understanding the nature of literary patronage in this period.

Here we need to return to the early activity of Maecenas as patron of writers, and take Horace as the paradigm, since he has left what purports to be a detailed account of how he came to be a friend of Maecenas. In *Satires* 1.6, addressed to Maecenas, the context is the envy that people feel toward Horace for his intimacy with the great man (52–62):

> felicem dicere non hoc
> me possim, casu quod te sortitus amicum;
> nulla etenim mihi te fors obtulit: optimus olim
> Vergilius, post hunc Varius, dixere quid essem.
> ut veni coram, singultim pauca locutus,
> infans namque pudor prohibebat plura profari,
> non ego me claro natum patre, non ego circum
> me Satureiano vectari rura caballo,
> sed quod eram narro. respondes, ut tuus est mos,
> pauca. abeo. et revocas nono post mense iubesque
> esse in amicorum numero.

"I could not say that I am lucky because I happened to acquire you as my friend; for it was no chance that brought me to your attention. My very dear friend Virgil, and then Varius, told you all about me. When I came into your presence, gulping out a few scattered words (for bashfulness robbed me of speech and prevented my saying more), I did not tell you that I was born of a

---

11. Repeated in G. Williams, *Change and Decline: Roman Literature in the Early Empire* (Berkeley and Los Angeles 1978) 57–58.

distinguished father, nor that I rode around my country estates on a Tarentine nag, but I told you simply what I was. You answered, as is your way, very briefly. I left. Nine months later you invited me back and ordered me to be numbered among your friends."

The features of Roman patronage all appear here. It was in general a relationship between an inferior and a superior. Horace could not take the initiative; Virgil and Varius, who were already in the circle of Maecenas, had to introduce him. Maecenas is totally in charge of the very formal interview, and the poet finds himself nervous and tongue-tied. Maecenas makes no immediate decision. There is a delay of nine months, and then the poet is "ordered" to join the number of Maecenas' friends. The verb *iubere* is not chosen at random; other verbs used of the relation between patron and poet are *cogere* and *iniungere*.[12] In a real sense the inferior came within the control of the superior. When Priam accepts Sinon on the Trojan side, he says *noster eris* (*Aen.* 2.149), and phrases like *noster esto* in comedy are straight from the language of Roman patronage.[13] The relationship was coercive. For all that the patron felt obligations toward his client and never referred to him as *cliens,* but always as *amicus,* the relationship was founded on a carefully balanced exchange of *beneficia,* and, naturally, a writer had nothing to offer but his writings. Virgil, Horace, and Propertius were citizens of honorable status (they were *equites Romani*), but all three had lost their estates in the civil wars and needed a patron who would enable them to continue their way of life. Virgil, as the opening to *Eclogue* 8 shows, had had C. Asinius Pollio as an earlier patron, and Horace certainly needed the help of a patron to obtain pardon for his part at Philippi and the office of *scriba* (that too may well have been Pollio).[14] But Pollio had little opportunity—and perhaps less inclination—for literary patronage after 40 B.C.; so Maecenas supervened.

It would be naive to attempt to dissociate this move by Maecenas from the general and widespread propaganda war of the thirties between Octavian and Antony. Consequently, there is a totally new element to be recognized here: whereas Pollio and Valerius Messalla and others patronized writers, each for his own personal aggrandizement and interest, Maecenas was exercising his patronage in the political in-

12. See further infra.
13. Ter. *Ad.* 951. In Plautus the phrase is often used comically by an inferior to a superior: *Miles* 899; *Truc.* 207, 953.
14. In that case, Horace rendered thanks in the impressive *Odes* 2.1. But it might have been M. Valerius Messalla Corvinus, to whom *Odes* 3.21 is addressed.

terest of Octavian. Herein lay his special genius, for he did it in such a way as to allow each poet to develop his own particular style and his own personal technique for dealing with political themes. There is a distinct note of independence in each poet and a total avoidance of *adulatio;* each poet expresses a sense of personal value, the possession of a vision not given to ordinary men, an authority that comes from potent sources of inspiration. What Maecenas had to work on was the very fact that the situation of these writers was the direct result of the social and political evils that issued in the civil wars. In this respect, their own interests coincided exactly with those of the state. They needed only to be persuaded that Octavian, and Octavian alone, was capable of saving the state. That was Maecenas' task—though it was not as simple as it now seems; for as late as 32 B.C. three hundred senators left Rome to join Antony (clearly unconvinced that Octavian was a savior).[15] Yet it was as inconceivable that Maecenas should fail in this endeavor as it was that any of these poets should write attacking his views.

That he was acting not in his own interests but in those of Octavian emerges from a striking feature of the poetry of this period. All three poets address Maecenas, dedicate their works to him, and express the utmost admiration for him and gratitude for his interest in them. But always behind Maecenas, never absent, though only most exceptionally addressed, there is the figure of Octavian and later of Augustus. He is always signified and represented as something beyond the ordinary level of humanity, like the mysterious young man of *Eclogue* 1 or the god-to-be or the victorious leader of the *Georgics* or the heroic warrior of *Epodes* 1 and 9 or the god in human disguise of *Odes* 1.2 or the victor whose accomplishments elude the grasp of the puny poet in Propertius 2.1. This is a figuration unique to this period, and it has the special and very important significance that thereby these writers acknowledge a greater than Maecenas, who is at least as relevant to their poetry and to whom, in some sense, their writing is directed. A similar figuration can be seen in a Greek epigram by Antipater of Thessalonica addressed to L. Calpurnius Piso Frugi, cos. 15 B.C. (*Anth.Pal.* 10.25):

Phoebus, harbor watchman of the Cephallonians, dweller on the beach of Panormos opposite rough Ithake, grant that I travel toward Asia through seas fair for sailing, following the long ship of Piso. And make my powerful monarch well disposed to him, well disposed also to my poetry.

15. Dio 50.2.4–6; 20.6; *RG* 25.3; Syme (1939: supra n. 2) 278–79. However, some seven hundred senators were left to support Octavian.

What Antipater is doing here is looking beyond his immediate patron Piso to the greater patron Augustus, who is *ex officio* the patron of Piso. This is all self-serving on the part of the Greek poet in a manner totally alien from that of the three Roman poets, but it serves to suggest a basic feature of Roman patronage. If B was a patron of C, and A was a patron of B (where the prestige of A was greater than B's), then *a fortiori* A was a patron of C. This is nowhere attested specifically in the ancient sources, but it makes good sense, and there are certainly examples attested where on the death of B, A takes over patronage obligations to C.[16] What is involved here is the hypothesis that a superior patron had claims on the resources (including *amici* and *clientes*) of an inferior patron. This is clearly inherent—even if not explicitly attested—in the nature of Roman patronage. The basic principle can be illustrated in a remark of Velleius Paterculus on Agrippa (2.79.1): *parendi sed uni scientissimus, aliis sane imperandi cupidus* ("most skilled in obedience—but to the one single individual; eager assuredly to command everyone else"). It can also be seen clearly in a letter from Augustus to Maecenas, quoted by Suetonius in his *Vita Horati*. Augustus had requested Maecenas to arrange that Horace should become his secretary, and he explains: *veniet ergo ab ista parasitica mensa ad hanc regiam et nos in epistulis scribendis adiuvabit* ("He will consequently be promoted from that parasite's table of yours to this patron's table of mine, and he will assist me in writing letters"). That is, since Augustus is Maecenas' patron, Maecenas is a parasite. This is, as Eduard Fraenkel anxiously insisted,[17] a joke (on the terms *rex* and *parasitus* as used in Roman comedy); but, as is customary with the jokes of the powerful, it is a joke that is itself an exercise of that power. It cleverly reproduces the reality of the relationship between Augustus and Maecenas, and shows Augustus poised to exercise a superior patron's right over Horace. In fact, Horace got out of this burdensome honor, and that must have been tactfully negotiated by a Maecenas who convinced Augustus that Horace had more important services to render him than secretarial.

This situation can be contrasted with that of Tibullus, who had no access to Augustus; or—to put it differently—M. Valerius Messalla

16. The evidence needs more discussion than is possible here. But the pattern of moving to a more important patron is clearly envisaged in Antipater's poem to Piso (supra), or by Ennius going from Cato to M. Fulvius Nobilior. Suetonius (who had an eye for such movements) notes Aurelius Opillus, "the freedman of some Epicurean," transferring to Rutilius Rufus (*Gram.* 6); and—a very interesting case—C. Melissus, born free but exposed as an infant and then given as a gift to Maecenas, preferred his servile status (though his mother claimed him as freeborn), but, soon manumitted, *Augusto etiam insinuatus est* (*Gram.* 21).

17. E. Fraenkel, *Horace* (Oxford 1957) 18.

Corvinus was not acting for Augustus in his patronage of writers—
though it looks as if, after 2 B.C., the situation changed, and Augustus
could then exert pressure on Ovid (perhaps through Messalla, perhaps
directly). Consequently Tibullus does not look past Messalla to Augustus.

The new hypothesis that is required, therefore, is this: the literary
patronage exercised by Maecenas was unique in that it was exercised
for the political benefit of Augustus, and, from the very beginning, it
envisaged that when the right time came, Augustus would take it over,
and Maecenas would fade into the background. The arrangement
proved useful. In the thirties Octavian was probably too occupied with
his own precarious situation to be able to devote the long hours needed
to cultivate writers and inspire them with hopes for a better future; and,
in any case, the task clearly suited the life-style of Maecenas and evoked
from him a rare talent for that delicate work. During the twenties the
new regime was trying to establish itself against opposition, and the
rhetoric of indirection that all three writers in different ways constructed served to focus attention on the seriousness of the political
problems rather than on personalities, and the strategy of address to
Maecenas avoided the inanities of premature celebration and panegyric.

But by 18 B.C. the scene had changed.[18] Augustus had become de
facto ruler of the state, his power was precisely guaranteed by constitutional safeguards, and he was actively planning to make his position
heritable by a designated successor. Spain was pacified, and the Parthians had returned the legionary standards disgracefully lost to them in
53 B.C. Above all, the moral legislation, blocked by opposition in 28
B.C.,[19] was passed in all its unprecedented complexity, on Augustus'
own authority in 18 B.C. The time for explicit acknowledgment of his
supremacy and for celebration of his achievements had come. The Roman state had been put on a new basis, and the possibility of civil war
had been eliminated. These extraordinary achievements called for identification of Augustus as the sole benefactor, and even for direct address
to him by a poet of eternal fame to replace the indirection of address to
Maecenas. Given such a list of concrete accomplishments, no Roman
poet could give the impression of relapsing into Hellenic sycophancy,
and so lay the majesty of the *princeps* open to mockery; that had been

18. On 18 B.C. as the point of change, see E. Badian, "'Crisis Theories' and the Beginning of the Principate," in G. Wirth, ed., *Romanitas-Christianitas: Untersuchungen zur
Geschichte und Literatur der römischen Kaiserzeit, Johannes Straub zum 70. Geburtstag
gewidmet* (Berlin and New York 1982) 18–41, esp. 37–38.
19. Denied by E. Badian, "A Phantom Marriage Law," *Philologus* 129 (1985) 82–98;
his argument needs (and will receive) a reply.

the danger earlier. Augustus himself celebrated his *res gestae* in a style marked by lapidary brevity and virile absence of emotion and ornament. Horace now invented a new rhetorical technique, suitable to the celebration of solid Roman achievement—the poetic list, free of flowery circumlocution, but hospitable to the stark realism of prosaic legal language. It was a perfect lyric responsion to the style used by Augustus.

There is no reason to deny the likelihood that it was the astute Maecenas himself who advised Augustus the right time had come in 18 B.C. to take over literary patronage and who gave the two surviving poets the instruction to desist from addressing him in their work. (It would be typical of Horace to honor the letter of that instruction, but breach its spirit by the affectionate celebration of his friend's birthday—properly confined to the third person—in the center of *Odes* 4.11.) Maecenas was, after all, the one person who had devised the new system whereby writers could be organized to give powerful literary support, not, as hitherto, to an individual through panegyric, but to a political program through discussion of issues. That program, of course, was recognized to be in the control of, and dependent on, a single individual. Maecenas had an agenda that can be discerned at least in general terms: it was to focus on the program until the new political system had been safely established and to shift the focus onto the great leader only after the program could be regarded as enacted. Such is the consequence of the hypothesis put forward in this essay: Maecenas shaped the traditional Roman institution of patronage into a new form so that literature could be pressed into service to what could be recognized, when it was successfully implemented, as a national political program, not the self-serving ambition of an individual. It was only when the moment of success had arrived that a change was then needed to channel national pride in the achievement and its great author into the effort to maintain it.

That change was great, and even Maecenas may not have foreseen its full consequences and dangers. There is no direct evidence for how the system worked under Maecenas, but it is highly implausible to suppose that, for instance, in 25 B.C. Horace suddenly felt inspired by the marriage of Julia and Marcellus to write the great "Pindaric" ode 1.12. Although there is nothing of the epithalamium about it, that ode may be regarded as written in celebration of that marriage. A precedent was provided by *Eclogue* 4, which was written to celebrate, in some sense, a marriage, but a marriage whose political implications were what mattered. The marriage of Julia and Marcellus was certainly of that nature, and Maecenas must be envisaged as having requested—or suggested in the right way—an ode for the occasion. He would have explained the political significance of the event, but it would have been left to Horace's genius to devise the technique of indirection whereby the idea that Augustus must have a successor, with the proper training and character and political ideals, could be accommodated within a view of Roman history to which, otherwise, the idea would be utterly repugnant. Virgil and Propertius cope with the same problem from a different perspective in their lamentations on Marcellus' death in 23 B.C.: the man had achieved nothing, but had been destined to achieve so much. This general pattern of imperative suggestion on the part of Maecenas should be seen as the main generative force in the production of political poems in the thirties and twenties. The poet was then free to exercise his genius within the constrictions of his chosen genre. There is good evidence to support this picture, for Augustus is clearly seen in Suetonius' account in the *Vita Horati* to be requesting poems on specific topics, and it is obvious that, in the case of the *Carmen saeculare,* not only was Horace given an account of the form the ceremonies would take, but he was also instructed as to the particular achievements of Augustus that were to be emphasized in the hymn.

Augustus took over from Maecenas; there is no reason to suppose that he made deliberate changes in the procedure, and so his activity can in general be used as evidence for Maecenas'. But there were important changes that he simply could not avoid causing. One derived from his being who he was. He was not only Maecenas' superior, he was every Roman's superior. Consequently, a request for a poem from Augustus had the force of a command that could not be refused. Suetonius used the verbs *cogere, iniungere,* and *exprimere* of Augustus' requests, and Horace himself, in the very epistle in which he acceded to Augustus' complaint, used the verb *cogere* to express writers' hopes for commands from Augustus (*Epist.* 2.1.226–28):

> cum speramus eo rem venturam ut, simul atque
> carmina rescieris nos fingere, commodus ultro
> arcessas et egere vetes et scribere cogas.

"When we hope things will come to the point that, as soon as you find out that we are composing poetry, you obligingly of your own accord summon us and order us to cease being in need and compel us to write."

Eduard Fraenkel anxiously explained that Suetonius was seeing things from the perspective of post-Domitianic Rome and that the verbs must not be understood literally.[20] But that well-intentioned explanation should not be accepted. Suetonius recognized the reality of power, and Horace, however jokingly, has the same point of view: if Augustus requests, there is no possibility of refusal. The verb *cogere* signifies the application of superior power, and other verbs used of the same activity have a similar force. Patronage constituted a power relationship, and Romans were conditioned from birth to accommodating themselves to it. An important element in this accommodation was disguise of the naked reality in various conventional ways. The most visible was that the great man carefully treated—and addressed—his *clientes* as *amici*. This was what Augustus was doing when he wrote to Horace: "Please understand that I am angry with you, because, amid very many compositions of this sort, you do not address yourself to me particularly. Are you afraid that the appearance of being on familiar terms with me will bring you infamy with posterity?" Augustus means that in inviting Horace to address poetic epistles to him he is thereby admitting the poet to the circle of his *amici,* and, of course, that would add greatly to Horace's distinction (even with posterity). So Augustus is again joking; the joke is that, as Augustus sees it, the opposite is true: Horace could not conceivably think that the friendship of Augustus would earn him infamy with posterity. The question is *a fortiori* ironic, but again the joke by the powerful man is an exercise of his power. Friendship was, of course, possible between Horace and Augustus, but it was an even more unbalanced relationship than friendship with Maecenas. That is shown by a significant fact. Horace constantly represents his friendship with Maecenas in poetic forms that depend on a social occasion, like, for instance, the invitation to a drinking party or the actual representation of himself and Maecenas drinking together, with the poet in charge and giving advice. Such intimacy was out of the question in addressing the *princeps*.

   Another poetic form that fell victim to the change in the nature of the relationship was the *recusatio*. Augustan poets (with Virgil leading the way) had cleverly reshaped Callimachus' refusal to write large-scale epic into a type of poem in which the poet could modestly assert that his talent was unfortunately too minor to give adequate treatment to political themes such as the great achievements of Augustus, while, in fact, doing exactly that in an indirect way. But any suggestion even of a

---

20. Fraenkel (supra n. 17) 364, 383. But, in saying this, Fraenkel forgot that Horace himself uses the verbs *cogere* and *iubere* of the process.

conventional poetic refusal was inappropriate to the head of state; his every request was a command, not to be turned aside by a rhetorical strategy that was perfectly appropriate when Maecenas was in the foreground and Augustus a grand figure barely glimpsed in the background. The closest Horace comes to the old form is *Odes* 4.2, where the absence of Augustus with the army allows the poet to insinuate that the suggestion of an ode on Augustus' triumphant return had been made by Iullus Antonius, and the poet deflects that suggestion back onto the maker in a grand and elaborate ode that superbly executes what he alleges his addressee could do better.

Odes 4.15 is always treated as a traditional *recusatio*, but this interpretation needs to be questioned. The poem opens (1–16):

> Phoebus volentem proelia me loqui
> victas et urbis increpuit lyra,
>   ne parva Tyrrhenum per aequor
>   vela darem. tua, Caesar, aetas
>
> fruges et agris rettulit uberes,
> et signa nostro restituit Iovi
>   derepta Parthorum superbis
>   postibus et vacuum duellis
>
> Ianum Quirini clausit et ordinem
> rectum evaganti frena licentiae
>   iniecit emovitque culpas
>   et veteres revocavit artis,
>
> per quas Latinum nomen et Italae
> crevere vires, famaque et imperi
>   porrecta maiestas ad ortus
>   solis ab Hesperio cubili.

Phoebus, when I wanted to speak of battles and of the conquest of cities, warned me with his lyre not to set my tiny sails across the Tyrrhenian sea. Your age, Caesar, has both restored bountiful crops to our fields and returned to our Jupiter our standards torn from the arrogant pillars of the Parthians and closed Quirinal Janus freed from warfare and clapped reins on licentiousness that strays beyond proper bounds and expelled crime and reintroduced the ancient skills by which the Latin state and the strength of Italy grew great and the fame and majesty of our empire was extended from the sun's bed in the West to his Eastern rising.

If this is a *recusatio*, from what is the poet excusing himself? Perhaps from martial epic poetry? But obviously the age of Augustus, marked by universal peace, has now made that kind of poetry irrelevant. When did Phoebus warn the poet? If this were a normal *recusatio*, the warning would have come when the poet tried to write a different poem from *Odes* 4.15. But the only different poem suggested is an epic on war, and that would have been ridiculously inappropriate. The warning of Phoebus here is more like a primal command, the basic inspiration and sense of his own talent that made Horace a lyric, rather than an epic, poet. So the *recusatio* here does not explain or excuse the present poem; instead it establishes Horace as essentially a lyric poet, and the rest of the ode praises the achievements that have made the present age the perfect setting (as well as the perfect subject) for such a lyric poet, since Augustus has abolished war and crime and anything that could disturb peace. All that remains to do is to celebrate without cease a great past brought to life again in the present (25–32). I have suggested that this ode was written to celebrate the dedication of the Ara Pacis in 9 B.C.[21] If so, it is one of Horace's latest odes, and it makes a statement about his own poetry that corresponds—with changes appropriate to the new situation—to *Odes* 3.30. Horace's kind of poetry has at last found its place and justification, not (as with *Odes* 3.30) in the achievement of personal fame, but within, and totally dependent on, the new political order. And that recalls another striking change: in *Odes* 1–3 (and going back, indeed, to the *Epodes*) Horace's political poetry was dependent on his own peculiar status as *vates,* as someone with a vision of his own society that was inspired and who was consequently in a position to speak with authority. His poetic achievement in consequence brought him eternal fame (*Odes* 3.30). There is nothing of that in *Odes* 4. He is indeed famous and grateful to his sources of inspiration (*Odes* 4.3 and 6), but there is not a word about his possession of a special status; his poetry has acquired a new capacity—to confer immortality on others (*Odes* 4.8 and 9).

One other supposed *recusatio* needs notice: that is Propertius 4.1. The first half of that programmatic poem is taken up with the poet's declaration that he will compose a new patriotic poetry to celebrate the greatness of Rome; the second half has an Egyptian astrologer called Horus presenting his credentials as an accurate prophet and asserting that the poet will never be able to shake himself free from the domination of Cynthia as a subject for poetry—nor should he. This strategy does indeed serve to explain—and justify—the inclusion of three poems about Cynthia among all the patriotic poems. But this is a total reversal

---

21. G. Williams, *Horace,* Greece and Rome: New Surveys in the Classics 6 (Oxford 1972) 47–48.

of earlier procedure. In Books 1–3 Propertius created his own special adaptation of the Callimachean *recusatio*. It took the form of asserting that unfortunately he could not deal adequately with political topics since his whole attention was riveted exclusively on Cynthia; later he would rise to the praise of Augustus' achievements, but for now his lifestyle and his poetry precluded that. Propertius 4.1 reverses that and, instead of excusing his inability to write anything but love poetry, apologizes for incorporating some love poems among the serious ideological poems. But, as appears from 4.7, Cynthia is now dead and the poet can only reminisce about the past; this consequently marks the end of his love poetry in the only way that could falsify Horus' prediction. It is to be noted that the addressee is not someone of the stature of Maecenas, still less of Augustus; it is a disreputable foreign astrologer who prescribes a continuation of the poet's disgraceful type of writing—though fortunately he is shown, in the sequel, to be wrong. The idea cannot be dismissed that this was Propertius' way of asserting a modest degree of freedom for himself and a consistency with his own past at the same time as he acknowledged that the moral legislation of 18 B.C. precluded such adulterous poetry. Defiance is put in the mouth of the disreputable Horus. But in his own voice, though he does not address him directly, the poet assures Augustus that his own desire is for a poetry of patriotic celebration. This is a deft strategy for dealing with the type of pressure that Augustus could exert on a poet, after he took over from Maecenas. Horace can be seen doing something of the same sort in *Odes* 4.1 when he directs Venus away from himself to Paullus Fabius Maximus, yet discovers to his own discomfiture that his bravado was false, and is in tears over the recalcitrance of Ligurinus. The poem is programmatic, as is Propertius', and the center of *Odes* 4 is occupied by four poems (10–13) that hark back to the more frivolous and private aspect of *Odes* 1–3. Both poets are coping with the same change in their situation.

What was the importance of the change to Augustus? The whole question of the value of literary support needs more examination than is possible here. But the thesis put forward in this essay is that a new type of literary patronage was planned from the start, to be initiated by Maecenas and then taken over by Augustus when the time was right. The aim was not to immortalize Maecenas or even Augustus, but to support a political program. It was expedient in the early years of struggle for Augustus to remain in the background. To have allowed himself to become more conspicuous and to draw attention to the reality of his power (rather than to the plight of the state and the necessary remedies) would have been to repeat the arrogant errors of Julius Caesar. This caution can be seen in Augustus' reluctance to accept general honors, such as the title of *pater patriae*. That title was hinted at in an ode of Horace that belongs to about 28 B.C. (*Odes* 1.2.50 *hic ames dici pater atque princeps*); it takes another form on coins of 19–16 B.C.;[22] it was offered by a plebeian delegation at Antium, and again in the theater (dates unknown; Suet. *Aug. 58*); and it was conferred formally only in 2 B.C. The same motivation lies behind the poets' indirect address of Augustus through Maecenas. It was only when Augustus' power was assured and accepted and the program was established that the uniqueness of the man and the solid political achievements represented by the program could be celebrated, and that celebration was not so much to immortalize the individual as to immortalize the program and ensure that it became the permanent form of the Roman polity. That was the unstated purpose of the widespread promulgation of the *Res Gestae:* any successor as well as succeeding generations were to be made to feel obliged to maintain Augustus' achievements. That idea lay behind Augustus' restoration of the statues of great army commanders and his dedication of statues of *triumphatores* in both porticoes of his own forum. The edict stated the purpose (Suet. *Aug. 31.5*): *commentum id se ut ad illorum 〈vitam〉 velut ad exemplar et ipse, dum viveret, et insequentium aetatium principes exigerentur a civibus.* "He had designed this so that the citizens could measure both him himself, as long as he lived, and the great men of following ages by the life of these men [of the past] as by a template." The same motive lay behind the emphasis he laid on educational reform, which is echoed in Horace's addressing his poetry to the next generation: Augustus' successors must be educated in the necessity to conserve what he had achieved, without change. The *Res Gestae* established the record for all to see. Augustus expressed the same motive in an undated edict (not earlier than 17 B.C.) reported by Suetonius (*Aug. 28.2*): "May I be permitted to establish the state safe and sound on its own foundation, and therefrom reap the reward I want—to be named as the author of the best constitution and, dying, to take with me the expectation that the foundations of the state laid down by me will stay fixed firmly in their place." Then Suetonius comments: "And it was he who achieved his own wish for himself by making every effort that no one should regret the new constitution."

22. *SPQR parenti conservatori suo* (see Nisbet and Hubbard [supra n. 7] on Horace *Odes* 1.2.50).

The danger always was that literary support could degenerate into mere panegyric; and, since panegyric is easily reversible by the malicious, could then actually injure the man and his program. It is instructive to compare *Odes* 3.14 and 4.5. Both poems celebrate a victorious return of Augustus to Rome. Neither should be taken to be composed at the sudden onset of grateful inspiration in the poet; the earlier should be regarded as suggested by Maecenas in 24 B.C., the later requested by Augustus in 13 B.C. The earlier poem swerves unexpectedly, after a central transitional stanza, into a private celebration by the poet, with erotic overtones and deftly managed political undertones.[23] It is a fine example of the earlier strategy of indirection. The later poem is on a far grander scale, and it contains a large-scale example of the new technique of celebrating Augustus' achievements by itemized factual listing (17–28); but the strategy throughout is for the poet to address Augustus not in his own voice and on his own behalf, but as a spokesman for the people of Italy as a whole; and when he deviates into private celebration at the end, it is not on his own account, but as one of innumerable loyal citizens, all content with the new Rome. In that way panegyric was deftly avoided. It was only with Ovid, and as Augustus became more autocratic in the assertion and use of his powers, and as he moved toward becoming censor instead of patron, that panegyric became the only possible literary response to pressure from the emperor.

23. Fraenkel (supra n. 17) 290.

The City Adorned:
Programmatic Display
at the *Aedes Concordiae Augustae*

Integral to the transformation of the Roman state in the Augustan period was the transformation of the city of Rome itself. In clothing the
city in marble,[1] Augustus and his program designers did more than
simply beautify the environment. Through the display of statues, paintings, and natural wonders in each structure, they created a system of
meaning that represented continuity and difference. This was no transparent system of propaganda; it was a complex system of familiar signs
that were manipulated for specific purposes. The protean nature of this
living mythology of the *princeps* can best be observed through the analysis of one of the last buildings to be completed during Augustus' reign
and one of key importance to the system as a whole—the *aedes Concordiae Augustae*. The temple was dedicated on 16 January A.D. 10 by Tiberius, the heir apparent, in his own name and that of his dead brother,
Drusus.[2] Located on the slopes of the Capitoline, overlooking the
Forum Romanum, the temple served as a dramatic centerpiece in the
Augustan orchestration of the city (figs. 1, 2).

1. Suet. *Aug.* 28.3.
2. Ov. *Fast.* 1.640, 643–48; Dio 56.25. See J. Gagé, ed., *Res Gestae* (Paris 1977) 164–
65.

The very site was, of course, significant. It was where Camillus had purportedly vowed the first Temple of Concord in 367 B.C. during the patrician-plebeian struggles over the Licinian-Sextian rogations (Ov. *Fast.* 1.641–44; Plut. *Cam.* 42). Restored by L. Opimius after the death of Gaius Gracchus (App. *BCiv.* 1.26; Plut. *C. Gracch.* 17), the building had remained, for better or worse during the Republic, a symbol of the ever vulnerable *concordia ordinum*. It had been here that Cicero had gathered the senate to try the Catilinarian conspirators (Cic. *Cat.* 3.21; Sall. *Cat.* 9.2), here that the verbal warfare between Antony and Cicero had been waged (Cic. *Phil.* 3.31, 5.20).[3]

It was this site, with its multiple associations, that Tiberius was to transform into a temple of Concordia with a decisive difference—it was to be a *templum Concordiae Augustae,* a Concordia "at once the deity and the work of the pacific chief" (i.e., Augustus).[4] The location bespoke continuity, but, at the same time, the architectural realization of the temple asserted difference. It was only in the Augustan period that the building assumed its distinctive shape, with a façade longer than it was wide (45 × 24 m), taking full advantage of the narrow site it occupied.[5] Moreover, it was embellished with the full coloristic vocabulary of Augustan buildings: the walls and floors were veneered with pavonazzetto, giallo antico, cipollino, and africano.[6] The architectural decoration was boldly undercut and closely related to that in the Temple of Castor in the Forum Romanum below, which had been refurbished by Tiberius in A.D. 6 and dedicated in his name and that of his dead brother, Drusus.[7] This again linked the two buildings, for the Temple of Concordia Augusta was also inscribed with the names of Tiberius and Drusus[8]—truly the *concordia sidera* themselves (*Consolatio ad Liviam* 283).

Even the dedication of the temple was an assertion of continuity and difference. To a certain extent, *concordia* had always had a familial as well as a political aspect. In 35 B.C., for example, the young Octavian

3. H. F. Rebert and H. Marceau, "The Temple of Concord in the Roman Forum," *MAAR* 5 (1925) 53–55; A. Momigliano, "Camillus and Concord," *CQ* 36 (1942) 111–20; B. Levick, "Concordia at Rome," in R. A. C. Carson and C. M. Kraay, eds., *Scripta Nummaria Romana: Essays Presented to Humphrey Sutherland* (London 1978) 217–24.

4. Ov. *Fast.* 2.631 (all translations are from the Loeb Classical Library); J. C. Richard, "Pax, Concordia et la religion officielle de Janus à la fin de la république romaine," *MEFRA* 75 (1963) 303–86.

5. C. Gasparri, *Aedes Concordiae Augustae* (Rome 1979) 62–72; F. Coarelli, *Roma³,* Guide archeologiche Laterza (Rome 1983) 63.

6. Rebert and Marceau (supra n. 3) 75.

7. Suet. *Tib.* 20; Dio 55.27.4; Ov. *Fast.* 1.707–8.

8. Ov. *Fast.* 1.640, 643–48; Dio 56.25.

had deftly pointed to Antony and Cleopatra as the source of discord in
the state by ostensibly honoring Antony with statues in the Temple of
Concord and by extending to him the right to banquet in that same
temple with his wife and children (Dio 49.18.6)—that is, of course,
with his legal Roman wife, Octavia, whom he had left to join Cleopatra
in 37 B.C. In the Augustan era, however, the concord of the state and the
concord of the imperial family became one and the same. From the beginning, the Augustan refurbishment of the Temple of Concord was a
family affair. The Temple of Concordia Augusta was vowed by Tiberius
on 1 January 7 B.C. in the Curia of Octavia (Dio 55.8.1–2). The Curia
of Octavia was outside the *pomerium* and was appropriate since Tiberius was about to celebrate a triumph over the Germans, but it was also
conveniently located in the Porticus of Octavia, which surrounded the
Temples of Jupiter Stator and Juno Regina and was filled with a panoply
of monuments celebrating Octavia, sister of the *princeps,* mother, and
loyal Roman wife. On the same day, Tiberius and his mother, Livia,
dedicated the Porticus of Livia, which contained its own shrine to Concord presented by Livia to her dear husband, Augustus (Ov. *Fast.*
6.637f.; cf. 1.649). Finally, well after Tiberius' adoption by the *princeps,* the *aedes Concordiae Augustae* was dedicated in A.D. 10 on 16
January, the anniversary of Augustus' assumption of his cognomen.[9]
This was no coincidence. Since at least 11 B.C., when Augustus had ordered that the money contributed by the senate and people for statues
of him be used instead to set up statues of Salus Publica, Concordia, and
Pax,[10] Augustus' name and theirs had been virtually synonymous.

I. *Program of Sculpture and Painting*

The harmony of the imperial family implied in the vowing and dedicat-
ing of the Temple of Concordia Augusta was also reflected in the program of objects on display. Tiberius, as dedicator, provided a statue of
Vesta from Paros;[11] bronzes of Apollo and Juno by Baton; of Latona
and her infants, Apollo and Diana, by Euphranor; of Asclepius and
Hygieia by Niceratus; of Mars and Mercury by Piston; and of Ceres,
Jupiter, and Minerva by Sthennis;[12] as well as a painting of Marsyas

9. Ov. *Fast.* 1.640, 643–48; Dio 56.25. See Gagé (supra n. 2) 164–65.
10. Dio 54.35.1–2; Ov. *Fast.* 3.881–82.
11. Dio 55.9.6.
12. Pliny *HN* 34.73, 77, 80, 89, 90; G. Becatti, "Opera d'arte greca nella Roma di
Tiberio," *ArchCl* 25–26 (1973–1974) 18–53, on the basic stylistic unity of these bronzes
by Greek masters of the fourth and third centuries B.C. in relation to Tiberius' own reputed
taste (cf. Pliny *HN* 34.62).

bound by Zeuxis; of Liber Pater by Augustus' favorite painter, Nicias; and of Cassandra by Theoros.[13] Augustus himself dedicated four obsidian elephants *pro miraculo* (Pliny *HN* 36.196), and Livia presented for the gem collection housed in the temple a famous sardonyx that had once belonged to Polycrates, tyrant of Samos, now set in a golden horn (Pliny *HN* 37.4) and thus transformed into a gift from Fortuna (or Concordia). It is not only the participation of all three imperial family members in the dedication that is significant here. The seemingly disparate objects on display, including the four obsidian elephants, are parts of a harmonious thematic whole.

The sculptures and paintings provided the visual equivalent of Concordia Augusta. This was not just the old republican *concordia ordinum,* but rather a new world order, which, as Manilius was to claim in his *Astronomica,* was reflected in the ordering of the cosmos itself.[14] The four seasons and the four elements were embodied in the gods present,[15] but more important, they typified a Concordia who—like the Greek Harmonia, a daughter of Venus and Mars, of Love and Strife—represented a new balance.[16] This new balance was ruled by the good, by the blessings of Peace, and was inextricably intertwined with Concord like the two snakes that encircled the caduceus of Pax, a bronze example of which was worked into the steps of the temple itself. The gods here are gods of healing and plenty: Asclepius, the son of Apollo, with his daughter Hygieia (the statues by Niceratus may be the inspiration for later imperial family portrait types [fig. 3]);[17] Ceres, the nursling of Pax (Ov. *Fast.* 1.704); and Ceres' sister Vesta (Ov. *Fast.* 6.285–86).[18] On 6 March, the day Augustus became *pontifex maximus,* Ovid refers to Vesta, goddess of hearth and home, "over whose eternal fire the divinity of Caesar, no less eternal doth preside" (*Fast.* 3.421–22).

---

13. Pliny *HN* 35.66, 131, 144.

14. Manil. *Astron.* 1.7–10, 247–57; 2.60–83; 3.48–55.

15. Seasons: spring (Aries; Minerva rules Aries; Manil. *Astron.* 2.445), summer (Gemini; Apollo rules Gemini; Manil. *Astron.* 2.440), autumn (Virgo; Ceres rules Virgo; Manil. *Astron.* 2.442), winter (Sagittarius; Diana rules Sagittarius; Manil. *Astron.* 2.444). Elements: earth (Ceres), air (Mercury), fire (Mars), water (Juno; Juno rules Aquarius; Manil. *Astron.* 2.446).

16. L. Spitzer, "Classical and Christian Ideas of World Harmony: Prolegomena to an Interpretation of the Word 'Stimmung,' " Part 1, *Traditio* 2 (1944) 415–23.

17. Ny Carlsberg Glyptotek I.N.714 and I.N.1615 found together. See V. Poulsen, *Les portraits romains,* vol. 2, Publications de la Glyptothèque Ny Carlsberg no. 8 (Copenhagen 1974) 103–104, nos. 88–89, pls. CXLIV–CXLIX.

18. Augustus had erected an altar to Ceres Mater and Ops Augusta in the *vicus Iugarius* on 10 August A.D. 7 (*CIL* I², pp. 240, 324), probably in honor of Livia (G. Grether, "Livia and the Roman Imperial Cult," *AJP* 67 [1946] 226–27).

Deities long associated with a variety of social factions—the god of the merchants, Mercury,[19] who like Pax carried the caduceus; the gods of the plebeians, Ceres and Liber Pater—were brought together here with the traditional gods of the state. Furthermore, the ensemble represented an absolute accord between the old pantheon of the state and the new. Here Jupiter, Juno, and Minerva were joined by Mars, Mercury, and the new divine triad, Apollo, Diana, and Latona.

Just as the statues of Asclepius and Hygieia by Niceratus were probably paired, so too were the bronzes of Mars and Mercury (fig. 4), the only two works in the Temple of Concord by Piston, the sculptor of the early third century B.C. The two may well have been displayed together and would likely have been recognizable as the work of the same hand, a fact surely underscored by an inscription. The statues are reproduced as they stood in the Temple of Concord on a Hadrianic relief and on two gemstones: Mercury with his caduceus and money bag and a Mars Ultor, the two on the same statue base. Though a pairing of the god of war and the god of commerce may seem inherently antithetical, that was precisely the point. In Augustan Rome, where Mars had become more fatherlike than furious,[20] he and his half brother Mercury could coexist. Though wars were waged in the far-off corners of the empire, the Mediterranean was at peace, and many citizens would likely have joined with the crew of the Alexandrian grain ship that greeted Augustus on one of the last days of his life, "saying that it was through him that they lived, through him that they sailed the seas, and through him that they enjoyed their liberty and their fortunes."[21] The same connection was reinforced by the pairing of Mercury and Mars in the Temple of Concordia Augusta.

The Apollo and Juno by Baton were also probably displayed together. Here was a combination that for any reader of the *Aeneid* would have proclaimed a major reconciliation: Apollo was Aeneas' mainstay, and Juno, throughout most of the epic, was the archnemesis of the Trojans. The *Aeneid* itself, however, revolves around the axes of Concord and Discord,[22] and in Book 12 Juno lays aside her wrath, reestablishes concord with her brother/husband, Jupiter, and paves the way for con-

19. B. C. Farnoux, "Mercure romain, les 'Mercuriales' et l'institution du culte impérial sous le Principat augustéen," *ANRW* 2.17.1 (1981) 458–501.

20. Ov. *Ars am.* 1.203.

21. Suet. *Aug.* 98; cf. Hor. *Carm.* 4.5, 4.15.

22. F. Cairns, "Concord in the *Aeneid* of Virgil," *Klio* 67 (1985) 210–15.

cord among mankind (Virg. *Aen.* 12.820–40). The statuary grouping by Baton in the Temple of Concordia Augusta gave three-dimensional reality to the results of that reconciliation and, in so doing, demonstrated again the benefits of the new order.

Only one god is represented twice in the program of the Temple of Concordia Augusta, Augustus' god Apollo. He appeared as an adult in the Baton grouping and as an infant in the famous grouping by Euphranor. This repetition is not surprising in itself. Apollo, closely identified with Augustus, had long been looked upon as the chief divine agent in the establishment of the new age.[23] As possessor of both the bow and the lyre Apollo typified the balance struck by Concordia Augusta: warlike when necessary, but inherently peace-loving.

The famous paintings displayed in the temple also have Apollo as their common denominator. The first is a painting of Apollo's beloved Cassandra by Theoros (Pliny *HN* 35.144). As Juliette Davreux realized long ago, since no male hero is mentioned by Pliny, the painting that hung in the Temple of Concordia Augusta probably showed Cassandra making the prophecy to her family.[24] Just such a representation, Cassandra stage center and Apollo's tripod visible in the background, is found in several Pompeian wall paintings (fig. 5), and as was often the case with works of art in Augustan Rome, it is also replicated on Arretine ware (fig. 6).[25] Cassandra foretells the fall of Troy, though she is destined not to be believed by her family or anyone else. A linear thematic connection can be drawn here to the other well-known works of Theoros in Rome—a series on the Trojan War displayed in the Augustan Porticus of Philippus (Pliny *HN* 35.144). But in the context of the Temple of Concordia Augusta, a viewer was likely to remember, as Anchises does in *Aeneid* 3.182–87, that Cassandra's prophecy of Troy's doom was balanced by her prediction of the Trojans' new home in Hesperia, the origin of Augustan Rome itself.

The Marsyas Bound by Zeuxis (Pliny *HN* 35.66) strongly implies, if it did not include, an image of the victorious Apollo. In Pompeian wall

23. Hor. *Carm. saec.*, esp. 61–68.

24. J. Davreux, *La légende de la prophétesse Cassandre d'après les textes et les monuments,* Biblio. de la Faculté de Phil. et Lettres de l'Université de Liège 94 (1942) 124, no. 46.

25. The best example: Pompeii, Reg. I, ins. 2, no. 28, now Naples, Museo Nazionale; see P. Hermann, ed., *Denkmäler der Malerei des Altertums* (Munich 1934–1950) 245–46, pl. 179. The Arretine ware fragment, now in the Antiquarium of the Staatliche Museen, Berlin, is from Puteoli.

painting, and in gem carving, the two are often juxtaposed, and it is tempting to see in the finest examples of these a reflection of Zeuxis' original composition.[26]

Finally, the painting of Liber Pater by Augustus' favorite painter, Nicias (Pliny *HN* 35.131), adds yet another dimension to the nexus of Apollo and Augustus references in the Temple of Concordia Augusta. To us, living in a post-Nietzschean world, this may at first seem contradictory, since Liber Pater's iconography is that of Dionysos,[27] and we tend to think of the Dionysian and the Apollonian as inherently antithetical. Not so in Augustan Rome. True, in building the early Temple of Apollo on the Palatine in honor of the Actian Apollo, Augustus and his builders played on defeated Antony's identification as the new Dionysos by using as repeated antefix decorations drunken Silenus masks,[28] hung like victory trophies on the exterior of the temple, but that did not rule out the appearance of Dionysos, in the form of Liber Pater, in the Augustan dispensation. After all, Dionysos had reputedly deserted Antony the night before Augustus took Alexandria (Plut. *Ant.* 75.3), and Liber Pater in Rome had long been associated with Ceres in their temple on the Aventine. The temple, the traditional headquarters of the plebeians during the Republic, was restored during the Augustan period and dedicated by Tiberius in A.D. 17.[29] In addition, Liber Pater was evoked throughout Augustan poetry in positive terms as a god of wine, fertility, and abundance.[30] Indeed, Horace compares Augustus to "Romulus, Liber Pater, Pollux and Castor, who, after mighty deeds were welcomed into the temples of the gods" (Hor. *Epist.* 2.1.5–6). In the Temple of Concordia Augusta, Liber Pater was no god of drunken excess, rather one who "had care for the earth and human kind" (Hor. *Epist.* 2.1.7). As such, he was also identified with Apollo.[31] Attic vase paintings made during Nicias' own century, the fourth century B.C., show Apollo and Dionysos coexisting in divine harmony at Delphi. On one magnificent crater, now in the Hermitage Museum, Apollo and Dionysos, standing near the *omphalos*, in front of a palm tree, join right hands in a solemn

26. See, for example, G. M. A. Richter, *Engraved Gems of the Greeks, Etruscans, and Romans,* vol. 2 (London 1978) 58 no. 251.

27. A. Bruhl, *Liber Pater: Origine et expansion du culte dionysiaque à Rome et dans le monde romain,* BEFAR 175 (Paris 1953) passim.

28. G. Carettoni, "Terracotte Campane dallo scavo del tempio di Apollo Palatino," *RendPontAcc,* ser. 3, 44 (1971–1972) 135–37 and fig. 10.

29. Dio 50.10; Tac. *Ann.* 2.49.

30. E.g., Virg. *G.* 1.7; Hor. *Carm.* 4.15.26.

31. Plut. *De Is. et Os.* 35, *De E apud Delphos* 9; Serv. *ad Aen.* 3.93, *ad Georg.* 1.5, *ad Ecl.* 5.66.

gesture that connoted concord. The gesture alone (or with the caduceus) had served as a symbol of concord on republican coinage[32] and continued as such on Augustan coinage.[33] Unfortunately, we do not know with certainty what Nicias' composition looked like. Liber Pater, however, appears only once as an obverse type in Augustan coinage, and it is in the company of a suggestive reverse type—Augustus in an elephant biga, holding a sprig of laurel in his right hand and a scepter in his left.[34] The coins are those of P. Petronius Turpilianus, a moneyer of 19 B.C., and both obverse and reverse are likely a flattering allusion to Augustus' triumphant return from the East in relation to its mythological counterpart, Dionysos'/Liber Pater's return from India. The Indian triumph of Dionysos/Liber Pater, showing the god in an elephant biga, became a popular motif on later Roman sarcophagi; it remains a tantalizing possibility that Nicias' painting of Liber Pater was a prototype for the later relief images. Nevertheless, however Liber Pater was depicted, his very presence in his beneficent aspect—at one with his old associate Ceres, his sphere overlapping that of Apollo, as at Delphi—added yet another dimension to Concordia Augusta.[35]

II. Four "Obsidian" Elephants

Though at first they may seem anomalous to the program as a whole, the four obsidian elephants dedicated *pro miraculo* by the emperor Augustus are of integral importance to it.[36] The association of elephants with kings and triumph was a strong one.[37] In Augustan Rome, the elephant-head antefixes of the sumptuous Temple of Apollo on the Palatine may well have celebrated Augustus' and Apollo's victory at Actium,[38] but if so, even in this early example, they served a dual purpose, for elephants were popularly known to be devout worshipers of the Sun

32. M. H. Crawford, *Roman Republican Coinage* (London 1974) 466, no. 450 and 491, no. 480/24, for example.

33. C. H. V. Sutherland, *The Roman Imperial Coinage*, rev. ed. by C. H. V. Sutherland and R. A. G. Carson, vol. 1 (London 1984) Augustus no. 423 (pl. 7).

34. Ibid., Augustus no. 283 (pl. 5).

35. Cf. Virg. *Ecl.* 5.65–80.

36. Pliny *HN* 36.196. In all likelihood, given the difficulties of carving obsidian, the statues were of highly polished diorite (cf. the statues of Augustus and the statue of Menelaus at Heliopolis, Pliny *HN* 36.196–97).

37. A. B. Brett, *Catalogue of Greek Coins*, Museum of Fine Arts, Boston (Boston 1955) nos. 2237, 2248–57, 2259–60; Plut. *Alex.* 60.7; Dio 18.27; see, in general, H. H. Scullard, *The Elephant in the Greek and Roman World* (Ithaca, N.Y. 1974).

38. Carettoni (supra n. 28) 137–38, fig. 11.

and beloved by the god.[39] At the Temple of Concordia Augusta, the very number of elephants on display, four, would have suggested an association with the sun to an erudite Augustan observer. He would have recognized with a smile that Augustus had wisely avoided, and was perhaps playing upon, Ptolemy Philopator's grave error of making a victory sacrifice of four large elephants to the Sun. Ptolemy had had threatening dreams until he placated the god by having four elephants made in bronze to replace those he had slaughtered.[40]

An Augustan four elephant-head figural capital (fig. 7) and the four elephant support from the large *oecus,* House of the Vettii, at Pompeii, suggest that the four elephants in the Temple of Concordia Augusta may have stood addorsed.[41] Such groupings of four elephants also appear on monuments in India from the second century B.C. on and were thought of as supporting the earth and presiding over the four cardinal directions.[42] Here in the Temple of Concord, with its program that reflected the harmony of the universe and located itself overlooking the Mundus and the Golden Milestone as well as near the crossing point of true east/west and north/south within the city, the four elephants may well have carried some of the same implications. Augustus prided himself on being the first Roman to receive frequent embassies from the kings of India (*RG* 5.31) and may even have received a rare white elephant as a gift from them.[43]

Indeed, the emperor seems to have been genuinely fond of elephants. In one of his witticisms, preserved in several sources, he readily compared himself to one. He teased a nervous petitioner by saying, "Do you think you are handing a penny to an elephant?"[44] Augustus was certainly not alone in his affinity. The Roman populace had seen elephants in one other situation in the late Republic, and it seems to have been a decisive one in the formation of public opinion. Both Pompey and Julius Caesar had staged large-scale elephant fights in the circus. In Pompey's case, the fights backfired, for though the elephants fought bravely

39. Pliny *HN* 8.1–2; Ael. *NA* 7.44.

40. Ael. *NA* 7.44; Plut. *De soll. an.* 17.972B–C.

41. Henner von Hesberg, "Elemente der frühkaiserzeitlichen Aedikulaarchitektur," *ÖJh* 53 (1981–1982) 43ff.; for column capital, provenance unknown, now Vatican, Cortile Belvedere, K. Schefold, *Die Wände Pompejis* (Berlin 1957) 147.

42. See, for example, the Great Stupa, North Torana (gate), Sanchi, India. I thank my colleague Marilyn Rhie for drawing these parallel groups to my attention. See also G. B. Walker, *The Hindu World,* vol. 1 (New York 1968) 326; J. Irwin, *Burlington Magazine* 118 (1976) 746–47.

43. Hor. *Epist.* 2.1.96; cf. Florus 2.34.

44. Macrob. *Sat.* 4.3; Suet. *Aug.* 53; Quint. *Inst.* 6.3.59.

against the javelin throwers, in the end, when all hope was lost, the huge beasts

> tried to gain the compassion of the crowd by indescribable gestures of entreaty, deploring their fate with a sort of wailing, so much to the distress of the public that they forgot the general and his munificence carefully devised for their honor, and bursting into tears rose in a body and invoked curses on the head of Pompey.[45]

As Cicero discerned, the crowd had "a kind of feeling that the huge beast had a fellowship with the human race" (*Fam.* 7.1.3–4). It is exactly that empathy between mankind and elephants that I think is essential to an understanding of the grouping of four obsidian elephants in the Temple of Concord.

Like Apollo himself, possessor of both the arrow and the lyre, and, by extension, like all righteous men, especially Apollo's son Augustus, elephants had a dual nature. Though they could be fierce fighters when necessary, they were also inherently gentle and peace-loving. This duality is clear in one of the earliest images of elephants we have from the Roman world: on a plate of the third century B.C. from Capena, an elephant, war machine nonetheless, has her baby lovingly in tow (fig. 8).[46] Significantly, the element that turns the elephant into a war machine—the turret—is man-made. As Lucretius emphasizes, mankind can turn elephants into agents of Discord, "Lucanian oxen with turreted backs, hideous creatures, snake handed," [47] but in the right environment it was the inherent goodness of elephants that came shining through. As Pliny enthuses, basing his text largely on his Augustan source, Juba,

> the largest land animal is the elephant and the nearest to man in intelligence: it understands the language of its country and obeys orders, remembers duties that it has been taught, is pleased by affection and by marks of honor, wisdom, justice, also respect for the stars and reverence for the sun and moon.[48]

Moreover, elephants "always travel in a herd" with "the oldest lead[ing] the column," and special concern is manifested by all for their young and for the elderly and the infirm.[49] Elephants venerate their ancestors, are modest and monogamous, abhorring adultery so much that, although gentle creatures, they punish the crime when they recog-

45. Pliny *HN* 8.21.
46. Helbig[4] 2754.
47. Lucr. 5.1302–5.
48. Pliny *HN* 8.1–2.
49. Pliny *HN* 8.11; Ael. *NA* 7.15, 9.8, 6.61.

nize it in humans.[50] Elephants were said to live to be two or three hundred years old, and their adult life was thought to begin at age sixty (Pliny *HN* 8.28)—a fact that must have appealed to Augustus, who was seventy-two years old when the Temple of Concordia Augusta was dedicated. In short, elephants prospered in a time of peace, just like the good, responsible married men and fathers whom Augustus praised in his speech in the Forum in A.D. 9, proclaiming that they had it within their power, through their children, to "render even mortality eternal,"[51] and, not incidentally, the Augustan state as well.

It therefore seems significant that elephants, like Concordia and Pax, underwent a metamorphosis in the Augustan era. They became imperial possessions,[52] and though other wild beasts were slaughtered in the Roman arena,[53] not one elephant was. The one recorded appearance of elephants in a show is of a markedly different nature from the beast slaughters of Pompey or Julius Caesar. In the games given by Germanicus Caesar, possibly in A.D. 10, six male and six female elephants, trained by a dancing master, entered the stadium in two chorus lines, swaying to the music and wheeling in a circle to a rhythmic beat. For the second act, banqueting couches with embroidered coverlets and golden goblets and bowls were laid out, and the elephants, dressed as men and women, entered, took their places, and dined with the greatest decorum.[54] The performance piece once again underscores that analogy between elephants and humans, and the benefits to each that the new order promised.

The harmony reflected in the statues of gods on display at the *aedes Concordiae Augustae* emanated equally from the grouping of four obsidian elephants that Augustus dedicated in the temple. From agents of Discord, as Lucretius described elephant war machines in the late Republic, elephants were transformed into *exempla* of concord and at the same time embodied that peace-loving morality that would insure the *aeternitas* of the whole. It was no coincidence that four living members of the breed were chosen to power the chariot of *divus Augustus* in the *pompa circensis* forevermore. The crucial transformation is described in the *Palatine Anthology* 9.285:

50. Pliny *HN* 8.13; Ael. *NA* 5.49, 7.2, 11.15.
51. Dio 56.2.4–5.
52. Juv. 12.102f.
53. Dio 55.10.6–7.
54. Ael. *NA* 2.11; Pliny *HN* 8.4–5.

No longer does the mighty-tusked elephant, with turreted back and ready to fight phalanxes, charge unchecked into the battle; but in fear he hath yielded his thick neck to the yoke, and draws the car of divus Augustus. The wild beast knows the delight of peace; discarding the accoutrement of war, he conducts the father of good order.

As Tiberius and Augustus certainly were well aware, "the hopes . . . for the perpetual security and the eternal existence of the Roman empire"[55] that all citizens were said to entertain on the day of Tiberius' adoption were contingent upon the *aeternitas* of the idea of Augustus and of the system of world order represented by Pax Augusta and Concordia Augusta brought together in the *aedes Concordiae Augustae*. This awareness resonates in every harmonious chord struck in the temple's program of display: the concord of Apollo and Juno, of Apollo and Liber, of Apollo and his elephants. Alike in their dual nature, all flourish in the environment of Concordia Augusta.

*III.   Mercury's Caduceus and the Capitals of the
        Interior Order*

In this context, the image of Mercury may also have attracted a contemporary viewer's eye. Unlike his half brother Apollo, Mercury, so far as we know, was represented only this one time in the official program of Augustan Rome. The first emperor was popularly identified with Mercury,[56] but so too was Tiberius, as was Livia with Mercury's mother, Maia.[57] Within the context of the Temple of Concordia Augusta, dedicated by Tiberius to honor Augustus and the new system of world order, the statue of Mercury by Piston must, then, have played a pivotal role. First, paired as we have seen with the statue of Mars by the same artist, Mercury would have served as one half of the Augustan reconciliation of the gods of commerce and war. Second, in association with his half brother Apollo—the statue of Apollo by Baton was, I believe, just across the room—the statue of Mercury may well have brought to mind a story chuckled about since the post-Homeric period. On the day of his birth Mercury had both invented the lyre and stolen the cattle of

55. Vell. Pat. 2.103.3–5.
56. Hor. *Carm.* 1.2.41–44; Farnoux (supra n. 19) 457–501.
57. *CIL* XIII.1769; J. Chittenden, "Hermes-Mercury, Dynasts, and Emperors," *NC*, ser. 6, 5 (1945) 49, n. 55.

Apollo.[58] Apollo and Mercury quarreled over the latter, but made peace with one another, Mercury giving Apollo his lyre as a token of their newfound harmony, and Apollo giving Mercury the caduceus.[59] By analogy, could not the mythological grouping of Apollo and Mercury in Tiberius' *aedes Concordiae Augustae* be a tacit acknowledgment that Augustus and Tiberius might not always have seen eye to eye in the past but that their harmony now was nonetheless complete, the balance had been struck, and their union was the better for it, just as for Apollo and Mercury (cf. *Hymn. Hom.* 4.523ff.)? If so, it was like the best of Augustan messages, subtly suggested rather than brutally inculcated. As gods of thresholds, of new beginnings, their harmony was all the more apt.[60]

The actual bronze caduceus inlaid in the front steps of the temple affirms the point. Mercury's magic staff, the gift of Apollo,[61] was a readily recognizable symbol. It had appeared on Rome's earliest coinage,[62] and, by the late Republic, when displayed between clasped right hands had become the visual sign for *concordia,* especially among the triumvirs.[63] In the Augustan period, though it continued to have this significative function,[64] the caduceus became an attribute of Pax as well.[65] The caduceus had long been the herald's *signum pacis,* as the spear was the *signum belli* (Gell. *NA* 10.27.3). However, it is the visual link established in Augustan coinage between this embodiment of Pax, holding the caduceus in her right hand, and the symbol of Concord, the caduceus between two right hands, that is also important here. The shared attribute, the caduceus, underscored the interdependence of Pax Augusta and Concordia Augusta: the perpetuation of the cherished Peace required the continuation of harmonious sociopolitical relations on all

---

58. *Hymn. Hom.* 4; cf. Ov. *Fast.* 5.691–92; Hor. *Carm.* 1.10.9–12.

59. *Hymn. Hom.* 4.475ff., 525ff. For statuary representation of the quarrel, Paus. 9.30.1.

60. Wall paintings from Pompeii representing Apollo and Mercury at thresholds: Real Museo Borbonico (Naples, 1824–58), X, pl. 37; cf. I, pl. 8; VII, pl. 3; IX, pl. 2. See DarSag I¹, 168, fig. 192.

61. *Hymn. Hom.* 4.525ff.

62. Crawford (supra n. 32) 133, no. 11/1 (pl. 6); Crawford (718) believes the pairing of a trident (on one side) and a caduceus (on the other) refers to a naval victory; but see also Livy 5.13.6 for the pairing of Neptune and Mercury at the first *lectisternium* (399 B.C.).

63. Crawford (supra n. 32) 508, nos. 494/41 (pl. 60); cf. 532, 529/4a,b (pl. 63); 450/2 (pl. 53).

64. Sutherland (supra n. 33) Augustus no. 423 (pl. 7).

65. Ibid., Augustus no. 476 (pl. 8); C. H. V. Sutherland, *The Cistophori of Augustus,* Royal Numismatic Society, Special Publication no. 5 (London 1970). Cf. the unidentified goddess with scepter and caduceus on a *denarius* of 43 B.C. of L. Flaminius Chilo; the goddess may be Venus or Pax (Crawford [supra n. 32] 496, no. 485 [pl. 58]).

levels. Indeed, the balance struck, the Augustan system of world order celebrated in every display element of the *aedes Concordiae Augustae* could have no better abstract symbol than the caduceus that was inlaid in the steps of the temple itself. Inherent in the very form of the caduceus—two snakes entwined around a staff—is unity. This is usually conceived of as a unity of opposites, either of male and female (Macrob. *Sat.* 1.19.16) or of the two warring snakes whose battle has been arrested by the intervention of Mercury's once plain staff (Hyg. *Poet. astr.* 2.7). The appeal of such a symbol for Augustus the pacifier, the mediator, the moralist, is apparent.

It is altogether appropriate, then, that, like Pax on the coins of 28 B.C., the so-called herald of the *ludi saeculares* wields the caduceus on coins beginning in 17 B.C. (fig. 9).[66] Heralds carried the caduceus, as their protector Mercury did, but whether or not the figure represented is the herald of the secular games, he epitomizes the herald's formula for summoning people to the games. He himself is that "which no one has ever seen or would see again." [67] His costume is an amalgam of things past: his short columnar robe, his small round shield, and his helmet with two long feathers resemble archaic Greek and Etruscan examples;[68] yet the same figure is shown on an analogous Augustan coin attendant at a contemporary sacrifice made at an altar labeled *ludi saecul[ares]*, celebrating the end of one *saeculum* and the beginning of another.[69] The mediation point was, of course, the Augustan present, and more specifically *Augustus Caesar, Divi genus, aurea condet saecula* (Virg. *Aen.* 6.792–93). When Virgil wrote this passage in Book 6 of the *Aeneid*, he was certainly aware of Augustus' plans to celebrate the beginning of a new age. The moneyers of 17 B.C. may also have been reflecting on Virgil's words when they chose, in turn, to give their "herald" a distinctive helmet with two towering feathers atop, so like the *geminae vertice cristae* of Romulus' helmet, described in the same passage:

> Seest thou how the twin plumes stand upon his crest, and how his father himself by his own token even now marks him for the world above? Lo!

66. Sutherland (supra n. 33) Augustus no. 340 (pl. 6); for a complete description, see *BMCRR* II, 78–79 (nos. 4583–87), pl. lxviii.3.

67. Suet. *Claud.* 21.2.

68. Hermes in archaic Greek vase painting: Roscher, *Ausführliches Lexicon der griech. und röm. Mythologie* I.2, col. 2403 (C. Scherer); cf. J. E. Harrison, "The Judgment of Paris," *JHS* 7 (1886) 198. Cf. E. Richardson, *Etruscan Votive Bronzes: Geometric, Orientalizing, Archaic* (Mainz 1983) fig. 539 (for costume), fig. 441 (for shield). Helmet: Val. Max. 1.8.6; DarSag II², 1437.

69. Sutherland (supra n. 33) Augustus no. 138 (pl. 3).

under his auspices, my son, that glorious Rome shall bound her empire by earth, her pride by heaven, and with a single city's wall shall enclose her seven hills, blest in her brood of men . . . all denizens of heaven, all tenants of the heights above. (*Aen.* 6. 778–84, 787)

Ultimately, Romulus in the text, like the archaistic "herald" on the coins, serves to proclaim not only the new Golden Age, but also the animating force that informs it:

This, this is he, whom thou so oft hearest promised to thee, Augustus Caesar, son of a god, who shall again set up the Golden Age amid the fields where Saturn once reigned, and shall spread his empire past Garamant and Indian, to a land that lies beyond the stars, beyond the paths of the year and the sun, where heaven-bearing Atlas turns on his shoulders the sphere, inset with gleaming stars. (*Aen.* 6.791–97)

The world order of Concordia Augusta was manifest in the caduceus inlaid in the temple steps every bit as much as in the program as a whole, simultaneously reminding the Augustan viewer of Mercury the mediator and of the association of both Augustus and Tiberius with him, of the interdependence of Concordia and Pax who shared this symbol, and finally of the unified spirit of the new age, epitomized in the figure of the "herald" of the secular games with his archaizing costume and caduceus in hand—connected with the past, but conjuring up the future. The caduceus, given as a token of the concord established between Apollo and Mercury, Augustus and Tiberius, similarly represented the harmony of opposites fundamental to the system of world order of Concordia Augusta and to the temple's program as a whole.

Even the smallest details echoed the refrain. The paired rams that leap from the acanthus foliage of the temple's interior order (fig. 10) are so beautifully integrated into the design that this unique choice could have been made for purely aesthetic reasons,[70] and, like the acanthus, the rams' presence is one more indication of the burgeoning life of the new age.[71] But for the Augustan viewer, the rams may well have conveyed additional meanings. Rams were closely associated with Augustus' god Apollo and with Augustus' and Tiberius' god Mercury.[72] Indeed, sheep had a basic significance for all Romans:

70. E. von Mercklin, *Antike Figuralkapitelle* (Berlin 1962) 184–86, no. 446, fig. 864, for late Hellenistic capital with single sheep protomes; cf. 201–3, no. 494, figs. 943–45 on Temple of Concord examples. For capitals and fragments, Gasparri (supra n. 5) 103–5 and pls. 18–22.
71. Cf. Virg. *Ecl.* 4.43; Macrob. *Sat.* 7.1. In all likelihood the rams on the column capitals were highlighted with paint.
72. Apollo Karneios: Pind. *Pyth.* 5.80; Herod. 7.206. Hermes Epimelius: Paus. 9.34.3; see also 2.3.4, 5.27.8, 9.22.1.

> Does not everyone agree that the Roman people is sprung from shepherds? Is there anyone who does not know that Faustulus, the foster father who reared Romulus and Remus, was a shepherd? (Varro *Rust.* 2.11–13)

The very fact that it was two identical horned rams that leapt from each corner of the capitals may well have suggested the notion of twins to the viewer on some level. If so, in the context of the Temple of Concordia Augusta it was not likely the still fratricide-tinged Romulus and Remus who came to mind.[73] The temple was dedicated, after all, in the names of the *concordia sidera,*[74] Tiberius and Drusus, the one alive, the other dead, like Castor and Pollux, whose temple in the Forum Romanum had also been dedicated in the names of Tiberius and Drusus.[75]

Augustus had long been compared to Pollux, who at his death was raised to the "starry citadels" on account of his merit, as Augustus himself would one day be.[76] The frontal view of any of the corners of the capitals would have revealed that though they leapt in tandem, each of the rams emanated from a separate calyx (fig. 11). Though originally from a separate family, since his adoption by the *princeps* in A.D. 4, Tiberius had been joined together with Augustus, sharing as well the all important *tribunicia potestas* and *imperium proconsulare.*[77] The paired rams, like so many other elements of the program, underscored the concord between Augustus and his heir apparent. In conjunction with the dedication of the temple in the names of Tiberius and Drusus, and through it to the original *concordia sidera,* Castor and Pollux themselves, there was also a tacit assurance here that even when one member of the pair went to join his heavenly counterparts, his spirit would live on in the other.[78] Not coincidentally, the constellation that Castor and Pollux constituted was Gemini, ruled over by Apollo, and the very embodiment of brotherly concord, depicting their arms "forever linked in mutual embrace" (Manil. *Astron.* 2.440; see also 164).

Male lambs were an appropriate sacrifice for Castor and Pollux and were to be the canonical sacrifice for all emperors who became *divi.*[79] Moreover, just as a ram was sacrificed to Jupiter and one to Janus to

---

73. Hor. *Epodes* 7.17–20 and Suet. *Aug.* 7; despite Virg. *Aen.* 1.292 and Ov. *Fast.* 4.809ff. See R. Schilling, "Romulus l'élu et Rémus le réprouvé," *REL* 38 (1960) 182–99.

74. Cf. Ov. *Cons.* 283.

75. Suet. *Tib.* 20; Dio 55.27.4. For the alternating life/death of Castor and Pollux, Cypr. 1; Ov. *Fast.* 5.693ff.

76. Hor. *Carm.* 3.3.9–12.

77. R. Syme, *The Roman Revolution* (Oxford 1939) 336–37; Tac. *Ann.* 3.56.

78. Cf. Ov. *Fast.* 1.613–16.

79. *Hymn. Hom.* 33.10; Prudent. *C. Symm.* 1.245–50.

mark the beginning of each year, the *flamen dialis* sacrificed a gelded ram in the Temple of Jupiter each year to commemorate the day on which Augustus assumed his cognomen, 16 January, the same day that the *aedes Concordiae Augustae* was dedicated.[80] A visual link between rams and Augustus had already been made on an important series of *aurei* and *denarii* of 17 B.C. with a reverse type of a tripod candelabrum ornamented with rams' heads, surrounded by a wreath, bucrania, and paterae and labeled AUGUST (fig. 12).[81] The association of Augustus and the ram is significant. Astronomically, in tracing the course of the sun through the year, the constellation of the Ram (Aries) "heads the procession of the skies," his stars "allotted a place in the middle of the firmament, where with even balance the sun levels night and day in springtime." [82] Writing at the time of the Temple of Concordia Augusta's dedication, Manilius did not miss the point, as his words about Aries as the protector of the human head make clear: *Aries caput est ante omnia princeps.* Equally, on the coins of 17 B.C. the association of the august *princeps* with the ram, Aries, the leader of the zodiac, and the close alliance of the two with the light of the Sun, Apollo, so deftly alluded to in the tripod-shaped candelabrum, becomes clear.[83] Within only a few years' time the poet Horace would allude in verse to these associations:

> To thy country give again, blest leader, the light of thy presence! For when, like spring, thy face has beamed upon the folk, more pleasant runs the day, and brighter shines the sun.[84]

IV. The Program and Its Designer

This association of Augustus with light and Apollo, the Sun, was to be a part of Tiberius' inheritance, or so it would appear from a passage in Book 4 of Manilius' *Astronomica*, written after Augustus' death in A.D.

---

80. Macrob. *Sat.* 1.16.30; Ov. *Fast.* 1.318 (cf. Varro *Ling.* 3.12); Ov. *Fast.* 1.587ff. (by mistake, the thirteenth instead of the sixteenth, see Gagé [supra n. 2] 164).

81. Sutherland (supra n. 33) Augustus no. 539 (pl. 10). See also C. H. V. Sutherland, "The Date and Significance of the 'Candelabrum' Coins of Augustus," *CR* 58 (1944) 46–49.

82. Manil. *Astron.* 2.945b, 743–45.

83. For actual candelabra with ram protomes, H.-U. Cain, *Römische Marmorkandelaber,* Beiträge zur Erschließung hellenistischer und kaiserzeitlicher Skulptur und Architektur 7 (Mainz 1985) 57–58. For the coin type, L. R. Taylor, *The Divinity of the Roman Emperor* (Middletown, Conn. 1931) 195–96.

84. Hor. *Carm.* 4.5.5–8. See M. C. J. Putnam, *Artifices of Eternity: Horace's Fourth Book of Odes* (Ithaca, N.Y. 1986) 104–5.

14 (4.548ff.). He is describing the zodiacal geography of the constellation Virgo, watched over by Ceres:

> Beneath chaste Virgo Rhodes prospers on land and sea, the erstwhile abode
> of him who was to rule the world as emperor: the whole island is consecrated
> to the Sun, and Rhodes was in very truth its house at the time when it re-
> ceived into its care the light of the mighty universe in the person of Caesar.
> (4.763–66)

In one fell swoop, Manilius not only equates Tiberius with light and the
Sun, but also transforms the most problematic period in Tiberius' career, his retirement/exile to Rhodes from 6 B.C. to A.D. 2, into an auspicious beginning.[85]
This passage is to be coupled with the descriptions of the portents
sent to Tiberius as he was about to be recalled from Rhodes, portents
interpreted successfully by one man as signs of Tiberius' imperial destiny.[86] That man was to remain one of Tiberius' closest friends and was
to be his astrological adviser from that moment forward.[87] His name
was Thrasyllus. Thrasyllus was an Alexandrian scholar who had published a definitive edition of Plato's works and was well known for his
own Neopythagorean writings on numerology and the seven tones.[88]
Though trained in matters arcane, he seems to have had a wily sense for
current Roman politics.[89] He was also, I believe, the chief designer of
the program of the *aedes Concordiae Augustae*.
The program was organized as the cosmos was conceived to be organized (fig. 14). The interior of the temple had a continuous dado 2 m
high projecting from the wall and supporting the freestanding columns
of the interior order. The back wall had a central projecting statue base,
and the side walls had narrower central projecting bases. The groupings
of Apollo and Juno by Baton and Mercury and Mars by Piston would
have stood, I suggest, on the two side-wall bases, so that Mercury on
the left and Apollo on the right were the first statues that the visitor
encountered on entering the temple. The wide central statue base on the
rear wall probably accommodated seated statues. It has often been
thought to have supported a statue of Concordia Augusta; yet we have
no record of such a statue, nor any depiction of Concordia Augusta as

85. Vell. Pat. 2.99.1–3; Suet. *Tib.* 10–13, 59.1; Dio 55.9.5–8.
86. Suet. *Tib.* 14.4; Tac. *Ann.* 6.21; Dio 55.11.2–3.
87. Suet. *Aug.* 98.4, *Tib.* 62.3, *Calig.* 19.1.
88. F. H. Cramer, *Astrology in Roman Law and Politics,* Memoirs of the American
Philosophical Society 37 (Philadelphia 1954) 92–108.
89. Cf. Suet. *Aug.* 98.4.

a seated deity with cornucopia and patera until the reign of Nero.[90] Instead, the central base was occupied by seated statues of the two goddesses that best epitomized the blessings of Concordia Augusta. One of the statues was Vesta; it had been brought by Tiberius from Paros and was depicted in the cella of the temple on the Tiberian *sestertius*. Vesta as goddess of hearth and home was of central importance in the Augustan scheme,[91] and was, moreover, in Neopythagorean terms, the goddess of light who stood at the center of the universe.[92] Her sister, Ceres, represented all the fruitfulness of the new era. Ceres had already been identified with Livia in the *vicus Jugarius* altar, dedicated in A.D. 7,[93] and the restoration of Ceres' Aventine temple was to be Tiberius' next dedication after the Temple of Concordia Augusta.[94] Ceres' central position here may also have reflected—and perhaps insured—Tiberius' own faith in his imperial destiny, which was first realized at Rhodes in the astrological province of Ceres' constellation Virgo (Manil. *Astron.* 4.763ff.).

As graphically depicted on a ring stone that may date as early as the Augustan period, the signs of the zodiac revolve around the figure of Apollo (fig. 13). As has already been demonstrated, the program of the *aedes Concordiae Augustae* was also Apollo-centric, but if the statues were distributed on the bases as just described, the correlation would be an even closer one. It is here that the hand of Thrasyllus as a program designer can be detected; he may have been assisted by Manilius, who was certainly a member of the same court circle.[95]

It is not just individual zodiacal signs but the relationships between them that are of central importance in the astrological system. The most powerful of these groupings is the trigon, formed by drawing equilateral triangles between signs (Manil. *Astron.* 2.270ff.). When judged by the principles of Manilius' schema, the paired statues on the main bases of the Temple of Concordia Augusta are each partners in a distinctive trigon: Vesta rules Capricorn, Ceres rules Virgo, and Capricorn and Virgo

90. Sutherland (supra n. 33) Nero no. 48 (pl. 18); cf. Drusilla, standing, with attributes of Concordia, ibid., Gaius no. 33 (pl. 13).
91. Ov. *Fast.* 4.951, *Met.* 15.864.
92. Pythag. *Philol.* frag. 7; R. E. Siegel, "On the Relationship Between Early Greek Scientific Thought and Mysticism: Is Hestia, the Central Fire, An Abstract Astronomical Concept?" *Janus* 49 (1960) 1ff., 16ff.; Tac. *Ann.* 6.20–21; Gell. *NA* 15.7.3 (Augustus and Neopythagorean "climactic").
93. *CIL* I², p. 324; cf. X.7501.
94. Tac. *Ann.* 2.49.
95. Manilius dedicated the *Astronomica* to Augustus, "who inspires my design." See also Cramer (supra n. 88) 95–99.

are in the same trigon;[96] Mars rules Scorpio, Mercury, and Cancer, and Scorpio and Cancer are members of another trigon;[97] Juno rules Aquarius, Apollo rules Gemini, and Aquarius and Gemini are members of the third trigon (fig. 15).[98] Significantly, Manilius points out that relations within a trigon were not always untroubled, but ultimately harmony prevailed and balance was maintained.[99] On many levels, then, the pairings of Juno and Apollo, Mars and Mercury, and Vesta and Ceres in the temple would have served to represent the newly harmonious world order of Concordia Augusta.

The balance struck, the balance of Concordia Augusta that resonated in all the objects on display within the temple might well have suggested one last cosmic association for the viewer. Italy, Rome, Augustus, and Tiberius all had one zodiacal sign in common: Libra, the Balance. In terms of zodiacal geography "Italy belongs to Libra" (Manil. *Astron.* 4.773), and Rome was founded beneath the sign of Libra (4.773–74): that is, the Moon was in Libra at the foundation of Rome.[100] Likewise, though his Moon sign was Capricorn (2.509), Augustus' natal Sun was in the sign of Libra (4.547f.; 23 September 63 B.C.). Opposite, but equal, Tiberius' Moon sign, like that of the city of Rome itself, was Libra (4.774). Augustus had had his horoscope published, and "astrology was becoming all the rage" in Rome;[101] such a correlation between the balanced world order of Concordia Augusta and the world orderers themselves would not likely have been missed.

From whatever angle it was approached and on every level, the program of the temple was Concordia Augusta manifest. As had been true in earlier programs, it was Augustus' god Apollo around whom every painting and sculpture—even the seemingly anomalous "obsidian" elephants—revolved. Yet this program, including its pairs of reconciled opposites, in which Apollo himself took part (Apollo and Juno by Baton), was also uniquely suited to convey the particular message of the *aedes Concordiae Augustae.* That message was of *pax deorum,* the very essence of Concordia Augusta, mirroring the balance struck between members of the imperial family, between social orders within the state,

96. Manil. *Astron.* 2.445, 442, 281.
97. Ibid. 2.443, 440, 282ff.
98. Ibid. 2.446, 440, 282ff. Minerva rules Aries (2.439), and Jupiter Leo (2.441), so the statues of Minerva and Jupiter by Sthennis (Pliny *HN* 34.90) would have represented the fourth and last trigon of the system (Manil. *Astron.* 2.279–80).
99. See esp. Manil. *Astron.* 2.608ff.
100. Cf. Cic. *Div.* 2.98.
101. Suet. *Aug.* 94.12; cf. Dio 56.25.5. See also B. Levick, *Tiberius the Politician* (London 1976) 18.

and ultimately reflecting the order of the cosmos as a whole.[102] Just as the Ara Pacis Augustae had transformed the Field of Mars, so too the *aedes Concordiae Augustae* transformed not only a venerable republican site, but also the oldest home of the gods in Rome, the Capitoline, into a distinctively Augustan entity. By its very nature, the program at once reaffirmed the past, celebrated the present, and affirmed its dedicator as the future rightful heir of Augustus and the city "filled with miracles." [103]

102. Cf. Manil. *Astron.* 1.247ff., 5.726ff.
103. Cf. Pliny *HN* 36.101f.

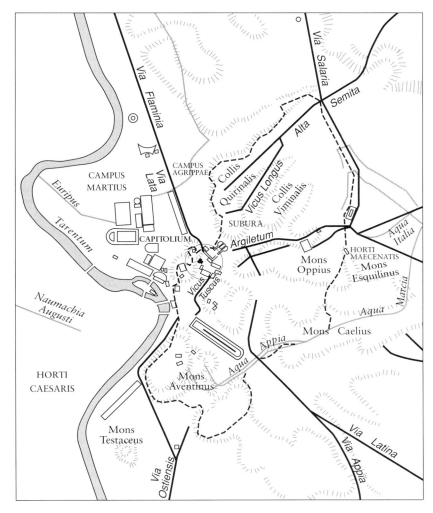

Figure 1. Map of Augustan Rome. *Aedes Concordiae Augustae* circled at center.

Figure 2. *Aedes Concordiae Augustae. Sestertius* of Tiberius (Fototeca Unione 3549).

Figure 3. Hygieia and Asclepius (Avidia? and Lucius Verus). Ny Carlsberg Glyptotek I.N. 1615, 714 (V. Poulsen, *Les portraits romains,* vol. 2, pls. CXLVII, CXLIV).

Figure 4. Above, Mercury and Mars Ultor. Carnelian. Hamburg, Museum für Kunst und Gewerbe M 891n (*LIMC* II.2, pl. 407.336). Figure 6. Below, Cassandra predicting the future to her family. Arretine ware, found at Puteoli. Staatl. Museen zu Berlin (P. Hermann, *Denkmäler,* ser. 1, text, 246, fig. 73).

Figure 5. Cassandra predicting the future to her family. Pompeii, Reg. I, ins. 2, no. 28; Naples, Museo Nazionale (P. Hermann, *Denkmäler,* ser. 1, pl. 179).

Figure 7. Porphyry four elephant-head capital, Augustan. Vatican, Cortile Belvedere (photograph by Barbara Bini).

Figure 8. Elephant plate from Capena, ca. 280–270 B.C. Rome, Villa Giulia Inv. 23949 (*Roma medio repubblicana,* front cover).

Figure 9. Obverse: "herald" in long robe with feathered helmet, holding caduceus. Reverse: youthful Divus Julius. *Denarius* of M. Sanquinius, 17 B.C. (*BMCRE,* vol. 1, pl. 2.20).

Figure 10. Above, Ram capital, interior order, *aedes Concordiae Augustae* (C. Gasparri, *Aedes Concordiae Augustae*, pl. 18). Figure 11. Below, Ram capital, interior order, *aedes Concordiae Augustae*, corner view (H. F. Rebert & H. Marceau, *MAAR* 5 [1925] pl. 48, fig. 1).

Figure 12. Obverse: youthful head, oak wreath. Reverse: candelabrum ornamented with rams' heads. *Aureus* ca. 17 B.C. (*BMCRE*, vol. 1, pl. 17.14).

Figure 13. Bust of Apollo encircled by the signs of the zodiac, carnelian ring stone. Munich, Staatliche Münzsammlung A 2151 (*LIMC* II.2, pl. 310.129).

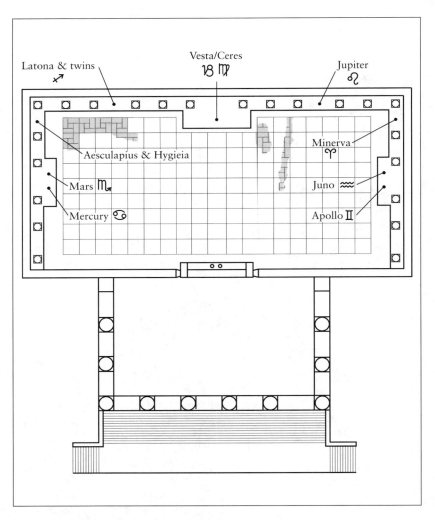

Figure 14. Reconstruction of statuary program at the *aedes Concordiae Augustae* (plan only, C. Gasparri, *Aedes Concordiae Augustae*, pl. 24).

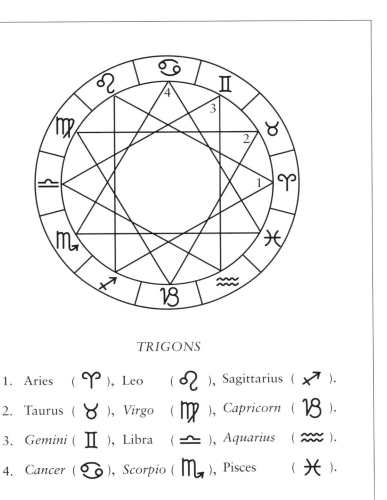

TRIGONS

1. Aries   (♈), Leo   (♌), Sagittarius (♐).

2. Taurus (♉), *Virgo* (♍), *Capricorn* (♑).

3. *Gemini* (♊), Libra   (♎), *Aquarius* (♒).

4. *Cancer* (♋), *Scorpio* (♏), Pisces   (♓).

Figure 15. Trigons of the zodiac according to Manilius (*Astron.* 2.273–86) (G. P. Goold, trans. and ed., Loeb Classical Library [Cambridge, Mass., 1977] xlii, fig. 3).

Augustan Building Programs
in the Western Provinces

Introduction

The western provinces in Gaul and Iberia figured prominently among the concerns of the emperor Augustus.[1] Augustus himself was responsible for the pacification of the Cantabrian coast, thus finishing the conquest of the western part of Europe.[2] He must have realized the potential political force of the western regions during his struggle with Antony. The West formed his base as he drew on the support of western provincials still loyal to Caesar.[3] After he had gained control of the empire, he redrew the administrative lines of the provinces and redistrib-

1. Research was made possible with grants from the American Philosophical Society (summer 1987) and the Joukowsky Foundation (1983–1984). The paper was first presented at Brown University on 14 March 1987. Rolf Winkes, Fred S. Kleiner, Kurt Raaflaub, and Stephen Dyson kindly read and commented on a draft version. All errors and opinions remain mine.

2. For recent studies and bibliographies on the conquest and Romanization of the West under the Republic, see S. L. Dyson, *The Creation of the Roman Frontier* (Princeton 1985); J. S. Richardson, *Hispaniae: Spain and the Development of Roman Imperialism, 218–82 B.C.* (Cambridge 1986); J. F. Drinkwater, *Roman Gaul: The Three Provinces, 58 B.C.–A.D. 260* (Ithaca, N.Y. 1983); J. P. Clébert, *Provence antique: L'époque gallo-romaine* (Paris 1970).

3. R. Syme, *The Roman Revolution* (Oxford 1939) 292.

uted them. The peaceful and more civilized Gallia Narbonensis and Baetica were left ungarrisoned and were placed under the control of the senate. Lusitania, Tarraconensis, Gallia Aquitania, Gallia Belgica, and Gallia Lugdunensis, which were still being pacified or had only recently been brought under Roman control, were garrisoned and made imperial provinces. Moreover, the emperor kept careful watch over the senatorial visits to these regions. The western provinces were removed as a potential power base for any of Augustus' enemies.[4]

The neat administrative system that Augustus designed for the West belied the reality of the cultural and ethnic heterogeneity of the regions. There were several distinct native peoples, and the Mediterranean coasts of France and Spain had been heavily colonized by Phoenicians and Greeks. Republican interest in the areas had been confined mostly to exploitation, but Roman and Romanized native populations were to be found in Gallia Narbonensis, Tarraconensis, and Baetica. It fell to Augustus to provide the basis for a true cultural unification of the western provinces and to integrate the provincial populations, Roman and native, into the empire. Many great public building projects and sculptural commissions begun on Gallic and Iberian soil during Augustus' reign, some with his specific promotion, were elements in a larger policy that stressed the newly established political unity of the West and strove to provide the provincials with a sense of being participants in the greater scope of the Roman world. In areas that had only recently been exposed to strong Mediterranean influences, new cities were founded and established with major pieces of architecture that often employed construction techniques and designs that were distinct from the local building methods. The urban plan and its architectural embellishment were vivid statements of a new order. In more Hellenized Gallia Narbonensis, the means for expressing the message was more subtle and took the form of sculptural displays on arches and trophies. The most visible symbol of unity and integration throughout the western provinces was the person of Augustus himself. His presence was constantly asserted by means of direct patronage, the establishment of cult places, and the appearance of his image on coinage and statuary.

Augustus and Provincial Urbanization

Augustus' strongest device for fostering unity was the founding of new cities and the redesign of older centers that were intended to serve as

4. Ibid. 405.

provincial capitals (Augusta Emerita, Lugdunum), *conventus* capitals (Caesaraugusta, Augusta Raurica), or local Romanized centers (Augustodunum, Colonia Julia Augusta Paterna Faventia, Conimbriga, Lugdunum Convenarum).[5] Where Roman urbanization had already become common in southern and eastern Iberia and Gallia Narbonensis, Augustus' actions did not impact on the pattern of life.[6] However, in the more recently pacified regions, the traditional settlements, *oppida*, were changed. The natives were encouraged to move from their defended heights to the nearby flatlands.[7] These new cities, relocated towns, and redesigned native villages began to look alike. They were laid out on a regular pattern of crossing streets around a forum. Boersma has argued that the plans for these new centers were taken from late republican models that had been developed in northern Italy and made use of large, wide *insulae*.[8]

Local pride in Romanness was encouraged with symbolic references to the foundation ceremony. The Iberian cities of Mérida (Augusta Emerita) and Zaragoza (Caesaraugusta) commemorated the event on issues of their local bronze coinages. The images for the reverse types are similar and show a priest plowing a furrow, the *pomerium*. The reference is to an Italic practice with roots in the *etrusca disciplina*.[9] The

5. Augusta Emerita: M. Almagro Basch, "Augusta Emerita," *150 Jahre Deutsches Archäologisches Institut, 1829–1979* (Mainz 1981) 143–63; *PECS* 114–16. Lugdunum: P. Grimal and M. Woloch, *Roman Cities* (Madison, Wis. 1983) 175–81; Augusta Raurica: *PECS* 116–18; Augustodunum: Grimal and Woloch (supra) 126–28; Lugdunum Convenarum: ibid., 244–46; Colonia Julia Augusta Paterna Faventia (Barcelona): J. Gimeno Pascual, "Barcino Augustea: Distribución de espacios urbanos y áreas centrales de la ciudad," *Boletín del Museo Arqueológico Nacional-Madrid* 1 (1983) 9–30; Conimbriga: J. Alarcão and R. Etienne, *Fouilles de Conimbriga*, vol. 1, *L'architecture* (Paris 1977).

6. Spain at the time of Augustus: J. M. Blázquez, "Ciudades hispánicas de la época de Augusto," in *Simposium de las ciudades augusteas de Hispania* 1 (Zaragoza 1976) 76–136; France: R. Hodson and R. M. Rowlett, "From 600 B.C. to the Roman Conquest," in S. Piggott, G. Daniel, and C. McBurney, eds., *France before the Romans* (London 1973) 157–91; N. J. DeWitt, *Urbanization and the Franchise in Roman Gaul* (Lancaster 1940).

7. DeWitt (supra n. 6) 29–30; Autun: Drinkwater (supra n. 2) 11–12, 131; Barcelona: A. Balil, *Colonia Iulia Augusta Paterna Faventia* (Madrid 1964) 43–48; Saint-Bertrand-de-Comminges: Grimal and Woloch (supra n. 5) 244–46.

8. Gimeno Pascual (supra n. 5) 9–30; F. Pallares, "La topografia e le origini di Barcelona romana," *Revista di Studi Liguri* 36 (1970) 63–102; J. B. Ward-Perkins, "From Republic to Empire, Reflections on the Early Provincial Architecture of the Roman West," *JRS* 60 (1970) 1–19; J. S. Boersma, "Large-sized Insulae in Italy and the Western Roman Provinces," *Bulletin van de Vereeniging tot Bevordering der Kennis van de Antike Beschaving* 57 (1982) 38–51. Boersma bases his conclusions on the evidence from Britain and the German territories.

9. Coins: A. de Guadán, *La moneda ibérica: Catálogo de numismática ibérica e iberoromana* (Madrid 1980) nos. 323–26, 328, 987–89. For the origin of the ritual, see L. Bonfante, "Daily Life and Afterlife," in id., ed., *Etruscan Life and Afterlife* (Detroit 1986) 264–65. For the Italic versus Greek concept in urbanization, see E. Gabba, "Urbanizza-

reverses announced each city's pride in being Roman. The message was forceful, a symbol of the new order, and was circulated with the coins to the hamlets that were being changed from native settlements into Roman villages.

Augustus' promotion of urbanization as a means of achieving homogeneity in a region was not a new policy. After the Social War the same practice was used in central Italy as a means of replacing tribal identities with a sense of urban pride. The cities were founded, and laws were promulgated for their administration.[10] Caesar used a similar approach on the Iberian Peninsula, where he instituted governing charters for new and refounded towns.[11] Augustus formed a personal association with some of the western settlements. He may have served as the *patronus* for Carthago Nova as he did for some veterans' colonies in Italy.[12] Trier (Augusta Treverum) may have celebrated its foundation day as 1 August.[13] Grant has argued that the image of Augustus as *conditor* became increasingly more common on some of the provincial coinages.[14] On the Iberian Peninsula, Augustus promoted the striking of coinage by Roman cities. At the same time, the mints of the peregrine communities were suppressed.[15] Local identity such as might continue to be fostered in local autonomous coinage was discouraged in favor of homogeneity promoted in Romanized urban centers.

Architecture

Urban life, even in distant regions, began to assume a sameness in visual surroundings. Another reverse coin type from Mérida (fig. 1) depicts a gateway with two large, arched openings forming the lower story and with an inscribed architrave, the whole flanked by two towers. The in-

---

zione e rinnovamenti urbanistici nell'Italia centro-meridionale del 1 sec. a.C.," *Studi Classici e Orientali* 21 (1972) 78–79.

10. Gabba (supra n. 9) 81–82.

11. J. Henderson, "Julius Caesar and the *Latium* in Spain," *JRS* 32 (1942) 1–13. Also, for the charter of Osuna (Urso), E. G. Hardy, "Three Spanish Charters and Other Documents," in id., ed., *Roman Laws and Charters* (Oxford 1912) 760.

12. L. Keppie, *Colonisation and Veteran Settlement in Italy, 47–14 B.C.* (London 1983) 112–13; for a different view, see M. Grant, *From Imperium to Auctoritas*[2] (London 1969) 158–59.

13. H. Heinen, "Augustus in Gallien und die Anfänge des römischen Trier," in *Trier, Augustusstadt der Treverer: Stadt und Land in vor- und frührömischer Zeit* (Mainz 1984) 41.

14. Grant (supra n. 12) 292–93, 319.

15. Ibid., 296, 472–74.

scription reads AUGUSTA EMERITA.[16] It is a schematic representation that appears in several versions. However, the longevity of the series, about three decades, and the fact that the image is found as a reverse type for both *dupondii* and *asses* provide good reasons to believe that the structure being commemorated actually did exist at the city and was not a borrowing from some other source or the creation of a particular die engraver. It was the main city gate, for which no other remains have been found. Standing gates like that represented on the coin are known from Autun (fig. 2), Nîmes, and Barcelona.[17] These are great arched entryways constructed of cut and fitted stone and resembling the late republican or early imperial gates at Verona.[18] Once again, forms from northern Italy were brought into the western provinces to supply a basis for visual unity.

In those areas where Hellenistic and republican influences had been strong, an accommodation process began. The older forms continued, but new structures based on metropolitan Roman models now appeared. Certain specific decorative details on some of the Augustan buildings in Narbonensis, such as the arcade for the theater at Arles, show stylistic traits borrowed from Asia Minor and may reflect a local preference that still survived into the first century A.C.[19] At Glanum in southern France, Agrippa had the native sanctuary of Valetudo restored. The excavator, Rolland, has seen in the stylistic details of the structure a struggle between the older native-Hellenistic traditions and the imposed Roman forms, albeit republican.[20] The treatment of the column bases, which lack plinths and which have tori of equal dimensions, is republican. Republican profiles for the tori are also seen at the Temple of Augustus and Livia at Vienne.[21] However, the acroteria with their busts ornamented by a torc and surrounded by a palmette are a native Gallic feature and have no parallels outside the region.[22] Excavations at

16. De Guadán (supra n. 9) nos. 975, 976, 983–86, 996–1000.
17. Barcelona's gate is known only from some nineteenth-century drawings of the discovery; Pallares (supra n. 8) 86, fig. 15.
18. Verona's gates could date from 28–15 B.C., the time of the adoption of the orthogonal plan; Grimal and Woloch (supra n. 5) 280.
19. P. Gros, "Traditions hellénistiques d'orient dans le décor architectonique des temples romaines de Gaule Narbonnaise," *Atti del Colloquio sul tema: La Gallia Romana,* Academia Nazionale dei Lincei, no. 158 (Rome 1973) 170.
20. H. Rolland, *Fouilles de Glanum: 1947–1956,* Gallia Suppl. 11 (Paris 1958) 98–106.
21. J. B. Ward-Perkins, *Roman Imperial Architecture* (Harmondsworth 1985) 227.
22. G. Charles-Picard, "Glanum et les origines de l'art romano-provençal, première partie: architecture," *Gallia* 21 (1963) 123–24. Head capitals of Hellenistic inspiration

the Greek colonial site of Ampurias on the east coast of Spain have shown that the Roman forum, already in place and operative in the first century B.C., was altered in the third quarter of the first century B.C. to follow metropolitan models. The front of the temple was somewhat obscured behind a series of statue bases and extensions from the temple's front, and a flanking lateral staircase was added that gave access to the top of the podium at the pronaos (fig. 3), creating a structure that may have looked somewhat like the Temple of Venus Genetrix in Rome, one of the projects finished by Augustus.[23] In each of these examples the changes reflect the mixing of local versions of Hellenistic or republican building types with new ideas. However, the Maison Carrée at Nîmes, a structure built during Augustus' lifetime, displays no Gallic traits.[24] It is a totally Augustan building as might have stood in the capital. In the more civilized regions the process of bringing about visual harmony relied perhaps more on the prestige of the new forms. It may have been assumed that building or changing structures to reflect prototypes from the capital would stimulate the sophisticated provincials to imitate and emulate the models and forego the older local versions of Hellenistic and republican styles. However, the policy seems to have been one of gentle persuasion, as is shown by the persistence of old-fashioned elements in the sanctuary of Valetudo at Glanum or the Temple of Augustus and Livia.

Three temples on the Iberian Peninsula reveal the interweaving of stylistic elements that occurred in the process of creating a Roman style of architecture for the western provinces. They are worth examining in detail. The so-called Temple of Diana in Mérida and the forum temple at Barcelona have been dated to the first century A.C. The temple at Evora has been assigned a second-century date.[25] The dates are determined on stylistic grounds, since there is no external evidence, but there

are known from the earlier levels at the site; F. Salviat, "La sculpture préromaine en Provence," in *Au temps gaulois: Les dossiers de l'archéologie* 35 (June 1979) 31–51.

23. J. Aquilué, R. Mar Medina, J. M. Nolla i Brufau, J. Arbulo Bayona, E. Sanmartí i Grego, *El fórum romà d'Empúries* (Barcelona 1984) 99–100. For the Temple of Venus Genetrix, see R. B. Ulrich, "The Rostrum and the Fountain of the Temple of Venus Genetrix in the Forum of Caesar," abstract, *AJA* 90 (1986) 190; *AJA* 91 (1987) 283.

24. Ward-Perkins (supra n. 21) 226–27; H. Kähler, *The Art of Rome and her Empire* (New York 1963) 55–57.

25. Mérida: J. M. Alvarez Martínez, "El templo de Diana," in *Augusta Emerita* (Madrid 1976) 49–50; Barcelona: Balil (supra n. 7) 103–5; Evora: T. Hauschild, "Zur Typologie römischer Tempel auf der iberischen Halbinsel: Peripterale Anlagen in Barcelona, Mérida und Evora," in *Homenaje a Sáenz de Buruaga* (Madrid 1982) 155–56.

are reasons for arguing that the three buildings are all Augustan. The development of the urban plans at Barcelona and Mérida is late first century B.C. The Barcelona temple stood in the forum, and it is difficult to conceive of a city that would have allowed the forum to sit without its temple for any length of time, especially since the forum and temple pattern was already clearly established at nearby Ampurias. The temple at Mérida was not the main temple for the city, but it did occupy a prominent spot on the Kardo Maximus. There is no evidence to suggest an earlier building on the site, and considering that the other public features of the city (the theater, the forum, the main bridge) were all constructed during the city's first building phase, work on a major temple and its associated precinct must also have begun at this time.[26] Evora received its Latin name, Liberalitas Julia, and was given its *Latium vetus* about 27 B.C. The temple, located on the highest point of land, must have served as the city's main temple from the start.[27]

The most interesting point of comparison for the three temples is their hexastyle, peripteral plan modified by a single flight of stairs, which gives them a typical Roman axiality.[28] Vitruvius discussed the type and also the larger pseudodipteral form (3.2.5–6; 4.4.1–2). But he could cite only one example in Rome, the Temple of Jupiter Stator by Hermodorus. To this one can be added the remains of the two temples in the *forum holitorium*, one a small doric peripteral type, the other an ionic peripteral plan. The latter, temple B, probably dates to 90 B.C.[29] There is also the republican temple A in the Largo Argentina.[30] In addition to these temples there was a group of older temples that were rededicated by Augustus—the Temple of Castor and Pollux in the Roman Forum; the Temple of Neptune in Circo, which Gros has identified with the remains of a peripteral temple on the via di S. Salvatore in Campo[31]; and the Temple of Minerva on the Aventine, known from a small fragment of the *Forma urbis*.

Though limited in number, the temples, along with the descriptions in Vitruvius, share significant design features that Gros has examined in

26. Theater: M. Almagro, *Guía de Mérida* (Valencia 1965) 50–51.
27. J. Alarcão, *Portugal romano* (1983) 75.
28. Hauschild (supra n. 25) 145–56.
29. R. Delbrück, *Die drei Tempel am Forum Holitorium* (Rome 1907); L. T. Shoe, *Etruscan and Republican Roman Mouldings,* MAAR 28 (1965) 177, 184. For a more recent plan, see F. Coarelli, *Roma,* Guide archeologiche Laterza (Rome 1981) 319.
30. A. Boethius, *Etruscan and Early Roman Architecture* (Harmondsworth 1978) 157 and fig. 126.
31. P. Gros, *Aurea Templa: Recherches sur l'architecture religieuse de Rome à l'époque d'Auguste* (Rome 1976) 111.

detail.[32] It was the ionic peripteral plan, a type developed out of Pytheos' design for the Temple of Athena Polias at Priene, that was favored in the capital. The type has either a shallow opisthodomus in its Greek form or none at all in its Italian version. The temple on the via di S. Salvatore, as restored by Vespignani,[33] shows a Roman version that is still quite close to the Greek form, with the stereobate and stylobate rising in steps on all four sides and the antae of the pronaos aligned to the second columns of the peripteros. Temple B on the *forum holitorium* and temple A in the Largo Argentina display a marked directionality created by the podium with its single flight of stairs. This is the common Roman version of the ionic peripteral temple and is also seen in the plans of the Temples of Castor and Pollux and of Minerva on the Aventine. These last two structures display another feature, the enlargement of the peripteros in front of the cella by two inserted columns. The plan takes on more the appearance of a pseudodipteros as described by Vitruvius (3.2.6), though with one more column.

The relationship of the cella and the colonnade has been reconstructed for the temple plans of Barcelona and Evora.[34] In both cases the plan used was the Roman version of the modified ionic peripteral temple. Both have deep front porches, the antae aligned with the fourth columns on the side. Celles' plan for Barcelona shows the temple with a pronaos and two columns *in antis*. This is not a common pattern for the peripteral plans in the capital. The temple on the via di S. Salvatore does have a pronaos, but it is aligned with the second columns on the side. There are no columns *in antis*. The Evora plan, without any pronaos, follows the Roman norm and may well indicate the type that stood in Mérida.

These porches with a depth of four side columns are a distinctive feature of the Iberian and the Roman peripteral temples. They are also a common trait of the great republican temples of the *sine postico* type, such as that of Jupiter Anxur or of Hercules Victor at Tivoli.[35] The two

32. Ibid., 108–15.

33. Ibid., pl. XV, fig. 3.

34. Evora: A. García y Bellido, "El recinto mural romano de Evora," *Conimbriga* 10 (1971) 85–92. Barcelona: Celles' plan in J. Puig i Cadafalch, A. de Falguera, J. Goday, *L'arquitectura romana a Catalunya* (Barcelona 1934) fig. 92. See also J. Bassegoda Nonell, *El templo romano de Barcelona* (Barcelona 1974). The cella and pronaos is not really understood yet for the "Temple of Diana" at Mérida. The palace that was built into the temple remains has obscured the interior portions of the structure.

35. Temple of Jupiter Anxur: L. Borsari, "Terracina: Del tempio di Giove Anxur scoperto sulla vetta di Monte S. Angelo," *NSc* (1894) 96–111; G. Lugli, *Forma Italiae* I. 1: *Anxur-Tarracina* (Rome 1926). Temple of Heracles Victor: C. F. Giuliani, *Forma Italiae* 1. 6: *Tibur* I (Rome 1970).

major new temples that Augustus commissioned in Rome, the Temple
of Venus Genetrix and the Temple of Mars Ultor, were built with the
sine postico plan and also display this deep porch.[36] The three peripteral
temples on the Iberian Peninsula must be seen as the continuation of an
architectural form that developed in Rome, a combination of the ionic
peripteral plan and the republican *sine postico* type.

The exteriors of the podia of the three temples are constructed using
a conservative technique of cut and fitted local stone. This old-fashioned
approach to building is also seen in the capitals of the temple at Mérida
(fig. 4). These are composed of three separate blocks, which were covered with stucco.[37] The use of the army to build in the newly conquered
regions such as Lusitania could explain these local features, at least at
Mérida and Evora.[38] Army engineers would have worked with local materials and used familiar methods.

The decorative details of the capitals and the column bases of the
three temples exhibit evidence of two different trends that were being
blended together. The tori of the bases for the columns at Mérida and
Barcelona are equal, top and bottom, a republican profile also known
for the bases at the Temples of Valetudo at Glanum and of Augustus and
Livia at Vienne. This same republican element can be found in the structure of the capitals at Mérida and in the decorative treatment of the
capitals at Barcelona. The Barcelona capitals (fig. 5) have a flat, linear,
lacelike decorative pattern that resembles that of the capitals from the
Temple of Augustus and Livia at Vienne (fig. 6). This dry, linear approach to the foliage of the capitals developed out of late republican
styles.[39] Barcelona was in a civilized sector of the Iberian Peninsula.
There is no reason to assume that the army engineers built this temple.
It seems more probable that older and newer forms were mixed here
just as in Gallia Narbonensis.

The corinthian capitals of the temple at Evora (fig. 7) are composed
of single marble blocks, a technique that became common in buildings
after the republican period. The marble bases of the columns of the
temple have tori of markedly unequal diameters and thus present the
elegant profile found on metropolitan Roman bases during the classicizing Augustan period. These are the same refinements that can be noted

36. Coarelli (supra n. 29) 100–101; Ward-Perkins (supra n. 21) figs. 7 and 8; Gros
(supra n. 31) pl. XIII.
37. J. M. de la Barrera Antón, *Los capiteles romanos de Mérida* (Badajoz 1984) no. 1.
38. R. MacMullen, "Roman Imperial Building in the Provinces," *HSCP* 64 (1959) 210,
214.
39. Gros (supra n. 19) 168–69.

in the Maison Carrée (fig. 8). The capitals of the Lusitanian temple and the Maison Carrée exhibit similar flowing of the volutes and pronounced horizontal curvature of the abacus, emphasized by the central placement of the rosette above the meeting point of the helices. Three rows of acanthus leaves on the capitals curve to form a lip and flare out to give prominence to the shape of the capital.[40] The architect for the temple at Evora did not possess the sophistication or skill of his contemporary at Nîmes, nor had he the same quality materials to produce his work. The granite column shafts for the Evora temple are more crudely worked and have fewer flutes than the elegant and refined shafts of the columns of the Maison Carrée. In this respect, the temple at Evora more closely resembles the "Temple of Diana" at Mérida. The corinthian capitals at Mérida (fig. 4) are only roughly blocked out, since the refinements were done in plaster. But the profiles of the capitals, even in their rough state, resemble the capitals of the temple at Evora. There is the same flaring to the volutes. The capitals of the temples at Evora, Mérida, and Nîmes share a similar plasticity that can also be seen in the capitals of the Temple of Mars Ultor in Rome. These similarities among certain western temples suggest that local builders were working according to some officially prescribed system. Distinctive individual features indicate that the specific projects must have been guided by *Skizzenbücher.*

Where the government wanted to promote the new forms by example, such as in the Maison Carrée, or by force, as in the recently pacified provinces like Lusitania, army engineers may have been responsible for the selection of the sites and the choice of certain design elements.[41] The *Skizzenbücher* provided the information for refinements. Where Romanized populations already lived the new could be made to harmonize with the old.

The peripteral plan itself offered the image of prestige and grand classical style for imperial projects. Augustus chose not to exploit it in that way in the capital. During Augustus' reign no new peripteral temples were built in Rome. The only other peripteral temple to be worked on may have been the Temple of Athena at Ilium.[42] Augustus rededicated

40. For the basic study of the development of the corinthian capital, see W. D. Heilmeyer, *Korinthische Normalkapitelle: Studien zur Geschichte der römischen Architekturdekoration* (Heidelberg 1970).

41. See P. Gros, "Qui était l'architecte de la Maison Carrée?" *Histoire et archéologie* 55 (July–August 1981) 42.

42. E. Akurgal, *Ancient Civilizations and Ruins of Turkey* (Istanbul 1978) 62. Gros (supra n. 31) 109, n. 55.

the peripteral Temples of Castor and Pollux and of Minerva, but he did not necessarily rebuild them.[43] On the other hand, on the Iberian Peninsula the plan is combined with features most commonly found on republican temples in Italy: conservative building technique, the use of local stone, the presence of column bases without plinths and with tori of almost equal diameters. These hybrid provincial temples combined plans ultimately derived from eastern Greek sources with conservative Roman building practices and new and old decorative vocabulary. They gave visual form to the concept of Roman unity, which was now being stressed. In those regions of the West that had no traditional connections with the classical world, such as Lusitania, these new temples with decorative elements based on metropolitan prototypes stood out as novel structures. They announced the arrival of a new social order and displayed the grandeur that Rome could bestow on the provinces. More importantly, they provided a visual link between the provincial cities. The tribal or ethnic or cultural boundaries among the western peoples were not reinforced by the immediately obvious differences in building types and urban settings.[44] Elsewhere in Gaul and Iberia, where long-standing ties existed between native and Punic, Greek, or Roman colonists, these hybrid temples with their old-fashioned details reminded the locals of their traditional associations with the larger Mediterranean and promoted the notion of integration into the larger world.

Arches and Trophies

Urban plans and buildings provided backdrops for the practice of Roman life. The dramatic difference between the old traditions, still to be seen in the countryside, and the new grandeur of the cities served to heighten the native provincials' awareness of the arrival of a new system. Neither plans nor architecture could explain to the provincials their role in this new order of things, however. Sculptural programs were needed to illustrate the situation.

Several of the cities in Gallia Narbonensis were embellished with public sculpture on arches and trophies. The structures were intended to be imposing. The arches were placed prominently at the juncture of

43. Tiberius may have been responsible for rebuilding the Temple of Castor and Pollux: D. E. Strong and J. B. Ward-Perkins, "The Temple of Castor in the Forum Romanum," *BSR* 30 (1962) 1–30; Coarelli (supra n. 29) 43.

44. Native sanctuaries along with local building types and methods of construction did continue to be used as at Autun and in Gallia Belgica. However, visual homogeneity was to be the norm in the urban centers of the Roman West after Augustus.

the *pomerium* with the Kardo or Decumanus Maximus. The trophies stood on frontier crossroads at the east and west ends of the province.[45] The sculptural programs are alike in their emphasis on martial iconography and stock elements such as captured weapons, bound captives, and battlefield trophies. With the exception of the arch at Orange, which may have been rededicated by Tiberius to celebrate his suppression of a local revolt,[46] the monuments are all Augustan in date, though the internal chronology is not certain.

No uniform theme was promoted in these sculptural programs. At the veterans' colonies of Arles (Colonia Julia Paterna Sextanorum Arelate), Béziers (Colonia Julia Baeterrae Septimanorum), and Narbonne (Narbo Martius) the stress was placed on the conquest of the Gauls and Greeks, as shown by the presence of Greek and Gallic armaments on the reliefs. Caesar had captured Greek Marseilles, and two of his legions were settled at Narbonne and Arles. Silverberg-Peirce has dated these arches to the years immediately after Augustus assumed sole control, and the reference could be to Caesar's success.[47]

More complex and more complete programs can be found on the arches at Carpentras (Colonia Julia Meminorum Carpentorate) and Vienne (Colonia Julia Vienna).[48] The compositions display bound captives placed around trophies. On the arch at Carpentras, one figure wearing an animal fur has been identified as a German, while a second male figure in a tunic with a Phrygian cap could be either a Dalmatian or a Parthian.[49] The chained captives on the arch at Vienne are also wearing pointed caps and may be Parthians. In these instances the iconography speaks of Roman conquests outside the boundaries of Gallia Narbonensis. On the arch at Saint Rémy there is a figure of a captive

45. S. Silverberg-Peirce, "The Many Faces of the Pax Augusta: Images of War and Peace in Rome and Gallia Narbonensis," *Art History* 9:3 (September 1986) 311. The trophy at Saint-Bertrand-de-Comminges is technically in Gallia Aquitania. G. Charles-Picard, "La mythologie au service de la romanisation dans les provinces occidentales de l'empire romain," in L. Kahil and C. Augé, eds., *Mythologie gréco-romaine, mythologies périphériques: Etudes d'iconographie* (Paris 1979) 45–46, has argued that the mausoleum of the Julii at Saint Rémy may also have carried imperial (public) iconography in its decorative program. For additional studies of the arches, see F. S. Kleiner, *The Arch of Nero in Rome: A Study of the Roman Honorary Arch Before and Under Nero*, Archaeologica 52 (Rome 1985); G. Charles-Picard, *Les trophées romaines: Contribution à l'histoire de la religion et de l'art triomphal de Rome* (Paris 1957).

46. R. Amy, P. M. Duval, J. Formigé, J. J. Hatt, A. Piganiol, G. Charles-Picard, *L'arc d'Orange*, Gallia Suppl. 15 (Paris 1962) 148–54.

47. Silverberg-Peirce (supra n. 45) 310.

48. Silverberg-Peirce dates the Carpentras arch to ca. 7 B.C.; Charles-Picard (1957: supra n. 45) 283–84 to ca. 20 B.C.

49. Silverberg-Peirce (supra n. 45) 318–19.

Gallic warrior, but elsewhere on the arch there are other captive figures. One with a possible beard could be a German; the other, wearing trousers, may be an Alpine tribesman.[50] If that is the iconography, then again the emphasis is placed on troublesome natives outside the geographic sphere of Gallia Narbonensis.

The iconographic program for the trophy found at Saint-Bertrand-de-Comminges (Lugdunum Convenarum), in the province of Gallia Aquitania, has been reconstructed on three levels. The lowest celebrated Augustus' victory at Actium, recognized from the presence of a ship's prow and a fragment of a Victory figure. The middle recorded the Roman success in the Cantabrian wars, indicated by a grouping of a free-standing, unchained figure in native garb and a bound, kneeling captive. A similar grouping may have formed the top, which honored the Roman victories in Germany. The monument dates 20/19 B.C., toward the conclusion of the Cantabrian wars (28–19 B.C.).[51]

The complex iconographic program for the trophy at Saint-Bertrand again stresses the victories over and subjugation of peoples outside Gallia Aquitania. The unbound female figure and the unbound male figure with a torc must be personifications of the Romanized native populations that allied themselves with Rome. Their presence on the monument reinforces the concept of integration of provincial natives into the larger world of Rome, which is still in the process of expansion. The unfettered native is a protected member of the Roman Empire and is placed in apposition to the captive. The message is simple: Become a part of the empire and enjoy its protection, or remain bowed in defeat.

The monuments, like the temples, were new structures. The earliest may have been erected in Gaul during the Republic. The sources for the architectural types and the iconographic messages are probably to be found in the Hellenistic world.[52] The architecture, as much as the iconography, carried the notion of a Roman order. Silverberg-Peirce has argued that the tenor of the iconography of the sculptural programs remained always that of subjugation, and the natives must have been constantly reminded of their conquered status.[53] However, the messages were not uniform, and in the more complex programs the emphasis is placed not on local conquest but on conquest outside of the region—in

50. Ibid., 317; Charles-Picard (1957: supra n. 45) 196 disagrees and sees all the figures as Gallic.
51. Silverberg-Peirce (supra n. 45) 313–14; Charles-Picard (1957: supra n. 45): 270–73.
52. Charles-Picard (1957: supra n. 45) 144–56.
53. Silverberg-Peirce (supra n. 45) 319.

Germany, Dalmatia, or Parthia or on the Cantabrian coast. On the trophy at Saint-Bertrand and on the arch at Orange, the specific power and
success of the emperor Augustus is honored with references to the battle
at Actium.[54] The person of the emperor forms an important element in
the message of pacification and unification. At Saint-Bertrand, he is associated with the conquest of a border region and the integration of
other native areas. His importance is most clearly stated in the great
inscription that records the subjugation of the Alpine tribes on the Trophy of the Alps (Tropaeum Alpium) at La Turbie, dedicated in 6 B.C.
(Pliny *HN* 3.4.20; Strab. 6.1.3). The trophy was dedicated to the emperor by the senate and the people of Rome; he is responsible for the
security of the province, because under his rule the Alpine peoples have
been pacified. Picard has suggested that the trophy was more than just a
standing monument; it included a sacred area with an altar surrounded
by a temenos.[55] While the message of Roman might and subjugation
could never have been distant from these arches and trophies, it may be
risky to assume that their references to the conquest and subjugation of
peoples outside the borders of the province were not recognized by their
provincial viewers. They served as much to incorporate Romanized
Gaul with Rome herself in opposition to the still unpacified, native regions as they did to kindle memories of Roman conquest. The Romanized native was intended to see his or her benefits as coming from the
association and protection of Rome.

The Gallic monuments stand out as distinct from most of the Italian
arches, such as Augustus' Parthian arch, which may commemorate military matters but tend to be devoid of the violence that is the basic theme
of the sculptural programs on the Gallic examples.[56] Yet the militaristic
theme fits comfortably into the larger propaganda campaign that Augustus was promulgating in the western provinces. Augustus did not
promote the virtue of long-lasting *pax*, but rather of peace achieved
through the agency of military might. Gruen has argued that *pax* was

54. Ibid., 315–16. The arch at Orange was probably reworked under Tiberius to celebrate his suppression of a local revolt with references to both Caesar's conquest of Marseilles and Tiberius' victory in the region: Amy et al. (supra n. 46) 148–54.
55. Charles-Picard (1957: supra n. 45) 292–93; Charles-Picard reproduces Mommsen's reconstruction of the inscription. See also J. Formigé, *La trophée des Alpes (La Turbie)*, Gallia Suppl. 2 (Paris 1949).
56. One of the gates into Saepinum in southern Italy was an arch that carried sculpted
figures of barbarians. However, the arch may date to the period of Tiberius and could
reflect the return to militaristic themes such as have also been noted for the arch at Orange.
See F. Coarelli and A. La Regina, *Abruzzo Milise,* Guide archeologiche Laterza 9 (Rome
1984) 216–17; *PECS* 781. I want to thank Stephen Dyson for making me aware of this
gateway.

not a republican virtue, and Augustus did not raise its prestige. It does not appear as a common coin type for the emperor, nor was it employed as an element in the imperial iconography. Instead, peace was seen as the result of a Roman victory over the agents of discord. It is this iconography that was developed on the sculptural decoration of the provincial arches and trophies. Roman armies conquered, and in their wake came peace. With peace came the flowering of Roman civilization on new soil, the civilization manifested in the Roman cities in which stood the arches.[57]

Augustus

Augustus, the emperor, became the icon that bound the western territories together. The importance of the icon is seen in the change that took place in the autonomous coinage of the western mints. The emperor's portrait was the only obverse type. Local references were limited to the reverse types. The local styles of die cutting, which were still quite noticeable in the later republican and early Augustan coinage, disappeared, subsumed in a more general imperial style of die treatment that reflected prototypes coming out of the mint at Rome.[58]

The circulation of the imperial portrait on local coins often in association with a well-known local monument as the reverse type served as a constant reminder of the Romanness of the region. In the same way, Augustus' official portraits, which could be found in any provincial city, underscored the individual nature of this patron of the western territories. In certain instances, the imperial portrait could also carry the message of Roman culture. A portrait of Augustus from Mérida shows the emperor *velato capite*, his head covered by the hem of his toga.[59] He is depicted in the act of sacrificing. The image is both traditional and distinctly Roman, for it was a Roman practice to make sacrifices with a veiled head.[60] Among the earliest public sculptural groupings in the newly Romanized cities were figures of the imperial family, especially Lucius and Caius.[61]

57. E. S. Gruen, "Augustus and the Ideology of War and Peace," in R. Winkes, ed., *The Age of Augustus*, Archaeologica Transatlantica 5 (Providence and Louvain-la-Neuve 1986) 51–72.

58. W. H. Gross, "Ways and Roundabout Ways in the Propaganda of an Unpopular Ideology," in Winkes (supra n. 57) 38.

59. Almagro (supra n. 26) 50, pl. XLVI.

60. Gross (supra n. 58) 36.

61. Trier: Heinen (supra n. 13) 38; for a coin image of a possible grouping in Caesaraugusta, A. Beltrán, "Los monumentos en las monedas hispano-romanos," *ArchExpArq*

The most important statements of the tie that bound the provinces to the emperor were made in a series of large altars erected throughout the West. These were dedicated to Roma and Augustus and later to Augustus alone. They included the state-initiated altars on the banks of the Elbe (Tac. *Ann.* 1.39.1, 57.3; Dio 55.10a.2); at Lyon (Lugdunum) (fig. 9), inaugurated by Drusus in 12 B.C. (Strab. 4.3.2; Livy *Per.* 139) and serving as the focus for the meetings and ceremonies of the *concilium Galliarum;*[62] and at Cologne, the Ara Ubiorum, constructed between 8 B.C. and A.D. 5. There were also municipal cult altars at Tarragona (Colonia Julia Urbs Triumphalis Tarraco) and perhaps at Mérida.[63]

The altars were erected under Augustus, who obviously promoted the revival of the Hellenistic altar type in Rome, as evidenced by the Ara Pacis. Their appearance in the native areas of the West is another instance of the imposition of a metropolitan design on the provinces. The altars were important; their images figured as reverse coin types, indicating some civic prominence. They can also be regarded as another attempt to create with architecture and sculpture an urban unity.

Some recent discoveries made at some of the western sites suggest that other novel architectuural changes were made during the reign of Augustus. At Arles a portico was constructed that copied aspects of the Portico of Octavia in Rome.[64] In Nîmes the major native sanctuary with its fountains was redesigned perhaps to form the precinct for the city's municipal altar to Roma and Augustus. There may have been a theatrical area established for ceremonies similar to those the emperor had initiated in Naples in A.D. 2 (Strab. 5.4.7; Suet. *Aug.* 59.3; Dio 55.10.9, 56.29.2).[65] Nowhere was this copying carried farther than at Mérida, where the pattern of caryatids and medallions from the attic story of the

---

26:87 (1953) 63–65; for a grouping of members of the Julio-Claudian family of Tiberian date from the theater at Tarragona (Tarraco), E. M. Koppel, *Die römischen Skulpturen von Tarraco* (Berlin 1985) 28–29.

62. The altar at Lyon is known from a coin image struck between 11 and 9 B.C. See O. Brogan, "The Coming of Rome and the Establishment of Roman Gaul," in Piggott, Daniel, and McBurney (supra n. 6) 204; A. Audin, *Essai sur la topographie de Lugdunum* (Lyon 1964); A. Audin and P. Quoniam, "Victoires et colonnes de l'autel fédéral des Trois Gaules—données nouvelles," *Gallia* 20 (1962) 103–16; D. Fishwick, "The Development of Provincial Ruler Worship in the Western Roman Empire," *ANRW* 2.16.2 (1978) 1201–53; id., "The Temple of the Three Gauls," *JRS* 62 (1972) 46–52.

63. The Tarraco altar is known from a reference in Quint. *Inst.* 6.3.77 and from coin images struck during the reign of Tiberius; see D. Fishwick, "The Altar of Augustus and the Municipal Cult of Tarraco," *MM* 23 (1982) 222–37; E. Hübner, "Tarraco und seine Denkmäler," *Hermes* 1 (1866) 110. The altar at Mérida (Augusta Emerita) is known solely from a coin image also struck by Tiberius; de Guadán (supra n. 9) nos. 997, 1001–3.

64. Gros (supra n. 19) 168.

65. P. Gros, "L'Augusteum de Nîmes," *RANarb* 17 (1984) 129–31.

Forum of Augustus was recreated in the precinct of the "Temple of Diana." [66] The copies of the caryatids (fig. 10) have been changed from supporting members of the trabeation to high-relief decoration. The medallion heads of Jupiter Ammon and Medusa (figs. 11, 12) show local sculptural traits. The heads occupy the central portion of the tondo and are surrounded by the tongue pattern of the outer border. The imbricated leaf pattern that forms the bed on which the heads rest in the versions from the Forum of Augustus is totally lacking on the Mérida pieces. The drill work is similar in both the Roman and provincial works, though on the latter the treatment of the beard where it meets the border seems more patterned. The hair of the Mérida Gorgons appears to have been arranged into more arbitrary parallel linear plays. Nonetheless, there can be no doubt of the source for the decorative program. Though the sculptural remains were not found *in situ,* it has been postulated by Alvarez Martínez, among others, that they decorated a structure in the vicinity of the "Temple of Diana." It is not possible to tell whether the structure was a building or something akin to the portico of the Forum of Augustus. The "Temple of Diana" did occupy a prominent position in the urban plan of the new colony. It also must have been standing by the end of Augustus' reign, if not earlier. By the second century it was a temple to the imperial cult,[67] and it seems likely that even during Augustus' lifetime the precinct was already the focus of an incipient cult to the emperor. It would not have been state sanctioned, but, like that at the rival provincial capital at Tarraco, municipal. There now does seem to be evidence, scant as it is, from elsewhere in the West to indicate that among the other projects sanctioned by the emperor some tentative steps were taken to establish architecturally formulated cult spaces for ceremonies that were completely Roman. By the time of Tiberius, the cult did exist at Mérida and was commemorated on a coin.[68] The fragments of sculpture from Mérida have been dated to the middle of the first century, which must indicate the date for the conclusion of work on the project. At the time of the end of the project a large relief was carved and set up in the same area. It showed Agrippa

66. M. F. Squarciapino, "Ipotesi sul gruppo di sculture da Pan Caliente," in *Augusta Emerita* (Madrid 1976) 55–62; id., "Cultura artística di Mérida romana," in *Homenaje a Sáenz de Buruaga* (Madrid 1982) 33–52; P. Zanker, *Forum Augustum: das Bildprogramm* (Tübingen 1968).
67. Alvarez Martínez (supra n. 25) 50–51; id., "El foro de Augusto Emerita," in *Homenaje a Sáenz de Buruaga* (Madrid 1982) 53–68.
68. The coin image, a tetrastyle temple, does not resemble the standing remains of the temple; however, the question of whether coin images can accurately reproduce real buildings is still a much debated subject; see de Guadán (supra n. 9) no. 1011; A. Vives y Escudero, *La moneda hispánica* (Madrid 1926) pl. CXLVI, nos. 6, 9, 10.

in the act of performing a sacrifice and must represent an official restate-
ment of the city's association with Augustus.[69]

Conclusion

Much of what was built during the Augustan decades had no specific
imperial associations. But there was an imperial interest in the West. It
can be seen in the amount of time the emperor spent in the provinces, in
the administrative decisions that he made in regard to the provinces,
and in the kinds of architecture and public sculpture that began to pre-
dominate in the western cities. The concern was to generate a visual
image of Romanness that could give encouragement to the idea of assimilation and promote a sense of common unity and shared values in a
heterogeneous mix of peoples. There remain unanswered questions:
Where might the architecture and sculpture have been the result of an
official policy, and where was it the response of the local population?
Picard thought that the Trophy of the Alps was probably built and decorated by local craftsmen but used cartoons sent from Rome.[70] The
temples at new foundations like Augusta Emerita may have been designed and built under the direction of army engineers following some
type of standard, official plan, but what underlies the choice of temple
plan at a small town such as Barcelona or even a city like Ampurias is
not so obvious. It may reflect the increasing sense of Romanness in the
local population. It would be helpful to be able to isolate the possible
agents who must have encouraged the adoption of forms that broke
with local traditions and emulated mainstream Italian and Greek models. The success with which the new was able to replace the old is striking. With the exception of some small sanctuaries in Gaul and some
outdoor, natural shrines in southern Spain, the pre-Roman native identities of the peoples of the West, as earlier given form in the visual arts,
disappeared after Augustus. By the end of the Julio-Claudian dynasty,
the western provinces were providing Latin writers, politicians, and
eventually emperors. The Romanization of the West did not take the
form of a thin veneer covering stronger native or tribal sensibilities. Roman identity replaced the older concepts of self. The process began
under Augustus, and the building projects were one of the means by
which the new sense of Romanness was encouraged to take root.

---

69. W. Trillmich, "Ein historisches Relief in Merida mit Darstellung des M. Agrippa
beim Opfer, ein Rekonstruktionsversuch," *MM* 27 (1986) 279–304.
   70. Charles-Picard (1957: supra n. 45) 293.

Figure 1. Gate at Mérida (Augusta Emerita). Coin reverse from mint of Augusta Emerita. Courtesy of the American Numismatic Society, New York.

Figure 2. Gate of Saint-André at Autun. Courtesy of Virginia Raguin.

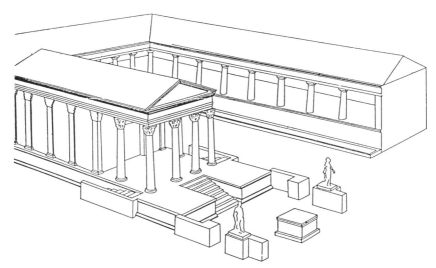

Figure 3. Reconstruction of the temple region of the forum at Ampurias, late first century B.C. After plan 15 in J. Aquilué Abadias, et al., *El fórum romà d'Empuries* (Barcelona, 1984).

Figure 4. Above, Capital from the Temple of Diana at Mérida (Augusta Emerita). Photo by author.

Figure 5. Capitals of the forum temple at Barcelona. Photo by author. Figure 6. Below, Capitals from the Temple of Augustus and Livia at Vienne. Photo by author.

Figure 7. Capital from the Temple of Diana at Evora. Photo by author.

Figure 8. Detail of the southeast corner of the entablature, Maison Carrée, Nîmes. Courtesy Marburg/Art Resource, New York.

Figure 9. Altar of Roma and Augustus at Lyon (Lugdunum). Coin reverse from mint at Lugdunum. Courtesy of the American Numismatic Society, New York.

Figure 10. Above and left, Caryatids from Mérida (Augusta Emerita). Courtesy of the Museo Nacional de Arte Romano, Mérida.

Figure 11. Clipeus with head of Jupiter Ammon from Mérida (Augusta Emerita). Courtesy of the Museo Nacional de Arte Romano, Mérida.

Figure 12. Clipeus with head of Gorgon (Medusa) from Mérida (Augusta Emerita). Courtesy of the Museo Nacional de Arte Romano, Mérida.

Man or God:
Divine Assimilation and Imitation
in the Late Republic and Early Principate

An important feature of religious belief and political rhetoric in the late Republic and the principate is the special relationship that individual leaders claimed to enjoy with the gods, an idea which served to enhance the leader's position in the state and to validate his acts.[1] In the visual arts an association with the divine could be expressed most directly

1. This paper is a somewhat reworked and enlarged version of the one that I delivered at colloquia at Brown University and the University of California, Berkeley. I have profited greatly from discussions of these and related subjects at both colloquia. Special thanks are owed to K. Raaflaub and R. Winkes of Brown University and to E. Gruen of the University of California at Berkeley. After the original version of this paper was completed, there appeared two contributions in particular that are concerned to some extent with the imagery on Augustan coinage: W. Trillmich, "Münzpropaganda," in *Kaiser Augustus und die verlorene Republik,* Exhibition Catalogue (Berlin 1988) 474–528 and P. Zanker, *Augustus und die Macht der Bilder* (Munich 1987). Of the two, only Zanker deals with Augustus' changing image on coinage. I disagree with his conclusions about divine imitation, especially prior to Actium, but the limitations of space preclude my discussing here fully the problems with his interpretations. I shall return to these matters in my forthcoming book, *The Image of Augustus: Art and Ideology,* in which I consider not only the coinage but also other artistic media of an official and unofficial nature.

For a general treatment of the Roman leader's relationship with the divine, see L. R. Taylor, *The Divinity of the Roman Emperor* (Middletown, Conn. 1931); L. Cerfaux and J. Tondriau, *Un concurrent du Christianisme: Le culte des souverains dans la civilisation gréco-romaine* (Tournai 1957); F. Taeger, *Charisma: Studien zur Geschichte des antiken Herrscherkultes,* vol. 2 (Stuttgart 1960); J. R. Fears, *Princeps a Diis Electus: The Divine*

through assimilation or imitation of a divinity. Divine assimilation comprises either the alteration of an individual's portrait so that he looks like a god, or the representation of a god with some degree of physiognomic resemblance to a specific individual. In either case, there may be ambiguity as to whether a man is portrayed like a god, or a god like a man. I would define divine imitation as the representation of an individual with divine symbols or attributes and often nude or seminude. The nature and meaning of such assimilation and imitation are still not well understood because of the many complex issues involved. Misunderstandings, for example, have often resulted from a fundamental failure (1) to distinguish between official and unofficial modes of representation,[2] (2) to consider whether a work was created during or after the lifetime of the individual portrayed, and (3) to take into account changes in political situations and ideology over a period of time.

I shall focus here primarily on artistic images of an official nature in the period of transition from republic to principate, more precisely from about 45 B.C. to the death of Augustus in A.D. 14.[3] This period presents particular difficulties because it was a time of great experimentation in the formulation and visual expression of political ideology. Since so few

---

Election of the Emperor as a Political Concept at Rome, PAAR 26 (Rome 1977); H. Gesche, "Die Divinisierung der römischen Kaiser in ihrer Funktion als Herrschaftslegitimation," *Chiron* 8 (1978) 377–90. For the coinage, see especially D. Mannsperger, "ROM ET AUG: Die Selbstdarstellung des Kaisertums in der römischen Reichsprägung," *ANRW* 2.1 (1974) 919–96. For a survey of important anthropological work on divine kingship, G. Feeley-Harnik, "Issues in Divine Kingship," *Annual Review of Anthropology* 14 (1985) 273–313. On the background and evolution of the Roman imperial cult, R. Etienne, *Le culte impérial dans la péninsule ibérique d'Auguste à Dioclétien,* BEFAR 191 (Paris 1958); C. Habicht, "Die augusteische Zeit und das erste Jahrhundert nach Christi Geburt," in *Le culte des souverains dans l'empire romain,* Entretiens sur l'ant. class. 19 (Vandoeuvres and Geneva 1973) 41–100; R. Turcan, "Le culte impérial au IIIe siècle," *ANRW* 2.16.2 (1978) 996–1084; D. Fishwick, "The Development of the Provincial Ruler Worship in the Western Roman Empire," ibid., 1204–10; id., *The Imperial Cult in the Latin West* (Leiden 1987); S. R. F. Price, *Rituals and Power: The Roman Imperial Cult in Asia Minor* (Cambridge 1984). For an exhaustive bibliography on various aspects of the imperial cult, P. Herz, "Bibliographie zum römischen Kaiserkult (1955–1975)," *ANRW* 2.16.2 (1978) 833–910.

2. By "official" I mean those modes of representation sanctioned by the Roman state rather than by a local government having some measure of autonomy.

3. For the arts of this period, see especially I. S. Ryberg, *Rites of the State Religion in Roman Art,* MAAR 19 (Rome 1955) 23–63; J. Pollini, *Studies in Augustan "Historical" Reliefs* (Diss. Univ. of Calif. at Berkeley 1978); P. Zanker and K. Vierneisel, *Die Bildnisse des Augustus* (Munich 1979); A.-K. Massner, *Bildnisangleichung. Das römische Herrscherbild IV* (Berlin 1982); T. Hölscher, *Staatsdenkmal und Publikum.* Xenia 9 (Konstanz 1984); T. Pekáry, *Das römische Kaiserbildnis in Staat, Kult und Gesellschaft. Das römische Herrscherbild III* (Berlin 1985); N. Hannestad, *Roman Art and Imperial Policy* (Aarhus 1986) 15–92 (with an excellent topically arranged bibliography); E. Simon, *Augustus, Kunst und Leben in Rom um die Zeitenwende* (Munich 1986); *Kaiser Augustus* (supra n. 1); Zanker (supra n. 1).

state monuments reflecting the official view have come down to us, I shall concentrate on the official coinage in examining the general line of development and the significance of divine assimilation and imitation. Varying and conflicting statements have been made in the past about these matters, which have never been dealt with in a comprehensive way.

For the artistic imagery of the period under consideration, the major turning points were the victories at Actium and Alexandria in 31 and 30, respectively, and the establishment of the principate in 27 B.C., resulting in what is called today the "first constitutional settlement." At that time Octavian claimed in his *Res Gestae* (34.1): *rem publicam ex mea potestate in senatus populique Romani arbitrium transtuli*. Having reestablished a form of constitutional government, Octavian (renamed Augustus) began to propagate a new ideology, one of the aims of which was the reconciliation of Rome's nobility, whose cooperation and support were needed to maintain peace and stability within the empire after a century of foreign war and civil conflict. As its essential feature, the new ideology held that Augustus' position in the state was that of *princeps*, or "first citizen", with various offices and powers voted to him by the senate and people. A "second constitutional settlement" in 23 brought about further modifications in his position. For the most part, he now exchanged political office for equivalent and additional political powers. It has generally not been recognized that in official art there were important changes and modifications in modes of representation after 31/30 and then again after 27, with additional modifications in some of the coinage between about 19 and 12, while in private art forms there was a continuity in imagery.[4] In my opinion, the period from 31/30 to 27 was a time of considerable experimentation in which association with the divine was expressed more directly in Octavian's official artistic program than it had been previously. Prior to 31 Octavian seems to have projected officially an image that would not give open offense to old republican sensibilities.[5]

When used with caution, the artistic record, especially numismatic evidence, can be a valuable resource in assessing historical situations.[6] More often than not, however, historians either do not utilize artistic

4. Those who would see an important change in official imagery generally place the turning point in 27 B.C., but do not recognize the change before and after 31/30 or after ca. 19.

5. Contra Zanker (supra n. 1) 46–52, 61–65.

6. On the interpretive value of coinage, see the critical remarks of A. H. M. Jones in "Numismatics and History," in *Essays in Roman Coinage Presented to H. Mattingly* (Oxford 1956) 15f., with response by C. H. V. Sutherland, "The Intelligibility of Roman Im-

evidence or treat it only superficially. Even R. Syme in his highly influential *Roman Revolution,* published half a century ago, did not give sufficient attention to numismatic evidence; he also did not clearly distinguish between official and private art or give any sense of changes and modifications of Augustus' image in the visual arts in response to changes in political situations.[7] That Augustus monopolized all forms of artistic expression has often been indicated or implied by Syme and other historians without considering the actual evidence—or lack of evidence—for control or intervention by the *princeps* or his aides.

Before examining the official coinage of the period under discussion, let us briefly consider two important works of Augustan art that point up the essential differences between official and unofficial modes of representation. The official view is best expressed in the Ara Pacis Augustae, constructed between 13 and 9 B.C.[8] In keeping with the ideology of the principate, Augustus is portrayed in the south processional frieze without divine trappings: he appears here as *primus inter pares,* or "first among equals," performing an act of religious ritual. He therefore functions as mediator between gods and man—a means of implying rather than expressing directly a special relationship with the divine.[9] Significantly, at this stage in the evolution of Roman state art there is no casual mingling of living humans and divinities within the same scene.[10] Such

---

perial Coin Types," *JRS* 49 (1959) 46–55; for a more current survey of the problem, Mannsperger (supra n. 1) 920–28.

7. For a recent comprehensive historical treatment of Augustus, with extensive bibliography, see D. Kienast, *Augustus: Prinzeps und Monarch* (Darmstadt 1982). Though Kienast notes in general the difference between official and court art (*Hofkunst*), he does not discuss the problems inherent in representing Augustus in different artistic media and for different audiences.

8. The bibliography on the Ara Pacis is vast. Fundamental is G. Moretti, *Ara Pacis Augustae* (Rome 1948). Among others who deal with major aspects of this monument are E. Simon, *Ara Pacis Augustae* (Greenwich, Conn. 1967); Pollini (supra n. 3) 75–172; D. E. E. Kleiner, "The Great Friezes of the Ara Pacis Augustae. Greek Sources, Roman Derivatives, and Augustan Social Policy," *MélRome* 90 (1978) 733–85; M. Torelli, *Typology and Structure of Roman Historical Reliefs* (Ann Arbor, Mich. 1982) 27–61; E. La Rocca, *Ara Pacis Augustae* (Rome 1983); G. Koeppel, "*Maximus Videtur Rex:* The Collegium Pontificum on the *Ara Pacis Augustae,*" *ArchNews* 14 (1985) 17–22; Simon (supra n. 3) 29–46, 74–79, and passim; Hannestad (supra n. 3) 62–78; and S. Settis in *Kaiser Augustus* (supra n. 1) 400–26 with annotated bibliography on all aspects of the monument.

9. As already noted by Pollini (supra n. 3) 126f.

10. Augustus appears with a divinity in only three official coin types of his principate, and in each of these cases the divinity is victory personified. He is represented crowned by Victoria in two closely related reverse types on *aurei* and *denarii* minted in Spain in the first decade of his principate (*BMCRE* I, 75 [nos. 432–34], pl. 10.6–8; *RIC*[2] I, 50 [nos. 140–41, 144]) and in another type on the obverse of medallic-like coins of 7 B.C. (*RIC*[2] I, 75 [no. 433], pl. 8; *BMCRE* I, 41–43 [nos. *, 217–19, 224–25], pl. 20.4–6). In these examples Victoria appears symbolically almost as a part of Augustus' charisma, that is, as *Victoria Augusti*. Cf. T. Hölscher, *Victoria Romana* (Mainz 1967) 173–77; Fears (supra

mingling becomes common in the second half of the first century A.C., as in the famous Domitianic reliefs from the Palazzo della Cancelleria.[11] In the relief program of the Ara Pacis, Augustus' association with divine and heroic figures is indicated indirectly by the representation of such figures within the context of the monument, but—appropriately—in separate panels at the front and back of the altar.

By contrast, in private works of art created throughout his lifetime, Octavian/Augustus is commonly depicted as godlike. For example, in the Gemma Augustea,[12] a large cameo dated toward the end of his life, Augustus appears not *as* Jupiter, as some have claimed in the past, but rather *like* Jupiter—a subtle yet important distinction.[13] The fact that he holds the *lituus,* the crook-shaped staff of the augur, indicates that he has the power to interpret the will of Jupiter and is therefore subordinate to the supreme god of the Roman pantheon. Augustus' otherwise godlike manner of representation, which is in keeping with the encomiastic traditions of Hellenistic kingship, cannot be considered indicative of official Augustan ideology because of the private nature of the cameo. Similarly, in evaluating the evidence of literature and inscriptions, it is important to distinguish between pronouncements or views that are official and those which are essentially private or personal in nature. As A. D. Nock warned long ago, "We must distinguish sharply between a) the normal working theory of the principate, and the implications of what the princeps officially says or does and b) the metaphorical language used by men of letters or the corresponding expressions in arts."[14]

n. 1) 193. In any case, the medallic-like nature of the coin type of 7 B.C. indicates that this issue was not intended for wide distribution: M. Grant, *Roman Imperial Money* (London 1954) 101–3.

11. Fundamental is F. Magi, *I rilievi flavi del Palazzo della Cancelleria* (Rome 1945). See also G. Koeppel, "Profectio und Adventus," *BonnJbb* 169 (1969) 130–94; A. M. McCann, "A Re-Dating of the Reliefs from the Palazzo della Cancelleria," *RM* 79 (1972) 249–76, with response by F. Magi, "Brevi osservazioni su di una nuova datazione dei rilievi della Cancelleria," *RM* 80 (1973) 289–91; M. Bergmann, "Zum Fries B der flavischen Cancelleriareliefs," *MarbWPr* (1981) 19–31; E. Simon, "Virtus und Pietas: Zu den Friesen A. u. B. von der Cancelleria," *JdI* 100 (1985) 543–55; Hannestad (supra n. 3) 132–39; F. Ghedini, "Riflessi della politica domizianea nei relievi Flavi di Palazzo della Cancelleria," *BullCom* 91 (1986) 291–309.

12. The principal study on the Gemma Augustea is H. Kähler, *Alberti Rubeni Dissertatio de Gemma Augustea,* Monumenta Artis Romanae 9 (Berlin 1968). See also Pollini (supra n. 3) 173–254; id., "The Gemma Augustea: Ideology, Rhetorical Imagery, and the Creation of a Dynastic Narrative" (forthcoming in a collection of essays entitled *Narrative and Event in Ancient Art*); Hannestad (supra n. 3) 78–82; E. Simon, "Die drei Horoskope der Gemma Augustea," *NumAntCl* 15 (1986) 179–96; id. (supra n. 3) 156–61.

13. See further Pollini (supra n. 3) 188–92. See also Fears (supra n. 1) 208.

14. A. D. Nock, "A Diis Electa," *HThR* 32 (1930) 263f. (reprinted in Z. Stewart, ed., *Essays on Religion and the Ancient World* [Oxford 1972] 262); Fears (supra n. 1) 10f., 121–23, and passim; Pollini (supra n. 3) 256–342.

The most complete and continuous picture of the official view in the visual arts for the period from about 45 B.C. to A.D. 14 is provided by state coinage, which survives in abundance and can often be closely dated. State coinage is considered to be that minted by authority of the Roman senate or by individuals who had the right to mint by virtue of their consular or proconsular *imperium*.[15] This coinage—whether minted at Rome or in the provinces—comprises *aurei* and *denarii*, that is, gold and silver issues that generally circulated throughout the empire, as well as certain *aes,* or base metal coinage, which had a fairly large regional distribution. Such state issues should be distinguished from civic, or local, base metal coinage, which had limited geographic distribution and may be regarded as unofficial from the point of view of the Roman state government.[16]

As regards Roman state coinage, there has been a great deal of debate in recent years about how much input the *princeps* or his chief agents actually had in the choice of coin types, as well as about the degree to which the final image may have reflected the desires of this authority.[17] The ultimate issue is, of course, whether the coin imagery expressed the rhetoric of the *princeps* and was meant to serve a persuasive purpose.[18] Some recent thinking on this subject has suggested that those officials directly responsible for the creation of coin types were merely offering tokens of respect to the *princeps*.[19] I would like to suggest that although this assessment is correct in part, the *princeps* or senate would, in any officially sanctioned work, bear ultimate responsibility for what was produced, if only by the tacit acceptance of it. After all, if a coin image were deemed somehow inappropriate or offensive, an effort could have been made to withdraw it from circulation.[20]

15. A. M. Burnett, "The Authority to Coin in the Late Republic and Early Empire," *NC* 137 (1977) 37–55; A. Wallace-Hadrill, "Image and Authority in the Coinage of Augustus," *JRS* 76 (1986) 66–87.

16. See in general C. H. V. Sutherland, *The Emperor and the Coinage* (London 1976) 11–30, 34–36, 77.

17. See especially, recently, Burnett (supra n. 15) 37–55; Wallace-Hadrill (supra n. 15) 66–87; Sutherland (supra n. 16) 96–101; M. Crawford, "Roman Imperial Coin Types and the Formation of Public Opinion," in C. N. L. Brooke et al., eds., *Studies in Numismatic Method Presented to Philip Grierson* (Cambridge 1983) 47–64.

18. The question of the use of coinage as an instrument of propaganda is a difficult one, in part dependent on one's definition of propaganda. For the different points of view, see especially G. Belloni, "Significati storico-politici delle figurazioni e delle scritte delle monete da Augusto a Traiano," *ANRW* 2.1 (1974) 999f.; and more recently, Hannestad (supra n. 3) 9–14.

19. See, for example, B. Levick, "Propaganda and the Imperial Coinage," *Antichthon* 16 (1982) 107. For a more balanced view, Wallace-Hadrill (supra n. 15) 67–70.

20. Cf., for instance, the senatorial decree after Caligula's death that the bronze "senatorial" coinage bearing his image be melted down (Dio 60.22.3); see also comments by Burnett (supra n. 15) 55f.

The earliest clear numismatic example of divine assimilation or imitation is found on *asses,* or base metal coins, minted in Spain and Sicily around 45–44 by Sextus Pompey, son of Pompey the Great (fig. 1).[21] This military issue was not, however, part of the state coinage and was not regarded as legal by the Roman senate, since Sextus did not at this time hold a legal military command.[22] In this coin type, Janus is consistently shown without his characteristic beard and with the distinctive mature features of Sextus' father, Pompey the Great (fig. 2).[23] In literature, divinities occasionally take on the appearance of specific humans: in the *Aeneid* (1.658f.), for example, Cupid takes the form of Ascanius when he goes to meet Dido for the first time. Between 42 and 40 Sextus also issued illegally a series of *denarii* on which Neptune is sometimes represented simply as a divinity (fig. 3)[24] and sometimes portrayed with the features of Sextus' father (fig. 4).[25] Since the Neptune in this coinage is not consistent in its resemblance to Pompey the Great, it is likely that individual die engravers independently represented Neptune looking like Pompey. Nevertheless, the mere fact that a number of examples showing assimilation have come down to us constitutes de facto approval of this image by Sextus Pompey. Although the depiction on Roman coinage of a divinity with human features represents a major departure from what had preceded, Pompey the Great was already dead at the time of issuance of both coin types. Like any deceased individual, Pompey therefore belonged to the divine sphere, even though his divinity was not officially recognized.

The first representation of a god with features assimilated to those of a *living* individual[26] appears on *denarii* issued in 42 B.C. by a mint traveling with the triumvir Marc Antony in the East. These coins, which

21. *BMCRR* II, 371–72 (nos. 95–103), III, pl. ci. 13–14; M. Crawford, *Roman Republican Coinage* (Cambridge 1974) 487 (no. 479); A. Banti and L. Simonetti, *Corpus Nummorum Romanorum* (Florence 1972) I, 250–53 (nos. 34–36).

22. Sextus held legal power, as *praefectus classis et orae maritimae,* only from April 43 B.C. until August of the same year, when he was outlawed under the *Lex Pedia:* Vell. Pat. 2.69.5, 2.73.2. See also R. Syme, *The Roman Revolution* (Oxford 1939) 187; C. H. V. Sutherland, *Roman Coins* (New York 1974) 103.

23. Cf., however, R. Albert, *Das Bild des Augustus auf den frühen Reichsprägungen* (Speyer 1981) 31 with n. 73, who identifies this figure as Sextus Pompey himself. Compare the facing portraits of Pompey the Great and Sextus on the reverse of an *aureus* of ca. 40 B.C.: J. P. C. Kent, *Roman Coins* (New York 1978) fig. 102R. Moreover, at the time the Janus coin type was in production, Sextus was only twenty-two years old.

24. See, for example, Banti and Simonetti I (supra n. 21) 232–34 (nos. 1, 4/3, 5/1).

25. Ibid. 232f. (nos. 2/1, 4/2); Sutherland (supra n. 22) fig. 176.

26. Cf. the obverse bust of Victory on gold *quinarii* minted for Marc Antony at Lugdunum in 43–42: *BMCRR* II, 394f. (nos. 40–45), III, pl. ciii.10; Crawford (supra n. 21) 499 (no. 489/5). The individualized features and hairstyle may be those of Antony's wife Fulvia, but we have no known likenesses of her with which to compare it. The assimilation in this case is therefore uncertain.

may be regarded as official by virtue of his *imperium,* represent Antony on the obverse and the sun-god Sol on the reverse. As on the Neptune coinage of Sextus Pompey, the god on these coins in some instances bears a striking resemblance to the obverse image of Antony (cf. figs. 5 and 6),[27] while in other cases (e.g., fig. 7)[28] the god lacks Antony's distinctive features. This inconsistency suggests that assimilation was probably not dictated from above; however, as in the case of the Neptune coinage of Sextus Pompey, the existence of a number of examples showing this rather striking assimilation indicates Antony's acceptance of this divine imagery. It is important to remember that although such direct association with the divine was acceptable among eastern peoples, these *denarii* were primarily intended to pay Antony's Roman soldiers.

When divinities are imitated on coinage, the small size of the image sometimes makes it difficult to determine the identity of the individual appearing with divine trappings. For example, a reverse type on *denarii* minted for Sextus Pompey in 42–40 shows a Neptune-like figure, wearing a wreath, placing his right foot on a prow, and holding an *aplustre* in his right hand with *chlamys* wrapped around his left arm (fig. 8).[29] The beardlessness of this figure indicates that he is to be seen as a human in divine guise. Flanking him are the Catanaean brothers, each bearing his father (thus shown twice) on his shoulders—an emblem of *pietas.* The visual reference to *pietas* and the appearance of the head of Pompey the Great on the obverse suggest that the Neptune-like figure might very well be Pompey the Great.[30] In fact, coinage of 44–43 from a mint moving with Sextus had already represented the head of Pompey the Great with trident, dolphin, and the legend NEPTVNI.[31] Associated with this equation of the dead Pompey with Neptune is Sextus' styling himself in 40 the "son of Neptune": δόξαν τέ τινα καὶ φρόνημα ὡς καὶ τοῦ Ποσειδῶνος παῖς ὤν, ὅτι πάσης ποτὲ ὁ πατὴρ αὐτοῦ τῆς θαλάσσης ἦρξε, προσέθετο, "and he assumed a certain additional glory and pride by representing himself to be the son of Neptune, since his father had once ruled the whole sea" (Dio 48.19.2).

Particularly problematic is a reverse type associated with *denarii*

27. See especially Banti and Simonetti (supra n. 21) II, 44f. (nos. 115/1, 115/2, 115/3).
28. Ibid., 44f. (nos. 115, 115/4).
29. *BMCRR* II, 560f. (nos. 7–11), III, pl. cxx.5–7; Crawford (supra n. 21) 520 (no. 511/3a–c), 742.
30. An identification as Sextus Pompey cannot be ruled out entirely, however. Cf. Zanker (supra n. 1) 49; there is no evidence for an actual statue—as Zanker supposes—behind this coin image.
31. Crawford (supra n. 21) 495f. (nos. 483/1–2).

from a mint moving with Octavian in 41. Represented is a galloping equestrian statue, below which is the legend POPVLI IVSSV (fig. 9).[32] The poor quality of the image in this small issue makes it difficult to determine whether the rider is bare-chested or whether vertical folds of drapery hang from the left shoulder over the chest. Nevertheless, because both horse and rider are very similar in pose to the equestrian figure on the reverse of an issue of *aurei* and *denarii* with the legend CAESAR DIVI F (fig. 10), dated in all probability to the period just after the victory at Actium in 31,[33] it has recently been proposed that both figures represent a statue of Octavian, set up *populi iussu*.[34] Since in the later type the rider appears to be nude above the waist and the horse is galloping, it has also been suggested that in both the earlier and later issues Octavian appears like one of the Dioscuri.[35] But even if the pose were reminiscent of a statue type associated with the twin gods, the equestrian figures on the two issues of Octavian lack any attributes of the Dioscuri, who were customarily represented on earlier Roman coins carrying lances and wearing *pileus* with star above and armor with *chlamys* billowing behind.[36] Furthermore, seminudity without divine attribute(s) need not imply anything other than heroization. As for the proposed statue of Octavian erected *populi iussu* corresponding to the image on the coin of 41, there is no corroborative literary or epi-

32. *BMCRR* II, 405f. (nos. 79–80), pl. civ.13; Crawford (supra n. 21) 526 (no. 518/2), 742; Banti and Simonetti (supra n. 21) V, 267f. (nos. 701–701/10).

33. *BMCRE* I, 98 (nos. 594–95), pl. 14.13; RIC^2 I, 59 (no. 262), pl. 5; *BMCRR* II, 9 (nos. 4325–26), III, pl. lix.5; J.-B. Giard, *Catalogue des monnaies de l'empire romain*, vol. 1, *Auguste* (Paris 1976) 71 (nos. 82–84), pl. IV; Banti and Simonetti (supra n. 21) IV, 82–84 (nos. 46–48). For the most comprehensive treatment of the dating of the CAESAR DIVI F coinage and the related IMP CAESAR series on the basis of a combination of evidence, including style of portrait and interlinking and internal linking of dies, see C. H. V. Sutherland, "Octavian's Gold and Silver Coinage from c. 32 to 27 B.C.," *NumAntCl* 5 (1976) 129–57; see also T. Fischer, "Zahlenmystik in der Goldprägung des CAESAR DIVI F," *NumAntCl* 13 (1984) 163–71. D. Mannsperger, "Annos underviginti natus: Das Münzsymbol für Octavians Eintritt in die Politik," in *Praestant Interna, Festschrift für Ulrich Hausmann* (Tübingen 1982) 331–37, views the CAESAR DIVI F coinage as dating as early as 36/35 and referring to Naulochus rather than Actium. Mannsperger's hypothesis is characterized as "ingénieuse mais mal fondée" by J.-B. Giard, "La monnaie coloniale d'Orange: une attribution en question," *RN* 26 (1984) 79, n. 7; Giard (78f.) believes both series begin in 31 B.C. (or slightly before), differing in this respect from Sutherland, who argues that the CAESAR DIVI F coinage was succeeded in 29 B.C. by the IMP CAESAR group.

34. Mannsperger (supra n. 33) 332–37.

35. Zanker (supra n. 1) 47.

36. For good representations of this common type, see, for example, Kent (supra n. 23) figs. 17–19, 22, 24, 26–28. For the full range of representations of the Dioscuri on republican coinage, see Crawford (supra n. 21) s.v. Dioscuri 861f. On the gesture of the rider on the coin type of 31, see R. Brilliant, *Gesture and Rank in Roman Art*, Memoirs of the Connecticut Academy of Arts and Sciences 14 (New Haven 1963) 57f.

graphical evidence for such a figure of Octavian. In fact, the only sculptural image of him mentioned in ancient literary sources as having been set up during the period 44–37 B.C. is the gilded equestrian statue erected on or near the Rostra by order of the senate in 43.[37] As represented on *aurei* and *denarii* of around 43–42, the statue (inscribed S C) was a stationary equestrian figure,[38] very like the image of Sulla on horseback that also adorned the Rostra.[39]

Since the equestrian figure on Octavian's coinage of around 43–42 is clearly different from the one that appears on his coinage of 41, it is by no means certain that the rider in the later issue (with the inscription *populi iussu*) is Octavian himself. It is difficult to believe, in any case, that the people would have erected a statue in Octavian's honor in 41, given his great unpopularity with the people at this time because of land settlement disputes and famine. But if, for the sake of argument, such a statue had been decreed,[40] it is unlikely that it would have been represented on this coinage, which was produced by a mint moving with Octavian while on campaign in northern Italy and was intended for the

37. Vell. Pat. 2.61.3; App. *BCiv.* 3.51; Dio 46.29.2; Cic. *Ad Brut.* 24.7. The phrase *in Rostris* need not mean on the Rostra; it could also mean in the area of the Rostra: G. Lahusen, *Untersuchungen zur Ehrenstatue in Rom* (Rome 1983) 16.

38. On *denarii* of 43 the statue that was voted by the senate was represented before it was actually erected: *BMCRR* II, 399f. (nos. 63–64), 406 (nos. 81–82) III, pl. civ. 1, 14; Crawford (supra n. 21) 499f. (no. 490/1, 490/3). The inscription S C presumably refers to the senatorial decree for this monument. On *aurei* of 42 the same statue type appears again, but instead of raising his right hand, Octavian holds a *lituus* symbolizing his *imperium;* the *rostrum* below the figure and between the S and C alludes to the statue's location on the Rostra: *BMCRR* II, 409 (no. 95), III, pl. cv. 3; Crawford (supra n. 21) 512 (no. 497). In my opinion, this "revised" type probably reflects the statue that was actually created, most likely when Octavian returned to Rome after the victory over Caesar's assassins at Philippi in 42. Mannsperger (supra n. 33) 334 postulates that the POPVLI IVSSV type represents yet a third revision of the original statue of Octavian voted by the senate: "die Durchsetzung eines Volksbeschlusses zur Realisierung der alten Ehrung [i.e., S C]." However, a decree *populi iussu* is not needed for the realization of a *senatus consultum.* Statues were set up independently by the senate or by the people, as is evident from Pliny the Elder's comment *statuae populi aut senatus sententia statutae* (*HN* 34.14.30); see now Lahusen (supra n. 37) 107f. and esp. n. 72.

39. This statue, in which Sulla wears the *trabea* with the right side of his chest bare, appears on *aurei* of 80 B.C.: *BMCRR* II, 463 (no. 16), III, pl. cx.11; Crawford (supra n. 21) 397 (no. 381/1a); Sutherland (supra n. 22) fig. 77. I disagree with Crawford that Sulla wears the *sagum,* since the *sagum* is fastened with a *fibula* over the right shoulder: L. M. Wilson, *The Clothing of the Ancient Romans* (Baltimore 1938) 104–9. For Sulla in *trabea,* A. Alföldi, *Der frührömische Reiteradel und seine Ehrenabzeichen* (Baden-Baden 1952) 45f.

40. There is no mention of statues among the honors that were reluctantly voted to Octavian as one of the victors of Philippi by the senate and/or people in 42. In this period it is reported that the people prayed for Octavian's death (Dio 48.3.1–5). If any statue were set up at this time, it was probably the one already voted by the senate in 43: see supra n. 38.

payment of his soldiers, especially in the Perusine War (Dio 48.12.4–5). The problem of land settlement had led to bloody conflict between the soldiers and the people and was even causing the soldiers to become disaffected with Octavian (Dio 48.4–14; App. *BCiv.* 5.12–49). Under these circumstances, the equestrian figure on the issue of 41 is perhaps best explained as an image of Divus Iulius, to whom we know statues were erected *populi iussu* under the *Lex Rufrena,* probably in 42 in consequence of Caesar's consecration as a *divus.*[41] The representation on the coinage of Divus Iulius would have been an apt reminder of Octavian's special status as *divi filius* and heir to a great military tradition. The continued affection of the soldiers for Caesar, with whom many of them had served, is demonstrated by the inscription DIVOM IULIUM on the lead shots (*glandes plumbeae*) used in the siege of Perusia in 41.[42] On coinage just prior to this time Octavian had emphasized his special relationship to Caesar in order to promote his own popularity.[43] On the much later issue of around 31 the equestrian image, presumably of Octavian because of the legend,[44] might have been intended to recall the equestrian figure of Caesar set up *populi iussu,* in much the same way that the statue type of Octavian originally intended for erection on or near the Rostra "cited" the equestrian statue of Sulla *in Rostris.*

The intention to imitate the divine is clear in a reverse type associated with *sestertii* minted for Antony in 36–35 (fig. 11).[45] Here a male and female appear to embrace one another while riding in Neptune's *quadriga* drawn by hippocamps. With no other divine attributes and fully clothed, rather than nude or seminude, they are not to be regarded as the gods Neptune and Amphitrite:[46] although we cannot distinguish

41. *Lex Rufrena: ILS* 73 (= *ILLRP* 409), 73a; A. Degrassi, *Inscriptiones Latinae Liberae Rei Publicae Imagines* (Berlin 1965) no. 173. These statues probably took different forms, with some of them being of the *statua pedestris* type, to judge from the size of the base illustrated in Degrassi. On Caesar's consecration, see App. *BCiv.* 2.148; Dio 47.18.3–19.3; S. Weinstock, *Divus Julius* (Oxford 1971) 386–98; cf., however, H. Gesche, *Die Vergottung Caesars* (Kallmünz 1968) 87–91. On the date of Caesar's consecration and the *Lex Rufrena* in 42, see further J. P. Rollin, *Untersuchungen zu Rechtsfragen römischer Bildnisse* (Bonn 1979) 76–93. Seminudity—if true in the case of the coin type of 41— would also be explicable in light of Caesar's status as a *divus.*

42. *EphEp* 6.59 no.64 = *ILLRP* 1116.

43. On this coinage, see L. Morawiecki, *Political Propaganda in the Coinage of the Late Roman Republic, 44–43 B.C.* (Warsaw 1983) 100–3.

44. There is, however, no corroborative evidence that this coin image copied an actual statue of Octavian.

45. Banti and Simonetti (supra n. 21) II, 105–6 (nos. 24–25), 109 (no. 33), 111–12 (nos. 37–38); *BMCRR* II, 515 (no. 151), 517 (nos. 152–53), III, pls. cxiv.14, cxv. 1–2.

46. For the ways in which these divinities would typically have been represented, see the wall mosaic from the House of Neptune and Amphitrite at Herculaneum: A Maiuri,

their features, they are surely Antony and his wife Octavia represented *like* Neptune and Amphitrite by virtue of the appropriation of the sea chariot of these divinities. On the obverse of these coins the facing portraits of Antony and Octavia do not appear in any way divine. Only in a series of "cistophoric" silver tetradrachms minted in 39 B.C. for regional distribution in the province of Asia was Antony represented with a divine attribute; namely, the ivy crown of the god Dionysos (fig. 12).[47] His representation in this manner, though without the long hair of the god or any other indication of divinity, would have lent support to Octavian's accusation that Antony was behaving like the god Dionysos in the East.[48] In the vicious war of propaganda during the second triumviral period, Antony in turn accused Octavian of acting like Apollo at a dinner party (Suet. *Aug.* 70),[49] almost certainly the banquet of 39 or 38 at which Livia was betrothed to Octavian by her first husband. The story that the dinner guests dressed as gods and goddesses and that Octavian himself masqueraded as Apollo is probably a fiction, since so many fabricated and distorted stories—which were often used uncritically by later biographers and historians—were being circulated in the triumviral period by the opposing leaders and their supporters. As A. D. Nock observed long ago, had Octavian played Apollo, who would have played the part of Jupiter?[50] Moreover, since this was a time of a severe grain shortage, it would have been particularly unwise politically to have acted in such a manner in the context of a banquet, as though lording it over the people like a god. By the same token, a time of famine would have offered the opposition the ideal opportunity to spread such a rumor, given the human tendency to seek scapegoats in times of crisis. Significantly, in none of his pre-Actium coinage or known official monuments from this period does Octavian appear like a god or with divine attributes. Instead, he seems to have contented himself with the special distinction of being the son of the new state divinity Divus Iulius, a fact

Ercolano, I nuovi scavi, 1927–1958 (Rome 1958) 393–403, figs. 336–37; G. M. A. Hanfmann, *Roman Art* (New York 1975) 254, pl. XX. See further *LIMC* I, 724–35 (S. Kaempf-Dimitriadou).

47. Sutherland (supra n. 22) figs. 171–72; *BMCRR* II, 502f. (nos. 133–37), III, pl. cxiv. 1–4; C. H. V. Sutherland, *The Cistophori of Augustus,* Royal Numismatic Society, Special Publication no. 5 (London, 1970) 86–88.

48. For Antony as Neos Dionysos: Dio 48.39; cf. Plut. *Ant.* 75.4. See also K. Scott, "The Political Propaganda of 44–30 B.C.," *MAAR* 11 (1933) 32; D. Mannsperger, "Apollon gegen Dionysos," *Gymnasium* 80 (1973) 381–404.

49. See also Scott (supra n. 48) 30–32.

50. To M. P. Charlesworth in "Some Fragments of the Propaganda of Marc Antony," *CQ* 27 (1933) 175, n. 2.

that was proclaimed by the legend DIVI IVLI F on gold and silver coinage beginning about 40 B.C.[51]

With his important victory at Actium in 31 and his conquest of Alexandria in the following year, Octavian became at the age of thirty-three the undisputed leader of the Roman world. No doubt impressed with his own success in overcoming Antony and Cleopatra (a sure sign of divine approval!), Octavian now began to be represented as godlike on coinage issued in the West, including almost certainly Italy.[52] On the reverse of *denarii* with the legend CAESAR DIVI F, most likely minted shortly after Actium, Octavian appears like the god Neptune (fig. 13).[53] It is clear that this figure holding the *aplustre* of Neptune in his right hand is not simply the sea god, for Neptune would not have been portrayed beardless, with short hair, wearing a sword, and holding a spear or scepter (rather than a trident, Neptune's usual symbol). Recently an attempt has been made to interpret this image as representing a statue set up in connection with Octavian's defeat of Sextus Pompey at Naulochus.[54] It is argued that it must be a statue because it appears in the same series with other coin types depicting monuments erected in Rome. In this series, however, it is by no means clear that all or even most of the figures are based upon plastic or glyptic images. There is, in addition, no literary or inscriptional evidence describing a Neptune-like statue of Octavian. In fact, of the "excessive honors" (τιμὰς ἀμέτρους) voted him by the senate after Naulochus, the only statue that he expressly accepted was a golden image to be set atop a rostral column in the Forum and representing him "in the dress he wore when he entered the city" (μετὰ σχήματος οὗπερ ἔχων εἰσῆλθε: App. BCiv. 5.130)— hardly a Neptune-like figure! Octavian therefore showed restraint in the honors that he accepted at this time. In any case, in his war with Sextus he was not favorably disposed toward Neptune, the patron god of Sex-

51. Issued for Octavian first by the moneyers T. Sempronius Gracchus and Q. Voconius Vitulus: Crawford (supra n. 21) 529f. (nos. 525–26). See also W. H. Gross, "Ways and Roundabout Ways in the Propaganda of an Unpopular Ideology," in R. Winkes, ed., *The Age of Augustus*, Archaeologia Transatlantica 5 (Louvain-la-Neuve and Providence 1985) 31f.

52. On the western origin of this coinage, which was once thought to have been minted in the East: K. Kraft, *Zur Münzprägung des Augustus* (Wiesbaden 1969) 206–25; M. Crawford, review of Kraft, *JRS* 64 (1974) 246.

53. *RIC*[2] I, 59 (no. 256); *BMCRE* I, 100 (no. 615), pl. 15.5; Giard (supra n. 33) 66 (nos. 13–18), pl. I.13–17; A. S. Robertson, *Roman Imperial Coins in the Hunter Coin Cabinet* (Oxford 1962) I, 48 (no. 248), pl. 8; Banti and Simonetti (supra n. 21) V, 60–64 (nos. 399–401). On the dating of the CAESAR DIVI F coinage, see supra n. 33.

54. Zanker (supra n. 1) 48–50.

tus (Suet. *Aug.* 16.2). It was Diana Siciliensis who assisted Octavian at Naulochus, and it is she who is represented in his later coinage to celebrate his victory over Sextus.[55] Only after Octavian's sea victory at Actium was he "reconciled" with Neptune, as is evident from the fact that he consecrated the site of his camp near Nicopolis to Neptune and to Mars. Here he set up a monument that was adorned with the *rostra* of the captured ships (Suet. *Aug.* 18.2) and presumably with statues to Neptune and Mars (Suet. *Aug.* 18.2).[56] In the Neptune-like Octavian coin type, the image of world rule evoked by the globe on which the figure places his foot would also have been far more appropriate for Actium than for Naulochus, which lacked the "global" significance of Actium.

Octavian's Neptune-like image may have been inspired by a reverse type on handsome silver tetradrachms of Demetrios Poliorcetes. The basic pose of Octavian with foot resting on globe and long scepter in hand seems to "cite" Demetrios' Poseidon, who rests his foot on a rock while holding a trident[57]—an image that was itself undoubtedly modeled on a popular lost sculptural original often attributed to Lysippos and best known now in a Greco-Roman copy in the Lateran Museum.[58] Since this coin type of Demetrios celebrates his great victory in 306 B.C. over Ptolemy of Egypt at Salamis off Cyprus, it is possible that Octavian intended to adapt Demetrios' coin type to publicize his own great victory over Egypt, an event that culminated in world rule. I would like to suggest that this thesis is further supported by the fact that Augustus frequently looked to the past for *exempla* to emulate[59] and that he was a collector of coins, especially old regal issues (Suet. *Aug.* 75). If the Poseidon coin type of Demetrios did indeed influence that of Octavian, it

55. *BMCRE* I, 84 (nos. 489–91), pl. 12.11–12; *RIC²* I, 53–55 (nos. 194–97, 204), pl. 4.
56. Suetonius is borne out by inscriptions mentioning Neptune and Mars that once decorated this monument: W. M. Murray and P. M. Petsas, "The Spoils of Actium," *Archaeology* 41 (1988) 28–35.
57. E. T. Newell, *The Coinage of Demetrius Poliorcetes* (London 1927) no. 115; C. M. Kraay, *Greek Coins* (New York 1966) 349, 351 (no. 573), pl. 174. The association between Octavian's coin type and that of Demetrios was first proposed by G. F. Hill, *History of Roman Coins* (London 1909) 134f., and elaborated upon by W. W. Tarn, "The Battle of Actium," *JRS* 21 (1931) 179–81 (for these two references I thank R. A. Gurval, who is himself sceptical of the connection).
58. Helbig⁴ I, 798f., no. 1118 (W. Fuchs). The Lysippan type was also adapted for the image of Pompey the Great or (less likely) Sextus Pompey in the guise of Neptune in Sextus' reverse type of 42–40: see supra n. 29.
59. See, for instance, Suet. *Aug.* 31.5, 89.2; Dio 55.10.7. See also T. Hölscher, "Actium und Salamis," *JdI* 99 (1984) 187–264.

would be another piece of evidence for Octavian's personal input—at lease on certain occasions—in the selection of coin types.[60]

In two other issues of *denarii* minted between 31 and 27, Octavian can be identified less reliably as godlike. Some have considered the naked figure seated on a rock and playing the lyre to be Octavian in the guise of Apollo or Mercury (fig. 14).[61] The *petasus* hanging down on his back and the *talaria,* or winged sandals, which are visible on his feet in some examples, clearly identify this figure as Mercury, not Apollo. However, no label or distinguishing feature indicates that Octavian should be seen here imitating the god, even though one might infer that. The other issue depicts a rostral column topped by a statue (fig. 15).[62] Presumably this is one of the rostral columns that Servius (*ad Georg.* 3.29) indicates were set up after Actium. The figure on the column is naked except for a billowing cloak. In one hand he carries a sword and in the other a spear, both attributes of the god Mars.[63] However, since this figure does not wear a helmet, another distinguishing attribute of Mars at this time, it is possible that Octavian is meant to be represented here as godlike, perhaps specifically like Mars, whom Octavian honored in connection with his victory at Actium.[64]

Direct association with the divine is unambiguously expressed in two series of *denarii* minted between 29 and 27. On the obverse of one is a laureate bust of Octavian in the form of a herm, as indicated by the square post at the level of the shoulder (fig. 16).[65] This head, with a thunderbolt behind it, is surely that of the ithyphallic herm that appears laureate above a thunderbolt on another issue (fig. 17).[66] In both coin

60. Cf. Augustus' choice of the Capricorn as a coin type: Suet. *Aug.* 94.12.

61. *RIC*² I, 59 (no. 257), pl. 5; *BMCRE* I, 98 (nos. 596–98), pl. 14.15; Robertson (supra n. 53) I, 49 (no. 251), pl. 8; Giard (supra n. 33) 70 (nos. 73–77), pl. LV. 73–77; Banti and Simonetti (supra n. 21) V, 64–69 (nos. 404–9). See also Kraft (supra n. 52) 214–19; Albert (supra n. 23) 25f.

62. *RIC*² I, 60 (no. 271), pl. 5; *BMCRE* I, 103 (no. 633), pl. 15.5; Robertson (supra n. 53) 52 (no. 267), pl. 9; Giard (supra n. 33) 69f. (nos. 68–71), pls. II–III; Banti and Simonetti (supra n. 21) V, 162–66 (nos. 543–47); Albert (supra n. 23) 26, 149f.

63. Some have claimed that this figure also wears greaves, another attribute of Mars, but this detail is not apparent to me.

64. E.g., Suet. *Aug.* 18.2; Pliny *HN* 32.3. See also *denarii* of 29–27 B.C. with the head of Mars: *BMCRE* I, 105 (nos. 644–46), pl. 15.18; Sutherland (supra n. 33) 154f., pl. II.18.

65. *BMCRE* I, 104 (no. 637), pl. 15.16; Robertson (supra n. 53) I, 52 (no. 268), pl. 9; Giard (supra n. 33) 68 (nos. 43–47), pl. II; Banti and Simonetti (supra n. 21) V, 142–44 (nos. 518–21).

66. *RIC*² I, 60 (no. 269a), pl. 5; *BMCRE* I, 102 (nos. 628–30), pl. 15.10–11; Robertson (supra n. 53) I, 51 (no. 264), pl. 8; Giard (supra n. 33) 68 (nos. 49–51), pl. II; Banti and Simonetti (supra n. 21) V, 133–37 (nos. 508–14).

types Octavian is represented like a divinity, variously interpreted as the god Terminus, Veiovis-Terminus, or Jupiter-Terminus.[67] The thunderbolt of Jupiter would be an allusion to the supreme god's divine assistance in Octavian's victories. The Terminus form, which served as a boundary marker, most likely commemorates here Octavian's divine mandate to increase the boundaries of empire. This task he accomplished through his victories, symbolized by the *victoriola* that he holds on the reverse of the issue with the terminal bust. To my mind, the imagery implied in the two coin types with Terminus recalls in part the dreams that Jupiter reportedly sent to Catulus, Cicero, and Octavius, the father of Octavian (Suet. *Aug.* 94.5–9). All of these dreams proclaimed Octavian's predestination for empire. I should also like to suggest that the ithyphallic nature of the herm may have been intended to allude to the formal worship of Octavian's *genius,* or divine procreative spirit. In 30 B.C. the senate had already decreed that his *genius* be worshiped at all public and private banquets.[68] Suggestive of a connection between the *genius* and the ithyphallic herm form is a herm from Pompeii representing Lucius Caecilius Iucundus, whose *genius* is mentioned in the dedicatory inscription on the front of the pillar.[69]

On another series of *denarii* minted in the West, probably at Rome, between 29 and 27, some have suggested that Octavian appears as the long-haired god Apollo.[70] In several coins of this type (e.g., fig. 18) there is indeed a resemblance to Octavian in the facial features of Apollo. Yet in other examples of this type (e.g., fig. 19) Apollo's features are more idealized than Octavian's usual numismatic image. Further complicating the picture are coin portraits of Octavian that show a greater degree of idealization and that therefore may approximate images of Apollo that are neither wholly idealized nor especially individualized.[71] In the debate as to whether or not Apollo has the features of Octavian in this

67. J. Liegle, "Die Münzprägung Octavians nach dem Siege von Actium und die augusteische Kunst," *JdI* 56 (1941) 91–119; Kraft (supra n. 52) 209f.; Albert (supra n. 23) 148–50; Weinstock (supra n. 41) 8–12 (for a discussion of the connection of Veiovis and Jupiter to the gens Iulia).

68. Dio 51.19.7; Hor. *Odes* 4.5; Taylor (supra n. 1) 181–83.

69. A. de Franciscis, *Il ritratto romano a Pompei* (Naples 1951) 31, figs. 17–20; H. Kunckel, *Der römische Genius, RM* EH 20 (1974) 33, 100 (F VIII.1), pl. 65.

70. *RIC*² I, 60 (no. 272), pl. 5; *BMCRE* I, 104 (nos. 638–43), pl. 15.7; Robertson (supra n. 53) I, 50 (no. 258), pl. 8; Giard (supra n. 33) 72 (nos. 92–96), pl. IV; Banti and Simonetti (supra n. 21) V, 145–49 (nos. 522–25).

71. Cf., for example, *RIC*² I, 60 (nos. 271, 272), pl. 5; C. H. V. Sutherland and C. M. Kraay, *Catalogue of Coins of the Roman Empire in the Ashmolean Museum* (Oxford 1975) nos. 232, 233.

coin type, due consideration has not been given to the range of idealization within both the Apollo type and portraits of Octavian minted at
this time. There may, of course, have been a tendency to see Octavian in
some of these images of Apollo because Octavian had claimed Apollo
as his patron divinity and because rumors had circulated earlier that
Octavian was really the son of Apollo (Suet. *Aug.* 94.4). Any similarity
in physiognomic features might therefore have been interpreted as a "familial" resemblance. Nevertheless, the inconsistencies of die images in
showing assimilation indicate that the issuing authority was not claiming that Octavian was to be seen as Apollo. Interestingly, the head of
Apollo does not appear on state coinage after 27 B.C., perhaps to avoid
any possibility of seeing Augustus' features in the head of his patron
god—imagery that might have recalled Antony's presumably false claim
that Octavian had impersonated Apollo. Throughout the Augustan
principate, the state coinage continued to represent full figures of divinities, but there is no hint that Augustus is to be seen imitating any of
these divinities. Some, however, have considered Augustus' wife Livia
to be represented in divine guise on *aurei* and *denarii* minted at Lugdunum toward the end of his principate (fig. 20).[72] In this coinage a
seated female figure holds a scepter and either a branch or ears of wheat,
attributes associated with various female divinities. A positive identification of Livia in the guise of a goddess cannot be made here because of
the small size of the facial features, the generalized nature of the hairstyle, and the absence of a legend making any claim of divine association.

After 27 B.C., moreover, divine symbols rarely appear in direct association with the head of Augustus on state coinage. And even then, they
do not signify that Augustus is meant to appear like a god. For example,
a caduceus is represented behind the head of Augustus and a palm
branch in front on *dupondii* and *asses* dated about 26–25 from an unknown mint in Spain (fig. 21).[73] This coinage was presumably minted

72. *BMCRE* I, 91 (nos. 544–46), pl. 14.8–9 (Livia? as Ceres); *RIC* I, 90 (no. 352), pl.
III.48 (Livia?); *RIC*² I, 87 (no. 219) (draped female figure); J.-B. Giard, *Le monnayage de
l'atelier de Lyon* (Wetteren 1983) 106f. (nos. 93–94), pl. XXIV (Justice); Banti and Simonetti (supra n. 21) IV, 162–64 (nos. 162–63) (female figure); Kraft (supra n. 52) 242–44,
250f. (Concord likened to Pax); Mannsperger (supra n. 1) 945–47 (Livia in divine guise).
73. Banti and Simonetti (supra n. 21) VII, 142–45 (nos. 1369–72); Giard (supra n. 33)
160 (nos. 1023–27), pl. XLI; A. Heiss, *Description générale des monnaies antiques de
l'Espagne* (Paris 1970) pl. LXV. 1–3; M. Vasques Seijas, "Posibles emisiones de Augusto
en Lugo," *Numisma* 70 (1964) 37–40; Sutherland and Kraay (supra n. 71) 1077–79, pl.
26.

on Augustus' authority to pay the troops in the Cantabrian wars of 26–25. Because Augustus does not wear a winged *petasus* on these coins, he is not to be seen here as the god Mercury. Moreover, by this time the caduceus had been adopted as a symbol of Pax, who is represented holding a caduceus on Augustan *cistophori*.[74] In my view, the shorthand language of the Spanish issues is clear: the caduceus symbolizes peace; the palm branch, victory—that is, peace through victory, a familiar theme in Augustan and later Roman art. Augustus is therefore to be seen here as victor and *pacifer*.

In view of the absence of divine imitation and symbols in Augustan official imagery, it might seem rather surprising that divine assimilation continues to occur under special circumstances in gold and silver issues from the mint of Rome, which resumed coining in precious metals around 19 B.C., when Augustus returned to Rome from the East. This coinage was produced under the ostensible authority of the *tresviri monetales*, a republican position revived for the minting of base metal coinage about 23 B.C. In that year a conspiracy against Augustus and his near death from natural causes led to a series of significant changes in the management of government, known as the "second constitutional settlement." From 23, Augustus gave up holding the consulship except on rare occasions and gained instead various political powers: having power without holding office was to be the essential feature of the rest of Augustus' principate. Although greatly diminished in authority under Augustus, the consulship remained the highest office attainable and was eagerly sought by many. It was probably in keeping with the "opening up" of the consulship that Augustus also decided to revive the office of the *tresviri monetales*. In gold and silver issues these moneyers initially employed some types that alluded to their own lineage, in accordance with old republican tradition. Soon, however, the types came to pertain exclusively to the concerns of the *princeps*, reflecting the reality of the situation; namely, that Augustus ultimately controlled all state coinage. Yet it was probably because the moneyers were the nominal minting authority that a certain latitude was allowed in the matter of divine assimilation, especially when that assimilation was not apparent in all or most coins of a given type. For example, in certain *denarii* minted at Rome by L. Aquillius Florus, one of the moneyers of 19 or 18, the features of the sun-god Sol compare favorably with those of Augus-

74. Sutherland (supra n. 47) 40–44, 88–90, pls. 15–17; *RIC*[2] I, 79 (no. 476), pl. 8; *BMCRE* I, 112 (nos. 691–93), pl. 17.4; Giard (supra n. 33) 144 (nos. 908–10), pl. XXXV.

tus (fig. 22),[75] although this resemblance is not apparent in other examples of this type (e.g., fig. 23).[76] A similar diversity is found on *denarii* of Marcus Durmius, another moneyer of 19 or 18. In some cases, the head of Honos on this coinage bears a marked resemblance to Augustus (fig. 24),[77] while in others there is little similarity (fig. 25).[78]

Because of the variability both in Florus' issue with the head of Sol and Durmius' issue with the head of Honos, it is reasonable to conclude that the die engravers were not provided with models or sketches of these divinities with the features of Augustus, nor were they otherwise directed to represent Sol and Honos looking like Augustus. Moreover, I do not think that the resemblance to Augustus apparent in some images is merely a result of the technical process of "hubbing" by which "virgin" dies were first stamped with a hub, or master punch, containing a general outline of the desired image, and then finished by hand-engraved details. In those examples in which divinities have Augustus' features, the individual images do not show an identity from die to die in mass and proportions consistent with the employment of the hubbing process.[79] In any case, because Augustus' own portrait was often quite idealized, in part to suggest the divine quality with him, the representation of a divinity with features like those of the *princeps* might easily have gone unnoticed by most people. The assimilation may therefore have been regarded as too subtle to warrant stopping coin production from such dies or recalling coins that had already been distributed.

There is only one coin type in which the head of a male divinity consistently and dramatically appears with assimilated features of Augustus—and this constitutes a special case. In the portraits of the deified Julius Caesar on the reverse of *aurei* and *denarii* of the moneyer Marcus Sanguinius minted around 17 B.C., the *sidus Iulium* appears over Caesar's head as a symbol of his divinity (fig. 26).[80] The resemblance of

75. *BMCRE* I, 8 (no. 39), pl. 2.1; Robertson (supra n. 53) I, 3 (no. 12), pl. 1; Banti and Simonetti (supra n. 21) II, 183f. (nos. 44–45); Giard (supra n. 33) 79 (no. 174), pl. VIII.

76. Banti and Simonetti (supra n. 21) II, 182 (no. 40), 183 (no. 44/1); Giard (supra n. 33) 79 (no. 173), pl. VIII.

77. Robertson (supra n. 53) I, 4 (nos. 15, 17), pl. 1; Banti and Simonetti (supra n. 21) II, 281 (nos. 184/1, 185/4); Giard (supra n. 33) 81 (no. 203), pl. IX.

78. *BMCRE* I, 11 (no. 58), pl. 2.11; Banti and Simonetti (supra n. 21) II, 283 (nos. 187/9, 187/10).

79. For the possibility of hubbing in ancient minting, see G. F. Hill, "Ancient Methods of Coining," *NC* 5.2 (1922) 19–22, who indicates that much time would have been saved in the reproduction of a repetitive series if a hubbing process had been used.

80. *BMCRE* I, 13 (nos. 69–73), pl. 2.19–20; Robertson (supra n. 53) I, 5 (nos. 25–26), pl. 1; Giard (supra n. 33) 88 (nos. 278–80), pl. XIII; Sutherland and Kraay (supra n. 71) nos. 284–85, pl. 6; Banti and Simonetti (supra n. 21) I, 154 (nos. 7–8).

Caesar to Augustus on the obverse (fig. 27) is quite striking and goes far beyond the family resemblance that is stressed (apparently by individual die engravers) in some of Octavian's coinage in the triumviral period.[81] Caesar's assimilated portrait on the issue of about 17 is very different from his image on other coins (like that on *denarii* minted just after his death [fig. 28]), as well as from both veristic and idealized portraits in the round.[82] Representative of his veristic image is the head from Tusculum in the Museum of Antiquities in Turin, which is thought to have been created shortly before his death;[83] exemplifying his idealized portrait is the so-called Chiaramonti head in the Vatican Museum, which reflects a type created only after his death and deification.[84] At the time the *aurei* and *denarii* of Marcus Sanguinius were being minted, both Caesar's veristic and classicizing portrait image would have been on display, and his earlier numismatic images would still have been in circulation. Sanguinius' coin portraits of Caesar would therefore have been a means of expressing visually Augustus' filial relationship with the deified Julius Caesar and, given his near death in 23, possibly even of implying now Augustus' own eventual apotheosis. The consistency of the resemblance to Augustus in the coinage in question suggests that it was intended by the moneyer or by a still higher authority.

The only other case of apparently authorized assimilation is found on *denarii* of the moneyer Gaius Marius Tromentinus (or Trogus), who probably minted in 13 B.C. In coins of this type the goddess Diana, identifiable by the quiver slung over her back, appears with rather personalized features and a hairstyle that resembles to some extent those worn by prominent females of the period (fig. 29).[85] It has often been sug-

81. Cf., for instance, the similarity between the obverse portrait of Octavian and reverse image of Divus Iulius in certain examples of a bronze issue variously dated between 41 and 38: A. Alföldi and J.-B. Giard, "Guerre civile et propagande politique: l'émission d'Octave au nom du Divos Julius (41–40 avant J.C.)," *NumAntCl* 13 (1984) 147–61, e.g., pl. II.6, 18–19; other examples of this issue show little or no similarity.

82. On the portraiture of Julius Caesar, see F. Johansen, "Antichi ritratti di Caio Giulio Cesare nella scultura," *AnalRom* 4 (1967) 7–68; J. Frel, "Caesar," *GettyMusJ* 5 (1977) 55–62; J. M. C. Toynbee, *Roman Historical Portraits* (Ithaca, N.Y. 1978) 30–39. On coinage, see further A. Alföldi, "Die stadtrömischen Münzporträts des Jahres 43 v. Chr.," *Eikones*, AntK Suppl. 12 (1980) 17–28.

83. M. Borda, "Il ritratto tuscolano di Giulio Cesare," *RendPontAcc* 20, 1943–1944 (1945) 347–82; E. Simon, "Das Caesarporträt im Castello di Aglie," *AA* (1952) 123–38; Johansen (supra n. 82) 34f., pl. XVI; Frel (supra n. 82) 57; Toynbee (supra n. 82) 39, figs. 34–35.

84. This portrait, formerly in the Museo Chiaramonti, is now in the Sala dei Busti of the Vatican Museum, inv. 713: Helbig⁴ I, 120, no. 158 (H. v. Heintze); Johansen (supra n. 82) 25f., pl. 1; Toynbee (supra n. 82) 34, fig. 33.

85. *BMCRE* I, 21 (nos. 104–5), pl. 4.2 [Diana (Julia)]; *RIC*² I, 72 (no. 403), pl. 7 (Diana); Robertson (supra n. 53) I, 9 (no. 46) [Diana (Julia)]; Giard (supra n. 33) 111

gested that Augustus' daughter Julia is meant to be represented here in the guise of Diana.[86] However, we have no securely identified sculptural portraits of Julia with which to compare it, because of her banishment in 2 B.C. and consequent de facto *"damnatio memoriae."*[87] And the few labeled coin images of her do not permit a positive identification of Julia *as* Diana. Julia appears on state coinage only once, on *denarii* of about 13 B.C. flanked by heads of her sons Gaius and Lucius, who were then about seven and four (fig. 30).[88] Since all three heads are extremely small and since the images of the boys in any case bear no relation to their known portraiture,[89] the accuracy of Julia's image in this coin type is open to question. The best available numismatic portrait of Julia is found on a local bronze issue of Pergamon (fig. 31).[90] As is sometimes the case in coinage and other artistic works *not* sanctioned by the senate or *princeps,* divine honors are paid to the living individual who is represented. Thus Julia is called Julia Aphrodite in this issue. If the image on the Pergamene coin is at all an accurate likeness, Julia's distinguishing features here are not like those of Diana. Furthermore, Julia's hairstyle on the Pergamene issue has a prominent hair knot at the front of her head and a short "ponytail" curled under at the nape of the neck.

(nos. 522–25), pl. XXV [Diana (Julia)]; Banti and Simonetti (supra n. 21) VIII, 177–80 (nos. 1–4) [Diana (or Julia)].

86. See supra n. 85. See also Mannsperger (supra n. 1) 944, 947; M. D. Fullerton, "The *Domus Augusti* in Imperial Iconography of 13–12 B.C.," *AJA* 89 (1985) 476, pl. 55, fig. 10; M. L. Anderson, "The Portrait Medallions of the Imperial Villa at Boscotrecase," *AJA* 91 (1987) 133, n. 38; Zanker (supra n. 1) 218, fig. 167c.

87. On the matter of Julia's portraiture, see G. Grimm, "Zum Bildnis der Iulia Augusti," *RM* 80 (1973) 279–82 (who rejects an identification of Julia in the coin type in question); Anderson (supra n. 86) 127–35 (who sees Julia in this type and compares this image with a painted portrait medallion ca. 7 cm in diameter in the central panel of the north wall of the Black Room of the imperial villa at Boscotrecase [figs. 1–2]). In my opinion, the features of the head in the medallion do not compare well with Julia's labeled coin images, and the free-flowing locks find no parallel with her hairstyle (cf., on the other hand, the facial features and hairstyle of the head in the medallion on the right with these aspects of Livia's portrait). Anderson does not consider the possibility that there may have been facing medallions on each of the three main walls and that Julia and perhaps Augustus' sister Octavia Minor might have been represented paired with a divinity on the other walls. In any case, notwithstanding Anderson's suggestion that this villa might have been administered by freedmen for the imperial family after Julia's banishment in 2 B.C., it is likely that any portrait of Julia would have been eradicated or painted over, especially since the property would have passed into the hands of Augustus, as Anderson himself notes (130).

88. *RIC*[2] I, 72 (no. 404), pl. 7; *BMCRE* I, 21f. (nos. 106, 108–9), pl. 4.5; Robertson (supra n. 53) I, 9 (no. 47), pl. 2; Giard (supra n. 33) 111 (nos. 526–29), pl. XXV.

89. On the portraiture of Gaius and Lucius, see J. Pollini, *The Portraiture of Gaius and Lucius Caesar* (New York 1987).

90. Sutherland and Kraay (supra n. 71) nos. 1229–34, pl. 29; *BMC Mysia,* 139 (no. 248), pl. XXVIII.6.

By contrast, Diana's hair is decorated with large pearls or other jewels at the front and is tightly bound into a small, braided bun at the back. A comparison of various obverses and reverses of the same coin often shows a marked similarity between the facial features of Augustus and Diana (cf. figs. 29a, b)—a resemblance that to my knowledge has not previously been noted. Obviously Augustus is not meant to be represented like Diana; rather Diana appears as an *Augustan* divinity. This interpretation, which has not been discussed in the literature on these coins, can be supported by epigraphic evidence. For example, an unofficial inscription dated about 6–5 B.C. mentions a *Diana Augusta*.[91] The tendency to associate divinities with the *princeps* in this way is also evident in the list of over a hundred different deities with the epithet *Augustus* or *Augusta* or the less common genitive form *Augusti* in the *Thesaurus Linguae Latinae*. The personalization of a particular god or goddess had a long history under the Republic, when gentilicial adjectives were added to the names of divinities, as in *Victoria Mariana, Diana Valeriana,* and *Hercules Iulianus*. As Duncan Fishwick has rightly shown in an article entitled "Augustus Deus or Deus Augustus," the intention behind all this seems to have been to adopt the divinity as a helper or protector, to appropriate his or her *numen* for the family.[92] The consistent representation of Diana with features like those of Augustus could therefore be seen as a means of recalling Diana's past aid to Augustus and of insuring her future favor.

Some similarity in features, though with less consistency, can also be perceived in images of other female divinities on state coinage issued during Augustus' principate.[93] For example, on *denarii* of Publius Petronius Turpilianus, a moneyer of 19 or 18 B.C., there is some resemblance between certain images of Feronia (e.g., fig. 32) and of Augustus,[94] especially on coins by the same moneyer. Analogous too are

91. *CIL* VI.1.128; *ThLL* II, 1395.

92. In M. B. De Boer and T. A. Erdridge, eds., *Hommages à Maarten J. Vermaseren,* vol. 1 (Leiden 1978) 375–80.

93. For an analogous case of assimilation during the principate of Trajan, see *denarii* dated ca. 107 that show Moneta (so labeled) with the portrait features of Trajan: R. Göbl, "Antike Darstellungen zur Münzprägung im Numismatisch-Sphragistischen Material," in *Mélanges de numismatique, d'archéologie et d'histoire offerts à Jean Lafaurie* (Paris 1980) 106 (no. 4), pl. 9; *BMCRE* III, 136 (no. 688), pl. 23.5; J. MacIsaac, *The Location of the Republican Mint of Rome and the Topography of the Arx of the Capitoline* (Diss. Johns Hopkins Univ. 1987) 33f., fig. 10.

94. *BMCRR* II, 64 (no. 4524), pl. lxvi.9; *BMCRE* I, 2 (no. 6), pl. 1.4; Giard (supra n. 33) 74–76 (nos. 109, 116–17, 136), pls. V, VII; Banti and Simonetti (supra n. 21) III, 78 (no. 327). Cf. esp. *BMCRE* I, 5 (no. 22), pl. 1.13; *BMCRR* II, 65 (no. 4530), III, pl. lxvii.11.

certain images of Venus (e.g., fig. 33) and Augustus on *denarii* of Gaius
Antistius Vetus, a moneyer of 16 B.C.[95] But whether a resemblance to
Augustus is consistent, as in the Diana coinage, or sporadic, as in the
Honos type, the ancient viewer—like the modern—was free to regard
such images of gods and goddesses in a variety of ways: first, simply as
the divinities themselves; secondly, as Augustus in divine guise (in the
case of male divinities); or thirdly, as a *deus Augustus* or *dea Augusta*
(i.e., not Augustus as a divinity, but rather an Augustan god or goddess).
Divine assimilation, at any rate, comes to an end just before 12 B.C.,
when an abundance of gold and silver coinage produced by the moneyers of the Rome mint was then in circulation in this area, thereby pre-
cluding the need for further minting in precious metals in Rome for
some years to come.[96]

In summary, we have seen that in the late 40s B.C. divinities begin to
appear on state coinage with the features of a living leader, and the living in turn begin to be represented imitating divinities. Significantly, Octavian appears to have avoided this assimilation and imitation in official
artistic media before his victories over Antony and Cleopatra at Actium
and Alexandria, a fact that has not been fully appreciated. With his
great victories, however, Octavian also begins to be represented like a
god, and divinities are portrayed with features like those of Octavian on
coinage issued under Octavian's direct *imperium*. Whether any of these
types was personally chosen by Octavian or simply permitted by him,
this imagery suggests that once he was in full control of the Roman
state, Octavian was considering the possibility of creating a government
more openly autocratic in form than was ultimately decided upon. That
there had been some debate about the type of government to be established is reflected in the famous speeches that Cassius Dio (52) puts in
the mouths of Agrippa and Maecenas.

With the establishment of the principate in 27 B.C., unambiguous imitation of divinities ceases altogether in state art. Divine assimilation can
be seen only on issues of named moneyers during the period from about
19 to 13 B.C., and then only rarely and inconsistently except in the special case of coin types showing his patron goddess Diana and his adoptive father, Divus Iulius. One has the impression that the sporadic ap-

95. *RIC*[2] I, 69 (no. 367), pl. 7; *BMCRE* I, 20 (no. 98), pl. 3.18; Giard (supra n. 33) 97
(no. 370), pl. XVII; Banti and Simonetti (supra n. 21) II, 166 (nos. 21, 22, 22/1). Cf.
especially *BMCRE* I, 18f. (nos. 95–99), pl. 3.15–17.
96. On the dates of the production of this coinage, see Sutherland (supra n. 16) 40–
42, 47–49.

pearance of divinities with facial features similar to those of Augustus
was permitted on issues by named moneyers only because the moneyers
by tradition had the right to select coin types. It is perhaps significant
that coinage issued in the provinces under Augustus' proconsular *imperium,* including the enormous output of the mint at Lugdunum, represents no heads of divinities. Was it perhaps to avoid any possibility of
a die engraver's representing a god with Augustus' features or anyone's
reading such a message in a god's image on coinage under Augustus'
direct control? When divinities do appear on this coinage, they are in
full figure on the reverse, with the head of Augustus usually on the obverse. Association with the divine is therefore suggested only indirectly,
as in the Ara Pacis, in which divinities are represented within the context
of the monument, but in scenes apart from those in which Augustus and
other contemporary historical figures appear.

Finally, the changes in divine imagery in official media after Actium
and then again after the establishment of the principate provide new
evidence of input from above, if only in the form of general directives
and injunctions concerning that imagery. An assessment of divine assimilation and imitation—both in terms of what is represented and what is
not—can also contribute to our understanding of the role of official art
in influencing and/or reflecting public perceptions of the leader in this
important period of transition from republic to principate.

Figure 1.   Janus with features of Pompey the Great (obv., *as*, ca. 45–44
B.C.). London, British Museum 195150. Figure 2.   Pompey the Great
(obv., *denarius*, ca. 42–40 B.C.). London, British Museum 096597. Fig-
ure 3.   Neptune (obv., *denarius*, ca. 42–40 B.C.). Frankfurt am Main,
Seminar für griechische und römische Geschichte, Johann Wolfgang
Goethe-Universität (Sammlung Niggeler, Teil II, Nr. 963). Figure 4.
Neptune with features of Pompey the Great (obv., *denarius*, ca. 42–40
B.C.). London, British Museum 195151. Figure 5.   Marc Antony (obv.,
denarius, 42 B.C.). *Corpus Nummorum Romanorum* II, 44.115/1. Figure
6.   Sol with features of Marc Antony (rev. of no. 5).

Figure 7. Sol (rev., *denarius,* 42 B.C.). Frankfurt am Main, Seminar für griechische und römische Geschichte, Johann Wolfgang Goethe-Universität (L 245, Juli 1964, Nr. 22). Figure 8.   Neptune-like figure of Pompey the Great (or Sextus Pompey) (rev., *denarius,* ca. 42–40 B.C.). From P. Zanker, *Augustus und die Macht der Bilder* (Munich, 1987), 49, fig. 31b. Figure 9.   Equestrian figure (rev., *denarius,* 41 B.C.). From P. Zanker, *Augustus und die Macht der Bilder* (Munich, 1987), 47, fig. 29c. Figure 10.   Equestrian figure (rev., *denarius,* ca. 31–29 B.C.). From P. Zanker, *Augustus und die Macht der Bilder* (Munich, 1987), 47, fig. 30a. Figure 11.   Neptune-like Marc Antony and Amphitrite-like Octavia (rev., *sestertius,* ca. 36–35 B.C.). *Corpus Nummorum Romanorum* II, 105.24. Figure 12.   Marc Antony with crown of Dionysos (obv., tetradrachm, 42 B.C.). London, British Museum 195152.

Figure 13.   Neptune-like figure of Octavian (rev., *denarius*, ca. 31–29 B.C.). Frankfurt am Main, Seminar für griechische und römische Geschichte, Johann Wolfgang Goethe-Universität (Sammlung Niggeler, Teil II, Nr. 1010). Figure 14.   Mercury seated on rock (rev., *denarius*, ca. 31–29 B.C.). London, British Museum 195154. Figure 15.   Statue on rostral column (rev., *denarius*, ca. 29–27 B.C.). London, British Museum 096494. Figure 16.   Terminal bust of Octavian (obv., *denarius*, ca. 29–27 B.C.). London, British Museum 134202. Figure 17.   Herm of Octavian/Terminus (rev., *denarius*, ca. 29–27 B.C.). London, British Museum 195155. Figure 18.   Apollo resembling Octavian (obv., *denarius*, ca. 29–27 B.C.). Paris, Bibliothèque Nationale 88A 60412.

Figure 19. Apollo (obv., *denarius*, ca. 29–27 B.C.). *Corpus Nummorum Romanorum* V, 145.522/12. Figure 20. Goddess of fertility (Ceres?) (rev., *aureus*, ca. A.D. 11–13). London, British Museum 096474. Figure 21. Augustus with caduceus and palm branch (obv., *dupondius*, ca. 26–25 B.C.). Paris, Bibliothèque Nationale 88A 60414. Figure 22. Sol resembling Augustus (obv., *denarius*, ca. 19–18 B.C.). From J.-B. Giard, *Bibliothèque Nationale. Catalogue des monnaies de l'empire romain* I (Paris, 1976), pl. VIII.174. Figure 23. Sol (obv., *denarius*, ca. 19–18 B.C.). Paris, Bibliothèque Nationale 88A 60416. Figure 24. Honos resembling Augustus (obv., *denarius*, ca. 19–18 B.C.). Paris, Bibliothèque Nationale 88A 60412.

Figure 25.   Honos (obv., *denarius,* ca. 19–18 B.C.). London, British Museum 142145. Figure 26.   Augustus-like Julius Caesar (rev., *denarius,* ca. 17 B.C.). Paris, Bibliothèque Nationale 88A 60421. Figure 27. Augustus (obv. of no. 26). Paris, Bibliothèque Nationale 88A 60420. Figure 28.   Julius Caesar (obv., *denarius,* ca. 40 B.C.). Vienna, Bundessammlung von Medaillen, Münzen (courtesy M. Schwarz). Figure 29a. Augustus (obv.). 29b. Diana resembling Augustus (rev.): *aureus,* ca. 13 B.C. From J.-B. Giard, *Bibliothèque Nationale. Catalogue des monnaies de l'empire romain* I (Paris, 1976), pl. XXV.524.

Figure 30.   Julia, Gaius, and Lucius (rev., *denarius,* ca. 13 B.C.). London, British Museum 177072. Figure 31.   Julia (rev., bronze issue of Pergamon, before 2 B.C.). London, British Museum 096524. Figure 32.   Feronia resembling Augustus (obv., *denarius,* ca. 19–18 B.C.). Paris, Bibliothèque Nationale 89A 61678. Figure 33.   Venus resembling Augustus (obv., *denarius,* ca. 16 B.C.). Paris, Bibliothèque Nationale H37332.

The *Augustales*
in the Augustan Scheme

The *Augustales* were members of collegial associations officially devoted to the imperial cult.[1] From the time of Augustus until the mid-
third century we find them in hundreds of towns across Italy and the
western Roman world—though not in Rome itself, and only very rarely
in the East. Their ranks were composed overwhelmingly (some 85 to 95
percent) of former slaves, especially wealthy ones. What we know of
them we owe largely to the evidence of some 2,500 inscriptions, mostly
tombstones or honorary dedications, such as statue bases, although a
few inscriptions actually give us partial membership lists. In their own
towns individual *Augustales* were commonly, though not always, designated for membership by the local decurions. While we are not informed of any particular minimum census required of candidates for
membership (or even that any such requirement was anywhere imposed), it is abundantly clear that comparatively wealthy persons were
favored for the role. Not only do the inscriptions frequently attest the

1. I warmly thank participants in the colloquium on Augustus held at Brown University on 14 March 1987 for their observations on an earlier version of this paper. I am
especially grateful to K. Raaflaub and S. Treggiari for their helpful comments, generously
offered.

obligatory payment of a *summa honoraria* to mark one's entry into the post of *Augustalis,* but we hear often as well of large additional payments made by *Augustales ob honorem, pro seviratu, pro honore.*[2] Campania offers important early examples of their architectural achievements,[3] but the *Augustales* are scarcely mentioned in all of Roman literature. Petronius is the only exception, for Trimalchio and two of his dinner companions proudly claim to be members.[4]

To understand the role of *Augustales* as well-to-do freedmen at the municipal level, we must recall that the freed slave, though a citizen, was barred from an active role in the political life of his town. He could hold neither any magistracy nor a seat on the town council. For the wealthy freedman in particular, recognition of this fact must often have been a troubling realization indeed. But inscriptions make clear, from their frequent mention of the various public honors accorded to individual *Augustales,* that the institution aimed in part to provide successful municipal freedmen with a path to civic esteem that all but equaled the prestige of the local ruling classes themselves. The newly selected *Augustalis* will have paid for his privilege with expensive public benefactions (food, temples, public entertainments), but he will at last have achieved the satisfaction of a surrogate public career.[5]

All these matters have received considerable scholarly scrutiny, some of it very recent. But much remains to be explored. The *Augustales* constitute one of the most pervasive of all Augustan institutions in the West, one that touched countless lives within a modestly prosperous population at the level of municipal life, and yet a systematic examination of how closely the *Augustales* were woven into the overall social and political fabric of the Augustan Age has not been undertaken thus far.[6] I

2. On all of this, see R. Duthoy, "La fonction sociale de l'augustalité," *Epigraphica* 36 (1974) 134–54; id., "Les *Augustales," *ANRW* 2.16.2 (1978) 1254–1309 (specifically on the payment of the *summa honoraria* and the like, 1266–67, 1281–82; on selection by the decurions, 1266, 1277). But P. Kneissl has now effectively shown that at least in the earliest years of their institutional existence, the *Augustales* may often well have been genuinely autonomous representatives of the local *plebs* in a given town, who themselves would have selected the *Augustales* to serve their interests against those of the town's governing class. Cf. Kneissl, "Entstehung und Bedeutung der Augustalität: Zur Inschrift der ara Narbonensis (CIL XII 4333)," *Chiron* 10 (1980) 291–326, esp. 293, 322–25.
    3. Cf. S. E. Ostrow, "*Augustales* along the Bay of Naples: A Case for Their Early Growth," *Historia* 34 (1985) 64–101, esp. 75–81 (Misenum, Herculaneum).
    4. On Trimalchio as *Augustalis,* see now J. H. D'Arms, *Commerce and Social Standing in Ancient Rome* (Cambridge, Mass. 1981) 97–120.
    5. Cf. Ostrow (supra n. 3) 70–72.
    6. It may be useful to note here that the inscriptions are very clear in setting the origins of the institution of the *Augustales* in Italy within the lifetime of Augustus. The earliest

propose to make a start of that investigation here, with the ultimate aim that both the *Augustales* and other Augustan developments may emerge in a clearer light. I speak of Augustan "developments," not "policies" or "programs," and I realize that my very choice of title, including the expression "The Augustan *Scheme*," may mislead. The word *scheme* suggests deliberate planning (or worse), and that may be to exaggerate what actually happened under Augustus. In his review of important recent work on Augustus, A. Wallace-Hadrill has cautioned that "anyone who tries to grapple with Augustus finds [himself] grappling with the whole principate," and he urges us to consider "the question of whether Augustus *had* formulated policies—or whether anything is gained by reading back from events to the 'intentions' of the ruler." [7] In a consideration of the *Augustales* in particular, these warnings must sound loud, clear, and often. Absent any explicit testimony from epigraphy or from ancient authors, and given the sheer variety of organizational structure and activity that we find among the different local groups of *Augustales,* we must be wary of claiming a direct role on the part of Augustus in "inventing" the very idea of the *Augustales* generally or in setting them up in any given town. At the very least we can be certain that no single prescription (if any) arrived from Rome in the municipalities to establish the local body of *Augustales.* On the other hand, in view of the presence of the *Augustales* in numerous towns already within Augustus' lifetime, it is unthinkable that their existence could have remained unknown to him and to the political circle around him and, consequently, that the institution could have flourished without at the very least the tacit approval of the *princeps* himself. Although the precise origin of the institution must thus continue to elude us (in the absence of pertinent new evidence such as epigraphy may be able one day to supply), it may be useful to distinguish between two possible levels of involvement on the part of the emperor. Specific *initiative* on the part of Augustus was surely not required for the original "*Augustales* idea"—and even perhaps its first concrete manifestations on the municipal scene—to come into being. But considering how intricately involved the *Augustales*

---

firmly dated notice stems from Nepet in Etruria (*CIL* XI.3200 = *ILS* 89; 13/12 B.C.). Several other inscriptions from Italy's Regio VII are likewise Augustan: *CIL* XI.3083 = *ILS* 5373 and *CIL* XI.3135 (both from Falerii); *NSc* (1938) 5 = *AEpigr* (1939) 142 (Telamon); and *CIL* XI.3782 (Veii). Cf. the observations of Duthoy (1978: supra n. 2) 1291, 1299.

7. A Wallace-Hadrill, *JRS* 75 (1985) 245, 246.

were with the very delicate matter of the imperial cult, *permission* at the level of the emperor himself surely must have been gained.[8]

If we wish to speculate as to just what was the manner in which the particular innovation of the *Augustales* spread so rapidly and to so many places, three useful analogies are at hand, each of them the focus of current scholarly attention: the development of the local coinages of Augustus' reign, the way in which public honors paid to members of the senatorial aristocracy were curtailed, and the rise of the imperial cult itself in the Greek world. In another recent article, pointing to the great variety of local civic coinages across the empire, all seeking to honor Augustus, Wallace-Hadrill suggests that we seek to understand them by positing a spectrum, "from direct involvement of the emperor in the issue at one end to an unsolicited honour at the other." Many "of these independent local authorities, which had, almost without exception, no tradition of portraying living Romans on their coins, and remained under no legal obligation to do so, increasingly chose to represent Augustus."[9] A similar spectrum seems the most useful model to suggest how the "*Augustales* idea" too many have spread, resulting in so many diverse local "signatures," all of which shared certain general patterns of organization and underlying purpose. W. Eck, charting the slow but steady reduction under Augustus in the public honors traditionally paid to senatorial aristocrats, concludes that the *gradual* "fading away proves that it was in no way a matter of direct intervention on the part of Augustus. It is rather that a degree of caution . . . developed."[10] That, again, is suggestive of just the kind of process we may imagine for the *Augustales:* a piecemeal, step-by-step evolution responding as much to local developments in the towns as to events in Rome. And, finally, in his account of the earliest growth of the imperial cult in the Greek East, G. Bowersock has traced something very similar at work: "What happened was undoubtedly what [Augustus] wished, but there was nothing he had to do to make it happen, except to defeat Antony. . . . Initiative from Rome was not required, only modification and adjustment."[11]

8. I am indebted to K. Raaflaub for the foregoing observation. On the cult, see pp. 377–78.

9. A Wallace-Hadrill, "Image and Authority in the Coinage of Augustus," *JRS* 76 (1986) 66–87, at 73 and 72, respectively.

10. W. Eck, "Senatorial Self-Representation: Developments in the Augustan Period," in F. Millar and E. Segal, eds., *Caesar Augustus: Seven Aspects* (Oxford 1984) 129–67, at 154, n. 16.

11. G. W. Bowersock, *Augustus and the Greek World* (Oxford 1965) 115, 121. On the whole question of the origins and promulgation of an "Augustan ideology," cf. now A. Wallace-Hadrill, "The Golden Age and Sin in Augustan ideology," *P&P* 95 (1982) 19–36.

What then are the specific areas of Augustan policy making—if we may use the term—with which the *Augustales* can most appropriately be compared so as to reveal a consistent Augustan intention at work? Although we lack any mention of the *Augustales* in contemporary literature, we must assume that there is a significant Augustan context, and we must seek it in order to understand the *Augustales*. That is our aim in this paper. We must at the same time avoid the temptation to multiply such areas unnecessarily in a fruitless search for merely superficial similarities with the *Augustales*.

I propose four distinct aspects of the Augustan "program" for our consideration: the emperor's concern with redefining and rebuilding the senatorial and equestrian orders; the reorganization of those lesser officials—the *apparitores*—who attended the magistrates of the Roman people; the attention paid to matters touching on slavery and, especially, freedmen; and, within the immense sphere of matters pertaining to Augustan religious policy as a whole, the establishment of the imperial cult.

As for the orders, the *Augustales* were one themselves, designated precisely as *ordo* in a number of inscriptions—though an order visible not in Rome itself, of course, but only in the towns (colonies and *municipia* alike) of Italy and the provinces. Membership clearly was conferred on the basis of credentials of social and economic status.[12] Recently C. Nicolet has carefully focused our attention on Augustus' efforts to reshape the two preeminent orders in Rome itself, thereby to enhance their prestige and utility.[13] What happened in Rome is most suggestive for the case of the *Augustales* as well, and in what follows I am much indebted to Nicolet's account.

First, the senate.[14] On at least three occasions (in 28 B.C., 8 B.C., and A.D. 14) a great census was carried out; the senate was purged, and purged again. A whole series of moral and civil legislation was begun in 19 B.C., entailing various disqualifications in matters of marriage and the making of wills and thus requiring that there be a precise definition of the senatorial order. In order to reinforce the existing social and political hierarchy and to distinguish more clearly the two orders, the minimum census qualification for senators was raised, in stages, to one million sesterces; the emperor himself was willing to contribute the

12. Cf. esp. Duthoy (1974: supra n. 2) 141–50.
13. Cf. C. Nicolet, "Augustus, Government, and the Propertied Classes," in Millar and Segal (supra n. 10) 89–128.
14. On what follows, see Nicolet (supra n. 13) esp. 91–92.

necessary funds "to those who seemed to deserve it." [15] And, finally, Augustus took several measures aimed at firmly establishing the hereditary nature of the order. With regard to the emperor's apparent generosity in making good the required census to those who lacked it, Nicolet insists that the "aim was not personal. It was not to reward wealth with the gift of political responsibilities, but, on the contrary, to restore a body politic to its traditional greatness and prestige." [16] And the ultimate purpose, as we shall see also for the equestrian order, was utilitarian in the highest degree: to provide the numbers of "suitable" candidates required for important offices in the state.

In the great speech that he fashioned for Maecenas, Dio Cassius suggests the same standards should apply for recruitment both to "Senate and to the equestrian order: birth, individual merit, and wealth" (52.19.2).[17] And Augustus followed just that prescription. Thus he revived some of the traditional modes of reviewing the qualifications of knights, including the famous mid-July inspection of their parade in military garb, and carried out a series of purging operations similar to those performed on the senate. For equestrians too a minimum census— 400,000 sesterces—was fixed from the Augustan Age on, if not already before, and the purpose was the same: to make ever more visible the existing hierarchy. As a senator was distinct from a knight, so a knight from a plebeian. But the census requirement—which might even be waived on occasion by Augustus—was not usually in itself enough, for the review of equestrian ranks looked again, as in the case of senators, at "origins, respectability, and fortune all at once." Free birth was required, and the way in which one's fortune was made was carefully scrutinized: already from the mid-first century B.C. actors and gladiators, as well as bankrupts, were, by law, excluded.[18]

And just how was this reformed order in the state to serve the public interest? Nicolet documents the military and judicial functions, and those involving the still important contracts for the farming of provincial taxes, services that, inherited from the Republic, were now again sought from the *equites* by the Augustan regime.[19] In addition, the

15. Ibid., 94.
16. Ibid., 95. For the (not insignificant) degree to which the senate retained its prior "freedom" to act under Augustus (and Tiberius as well), cf. P. A. Brunt, "The Role of the Senate in the Augustan Regime," *CQ* n.s. 34 (1984) 423–44.
17. Nicolet (supra n. 13) 92.
18. Ibid., 96–98; the quotation at 97.
19. Ibid., 99–103.

equestrian order was no doubt seen, in Livy's phrase,[20] as a *seminarium*—a kind of seedbed or training ground—for future members of the senate itself, a "huge reservoir" of "suitable candidates for various essential offices."[21] Not that all equestrians were well disposed to serve in this way. Nicolet cites Ovid as an example of the "reluctance to hold magistracies" that endured throughout the principate.[22]

What then, viewed as a whole, was the "logic of the reorganization of the higher orders by Augustus," as seen by Nicolet? "[It] was not in their own interests, individual or corporate, that [Augustus] took pains, by a great many touches, to regulate the qualifications and functions of senators and knights: it was to encourage them to aim at a career of service to the state."[23]

But when we look again at the *Augustales*, it is just this picture of the senatorial and equestrian orders—in their overall dimensions—that is called to mind: the *Augustales* are themselves an order defined by social origins, financial fortune, and "worthiness"—a *dignitas* of a sort. Our very limited evidence, we are reminded, does not offer any trace of legislation to define their institutional form, nor of census machinery to comb their ranks, but in their essential profile the *Augustales* represent just the kind of "*ordo* making" in the age of Augustus that we have seen for the senate and *equites*—and for fundamentally similar purposes: to serve, at the municipal level, as an additional "reservoir" of financially qualified and morally deserving persons (alongside the order of decurions themselves) who were willing to make substantial contributions to the everyday business (religious, architectural, entertainment) required in their towns. And even as the equestrians proved a *seminarium* for the senate, so the *Augustales* may well have served that role with respect to the local municipal ruling classes. At least at Ostia a plausible argument has been made, after careful scrutiny of the epigraphical evidence, that by the late second century the local town council did indeed include descendants of freedmen from a century earlier who had been *Augustales*.[24] It may be worth noting that the *Augustales* too could claim parallels to the reluctant Ovid among their ranks: an Antonine inscription from Petelia in southern Italy points unambiguously to hesitation within local freedmen circles to "leap at" (*prosilio*) the honor of *Augus-*

20. 42.61.5, quoting King Perseus in 169 B.C.: cf. Nicolet (supra n. 13) 103, n. 56.
21. Nicolet (supra n. 13) 99.
22. Ibid., 104.
23. Ibid., 103.
24. Cf. D'Arms (supra n. 4) 134–39.

talis.[25] Nicolet observes that there are two sides to the notion of *ordo*—privilege *and* obligation[26]—and the *Augustales* reveal both facets every bit as much as do the two great orders in Rome.

I do not wish to claim, as I said earlier, that such parallels prove specific initiative on the part of the emperor or his circle in either the original establishment of the *Augustales* or their subsequent evolution—though surely such intervention, on occasion, is more than plausible. A likely instance is found at Narbo. P. Kneissl has convincingly argued that a familiar inscription from the town is none other than the very "founding charter" of the local *Augustales* and that the occasion was probably intended to celebrate the personal role of Augustus in settling a dispute between the local *plebs* and the local decurions.[27] At all events the parallels between the orders at Rome and those in the towns are

25. *CIL* X.114 = *ILS* 6469. Cf. Duthoy (1978: supra n. 2) 1283, n. 223; cf. R. P. Duncan-Jones, *The Economy of the Roman Empire: Quantitative Studies*[2] (Cambridge 1982) 269–70, 284, 286.

26. Nicolet (supra n. 13) 122, n. 39.

27. *CIL* XII.4333 = *ILS* 112 = V. Ehrenberg and A. H. M. Jones, *Documents Illustrating the Reigns of Augustus and Tiberius*[2] (Oxford 1955) 85–86, no. 100. Cf. Kneissl (supra n. 2) esp. 305–6. (Translations of the inscription may be found in the following sourcebooks: N. Lewis and M. Reinhold, *Roman Civilization*, vol. 2 [New York 1966] 62–64; B. Levick, *The Government of the Roman Empire* [London and Sydney 1985] 119–20, no. 116; D. C. Braund, *Augustus to Nero* [Totowa, N.J. 1985] 61–62, no. 125.) Although the inscription makes no mention of *Augustales* by that (or a similar) title, Kneissl argues that the social character and religious and political functions of the *tres equites Romani a plebe et tres libertini* who are featured on the stone correspond closely with the profile of the well-known colleges of late republican *magistri* on Delos and at Capua. He further shows that the similarities between the *magistri* and the *Augustales* were closer still, and so plausibly concludes that the inscription marks the very moment that the *Augustales* were established at Narbo. On the *magistri* and their parallels with the *Augustales*, cf. also Ostrow (supra n. 3) 91–95. We must caution that among the many dozens of inscriptions explicitly attesting the presence at Narbo of *Augustales*—or, more precisely, of *seviri Augustales,* the other of the two most frequently occurring variants of the title among some forty thus far identified across the empire—very few (perhaps only three) can be securely dated, and the earliest of these is put at the end of the first century A.C.: cf. R. Duthoy, "Recherches sur la répartition géographique et chronologique des termes sevir Augustalis, Augustalis et sevir dans l'Empire romain," *Epigraphische Studien* 11 (Cologne and Bonn 1976) 143–214, at 182. On the complex matter of the varying titulature associated with the *Augustales,* cf. Duthoy (supra) passim; id. (1978: supra n. 2) 1254, introductory footnote; and Ostrow (supra n. 3) 64, n. 2, and 65. The ambiguous wording of the inscription that points to the emperor's role is found at 11.30–31: *iudicia plebis decurionibus coniunxit.* After painstaking discussion of the several possibilities (see, for example, the divergent translations cited above), Kneissl plausibly suggests (306) that the words mean " 'Weil er (sc. Augustus) . . . die Vorstellungen, die Beurteilungen der *plebs* mit den Dekurionen vereinte', oder genauer: 'Weil er . . . die Vorstellungen der plebs mit denen der Dekurionen in Einklang brachte.'" Hence, Kneissl concludes, Augustus must have intervened as mediator in a dispute between the *plebs* and the decurions—a dispute the origin of which remains quite unknown, though its outcome was marked with the foundation of a new municipal institution focused on the imperial cult.

remarkable, and in three respects: in the criteria (social, financial, and presumably also moral) by which the respective orders were defined; in the aim of public service they were meant to achieve; and very possibly in the similar shared intention that the more modest *ordo* in each case (*equites, Augustales*) should, in time, serve to prepare some of its own members as suitable candidates for the more prestigious order (senate, decurions). These similarities testify to the obviously enormous prestige of the two orders in the capital and of Augustus' reshaping of them, and to their corresponding stature as models available for municipal imitation—whether at the prompting of the local *plebs* (as at Narbo) or of the town councillors. In other words, these were the Augustan formulas that were "in the air," and they were, evidently, very well publicized, however exactly they arrived at one town after another. We can easily imagine that the paths of transmission—from the center of power outward or from spontaneous local initiatives or admixtures of both— were multiple, but the resulting similarities evidenced in hundreds of Roman towns are truly striking. More and more, from the age of Augustus onward, with respect to the town councils, local *Augustales* must have looked and played the part of Roman knights vis-à-vis the Roman senate.

And not only senators and knights, but another group of public servants too shows signs of wholesale reorganization in the Augustan period. These, the so-called *apparitores,* or attendants of the magistrates of the Roman people, have been the subject of yet another recent and most revealing investigation, by N. Purcell.[28] Here, at what is clearly a still reputable, if less exalted, step of the social pyramid in Rome, we find scribes, lictors, heralds, and the like. Horace was one of them.[29] The more than five hundred inscriptions that constitute the bulk of our evidence for them naturally cluster in Rome and in her neighboring towns. The *apparitores* show close similarities with the *Augustales* in their social origins and, especially, in their social function. Most of them are freedmen, although none of their several grades was reserved exclusively for freedmen. Some are even *Augustales.*[30] It is precisely under Augustus that "much of the tremendous complexity of the apparitorial organisation, with its numerous honorific positions and well-regulated hierarchy, develops." Along with the tribes, the order of the *apparitores* constituted one of the chief institutions of the Urban *plebs*. The scribes

28. N. Purcell, "The *Apparitores:* A Study in Social Mobility," *BSR* 51 (1983) 125–73.
29. Purcell (supra n. 28) 138–39, n. 82.
30. Ibid., 137.

among them were "recognised as standing on the edge of equestrian status," [31] and indeed that status might well be gained by the *apparitor* himself, or by his son. We are reminded of the son of the freedman, and presumably all the more of the son of the *Augustalis,* at the municipal level, for whom—but not for whose father—the path to local political honors *did* lie open.

There are indeed significant structural differences. The *apparitores* had a professional basis, and they were salaried (though for some the position may have been a sinecure), whereas the *Augustales,* as members of a council-like body, behaved on occasion as quasi magistrates, not without a flavor of the priest as well. And the *Augustales,* far from receiving a salary, were expected to pay out, and generously. But in their essential function the two institutions were very similar. The world of the *apparitores* was "the world of the social climber," in which their positions offered nothing less than "a route by which the freedman and the outsider might be admitted to the society of the city of Rome." [32] We might have said the same for the *Augustales* with respect to social life in the towns of Italy and the Roman West. And surely the ties were even closer than that, for it is just such persons as the *apparitores,* with family roots in the towns near Rome and, in Purcell's phrase, "schooled in the capital in the ways in which loyalty could most profitably be demonstrated," [33] who are likely to have been instrumental in spreading the institution of the *Augustales* in the Italian towns.

There thus seems good reason to consider the *Augustales* against the backdrop of Augustus' redefinition of the greater and lesser orders in the state. But since the *Augustales* constitute a predominantly freedman institution, there is all the more reason to observe them in the context of the emperor's preoccupation with matters of slavery, and with the numbers and social status of freed slaves. We emphasize here but a few salient features of the subject that especially touch on the *Augustales.*

That a problem, indeed a crisis, involving slaves and freedmen haunted the final century of the Republic will not be disputed. The promise or fact of the manumission of slaves en masse, for military and political ends, by one great politician or general after another, from the time of the Gracchi to that of Octavian himself, needs little review.[34]

31. Ibid., 133–36; the quotations occurring at 133 and 136, respectively.
32. Ibid., 136, 138.
33. Ibid., 163.
34. Cf. K. R. Bradley, *Slaves and Masters in the Roman Empire: A Study in Social Control,* Coll.Latomus 185 (Brussels 1984; reissued, New York 1987) 84–85 with nn. 11–12, citing some of the numerous sources, including App. *BCiv.*1.26 (offer of freedom to

Nor does the continued addition of many tens, perhaps even hundreds, of thousands of war captives to Rome's slave population as a result of military campaigns fought abroad in the same period. The hordes of slaves taken by Caesar in Gaul may serve as a useful reminder.[35] In reviewing these conditions in his recent survey of Roman slavery under the empire, K. Bradley has observed that "there was no stable basis on which slaves could put their expectations [of manumission] and the impact on slave psychology must have been severe."[36] The famous Augustan legislation that sought to control the manumission of slaves was surely intended in part to restore just such a secure basis for slaves' expectation of their freedom—not, of course, for the benefit of the slave, but, ultimately, in order to reinforce the entire system of Roman slavery.

Two laws stand out for their importance. The *Lex Fufia Caninia* of 2 B.C. fixed precise limits on the number of slaves—up to a maximum of one hundred—that might be freed at the master's death. The *Lex Aelia Sentia* of A.D. 4 set minimum ages of thirty for a slave and twenty for an owner before the slave could be manumitted and receive Roman citizenship.[37]

It seems that Augustus' aim in both laws was not merely "to halt the numerical flow of emancipations."[38] Rather, the chief aim of the *Lex Fufia*—in Bradley's view—was to curb the current "tendency on the part of the Roman élite to free slaves by will as a form of social ostentation." The law thus was one in a series of efforts by Augustus, including sumptuary laws, to suppress "the luxurious . . . practices of the ruling classes." There was a particular effect of the *Lex Fufia,* however, in the state of mind that it must have induced in many slaves themselves: in brief, the limitation upon the number of slaves who might be freed by the master's will gave this form of manumission the "character of a competition," in which the slave who was to succeed in gaining manumission ahead of his companions would be the one who better adhered

---

slaves by Gaius Gracchus and Fulvius Flaccus), 1.54 (offer from the senate as a whole in 89 B.C.), 1.58 (offer from the supporters of Marius), 1.65 and 69 (two separate offers from Cinna; cf. 1.74), 1.100 (Sulla's famous offer of freedom to upwards of ten thousand slaves of the proscribed); also 4.7 and 11 (offer from the second triumvirate), 4.36 (offer from Sextus Pompeius), 4.73 (offer from Cassius); and Suet. *Aug.* 16.1 (offer from Octavian). Bradley notes (85) that of course by no means all of these offers were accepted by the slaves involved (App. *BCiv.* 1.26, 54, 58, 65). Cf. also W. L. Westermann, *The Slave Systems of Greek and Roman Antiquity* (Philadelphia 1955) 66–67.

35. On Caesar's war captives, cf. Bradley (supra n. 34) 86, n. 16; Vell. Pat. 2.47.1.

36. Bradley (supra n. 34) 85.

37. Ibid., 87. On these laws, cf. also G. Boulvert and M. Morabito, "Le droit de l'esclavage sous le Haut-Empire," *ANRW* 2.14 (1982) 98–182, at 112–13.

38. Bradley (supra n. 34) 89 and (for what follows in this paragraph) 91.

to the rules of "compliant behaviour, loyalty and obedience." The parallel with the *Augustales* is not far to seek.

When we turn to the *Lex Aelia* of five years later and inquire as to its primary purpose, the answer is again revealing for its tendency toward the same kind of "social engineering" that we may posit for the institution of the *Augustales* itself. By setting minimum age limits for both slave and master before manumission with full citizenship could be granted, a more or less lengthy period of waiting for his possible freedom was imposed upon the slave—especially, of course, upon the home-born slave. This was a time in the slave's life during which all criminal behavior must be avoided and when at least some of the values of Roman morality and some sense of the patterns of Roman civic life could be inculcated to prepare the slave for his potential future role in free society. In Bradley's useful summary, the purpose of the *Lex Aelia* "was to inform slaves as much as their owners of the qualifications required for citizenship, and to create potential for harmony between privileged and non-privileged sections of Roman society by offering slaves the prospect of eventual release from their condition in a way which meantime guaranteed without resistance the continuation of the servile system." [39]

But is this aim not precisely analogous to that of the *Augustales*, making necessary allowance for the different social levels and incentives involved? To hold out to well-to-do freedmen the prospect of meaningful activity and high prestige in their towns, alongside the local town councillors themselves—this was surely to forge a more stable harmony with Roman municipal life through a mechanism of well-controlled social mobility. The Augustan laws that regulated the freeing of slaves seem, in other words, all of a piece with the overall pattern of social reorganization represented also by the establishment of the *Augustales* and, for that matter, by the reshaping of the senatorial and equestrian orders and of the *apparitores* as well.

It is not, once again, that we must read back into the original setting up of the *Augustales* a direct initiative on the part of Augustus, but that such ideas were the common currency of the age. Whatever the initial impulse—and there may have been many varying ones in different towns—we can be sure that once the *Augustales* had been established and become widespread across Italy and the West, the promise they offered of promoting social stability at the local level must have been

---

39. Ibid., 93.

warmly encouraged by the powers in the capital. Their rapid development, especially in Latium and Campania, already within the reign of
Augustus suggests that the first *princeps* himself must have been foremost among their early sponsors.

Just how may social stability have been enhanced by the institution
of the *Augustales?* May we not fairly conjure up a vision of likely re-
sentment, even potentially violent civil unrest, on the part of wealthy
municipal freedmen as a reaction against their exclusion from political
life in the towns? The very existence of the *Augustales* must have served
in part to defuse this potential danger by opening up a useful outlet for
the energies and ambitions of these persons. The objection may be
raised that wealthy freedmen had such a clear economic stake in maintaining the status quo that they were most unlikely to do anything to
upset it.[40] But should we not then remind ourselves of the bloody disturbances in Rome in 31 B.C., as described by Dio Cassius (50.10.4–6), by
which freedmen expressed their disapproval of Octavian's harsh imposition of taxes—taxes levied not against impoverished freedmen souls,
but on those with a minimum property assessment of 200,000 sesterces?[41] Granted, those were especially troubled times, on the eve of
Actium. But may we not credit Augustus (and others both in his regime
and in the ruling classes of the local towns) with a sharp enough memory of events such as these to realize the enormous social (and even economic) advantages that would accrue to them all by channeling the talents (and money) of the wealthy municipal freedman into the socially
prestigious role of civic benefactor? That was, after all, precisely the
role played by the *Augustales.* And how sharp *must* their memory have
been in any case, since Dio, for the episode in 31, records murder, riots,
and so many buildings damaged by arson that the fires were counted
among the portents (*terata*) of the year? With this upheaval in mind, as
well as the earlier role of freedmen among the supporters of Catiline
and Clodius in midcentury,[42] and the series of violent disturbances during the late Republic and early decades of the empire even in a region

40. When I first suggested this particular aim of social stability for the *Augustales,* at a
meeting of the New England Ancient History Colloquium held at Tufts University in April
1983, precisely this objection was raised by several participants, whom I thank at this late
date for their generous hearing and stimulating questions.

41. On the whole episode, cf. R. Syme, *The Roman Revolution* (Oxford 1939) 284, n.
1, 354; D. Kienast, *Augustus: Prinzeps und Monarch* (Darmstadt 1982) 210.

42. On which cf. S. Treggiari, *Roman Freedmen during the Late Republic* (Oxford
1969) 168–77, esp. 175.

like Campania,[43] with all these factors in view, it still strikes me as reasonable that one prime motivation behind the institution of the *Augustales* was precisely that of preventing the disgruntlement of unhappy but well-to-do local freedmen from getting out of hand. And whether, in any given town, the first inspiration came from Rome or from local initiative or from any other source (as, for example, the report of an enterprising freedman trader on what he had seen in his travels abroad), we can be sure that the role played by the *Augustales* in building social harmony must soon have been equally well appreciated by all parties concerned: the emperor and the governing class at Rome, the leading circles in the towns and in the provinces, and above all, of course, the better-placed freedmen themselves.

If there is any one aspect of the *Augustales* that has indeed been thoroughly treated by scholars, it is their relationship to the imperial cult. Thus we may be brief. It is all but universally agreed that the one essential assignment that fell to the *Augustales* was to see to the needs of this most notorious of Augustan innovations.[44] More notorious by the year, we might add; for there now thrives a new (or rather newly reinvigorated) doctrine to the effect that there *was,* after all, real "religious content" to the imperial cult, a true depth of devotion in it; that it was *not* wholly devoid of feeling—not even for the elite within Roman society, let alone for the common folk. S. Price's new book on the imperial cult in Asia Minor is perhaps the most vigorous specimen to date.[45] So quickly overturned is the sceptic's viewpoint, the "naive rationalism" of earlier years,[46] to be replaced by newfound faith.

Whatever else the *Augustales* may tell us, they can scarcely shed light on this elusive problem of the genuineness of belief in the emperor's divinity. Enthusiasms of various sorts may surely be read behind the *Augustales* for Augustus himself, for institutions that he encouraged, for the very achievement of social mobility that the *Augustales* represent—and for the public display of that achievement in the performance of local benefactions. But as to belief in divinity, the *Augustales* are certainly not going to decide the issue for us.

Noting in his book that "many societies have the problem of making

43. See, for example, Ostrow (supra n. 3) 95–98.

44. Cf. Duthoy (1978: supra n. 2) 1293–1306; Kneissl (supra n. 2) 319; Ostrow (supra n. 3) 67.

45. S. Price, *Rituals and Power: The Roman Imperial Cult in Asia Minor* (Cambridge 1984).

46. As it is characterized by Purcell (supra n. 28) 167.

sense of an otherwise incomprehensible intrusion of authority into their world," Price has proposed that the imperial cult served in part to "construct" (in a social sense) the emperor and Roman power for the Greeks of Asia.[47] By means of the cult, which employed symbols drawn from their traditional religious system, these Greeks could represent "the emperor to themselves in the familiar terms of divine power."[48] May we not imagine that the *Augustales,* as one of the cult's chief manifestations in Italy and the West, served a similar function? Most of the freedmen members were, after all, either foreign-born slaves or were descended from such. These persons must have been conscious of having experienced a bewildering array of profound changes in their lives: not only the transition from slave to freedman and from political outsider to local citizen, but also from meager economic circumstances to a position of some wealth. For these *Augustales*—every bit as much as for Greeks of Asia—the imperial cult, and membership in a brotherhood devoted to it, must have gone a long way to help interpret *their* new world, including their own direct relationship to the emperor.

These, then, are the chief Augustan developments that mirror either the way in which the *Augustales* themselves evolved or the general concern of the age—indeed of Augustus himself—with the framing of social institutions for particular aims. The senatorial and equestrian Orders were shaped anew, their qualifications specified, their tasks multiplied, so that the state might be enriched with the talents of their respective members. Similarly the ranks of the *apparitores* were combed, their internal hierarchy restructured, so that the Roman *plebs* too might contribute profitably to the state. Matters of slavery, and especially the regulation of manumission and the status of freedmen, were of central concern to the Augustan regime, which attempted to reinforce social harmony with an ambitious program of legislation. And, finally, the imperial cult was established. Although it must have served multiple ends in various places, surely not the least of them in the Greek East was to help make comprehensible the novel presence of a Roman emperor. There are several other sides too—more subtle, perhaps, but still revealing—to the tale of how the *Augustales* "fit" into the full array of Augustan measures. Space permits me here to make bare mention of two that I hope to pursue elsewhere: the continuing process of Italian integration, which was so dear to the hearts of Augustus and several of his

47. Price (supra n. 45) 247 and, for social "construction" in this special sense, 242–43.
48. Ibid., 248.

first-century successors; and yet another theme now so usefully emphasized, again, by Nicolet,[49] the Augustan campaign for the protection of
property, the security of ownership—in the hands of the humble and
the exalted alike. With further study, the *Augustales* are likely to emerge
ever more clearly as emblematic of Augustan "policy," however we
understand that abstraction.

49. Nicolet (supra n. 13) esp. 107–17.

The Pontificate of Augustus

On the sixth day of March in the year 12 B.C. Augustus Caesar was declared *pontifex maximus* in succession to the recently deceased triumvir M. Aemilius Lepidus. The date of this event is securely attested on three of the great epigraphic calendars of the Roman Empire: on the *Feriale Cumanum,* for example, we read [*eo die Caesar Pontifex Ma*]*ximus creatus est, supplicat*[*i*]*o Vestae,* an entry that explicitly records the role of the *pontifex maximus* in the Vestal cult. Despite his program of reorganization and renewal and his desire to reinvigorate the religious life of Rome, Augustus had allowed the priesthood of the Vestals to lie unattended for nearly two decades. Lepidus, *pontifex maximus* from the troubled days of the forties, resided in ignominious confinement at Circeii but continued to hold the office, which not even Augustus chose to strip from him.

This, the highest and most august priesthood at Rome, had traditionally been conjoined with the office of *princeps senatus,* which Augustus already held. But the splendor of the pontificate seems to have kept Augustus from defiling it by arrogation, and he waited patiently for the old Lepidus to die. When this finally happened, he added the grandiloquent words *pontifex maximus* to his own titulature, and they then became a

standard part of the imperial titulature for all of his successors. Nothing
is more consistently or ostentatiously paraded by the Roman emperors
apart from their tribunician power. When one considers the enormous
labor that has been expended on interpreting the nature of the tribunician power, it can only seem surprising that the pontificate has attracted
so little attention.

A new assessment of Augustus could well take as one of its starting
points the circumstances that surround the assumption of the office of
pontifex maximus in 12 B.C. This was the time in which the design of
the great sundial of Augustus was laid out, the time in which the Ara
Pacis was being created, the time in which two obelisks were brought
from Heliopolis in Egypt to Rome, the time in which the fourth book of
Horace's *Odes* was first being circulated at Rome—to convey a sense of
the excitement of that age. To examine the long neglected pontificate
of Augustus we must look at the whole period from 13 to 9; in other
words, the period from the return of Augustus to Rome from Gaul and
Spain down to the dedication of the Ara Pacis on 30 January 9 B.C.

In any book on Augustus it would be hard to find much more than a
simple reference to the death of Lepidus and the emperor's assumption
of the office of *pontifex maximus*. In the *Oxford Classical Dictionary*
an excellent article on Augustus even omits the priesthood altogether.
The general impression conveyed is that Augustus did not really care
much about the position and therefore left it to the old triumvir. The
long wait appears to have been understood as an indication of disinter-
est on the emperor's part. In his *Roman Revolution*, Syme wrote: "The
official head of the state religion, it is true, was Lepidus, the *pontifex
maximus*, living in seclusion at Circeii. Augustus did not strip him of
that honour, ostentatious in scruple when scruple cost him nothing. He
could wait for Lepidus' death."[1]

And yet the extraordinary prominence of the title, once assumed,
both in the Augustan period and afterwards ought to have suggested the
opposite of such a view. The priesthood was simply too important to
tamper with. The whole survival of the Roman world seemed in some
sense to depend upon the Vestal cult, which traced its origins to Troy
and the flight of Aeneas. Readers of the last poem in the third book of
Horace's *Odes* will recall that the longevity of Roman civilization and
with it the renown of the poet are expressed by a reference to the *pontifex maximus* climbing the Capitoline Hill with a Vestal virgin: *dum*

1. R. Syme, *The Roman Revolution* (Oxford 1939) 477.

Capitolium / scandet cum tacita virgine Pontifex (*Carm.* 3.30.8–9). These words must have seemed all the more portentous when they were written in the twenties, since at that time the *pontifex* was not ascending the Capitolium at all but living out his life in a kind of internal exile.

Caesar Augustus had long displayed an exceptional interest in the revival of traditional religion and his own participation in priestly colleges. He had become a *pontifex* very early and subsequently became *augur, quindecimvir sacris faciundis, septemvir epulonum, frater arvalis, sodalis Titius,* and *fetialis.* It is inconceivable that he thought that the greatest of all priesthoods, the position of spiritual leadership of the Roman state, did not really matter. The high priest traditionally controlled the calendar and state sacrifices. He chose the *flamines.* Yet at the celebration of the secular games in 17 B.C. Augustus presided with Agrippa in the embarrassing absence of the *pontifex maximus,* but he dared not touch the incumbent. A newly discovered fragment of the great inscription describing the organization and celebration of those games now reveals Augustus' solemn prayer to the gods on that occasion.[2] He ought to have pronounced it as *pontifex maximus.* Neglect of the pontificate has kept an important part of the Augustan principate in the dark.

Augustus himself did not even believe that Lepidus had properly assumed the priesthood, but nonetheless he was unwilling to deprive him of it. Despite the attitude of modern historians, the emperor in his *Res Gestae* clearly indicates the significance he attached to the priesthood he assumed in 12: *pontif]ex maximus ne fierem in vivi [c]onle / [gae mei l]ocum, [populo id sace]rdotium deferente mihi quod pater meu[s] / [habuer]at, r[ecusavi. qu]od sacerdotium aliquod post annos, eo mor/[t]uo q[ui civilis] m[otus o]ccasione occupaverat, cuncta ex Italia / [ad comitia mea] confluen[te mu]ltitudine, quanta Romae nun[q]uam / [fertur ante i]d temp[us fuisse], recep[i] P. Sulpicio C. Valgio consulibu[s].* "I refused to become *pontifex maximus* as a successor to my colleague while he was still alive, even though the people offered me that priesthood, which my father had held. Some years later, after the death of the man who had seized this priesthood on the occasion of a civil war, a multitude from the whole of Italy came together to elect me, a crowd such as they say had never been seen at Rome before that time. I took the priesthood in the consulate of P. Sulpicius and C. Valgius."[3]

---

2. L. Moretti, "Frammenti vecchi e nuovi del Commentario dei Ludi Secolari," *Rend PontAcc* 55–56 (1982–1984) 361–79.

3. *RG* 10.2.

These words leave no doubt of Augustus' view of the high priesthood nor of his desire to guarantee the legitimacy of his assumption of it. The very date of the event was perceived as important by his successors, who regularly waited to take the office of *pontifex maximus* in the month of March, no matter when their actual power began. The date for the pontificate became as traditional as the December date for the assumption of the tribunician power.

In his *Fasti* (3.415–28) Ovid commemorated the event of 6 March in a series of couplets that emphasized the Trojan connections of the Vestal cult (*Iliacis tura pone focis*) and the role of Aeneas in rescuing the sacred objects of the cult that were still preserved at Rome. Because of the emperor's own Trojan ancestry through Venus, Ovid is able to declare that the right priest has assumed the right priesthood: "A priest sprung from Aeneas touches the divinities that are related to him (*cognata numina*)." Accordingly the poet beseeches Vesta to protect her *cognatum caput*. Both the Vestal fires and their priest are to live forever: *vivite inexstincti, flammaque duxque, precor*. Once again we see the importance of the Vestal cult and its priest for the symbolism of eternity and immortality.

Although both the epigraphic and the literary *fasti* are explicit on the date of Augustus' assumption of the pontificate, the historian Cassius Dio records the event under the year 13 B.C. This is evidently because it was in that year that Lepidus died. The entry in Dio begins simply, "On the death of Lepidus he was appointed high priest."[4] Although it is customary to say that Lepidus died either in 13 or in 12, the evidence as it stands would suggest that his death came in 13 and that Augustus allowed some time for the preparation of the formal assumption of the priesthood. The death of Lepidus in 13 has significant implications, for that is the year in which Augustus returned from Spain and Gaul, and it is also the year in which the Ara Pacis was begun. Although the Ara Pacis may well have been formally voted as an immediate expression of gratitude for the return of Augustus, it has long been evident that there must have been substantial discussions and preparations for such a major proposal.

The assumption of a preparatory phase is now made absolutely certain by the phenomenal discoveries of the German Archaeological Institute in the vicinity of San Lorenzo in Lucina in Rome. The publication of the German excavations by Edmund Buchner has revealed the full

---

4. Dio 54.27.2.

extent of the huge and complex sundial that was laid out in the Campus Martius, undoubtedly the largest sundial ever constructed anywhere at any time.[5] It is now clear not only that this monumental work was conceived at the same time as the Ara Pacis, but that the orientation of the altar itself was actually determined by the lines of the sundial.

This means that the sundial (or *solarium*) and the Ara Pacis were part of a single great plan designed in 13 B.C. in connection with the return of Augustus. The interdependence of these two projects is borne out as well by the grand inscription that appears on two sides of the base of an Egyptian obelisk, now on the Montecitorio, which served as the *gnomon*, or pointer, of the sundial. The text of this inscription records dedication to the sun (*soli donum dedit*) in the year 10/9 B.C.[6] Since we know that the Ara Pacis was dedicated on Livia's birthday, 30 January 9 B.C., Buchner has rightly brought the dedication of the sundial into conjunction with the dedication of the Ara Pacis, and he has seen the entire complex as dedicated on 30 January 9 B.C.

The preeminent role of the sun in the overall concept of the scheme for the Campus Martius is reinforced by the obelisk itself. This object was brought to Rome at some time between 13 and the end of 10 on the orders of Augustus and inscribed on two sides with the Latin dedicatory text. What was dedicated to the sun came from the city of the sun, Heliopolis, in Egypt. Furthermore, in precisely the year 13/12 B.C., as can be determined from inscriptions, two other obelisks were removed from Heliopolis and placed in front of the shrine of Caesar Augustus, the Caesareum, at Alexandria in Egypt.[7] This operation was obviously correlated with the design for the Campus Martius, which also honored the Augustan achievement. Finally, in the same period (between 13 and 10) a fourth obelisk was taken from Heliopolis and brought to Rome for erection in the Circus Maximus. The inscription on this obelisk,[8] which stands now in the Piazza del Popolo in Rome, was identical to the one that served as the *gnomon* in the Campus Martius.

Our understanding of the thinking of Augustus and his planners in 13 can be broadened still further if we survey the full text of the inscriptions on the obelisks at Rome and on those in Alexandria. The two at Rome begin in large letters with the emperor's name, *Imp. Caesar divi f.*

---

5. E. Buchner, *Die Sonnenuhr des Augustus* (Mainz 1982), incorporating articles in *RM* 83 (1976) 319–65 and 87 (1980) 354–73.
   6. *ILS* 91.
   7. *OGIS* 656; *CIL* III.6588. Cf. J. Klein, "P. Rubrius Barbarus," *RhM* 35 (1880) 634, with Pliny *HN* 36.69 (on the two obelisks).
   8. Cf. *ILS* 91.

Augustus / Pontifex Maximus. In the next line follows the titulature that establishes the date of 10/9 B.C., and after this the words *Aegypto in potestatem populi Romani redacta / soli donum dedit.* In other words, these obelisks, coming from Egypt, are memorials of Augustus' victory over Cleopatra and the fall of Alexandria. The prominence assigned to the title *Pontifex Maximus* is remarkable and new, for Augustus had held the office for only about two years. And he was not holding it at all when the scheme represented by these obelisks was designed.

The reference to Egypt ties the two obelisks in Rome to the two that were set up before the Caesareum in Alexandria in 13/12. There the two obelisks from Heliopolis, which stand today in London and New York, were set up on newly created bronze bases in the shape of crabs, and on each of these crabs was inscribed in both Latin and Greek the year of Augustus in which the objects were erected at Alexandria and the name of the prefect of Egypt. The bases were probably designed to represent the astrological sign of the Crab (Cancer). And to understand this some technical observations are required. It is astronomically impossible that Augustus' *horoscopos* was in the Crab (in other words, that this was the sign rising) at the moment of his birth, because we know from Suetonius that he was born shortly before sunrise on 23 September 63 B.C. The Crab was not ascendant at that time. But it could well have been rising at the moment, equally significant astrologically, of his conception.

Suetonius suggests that Augustus' vital dates of genesis and birth were irresistible to mathematicians and astrologers. When as a young man the heir of Caesar and future Augustus met the mathematician Theogenes at Apollonia and reluctantly revealed the dates of his coming into the world, Theogenes jumped up ecstatically and then bowed down before the youth. As a result Augustus later showed so much faith in his horoscope, according to Suetonius, that he published it widely and issued coins with the sign of Capricorn, under which he was born (*quo natus est*).[9] Now, the allusion to Capricorn here and on the surviving coins that confirm it have baffled commentators for a long time.[10] The emperor's birth date in September should place him in Libra, and a *horoscopos* in Capricorn is just as impossible at the time of birth as one in Cancer.

Capricorn as a zodiacal month came much earlier than Augustus'

9. Suet. *Aug.* 94.12: *exilivit Theogenes adoravitque eum. tantam mox fiduciam fati Augustus habuit, ut thema suum vulgaverit nummumque argenteum nota sideris Capricorni, quo natus est, percusserit.* Cf. also German. *Phaen.* 558–60.

10. Cf. *RIC* 61 (28–27 B.C.), 63 (19–18 B.C.), 83 and 85 (25–22 B.C.), 88 (12–11 B.C.).

birth date in September. But it came exactly nine months earlier. In other words, Capricorn ought to be considered the sign of his conception, and so it was by the excellent Bouché-Leclercq in his *L'astrologie grecque*.[11] But philologists like A. E. Housman could neither tolerate *quo natus est* as a reference to conception nor concede that Suetonius might have erred here.[12] This was in spite of the plain and multiple evidence that Augustus was born under Libra. Suetonius himself provides the correct calendar date in that sign, and Virgil in his first *Georgic* had long before located the birth of the future Augustus in Libra.[13] The astronomical poet Manilius, whose text Housman understood better than the Augustan world in which Manilius wrote, was able to name Capricorn as the emperor's sign in Book 2 and Libra as his sign in Book 4, leading not only Housman but George Goold, his successor in editing Manilius, into transparent contradictions.[14] It took Housman ten years to face up to the fact that Augustus had at least two signs, and unfortunately when he did so he misinterpreted the situation.[15] He assumed that the sun was in Libra but the moon in Capricorn at Augustus' birth, and yet anyone who was at all familiar with the importance of the sun on the obelisks and indeed generally in Augustan Rome would have found it odd that the emperor chose to advertise a zodiacal sign determined by the moon. The discovery of the sundial has now proved beyond any doubt, by means of its mathematical layout, that Augustus celebrated both conception and birth.

Conceived on the winter solstice, he was born on the autumnal equinox. It has now been demonstrated that in the great plan of the horizontal sundial the equinoctial line passes directly through the middle of the Ara Pacis and determines the openings on the eastern and western sides of the altar. Furthermore a circle described through the endpoints of the curved line of Capricorn passes directly through the midpoint of the Ara Pacis, there intersecting the equinoctial line. The conjunction of these lines fixes exactly the orientation of the altar within the *solarium*.[16]

11. A. Bouché-Leclercq, *L'astrologie grecque* (Paris 1899) 374, n. I am grateful to Otto Neugebauer for patiently instructing me in astrology and for emphasizing the enduring value of Bouché-Leclercq's book.

12. Manilius, *Astronomica*, ed. A. E. Housman (London 1903) vol. 1, lxix-lxxi.

13. Virg. G. 1.32–35.

14. Manil. *Astron.* 2.507–9 (Capricorn) and 4.773–77 (Libra). Cf. G. P. Goold, Loeb edition of Manilius' *Astronomica* (1977) 284, n. b.

15. Housman (supra n. 12), revised in "Manilius, Augustus, Tiberius, Capricornus, and Libra," *CQ* 7 (1913) 109–14, and reprinted in J. Diggle and F. R. D. Goodyear, eds., *The Classical Papers of A. E. Housman,* vol. 2 (Cambridge 1972) 867–72. Cf. the posthumous second edition of Housman's Manilius (Cambridge 1937), vol. 1, 93–95.

16. Cf. Buchner (1982: supra n. 5) 27 (= id. [1976: supra n. 5] 337).

Hence the position of the Ara Pacis was such that on Augustus' day of birth the shadow of the sun would traverse the equinoctial line and ultimately fall directly upon the center of the altar. The sun would signal its winter rising annually on the day of Augustus' conception by casting the shadow of the obelisk's point along the line of Capricorn, from the eastern end of which a perpendicular would intersect the equinoctial line at the very midpoint of the altar. The revelation of this symbolism at Rome tells us more about the mechanics of Augustan ideology than do centuries of scholarly speculation. And there is more: in the previous generation Varro's friend Tarutius had prepared retrospectively a horoscope for Romulus, and he had discovered that the founder of Rome had been conceived under Capricorn and born under Libra.[17]

This momentous parallel was not lost on Manilius. In Book 4 the poet puts the foundation of Rome under Libra, *qua genitus Caesar . . . nunc condidit urbem,* "under which sign Caesar was born who has now founded the city and curbs (*frenat*) the world."[18] It is hard to credit the pertinacity with which both Housman and Goold have clung to the view that the reference here to Rome's new founder and current ruler, described as born under Libra, is to Tiberius and thus that this part of the *Astronomica* was written after Augustus' death. Their error is rooted in the old mistake that Augustus was born under Capricorn, even though Housman finally knew better. The allusion is precisely to Augustus, still living, and with it the poem is authoritatively vindicated as a wholly Augustan achievement. When Manilius speaks earlier of Capricorn at the time of the *ortus Augusti,* he uses *ortus* in a broad sense to encompass conception.[19] Whether Suetonius used *natus* in the same way or simply misunderstood an earlier source that had *ortus* is unclear. But the importance of the date of conception is triumphantly affirmed both by the sundial and, with its help, by Manilius rightly understood. And so the possibility, raised earlier, of referring the Alexandrian crabs to the *horoscopos* showing the rising sign at the moment of conception becomes the most attractive explanation of their appearance in 13/12 B.C.

The interdependence of the projects and themes—*solarium,* Ara Pacis, the conquest of Egypt, the days of Augustus' conception and birth—now open up to us the whole process of planning that must have gone on in 13 in anticipation of Augustus' return. Although the projects took

17. Plut. *Rom.* 12. Cf. Bouché-Leclercq (supra n. 11) 369 with n. 1.
18. Manil. *Astron.* 4.773–77.
19. Manil. *Astron.* 2.509.

nearly four years to reach fulfillment, they were conceived as a whole; and the ideology that they represent is precise and interlocked. When the public monuments were ready, Augustus presented himself to the public on the obelisks as *pontifex maximus* before anything else, and in the great frieze on the right or southern side of the Ara Pacis he appears, as has been widely recognized and much discussed, in the guise of the *pontifex maximus*. It would appear, therefore, that his succeeding to this priesthood upon the death of Lepidus was an integral part of the overall plan. It would thus be legitimate to assume that Lepidus had already died when the preparations were under way to receive Augustus in Rome in 13 and to inaugurate the spectacular sequence of honors that followed.

The great voice that we can still hear today from that momentous time is that of Horace, reawakened to poetry in his early fifties. (He was less than two years older than the emperor.) It is scarcely necessary to argue here, despite an occasional dissenting opinion, that the fourth book of the *Odes* must be assigned to the year 13 or perhaps, as I am inclined to think, 13/12 B.C.[20] The anticipation of Augustus' return to Rome in the second and fifth poems and the account of Augustus' step-sons, Drusus and Tiberius, in the second and fourteenth poems can leave no doubt about the time of composition. Furthermore, as Michael Putnam has observed in his illuminating new book on these late odes of Horace, the poet proceeds chronologically from longing for the absent Augustus to hailing the present ruler, received in the city with honors and encompassed with evocations of his Trojan ancestry and the peace of the contemporary empire.[21] In other words, the earlier poems must precede the emperor's return and antedate 4 July 13, while the later poems must be dated after that day. It is hard to say whether the fourth book of *Odes* included pieces from early in 12, but there is a seasonal progression within the book as well as the progression from the absence to the presence of the emperor.

The marvelous poem to Torquatus on the inevitability of death begins with late winter and the retreat of the snows: *diffugere nives, redeunt iam gramina campis*. The same poem evokes the solemn procession of seasons and the helplessness of men before them. The ode to Phyllis is set exactly on Maecenas' birthday in April, and the following piece evokes the Thracian breezes of full springtime. Is it possible that

20. Cf. M. C. J. Putnam, *Artifices of Eternity: Horace's Fourth Book of Odes* (Ithaca, N.Y. 1986) 23, n. 6.
21. Ibid, esp. 24–25.

this obsession with the seasons and their progression is a reflection of the bold scheme to represent not only days and nights but seasons and the winds on the massive sundial in the Campus Martius? Horace seems, at any rate, to have been attentive to the solar theme in the plan worked out in 13 B.C. In his second ode he wants to cry out to the emperor, *o sol / pulcher, o laudande,* and in the fifth poem (*divis orte bonis*) he beseeches the ruler to give back his radiance to his homeland, *lucem redde tuae, dux bone, patriae,* "for when your countenance like the spring has shone upon the people, the day passes more agreeably and suns are more radiant (*et soles melius nitent*)."

In the penultimate poem of the book Horace invokes the efforts of the senate and people of Rome to immortalize the virtues of Augustus, *qua sol habitabilis illustrat oras,* "wherever the sun illumines the habitable shores." In those extraordinary lines with which the poem begins, Horace evokes the concerted efforts of the *patres* and the *Quirites* to pile up honors on Augustus, to make his virtues eternal forever, *virtutes in aevum / per titulos memoresque fastos / aeternet.* The placing of *aeternet* at the beginning of the second strophe and the choice of this preternaturally rare word gives it tremendous emphasis. The virtues of the emperor are immortalized *per titulos memoresque fastos.* The *fasti* are, of course, the calendars that prescribe annual celebrations such as the *anniversarium sacrificium* that is established along with the Ara Pacis. The *tituli* could either be inscriptions or honorific offices bestowed upon Augustus.

That the latter is what Horace means here is supported by a remarkably similar passage in Ovid's *Fasti.* The passage comes from the very lines that describe the assumption of the office of *pontifex maximus* in 12.[22] The pontifical honor (*pontificalis honor*), says Ovid, has been added to the innumerable *tituli* of Caesar, which he chose to accept. As a result the divine manifestation of eternal Caesar presides over the eternal fires of Vesta. The Latin is very striking: *Caesaris innumeris, quos maluit ille mereri, / accessit titulis pontificalis honor. / ignibus aeternis aeterni numina praesunt / Caesaris.* This close conjunction of the *tituli* of Caesar and the office of *pontifex maximus,* together with the explicit statement of eternity suggested by the Vestal cult, matches exactly the conjunction in Horace's ode. I am inclined to think, accordingly, that the fourteenth ode of the fourth book makes reference to the assumption of the pontificate and must be dated after 6 March 12. When the

22. Ov. *Fast.* 3.420–22.

long question with which that poem begins comes to an end in line 6, Augustus is addressed as *maxime principum*. This could well be the poet's way of referring to the reestablished union of the *princeps senatus* and the *pontifex maximus*.

The relation of the sundial and its obelisks to the commemoration of the conquest of Egypt is likewise recalled in the same poem of Horace. After a series of strophes concerned with the Claudii Nerones, the poet returns to Augustus in order to celebrate the peace that now reigns throughout the empire. And the peace begins with an evocation of the conquest of Alexandria and the end of the Ptolemaic dynasty: *nam tibi, quo die / portus Alexandrea supplex / et vacuam patefecit aulam, / Fortuna lustro prospera tertio / belli secundos reddidit exitus*, "for to you, on the day when Alexandria as a suppliant opened its harbors and its deserted palace, prospering fortune gave favorable outcome in war in the third lustrum."

After this poem comes the closing ode in the fourth book, beginning with Phoebus Apollo and ending with Troy, Anchises, and Venus. Peace, fertility, and good harvest dominate the poem and have long suggested to readers some kind of parallel with the motifs of the Ara Pacis, which was to be dedicated a few years later. In a valuable appendix to his book Michael Putnam has raised very plausibly the possibility that the inauguration of the Forum Augustum should also be dated to this period and seen as part of the overall grand scheme.[23] Since we know that Augustus and his planners included the Circus Maximus in the commemoration of his rule and his family, it is by no means impossible that the Forum Augustum, which could have been started in 12 or 11, was a part of the larger plan.

It has already appeared that the timing of these interlocked projects seems to have been due to the fortunate coincidence of Lepidus' death and Augustus' return from Spain and Gaul in 13. The centrality of the assumption of the high priesthood in 12 in the whole complex of honors must now be considered directly with reference to the Ara Pacis itself.

Augustus appears on the south wall as *pontifex maximus* in the great frieze with his family. Erika Simon's eccentric opinion that he appears as *rex sacrorum* need not detain us.[24] Augustus never held this inferior office, assiduously avoided the word *rex* in any context, and gave away the house of the *rex* presumably because there was no incumbent at

---

23. Putnam (supra n. 20) 327–39. Cf. P. Zanker, *Forum Augustum: das Bildprogramm* (Tübingen 1968).

24. E. Simon, *Ara Pacis Augustae* (Tübingen 1967) 17.

all.[25] He is unmistakably *pontifex maximus* on the frieze of the Ara Pacis. There has long been a temptation to assume that the scene represented there was the actual dedication of the altar on 30 January 9 B.C., when Augustus was indeed *pontifex maximus*. On the surface this seems a reasonable assumption in the light of the grand statement of the office on the obelisk inscriptions of the same date. But it cannot be. The frieze depicts Augustus' friend and counselor for many decades, M. Vipsanius Agrippa, as a member of the solemn procession. The veil he wears marks him as a priest, although this in itself poses no problem since as adjutant to the emperor he is more than likely to have served as a plebeian *pontifex* in the college of *pontifices*.[26] The problem is simply that the great man died at the end of March in 12 B.C., only a few weeks after Augustus had assumed the pontificate.

If, however, one opts for an identification of the procession with that of the *constitutio* of the Ara Pacis in 13 B.C, other serious obstacles obtrude. Not least of these, of course, is the appearance of Augustus as *pontifex maximus*. Furthermore, Drusus in military garb is clearly recognizable, and on 4 July 13 he was away in Gaul looking after the situation there when Augustus had returned to Rome. Agrippa too was probably absent, not yet back from Syria. An additional problem seems to be the fourth *flamen* who appears conspicuously in the procession with his distinctive cap with an *apex*, or point, on top. The appearance of four *flamines* means that one of them must be the *flamen* of Jupiter, the so-called *flamen Dialis*; and, according to present opinion, the office was vacant in that year and not filled until 11.[27]

Problems of this kind have forced scholars to assume that the frieze is to a greater or lesser extent fictional, representing some kind of ideal procession in which a *flamen Dialis*, Agrippa, Drusus, and Augustus as *pontifex maximus* could all be brought together at the same time. Here, for example, is Mario Torelli in his recent volume of Jerome Lectures on Roman historical reliefs: "Therefore the meeting of the *Ara Pacis Augustae* is entirely fictitious but is represented as 'the meeting that could have taken place.' The only possible truth of the representation is not the reality but the norm, i.e. how the *apantesis* should have been performed in 13 B.C. as in the future."[28]

25. Cf. M. W. Hoffman Lewis, *The Official Priests of Rome under the Julio-Claudians* (Rome 1955) 76–77. On the house of the *rex*, Dio 54.27.3.
    26. Lewis (supra n. 25) 68–71.
    27. By Ser. Cornelius Lentulus Maluginensis (*PIR*[2], C 1394).
    28. M. Torelli, *Typology and Structure of Roman Historical Reliefs* (Ann Arbor, Mich. 1982) 54.

It must be obvious, in view of the care and exquisite precision that went into the delineation of the *solarium Augusti* and the Ara Pacis, to say nothing of the work in Alexandria, in the Circus Maximus, and perhaps elsewhere, that so careless a representation that has nothing to do with reality on the south side of the Ara Pacis—the very side that looks toward the obelisk—is very difficult to accept or believe. All the more so when there is a date and an event that would accommodate perfectly the entire scene on the south side of the altar. That is a procession of the imperial family on the day that Augustus became *pontifex maximus*.

On that occasion the emperor was quite properly garbed as the high priest, and we know that Agrippa had already returned to Italy and thus could easily have been in Rome, close by his leader, on 6 March before retiring to Campania where he was soon to die. As for Drusus, Augustus had left him in Gaul to look after the German frontier in his absence. But it appears that relatively early in 12 B.C. the Sugambri and their allies opened a war. This probably means that Drusus had left the area at the time and provided an opportunity for hostile action in much the same way as the return of Agrippa from Illyricum led to an outbreak in that region. As we know, the Illyrian campaign was subsequently entrusted to Drusus' brother, Tiberius. But he too was present in Rome on 6 March, and he is almost certainly to be identified alongside Livia on the frieze of the Ara Pacis. So Drusus would have appeared with his brother at Rome on the occasion of Augustus' assumption of the pontificate and on a representation of that event.

The presence of the *flamen Dialis* is actually less of a problem than has been surmised. It disappears altogether in the light of what we now know about the plans of 13 and 12 B.C. The last *flamen* of Jupiter before the Augustan Age had been Cornelius Merula, who had died in 87. In recording the events of 11 B.C. Cassius Dio observes, in the characteristically vague expression "at about the same time" (*en tōi autōi toutōi chronōi*), that the priest of Jupiter was appointed for the first time since Merula.[29] The appointment is also mentioned by Tacitus in the *Annals*, where a specific number is given for the years intervening between Merula and his successor.[30] In all modern texts of the *Annals* the number appears as seventy-five, producing a date of 11, which coincides with the year under which Dio records the event. But it is time to insist that

29. Dio 54.36.1.
30. Tac. *Ann.* 3.58.

that number is nothing more than an emendation designed to harmonize Tacitus with Dio and that what survives in the Medicean manuscript of Tacitus is seventy-two, in other words, 14 B.C.

Nothing stands against this date, nor is it intrinsically unlikely that in the year before his return to Rome Augustus was already thinking about new appointments to strengthen his revival of the old traditions of Roman religion. By what procedures he secured the election of *flamines* in the lifetime of Lepidus is unknown, but we know that he did it. Thus the *flamen Dialis* on the south frieze of the Ara Pacis would also be no impediment to a date in 12 (nor, for that matter, should he have been even in 13). But there is no year other than 12 in which the entire group pictured as they are pictured could have assembled. It may well be, therefore, that we have on the Ara Pacis not only the precise commemoration of Augustus as a prince of peace, of Trojan ancestry, whose genesis and birth are remembered by the sun twice a year and whose peace was won by conquest commemorated by the great obelisk that cast the shadow; the altar was also an eternal reminder of an eternal cult, that of Vesta and her priest, the *pontifex maximus*.

It was in the majesty of the pontificate that Augustus presented himself as the conqueror who brought peace. The astronomical precision of the buildings and images associated with the assumption of the pontificate reveal with a clarity hitherto unexampled the reality of Augustan ideology. The crab, Capricorn, and the sun itself were components in a mathematical construct to honor the emperor by showing that his destiny was part of the universal order. The haunting verses in the fourth book of Horace's *Odes* faithfully mirror the spirit of that time, an era of *tituli, fasti,* and solar radiance that chronicled the ceaseless march of days, months, seasons, and years. Even the long poem of Manilius, all of which was composed when Augustus was still alive, can now be seen not as a bizarre by-product of the early empire but as an integral and authentic reflection of later Augustan culture. Manilius' world is the world of the great sundial: he must have seen it and understood its calibrations. He wrote to honor an emperor who published his own horoscope, and he had the leisure to write because the emperor had brought peace. *Hoc sub pace vacat tantum,* "Only in time of peace is there leisure for this task," Manilius declares in the proem to Book 1 of his *Astronomica.*[31]

A new vision of the Augustan Age has opened up under our scrutiny

31. Manil. *Astron.* 1.13.

of the commemorations that surrounded the assumption of the pontificate. The inscription that stands in large letters on the obelisks of Montecitorio and the Piazza del Popolo has long been familiar to those who
know Rome. But if we use our imagination to restore those spoils from
Egyptian Heliopolis to their original Roman setting—to the sundial and
to the Circus Maximus—and to read again the text they both bear, we
can now perhaps hear a resonance we had missed before: *Imp. Caesar
divi f. Augustus / Pontifex Maximus, imperator"* for the twelfth time,
consul for the eleventh, in the fourteenth tribunician power, having
brought Egypt into the power of the Roman people, dedicated this to
the sun (*soli donum dedit*)."

The Imperial Policy of Augustus

The contemporaries of Augustus issued high praise for conquest and empire. The theme is all-pervasive. The poet of the *Aeneid* has Jupiter forecast a Roman rule that will know no bounds of time or space. And Anchises' pronouncement from the underworld previews Augustus extending imperial power to the most remote peoples of the world. Livy characterizes his city as *caput orbis terrarum* and its people as *princeps orbis terrarum populus*. Horace asserts that the *maiestas* of the *imperium* stretches from one end of the world to the other.[1]

The phrases echo sentiments and expressions of the Roman Republic. Militarism marked much of its history. The exploits of the conqueror were envied, honored, and celebrated. Those precedents stimulated Augustus and helped shape the character of the Augustan years. Wars dominated the era; victories were repeatedly gained—or claimed. That distinction is important. The humbling of external foes was a prime catchword of the regime. But the difference between rhetoric and reality is a central feature of the Augustan years, and of Augustan imperial policy. It is that to which I want to call special attention.

1. Virg. *Aen.* 1.278–79; Livy 21.30.10, 34.58.8; Hor. *Carm.* 4.15.13–16.

The *princeps,* it appears, had no structured blueprint for empire. Nor did his actions adhere to a uniform pattern imposed on all sectors of the Roman world. Diverse circumstances in diverse areas provoked a variety of responses, sometimes cautious, sometimes bold, occasionally calculated, often extemporaneous. Augustus' directives do not reveal any systematic plan for world dominion. What the *princeps* did promote, I shall argue, was a systematic image of himself as world conqueror.

A brief paper, of course, will not permit one to do justice to this formidable subject, to survey Augustan advances from one end of his vast empire to another. Certain key examples, however, can highlight the process and illuminate the policy.

Armenia and Parthia

Rome's posture with regard to Armenia and Parthia is especially revealing. Parthia had inflicted defeat upon Roman armies, and Rome's influence in Armenia had proved ephemeral. Standards of the Republic's army captured at Carrhae and hostages taken in Antony's abortive campaigns remained in Parthian hands. After Antony's demise, the burden of restoring Rome's honor rested with the victor of Actium.

Octavian resisted the temptation to retaliate. And the restraint set a pattern. The *princeps* recognized that prudent diplomacy and discreet display of force were preferable to expensive and hazardous ventures across the distant Euphrates. Indirect suzerainty in Armenia and a *modus vivendi* with Parthia represented the means to preserve prestige and protect security.

But Augustus did not rest content with the status quo in the East. Parthia's retention of standards and captives taken from Roman armies remained an open sore and an implicit denial of Rome's omnipotence. The year 20 B.C. proved to be a year of reckoning. Augustus traveled personally to the East, adjudicating disputes in Greece, Asia Minor, and Syria and exhibiting the authority of the suzerain by reassigning lands to dynasts from Cilicia to Armenia Minor.[2] The *princeps'* presence in the Near East may have provided the occasion for upheaval in Armenia. The citizenry expelled their king and requested a new ruler from Rome, namely, a member of the Armenian ruling house resident at Augustus' court. The *princeps* was happy to comply: Tiberius, at the head of a

2. Dio 54.7, 54.9.1–3.

Roman army, delivered Tigranes to the vacant throne.[3] No force was used, and none was needed. Presentation of the event in Rome, however, took another form. It endeavored to simulate military victory. The coinage blared slogans of *Armenia capta* and *Armenia recepta*.[4]

In the East generally Augustus affected war but practiced diplomacy. The *princeps'* presence in Syria and the settlement in Armenia also put pressure on Phraates IV, monarch of Parthia. In 20 B.C. the king yielded up at last the standards and captives held for a generation as Parthian prizes, thereby allowing Augustus to claim credit for wiping out a longstanding stain on Roman honor.[5] Negotiation had brought about that result. Phraates evidently received assurances of noninterference in his own realm. And Parthia acknowledged the Roman interest in Armenia. An informal accord arose from the bargaining, even an acceptance, tacit or overt, that the Euphrates would serve as boundary between the zones of influence.[6] But the message delivered in Rome was rather different. Augustus proclaimed victory, conquest, and martial supremacy for consumption at home. The *Res Gestae* declared that he had compelled the Parthians to surrender trophies and beg for Roman friendship. The senate offered to vote a triumph, and a triumphal arch was erected in the Forum. Numismatic representations repeatedly called attention to *signis receptis*. And the central scene of the cuirass of the Prima Porta statue depicted the transfer of the standards.[7] Augustus made the most of his diplomatic success. A compact of mutual advantage and mutual agreement took on the glow of military mastery.

Two decades later, Rome faced a similar situation. A struggle for the throne gripped Armenia, and the new Parthian monarch, Phraataces,

---

3. Dio 54.9.4; Vell. Pat. 2.94.4; *RG* 27.2; Tac. *Ann.* 2.3; Strab. 17.1.54 (c821); Joseph. *AJ* 15.105; M. Chaumont, "L'Arménie entre Rome et l'Iran I: de l'avènement d'Auguste à l'avènement de Dioclétien," *ANRW* 2.9.1 (1976) 73–75.

4. *BMCRE* I, Augustus, nos. 671–78; *RIC* I², nos. 513–20; cf. Hor. *Epist.* 1.12.26–27; Vell. Pat. 2.94.4.

5. *RG* 29.2; Vell. Pat. 2.91.1; Dio 54.8.1–2; Ov. *Fast.* 5.579–84; Suet. *Aug.* 21.3; *Tib.* 9.1, probably wrongly, has the standards turned over to Tiberius, a tale defended by R. Seager, "Horace and the Parthians," *LCM* 2 (1977) 201–2.

6. Sources report an *amicitia* or even *foedus* and *societas*: *RG* 29.2; Strab. 16.1.28 (c748–49); Vell. Pat. 2.100.1; Oros. 6.21.24. The discussions of F. H. Ziegler, *Die Beziehungen zwischen Rom und dem Partherreich: Ein Beitrag zur Geschichte des Völkerrechts* (Wiesbaden 1964) 47–50, and M. R. Cimma, *Reges socii et amici populi Romani* (Milan 1976) 319–24, are too legalistic. Parthia's acknowledgement of Roman interest in Armenia: Suet. *Aug.* 21.3; cf. Vell. Pat. 2.100.1; Eutrop. 7.9. The Euphrates as boundary: Strab. 16.1.28 (c748).

7. *RG* 29.2; Dio 54.18.1–3; *BMCRE* I, Augustus, nos. 410–23, 679–81; *RIC* I², 521–26. The propaganda may be reflected also in the report that Phraates gave up the standards out of fear of a Roman invasion; Dio 54.8.1; Justin 42.5.10–11.

took the occasion to intervene.[8] Augustus could not permit Rome's prestige to deteriorate. His own prestige at home was at stake. The *princeps* staged a public demonstration to reassure the citizenry that Roman power would again make itself felt, undiminished, in the lands of the East. Augustus' grandson Gaius took command of troops to head for the Euphrates, intimidate Parthia, and settle accounts in Armenia. The young prince received a handsome send-off, amidst considerable pageantry, with talk in the air of conquest, vengeance against Parthia, new triumphs, and expansion of the Roman Empire.[9]

Augustus' intentions, in fact, were considerably more modest than this. But public perception was what counted. There was some sharp exchange of letters, no doubt meant for domestic constituencies—on both sides. But no fighting, not even a hostile confrontation. In A.D. 2 Gaius and Phraataces, each with impressive and equal entourage, met on an island in the Euphrates. The king dined with Gaius on Rome's side of the river, and then Phraataces hosted a banquet on the Armenian side. The whole scene had been carefully orchestrated in advance. Phraataces now officially acknowledged Rome's interests in Armenia, and Augustus consented to leave Phraataces undisturbed.[10]

The pattern of the emperor's policy in that region remained consistent thereafter and throughout. Two or three more changes of rulers came in Armenia, and comparable struggles for the throne in Parthia. The *princeps* neither promoted nor abetted them, but he did profit from them. He pursued the twin goals of hegemony via client-rulers in Armenia and amicable relations, with mutually acknowledged spheres of influence, toward Parthia. The behavior was marked with restraint, but the public posture was one of aggressiveness. So Augustus presented the endorsement of a client-king as the capture of Armenia, the recovery of the standards as Parthian submission, and the assignment of Gaius as an imperialist venture. The *princeps* knew the limits of Rome's effective authority in the East and stayed within them. But keeping up appear-

8. Dio 55.10.18; Vell. Pat. 2.100.1.

9. The pageantry and expectations are reflected in Ov. *Ars am.* 1.177–86, 201–12—surely not his own invention, though he uses them for his own purposes; cf. Dio 55.10a. 3; A. S. Hollis, *Ovid, Ars Amatoria, Book I* (Oxford 1977) 65–73; R. Syme, *History in Ovid* (Oxford 1978) 8–11. Gaius' appointment is recorded also by Tac. *Ann.* 2.4; Dio 55.10.18–19; Vell. Pat. 2.101.1.

10. Dio 55.10.20–21, 55.10a.4; Vell. Pat. 2.101.1–3. Among modern discussions, see, for example, Ziegler (supra n. 6) 53–56; M. Pani, *Roma e i re d'Oriente da Augusto a Tiberio* (Bari 1972) 45–46; Cimma (supra n.6) 324–28; Chaumont (supra n.3) 77–80; F. E. Romer, "Gaius Caesar's Military Diplomacy in the East," *TAPA* 109 (1979) 203–4, 208–10.

ances was no less important than keeping within limits. Augustus projected the image of a conqueror who extended Roman sovereignty to the East.

Spain

Circumstances were very different in the West—but the principles were much the same. The Iberian Peninsula serves as a valuable illustration. Here too the reputation of Augustus played a major part in determining the extension of imperial power to northwest Spain. That region, home of the fierce Cantabrians and Asturians, remained outside Rome's control, despite more than two centuries of Roman presence in the peninsula. Augustus led his forces in person, the last time he was to do so, in 26 B.C. The matter was evidently deemed to be of high importance. Tales made the rounds of the ferocious nature of the Cantabrians and the Asturians, and of their fanatic resistance to any infringement on autonomy. Augustus threw open the gates of Janus, a symbolic means of proclaiming a crusade against the foe. And his personal leadership of the army would reinforce martial credentials, a check on actual or potential rivals with military claims of their own.[11]

As in the case of Parthia, however, battlefield exploits in Spain did not match their publicity in Rome. Augustus' sole campaigning season in 26 B.C., in fact, produced few successes. More substantial victories followed, but they came at heavy cost in lives.[12] And even those victories were superficial. Both the Cantabrians and the Asturians exploded into revolt as soon as Augustus left the province in 24. The legate of Tarra-

11. Augustus' announced resolve for subjugation: Dio 53.13.1. The ferocity of the foe: Strab. 3.4.17–18 (c164–65); Oros. 6.21.8. The opening of the gates: Oros. 6.21.1. The connection with domestic affairs is rightly stressed by W. Schmitthenner, "Augustus' spanischer Feldzug und der Kampf um den Prinzipat," *Historia* 11 (1962) 29–43, though he exaggerates the actual threat to Augustus' position.

12. Suet. *Aug.* 26, 81; Dio 53.23.1, 53.25.5–8; Florus 2.33.48–58; Oros. 6.21.3–10. Among numerous scholarly discussions, see D. Magie, "Augustus' War in Spain (26–25 B.C.)," *CP* 15 (1920) 325–39; R. Syme, "The Spanish War of Augustus (26–25 B.C.)," *AJP* 55 (1934) 293–317; A. Schulten, *Los Cantabros y los Astures y su guerra con Roma* (Madrid 1943); J. Horrent, "Nota sobre el desarollo de la guerra Cántabra del año 26 A.C.," *Emerita* 21 (1953) 279–90; Schmitthenner (supra n.11) 54–60; R. Syme, "The Conquest of North-West Spain," in *Legio VII Gemina* (Leon 1970) 83–103. A recent summary of scholarship appears in N. Santos Yanguas, "La conquista romana del N.O. de la Península Ibérica," *Latomus* 41 (1982) 16–26. See also F. D. Santos, "Die Integration Nord- und Nordwestspaniens als römische Provinz in der Reichspolitik des Augustus," *ANRW* 2.3 (1975) 531–36; F. J. Lomas Salmonte, *Asturia prerromana y altoimperial* (Seville 1975) 103–27; J. M. Solana Sainz, *Los Cantabros y la ciudad de Ireliobriga* (Santander 1981) 97–142; A. Tranoy, *La Galice romaine* (Paris 1981) 132–44; E. Martino, *Roma contra Cantabros y Astures: Nueva lectura de las fuentes* (Santander 1982) 41–104.

conensis resorted to brutality in suppressing the rebellion.[13] Two further uprisings by the Cantabrians occurred in 22 and 19, bringing more ruthless repression and subjugation. It took M. Agrippa to flush the Cantabrians out of their strongholds and compel them to settle in the plains—but at heavy cost and severe losses.[14] Augustus was finally able to make a more peaceful tour of Spain in 15/14 B.C., organizing colonial foundations and exhibiting generosity.[15]

Here, as elsewhere, public presentation and reality diverged. As the opening of Janus' gates declared Augustus' purpose, so their closing advertised its accomplishment. The *princeps* made certain to have that ceremony conducted to commemorate his success in 25 B.C., only the fourth time in Roman history that Janus' gates were shut—but the second time in five years.[16] He declined a triumph, but accepted a more enduring distinction: the privilege of wearing garlands and triumphal dress on the first day of every year.[17] He plainly intended to make the event memorable, a fact underscored by the composition and publication of Augustus' own autobiography. That work concluded with the successful close of the Cantabrian War.[18] The portrayal is reflected in the Livian tradition and embellished by Velleius Paterculus. In this version, Caesar Augustus' campaigns, after two centuries of bloodshed in that violent and savage land, finally imposed a lasting peace that not only crushed armed resistance but even wiped out brigandage.[19] Augustus further authorized the establishment of a veteran colony, *colonia Augusta Emerita,* as a symbol of the settled status of the land.[20] An ode of Horace welcomed home the returning conqueror, comparing him to Hercules, and rejoicing in a new security.[21]

Augustus had entered Spain to claim victory and to announce pacification—and so he did. Never mind that the real victory did not match his boast. It came slowly, a bloody and brutal process that endured well beyond the *princeps'* declaration of success. The Ara Pacis was duly decreed to herald Augustus' return from Spain. Not, however, in 25 B.C.,

13. Dio 53.29.1–2.

14. Dio 54.5.1–3, 54.11.2–6; cf. J. M. Roddaz, *Marcus Agrippa* (Paris 1984) 402–10.

15. Dio 54.23.7, 54.25.1, 56.43.3; *RG* 12.2.

16. Dio 53.26.5; Oros. 6.21.11; *RG* 13.

17. Dio 53.26.5; cf. Florus 2.33.53; T. D. Barnes, "The Victories of Augustus," *JRS* 64 (1974) 21.

18. Suet. *Aug.* 85.1.

19. Livy 28.12.12; Florus 2.33.59; Vell. Pat. 2.90.2–4.

20. Dio 53.26.1.

21. Hor. *Carm.* 3.14; cf. 4.14.50. A darker interpretation of the poem is offered by U. W. Scholz, "*Herculis ritu, Augustus, consule Planco,*" *WS* 84 (1971) 123–37.

when Janus' doors were prematurely closed and triumphal honors bestowed. Rather in 13 B.C., after more than a decade of intermittent insurrection, costly casualties, and terrorism.

The Balkans

In the Balkans different circumstances prevailed, and different goals—but similar public relations. Strategy and politics combined to motivate Roman action in Illyricum. Octavian's thrust into the area from 35 to 33 B.C. had specific ends in view. The rugged lands across the Adriatic would provide good training and discipline, a hardening of the sinews, as Velleius Paterculus put it, that might otherwise grow soft with idleness.[22]

The memoirs of Augustus expounded at length on the Illyrian adventure and provided due justification for the war. The Illyrians had periodically plundered Italy, had destroyed Roman armies in the forties, and held the captured standards of Roman legions. That provided adequate reason for retaliation and restoration of national honor.[23] A harsher assessment comes from the pen of Dio Cassius. He notes correctly that no Illyrian provocation prompted the war: Octavian lacked legitimate complaint and sought a pretext to give practice to his legions against a foe whose resistance was likely to be ineffective.[24] In fact, neither the cynical judgment nor the self-serving explanation gets to the heart of the matter. Octavian needed to enhance his military reputation, to match the accomplishments of his partner and rival M. Antony. It is no coincidence that Octavian took conspicuous personal risks and twice suffered injury in Illyricum.[25] Those badges of courage could be useful. And upon completion of the contest he delivered a speech to the senate, making a pointed contrast between Antony's idleness and his own vigorous liberating of Italy from incursions by savage peoples.[26]

Actual accomplishments in the Illyrian campaigns of 35–33 B.C. were modest. Octavian drove as far as Siscia on the Save, and displayed Roman power to the Dalmatians, thus retaliating against peoples who

22. Vell. Pat. 2.78.2.
23. App. *Ill.* 12–13, 15, 18, *BCiv.* 5.145; cf. Dio 49.34.2.
24. Dio 49.36.1.
25. App. *Ill.* 27; Suet. *Aug.* 20; Pliny *HN* 7.148; Florus 2.23; Dio 49.35.2.
26. App. *Ill.* 16. Larger strategic considerations have also been postulated: R. Syme, *Danubian Papers* (Bucharest 1971) 17, 137; J. J. Wilkes, *Dalmatia* (Cambridge, Mass. 1969) 48–49. A healthy scepticism is expressed by W. Schmitthenner, "Octavian's militärische Unternehmungen in den Jahren 35–33 v. Chr.," *Historia* 7 (1958) 193–200.

had raided Roman territory or vanquished Roman troops in the past.[27] What really mattered, however, was the presentation of events in Rome. Octavian spoke to the senate and rattled off the names of nearly thirty tribes that his forces had coerced into submission, surrender, and payment of tribute. He proudly set up the recovered standards in the Portico of Cn. Octavius, thus linking his success to earlier republican victories. And he elevated the prestige of his family through the award of statues and the privilege of tribunician sacrosanctity for Livia and Octavia. Propaganda value, as so often, counted for more than tangible achievement.[28]

A major advance in the region did not come for two decades. The advantages of a push to the Danube that would control the land route from northern Italy to the lands of the East became increasingly evident. Tiberius conducted four intensive campaigns in the Balkans between 12 and 9 B.C. The *imperator* reduced recalcitrant tribes in Dalmatia and Pannonia, pacified the region, and won an *ovatio*. Augustus himself paid signal tribute to his stepson's achievements in the *Res Gestae:* he had subjugated the previously unconquered peoples of Pannonia and extended the frontiers of Illyricum to the Danube.[29] Augustus boasts hyperbolically of smashing the Dacians and compelling them to submit to Roman orders, a claim echoed but modified by Strabo.[30] The situation seemed secure.

But that confidence proved to be premature. National pride came to the surface, intensified by harsh exactions of tribute by Roman officials and the fierce spirit of a new generation of Illyrian warriors. The great Pannonian revolt exploded in A.D. 6 and nearly shook the empire to its foundations. Four bloody years were consumed in suppressing this

27. App. *Ill.* 18–28; Dio 49.37.1–49.38.4, 49.43.8; Strab 7.5.5 (c315).
28. Announcement of tribes subjugated: App. *Ill.* 16–17. The standards: App. *Ill.* 28; cf. Dio 49.43.8. Honors for Livia and Octavia: Dio 49.38.1. The political implications are rightly noted by Schmitthenner (supra n. 26) 218–20, 231–33. Useful summaries of the campaigns can be found in *RE* Suppl. 9 (1962) 538–39, s.v. Pannonia (A. Mocsy); Wilkes (supra n. 26) 49–57. Sweeping statements by Appian (*Ill.* 28) and Dio (49.37.6) give the misleading impression of extensive conquests, inducing some to believe that Octavian advanced Roman holdings as far as Moesia, encompassing most of the later provinces of Dalmatia and Pannonia; so, most notably, E. Swoboda, *Octavian und Illyricum* (Vienna 1932); cf. N. Vulić, "The Illyrian War of Octavian," *JRS* 24 (1934) 163–67. That idea is persuasively refuted by Syme (supra n. 26) 13–18, 135–42, pointing to App. *Ill.* 22 and Strab. 7.5.3 (c314); cf. Schmitthenner (supra n. 26) 201–17. Further bibliography in Roddaz (supra n. 14) 140–45.
29. *RG* 30.1; Dio 54.31.2–4, 54.34.3–4, 54.36.2, 55.2.4; Vell. Pat. 2.90.1, 2.96.3; Florus 2.24.8; Suet. *Tib.* 9; Festus *Brev.* 7; Frontin. *Str.* 2.1.15. See Syme (supra n. 26) 18–22; *RE* (supra n. 28) 540–41; Wilkes (supra n. 26) 63–65.
30. *RG* 30.2; Strab. 7.3.11, 7.3.13 (c304–305). The defeat of the Dacians may have been spurred by a Dacian invasion of 10 B.C.: Dio 54.36.2.

mighty challenge to Roman authority. Tiberius brought the Pannonians to full surrender in A.D. 8.[31] Germanicus was delegated to help reduce Dalmatia, but the inexperienced young prince made little headway. Augustus had to send Tiberius back to resume command, thereby sealing the fate of Dalmatia in A.D. 9.[32]

Military success, as usual, would be translated into political distinction. Augustus exploited the victory to bestow honors on his family. Germanicus made a public announcement of the result. Augustus and Tiberius both celebrated triumphs in A.D. 10 and received triumphal arches in Pannonia, as well as other distinctions. Germanicus gained triumphal insignia and praetorian rank. And even Tiberius' son Drusus, though he played no part in the war, obtained the right to attend the senate and to hold praetorian status as soon as he reached the quaestorship.[33]

All this is not to deny the important geopolitical consequences of the expansion. Roman power extended to the Middle Danube, a critical link in the connection that now ran from northern Italy through the Balkans to the provinces of the East. At some time after A.D. 8, the *princeps* set in place the two great military commands that would become the new provinces of Dalmatia and Pannonia. It was a solid and enduring achievement. But it had also involved severe setbacks and substantial losses obscured by the honors and distinctions conferred upon members of the imperial family.

The Alps

The imperial family benefited further from publicity generated by the conquest of the Alps. The major campaigns came in 16 and 15 B.C. Augustus' stepsons earned the chief accolades. Tiberius marched eastward from Gaul, Drusus northward through Alpine passes to the Valley of the Inn. The brothers achieved their goals, subduing the formidable Raeti and Vindelici of eastern Switzerland, the Tyrol, and southern Bavaria.[34] Roman dominion in the Alps would be solid.

31. Suet. *Tib.* 16; Dio 55.29.3–55.31.4, 55.33.1–3, 55.34.3–7; Vell. Pat. 2.110.3–2.113.3, 2.114.4.
32. Dio 56.11–16; Vell. Pat. 2.115.1–4. See the analyses of E. Koestermann, "Der pannonisch-dalmatinische Krieg 6–9 n.Chr.," *Hermes* 81 (1953) 368–76; J. J. Wilkes, "Splaunon-Splonum Again," *ActaAntHung* 13 (1965) 111–25.
33. Dio 56.17.1–3.
34. Dio 54.22.1–4; Vell. Pat. 2.95.1–2; Strab. 4.6.9 (c206); Suet. *Aug.* 21; *Tib.* 9; Florus 2.22; Livy *Per.* 138; *Consolatio ad Liviam* 15–16, 175, 385–86. Cf. the discussions of K. Christ, "Zur römischen Okkupation der Zentralalpen und des nördlichen Alpenvor-

The strategic objectives are matters of dispute. Moderns often conjecture a long-range imperialist plan: the Alpine campaigns set the stage for major offensives against Germany, to effect subjugation of that land all the way to the Elbe.[35] Perhaps. But that ambitious scheme may not have been in prospect at the outset. Other motives sufficed. The reduction of Raetia and the occupation of Noricum provided essential links between legions on the Rhine and the armies of Illyricum. Ease of communications rather than future expansionism may have been the chief stimulus.

Concrete objectives, in any case, coincided with political motives and public relations. Augustus utilized the Alpine campaigns to hone the talents and advance the claims of his stepsons. Horace sang of the exploits in two *carmina,* celebrating Drusus' routs of Alpine tribes and Tiberius' decisive conquests of the Raeti.[36] The *Consolatio ad Liviam,* composed later in the reign of Augustus, also extolled the accomplishments of the brothers and the thorough defeat of the barbarians.[37] A monument was erected to commemorate these events, the Tropaeum Alpium, installed at La Turbie in the Maritime Alps and listing no fewer than forty-five tribes brought under subjection by the *princeps.*[38] And Augustus boasts in the *Res Gestae* that he had pacified the Alps all the way from the Adriatic to the Tuscan Sea—adding the questionable corollary that every campaign had been legitimate and justified.[39] The *princeps,* as ever, cultivated the image of the successful and rightful conqueror.

Germany

That image was closely bound up with the most celebrated of Augustus' imperial ventures. The confrontation of Rome and Germany created high drama in the age of Augustus. Caesar had conquered Gaul but had not fully pacified it. Uprisings and unrest persisted among Gallic

---

landes," *Historia* 6 (1957) 416–28; J. A. Waasdorp, "*Immanes Raeti:* A Hundred Years of Roman Defensive Policy in the Alps and Voralpenland," *Talanta* 14–15 (1982–1983) 40–47; F. Schön, *Der Beginn der römischen Herrschaft in Rätien* (Sigmaringen 1986) 43–56.

35. See especially K. Kraft, *Gesammelte Aufsätze zur antiken Geschichte und Militärgeschichte,* vol. 1 (Darmstadt 1973) 181–208; cf. also C. M. Wells, *The German Policy of Augustus: An Examination of the Archaeological Evidence* (Oxford 1972) 5ff.; D. Kienast, *Augustus: Prinzeps und Monarch* (Darmstadt 1982) 297.

36. Hor. *Carm.* 4.4.17–18, 4.14.7–19.

37. *Consolatio ad Liviam* 15–16, 175, 384–86.

38. Pliny *HN* 3.136–38.

39. *RG* 26.3.

peoples, often with support of trans-Rhenane tribes through the thirties, twenties, and teens.[40] The Rhine was an artificial and largely ineffectual barrier. Germanic tribes dwelled on both sides of the river. It represented at best a frontier zone, certainly not a demarcated border.

In 17 or 16 B.C. the Sugambri, Usipetes, and Tencteri spilled over the Rhine, plundered Gallic territory, ambushed Roman forces, and inflicted an ignominious defeat upon the legate M. Lollius.[41] The *princeps* himself hastened to Gaul in 16 B.C. to repair the damage. The cost in prestige outweighed any material losses. Augustus effected a peace settlement, but it is no accident that he appeared in the region, prepared to lead forces in person.[42] It was essential to present a bold face to the public.

Augustus stayed in the West for three years.[43] That period marks the beginning of a more aggressive posture to assure ascendancy in Gaul and to intimidate tribes across the Rhine. When Augustus returned to Rome in 13 B.C., his stepson Drusus launched the first of four major offensives against tribes on the far side of the Rhine.[44] They illustrate a continued connection, made explicit by the sources, between suppression of Gallic unrest and the terrorizing by Rome of Germanic peoples who had contributed or might contribute to that unrest. The altar of Augustus at Lugdunum, erected by Drusus, had as its aim the rallying of Gallic loyalty to the regime.[45]

Drusus' fourth and final campaign, in 9 B.C., produced the most far-reaching successes. Drusus attacked the Chatti, defeated the Marcomanni, and got as far as the Elbe. But that proved to be the terminus. Drusus turned back, suffered the misfortune of a broken leg, and died en route to the Rhine.[46] What stayed his advance at the Elbe is unspeci-

40. App. *BCiv.* 4.38, 5.92; Dio 48.49.2–3, 51.20.5, 51.21.5–6, 53.22.5, 53.26.4–5, 54.11.2; Livy *Per.* 134; Eutrop. 7.5; Tib. 1.7.3–12, 2.1.31–36; *ILS* 895; *CIL* I², pp. 50, 77. Cf. Roddaz (supra. n. 14) 66–75; J. F. Drinkwater, *Roman Gaul: The Three Provinces, 58 B.C.–A.D. 260* (Ithaca, N.Y. 1983) 20–21, 95.

41. Dio 54.20.4–5; Vell. Pat. 2.97.1; Suet. *Aug.* 23; Tac. *Ann.* 1.10; Obsequens. 71.

42. Dio 54.19.1, 54.20.6; Vell. Pat. 2.97.1; Suet. *Aug.* 23. It is presumptuous to regard the *clades Lolliana* as prompting the Roman offensive in the Alps, as preliminary to a broad concerted plan for conquest and occupation of Germany; so Kraft (supra n. 35) 181–208. See the refutation by K. Christ, "Zur augusteischen Germanienpolitik," *Chiron* 7 (1977) 184–89.

43. Dio 54.25.1.

44. Dio 54.25.1. See R. Frei-Stolba, "Die römische Schweiz: Ausgewählte staats- und verwaltungsrechtliche Probleme im Frühprinzipat," *ANRW* 2.5.1 (1976) 355–65.

45. Livy *Per.* 139; Dio 54.32.1; *ILS* 212, II, lines 36–39; D. Timpe, "Zur Geschichte der Rheingrenze zwischen Caesar und Drusus," in E. Lefèvre, ed., *Monumentum Chiloniense: Kieler Festschrift für E. Burck* (Amsterdam 1975) 142; S. Dyson, "Native Revolt Patterns in the Roman Empire," *ANRW* 2.3 (1975) 155–56.

46. Dio 55.1.2–5; Florus 2.30.23–27; Strab. 7.1.3 (c291); Livy *Per.* 141; Suet. *Claud.* 1.2.

fied—but Augustan policy demanded that the best face be placed upon events. Drusus, like Alexander the Great at the Hyphasis, set up trophies at the Elbe to signify progress rather than setback. And a story conveniently circulated that Drusus was halted by a vision delivering a divine pronouncement about the fate of the mission.[47] Hence the gods, not Roman failures, accounted for withdrawal. And elaborate honors were showered upon the memory of Drusus and his deeds.[48] Whatever the reality of the situation, Augustus, here as elsewhere, insisted on the appearance of success.

How much had been accomplished in fact? Drusus' campaigns had been invasions rather than conquests, the Germans intimidated rather than subdued. Archaeology discloses important legionary bases on the Lippe and other garrisons elsewhere, but does not permit a precise chronology that would fix them to the time of Drusus' incursions. Tiberius rushed to the scene and repaired the damage with vigorous campaigning in 8 B.C. Among other actions he deported forty thousand Germans to the Gallic side of the Rhine.[49] The exhibition of Roman power is clear, a necessary demonstration in the wake of Drusus' death. But it is rash to speak of Germany organized as a province of the empire, with Roman authority extended to the Elbe.[50] Even Velleius Paterculus, who would hardly minimize Tiberius' accomplishment, speaks only of reducing Germany "almost to the form of a tributary province." And Florus acknowledges that Germany was defeated rather than subdued.[51] Rome held only selected portions of German soil.[52] As so often, the appearance of Roman success outstripped the reality of Roman control.

The need to maintain a posture of strength continued to mark Augustan policy. An altar to Augustus was erected among the Ubii who had settled on the Rhine bank at Cologne. Appointment of a priest to the cult from the Cherusci was clearly meant to signal German allegiance to the *princeps* and his regime.[53] At some time before A.D. 1, L. Domitius Ahenobarbus crossed the Elbe without any resistance, made an alliance with people on the farther bank of that river, and planted a new altar to

47. Dio 55.1.3; cf. Suet. *Claud.* 1.2. On the tale and its significance, see D. Timpe, "Drusus' Umkehr an der Elbe," *RhM* 110 (1967) 289–306.

48. Dio 55.2.1–3; Livy *Per.* 142; Suet. *Claud.* 1.3–5; Tac. *Ann.* 2.7.

49. Dio 55.6.2–3; Suet. *Aug.* 21; *Tib.* 9; Tac. *Ann.* 2.26, 12.39. On the archaeological evidence, see H. Schönberger, "The Roman Frontier in Germany: An Archaeological Survey," *JRS* 59 (1969) 147–49; Wells (supra n. 35) 161–233.

50. As, for example, do Wells (supra n. 35) 156–57; Kienast (supra n. 35) 300–301.

51. Vell. Pat. 2.97.4; Florus 2.30.29–30. Florus' claim (2.30.22) that Augustus sought to make Germany a province in order to honor Julius Caesar is not to be taken seriously.

52. Dio 56.18.1; cf. Christ (supra n. 42) 189–98.

53. Tac. *Ann.* 1.39.1, 1.57.2.

Augustus on the site, a symbol that loyalty extended even to that distant region. The idea that his expedition prepared the way for a Roman invasion of Bohemia is unnecessary conjecture. It supplied a means to reassert Roman influence without taking undue risks. Domitius even became embroiled in intratribal disputes among the Cherusci. But he made sure to winter his men back in the safer quarters on the Rhine.[54]

In A.D. 4 Tiberius returned to Germany and launched an ostensibly even more vigorous expedition. If Velleius Paterculus be believed, Tiberius was victorious everywhere, his army unscathed; the victories left nothing unconquered in all Germany except the Marcomanni.[55] Dio Cassius, by contrast, provides a curt and sober assessment: Tiberius advanced to the Weser and the Elbe, but accomplished nothing worthy of record.[56] Only peace treaties resulted, but the legate got triumphal honors, and the *princeps* and his son were hailed as *imperatores*.[57] The contrast between appearance and reality persists.

Five legions remained in the Rhine command. But the hand of Rome, it seems, was felt only lightly in Germany. Roman authority extended to parts of the nation, but by no means all. The process of urbanization, establishment of markets, and encouragement of peaceful assemblies that came with the Roman presence advanced without apparent resistance.[58] The new legate, P. Quinctilius Varus, was a man more accustomed to peace than to war.[59] His activities concentrated on the imposition of rules, the exercise of judicial powers, and the collection of revenues—a practice not hitherto implemented in Germany. Dio Cassius appropriately notes that Varus behaved *as if* the Germans were subject peoples.[60] They were not—as the rebellion of Arminius demonstrated. The Cherusci lulled Varus into complacency, then lured him into an ambush. In the vicinity of the Teutoburg Forest in September A.D. 9, Varus lost his life and Rome lost three legions—a disaster unparalleled

54. Dio 55.10a. 2–3; Tac. *Ann.* 4.44. The conjecture on Domitius' purpose is that of R. Syme in *CAH* X, 365–66. The starting point of his expedition remains in dispute: Syme (supra); D. Timpe, "Zur Geschichte und Überlieferung der Okkupation Germaniens unter Augustus," *Saeculum* 18 (1967) 280–84; Wells (supra n. 35) 158–59; Christ (supra n. 42) 181–83.

55. Vell. Pat. 2.106.1–3, 2.107.3, 2.108.1. Similarly, Aufidius Bassus, in Peter, *HRRel* II, 96, 3.

56. Dio 55.28.5; cf. Timpe (supra n. 54) 284–88. Note that after the campaign of A.D. 5 Tiberius evidently returned to winter quarters on the Rhine: Vell. Pat. 2.107.3.

57. Dio 55.28.6.

58. Dio 56.18.1–2. On this passage, see the astute remarks of Christ (supra n. 42) 194–98 as against Timpe (supra n. 54) 288–90 and id., *Arminius-Studien* (Heidelberg 1970) 81–90.

59. Vell. Pat. 2.117.2.

60. Dio 56.18.3. Other sources, eager to blame the legate for future calamity, stress his combination of greed and ineptitude: Vell. Pat. 2.117.2–2.118.1; Florus 2.30.31.

in the Augustan years.[61] The news shocked and dispirited the *princeps*. Augustus reportedly let his hair and beard grow for months as a sign of mourning, and more than once let fly the celebrated lament, "Varus, give me back my legions!"[62] Those histrionics buttress the common view that Varus' defeat marked the major turning point in Augustus' German policy: the plan to pacify all of Germany to the Elbe was given up, and the empire's borders were withdrawn to the Rhine.[63]

It might be more accurate, however, to point to the continuities than to stress the break. Augustus made no public move to surrender. Quite the contrary. Tiberius returned to take command on the Rhine. Roman forces in the area were rebuilt to a total of eight legions, a far larger army than before. Augustus would not give even a suggestion of retreat. Tiberius restricted himself to cautious raids and demonstrations in A.D. 10 and 11. But the demonstrations themselves were important. In the presentation of Velleius Paterculus, they were dynamic offensive maneuvers and aggressive warfare—and that is doubtless the impression Augustus wished to deliver.[64] And in A.D. 13 Augustus appointed Germanicus to supreme command on the Rhine. Germanicus would lead conspicuous offensive campaigns into the interior of Germany. Tacitus pinpointed the motives with accuracy: war on the Germans derived less from the desire to extend the empire or to achieve tangible gain than to wipe out the disgrace of Varus' defeat. The *princeps* would not allow that calamity to stain Rome's reputation.[65]

The campaigns of Germanicus in A.D. 15 and 16 follow a long familiar pattern. Germanicus claimed major victories and accomplished very little. Despite—or perhaps in consequence of—that fact, he enjoyed lavish honors. Germanicus celebrated a handsome triumph, and his legates received *ornamenta triumphalia*.[66] When Tiberius recalled Ger-

61. Vell. Pat. 2.118.2–2.119.5; Dio 56.18.4–56.22.2; Tac. *Ann.* 1.57–61; Suet. *Aug.* 23; *Tib.* 17. The account of Florus (2.30.32–38) is unreliable. On the site of the battle, see E. Koestermann, "Die Feldzüge des Germanicus 14–16 n.Chr.," *Historia* 6 (1957) 441–43. On Arminius, see Timpe (1970: supra n. 58) 11–49; S. Dyson, "Native Revolts in the Roman Empire," *Historia* 20 (1971) 253–58. Tacitus' description of Arminius as *liberator Germaniae* (*Ann.* 2.88) does not imply that Rome had previously annexed the land as a province.

62. Suet. *Aug.* 23.2; Oros. 6.21.27.

63. Cf. Florus 2.30.39.

64. Vell. Pat. 2.120.1–2, 2.121.1; Dio 56.24.6, 56.25.2–3; Suet. *Tib.* 18. The eight Rhine legions are listed in Tac. *Ann.* 1.37.

65. Tac. *Ann.* 1.3.6; cf. Vell. Pat. 2.123.1. The motive is confirmed by Strab. 7.1.4 (c291–92).

66. Tac. *Ann.* 1.55.1, 1.72.1, 2.41.2–4; Strab. 7.1.4 (c291). On Germanicus' campaigns, see Koestermann (supra n. 61) 429–79; cf. the analyses by D. Timpe, *Der Triumph des Germanicus: Untersuchungen zu den Feldzügen der Jahre 14–16 n. Chr. in Germanien* (Bonn 1968) 41–77; and K. Telschow, "Die Abberufung des Germanicus (16 n.Chr.): Ein

manicus in A.D. 16, the young general expressed disappointment and asserted that another season's campaigning would have brought the war to an end.[67] Whatever the plausibility of those claims, they were bound to be made. Nor did Tiberius dispute them. Rome halted offensive operations across the Rhine. But Rome also let it be known that it could have subjugated Germany in a year—had it wished.[68] Germanicus' campaigns exemplify once again the repeated discrepancy between achievement and advertisement.

A definition of a general "Augustan policy" in Germany would be difficult to formulate and probably pointless to attempt. To designate it either as defensive or as imperialistic risks oversimplification.[69] And it would be erroneous to consider Roman actions in Germany as following a static or consistent plan. But, despite shifts in behavior and action, continuities prevailed: the emphasis on Rome's international authority and its ascendancy over all rivals. The emphasis emerges in the swift retaliation after each challenge, timely appearance of the *princeps* and his stepsons, establishment of garrisons, promotion of the imperial cult, expeditions (however brief and temporary) to the Elbe, triumphal honors and imperial salutations repeatedly awarded, display of Roman magisterial symbols, introduction of administrative regulations, and drive to compensate publicly for every setback. The reference to Germany in the *Res Gestae* suitably completes the picture. Augustus ignores precision for propaganda. He includes Germany and Spain as evidence of his pacification of Europe from Gades to the Elbe.[70]

Imperial Ideology

The assessment of Augustus' imperial policy has long divided scholars. Was he a relentless expansionist, or a prudent leader who set bounds to the empire? Did he conduct an aggressive imperialism or follow a defensive scheme? Was he military conqueror or bringer of peace?

Augustus, it is often alleged, placed limits on the extension of territory and advised that the empire be held within fixed bounds. But evi-

Beispiel für die Kontinuität römischer Germanienpolitik von Augustus zu Tiberius," in Lefèvre (supra n. 45) 148–82.
67. Tac. *Ann.* 2.26.
68. Strab. 7.1.4 (c291), written after Augustus' death, implies that the *princeps* never relinquished claims on Germany west of the Elbe.
69. For an extensive rehearsal of opinions through the early twentieth century, see W. A. Oldfather and H. V. Canter, *The Defeat of Varus and the German Frontier Policy of Augustus* (Urbana, Ill. 1915) 9–20, 35–81. A more recent survey has been made by Christ (supra n. 42) 151–67.
70. *RG* 26.2.

dence for that conclusion is slim and dubious. The recovery of the standards from Parthia in 20 B.C. induced the *princeps* to announce that the realm could remain at its present extent—a posture that, at best, was only temporary and brief.[71] He issued instructions directing generals not to pursue enemies beyond the Elbe, but that too was a temporary restraint designed to allow concentration on another conflict, not a delineation of boundaries.[72] More significant, or so it would seem, was a document read to the senate after Augustus' death and purporting to contain his advice that the empire be held within its present frontiers.[73] The authenticity of that item remains in doubt. Tiberius may have had cause to seek posthumous Augustan sanction for policies he intended to promote. And the statement attributed to Augustus by Dio that he had never added possessions from the barbarian world is preposterous.[74]

The martial accomplishments of Augustus themselves mock any notion of restrained limits or pacific intent. The *princeps'* appointees penetrated beyond the First Cataract in Egypt, extended influence to Ethiopia, and invaded Arabia. He converted Judaea into a province, rattled sabers at Parthia, and maintained an indirect hegemony in Armenia. Roman forces subjugated northwest Spain and carried campaigns against tribes in North Africa. Augustus or his surrogates fought the Dalmatians and Pannonians, mounted a force against the Marcomanni, and laid the groundwork for Roman provinces along the Danube. He routed Alpine peoples, opened passes in the mountains, reduced Raetia, and occupied Noricum. Romans crossed the Rhine, established garrisons in Germany, and dispatched armies to the Elbe. The record of conquest eclipsed that of all predecessors. The regime thrived on expansionism—or at least the reputation of expansionism.

Augustus left the impression of aggressiveness even where he had no intent to undertake aggression. Britain is a prime example. On three occasions, the *princeps* let it be known that he was on the point of mounting an expedition against that remote island: in 34, 27 and 26 B.C. Each time other pressing needs conveniently intervened to postpone the venture: a rising in Dalmatia, unsettled conditions in Gaul, and the Cantabrian War, respectively.[75] In the eyes of contemporaries in the thir-

71. Dio 54.9.1; cf. 53.10.4–5.
72. Strab. 7.1.4 (c291).
73. Tac. *Ann.* 1.11.4; Dio 56.33.5–6.
74. Dio 56.33.6. Suetonius' assertion that Augustus had no ambition for empire or martial glory (*Aug.* 21.2) is nonsense. On these matters, see now J. Ober, "Tiberius and the Political Testament of Augustus," *Historia* 31 (1982) 306–28.
75. Dio 49.38.2, 53.22.5, 53.25.2.

ties and twenties, the invasion of Britain was a sure thing—as was the conquest. Repeated allusions in the poems of Virgil, Horace, and Propertius attest to that public perception.[76] Augustus could later abandon the idea altogether by producing a plausible justification. British kings had sent embassies, made offerings on the Capitol, and formally acknowledged the *princeps'* authority. It was as good as a conquest—and much cheaper.[77] Britain could subsequently be ignored, a matter of policy, as Augustus explicitly characterized it.[78] The earlier projection of an aggressive pose had equally been a matter of policy.

Martial reputation held a preeminent place in the realm of Augustus.[79] After the defeat of Antony and Cleopatra, he may have sought to bind up the wounds of civil war. But he also made certain to commemorate the victory—and to institutionalize reminders of it. Two new cities rose as memorials to the achievement, each bearing the imposing designation of Nicopolis, one on the site of Octavian's camp at Actium, the other to mark the battle near Alexandria that completed the conquest.[80] And in 29 B.C. Octavian celebrated a triple triumph, a spectacular event that stretched over three days, to signal his successes in Illyria, Actium, and Alexandria.[81] The monuments and the ceremonies spelled out these messages clearly: they exalted not *pax* but the *gloria* of the conqueror. Those celebrations set a pattern for the imagery, both written and visual, that characterized the self-representation of the *princeps* and his government. The preamble of the *Res Gestae* sums up neatly the contents of that document: "The achievements of the divine Augustus, whereby he subjected the world to the power of the Roman people."

The poets of the era reinforce that impression. I offer only a small sample as illustration. Vergil's *Aeneid* forecasts world dominion in the age of Augustus. Jupiter promises imperial holdings without limits. And

76. Virg. *Ecl.* 1.67, *G.* 1.29, 3.25; Hor. *Epod.* 7.7, *Carm.* 1.21.13, 1.35.29, 3.4.34, 3.5.2–4, 4.14.47; Prop. 2.27.5, 4.3.7; cf. A. Momigliano, "Panegyricus Messalae and 'Panegyricus Vespasiani': Two References to Britain," *JRS* 40 (1950) 39–41.

77. Strab. 4.5.3 (c200). These embassies need to be kept distinct from the arrival of British refugee princes as suppliants at the court of Augustus; *RG* 32.1.

78. Tac. *Agr.* 13.

79. On what follows, see the fuller treatment in E. S. Gruen, "Augustus and the Ideology of War and Peace," in R. Winkes, ed., *The Age of Augustus: Conference held at Brown University in Providence, R.I., 1982,* Archaeologia Transatlantica 5 (Louvain and Providence 1986) 51–72.

80. Epirote Nicopolis: Strab. 7.7.5–6 (c324–25), 10.2.2 (c450); Pliny *HN* 4.1.5; Paus. 10.38.4; Dio 51.1.2–3; Suet. *Aug.* 18. Alexandrian Nicopolis: Strab. 17.1.10 (c795); Dio 51.18.1; see A. E. Hanson, "Juliopolis, Nicopolis, and the Roman Camp," *ZPE* 37 (1980) 249–54.

81. Suet. *Aug.* 22; Dio 51.21.5–9.

the shield of Aeneas depicts the *princeps* as sitting in proud splendor while long rows of conquered peoples from Africa to the Euphrates pass in array before him.[82] Comparable indications recur in the songs of Horace. The *princeps* obtained standards from Parthia, without battle, trophies, or triumphs. But in Horace's lines, the Parthians, stripped of their spoils, bend to the dictates of Rome and venerate Augustus. The taking of the standards is juxtaposed to the exercise of Roman sway throughout the world.[83] Propertius too alludes to victories abroad, kings led in triumph, distant lands trembling and obedient to the authority of the *princeps*.[84] Ovid's *Metamorphoses* and *Fasti* speak of the subjugation of barbarian peoples and the deep penetration of Roman power. Jupiter surveys a world where Roman dominion is universal. The earth lies under the heel of the conqueror.[85] Even in the poems from exile, late in Augustus' reign, Ovid's praise of the *princeps* places stress upon victory; the garnering of military laurels; the conquest of Pannonia, Raetia, and Thrace; awestruck Germany; and imperial holdings now at their greatest reach.[86]

The Forum Augustum gave the most visible and prominent display of Augustan ideology. The imposing Temple of Mars Ultor, completed in 2 B.C., held a conspicuous place. It would be the locus of assemblage for the senate for all declarations of war or awards of triumph, and the symbolic starting point from which every general would lead his troops abroad. The Forum Augustum served as a repository of weapons of all sorts and for arms seized as booty from the defeated foes of Rome.[87] A statue of the *princeps* himself stood in the center of the Forum, set in a triumphal chariot that contained a record of his conquests.[88] The flanks of the Forum held two rows of statues. In the niches of one side Augustus installed representatives of the great men of Rome's past, with inscribed *elogia* attesting, among other things, to military achievements and triumphal honors. Opposite that array of heroes stood the figures of Aeneas and all the key members of the Julian line.[89] The *princeps* thus linked himself and his family to a gallery of Republican *duces, trium-*

82. Virg. *Aen.* 1.278–79, 3.714–18; cf. 1.286–90, 6.791–800, 7.601–15.
83. Hor. *Epist.* 1.12.27–28, 1.18.56–57, 2.1.256; *Carm.* 4.14.41–52, 4.15.6–8, 4.15.21–24; *Carm. saec.* 53–56.
84. Prop. 2.1.25–36, 2.10.13–18; cf. 4.4.11–12.
85. Ov. *Met.* 15.820–31, 15.877; *Fast.* 1.85–86, 1.717, 2.684, 4.857–62.
86. Ov. *Tr.* 2.169–78, 2.225–32, 3.12.45–48.
87. Ov. *Fast.* 5.550–62; Suet. *Aug.* 29.2; Dio 55.10.2–3.
88. *RG* 35.1; Vell. Pat. 2.39.2.
89. Ov. *Fast.* 5.563–66; Suet. *Aug.* 31.5; Dio 55.10.3; *SHA* Alex. Sev. 28.6; P. Zanker, *Forum Augustum: das Bildprogramm* (Tübingen 1968); P. Frisch, "Zu den Elogien des Augustusforums," *ZPE* 39 (1980) 91–98.

phatores, and *summi viri,* as heir to the grandest martial traditions of the state.

The *gloria* of the conqueror held a central place in the advertisement of the regime. Augustus attached special importance to it for reasons not difficult to discern. His military reputation in the early years had been dubious and tainted, subject to the ridicule of his enemies.[90] That stain needed to be wiped out. The defeat of Antony settled the contest for mastery of the Roman world. But triumph in the ruins of civil war carried troublesome connotations. The slaughter of fellow citizens brought little joy and left bitter memories. It was better to divert attention from the results of fratricidal strife by urging the claims of foreign conquest and the subjugation of external foes. And, above all, the man who fashioned a new government out of the wreckage of republican institutions had compelling reason to stress continuity with the past. The *novus status* would be more palatable if directed by one who championed the imperialist legacy of the Republic.

◆   ◆   ◆   ◆   ◆

A survey of territorial expansion under Augustus tempts conclusions about strategic designs, all-inclusive policy, and imperialist ambitions. Various theories endeavor to reconstruct Augustus' purpose and to discern an encompassing plan. A recent interpretation argues that the *princeps* adopted and refined a pattern of hegemonic rule. The organization rested on a network of client-states that shouldered the task of peripheral security. Roman forces took up station in frontier regions, economically deployed, with the mobility for transfer to areas of trouble whenever needed. The system had consistency and worked with efficiency.[91] Augustus' push to the north has often been reckoned as a carefully conceived and sweeping plan that linked the Alpine, Balkan, and German campaigns and aimed to establish a secure boundary of the empire that ran along the line of the Danube and the Elbe.[92] In a different formulation, the *princeps* had unlimited territorial aspirations. His objective was conquest of the known world, the inspiration coming from Alexander and the expectation grounded in geographic ignorance: erroneous calculations postulated a small *orbis* whose subjugation could

90. Cf. Suet. *Aug.* 16.2.
91. E. N. Luttwak, *The Grand Strategy of the Roman Empire* (Baltimore 1976) 13–50, 192. On client-states, see further Kienast (supra n. 35) 407–10; D. C. Braund, *Rome and the Friendly King* (London 1984) 91–103.
92. See the list of scholars in Oldfather and Canter (supra n. 69) 9–10 and note especially Syme (supra n. 54) 351–54; Kraft (supra n. 35) 181–208.

readily come within his lifetime. Only the Pannonian revolt and the defeat of Varus obliged him to check his ambition and bequeath a defense policy to his successor.[93] Augustus, it is claimed, had a sense of the totality of Rome's empire, strove to consolidate his realm, and bound together the various parts into an integral unity.[94]

The diverse theses share a common ground: they presume an empire-wide policy on the part of the *princeps*. The presumption may contain truth on a theoretical level. Augustus spoke of *pax* obtained by conquests *per totum imperium*.[95] And he was hailed as *custos imperii Romani totiusque orbis terrarum praeses*.[96] One will not doubt that he had certain broad aims and a vision of how it might all hold together. A need to achieve secure frontiers provided motivation. The determined effort to construct and extend roads and the creation of the *cursus publicus* reveal a drive to facilitate communications between armies and links among provinces. Control of restive populations within and intimidation of foes outside the imperial boundaries remained consistent objectives. Augustus intended to quell resistance and enforce allegiance, to overawe troublesome neighbors and to reassert the might of Rome in areas beyond its direct control.

General considerations and the notion of an overall scheme, however, misplace the emphasis. The diversity and flexibility of Augustus' foreign ventures stand out. No uniform plan or single-minded goal determined his moves. Location, circumstances, and contingencies guided decisions. Pragmatism took precedence over policy.

The eastern realms provoked varied responses. In Asia Minor and Judaea Augustus cultivated client-princes, generally keeping in place those already established, regardless of prior allegiances. But he was not averse to deposing dynasts (e.g., in Commagene), intervening in royal dispensations (as with Herod), or even converting principalities into provinces (Galatia and Judaea) when unexpected developments called for it. The principal garrisons of Roman power in the East stood in Egypt and Syria—but for very different purposes. Egypt held a special place for Augustus, its economic resources a mainstay of the empire and its territory a staging ground for military adventures in Ethiopia and

93. P. A. Brunt, review of *Die Aussenpolitik des Augustus und die augusteische Dichtung*, by H. D. Meyer, *JRS* 53 (1963) 170–76; Wells (supra n. 35) 3–13; R. Moynihan, "Geographical Mythology and Roman Imperial Ideology," in Winkes (supra n. 79) 149–62.

94. Kienast (supra n. 35) 368–70, 410–20.

95. *RG* 13: *cum per totum imperium populi Romani terra marique esset parta victoriis pax.*

96. *ILS* 140, lines 7–8.

Arabia. The troops in Syria, by contrast, served to signal stability rather than advance, a means of showing the flag and discouraging Parthian ambitions. The *princeps* kept a hand in the dynastic affairs of Armenia and a careful watch on vicissitudes in the royal house of Parthia. Recovery of the standards held priority in policy and propaganda. But dealings with Parthia relied on diplomacy—alternate displays of resolve and negotiated settlements—rather than force. The kingdom supplied occasions for posturing; it was not a menace against which to devise a strategy.

Different motives and different actions prevailed in the West. The *princeps* or his generals conducted vigorous campaigns in Illyria and Spain in the thirties and twenties B.C. Strategic purposes, however, played at best a secondary role. Octavian used the Illyrian adventure to shore up his reputation vis-à-vis Antony and brought northwest Spain under subjection to demonstrate Roman might throughout the Iberian Peninsula. Roman involvement in North Africa had a still different character (or characters): the *princeps* experimented with client-kings, warfare, and colonial foundations at various times and places in that area—with no consistent results.

The great northern campaigns may assume coherent shape in retrospect—but hardly at the time. Divergent aims dictated action; Roman response occurred as often as Roman initiative; political and ideological purposes frequently took precedence over strategic goals. Control of the Alpine regions expedited communications between the Rhine forces and the troops in Illyricum. The push to the Danube held out many advantages: the disciplining of recalcitrant tribes that had damaged Rome's repute, military laurels for members of Augustus' family, and the opening of a land route from northern Italy to the eastern dependencies. The heaviest fighting, however, came in reaction to rebellion rather than as part of an imperial scheme. Advancement against the Germans derived from security and administrative needs in Gaul. Strikes across the Rhine advertised Roman might and authority without establishing a permanent presence. Prestige may have counted for more than strategy. Exhibitions of force occurred after the Varian disaster as before.

Diversity stands out far more boldly than uniformity. There was uniformity, however, in one key respect. The *princeps* need not have felt commitment to relentless conquest and indefinite extension of territory and power. But he represented such aspirations with regularity and conviction.

Representation and reality often diverged. Augustus made certain to maintain consistency in the former. Pragmatic considerations might on occasion dictate restraint or withdrawal. And defeat could sometimes mar the achievement. But the public posture remained uniform: a posture of dynamism, success, and control.

Bloodless negotiations allowed Augustus to recover the standards from Parthia, and diplomacy provided an acceptable settlement in Armenia. But the regime made menacing gestures, and the propaganda proclaimed defeat for Parthia and subjection for Armenia. The closing of Janus' doors and the triumphal honors awarded after a campaign in northwest Spain belied the superficiality of that achievement—to be followed by another decade of brutal fighting in the region and heavy losses for Rome. Modest successes in Illyria during the triumviral period became exaggerated in report and announcement so as to elevate Octavian's reputation at the expense of his rival. Victories and the honors of victory marked the advance to the Danube and even encouraged the mounting of a campaign against the Marcomanni. The Pannonian revolt, however, shattered the illusion of Roman mastery and required an enormous commitment of resources to restore control. The conquest of the Alps may have had strategic ends. But it also served to advertise the prowess of Augustus' stepsons and to summon public acclaim for the imperial house. Similarly, Drusus' thrusts across the Rhine called forth magnificent honors, out of proportion to solid accomplishments. And the termination of his advance at the Elbe was explained away as the consequence of divine intervention. In comparable fashion, Tiberius obtained high honors for victories in Germany, and his panegyrist, Velleius Paterculus, rhapsodized about his successes, though little of substance was accomplished. And when disaster did strike, in the form of Varus' crushing defeat, the *princeps* strove to stress continuity, appointing Tiberius and then Germanicus to resume aggressive campaigns across the Rhine, as if to deny any setback or interruption.

The imperial policy of Augustus varied from region to region, adjusted for circumstances and contingencies. Aggression alternated with restraint, conquest with diplomacy, advance with retreat. Acquisitions and annexations occurred in some areas, consolidation and negotiation in others. The insistence upon reputation, however, was undeviating. The regime persistently projected the impression of vigor, expansionism, triumph, and dominance. The policy may have been flexible, but the image was consistent.[97]

97. This paper is a condensation of a longer version that will appear as chapter 4 of the second edition of *The Cambridge Ancient History*, vol. X. Gratitude is due to the Cambridge University Press for permission to reproduce portions of that chapter.

Opposition to Augustus

nullo adversante
(Tac. *Ann.* 1.2)

That there existed opposition under Augustus and that much of it was aimed no less at the new system and individual solutions introduced by Augustus than at the *princeps* himself cannot be doubted.[1] Our sources confirm this, and historical experience indicates that such must indeed have been the case. Accordingly, it has often been taken for granted by modern scholars that the first *princeps* was more or less constantly threatened by the ever-present forces of opposition, that the known conspiracies as extreme forms of expressing such opposition are but the tip of an iceberg, that such opposition became visible whenever Augustus met with difficulty, and that many of his policies and reforms must be seen as reactions to such opposition.[2] Some of this may well be true. But

1. This paper presents the results of a collaborative effort of its authors that goes back to a graduate seminar on Augustus taught at Brown University by M. C. J. Putnam, R. Winkes, and K. A. Raaflaub in the spring of 1987. L. J. Samons is primarily responsible for part II, K. Raaflaub for parts I and III. Thanks for valuable suggestions is owed to C. W. Fornara, S. G. Nugent, M. Toher, J. Kennelly, W. Stevenson, and especially P. M. Swan and E. S. Gruen. The translations cited (sometimes in slightly adapted form) are those of the Loeb Classical Library and the Penguin Classics Series.
2. For a refutation of the last point, see E. Badian, " 'Crisis Theories' and the Beginning of the Principate," in G. Wirth, ed., *Romanitas-Christianitas: Untersuchungen zur Geschichte und Literatur der römischen Kaiserzeit, Johannes Straub zum 70. Geburtstag*

in view of questions raised by recent scholarship on the opposition to the emperors from Tiberius to Domitian this traditional picture needs to be reexamined.[3] It is the purpose of this paper to take a fresh look at the actions recorded by the ancient sources or interpreted by modern scholars as indicative of opposition to Augustus; we shall examine the motives, goals, and connections of the persons involved in such actions, determine how much and what kind of opposition confronts us in each case, and finally seek an explanation for the picture that will emerge.

The investigation has been limited to the period after Actium, when Augustus was in sole control of power,[4] and to two closely related types of opposition: the "political," which originated with senators and equestrians and surfaced mostly in the senate or in the form of (real or alleged) conspiracies, and the "intellectual," which was mainly expressed by orators and historians.[5]

I. Political opposition

A. GENERAL STATEMENTS OR LISTS OF OPPONENTS

Velleius Paterculus is our oldest source on the opposition to Augustus. He frames his glowing report of Augustus' achievement (2.89–90) with descriptions of the conspiracies of M. Aemilius Lepidus (30 B.C.: 2.88), L. Murena and Fannius Caepio (22 B.C.: 2.91.2), and Egnatius Rufus (19 B.C.: 91.3–4). The latter individuals are explicitly introduced as ex-

---

gewidmet (Berlin and New York 1982) 18–41. Among many others, R. Syme, P. Sattler, and, more recently, D. Kienast are representatives of such views; see also P. W. Ruikes, *Samenzweringen en intriges tegen Octavianus Augustus Princeps* (Diss. Nijmegen 1966; with German summary 235–41). To cite just one example: in 12 B.C. Augustus ordered all existing oracles and prophetic texts (*fatidici libri*) purged and the authentic Sibylline prophecies deposited under the base of the Palatine Apollo (Suet. *Aug.* 31.1). D. Kienast, *Augustus: Prinzeps und Monarch* (Darmstadt 1982) 196 n. 103, comments: "Der Grund für die Aktion des Augustus ist . . . sicherlich vor allem in der angespannten politischen Situation nach dem Tode des Agrippa zu suchen, welcher der stets vorhandenen Opposition gegen den Prinzeps neuen Auftrieb gegeben haben muss"; cf. infra nn. 62 and 116.

3. See K. Raaflaub, "Grundzüge, Ziele und Ideen der Opposition gegen die Kaiser im 1. Jh. n. Chr.: Versuch einer Standortbestimmung," in O. Reverdin and B. Grange, eds., *Opposition et résistances à l'empire d'Auguste à Trajan*, Entretiens sur l'ant. class. 33 (Vandoeuvres and Geneva 1987) 1–55 (with the literature cited there), and the other contributions in the same volume.

4. The extended power struggle during the age of the civil wars created conditions that were substantially different from those in peacetime and under the rule of the *princeps*. Thus the case of Q. Salvidienus Rufus (cf. Kienast [supra n.2] 40f.; R. Syme, *The Roman Revolution* [Oxford 1939] 217, 220) is not comparable to those of the conspirators after 31.

5. This distinction is, of course, somewhat artificial since most orators and historians were senators. See infra at n. 84 for the poets.

amples of those "who did not like this prosperous state of affairs" (2.91.2).

Describing the worries and responsibilities that made the emperor yearn for rest and retirement, Seneca relates that while Augustus was pacifying the empire and extending its boundaries,

> in Rome itself the swords of Murena, Caepio, Lepidus, Egnatius, and others were being whetted to slay him. Not yet had he escaped their plots, when his daughter and all the noble youths who were bound to her by adultery as by a sacred oath (*adulterio velut sacramento adacti*) kept alarming his failing years: Iullus and once again a woman to be feared in league with an Antonius. (*Brev. 4.5*)[6]

Elsewhere Seneca has Livia mention the plots of Lepidus, Murena, Caepio, and Egnatius in her plea for clemency toward another conspirator, Cinna Magnus (*Clem. 1.9.6*).

Pliny the Elder cites Augustus as a superb example of the limitations of human happiness. He lists numerous setbacks and disasters in Augustus' life, among them

> the many plots against his life, . . . his daughter's adultery and the disclosure of her plots against her father's life (*consilia parricidae palam facta*), . . . another adultery, that of his grand-daughter, then . . . the disowning of Agrippa Postumus after his adoption as heir. (*HN 7.149f.*)

Without necessarily being hostile to Augustus, this summary emphasizes the negative aspects of his life and reign. While it stresses the multitude of plots and is alone in explicitly attributing to the elder Julia the intention of assassinating her father, it fails, with this one exception, to substantiate the information with names and details.[7]

Tacitus begins his comments on Augustus in the *Annals* by pointing out the lack of opposition to the first *princeps* (*nullo adversante: 1.2*). But in his famous "debate about Augustus" (1.9–10) he presents the familiar contrasting views:

> Force had been sparingly used—merely to preserve peace for the majority; . . . there had certainly been peace, but it was bloodstained: there followed

6. Cf. P. Jal, "Images d'Auguste chez Sénèque," *REL* 35 (1957) 247–64, esp. 248–51.

7. For recent discussion, see H. Tränkle, "Augustus bei Tacitus, Cassius Dio und dem älteren Plinius," *WS* 82 (n.s. 3) (1969) 108–30, esp. 121–23 (suggesting Cremutius Cordus as a source); B. Manuwald, "Cassius Dio und das 'Totengericht' über Augustus bei Tacitus," *Hermes* 101 (1973) 352–74, esp. 372; K. Sallmann, "Plinius der Ältere 1938–1970," *Lustrum* 18 (1977) 172; R. Till, "Plinius über Augustus (nat. hist. 7.147–150)," *WürzJbb* N.F.3 (1977) 127–37, esp. 137; see also infra n. 46 and text. For Julia, see infra n. 49.

... the executions of men like Varro, Egnatius, and Iullus (*interfectos* ... *Varrones, Egnatios, Iullos*).

Suetonius reports the suppression of several conspiracies,

> all of them detected before they became dangerous. Involved in the conspiracies were Lepidus the Younger, Varro Murena and Fannius Caepio, Marcus Egnatius, Plautius Rufus and Lucius Paulus (the husband of Augustus' grand-daughter), and besides those Lucius Audasius, a feeble old man who had been indicted for forgery. (*Aug.* 19.1)

Suetonius goes on to mention the plan of Audasius and one Asinius Epicadus to abduct Julia the Elder and Agrippa Postumus from the islands to which they had been exiled and take them "to the armies"; the plot of a slave, Telephus, who was driven by delusions of grandeur; and the bizarre intrusion into the palace by an Illyrian camp orderly armed with a hunting knife (19.1f.). Presumably, this is meant to be a complete list; the omission of Julia the Elder and her paramours therefore seems significant.

In addition to reports of individual conspiracies, Dio Cassius makes several general statements on the frequency of plots against Augustus.[8] The most important of these follows Dio's report on the purge of the senate in 18 B.C. (54.15.1–4):[9]

> After these events many immediately and many later were accused, whether rightly or falsely, of plotting against both the emperor and Agrippa. It is not possible, of course, for those on the outside to have certain knowledge of such matters, for whatever measures a ruler takes for the punishment of men for alleged plots against himself, either personally or through the senate, are generally looked upon with suspicion as having been done out of spite, no matter how just such measures may be. For this reason it is my purpose to report in all such cases simply the recorded version of the affair, without . . . giving a hint as to the justice or injustice of the act or as to the truth or falsity

8. Cf. 54.12.3 (19 [or 18?] B.C.): "Augustus saw that the public business (*ta koina*) required most careful attention (*therapeia akribēs*) and feared that he himself might, as often happens to men of his position (thus for *en tois toioutois* E. Cary [Loeb] and I. Scott-Kilvert [Penguin]; or perhaps "to men carrying out such *therapeia akribēs* [M. Swan's suggestion]?), fall victim to a plot"; 54.18.1 (17 B.C.): After Lucius Caesar's birth "Augustus immediately adopted him together with his brother Gaius, . . . appointing them then and there successors to his office, in order that fewer plots might be formed against him" (cf. Kienast [supra n. 2] 97); 55.4.3 (9 B.C.): Despite making a point of being "democratic" (4.1–3), Augustus "punished others who were reported to be conspiring against him" (cf. B. Manuwald, *Cassius Dio und Augustus: Philologische Untersuchungen zu den Büchern 45–56 des dionischen Geschichtswerkes,* Palingenesia 14 [Wiesbaden 1979] 108; B. Levick, "Tiberius' Retirement to Rhodes in 6 B.C.," *Latomus* 31 [1972] 802). Cf. infra at n. 41.

9. For comments on this passage, cf. esp. F. Millar, *A Study of Cassius Dio* (Oxford 1964) 87–90; Manuwald (supra n.8) 102–8.

of the report. . . . As for the time of which we are speaking, Augustus executed a few men.

The historical value of these general remarks is questionable for several reasons. First, some of them resemble those in Dio's chapter on the difficulties of historiography in an autocratic state (53.19), and they recall the complaint attributed by Suetonius to Domitian that "all emperors are necessarily wretched, since only their assassination can convince the public that the conspiracies against their lives are real" (*Dom.* 21). Second, when dealing with conspiracies both here (where he continues with a reference to the plot of Lepidus of 30 B.C.) and elsewhere, Dio's chronology is so confused that some scholars assume a separate source that focused on the opposition to Augustus without attention to chronology.[10] Third, Dio does not provide any names or details in these general statements. They are similar, however, to observations made in the long advisory speeches by Maecenas and Livia, who both point out that a sole ruler simply has to expect such plots and must protect himself accordingly. Even more than the rest of his work, these speeches were clearly written by Dio on the basis of contemporary experiences and for the benefit of his own time.[11] Thus it seems reasonable to conclude that whatever special source Dio might have used, he dealt with the problem of opposition to Augustus from the point of view of one experienced with the monarchy of the late second and early third centuries. Consequently, unless confirmed by other sources, Dio's general remarks (as opposed to his comments on specific conspiracies or actions hostile to the *princeps*) should not be taken as evidence either of the existence of otherwise unattested conspiracies or of the fact that some of Augustus' actions were motivated by fear of plots or by opposition in general.[12]

10. Cf. Millar (supra n. 9) 87, referring to H. A. Andersen, *Cassius Dio und die Begründung des Principates* (Berlin 1938) 31, n. 74.

11. Maecenas: 52.31.5–10 (cf. Agrippa in 52.10.4); cf. Millar (supra n. 9) 102–18, esp. 104, 107f.; J. Bleicken, "Der politische Standpunkt Dios gegenüber der Monarchie," *Hermes* 90 (1962) 444–67. Livia: 55.14.2–21.4; cf. Manuwald (supra n. 8) 126f. Cf. in general the contribution to this volume by M. Reinhold and P. M. Swan.

12. An example might be helpful. Suetonius reports that during the purge of the senate in 18 B.C. Augustus wore a sword and breastplate under his tunic and was protected by a bodyguard of ten sturdy senators (*Aug.* 35.1; for the date, see infra n. 71). Dio mentions before this purge Agrippa's promotion to a position of co-rulership, which he explains by Augustus' work load and fear of plots (54.12.2f.: supra n. 8). The underlying thought must be (as in 54.18.1: supra n. 8) that the existence of two rulers makes it more difficult for the opposition to plot successfully against the monarchs; for, Dio continues, "as for the breastplate which he often wore beneath his dress, even when he entered the senate, he believed that it would be of but scanty and slight assistance to him" (12.3). Dio then reports the purge of the senate (13–14) and continues with the remark quoted above about

Thus the general and summary statements discussed so far present two basic facts. First, a few plots and scandals supposedly involving conspiratorial activities held a firm place in the historical tradition. They were connected with the names of M. Aemilius Lepidus, Varro Murena and Fannius Caepio, Egnatius Rufus, Julia the Elder and Iullus Antonius, L. Aemilius Paullus (the husband of Julia the Younger), Plautius Rufus, and finally Agrippa Postumus. Not all of them are mentioned by every source, but apart from this group there appears only one name, Cinna Magnus. Second, general statements emphasizing the frequency of plots and the intensity and constancy of Augustus' fear as a result of them fail to add any substance; most probably, they were based on the same list.

It is time now to look more closely at the individual cases, including a few that are not mentioned by the ancient authors as acts of opposition but have been considered as such by modern scholars.

B. INDIVIDUAL PLOTS

The conspiracy of M. Aemilius Lepidus (30 B.C.).   Lepidus, son of the former triumvir, was accused of planning Octavian's assassination and a new civil war and was either executed by Maecenas, who was in charge of affairs at Rome, or sent on to Octavian at Actium.[13] Save for his closest relatives, we know of no other person involved. There is no reason to consider the conspiracy of Lepidus as anything more than an isolated action of a young man who had sufficient grounds to hate Octavian and dream of restoring his family to its former glory.[14]

The affair of M. Licinius Crassus (27 B.C.).   Crassus, the grandson of the triumvir, had first supported Antonius but joined Octavian shortly before Actium. He was consul in 30 and as proconsul of Macedonia

---

the multitude of plots following that purge and occurring even later (15.1). It does not seem plausible that Dio's narrative is based here on a good source and therefore trustworthy (*pace* Kienast [supra n. 2] 96f.). On the contrary, operating with preconceptions of a very general nature (a monarch is constantly threatened by conspiracies; co-rulership or a well-publicized scheme of succession help to reduce this danger) and using basic information (there were a number of conspiracies during Augustus' reign), he or his source greatly exaggerated the fact that Augustus had to seek special protection during that particular purge of the senate.

13. Cf. Vell. Pat. 2.88.1–3; App. *BCiv.* 4.50.217–19. The other sources (e.g., Livy *Per.* 133; Dio 54.15.4) add no substance. For discussion, cf. P. Sattler, *Augustus und der Senat: Untersuchungen zur römischen Innenpolitik zwischen 30 und 17 v. Chr.* (Göttingen 1960) 29f. Despite its date, the affair still belongs to the civil war period.

14. Contra: Kienast (supra n. 2) 66: "eine offenbar weitverzweigte Verschwörung."

undertook successful campaigns for which he was awarded supplication and triumph. By virtue of having killed the king of the Bastarnae with his own hands he claimed the ancient right to offer the *spolia opima* to Jupiter Feretrius. Augustus refuted this claim on the strength of his own epigraphical research.[15] Crassus' triumph in the summer of 27 was both the high point and the end of his career; we have no knowledge of his later activities.[16] There is no reason to assume that Augustus refuted Crassus' claim because he saw in him a political enemy; rather, with his extraordinary achievement and demand Crassus challenged the monopoly of control over the armies that Augustus tried to establish and that was crucial for any lasting pacification of the empire.[17] That Crassus was ambitious and thus unhappy about the abrupt end put to his career is quite likely. But attempts to identify him as the driving force behind later opposition find no support in the ancient sources.[18]

The affair of C. Cornelius Gallus (27 B.C.).   Gallus, an equestrian, was one of Octavian's commanders in the Alexandrian war of 30 B.C. and became the first prefect of Egypt in the same year. He set up statues of himself, and a surviving inscription attests to his boasting about his achievements.[19] His fall in 27 or 26 has caused much debate.[20] The following conclusions seem safe enough. Our main sources do not speak of Gallus as a conspirator against Augustus. Suetonius (*Aug.* 66.2), in fact, distinguishes sharply between Salvidienus Rufus, who lost Augustus' friendship because of a plot (*res novas molientem*), and Gallus, who suffered this fate because he proved ungrateful and ill willed toward his friend and benefactor (*ob ingratum et malivolum animum*). The mis-

15. Livy 4.20.7 with R. M. Ogilvie, *A Commentary on Livy, Books 1–5* (Oxford 1965) 563f.

16. For details and sources, cf. E. Groag, *RE* 13.1 (1926) 283–85 s.v. Licinius (Crassus) no. 58, and the recent literature listed by Kienast (supra n. 2) 84f.

17. Cf. Syme (supra n. 4) 308f.; Badian (supra n. 2) 25–27; and, for Augustus' efforts to control the armies, K. Raaflaub, "Die Militärreformen des Augustus und die politische Problematik des frühen Prinzipats," in G. Binder, ed., *Saeculum Augustum,* vol. 1, *Herrschaft und Gesellschaft,* Wege der Forschung 266 (Darmstadt 1987) 246–307.

18. B. Levick, "Primus, Murena, and *Fides:* Notes on Cassius Dio LIV. 3," *GaR* 22 (1975) 158f., suggests Crassus and his friends as backers of the prosecution against M. Primus in 23/22.

19. Dio 53.23.5. For the inscription of Philae (*CIL* III. 14147.5 = *ILS* 8995), cf. J.-P. Boucher, *Caius Cornélius Gallus* (Paris 1966) 38–45; E. Bernand, *Les inscriptions grecques et latines de Philae,* vol. 2 (Paris 1969), no. 128, pp. 35–47.

20. Cf. Boucher (supra n. 19) 49–57 and the literature cited by Kienast (supra n. 2) 85, n. 68. For a recent discussion of the date, see L. J. Daly, "The Gallus Affair and Augustus' *lex Iulia maiestatis:* A Study in Historical Chronology and Causality," in C. Deroux, ed., *Studies in Latin Literature and Roman History,* vol. 1 (Brussels 1979) 289–311, esp. 292f.; Manuwald (supra n. 8) 111f.

deeds that initiated Gallus' downfall were disrespectful self-aggrandizement, inability to understand his position and its limits, and open support for Q. Caecilius Epirota, who had been expelled from Augustus'
house for gross moral violations. The punishment for these misdeeds
was strictly based on, and limited by, Augustus' position as *patronus*
and *amicus:* he expelled Gallus from his group of friends and prohibited
him from entering the imperial provinces. Politically, this was the end of
Gallus' career; socially, Gallus was ostracized. Hatred for the fallen upstart then (that is, in a second stage that followed Augustus' private
action) combined with political opportunism to produce a flood of accusations, most likely of extortion and provincial mismanagement. A
trial was scheduled; "the senate unanimously voted that he should be
convicted in the courts, exiled, and deprived of his estate . . . and that
the senate itself should offer sacrifices." Thus conviction was certain,
and Gallus committed suicide.[21]

In all this, there is no hint of treason or conspiracy. It is only in very
late sources that this charge figures explicitly and prominently.[22] Moreover, a recently found papyrus that mentions military and naval preparations in the context of a revolt, though without naming the agent, has
been interpreted as supporting this charge and providing the real cause
of Gallus' fall.[23] This interpretation is untenable for several reasons. It
raises serious textual problems, and the preparations referred to in the

21. Dio 53.23.5–24.3 (the quotation: 23.7); Suet. *Aug.* 66.2 (*accusatorum denuntia-
tionibus et senatus consultis*), *Gram.* 16 (*Epirota . . . ad . . . Gallum se contulit vixitque
una familiarissime, quod ipsi Gallo inter gravissima crimina ab Augusto obicitur*); Ov. *Tr.*
2.445f. See further infra with n. 22. P. M. Swan observed in his comments on a draft of
this paper: "The senate instructed the court(s) on what the verdict and punishment was to
be in the case. . . . Assuming a date of 29/26 and that a consul presided in the senate, either
Augustus or someone close to him had an important role in this remarkable procedure—
hapax as far as I know." However, given the precise instruction "that this estate should be
given to Augustus" (Dio 53.23.7), the latter's direct involvement seems doubtful (see W.
Kunkel, *Kleine Schriften* [Weimar 1974] 283), but the senate's action certainly is remarkable. On this case especially, cf. Kunkel (supra) 277–84; H. Volkmann, *Zur Rechtsprechung im Principat des Augustus* (Munich 1935) 105ff., esp. 113–17; W. Schmitthenner,
"Augustus' spanischer Feldzug und der Kampf um den Prinzipat," *Historia* 11 (1962) 29–
85, esp. 40f., 74f. For the effects of the *renuntiatio amicitiae*, see R. S. Rogers, "The Emperor's Displeasure—*amicitiam renuntiare*," *TAPA* 90 (1959) 224–37.
22. Amm. Marc. 17.4.5 indicates financial mismanagement and extortion in the province. Serv. *ad Ecl.* 10.1: *Gallus . . . cum venisset in suspicionem, quod contra eum con-
iuraret, occisus est;* cf. *ad Georg.* 4.1: *postquam irato Augusto Gallus occisus est.* We
should like to know what Suet. *Gram.* 16 meant by *gravissima crimina* (see supra n. 21).
In view of *Aug.* 66.2 (mentioned supra after n. 20) we must not think automatically of
conspiracy.
23. *POxy.* 2820, published by E. Lobel in *Ox. Pap.* 37 (1971) 98–100. Cf. M. Treu,
"Nach Kleopatras Tod (P.Oxy. 2820)," *Chiron* 3 (1973) 221–33, supported by W. Luppe,
"P.Oxy. 2820: Ein Bericht über die politische Tätigkeit des Cornelius Gallus?" *ArchPF* 26
(1975) 33–38.

papyrus are more plausibly attributed to Gallus' successor, Aelius Gallus, who undertook an expedition to Arabia Felix.[24] Finally, it is most improbable that the *princeps* would not have learned of conspiratorial plans and himself immediately and openly turned Gallus over to the senate or another court for trial.[25] Augustus' complaint that he alone was not allowed to determine himself to what extent he wished to be angry at his own friends and the prominence of personal motives attributed to the *princeps* by the early sources make sense only in the context of a violation of *amicitia*, not in that of a conspiracy or planned military revolt.[26]

If Gallus' Egyptian activities contributed to his downfall, his case is comparable to that of Crassus: both were high-ranking men who, deliberately or not, tested the limits of the powerful individual's freedom of action and self-advertisement under the new regime.[27] Whether the senators who attacked Gallus after he had lost Augustus' protection really aimed at hurting the *princeps* himself, thereby expressing their opposition against the new order inaugurated in 27 B.C., remains anyone's guess.[28]

The conspiracy of Murena and Caepio (23/22 B.C.). The literature on this conspiracy is immense; most of it focuses on the date and the identity of Murena.[29] It can now be safely stated that the conspiracy was discovered in late 23 or in 22, certainly after the settlement of 23; this eliminates the popular thesis that Augustus' hand was forced by the conspiracy and the strong opposition that supposedly stood behind it.[30] Of the apparent leader, Fannius Caepio, we know nothing except that

24. N. Lewis, "P.Oxy. 2820: Whose Preparations?" *GRBS* 16 (1975) 295–303.

25. As he had done in the case of Salvidienus Rufus and would do later in all cases of conspiracy originating outside of his family. This objection is even more valid if Gallus returned to Rome already in 28 or even late 29 (cf. Daly [supra n. 20] 296, n. 25) and if he was indeed received in Rome with great honor (as is possibly indicated by Dio 53.24.1).

26. Suet. *Aug.* 66.2; Ov. *Am.* 3.9.63f.: *temerati crimen amici.* Cf. Ruikes (supra n. 2) part V and 237.

27. Cf. E. A. Judge, "*Veni. Vidi. Vici*, and the Inscription of Cornelius Gallus," *Akten des VI. Internationalen Kongresses für griech. und lat. Epigraphik*, Vestigia 17 (Munich 1973) 571–73; W. Eck, "Senatorial Self-Representation: Developments in the Augustan Period," in F. Millar and E. Segal, eds., *Caesar Augustus: Seven Aspects* (Oxford 1984) 129–67, esp. 131.

28. Thus, for example, Schmitthenner (supra n. 21) 74f.; Daly (supra n. 20) 298–301 and 310f. In her comments on a draft of this paper, S. G. Nugent suggests an additional dimension, which, unfortunately, cannot be substantiated: Gallus was a poet, writing in a "morally" questionable genre and thus possibly at odds with Augustus' plans of moral reform.

29. Cf. the literature cited by Kienast (supra n. 2) 86, n. 72.

30. See Badian (supra n. 2) 29–36.

he is labeled as "very bad" and thus usually considered "Republican in family and sentiment."[31] Murena has often been thought to be identical with A. Terentius Varro Murena whom the consular *fasti* seem to list as *ordinarius* of 23 and who was replaced by Cn. Calpurnius Piso, supposedly because of his involvement in the conspiracy. It has been demonstrated conclusively, however, that this man must have died as consul designate, before entering office. Most likely the conspirator was his brother, L. Licinius Varro Murena.[32] At any rate, this was an important person as well, a member of a consular family with relatives in influential positions and numerous important connections. Unfortunately, we have no names of other persons involved, although Dio reports they existed. What the conspirators wanted beyond the assassination of Augustus is unclear.[33] Only for Murena is a motive given: he was upset because he felt that in a recent trial Augustus had betrayed his client, M. Primus, a former governor of Macedonia. In that trial Augustus had intervened of his own accord (*autepangeltos*), which provoked mixed reactions; some, Dio says, despised him. This may well be the reason why, despite the clear directions given from upon high, a number of jurors voted for acquittal.[34] The same happened in the court trial of Caepio and Murena after they had defaulted; given the charge of conspiracy against the *princeps,* this act of defiance was even more flagrant. Nevertheless, conviction *in absentia* in a *quaestio de maiestate* and sacrifices by the senate seem to underscore the significance of the event, although the extent of the conspiracy and the danger posed by it are beyond recovery.[35]

31. Vell. Pat. 2.91.2 (*Caepio et ante hoc erat pessimus*) is interpreted by Sattler (supra n. 13) 63 as indicating old hostility to Augustus, while Murena (*sine hoc facinore potuit videri bonus*) previously was trusted by Augustus. Cf. Syme (supra n. 4) 333: the quotation in the text; 334: "Fannius was a 'bad man' to begin with, a Republican."

32. For literature, see Kienast (supra n. 2) 86, n. 72. For the consul designate, M. Swan, "The Consular *Fasti* of 23 B.C. and the Conspiracy of Varro Murena," HSCP 71 (1966) 235–47; for the conspirator, G. V. Sumner, "Varrones Murenae," HSCP 92 (1978) 187–95.

33. Murena's sister was Maecenas' wife; his brother, C. Proculeius, a close friend of Augustus'. Dio 54.3.4 expresses doubts about Murena's involvement and alludes to other conspirators. Suet. *Aug.* 56.4 at least gives us the name of the informer, one Castricius; cf. D. Stockton, "Primus and Murena," *Historia* 14 (1965) 18–40, esp. 26f. Vell. Pat. 2.91.2: *occidendi Caesaris consilia;* all the other sources simply mention the conspiracy.

34. Dio 54.3.2–6; cf. Levick (supra n. 18) 159–62; Sattler (supra n. 13) 63f.; and, generally on Dio's report, Manuwald (supra n. 8) 115–20.

35. For the details mentioned, see Dio 54.3.5–8; Suet. *Tib.* 8.1. Syme (supra n. 4) 333f.; Sattler (supra n. 13) 63–65; Stockton (supra n. 33) 26f., and others all argue for the importance of the conspiracy (although assuming that the conspirator actually was consul in 23). Ruikes (supra n. 2), part VI.A and 237 is entirely speculative. Comments by E. S. Gruen and P. M. Swan have been particularly helpful in this section.

The conspiracy of M. Egnatius Rufus (19 B.C.).   Egnatius Rufus exploited a long-standing deficiency in the administration of the city of Rome by setting up his own fire brigade. Capitalizing on his popularity, he was able to advance rapidly (and illegally) from the aedileship to the praetorship. When he tried to move immediately to the consulship, he was prevented by the consul. In his impatience and frustration, we are told, he started a conspiracy with "men of his own kind" that was quickly brought down.[36] Otherwise we know nothing of the man and his background. Whatever the truth about his conspiracy, it is clear that he was a problem mainly because he challenged Augustus' attempts to monopolize patronage of the urban masses.[37]

Anonymous plots in 18 and 9 B.C.   For both these years Dio reports the accusation and punishment of several men for (real or alleged) conspiracy. Unfortunately, the historian mentions these events summarily, without giving any names or details. Thus the historical value of this information is questionable.[38]

The plot of Cn. Cornelius Cinna Magnus (16–13 B.C.?).   Cinna was the grandson of Pompey the Great. His plot is absent in all lists of conspiracies against Augustus. It is mentioned only by Seneca (with details that support a date between 16 and 13 B.C.) and, depending directly or indirectly on him, by Dio (under the year A.D. 4). Both authors present the case as an example of Augustus' clemency toward his opponents, thus illustrating one of the capital virtues of the sole ruler. Dio has expanded his report of this event into a major story, featuring a dialogue between Augustus and Livia and a long speech by the latter that most likely served the purpose of discussing matters of principal importance

36. Cf. Vell. Pat. 2.91.3–92.4 (describing Egnatius as a second Catiline); Dio 53.24.4–6 (who, however, does not mention the conspiracy). Suet. *Aug.* 19.1, Sen. *Brev.* 4.5, and Tac. *Ann.* 1.10 simply mention the name. For the chronological problems of Dio's report, see Manuwald (supra n. 8) 113f., arguing against Millar (supra n. 9) 87f.; Badian (supra n. 2) 20f. with n. 10, arguing against P. Badot, "À propos de la conspiration de M. Egnatius Rufus," *Latomus* 32 (1973) 606–15. Ruikes (supra n. 2) part VI.B and 237f. again is too fancy.

37. Which was a cornerstone of the recent settlement of 23: P. J. Cuff, "The Settlement of 23 B.C.: A Note," *RivFil* 101 (1973) 466–77, esp. 473–77. Cf. further Z. Yavetz, *Plebs and Princeps* (Oxford 1969; reprint New Brunswick, N.J. 1988) 93ff. Egnatius' initiative forced Augustus to take care of the problem of fires in more permanent ways: Dio 53.24.6; 54.2.4; 55.26.4f.; cf. Kienast (supra n. 2) 273f.

38. 18 B.C.: Dio 54.15.1 and 4; 9 B.C.: Dio 55.4.3. See supra nn. 8f. and text. The lack of confirmation of such plots by other authors (particularly Suetonius and Seneca, who were strongly interested in such events) is alarming.

for the historian's own time.[39] Accordingly, the authenticity of the whole episode has been doubted.[40] If it is genuine, we still are completely ignorant of Cinna's motives and connections. The same is true for other conspirators vaguely mentioned by Dio in the same context.[41]

The scandal of Julia the Elder and Iullus Antonius (2 B.C.).   The fall of Julia, Augustus' daughter, and her entourage, foremost among which was M. Antonius' son, Iullus, who by marriage to Augustus' niece also belonged to the imperial family, was a tremendous shock, following, as it did, the grand celebrations at the beginning of 2 B.C.[42] Julia and most of her associates were exiled; Iullus committed suicide.[43] The official charge, publicized in a letter to the senate, was adultery and excessive immorality. That this was only a pretext and that the real reason was conspiracy against Augustus was assumed in antiquity and has been the focus of many modern discussions.[44] However, the sources we should trust most (Tacitus and Suetonius, if not Velleius Paterculus, who was living when the events took place) do not even mention the conspiracy,[45] which occurs only in a secondary line of tradition (found in Seneca and

39. Sen. *Clem.* 1.9.2–12; Dio 55.14–22. On Dio, see Millar (supra n. 9) 78f.; Manuwald (supra n. 8) 120–27; M. A. Giua, "Clemenza del sovrano e monarchia illuminata in Cassio Dione 55, 14–22," *Athenaeum* 69 (1981) 317–37.

40. Cf. the literature cited by Kienast (supra n. 2) 116, n. 200. Seneca's date is more plausible (cf. Manuwald [supra n. 8] 122, against D. C. A. Shotter, "Cn. Cornelius Cinna Magnus and the Adoption of Tiberius," *Latomus* 33 [1974] 306–13), "though Seneca's main reference is so full of mistakes in names, dates, ages and even the sequence of other conspiracies that it would be hazardous to believe him" (Badian [supra n. 2] 21). Cf. Syme (supra n. 4) 414; id., *The Crisis of 2 B.C.*, SBMünch, 1974, no. 7, 20 (= id., *Roman Papers*, vol. 3 [Oxford 1984] 925); id., *Tacitus*, vol. 1 (Oxford 1958) 404, n. 2: "The episode is edifying fiction."

41. Dio 55.14.1f. (merely generalizing? cf. supra at nn. 8f.): "While he [Augustus] was thus occupied, various men formed plots against him, notably Cn. Cornelius . . .'"; cf. 55.22.1f.

42. Cf. Syme (1974: supra n. 40) 10–16 (= id. [1984: supra n. 40] 918–22); W. K. Lacey, "2 B.C. and Julia's Adultery," *Antichthon* 14 (1980) 127–42, esp. 128–36.

43. According to Velleius, who ought to have known; Tacitus and Dio have him executed. Cf. A. Ferrill, "Augustus and His Daughter: A Modern Myth," in C. Deroux, ed., *Studies in Latin Literature and Roman History,* vol. 2 (Brussels 1980) 332–46, esp. 343.

44. Cf. the titles cited by Kienast (supra n. 2) 111, n. 179 and the survey in Ferrill (supra n. 43) 333–37.

45. Vell. Pat. 2.100.2–5 (mentions sexual depravity; names Iullus and the other principal victims of the "purge"); Tac. *Ann.* 1.10 (death of Iullus), 1.53 (adultery as reason of exile of Julia and her "persistent adulterer," Sempronius Gracchus; entirely personal reasons for Tiberius' harsh treatment of both many years later), 3.18 (Iullus had violated the house of Augustus; since Tacitus mentions in the same sentence the elder Antonius' supreme crime of starting a civil war against the *patria,* the conspiracy was bound to be mentioned here if Tacitus believed in its existence), 3.24 (Augustus expelled the two Julias *ob impudicitiam* from the city "and executed or banished their adulterers. For he used the solemn names of sacrilege and treason [*gravi nomine laesarum religionum ac violatae maiestatis appellando*] for the common offense of misconduct between the sexes; this was inconsistent with traditional tolerance and even with his own legislation"; thus Tacitus

Dio and supported by Pliny the Elder).[46] Moreover, Syme, one of the leading architects of the conspiracy theory, considers this line of tradition unreliable in the case of Cinna Magnus.[47] Thus attempts to refute altogether the existence of a real conspiracy ought to be taken seriously.[48]

The truth may well be beyond recovery, but even if there was a "conspiracy," most probably in this case the goals of the "conspirators," though directed against some of Augustus' plans, were neither aimed at his life nor at the principate as such.[49] Rather, they should be seen as part of an ongoing conflict within the palace; their purpose was to influence the succession, the designated successors, and, possibly, the future course of the principate.[50] Since they ran counter to Augustus' most

---

considers the charge of *violata maiestas* inappropriate and does not believe in a conspiracy), 4.44 (adultery); Suet. *Aug.* 19.1 (not listed among the conspirators), 65.1–5, 101.3, and *Tib.* 11.4 (immorality).

46. Sen. *Brev.* 4.5 (cited supra in part A, before n. 6), but see *Ben.* 6.32.1f. (only immorality), *Clem.* 1.9.6 (not mentioned among conspirators); Pliny *HN* 7.149 (cited supra in part A, after n. 6), but see 21.9 (only immorality); Dio 55.10.12–16 (Julia banished for immorality; of her lovers, "Iullus Antonius, on the ground that his conduct had been prompted by designs upon the monarchy, was put to death along with other prominent persons, while the remainder were banished to islands"). On Dio, cf. Manuwald (supra n. 8) 108f.; on Pliny, see Levick (supra n. 8) 795, n. 3 ("this could be a later elaboration") with reference to Norwood (infra n. 61) 163, n. 33, who attributes the dramatizing background of this tradition and mentions the case of C. Silius and Messalina in 48 A.D. (cf. Tac. *Ann.* 11.12–38), which may have been perceived as an analogy by later generations. Indeed, is it implausible that the tradition we grasp in Seneca and Pliny was inspired by that experience and was amplified (as in the case of Cinna Magnus: supra at n. 39) by Dio? For amplification, see Syme (supra n. 4) 426, n. 7; id. (1958: supra n. 40) 404, n. 1.

47. For the case of Cinna Magnus, see supra n. 40. In his *Roman Revolution* (supra n. 4) 426f. Syme refers for his conspiracy theory to E. Groag, "Studien zur Kaisergeschichte III: Der Sturz der Julia," *WS* 40 (1918) 150–67 and 41 (1919) 74–88. But in a later article (1974 [supra n. 40] 20–26 [= 1984 (supra n. 40) 926–30]) Syme exploits Seneca and Pliny and expressly criticizes Tacitus: "It is seldom indeed that one must rebuke Cornelius Tacitus for a lack of insight" (23 = 928). Tacitus' remark in *Ann.* 3.24, however, does not necessarily mean that he would have adopted a political interpretation of the affair had he, as he intended, gone back to study it more closely.

48. Cf. recently Ferrill (supra n. 43). Which does not mean that Iullus Antonius' offense was not taken seriously by Augustus (see infra). As E. S. Gruen rightly stresses in his comments on a draft of this paper, "one does not engage lightly in adulterous liaisons with a daughter of the *princeps*." See also J. Linderski, "Julia in Regium," *ZPE* 72 (1988) 181–200, esp. 182, n. 2 (with more literature). Iullus' son was exiled (Tac. *Ann.* 4.44, who does not seem to consider this extraordinary).

49. Cf. Syme (1974 [supra n. 40] 24 [= 1984 (supra n. 40) 928]) on Pliny's *consilia parricidae*, "which passes belief"; Lacey (supra n. 42) 137 with n. 60: "a speculation and certainly a later fabrication." For an alternative explanation, see P. M. Swan, review of *Untersuchungen zur Geschichte der Julisch-Claudischen Dynastie*, by E. Meise, *AJP* 92 (1971) 740f.

50. Variations of this view seem to be accepted by most supporters of the conspiracy theory. See, for instance, T. A. Dorey, "Adultery and Propaganda in the Early Roman Empire," *Univ. of Birmingham Hist. Journ.* 8 (1961) 4–6; Levick (supra n. 8) 795–801; Syme

cherished intentions, their authors, once found out, had to be deprived of any possible influence—which was easy because their life-style had made them vulnerable.

Thus we meet here the first occurrence of a phenomenon that is well known from the later history of the Julio-Claudians: power struggles within the imperial family inevitably involved relatives and outside supporters who in case of failure were easily denounced to the outside world—or were perceived by it—as conspirators against the emperor.[51] Augustus, it seems, did not present the case of Julia and her friends in this way, and our better sources knew that; but once this pattern had become familiar, their case may well have been reinterpreted in this light. To some extent, it is a question of definition, when disagreement turns into opposition and scheming into conspiracy.[52] But between this kind of "conspiracy" and, say, that of Murena and Caepio, there is a clear qualitative difference that should not be masked by loose terminology.

The scandal of the younger Julia, the conspiracy of L. Aemilius Paullus, the affair of Plautius Rufus, and the fall of Agrippa Postumus (A.D. 6– 8). Several persons and events seem to be connected in this affair, which offers to the modern scholar a large and possibly insoluble puzzle due to the scarcity and unreliable nature of the extant sources.[53] Augustus' granddaughter, the younger Julia, was exiled in A.D. 8, according to all sources, because of adultery. Her lover, D. Iunius Silanus, was expelled from Augustus' friendship and went into exile.[54] The disgrace and exile of Ovid seems to be tied in with this affair.[55] Julia's husband, L. Aemilius Paullus, of illustrious background and related himself to the emperor's family, was convicted of *maiestas* at a date not specified in

---

(1974 [supra n. 40] 23–26 [= 1984 (supra n. 40) 928–30] and id. [supra n. 4] 426f.). For a different proposal, see Lacey (supra n. 42) 137–41.

51. Cf. Raaflaub (supra n. 3) 9–11, 23f., 40.

52. See Syme (1974: supra n. 40) 24 (= 1984 [supra n. 40] 928).

53. A large part of Dio is lost precisely for the year A.D. 8; the potentially important schol. Juv. 6.158 proves unreliable in its crucial information: cf. recently E. Meise, *Untersuchungen zur Geschichte der Julisch-Claudischen Dynastie* (Munich 1969) 40–42; R. Syme, *History in Ovid* (Oxford 1978) 209; id., *The Augustan Aristocracy* (Oxford 1986) 119f.; contra: e.g., B. Levick, "The Fall of Julia the Younger," *Latomus* 35 (1976) 307–9.

54. Tac. *Ann.* 3.24, 4.71; Suet. *Aug.* 65.2–5, 72.3, 101.3; Schol. Juv. 6.157f. The date is plausibly established on the basis of Tac. *Ann.* 4.71 and the gap in Dio (Syme [1986: supra n. 53] 118). Augustus' unrelenting anger, the destruction of Julia's house, and the stark difference in treatment between her and her lover have been interpreted as indicating more than adultery (cf. Meise [supra n. 53] 39f., 42, 46).

55. Cf. the literature cited by Kienast (supra n. 2) 121, n. 219; 251, n. 310; Levick (supra n. 53) 333f.; Syme (1978: supra n. 53) 215–29. See further infra nn. 118f. with text.

our sources; Suetonius mentions him in his list of conspirators and seems to link him with one Plautius Rufus.[56] This man is often identified with a Publius Rufus who, according to Dio, was accused of being the instigator of hunger riots and other revolutionary activities in A.D. 6, although the real responsibility may have rested with some conspirators in the background.[57] Probably by A.D. 7 Agrippa Postumus, only recently adopted by Augustus, had fallen into disfavor, as all sources agree, because of intolerable *mores,* and was exiled. At an unclear date there was a failed attempt (or at least a plan) to rescue him and Julia (probably the Elder) and bring them "to the armies." [58]

Scholars generally agree that the charges of adultery against Julia and of intolerable character flaws against Agrippa were only pretexts designed to conceal political and conspiratorial involvement of the two. Some leave it at that; others have made elaborate efforts to build one large and coherent scheme out of these scattered pieces.[59] Such constructions, however plausible in themselves, have been damaged by Syme's recent demonstration that Paullus was exiled not executed and that his fall is connected with that of Julia and must be dated to the year 8 as well.[60]

At any rate, most important for our purpose is that this again mostly seems to have been a *Palastrevolution,* a new version, or even continuation, of the struggle between factions in Augustus' family and entourage for influence and control over the succession and all that was connected with it.[61] To repeat, if this is correctly labeled "opposition," it is of an entirely different nature and ought to be distinguished sharply from those forms of opposition that are found in some of the other conspiracies.[62]

56. Suet. *Aug.* 19.1 (cited supra in part A); schol. Juv. 6.157f.: [*Iulia*] *quae nupta Aemilio Paullo, cum is maiestatis crimine periisset . . . relegata est.* For proposed dates and literature, see Meise (supra n. 53) 36–38; Kienast (supra n. 2) 120, n. 218.

57. Dio 55.27.1–3. For a discussion of the identity of the two Rufi, see Meise (supra n. 53) 46, n. 61.

58. Suet. *Aug.* 19.2, cf. 65.4; Vell. Pat. 2.112.7; Tac. *Ann.* 1.3.4; Dio 55.32.1f.; cf. the literature cited by Kienast (supra n. 2) 120, n. 217.

59. Cf. recently Levick (supra n. 53) 301–39; ead., *Tiberius the Politician* (London 1976) 54–61.

60. Syme (1978: supra n. 53) 206–11; id. (1986: supra n. 53) 115ff., esp. 118–27.

61. On this most seem to agree, whether they interpret the Julia-Paullus affair as a mere eruption of dissatisfaction with Augustus' arrangements after the death of his grandsons (thus, for example, Meise [supra n. 53] 35ff., esp. 44–48; Syme [1978: supra n. 53] 206ff., esp. 210; id. [1986: supra n. 53] 122) or as part of a much broader effort to continue the fight of Julia the Elder and her group to secure succession and power for members and friends of her immediate family (thus, for instance, F. Norwood, "The Riddle of Ovid's *relegatio*", *CP* 58 [1963] 150–63, esp. 153–55; Levick [supra n. 53] 301–39).

62. There is no evidence for generalizations like that by Kienast (supra n. 2) 145 (on all the crises in Augustus' family): "Dabei konnte es gar nicht ausbleiben, dass sich persön-

The evidence of the conspiracies. To what, then, does the evidence regarding the conspiracies against Augustus amount? Having eliminated the cases of Crassus and Gallus, we are left with a few summary references in Dio to a number of unspecified conspirators and with six more widely reported plots undertaken by specific groups or individuals. Two of these involve apparently isolated young noblemen; one of them (Lepidus) probably acted out of a family grudge and the emotions of the civil wars; of the other (Cinna Magnus) we know nothing—if his plot is even authentic. One conspiracy seems to have been the desperate last move of an ambitious upstart who had overplayed his cards (Egnatius Rufus). None of these three men seems to have enjoyed significant support. The scandalous affairs centered around the two Julias, although involving some members of the aristocracy, primarily mirror the ongoing rivalries within the family and entourage of the *princeps;* their objectives were control over power and succession within the dynasty, not the elimination of the *princeps* or the principate. There remains the case of Caepio and Murena, who appear to have attracted some sympathy, if not active support, among their fellow senators. In short, despite all the lists of conspirators and general remarks about frequent plots that we find in our sources, there is specific evidence for only one potentially serious conspiracy that could possibly be interpreted as indicative of widespread dissatisfaction and opposition among Rome's leading class—and even that evidence is thin and full of problems.

This, at least, is what our sources reveal. It is of course possible that they mislead us and that what we see is only the tip of an iceberg. But we have to work with what we have. For a regime that stretched over nearly half a century and brought about such fundamental changes, the evidence for conspiracies is extremely limited. No comparison is possible with the bloody reigns of Tiberius, Claudius, Nero, and Domitian.[63] Moreover, whether due to extraordinary vigilance and luck on the part of the intended victims[64] or to lack of cause and support, there is not the slightest indication of any large conspiracy of the scale that brought Caesar or Caligula down or was broken up by Nero in 65. Finally, all the plots originating outside of the center of power itself are concentrated roughly in the first twelve or fifteen years of the princi-

---

liche Motive mit einer grundsätzlichen Opposition mischten und dass umgekehrt eine stets vorhandene Opposition sich den persönlichen Ehrgeiz einzelner Angehöriger der *domus Augusta* für ihre Pläne dienstbar machte."

63. One might be tempted to attribute this to the different source situation: had Tacitus implemented his plan to write about Augustus (*Ann.* 3.24), things might look different. Not necessarily, if Suetonius is any indication! See also supra nn. 47 and 45.

64. Thus Suet. *Aug.* 19.1.

pate.[65] Afterwards, with two dubious exceptions, plots seem to have originated within the imperial family and entourage.[66]

Now it is obvious that "opposition" cannot be measured merely by the number and size of conspiracies. There must be, and there certainly are, other indications of resistance among the upper classes. The senate's relationship to Augustus has been studied carefully by various scholars.[67] It suffices to discuss a few aspects of that relationship.

C. RESISTANCE IN THE SENATE

Resistance in the senate seems to have arisen mainly in three contexts: against the "purges" of the senate, against the assumption of extraordinary offices by Augustus himself or his associates, and against legislation that negatively affected social or financial privileges of the senators.

To begin with the first, the purges of the senate were officially justified with the need to reduce the vastly inflated senate to a manageable size and to get rid of "unworthy elements." For both there certainly was reason enough. Modern scholars have often taken these official justifications as covers for the "real" purpose of eliminating political opponents.[68] The charge is probably correct to some extent. But since we do not have the records,[69] it is hard to verify, and the impact of the measure is impossible to assess with any certainty. At any rate, if it had significantly affected the upper echelons of the senate (whence any dangerous opposition was to be expected), we would probably know. That we find not a single reference to this political purpose in our sources (which certainly are not all friendly toward the first *princeps*) ought to make us

65. 30 (Lepidus)–19 (Egnatius) or 16/13 (if the case of Cinna Magnus is authentic).

66. Including the efforts by two lowly persons to free Julia and Agrippa Postumus (Suet. *Aug.* 19.2). Dio's references to the punishment of several conspirators in 9 B.C. (55.4.3: supra n. 8 and at n. 38) and in connection with the Publius Rufus affair in A.D. 6 (55.27.1–3: supra at n. 57) are too vague to make much of it.

67. Cf. esp. Sattler (supra n. 13); Syme (supra n. 4) chaps. 22–33; Kienast (supra n. 2) 126–51 with literature; A. Bergener, *Die führende Senatorenschicht im frühen Prinzipat: 14–68 n.Chr.* (Bonn 1965) 6–12; P. A. Brunt, "The Role of the Senate in the Augustan Regime," *CQ* n. s. 34 (1984) 423–44.

68. Cf. Aug. *RG* 8.2: *senatum ter legi* (the "laconic brevity" of this note has been interpreted as indicative of bad memories: Sattler [supra n. 13] 12); Vell. Pat. 2.89.4: *senatus sine asperitate nec sine severitate lectus;* Suet. *Aug.* 35.1 (mentions the *lectiones* of 29 and 18 in inverse order and gives the official reasons); Dio 52.42 (on 29 B.C.: cf. Sattler [supra] 31–34), 54.13–14 (on 18 B.C.: Sattler 95–99), 54.26.3–9 (on 13 B.C.), 54.35.1 (on 11 B.C.), 55.13.3 (on A.D. 4); cf. A. H. M. Jones, *Studies in Roman Government and Law* (London 1960) 21–26. Political reasons are suspected by, for example, Syme (supra n. 4) 349f.; Sattler (supra) 32f., 95–99; Kienast (supra n. 2) 128f., 134; M. A. Levi, *Augusto e il suo tempo* (Milan 1986) 259f., 287f.: "[The *lectio* of 18 B.C.] era una proscrizione incruenta, e con essa un nuovo colpo alla vecchia *nobilitas.*"

69. The few persons named in Dio are not known otherwise; cf. Sattler (as cited in the previous note).

cautious.[70] Understandably, however, these purges were unpopular among the potential victims, particularly in 18 B.C., when Augustus planned to eliminate no fewer than five hundred of the roughly eight hundred senators who had survived the earlier *lectio*. That was the year in which Agrippa was given the same powers as Augustus; emotions were running high anyway, and the announcement of a purge on such a large scale might very well have provoked threats of violence and fear of conspiracies.[71]

Second, extraordinary powers. Augustus proudly asserts in his *Res Gestae* (5f.) that he never accepted such powers. There was good reason. Caesar's last years and the triumviral period lingered as a bad memory, and in his efforts to gain acceptance for his new order Augustus had distanced himself from the former and condemned the latter as fraught with illegality.[72] Messalla Corvinus' early resignation from the newly created and powerful office of urban prefect in 26 was explained with the fact that the office was *incivilis*, incompatible with the rights of Roman citizens,[73] and may have been prompted by widespread resistance among the senators. Such resistance is attested for the plan, tumultuously supported by the urban masses, to endow Augustus with a dictatorship in 22; it may have been a factor in other instances too.[74]

Third, legislation. Two examples come to mind. Augustus' legislation on marriage and morals certainly was unpopular, particularly among the senators and *equites*, for whom it was primarily designed.[75] Such resistance even may have forced the *princeps* to withdraw an

70. Cf. the excellent review of the first *lectio* by Sattler (supra n. 13) 31–34. Dio 52.42.8 speaks rather against a massive political purge in 29. Contra: Syme (supra n. 4) 349f. Political motives are also completely absent in Maecenas' advice concerning this matter in Dio 52.19.1–3. By contrast, Sattler's discussion (supra) 95–99 of the procedures in the *lectio* of 18 B.C., which he considers politically manipulated throughout, appears unnecessarily one-sided. The evidence (e.g., Labeo's nomination of Lepidus, the disgraced triumvir: Dio 54.15.4–8) allows various interpretations.

71. Suet. *Aug.* 35.1; Dio 54.12–15. Suetonius links Augustus' fear of violence to the purge; Sattler (supra n. 13) 94f. follows Dio in connecting it with Agrippa's elevation: cf. supra n. 12. For a recent discussion of the date of the "breastplate episode" (18 and not, as is frequently proposed, 29 B.C.), see H. Tränkle, "Zu Cremutius Cordus fr. 4 Peter," *MusHelv* 37 (1980) 231–41 with literature.

72. Cf. Syme (supra n. 4) 307, 317f.; Sattler (supra n. 13) 35.

73. Cf. Sattler (supra n. 13) 59–61 with sources; Kienast (supra n. 2) 85 with literature in n. 69. Contra: Syme (supra n. 4) 403.

74. For discussion of this and other instances of extraordinary powers, see Sattler, (supra n. 13) 72–82, 87–93. One would expect resistance against the designation and extraordinary promotion of successors; except for the case of Marcellus (cf. Dio 53.31.1) such is not attested; cf. Syme (supra n. 4) 341–43; Kienast (supra n. 2) 87.

75. Cf. Syme (supra n. 4) 442–45; Kienast (supra n. 2) 137–39 with literature, 147, 230, n. 231; further, K. Galinsky, "Augustus' Legislation on Morals and Marriage," *Philologus* 125 (1981) 126–44; L. F. Raditsa, "Augustus' Legislation Concerning Marriage, Procreation, Love Affairs and Adultery," *ANRW* 2.13 (1980) 278–339.

early attempt at moral legislation in 28 B.C., and it may have contributed to the massive opposition he encountered on the part of the senate in 18.[76] Equally resented were the taxes imposed on all Roman citizens in A.D. 6 for the purpose of supporting the newly created military fund (*aerarium militare*). Opposition to the 5-percent inheritance tax was so strong among the senators that Augustus seriously considered alternative proposals; he prevailed only when these proved even less attractive.[77]

These are the only issues for which our sources explicitly attest strong senatorial resistance that occasionally forced Augustus to reconsider or compromise. No doubt there were others for which our evidence fails us. As it is, however, we have to conclude that the senators offered determined and open collective opposition only when the *princeps* interfered with their traditional privileges and immediate social and economic interests.

Naturally, dissatisfaction and criticism were expressed in other ways and quarters as well, as they had always been. The courts occasionally seem to have served as outlets for opposition on the part of those who did not dare to express their dissatisfaction openly and were thus limited to oblique forms of protest such as the secret ballot.[78] The masses did not hide their feelings. If there were floods, fires, food shortages, or other disturbances, demonstrations occurred, posters and graffiti appeared, and rumors of unrest or impending revolution pervaded the city.[79] There might even be calls, equally unwelcome to the *princeps*, to give him extraordinary powers to cope with the problems.[80] Criticism, or what was taken as such, was expressed, wittily or bluntly, at dinners, parties, and other social gatherings, and in the streets, markets, and parks, and was wisely ignored by the *princeps* whenever possible.[81] And there were the "intellectuals." They deserve a closer look.

76. 28 B.C.: cf. the literature cited by Kienast (supra n. 2) 139, n. 55; 234, n. 245; contra: E. Badian, "A Phantom Marriage Law," *Philologus* 129 (1985) 82–98. 18 B.C.: Syme (supra n. 4) 444.
77. Dio 55.25.4–6; 56.28.4–6; cf. Kienast (supra n. 2) 334–36 and, for the *aerarium militare*, the literature cited in 334, n. 92.
78. Suggestion by P. M. Swan. The trial of Caepio and Murena (supra at nn.34f.) provides a good example.
79. Thus in A.D. 6 (Dio 55.27.1–3) and the years after 23 B.C.: Kienast (supra n. 2) 92–94. Cf. Yavetz (supra n. 37) chaps. 2 and 5; and, e.g., T. Bollinger, *Theatralis licentia: Die Publikumsdemonstrationen an den öffentlichen Spielen im Rom der früheren Kaiserzeit und ihre Bedeutung im politischen Leben* (Winterthur 1969); R. Gilbert, *Die Beziehungen zwischen Princeps und stadtrömischer Plebs im frühen Principat* (Bochum 1976).
80. Cf. Sattler (supra n. 13) 72–81.
81. Cf. Syme (supra n. 4) 481. The material is collected (though for the entire first century A.C.) by G. Boissier, *L'opposition sous les Césars*[2] (Paris 1885).

II. Intellectual Opposition

Augustus had his detractors among the intellectuals of Rome—poets, orators, historians—some of whom found it difficult not to draw sharp distinctions between the Republic and Augustus' *res publica restituta*. Scholars have focused on the "republican" nature of such intellectual opposition and postulated a "republican camp" of intellectuals, including Asinius Pollio as the champion of *libertas,* opposed to the new regime and decidedly, if less than openly, non-Augustan.[82] Lacking a precise term for "republicanism," they are said to have massed under the name Pompeiani, by which title even Augustus recognized them.[83]

Who could doubt the existence of such a group? Were evidence lacking for its activity, one might justly infer its presence in the early principate. Yet upon close inspection most of the evidence for an "intellectual opposition" proves to be nothing of the sort. Indeed, the assumption that such an opposition *must* have existed has only led scholars to press the evidence and obscure the historical picture of opposition under Augustus. They have generally failed to emphasize the paucity of such evidence, preferring to concentrate on the same few and ambiguous cases, often focusing on the intricate legal questions with little general application.

Some measure of opposition, or at least reservation, among the Augustan poets is now widely recognized.[84] The poets, even those patronized by Maecenas, were not simply sycophants afraid to cast the slightest aspersion on the *princeps* and his "new age." However, as men of letters and not of affairs, the poets comprise a special group, and they

---

82. That Pollio was an active part of this group has been widely held. Cf. esp. Syme ([supra n. 4] vii, 166, 291, 320, 476–89, esp. 483–84; [1958: supra n. 40] 136, 138, 140; "Livy and Augustus," *HSCP* 64 [1959] 27–87 [= *Roman Papers,* vol. 1 (Oxford 1979) 400–54]) who, however, often sees him as the republican champion of *libertas,* the anti-Augustan adherent to neither party; see also E. W. Mendell, "The Epic of Asinius Pollio," *YCS* 1 (1928) 201–3; and E. Kornemann, "Die historische Schriftstellerei des C. Asinius Pollio," *Jahrb. für class. Philologie und Pädagogik* 22 Suppl. (1896) 590–600.

83. Tac. *Ann.* 4.34; Sen. Rhet. *Controv.* 10 *praef.* 5; Syme (supra n. 4) 464 and n. 2; id. (1958: supra n. 40) 140; and esp. id., "The Allegiance of Labienus," *JRS* 28 (1938) 125 (= id. [1979: supra n. 82] 75), where he describes both Livy and Augustus as Pompeians, "sham ones."

84. Cf. recently, for example, C. R. Phillips, "Rethinking Augustan Poetry," *Latomus* 42 (1983) 780–817; D. Little, "Politics in Augustan Poetry," *ANRW* 2.30.1 (1982) 254–370; E. Doblhofer, "Horaz und Augustus," *ANRW* 2.31.3 (1981) 1922–86; J. Griffin, "Augustus and the Poets: 'Caesar qui cogere posset,'" in Millar and Segal (supra n. 27) 189–218; F. Ahl, "The Rider and the Horse: Politics and Power in Roman Poetry from Horace to Statius," *ANRW* 2.32.1 (1984) 40–110; various contributions in T. Woodman and D. West, eds., *Poetry and Politics in the Age of Augustus* (Cambridge 1984); and, for a summary, Kienast (supra n. 2) 226–53. See also the contributions of M. C. J. Putnam and S. G. Nugent to the present volume.

will not concern us here.[85] We shall treat those men who constituted both an intellectual *and* political force in the Augustan Age—that is, the orators and historians.

That the orators were politically active and interested individuals needs no demonstration. However, the occupation of the historian was also a political one, and in fact, many eminent orators also wrote history; for unlike the Greek historians who customarily were professional men of letters, the Romans felt that only men who had participated in great deeds were capable and qualified to write about them. This tradition of "active historiography"[86] continued into the first century B.C., in which Sallust and Pollio perhaps best typified the statesman-historian. Consequently, Roman history was always the history of the ruling class, and Roman historiography as a literary genre was by its very nature *republican*.[87] Leading men of the Republic wrote accounts of the state that they governed. For them the forces that drove history were recorded in the *fasti* and the *annales maximi*—magistracies filled each year by a different set of Roman *nobiles* and providing the state with continuity and stability. Thus a change in the form of government and the emergence of a new center of power would necessarily create tensions in historiography. Sallust and others reflect the tendency to personalize history as predominance by a few *principes* became prevalent. By the time Tacitus composed his *Annales,* the annalistic format only superficially concealed the true organizing principle of his work: continuity in Roman government now depended on one individual, the *princeps.* The *res gestae populi Romani* had become the *res gestae imperatorum Romanorum*. Republican history was dead.

Under Augustus it was only moribund.[88] Appropriately enough, the age opened with Livy's composition of an account of the republic[89] and

---

85. Cornelius Gallus is an obvious exception: see supra at nn. 19–28. For his poetry, see the new fragment published in 1979 (R. D. Anderson, P. J. Parsons, R. G. M. Nisbet, "Elegiacs by Gallus from Qasr Ibrîm," *JRS* 69, 125–55). Discussion of this fragment has been vast; it is listed in *L'année philologique* since vol. 51 (1980).

86. I.e., history written by statesmen, participants in the political sphere. Polybius maintains that such men were best suited to write history (12.28.2–5). Cf. C. W. Fornara, *The Nature of History in Greece and Rome* (Berkeley and Los Angeles 1983) 49–55, esp. 54: "The requirement for writing the 'deeds of the Roman people' was *auctoritas*, the authority of offices held, of armies commanded."

87. B. W. Frier, *Libri Annales Pontificum Maximorum: The Origins of the Annalistic Tradition*, PAAR 27 (Rome 1979) esp. 205.

88. See, in contrast to Tac. *Hist.* 1.1 (*magna illa ingenia cessere*), *Ann.* 1.1 (*temporibusque Augusti dicendis non defuere decora ingenia, donec gliscente adulatione deterrerentur*).

89. Thus Livy has often been seen as the last of the republican historians; cf., for example, Syme, *Sallust* (Berkeley 1964) 289; E. Norden, *Die antike Kunstprosa*⁵, vol. 1 (Darmstadt 1958) 234–37.

closed with the publication of his final, one might say, imperial books.[90] Under Tiberius we have Velleius Paterculus' history—proof enough for any doubter that republican history had breathed its last.[91] During Augustus' reign, the tension created by the constraints of the prevalent genre of Roman—that is, republican—history must have increased rapidly. When Cremutius Cordus' history praised Brutus and called Cassius the last of the Romans, it was one of the last attempts to write history as it had traditionally been understood. Thus the expression of republican sentiments in histories of the Augustan Age need not be interpreted as attacks on Augustus himself,[92] but as indications of the historical contradiction that the principate presented for historians. The imprint of the principate on historiography was only gradually sufficient to change the nature of the genre.

Several factors, therefore, contributed to the highly political nature of the genre of historiography: its close relation to oratory, the intimate connection of both with republican and senatorial traditions, and the social prominence of most historians. That Pollio, rather than Livy, represented the typical Roman historian a priori put history in a special and, to some extent, protected position: Augustus, as *restitutor rei publicae*, would not be quick to trifle with the senatorial class.

Unfortunately, the desolate state of our extant sources does not permit detailed analysis of the effects of those tensions on historiography during the Augustan Age. Upon review one finds the list of Augustan historians littered with names that today are only that, names. Little of substance can be said, for example, about the work of T. Ampius Balbus, or of some of the others listed by Peter.[93] Many are all but lost. The categorization of these writers as "republican" or "Augustan" is extremely speculative and of questionable value; for, as we hope to show, the terms are not mutually exclusive.

Such a "republican" categorization may have been most harmful in the case of Asinius Pollio. A. B. Bosworth's article, however, has corrected the previous orthodoxy, for he firmly establishes Pollio's relation-

---

90. Frier (supra n. 87) 202–5; A. J. Woodman, *Velleius Paterculus: The Tiberian Narrative: 2.94–131*, Cambr. Class. Texts and Comm. 19 (Cambridge 1977) 37; cf. Syme (supra n. 82) 62–76; and infra n. 121.

91. See Woodman (supra n. 90) 30–56; C. Kuntze, *Zur Darstellung des Kaisers Tiberius und seiner Zeit bei Velleius Paterculus* (Frankfurt 1985).

92. Syme (supra n. 4) 317. On Cremutius, see Tac. *Ann.* 4.34f. and the discussion infra at nn. 105f. As is well known, even Augustus could resuscitate Pompey at the expense of Caesar (see infra at n. 120) and cover himself with "Catonism"; see L. R. Taylor, *Party Politics in the Age of Caesar* (Berkeley and Los Angeles 1949) 162–82.

93. Peter, *HRRel* II, LXXI–CXXIII.

ship as an *amicus* to Augustus.[94] Certainly Pollio, and probably others among Augustus' *amici*, fostered independence and, to some extent, republican sentiments. But that does not make him part of any supposedly "archrepublican" opposition group. He disagreed with the *princeps* on certain issues and dared to speak his mind, but he was not perpetually at odds with Augustus and his partisans, and thus out of favor with the *princeps*. That Pollio's fame as an historian of the Augustan Age today stands second only to Livy's is an amazing fact, considering the dearth of fragments from his histories (Peter, *HRRel* II, 67–70). Obviously Pollio the politician/statesman to some degree has been confused with Pollio the historian; for although he was certainly an eminent and important personage of his age, his worth as an historian is virtually indiscernible to moderns,[95] and there is little to be gained from tenuous speculation about Appian's use of Pollio as a source.[96]

With Pollio removed from the vanguard of the opposition, we must now examine the core of the so-called intellectual *Widerstand* to Augustus. Sadly, their works are as fragmentary as Pollio's. Titus Labienus exists only in a brief *testimonium* in Peter's collection (*HRRel* II, C–CI) with not a single quotation preserved. The fragments of Cremutius Cordus comprise a few pages (*HRRel* II, 87–90) but shed little light on the author's assessment of Augustus. Cassius Severus fails to appear at all in Peter, simply because there is nothing we can gather about his writings. It is unfortunate that we know more about these individuals' personalities and reputations as *oratores* than about the substance of their histories and their political persuasion.[97]

Titus Labienus was a man known for speaking his mind (Sen. Rhet. *Controv.* 10 *praef.* 4–5, 8). The reputation for genius he achieved with his invective style of oratory engendered also a great deal of hatred (*summum odium*). "His freedom of speech was so great that it passed the bounds of freedom, and because he savaged all ranks and men alike, he was nicknamed 'Rabienus.'" Moreover, he had refused to give up his republican sentiments (*Pompeiani spiritus*, 5). The elder Seneca relates

94. A. B. Bosworth, "Asinius Pollio and Augustus," *Historia* 21 (1972) 441–73 passim and esp. 441–52. Cf. also B. Haller, C. *Asinius Pollio als Politiker und zeitkritischer Historiker: Ein Beitrag zur Geschichte des Übergangs von der Republik zum Prinzipat in Rom, 60–30 v. Chr.* (Diss. Münster 1967). For the traditional assessment, see supra n. 82.

95. Fornara (supra n. 86) 75: "It is impossible to say whether he [Pollio] is the last of the republican writers or the first of the new age; in truth, he seems to be neither."

96. As in E. Gabba, *Appiano e la storia delle guerre civili* (Florence 1956) esp. 79–88 and 229–49. For literature on this issue, see Kienast (supra n. 2) 221, n. 204.

97. Labienus: infra in the text. Cassius Severus: Tac. Ann. 1.72, 4.21, *Dial.* 19, 26; Macrob. *Sat.* 2.4.9; Sen. Rhet. *Controv.* 3 *praef.*; Pliny HN 7.55; Jerome *Chron.* 2048; Quint. *Inst.* 10.1.116, 12.10.11, etc. Cremutius Cordus: Sen. *Ad Marc.* 1.3, 22.4, 26.1; Quint. *Inst.* 10.1.104; Tac. *Ann.* 4.34f.; Dio 57.24.

that Labienus once chose not to read aloud some parts of his history, saying that they would be read after his death. "How great must have been their outspokenness (*libertas*) if even Labienus was frightened of it" (*extimuit*, 8). Seneca's comment is perhaps telling, for it implies that Labienus acted out of some measure of fear. This, taken together with his *spiritus Pompeiani,* could lead one to conclude that his history was critical of Augustus or his regime and that Labienus, although the first man to undergo punishment for his writings (5), already felt that it was possibly dangerous to compose histories too critical of the regime and its adherents. One may not assume that Labienus chose to omit inflammatory sections merely to avoid stepping on toes, for Seneca states that he attacked all ranks (*passim ordines hominesque laniabat*, 5)—thus he must have nourished a special concern about these sections of his history.

It would clarify things if Seneca had gone on to say that it was Augustus who took action against Labienus for his radical writings. Yet this is not the case. Seneca explicitly reports that Labienus' books were burned at the initiative of his enemies (*per inimicos*) and by senate decree (*senatus consulto*, 5, 8). Moreover, the assumption that Augustus not only tolerated and supported but even initiated this action is rendered unlikely by another statement of Seneca's on the emperor's policy in such matters.[98] In *Controv.* 2.4.13 he relates that freedom of speech (*libertas*) was so great under Augustus that there was no lack of critics of Marcus Agrippa's low birth, although Agrippa was *praepotens* at that time. In fact, writes Seneca, "the deified Augustus deserves admiration if such license was permitted in his reign!"

The date of the proscription of Labienus' works is uncertain. Conveniently for those who wish to make this an example of what they see as Augustus' increasing censorship in the latter, "oppressive" part of his reign, the event seems to fall between A.D. 8 and 12 and thus to follow upon a series of crises and disturbances in Rome and the empire.[99] But the argument tends to be circular here, for our sources fail to make any

98. See Syme (supra n. 4) 486f. and (supra n. 82) 72 (although originally taking a different view: [supra n. 83] 113); F. H. Cramer, "Bookburning and Censorship in Ancient Rome: A Chapter from the History of Freedom of Speech," *JHI* 6 (1945) 169–73.

99. E.g., the Pannonian revolt, famine in Rome, Agrippa's relegation, the conspiracy of the younger Julia and Paullus, Ovid's exile (see Dio 55.26–27.4; Suet. *Aug.* 65.1). The dating is common; see M. Schanz and C. Hosius, *Geschichte der römischen Literatur*[2], vol. 2 (Munich 1935) 345. Syme initially was cautious ([supra n.4] 486: "the last years of Augustus") but later argued for A.D. 8 ([1986: supra n. 53] 363f., 410–12), following R. A. Bauman, *Impietas in Principem* (Munich 1974) 28–31; see also D. Hennig, "T. Labienus und der erste Majestätsprozess *de famosis libellis*," *Chiron* 3 (1973) 254 on the date and 245–54 for the nature of the trial. Hennig's work is useful, although it cannot overcome the failure of Tacitus and Seneca to treat Labienus' case as a *Majestätsprozess*.

such connection, and the date alone cannot make up for the lack of evidence that it was primarily Augustus who wished Labienus' history burned. Of course, the senate must have known that its action would not meet Augustus' disapproval, but we have no reason to doubt Seneca's explicit report that Labienus' style had made him many enemies and that the senate thus was willing *sua sponte* to take action against him.[100]

Another author whose works were put to the flame was Cassius Severus. We cannot say whether or not his *scripta* (Suet. *Calig.* 16) included history; he was undoubtedly primarily an orator, delivering brilliant but highly caustic speeches.[101] The proscription of his writings has been linked to that of Labienus' by the apparent similarity of circumstances and, possibly, date (A.D. 8–12).[102] But in Severus' case we have the testimony of Tacitus that the emperor Augustus himself was provoked (*commotus*) by the *libido* of Severus, because "he had defamed distinguished men and women with brash writings" (*Ann.* 1.72). By his "unrestrained hostilities" (*per immodicas inimicitias*) he made many enemies and compelled the senate to banish him to Crete; later he died in exile on Seriphus (4.21). While Augustus clearly initiated Severus' punishment for his libelous writings, there is no evidence that the emperor himself or his family were the object of Cassius' criticism or that these *scripta* were politically inflammatory or unacceptably republican.[103] Thus one has to conclude that it was indeed Severus' slanders of illustrious men and women of Rome that provoked Augustus into action and compelled the senate to go along with him.[104]

---

100. The senate, however, could be fickle and capricious: the books of the (unnamed) sponsor of the *senatus consultum* proscribing Labienus' work were burned in turn (Sen. Rhet. *Controv.* 10 *praef.* 7); see C. A. Forbes, "Books for the Burning," *TAPA* 67 (1936) 114–25, esp. 122f.

101. Sen. Rhet. *Controv.* 3 *praef.*; Quint. *Inst.* 10.1.116, 12.10.11; cf. supra n. 97.

102. E.g., Syme (supra n. 4) 486f.; id. (1986: supra n. 53) 410–12. R. A. Bauman, *The Crimen Maiestatis in the Roman Republic and Augustan Principate* (Johannesburg 1967) 257–65, proposes two trials, the first (in A.D. 6) brought by Augustus (Tac. *Ann.* 1.72.4; Dio 55.4.3) in which Severus was acquitted, the second (ca. A.D. 8) resulting in the *senatus consultum* relegating him to Crete. Cramer (supra n. 98) 173 and n. 70 accepts Jerome's dubious testimony (*Chron.* 2048) that Severus died in A.D. 32, i.e., in the twenty-fifth year of his exile, which would then have occurred in A.D. 8. However, whenever we date the proscription of Cassius Severus' writings (A.D. 12 if Dio 56.27 indeed refers to this), Labienus' should have been burned sometime before, since Severus is said to have remarked after Labienus' works were burned that he knew them all by heart anyway (Sen. Rhet. *Controv.* 10 *praef.* 8); cf. Hennig (supra n. 99) 254.

103. *Pace* C. W. Chilton, "The Roman Law of Treason under the Early Principate," *JRS* 45 (1955) 73–81, esp. 73–76.

104. It should be pointed out that there existed a republican tradition of suppressing libel and slander. According to Cic. *Rep.* 4.12, the XII Tables provided the death penalty for the performance or composition of slanderous songs, and this proscription probably later applied to prose as well. Cf. P. R. Coleman-Norton, *The Twelve Tables* (Princeton

The historian Cremutius Cordus was prosecuted for treason in A.D. 25 under Tiberius, specifically for writing a history that praised Brutus and called Cassius the last of the Romans. We know that Cordus composed this work, or one of similar sentiments, during the reign of Augustus and that, in fact, Augustus had been present at a reading of the history.[105] On this point the sources are clear. Cremutius Cordus was free to write his "republican" history under Augustus, but under Tiberius these same writings provoked the charge of treason. Again, the writing of such a history need not imply enmity or opposition to the *princeps;* Augustus' *amici* Messalla Corvinus, Asinius Pollio, and Livy professed similar sentiments in their works.[106] If Cordus was involved in more serious acts of opposition, they have left no historical record. On the other hand, there is reason to believe that the prosecution of A.D. 25 was instigated by Sejanus, who held a personal grudge against Cordus.[107] Whether or not Cordus' speech in his own defense (Tac. *Ann.* 4.34f.) records his actual words taken from the *acta senatus,* it is a unique testimony to the freedom that historians of republican sentiment possessed in the Augustan Age. Tacitus (and his readers) undoubtedly had read their histories; it is highly unlikely, therefore, that his characterization of their work is untrustworthy.

Timagenes of Alexandria, one of the ranking historians of the age,

---

1948) 11, nn. 35–37; C. Wirszubski, *Libertas as a Political Idea at Rome during the Late Republic and Early Principate*[2] (Cambridge 1968) 18f. and n. 2; on possible developments in slander laws during the second century B.C., see OCD[2], 606, s.v. Libel and Slander (G. Williams). However, no example is known in which this severe penalty was applied, and defamatory literature certainly had its place in late republican social and political life. On the other hand, Suetonius (*Aug.* 55) reports that Augustus brought to account those who under false names published defamatory writings, a very un-Roman practice indeed (on Augustus' use of the XII Tables in this context, see Cramer [supra n. 98] 169f., who, however, takes a much different view of Augustus and censorship than is presented here). The ferocity and very personal nature of Labienus' and Severus' slander must have been unusual; they certainly ran counter to contemporary efforts to raise the social eminence and moral prestige of the senatorial and equestrian orders.

105. Suet. *Tib.* 61.3; Dio 57.24; Tac. *Ann.* 4.34f.

106. Tac. *Ann.* 4.34. See Bosworth (supra n. 94) 444 with n. 18. See further E. Rawson, "Cassius and Brutus: The Memory of the Liberators," in I. S. Moxon, J. D. Smart, A. J. Woodman, eds., *Past Perspectives: Studies in Greek and Roman Historical Writing* (Cambridge 1986) 101–19; G. Zecchini, "La morte di Catone e l'opposizione intellettuale a Cesare e ad Augusto," *Athenaeum* 58 (1980) 39–56, esp. 51–56. For a recent discussion of Livy's relationship to Augustus, see J. Deininger, "Livius und der Prinzipat," *Klio* 67 (1985) 265–72.

107. Cf. Sen. *Ad Marc.* 22.4–7; F. B. Marsh, *The Reign of Tiberius* (Oxford 1931) 290–93; R. S. Rogers, *Criminal Trials and Criminal Legislation Under Tiberius* (Middletown, Conn. 1935) 86f.; R. MacMullen, *Enemies of the Roman Order: Treason, Unrest and Alienation in the Empire* (Cambridge, Mass. 1966) 19–21 with literature; D. Hennig, *L. Aelius Seianus: Untersuchungen zur Regierung des Tiberius* (Munich 1975) 55–63.

enjoyed a close relationship with Augustus before his jibes against the emperor and his family and clashes with the academician Kraton forced the *princeps* to expel him from his house. Timagenes found a new home with Pollio and subsequently burned the portions of his histories containing the deeds of Augustus, "as though barring him, in turn, from access to his genius" (Sen. Rhet. *Controv.* 10.5.22). Nevertheless, there is every indication that Augustus endured Timagenes' attacks on himself, his wife, and Rome rather good-naturedly, and took no action to censure the irascible eastern historian. The whole matter seems to have caused no friction between Augustus and Pollio, whose offer to expel the Alexandrian if the emperor so desired was declined.[108]

As an easterner, Timagenes would have been anomalous as a detractor of Augustus and his regime. The tendency of Greek and other eastern historians was to sing the praises of the *princeps*.[109] It is important to remember the essential difference in *Weltanschauung* between these authors and the Romans who wrote during and about the reign of Augustus. The Hellenistic easterners had no republican tradition of nearly five centuries to uphold, no membership in a class that mandated service to the *res publica* and political achievement for the augmentation of power and status. Indeed, for them there was much to be gained from a monarch and very little to be lost. In any event, the treatment of Timagenes' case by Augustus indicates violation of *amicitia*, not serious political opposition to the regime.

Augustus did stop publication of the official minutes of the senate, which had only begun in the first consulate of Julius Caesar. The reasons are unclear.[110] In general, senators seem to have possessed a great measure of freedom in addressing the emperor and their colleagues in the *curia*, even those of as independent a mind as M. Antistius Labeo. Labeo's father had met his end under Brutus. His own failure to achieve the consulship resulted either from his refusal of the office or from a slight by Augustus. But Labeo was more a republican relic, an antiquar-

---

108. Cf. Sen. *Ira* 3.23.4–8, *Ep.* 91.13; Sen. Rhet. *Controv.* 10.5.22; Suda, s.v. "Timagenes." On his rank as a historian, Quint. *Inst.* 10.1.75. Cf. Cramer (supra n. 98) 165–67; and G. W. Bowersock, *Augustus and the Greek World* (Oxford 1965) 109f., 125.

109. Cf., for example, Strab. 6.4.2, the extremely laudatory *Bios Kaisaros* of Nicolaus of Damascus (cf. B. Z. Wacholder, *Nicolaus of Damascus* [Berkeley and Los Angeles 1962]; G. Dobesch, "Nikolaos von Damaskus und die Selbstbiographie des Augustus," *GrazBeitr* 7 [1978] 91–174), and Dionysius of Halicarnassus (cf., among others, E. Gabba, "The Historians and Augustus," in Millar and Segal [supra n. 27] 64–67).

110. Suet. *Jul.* 20, *Aug.* 36, 54. Cramer (supra n. 98) 161f. sees this as an attempt to bar publication of the antimonarchic outbursts that the emperor was compelled to endure in the senate; others see this act as favorable to the senate: e.g., Kienast (supra n. 2) 141.

ian fascinated by the origin of Latin words and given to caustic witticisms than an active opponent of the regime. He might embarrass the
emperor by nominating M. Lepidus for a senate seat in the purge of 18
B.C. and thereby assert his right to his own opinion, yet, as Suetonius
here reports, "Augustus never punished anyone for showing independence of mind on such occasions, or even behaving insolently." [111]

There is ample documentation of political and intellectual opposition
under Augustus' successors and of the increasing amount of censorship
that accompanied such opposition, especially in the form of *maiestas*
trials.[112] Thus it is all the more noteworthy that Augustus never undertook such a program of censorship and applied the *lex maiestatis* to
writings only in the case of the slanders of Cassius Severus. This is the
impression we are given by Tacitus. True, he contrasts this action with
the previous situation when "action had been taken against deeds,
words went unpunished" (*facta arguebantur, dicta impune erant*), and
he emphasizes that this case set a precedent that Tiberius and later emperors employed to abuse the law of *maiestas*. But he does not indicate
that Augustus frequently or even ever again invoked this law.[113] Although neither Augustus nor the senate was loath to enforce slander/
libel laws, there obviously was no need for politically repressive measures.

Suetonius emphasizes Augustus' clemency and tolerance. To this effect, he states that instead of listing all the opponents whom Augustus
pardoned, spared, or allowed to hold government positions, it would
suffice to say that Augustus considered it enough to punish two plebeians, one with a fine and the other with a light banishment, for their
slanders. The point of this passage is that Augustus was not given to
actions of this type. Of course, Suetonius was comparing Augustus to
his less tolerant successors. But he presents a consistent picture of a
princeps who was accustomed not to censuring but to pardoning. Such
an attitude, it seems, would have been unusual for a regime embattled
by opposition.[114]

111. Father: App. *BCiv.* 135; consulship: Tac. *Ann.* 3.75; Pompon. *Dig.* 1.2.2.47. Antiquarianism: Gell. *NA* 13.10.1–3; witticism: Dio 54.15.7–8; Porph. *ad* Hor. *Sat.* 1.3.82;
Lepidus: Suet. *Aug.* 54.
112. See the recent volume *Opposition et résistances à l'empire d'Auguste à Trajan*
(supra n.3) with various contributions and the literature listed there (46–55).
113. Tac. *Ann.* 1.72, though some would have the *lex maiestatis* as Augustus' tool of
preference in his alleged attempts at political censorship: e.g., Cramer (supra n. 98) 169–
71; cf. Hennig (supra n. 99) passim.
114. Of course, one might suggest that to be known for pardoning, there must be
crimes to pardon. Admittedly so. And yet we can little doubt that if those pardoned had

In fact, none of our sources relates that Augustus generally increased political or moral censorship in the later years of his reign by actions that might have indicated substantial intellectual or political opposition in that time. Dio's reference to censorship is short and cursory (56.27.1) and certainly does not imply that there was a drastic change in the emperor's policy. Perhaps there were other cases—if so, even the sources hostile to Augustus fail to recount them.[115] Nor can it be maintained that the *princeps* promoted censorship in response to state crises such as the famine or the Pannonian revolt of A.D. 6. Neither Suetonius nor Dio indicate in any way that Augustus reacted to such emergencies in this fashion.[116]

Severus, two plebeians, and Ovid: hardly sufficient warrant for Syme's description of "stern measures of repression against noxious literature" and "public bonfires."[117] And so finally we turn to Ovid; ultimately the case for increased censorship in the later years of Augustus' reign revolves, to a great degree, around the *relegatio* of this poet. It is curious to note that none of our sources except Ovid himself mentioned his exile.[118] But Ovid's banishment could scarcely have been indicative of a concerted policy on the part of Augustus to repress freedom of

---

constituted direct and significant threats (intellectual or otherwise) to the regime, at least their names would be known to us. Instead we have a short list of marginal cases. Plebeians: Suet. *Aug.* 51, cf. 55f. (two important chapters), esp. 56.1: *iocis quoque quorundam invidiosis aut petulantibus lacessitus contra dixit edicto. et tamen ne de inhibenda testamentorum licentia quicquam constitueretur intercessit.* Thus the proposal originated among the senators. As for the two plebeians, it should be remembered that Romans of the lower class never enjoyed the same freedom of speech exercised by the *nobiles* and that, in general, members of the upper order used libel and slander laws to protect themselves against members of the lower, and not against one another. This is a complex problem, but for a lucid and brief discussion, see G. Williams (supra n. 104) and A. Momigliano, "Review and Discussion: Robinson's *Freedom of Speech in the Roman Republic,*" *JRS* 32 (1942) 120–24.

115. See Cramer (supra n. 98) for a lengthier treatment of alleged cases of the suppression of free speech and censorship under Augustus, giving more emphasis to cases such as those of Suet. *Aug.* 36 and 51. Again, definitions and categories are important—e.g., is "opposition" appropriate in the case of a certain professor Corvus, who in public lecture discussed the merits of a debate on child rearing by married women (while Augustus adamantly discouraged celibacy and birth control), thus incurring a legal suit (Sen. Rhet. *Suas.* 2.21)?

116. Suet. *Aug.* 42.3; Dio 55.27; *pace* Cramer (supra n. 98) 168f.; see supra n. 99. Equally, the burning of unauthorized prophecies in 12 B.C., after Augustus took over the office of *pontifex maximus* (Suet. *Aug.* 31.1 [supra n. 2]), clearly must be seen as an effort to establish order in a chaotic situation, and thus as part of his religious duties; see Forbes (supra n. 100) 119; contra: Cramer (supra n. 98) 167f.

117. Syme (supra n. 4) 486 and (supra n. 82) 72.

118. Ov. *Tr.* 1.7.15–30, 2.345–61, 5.7.65–68; *Pont.* 2.9.71–80, 4.6.9–16; for references to Ovid but not to his exile, see, for example, Sen. Rhet. *Controv.* 2.2.12; Quint. *Inst.* 10.1.98.

speech and never have found its way into the extant sources. Modern scholarship is guilty of interpreting this event in a way the ancient authors never did.[119] We can only infer that the exile of Ovid was a singular event, and one of little import to ancient observers of the period; it gained significance only in modern times as evidence of Augustus' attempt to control Roman authors. The conclusion is inescapable and supported by the sources at all points: the cases of "censorship" listed above are rare exceptions in Augustus' reign. Although they are concentrated in its last phase, they represent isolated incidents and provide no sufficient foundation for a theory of heightened political censorship in this period.

In conclusion, since the works of Pollio, Labienus, Severus, and Cordus hardly constituted an intellectual opposition to the regime, the weakness of such opposition is mirrored in the failure of its historical record. The *princeps* was thus at leisure to practice his *clementia,* for he had little reason to institute measures of censorship against an "opposition" with few exponents and little importance. Moreover, how could he claim to have restored the Republic and then repress its laudation? In keeping with his theme of *res publica restituta* he may well have considered it to be in his best interest to foster prorepublican sentiments. Undoubtedly the memory of Pompey was revived at the expense of Caesar's with Augustus' full sanction.[120] Likewise, he was compelled to eschew the appearance of monarchy—legal action against detractors of his person or regime would have had a despotic appearance, especially if they were relatively few in number and politically insignificant. Horace's warning to Pollio early in Augustus' reign concerning his historical treatment of the civil wars can hardly have grown out of actual fear of retribution on the part of the emperor.[121] Such fear would not have led to open discussion of what should or should not be written.

Only an Augustus relatively free from concerns about a powerful and

119. For discussion, see the literature cited supra in n. 55. On Ovid's strategy in his poems from exile (esp. *Tr.* 2), see S. G. Nugent's contribution to the present volume.

120. Syme (supra n. 4) 317: "The tone of literature in the Augustan age is certainly Pompeian rather than Caesarian, just as its avowed ideals are Republican, not absolutist. Seeking to establish a continuity with a legitimate government, Caesar's heir forswore the memory of Caesar . . . [which] meant a certain rehabilitation of the last generation of the Republic, which in politics is the Age of Pompeius."

121. Hor. *Carm.* 2.1; for literature and discussion, see R. G. M. Nisbet and M. Hubbard, *A Commentary on Horace: Odes, Book II* (Oxford 1978) 7–31, esp. 7–9. One might entertain such speculation on retribution based on the heading of Livy *Per.* 121, which reports that Books 121–42 were *said* to have been published after the *princeps'* death (see, for instance, Syme [supra n. 82] 71f.). But even if they were, this does not necessitate that Livy intentionally withheld them out of fear of the emperor's reaction. Certainly Tiberius would not have welcomed a hostile treatment of his father's reign. That young Claudius

concerted intellectual opposition could advise Tiberius to endure personal criticism and even slander: "My dear Tiberius, you must not . . .
take it to heart if anyone speaks ill of me; let us be satisfied if we can
achieve it that nobody is able to *do* us any harm" (*satis est enim, si hoc
habemus ne quis nobis male facere possit,* Suet. *Aug.* 51.3).

III. Conclusion and Explanation

What emerges from our investigation is a clear and consistent picture.
There certainly was opposition and resistance to Augustus' regime, and
it was expressed in various forms and intensities, from riots in the
streets through criticism in oratory and literature to conspiracies of individuals and groups. Occasionally the senate, although generally willing to cooperate, refused to ratify Augustus' initiatives, and the secret
ballot in the courts offered an opportunity for silent defiance. In the first
fifteen years after Actium several conspiracies were uncovered and the
culprits punished. Later, Augustus' plans, dynastic and otherwise, provoked resistance and secret schemes in his own family and entourage.
Poets and historians initially were sceptical and focused on the dark
memories of civil strife and dictatorship; later, some were reconciled,
while others remained critical and suspicious. Both groups, no doubt,
expressed sentiments widespread among their contemporaries—and
not only for political reasons. And there were, mostly in the late years,
a few cases of censorship and oppression of outspoken intellectuals.

All this cannot and will not be denied. More importantly, it is not in
the least surprising. After all, Augustus rose to power through violence
and civil wars. In 31 B.C. he and his supporters assumed control over
the entire state. Despite the concessions and adjustments they made in
27 and repeatedly thereafter, power largely remained monopolized in
the hands of the *princeps* and those he trusted. Thus even in the *res
publica restituta* political life was only partially free. This is a truism
and must have been obvious to contemporaries. Later observers, judging on the basis of subsequent developments, were unable to recognize
in Augustus' principate anything but outright monarchy and despotism.[122] Moreover, the principate brought about deep changes in every
aspect of social and political life. Adjustments were necessary on every
level. Not everyone was happy about all the innovations, small and

---

was discouraged from writing, of all subjects, a history of the civil wars after 44 (Suet.
Claud. 41.2) was certainly understandable.
    122. Thus Tacitus in the opening chapters of the *Annals,* and Dio 53.17.

large, that made up the *novus status*. Inevitably, there were misunderstandings, tensions, collisions of interests and expectations, frustration,
anger, bitterness. As a logical consequence, there was defiance and resistance, even in stubborn and violent forms.

All this was to be expected. In fact, from the historian's point of view,
a social and political transformation of such magnitude and duration
should have produced much more opposition, whatever its appearance
and intention, than is reported by the sources. Sooner or later after the
end of the civil wars, sustained and determined efforts should have been
undertaken by substantial groups of senators to break the monopoly of
power established by the *princeps*. This is precisely what happened
under Augustus' successors. The ancient authors who were influenced
by the regimes of Claudius and Nero, Domitian, Commodus and the
Severans, and were therefore used to intense senatorial opposition to the
emperors, naturally judged Augustus' reign on the basis of these very
experiences. Yet the facts they report clearly indicate that under the first
princeps things were different. Whatever kind of resistance we focus on,
no comparison is possible between the principate of Augustus and that
of his Julio-Claudian successors. Thus what is surprising to the historian really is not the existence but the relatively small amount and low
intensity of opposition under Augustus.

The contrast between what we should expect and what we actually
find is even more stunning if, by way of a brief digression, we take a
more general look at the problem of "opposition" in the Greco-Roman
world before the establishment of monarchy in the Hellenistic East and
Augustan Rome. In our modern parliamentary democracies, "opposition" is a recognized, formalized, and organized component of political
life. This is the result of relatively recent developments, originating in
the enlightenment of the eighteenth century.[123] Such an accepted and
clearly defined concept of "political opposition" was unknown to the
ancient world; neither the Greeks nor the Romans even had a term for
it,[124] and in political life there was no proper place for it. Of course there
was plenty of resistance to individual programs and persons; there was
constant debate, serious disagreement, even civil strife and war; but an
institutionalized form of opposition did not exist. For example, Athenian democracy was perceived and presented by its supporters as encompassing the participation and will of all citizens and giving every-

123. Cf. W. Jaeger, "Opposition," in O. Brunner et al., eds., *Geschichtliche Grundbegriffe: Historisches Lexikon zur politisch-sozialen Sprache in Deutschland,* vol. 4 (Stuttgart 1978) 469–517, esp. 471, 474–80.

124. See Jaeger (supra n. 123) 472f.; and for Rome, Raaflaub (supra n. 3) 2f.

body, including those who disagreed with individual decisions or the system as a whole, full freedom to express their opinion—no matter how much the opponents of democracy contested this view and felt themselves a permanently excluded minority.[125] In republican Rome decisions were made in the senate and voted upon by the assembly on the basis of alliances and agreements among individuals and family groups.[126] Although the core of such factions might remain stable for some time, their composition constantly changed.[127] The majority carrying one issue differed from that prevailing on another; parts of the group one opposed in one case might be one's allies in the next. As long as there were several competing power centers, grouped around the *principes* in the senate, political give-and-take, even in an extreme form, balanced out over time. "Opposition," that is, was neither fixed nor organized, because all participated in all decisions and the constituents of opposing groups changed from issue to issue. Moreover, strong forces, centered in the eminent group of former consuls, aimed at (and normally succeeded in) establishing unity on the essential issues and decisions with long-term effects.[128]

This system, originally based on the principle of aristocratic equality, could not tolerate monopolization of power, whether by a group or an individual. Whenever such monopolization occurred, factional strife turned into a struggle of principle and survival and was fought with all available means, even with murder, conspiracy, and civil war.[129] But

125. Cf. K. Raaflaub, *Die Entdeckung der Freiheit* (Munich 1985) 264–72. For fifth-century discussions of this point, id., "Contemporary Perceptions of Democracy in Fifth-Century Athens," forthcoming in *ClMed* 40 (1989). For opposition to democracy, H. Wolff, "Die Opposition gegen die radikale Demokratie in Athen bis zum Jahre 411 v.Chr.," *ZPE* 36 (1979) 279–302; J. Bleicken, *Die athenische Demokratie* (Paderborn 1985) 261–68.

126. See, in general, M. Gelzer, *The Roman Nobility*, trans. R. Seager (Oxford 1969) (= *Die Nobilität der römischen Republik* [Leipzig and Berlin 1912]); C. Meier, *Res publica amissa* (Wiesbaden 1966; new ed., Frankfurt 1980) part I and "Einführung zur Neuausgabe 1980," XXXII–XLIII; T. P. Wiseman, "Competition and Co-operation," in id., ed., *Roman Political Life: 90 B.C.–A.D. 69* (Exeter 1985) 3–19; J. Paterson, "Politics in the Late Republic," ibid. 21–43 (with literature, 69–73).

127. For discussion of the impact of such factions, see Meier (supra n. 126) 174–200; E. S. Gruen, *The Last Generation of the Roman Republic* (Berkeley and Los Angeles 1974) 47–50.

128. For *princeps, principes,* see *RE* 22.2 (1954) 1998ff., esp. 2004–56, s.v. *Princeps (civitatis)* (L. Wickert). For the processes of decision making and enforcing unity, see Meier (supra n. 126) and id., "Die Ersten unter den Ersten des Senats: Beobachtungen zur Willensbildung im römischen Senat," in D. Nörr and D. Simon, eds., *Gedächtnisschrift für W. Kunkel* (Frankfurt 1984) 185–204.

129. Examples: the resistance of the *optimates* against the Gracchi, Bibulus' permanent obstruction in 59, Cicero's abstention from active participation in the senate in 48–46, the conspiracy against Caesar in 44, and the civil war of 49.

these were extreme and temporary devices, designed to restore the free play of political forces within the senatorial oligarchy with all its traditional possibilities and limitations.

Thus again, the monopolization of power by Augustus and his associates should have provoked continuous and violent opposition by many of those who did not belong to that group. Our investigation has demonstrated that this was the case only to a surprisingly limited extent. The importance of this result for our understanding and assessment of Augustus and his principate is obvious. An explanation is required. By necessity, in the present context such an explanation has to be both broad and selective, combining a number of mostly well-known factors.

Tacitus provides an answer to the problem: the sweetness of peace seduced everyone; the boldest (*ferocissimi*) had died in war or proscriptions, and the other *nobiles* found out that submission (*servitium*) led to wealth and honor; they all profited from the new state of affairs and preferred the security of the present arrangement to the dangers of the former. Hence, no resistance—or, at any rate, little.[130] There certainly is much truth in this—even though it might be formulated with less contempt for the *princeps* and the spineless senators who rushed into slavery.[131] In his *Roman Revolution* Sir Ronald Syme basically accepts Tacitus' explanation but explores and illuminates an additional crucial factor: the organization of power. He shows how Augustus skillfully and patiently broadened his base of support and built up faction and "party," relying for army commands and other powerful offices extensively on new men from outside of the old republican aristocracy, but tying the nobility to himself through marriage alliances and the distribution of honor and social distinction. All along, Syme insists, Augustus considered the *nobiles* his enemies, he did not trust them, he kept them away from the handling of power; ultimately, he was responsible for the "doom of the nobility."[132] To a large extent this undoubtedly is correct. But it throws us back to the same question: If there was such a large group of influential men who were permanently excluded from what had been the prerogative of their ancestors, why was there no stronger and more persistent opposition?

130. Tac. *Ann.* 1.2 with the modifications about violence in 1.9f.
131. As again in A.D. 14: Tac. *Ann.* 1.7.
132. This is the thrust of Syme's argument, abundantly documented throughout the last third of the book (supra n. 4), particularly in chaps. 22, 24–26, 32f. The *nobiles* as Augustus' enemies: 310, 328, and often.

They were exhausted, explains Syme, their spirits broken, their families all but extinguished; peace proved too attractive, they succumbed to their master.[133] Possibly, but the sons of the new *nobiles* who replaced the disappearing old families were treated no better by Augustus. And why were these same men involved in a long chain of acts of opposition to, and perpetually at odds with, his successors?[134] There must be reasons that go beyond the control of power and the organization of alliances, reasons that cannot be gleaned from the prosopographical study of individual careers, the composition of factions, and the changes undergone by an aristocracy.[135] Four points seem particularly important.[136]

First, few indeed remained in the senate, and particularly among its leading families, who had known the free play of political forces in the Republic.[137] More importantly, for the overwhelming majority of the senate such free play had never existed. For all those who did not belong to the ruling oligarchy of the late Republic, it did not matter much whether a few *principes,* three triumvirs, or finally one *princeps* exerted decisive influence over political decisions, whether in the senate or outside of it. But it mattered whether such a leader or leaders guaranteed peace, prosperity, and fair chances to all. Their situation and prospects actually improved dramatically under Augustus: there was no need to oppose that! Consequently, the *libertas* that was lost and lamented as incompatible with *principatus* by some was not that of the Roman people nor that of the senate as a whole but only that of the narrow oligarchy that had been in charge during the Republic.[138]

133. Syme (supra n. 4) 325, 368, 513–15, and often.
134. Sons of *nobiles:* Syme (supra n. 4) 435f. Opposition: for a general picture, Raaflaub (supra n. 3); for one specific example, id. (supra n. 17) 288f.
135. This is the approach taken explicitly by Syme (supra n. 4) e.g., vii, 4, 7f.
136. The following observations are offered as a mere sketch; the issue is far too complex to be dealt with so briefly. But any effort to supplement and, inevitably, modify Syme's assessment of Augustus' principate will have to aim in this direction. Such an effort is overdue: too many generations of historians have taken Syme's invaluable book for more than it wants to be (see also infra n. 138). For an alternative explanation of Augustus' success, see C. Meier, "Augustus: Die Begründung der Monarchie als Wiederherstellung der Republik," in id., *Die Ohnmacht des allmächtigen Dictators Caesar: Drei biographische Skizzen* (Frankfurt 1980) 223–87; id., *Caesar* (Berlin 1982) 584–86; and Meier's contribution to this volume.
137. Even fewer in A.D. 14: Tac. *Ann.* 1.3.
138. Tac. *Agr.* 3.1: *quamquam . . . Nerva Caesar res olim dissociabiles miscuerit, principatum ac libertatem.* On *libertas* under Augustus and his successors, see C. Wirszubski (supra n. 104) parts IV and V; the literature cited by Raaflaub (supra n. 3) 27, n. 66; Syme (supra n. 4) 154–56, 320f. It is both the strength and one of the decisive weaknesses of Syme's work that he attempts "to record the story of the Roman Revolution and . . . the Principate of Caesar Augustus . . . from the Republican and Antonian side" (6f.), that is,

Second, after twenty years of intermittent civil war the prospect of guaranteed peace undoubtedly was highly attractive even to the most hardened republicans. Moreover, after Caesar's perpetual dictatorship and thinly disguised attempts at establishing a monarchy, and after the violence and illegalities of the triumvirate, the alternative offered by Augustus must have appeared irresistible. Granted, the senate lost much of its power and independence. But it regained distinction and a meaningful role; in stark contrast to its situation under Caesar it was treated with respect and dignity. Its collaboration was sought and valued.[139] In short, the *res publica restituta* was much more than a mere façade; it contained enough republican substance to be credible and to encourage cooperation rather than resistance.

Third, long before the collapse it had been obvious to critical observers that the Republic was sick, the senatorial regime malfunctioned, and remedies were hard to find.[140] To a large extent, the Republic broke down because the senate—overextended and inflexible, morally corrupt and paralyzed by continuous factional strife, politically bankrupt and powerless in the face of the demands and aspirations of the generals with their armies—proved incapable of solving many of the urgent problems with which it was confronted. Augustus and his friends and associates tackled these problems, one after the other, with determination, patience, hard work, and, mostly, success. By establishing and guaranteeing domestic peace, they fulfilled the yearning of millions in Italy and all over the empire; by finally satisfying the needs of the professional soldiers, the exhausted provinces, the neglected municipal aristocracies of Italy, and the depressed urban masses in Rome, they largely eliminated the causes of widespread and long-standing dissatisfaction and thus many of those factors that had served as stimuli and instruments in the power struggle among the leading senators. Government thereby was stabilized, the initiative returned to Rome. The impact and significance of these efforts, and the popularity the *princeps* gained from them, must have influenced the attitudes of the senators as

---

from the point of view of the "doomed nobility" and the historians Sallust, Pollio and Tacitus, all senators, "deeply imbued with the traditional spirit of that order, . . . preoccupied with the fall of *Libertas* and the defeat of the governing class" (5). As the assessment of Tiberius by Tacitus, so that of Augustus by Syme is deeply influenced and, some might think, distorted by that *parti pris*. Fortunately, again like Tacitus, Syme provides us with most of the elements needed to balance his judgment; thus, in the case of *libertas et principatus*: Syme (supra) 2 and chap. 33.

139. See Brunt (supra n. 67); Kienast (supra n. 2) 126–51.
140. Cf. Meier (supra n. 126) 1–3 with sources.

well; at least it was more difficult to oppose those who knew their job and did it well.[141]

Fourth, whenever a radical political change occurs in a society, the group that carried and dominated the old system has to be ousted with it, and expectations and values must be adapted to the new realities. For good reasons—among them Caesar's negative example, his own desperate need of senatorial support in the final struggle against Antonius, and his belief in republican values and traditions[142]—Augustus chose to go only part of the way toward monarchy and to combine the necessary monarchic elements with the basic principles of republican government.[143] As it turned out, he thereby left the difficult process of social and "ideological" adaptation largely to his successors.[144] What he gained was credibility and support. And there was a possibly unexpected advantage: with the traditional forms of conducting politics in the senate there also returned competition, rivalry, disagreement on issues and principles. Unfortunately, our extant sources do not give us enough information about debates and decisionmaking in the senate.[145] But from Tacitus' reports on these matters under the Julio-Claudians it is clear that the *princeps* profited from factional strife and rivalries among the senators.[146] The same was probably true under Augustus.[147] Thus the potential opposition in the senate was fragmented; the groups involved tended to paralyze each other and to be threatened as much by

141. The serious disturbances during the years after 23 (Kienast [supra n. 2] 92–94; Sattler [supra n. 13] 72–93 passim) will have made that clear to everyone; cf. Syme (supra n. 4) 371. Later judgments (for example, by Vell. Pat. 2.89; Sen. *Clem.* 1.9–11; Tac. *Ann.* 1.9.3–5; Dio 56.43; Oros. 6.22.3) stress these aspects; they express a common tradition (strongly contradicted, perhaps for the first time, by Tac. *Ann.* 1.10), according to which the achievements of Augustus during his principate (i.e., after Actium) more than balanced the negative impression left by Octavian's violent rise to power; cf. (with earlier literature) Manuwald (supra n. 7) 352–74, esp. 373f. K. Galinsky, "Recent Trends in the Interpretation of the Augustan Age," *The Augustan Age* 5 (1986) 22–36, esp. 32f., usefully applies categories developed by modern political science in defining Augustus' leadership as "transforming" rather than "transactional." While the latter is preoccupied with establishing and organizing power, tying followers to the regime, and carrying out the government's daily business, transforming leadership goes beyond that in its effort to address the deeper issues and instill purpose: "It seeks to inculcate values, it seeks to satisfy the higher needs of the followers, and it may convert leaders into moral agents" (32).

142. Cf. W. Eder's contribution to this volume.

143. Cf. Meier (1982: supra n. 136) 585: "[Augustus] schlich sich gleichsam in die Republik ein. Er überholte den Senat an Konservativität, indem er sich der Restitution des Überkommenen—sowie dessen Fortbildung—annahm."

144. Cf. Raaflaub (supra n. 3) 43f.

145. Sattler (supra n. 13) 55–57.

146. Cf. Raaflaub (supra n. 3) 26, 40; B. Levick, "The Politics of the Early Principate," in Wiseman (supra n. 126) 45–68, esp. 55–60.

147. Labienus and Severus, who were brought down by their *inimici,* are good examples: supra at nn. 98–104.

their rivals as by those holding the power. It should not be overlooked that eventually most members of the Augustan senate owed their advancement in one way or another to him.

To all this we should add, on the one hand, the potential impact of the various *lectiones* of the senate and other mechanisms of control available to the *princeps;* on the other, his extraordinary political insight and skills—and his *humanitas.*[148] Only if we combine all these elements in a comprehensive system of interacting factors, shall we be able to understand fully why, contrary to all expectations, opposition to Augustus was scattered, isolated, ineffective, and, overall, minimal.

148. Rightly emphasized in the final section of Z. Yavetz's contribution to this volume, and by Galinsky (supra n. 141) 30–33: "The Age of Augustus, which was not perfect, speaks to us precisely because it emphasized . . . humanity amidst the power of empire and amidst the might of the ruler and the government machinery. . . . As Wolfgang Schadewaldt outlined many years ago, the need for the expression of humanity becomes especially acute when our daily lives, the economy, the government, domestic and foreign affairs become overstructured, unwieldy and bewildering in their complexity, and unresponsive to our simple instincts. . . . The Augustan reaction stands out . . . by being quintessentially humane—the relaxed humor, the bantering, the easy communication (devoid of its modern buzzword overtones), the nicety of discourse between human beings, and most of all, by incorporating this humaneness both informally and formally into the literary and artistic milieu of the time" (31–32).

Index of Subjects

Abacus, 317
Acanthus, 290, 317
Acta diurna, 173
Acta senatus. See Senate, senators
Acta triumphalia. See Triumph, *trium-phatores*
Actors, 369
Adfectatio regni, 110
Administration: provincial, 16; imperial, 155
Adulatio, 140, 153, 153n.53, 265
Adultery, 40, 261, 428–31
Aedes Concordiae Augustae, xx, 276–96; dedication of, 277–78; designer of, 293–94; ornamentation of, 278–92; program of, 293–96; site and shape of, 277
Aediles, aedileship, 96, 107, 112, 126, 130n.21, 132, 134, 427
Aeneid, 174–210, 250, 280–81; and *Iliad,* 184, 193n.24, 195n.27, 209; interpretations of, 178–82, 197n.29, 199n.31; Iulus and Aeneas in, 207–8; Pallas and Aeneas in, 200–202, 205–9; tenth book of, 200–205; Turnus and Aeneas in, 183–205, *See also* Augustus: and Aeneas; Augustus: and Vergil
Aerarium militare, 165, 167, 435
Aeternitas, 286–87
Alphabet, 33
Altars, 37, 175, 188, 237n.25, 279n.18, 289, 294, 321, 323, 405, 406–7. *See also* Ara Pacis
Alternative to Roman Republic, 65–70

Ambitio, 148n.35, 149
Amicitia, 142n.8, 223, 425, 443
Amicus, amici, 264, 266, 270, 424, 439, 442
Amor, 230
Ancestors, ancestry, 5, 6, 18, 126–27, 151, 174–78, 189, 192, 285
Anecdotes, 7, 260–61
Annales maximi, 135–36, 146, 437
Annalists, annalistic tradition, 134, 145–150, 152, 171–73. *See also* Historiography, Roman
Antae, 315
Anti-hero, 26
Antiquarianism, antiquarians, 5, 50, 135–36
Apologia, 150
Apophthegmata, of Augustus. See *Dicta,* of Augustus.
Apparitores. See Augustales: and *apparitores*
Aqueducts, 47, 96, 117
Ara Pacis, xiv, 119, 272, 296, 323, 337–38, 357, 381, 383, 384–93, 400–401; event depicted on, 390–93; and *solarium Augusti,* 384–97
Arcanum imperii, 47, 51, 78
Archaeology, xix, 23
Arches, 309, 311–12, 318–22, 397, 403
Architecture, 309, 311–18, 365; Hellenistic features of, 312–13, 320; native features of, 312. See also *Aedes Concordiae Augustae;* Provinces: Augustan building program in West
Architrave, 125–26, 311

455

Arena, 286
Aries. See Zodiac
Aristocracy, aristocrats, xvi, 10, 13, 17–
    19, 30, 37, 49, 60, 63, 143, 147, 149,
    260, 367, 432, 449, 450–52; munici-
    pal, 14, 17, 17n.66, 452
Army, xvii-xviii, 29, 48, 61, 316, 317,
    325, 341; and Augustus, xvii-xviii,
    14–15, 30, 38, 65–67, 75, 77, 78, 91,
    100, 102, 106, 157, 160–61, 164–
    65, 343–44, 423. See also Legions,
    Roman
Ars Amatoria, 243–45, 255
Art, xix. See Architecture; Images; Paint-
    ing; Statuary, statues
Arval brethren. See Fratres Arvales
Assassination, assassins, 426; of J. Cae-
    sar, 29–30, 32, 61, 63, 143, 153–54,
    175, 202–3, 210
Assembly. See Comitia
Assimilation and imitation, divine, 334–
    57; of Augustus, 341–57; in coinage
    of Antonius, 340–41, 344–45; de-
    fined, 335; of Sextus Pompeius, 340
Astrologers, 142, 173, 272–73, 385
Astrology. See Zodiac
Atrium Libertatis, 96
Auctoritas, 3, 16, 24, 62, 73, 120, 150,
    437n.86. See also Augustus: auctori-
    tas of
Augur, augurate, 131, 136, 188, 382
Augurium, 105
Augustales, xx, 120, 364–79; and appar-
    itores, 372–73; as factor in social sta-
    bility, 375–77; and imperial cult,
    377–78; and renewal of senatorial
    and equestrian orders, 368–72; and
    slavery, 373–76
Augustus: and Aeneas, 174, 175–76,
    177, 188–89, 192, 197, 208, 236;
    and Agrippa, 161–62, 259–61; auc-
    toritas of, 17, 24, 68, 73, 75, 101,
    118, 121, 150; and Augustales, 366–
    67, 370–72; autobiography of, 33,
    38, 156n.4, 261, 400, 401; and J.
    Caesar, 32, 33, 34, 63, 89–90, 95–
    96, 175, 344–46, 352–53, 434; cen-
    sorship by, 142–43, 275, 440, 444–
    46, 447; and M. Cicero, 32–33, 34,
    90–91; clementia of, 75, 167, 197,
    244, 253, 427, 444, 446; and coin-
    age, 341–57, 385; and consulship,
    107–9, 237n.25, 351; cult of, 324–
    25, 364, 367, 377–78, 406–7, 409; as
    defender of traditional Roman values,
    64–65, 95, 96–97, 100; dissimula-
    tion of, 35–36, 69, 166, 167–68; di-

vinity of, 15–16, 36, 105, 175, 245–
    46, 265, 337–38, 341–57; early
    career to Actium, 32–33, 63–64, 72,
    85, 89–101, 158–59, 160, 202–3,
    264–65, 267, 341–46; and elephants,
    284–86; and equites, 369–70; fu-
    neral of, 86, 127, 125n.6, 130n.20;
    funeral oration of Tiberius for,
    159n.14, 165, 166, 167, 170n.70;
    and historiography, 139–54, 437–38;
    and Horace, 40, 213–38, 262–63,
    268, 388–90, 400; horoscope of,
    385–87, 393; humor of, 36–38; ill in
    23 B.C. 237n.25, 351, 353; imperial
    ideology of, 409–13; and Italy, 64–
    65, 66, 100–101, 122, 378–79, 401;
    and literature, 37, 141–42, 249–57,
    258n.1, 269–70; and Livia, 251n.35;
    and Livy, 34, 128–34, 137–38, 144,
    151–53, 446n.121; and Maecenas,
    96, 161, 258–75; as military leader,
    160, 399, 401, 405, 413; moderate
    and conservative nature of, 30–31,
    33–34, 40, 41, 56–57, 68, 165;
    Mommsen on, 52–53; morality,
    moral legislation, 30, 142, 170n.70,
    216, 237n.25, 240, 247, 250–51,
    255–57, 261, 267, 286, 368, 424,
    425n.28, 434–35; and Ovid, 140,
    141, 142, 239–57, 412, 445–46; as
    patronus, 77, 101, 118, 309, 311,
    424, 427; personality of, 27–28, 30–
    41, 71, 75, 85; pontificate of, 88–89,
    380–94, 445n.116; and Propertius,
    178, 181–82, 210, 263; and prov-
    inces, 9, 15, 16, 64, 67, 105–7, 109,
    112, 308–25; and religion, 49, 119,
    382, 393; Republican traditionalism
    of, 71–122, 127; self-representation
    of, xx, 14, 33, 33n.50, 38–39, 72, 75,
    86–87, 103, 108, 118, 123, 126–28,
    175, 202–3, 268, 274, 336, 337–38,
    341–57, 397, 400–402, 404, 409,
    411, 415–16; and slavery, 374–75;
    tact of, 38, 40–41; and Tibullus,
    266–67; title "Augustus," 105, 224–
    25, 278, 292; tolerance of, 34–35,
    142; tribunicia potestas of, 14, 73,
    109–11, 114, 237n.25; and Vergil,
    34, 175–76, 177–78, 189, 202–3,
    210–11, 231–32, 411–12. See also
    Army: and Augustus; Crisis, of Ro-
    man Republic; Fiscus; Imperial pol-
    icy; Opposition to Augustus; Pater
    patriae; Personality: of Augustus;
    Senate: and Augustus; Solarium Au-
    gusti; Succession

Aurea mediocritas. See Moderation
Auspicium, 51
Autobiography, 148. *See also* Augustus:
  autobiography of
Autotelism, 227
Avaritia, 148n.35
Avenger. *See* Revenge, avenger

Ballots, secret, 435
Banishment. *See* Exile
Beneficia, 264
Berlin Academy, 53
Bimillennium of Augustus, xiv, 3n.5, 43,
  43n.4, 76
Biography, xiii, xiv, 30, 73, 149
Birthrate, 170n.70
Bodyguard, 115n.200
Books, burning of, 142, 440–41, 443
Bucrania, 292

Caduceus, 279, 280, 283, 288–90, 350–
  51
Calendar, 380
Calyx, 291
Camden professorship, 3n.7, 19
Cancer. *See* Zodiac
Candelabrum, 292
Cantabrian War. *See* Imperial policy: in
  Spain
Capitals, 290–91, 290n.70, 290n.71,
  312n.22, 316–17
Capricorn. *See* Zodiac
Captives, 319–20, 374
Caryatids, 323–24
Cassius Dio, 155–73, 421, 421n.12,
  427–28; on Augustus as monarch,
  159–69; career of, 155–56, 157, 161,
  162, 164, 165, 166, 169–73, 421;
  and duplicity of Augustus, 167–68;
  historicity of, 169–73; *History,* date
  of composition of, 155n.1; *History,*
  speeches in, 102, 157n.7, 170, 369,
  421; and imperial policy of Augustus,
  162–64; sources of, 156–57, 171–73;
  and Thucydides, 157–58, 171
Cella, 125, 294, 315
Censor, census, 7, 9, 103, 112, 113–14,
  122, 130n.21, 364, 368–69
Censoria potestas, 113n.194
Censorship. *See* Augustus: censorship by
Character. *See* Personality
Chiasmus, 225
Chlamys, 341–42
Chronicle, 147. See also *Annales maximi*
Circus, 14, 39, 134, 284
Circus Maximus, 384
Cistophoroi, 351

Civil wars, 13, 16, 28, 34, 48, 54, 56, 62,
  65, 69, 74, 92, 94, 97, 98, 101, 113,
  117, 139, 143, 149, 151–52, 158,
  177, 181, 192, 213–14, 235–38,
  264–65, 267, 448, 449, 452. *See also*
  Horace: and civil wars
Clades Lolliana, 405, 405n.42
Clementia, 170n.70, 197, 197n.29, 209,
  215, 236. *See also* Augustus: *clementia* of
Clientela, clientes, 11, 17, 59, 65, 77,
  101, 116, 118, 120, 264, 266
Clupeus aureus, 105, 215, 216
Coercitio, 51
Cogere, 264, 269, 270
Cognomen, 224, 278
Coinage, coins, xx, 67, 175, 177, 178n.7,
  274, 283, 288, 289, 292, 294, 309,
  310–12, 322, 324, 324n.68, 336–37,
  339–57, 385, 397; "hubbing," 352;
  local, 311, 322, 367; and propa-
  ganda, 339n.18; Roman state issue,
  338–40, 351–52. *See also* Assimila-
  tion and imitation, divine
Collegia, 120, 364. See also *Augustales*
Colonies, colonization, xviii, 78, 415
Comedy, Roman, 266
Comitia, 13–14, 92, 93, 94, 97, 114–16.
  See also Jurisdiction
Commentarii, 139, 143–44, 151
Commerce, 280, 287
Concilium Galliarum, 323
Concordia, concord, 149, 152, 153, 277–
  78, 279, 280–81, 283, 286–90
Concordia Augusta, 293–94, 295
Concordia ordinum, 277, 279
Concordia sidera, 277, 291
Conditor, Augustus as, 311
Confiscations of land, 164
Congiaria, 96. *See also* Donatives
Consensus universorum, 7, 17, 18, 99,
  100, 102, 121
Consilium, 215
Consilium principis, xviii, 46
Consolatio, 217n.5
Conspiracies, conspirators, 108, 112–13,
  168–69, 237n.25, 277, 351, 422–33.
  See also Assassination, assassins; Op-
  position
Constitution of Roman Republic, 54–60,
  77, 83, 93, 104, 105; and Stalin, xv,
  49, 76n.34
Consuls, consulship, consulates, 8, 13,
  29, 32, 93, 96, 98–99, 103,
  104n.159, 106, 112, 114, 116, 121–
  22, 124n.2, 132n.25, 133, 137, 148,
  149n.36, 155, 161, 171, 216,

Consuls, consulship, consulates *(cont'd)*
    424n.21, 426, 427, 443. *See also* Au-
    gustus: and consulship
Conubium, 95
Cornucopia, 294
Corona civica, 105, 109
Cosmos, 279, 293, 296
Courts, 424n.21, 435
Crab. *See* Zodiac: Cancer
Crater, 282
Crisis, of Roman Republic, xvii, 25, 40,
    48, 54–70; and Augustus, 63–68;
    and J. Caesar, 60–62; and senate,
    54–57; as "crisis without alterna-
    tive," 25, 40, 48, 55–56, 57–70. *See
    also* Alternative to Roman Republic
Cult: Egyptian, 118n.210; imperial, xviii,
    323–34, 364, 367, 377–78. *See also*
    Augustus: cult of
Cupido domandi, 158–59
Cura annonae, 111, 117
Cura aquarum, 47
Cura morum et legum, 114
Curia Octavia, 278
Cursus honorum, 5, 6, 109

Dado, 293
Debt, 131, 137
Decurions, 364, 370–71
Democracy, Athenian, 448–49
Dicta, of Augustus, 22, 31–38; authen-
    ticity of, 31–32
Dictator, dictatorship, xv, 3, 15, 22, 25,
    26, 35, 36, 40, 43, 48, 61, 75, 78,
    81n.57, 92–94, 97, 111, 116, 131,
    133, 136, 165, 434, 447, 452. *See
    also* Monarch, monarchy
Dignitas, 7, 17, 58, 60, 106, 232, 370
Dio Cassius. *See* Cassius Dio
Diplomacy. *See* Imperial policy
Disciplina, Etruscan, 310
Divinity, 337–38. *See also* Assimilation
    and imitation, divine; Augustus: di-
    vinity of
Dominatio, 28, 73–74
Donatives, 75, 96, 102, 107, 109, 117,
    121, 121n.219
Dreams, 171n.74
Duel, 201; of Aeneas and Turnus, 182–
    99, 205, 209
Dux, duces, 47, 101, 122, 133n.28, 412
Dyarchy, xiii, 25, 51–52, 77, 81n.57, 158
Dynasts, Roman Republican, 54, 59–60,
    67, 73, 148

Ekphrasis, 232
Elections, 13–14, 111–12, 115–16

Elegist, 219, 226–27, 229
Elegy, 222, 229, 231–32, 233
Elephant biga, 283
Elephants, 279, 283–87
Elogia, in *Forum Augustum*, xx, 123,
    124, 126–27, 129–38, 412; and Livy,
    129–34, 137–38
Encomium, xx, 212–38
Epic, 190, 210–11, 222, 229, 271–72,
    280
Epigram, 134n.29
Epigraphy. *See* Inscriptions
Epithalamium, 268
Epitomator, 144, 151
Epitomes, 141, 156n.2, 172
Equality, oligarchic, 59, 67
Equites, xviii, 4, 8, 13, 18, 58, 61, 67,
    68, 87, 113, 121, 122, 166n.49, 264,
    369–70, 434
Eulogy, 229, 233
Exedra, 123, 125–27
Exempla, 129, 148, 164, 261, 286, 347
Exempla exolescentia, 82
Exile, 354, 382. *See also* Ovid: exile of
Exordium, 245
Exprimere, 269

Factions, xvi–xvii, 4, 7, 10–11, 11n.38,
    77, 175, 177, 280, 449, 450–53
Famine, 111, 343, 345, 431, 435,
    440n.99, 445
Fasces, 103, 113
Fascism, 4
Fasti, 8, 10–11, 136, 382, 389, 393, 426,
    437
Fertility, 282
Fescenni, 36
Festina lente, 34
Festivals, 165, 171, 206
Fetialis, 382
Fides, 100, 101
Fire, 435; fire brigade, 112, 117, 427
Fiscus, finances, 46–47, 117, 157, 164–
    65, 167–68
Flamen, flamines, 382, 391; *Dialis*, 291,
    391, 392–93; *Quirinalis*, 132
Floods, of Tiber, 117, 435
Forma urbis Romae, 314
Forum, 310, 313–14
Forum Augustum, xiv, xx, 16n.59, 86,
    91, 119, 123–38, 274, 323–24, 390,
    412–13. See also *Elogia*
Fratres Arvales, 49n.36, 382
Freedmen, xx, 120, 266n.16, 364, 365;
    and social unrest, 375–77. See also
    Augustales

Freedom of speech. *See* Augustus: tolerance of; Opposition to Augustus
Frontiers, 172. *See also* Imperial policy
Funerals, 127n.13, 147. *See also* Augustus: funeral of

Games, 39, 96, 102, 118n.219
Garlands, 400
Gates. *See* Arches
Geistesgeschichte, 3
Gemini. *See* Zodiac
Gemma Augustea, 338
Gems, 279, 280, 282, 294
Genius, of Augustus, 120, 349
Gens, gentes, 6, 10–11, 17
Gens Romula, 117, 118
Georgics, 232–33
Gladiators, 369
Gnomon, 384
Golden Milestone, 284
Governors, provincial, xviii, 8–9, 31, 35,
46–47, 112, 161
Grain distributions, 107
Gravitas, 33
Guard, praetorian, 161, 170n.69

Harmonia, 279
Helices, 317
Hellenistic artistic traditions, 80. *See also*
Architecture: Hellenistic features of;
Kings, kingship: Hellenistic
Herald, 289–90, 372
Herm, 348–49
Heroization, 342
Hesperia, 281
Hippocamps, 344
Histoire totalisante, 25
Histoires de mentalité, 19–20
Historians: Greek, and Augustus, 153–
54, 443; Roman, and Augustus, 139–
41, 143–45, 150–54, 437–47
Historiography, Roman, 145–50, 437–
38; compared with Greek, 146, 147,
149, 150; characterization of individuals in, 147, 148; focus on community in, 147–51; *metus hostilis* in,
149, 152
History: legal, xiii, 3, 50–53, 77; narrative, 45–46; universal, 144
Homonoia, 153
Horace, 212–38; and Augustus, in first
three books of odes, 213–17, 235–
38; and Augustus, in fourth book,
237–38; and civil wars, 74, 213–14,
213n.2, 235–36, 238, 336, 411, 413,
446, 447; and context of *Carm.* 2.9,
227–30; eroticism and sexual imagery, 221–24, 229; foreign enemies
and conquest, 214, 215, 216, 223–
27, 229, 395, 404, 412; liminality in,
218–19; and Maecenas, 262, 263–
64, 269–70; meters of, 227–28; and
pontificate of Augustus, 388–90; Vergilian echoes in, 230–33. *See also* Augustus: and Horace
Horography, 146, 148
Horoscope, *horoscopos. See* Augustus:
horoscope of; Zodiac
Hospitality, 206
Hostis, 100
Humanitas, 39, 454
Hybris, 204
Hypocrisy. *See* Augustus: dissimulation
of
Hypotaxis, 225

Iliad, 250. See also *Aeneid*
Images: power of, 72–82, 84–85, 116–
20; on coins, 339. See also *Imagines;*
Propaganda
Imagines, 5, 86, 125n.6, 127, 130n.20
Imber, 220
Imitation, divine. *See* Assimilation and
imitation, divine
Imperator, 14–15, 47, 91, 94, 122, 162,
402, 407
Imperial cult. *See* Augustus: cult of; Cult:
imperial
Imperial policy, 34, 85, 121–22, 144–45,
151–53, 162–64, 395–416; in Alpine
region, 163, 321, 403–4, 416; in Armenia, 122, 396–99, 415–16; in Balkans, 33, 163, 172n.79, 172n.80,
401–3; 415–16; in Britain, 163, 410–
11; in Egypt, 101, 162, 347, 385,
390, 410; in Germany, xviii, 404–9,
415–16; in Parthia, xviii, 162,
172n.80, 396–99, 415–16; in Spain,
122, 144, 162, 267, 308, 350–51,
399–401, 415–16; and diplomacy,
396–98; and grand strategy, 404,
413–16; ideology of, 409–13; and rebellions, (Germany) 404–5 (Pannonia) 403–4, 414, 416, 440n.99,
445 (Spain) 399–40. *See also* Militarism; Propaganda
Imperialism, 179, 320–22. *See also* Imperial policy
Imperium, 51, 74, 86, 106–7, 109, 113,
116, 339, 341, 343n.38, 356
Imperium proconsulare, 93, 106–7, 111,
237n.25, 291, 339, 357
Imperium propraetore, 90–91
Inimicus, 100

Iniungere, 264, 269
Inscriptions, 6, 7–10, 22, 364–65, 370–
    71, 371n.27, 372, 382, 384–85, 391
Institutions, 166, 169–70; governmental,
    46–47, 57, 59, 128, 156
Insulae, 310
Intercessio, 104n.159
Interrex, 132, 133, 134
Ira, iusta, 198
Italy. *See* Augustus: and Italy; Oath: of
    tota Italia
Iubere, 270n.20
Ius auxilii, 109
Ius cum plebe agendi, 109
Ius cum senatu agendi, 109
Ius subselli, 109
Iustitia, 105, 215

Jokes. *See* Augustus: humor of
Jurisdiction, xviii, 106; of senate and
    comitia, 115–16

Kings, kingship, 3, 7, 36, 207, 283; Al-
    ban, 135; Hellenistic, 116, 338. See
    also *Rex, reges*

Lambs, 291
Lararia, 120
Lares comptiales, 120
Largo Argentina. *See* Temples
Laudatio, 234
Laudatio funebris, 207. *See also* Augus-
    tus: funeral oration of Tiberius for
Laurel, 283
Law, 23, 42, 47, 50–53, 60, 75, 77, 83,
    95, 103–5, 110, 116; and senatorial
    decrees, 115. *See also* History: legal;
    Lex, leges
Lectio senatus, 103, 115, 144n.20, 368,
    420, 421n.12, 433–34, 444, 454
Lectisternium, 288n.62
Legati, 106
Legions, Roman, 106, 164–65, 170
Legislation. *See* Law
Lepide et verecunde. See Augustus: tact
    of
Leve genus, 149
Levitas, 33
Lex, leges: Aelia Sentia, 374–75; *annalis,*
    104n.159; *de imperio abrogando,* 95;
    Fufia Caninia, 374; *Gabinia,* 98, 106;
    Juliae, 261; *Liciniae Sextiae,* 277;
    Manilia, 98; *Rufrena,* 344; *Titia,* 92,
    94, 97, 104
Libel, 142, 441, 444. *See also* Slander
Libertas, 17, 40, 157–58, 451
Libra. *See* Zodiac

Library. *See Atrium Libertatis*
Lictors, 372
Lists. *See Fasti*
Lituus, 338, 343n.38
Ludi comptiales, 120
Ludi saeculares, 88, 117, 237, 237n.25,
    262, 289, 382
Lyre, 285, 287–88, 348

Magister equitum, 130n.23, 133
Magistracies, magistrates, Roman Re-
    publican, 4, 7–8, 10–11, 16, 24, 51–
    52, 62, 71, 85, 106, 113–14, 116,
    134, 165–66, 437
Magistratus, 51, 51n.44
Maiestas, 169, 169n.67, 426, 430, 444
Maison Carrée. *See* Temples: Maison
    Carrée, at Nîmes
Manumission, 373–75
Marriage. *See* Augustus: morality, moral
    legislation
Masks, 282
Mausoleum, of Augustus, 100n.136, 127
Medallions, 323–24, 354n.87
Memoirs. See *Commentarii*
Menschheitsdichtung, 180
Merchants, 280
Metamorphoses (Ovid), 240, 242, 252,
    256–57, 412
Metastasis, 228
Meter. *See* Horace: meters of
Metus hostilis. See Historiography, Ro-
    man: *metus hostilis* in
Militarism, 179, 213–14, 226–27, 321–
    22. *See also* Imperial policy: ideology
    of
Mimes, 250
Moderation, 40
Monarch, monarchy, 1, 25, 51, 58, 59,
    61, 63, 67–70, 71, 78, 79–82, 84, 86,
    102, 108, 113, 117, 119, 155–172,
    356, 421, 443, 446, 447, 452–53. *See
    also* Cassius Dio
Moon, 295, 386
Mores, 128–29
Mostra Augustea. See Bimillennium of
    Augustus
Mundus, 284
Municipia, 364–79; social stability in,
    375–77. *See also* Aristocracy, aristo-
    crats.

Niches, 125–26
Nobilis, nobiles, xvi, 4, 5, 18, 45, 48, 58,
    65, 107–8, 109, 111, 114, 116, 120,
    261, 336, 437, 450–51
Nobility. See *Nobilis, nobiles*

Novus homo, 13, 17, 18, 18n.64, 108
Numen, 355
Numerology, 293

Oath, 99, 103n.158, 122, 188; of eastern
	provinces to Augustus, 101; of *tota
	Italia,* 100–101
Obelisks, 381, 384–88, 390–91, 394
Obnuntatio, 104n.159
Obsidian, 283n.36
Octavian. *See* Augustus
Oligarchy, 12–13, 48, 48n.28, 59, 60,
	81, 87, 451. *See also* Equality, oli-
	garchic
Omphalos, 282
Opisthodomus, 315
Oppida, 310
Opposition to Augustus, 34–35, 85,
	417–54; conspiracies, 422–33; intel-
	lectual, 436–47; political, 418–36;
	political, in pre-Hellenistic Greece
	and Rome before Augustus, 448–50;
	in senate, 433–35, 443–44
Optimates, 12, 449n.129
Oracles, 176–77, 418n.2
Oration, funeral. *See Laudatio funebris*
Orators, oratory, 139, 141, 418, 437–41
Ordinarius, 426
Otium, 58
Ovatio, 402
Ovid, 239–57; attitude toward Augustus,
	241–42; *carmen et error,* 142, 240,
	251, 256–57; exile of, 140, 239–40,
	252–53, 430, 440n.99, 445–46; sin-
	cerity of, 242. *See also* Augustus: and
	Ovid; *Metamorphoses; Tristia II*

Painting, 276, 281–83, 288n.60
Palmette, 312
Panegyric, 229, 246, 268, 275
Papyrus, 143n.10, 424–25
Parasitus, 266
Parataxis, 225
Parties, political. *See* Factions
Pater familias, 86
Pater patriae, 2–3, 16n.59, 73, 87, 89,
	118, 119–20, 125, 126, 257, 274
Patera, paterae, 292, 294
Patricians, patrician status, 9, 62, 109,
	132, 277
Patriotism, Roman, 87–88, 117, 119–20,
	150
Patronage, 24; literary, 96, 263–75, 436
Patronus, patrocinium, 17, 266. *See also*
	Augustus: as *patronus*
Pax, 85, 278, 279, 288, 289–90, 321–22,
	351, 411, 414

Pax Augusta, 117, 244, 287, 288
Pax deorum, 295
Pax Romana, 119
Peace. See *Pax*
Pediment, 125
Perestroika, 24, 24n.10
Periochae. See Epitomes
Peripeteia, 172
Personality, 25–41; of Antonius, 28–30;
	of Augustus, 27–28, 30–41, 71
Perusine War, 33, 85, 158n.8, 344
Petasus, 348
Philology, 23
Pietas, 80, 105, 215, 341
Pileus, 342
Plebiscitum, 98
Plebs, plebians, xvii, 13–14, 14n.50, 17,
	25, 39, 87, 95, 109, 110, 111–12,
	114, 130, 131–32, 274, 277, 280,
	282, 284, 372, 378, 427, 444, 452
Plinths, 312, 318
Poetry, poets, and Augustus, 31, 36–37,
	39, 68, 74, 96, 411–12, 436–37. *See
	also* Horace; Ovid; Patronage: liter-
	ary; *Tristia II*
"Political Catchwords," 15n.55, 22–23
Pomerium, 278, 310, 319
Pompa circensis, 286
Pontifex maximus, 88–89, 95, 119, 135,
	136, 167, 279, 445n.116. *See also*
	Augustus: pontificate of
Populares, 12
Population of ancient Rome, 21
Portents, 171n.74, 293, 376
Porticus, 126, 274, 323; of Livia, 278; of
	Octavia, 278, 323; of Cn. Octavius,
	402; of Philippus, 281
Portraits. *See Imagines*
Portum, 144n.16
Potestas, 51, 75, 83, 118; of triumvirs,
	93–94, 97–102, 104, 115, 116. See
	also *Tribunicia potestas*
Power, political, 62, 71–72; organization
	of, xvi, 84–85, 450
Praefectus urbi, 434
Praescripta, 224, 224n.13, 232
Praetors, praetorship, 8, 106, 108n.173,
	112, 114n.197, 126, 132, 134, 261,
	403, 427
Priests, priesthood, 7–8, 30, 49–50, 88–
	89, 119–20. See also *Pontifex maxi-
	mus;* Religion
Princeps. See Augustus
Princeps civitatis, 101
Princeps senatus, 15, 86, 131, 134, 380,
	390, 449
Principate, Augustan, xi-xx, 42–43, 48,

Principate, Augustan *(continued)*
  70, 71–122, 447–54; delimitation and
  division of, xii, 72–74, 88–89; historians' judgments on, xi-xvii, 3–4, 17,
  74–75; Mommsen on, 51–52; reassessment of, 22–24, 451n.136; as victory of "nonpolitical classes," 16, 24,
  25. *See also* Crisis, of Roman Republic: as "crisis without alternative";
  Dyarchy
Principes iuventutis, 121
Privatus, 98, 110–11
Probatio, 245
Proconsuls, 112, 116, 130n.21, 133
Procurator, 35
Pronaos, 313, 315
Propaganda, 15, 29–30, 70, 78, 88, 96–
  97, 158, 170n.71, 240, 264, 276,
  336, 345; in imperial policy, 319–20,
  395–416. *See also* Coinage, coins:
  and propaganda
Property, 120, 125–26, 165n.45
Prophecies, 175, 179; texts of, 142,
  418n.2, 445n.116
Prorogatio imperii, 98
Proscriptions, xi, 13, 18, 63, 85, 91, 94,
  158n.8, 160
Prosopography, prosopographical
  method, xv, xvii, 2, 4–12, 23–24, 42,
  44n.7, 44n.8, 48, 52–53, 77, 451; in
  antiquity, 5–6; and factions, 10–11;
  and inscriptions, 7–10; as method, 6–
  12; of the Roman Republic, 10
Protomes, 290n.70, 292n.83
Provinces, 9, 15, 29, 64, 172, 452; Au-
  gustan building program in West,
  308–25; urbanization of West, 310–
  11. *See also* Augustus: and provinces;
  Senate, senators: and provinces
Prudentes, 74n.18
Psychoanalysis. See *Psychohistory*
Psychohistory, psychohistorians, 25–26,
  31
Psychology. *See* Psychohistory
Puns. *See* Augustus: humor of
Purges. See *Lectio senatus*

Quadriga, 125, 344
Quaestor, quaestorship, 133, 134, 403
Quellenforschung, 134
Quindecimvir sacris faciundis, 382

Races, chariot, 165
Rams, 290–92
Ransom, 202, 205
Reassessment, of Augustan principate,
  xvi-xix, 22–24; in history, 21–24

Rebellion. *See* Imperial policy: and rebel-
  lions
Recusatio, 233–34, 234n.23, 270–73
Recusatio imperii, 166, 168, 170n.70,
  173n.84
Refutatio, 245
Relegatio, 445
Religion, *religio,* 49–50, 382
Republic, restored, 47, 48, 61, 66–68,
  69–70, 72, 86, 102–3, 110–11, 120–
  21, 151, 436, 446, 447, 452. *See also*
  Crisis, of Roman Republic
"Republican opposition." *See* Opposition
  to Augustus: intellectual
Res Gestae Divi Augusti. See Augustus:
  self-representation of
Res publica restituta. See Republic, re-
  stored
Revenge, avenger, 202–3, 209–10, 214
Revocatio, 237
Revolt, 131. *See also* Imperial policy: and
  rebellions
"Revolution," xvii, 12, 24, 44n.10
Rex, reges, 36, 81n.57, 266
Rex sacrorum, 390–91
Rhetoric (Aristotle), 243
Riots, 447
Roman Revolution, The, xiii, xiv-xvii,
  xix, 2–20, 22, 24–25, 27, 42, 43–50,
  76–77, 450–52; on army, 14–15, 46,
  78; coinage in, 337; composition and
  reception of, xv-xvii, 2–3, 43, 44–45,
  48, 76–77; on ideology, 15; on institutions, 46–47; and Mommsen, 43–
  44; on *plebs,* 13–14, 46, 46n.22; and
  term "revolution," 12; on senatorial
  elite, 16–19; Tacitean influence in, xv,
  43, 46, 50. *See also* Prosopography
Romanization. *See* Provinces: Augustan
  building program in West
Römisches Staatsrecht, 3, 42, 43, 45, 50–
  53, 77
Rostra, 343, 344

Sacrosanctitas, tribunician, 94, 109, 402
Salus Publica, 278
Sanctuary, 318n.44, 323, 325
Sardonyx, 279
Scepter, 283, 288n.65, 347, 350
Scriba, 264, 372–73
Sculpture, 119, 279, 309, 318–22, 323–
  25; iconography in West, 319–22. *See
  also* Images; Statuary, statues
Sebasteion, xiv
Secession, 131
Sella curulis, 113, 131
Senate, senators, xi, xiii, xviii, 4, 8, 9–10,

16–19, 29, 32, 33, 46–47, 55–62,
  67, 85, 87, 90, 96, 98–99, 104–5,
  114–15, 117–18, 119, 121, 122, 153,
  157, 166n.49, 172, 277, 278, 321,
  403, 410, 412, 424–25, 424n.21,
  432, 440–41, 448–54; *acta senatus,*
  172, 173, 442, 443; and Augustus,
  39, 51, 54, 64–69, 78, 85, 88, 98,
  101, 104–5, 107, 108n.173, 111,
  112, 113, 114–15, 166–69, 173n.84,
  265, 309, 343, 356, 367, 368–69,
  397, 401–2, 443–44, 448–54; and J.
  Caesar, 60–62, 114; and coinage,
  339, 343n.38; and historiography,
  146, 150–51, 154, 437; and provinces, 78, 102, 105, 112, 309; *senatus
  consultum ultimum,* 93. *See also* Jurisdiction; *Lectio senatus;* Opposition
  to Augustus: in senate
Sensibilité collective, 19–20
Septemvir epulonum, 382
Settlements, "constitutional": of 27 B.C.,
  88, 91, 101, 104–7, 166, 336; of 23
  B.C., 73, 88, 107–11, 113, 336, 351,
  425
Shield, of Aeneas, 232–34, 412
Sibylline books, 418n.2
Sidus Iulium, 352
Slander, 444, 447. *See also* Libel
Slavery, slaves, 24, 38, 48, 373–75, 420
Social War, 17, 124, 311
Sodalis Titius, 382
Sodalitates, 119
Solarium Augusti, xiv, 381, 383–97
Spanish Civil War, 3
Spiritus Pompeiani, 439–40
Spolia opima, 125, 128, 151, 201, 423
Stadium, 286
Staff. See *Caduceus*
Standards, Roman legionary, 401, 402;
  recovered from Parthia, 112, 125,
  237n.25, 267, 396–97, 398, 410, 412
Stasis, 153
Statistics, in history, 7
Statuary, statues, 80n.49, 85, 86, 102,
  125–27, 129n.19, 130n.23, 135–36,
  274, 276, 278, 279–81, 286, 287,
  293–94, 309, 341–44, 346–48, 397,
  402, 412. See also *Forum Augustum;*
  Images; Sculpture
Stereobate, 315
Stoicism, 171
Struggle of the Orders, 149
Stylobate, 315
Suasio, 217n.5
Succession, 47, 89, 108, 113, 120–22,
  259, 429–30, 431, 432

Suicide, 424, 428
Summi viri, 75, 86, 91, 119, 123, 127,
  129–34, 137, 274, 413
Sun, 283–84, 292–93, 384, 386
Sundial. See *Solarium Augusti*
Sycophancy, 267

Tabulae dealbatae, 135
Tabulae pontificum, 135
Taxes, 157, 164, 369, 376, 435; *vicesima,* 168, 435. See also *Aerarium militare; Fiscus,* finances
Temenos, 321
Temperantia, 215
Temples, 96, 102, 313–18; peripteral
  plan of, 314–18; of Apollo on Palatine, 95, 119, 283; of Castor and Pollux, 277, 314, 315, 318; of Ceres on
  Aventine, 282, 294; of Concord, 277,
  280; in *Forum Holitorium,* 314, 315;
  of Janus, 102, 399, 400–401, 416; of
  Juno Regina, 278; of Jupiter Stator,
  278, 314; in Largo Argentina, 314,
  315; of Mars Ultor, 16n.59, 119,
  123, 125–26, 202–3, 316, 317, 412;
  of Minerva on Aventine, 314, 315,
  318; of Neptune, 96; at Via di S. Salvatore en Campo, 314–15; of Venus
  Genetrix, 313, 316; at Ampurias,
  314, 325; at Barcelona, 313–18, 325;
  at Circo, 314; at Evora, 313–18; at
  Glanum, 316; at Ilium, 317; at Mé-
  rida (Augusta Emerita), 313–18,
  323–24, 325; Maison Carrée, at
  Nîmes, 313, 317; at Priene, 315; at
  Tivoli, 315; at Vienne, 316. See also
  Aedes Concordiae Augustae
Theaters, 14, 120, 274, 312, 314
Tori, 312, 316, 318
Tories, 4–5
Treasury, military. See *Aerarium militare*
Treaty, 188–93, 209
Tresviri monetales, 351
Trials, 260, 426
Tribes, Roman, 13, 372
Tribunes, tribunate: of the *plebs,* 14,
  104n.159, 109, 110, 114, 134; mili-
  tary, 130n.22, 132, 133
Tribunicia potestas, 110n.179, 121, 122,
  291, 381, 383. *See also* Augustus: *tri-
  bunicia potestas* of
Trident, 288n.62, 347
Trigon, 294–95
Tripod, 175, 281
Tristia II, 242–57; addressed to Augus-
  tus, 242–43; arrangement of, 243;

Tristia II (continued)
  and *Ars Amatoria,* 251–52; as chal-
    lenge to poetic sense of Augustus,
    249–57; double entendres in, 243–
    44; interpretations of, 245–49; pur-
    pose of, 243, 254–57. *See also* Au-
    gustus: and Ovid; Ovid
Triumph, *triumphatores,* xx, 95, 96, 101,
    112, 129, 130, 133, 148, 162, 231–
    32, 234, 274, 283, 397, 400–401,
    403, 407, 408, 409, 411, 412–13,
    416, 423, 451; *acta triumphalia,* 136
Triumvir coloniae deducendae, 134
Triumvirate, triumvirs, 10, 11n.38, 63–
    64, 75, 88, 92–103, 107, 115, 156,
    158–59, 160, 175, 288, 341, 345,
    353, 416, 434. See also *Potestas*
Tropaea, trophies, 219, 224, 231, 309,
    318–22, 325, 397, 404, 405
Turret, 285
Twelve Tables, 440n.104

Unrest, social, 88, 94–95, 111–12
Urban populace. See *Plebs,* plebians
Urbanization, 407. *See also* Provinces:
    urbanization of West

Vases, 289n.68; Arretine, 281; Attic, 282
Vates, 272

Vergil. See *Aeneid;* Augustus: and Vergil
Vesta, cult of, 380, 381, 383, 389, 393.
    See also *Pontifex maximus*
Vestals, 99, 130–31, 132n.25
Vestigare, 190
Veterans, army, xvii-xviii, 63–64,
    78n.40, 89–90, 344; settlement of,
    58–59, 63–64, 78, 85, 102, 160,
    343–44, 452
Vicesima. See Taxes: *vicesima*
Vicus lugarius, 279n.18, 294
Vietnam War, 26, 179
Virtus, 91, 105, 214–15, 223n.12
Vituperation, 150, 158
Volutes, 317

Water supply. *See* Aqueducts
Wealth, 9–10, 38, 40, 157, 164
Whigs, 4–5
Will: of Antonius, 99–100; of J. Caesar,
    89, 96; of Maecenas, 262
World War I, 36, 180
World War II, 2–3, 8n.30, 25, 26, 179,
    180

Zodiac, 49, 279n.15, 292–95, 385–87,
    393; Aries, 292; Cancer, 295, 385–
    86, 393; Capricorn, 295, 385–87,
    393; Gemini, 291; Libra, 295, 385–
    87

Index of Persons and Places

Achilles, 185, 193, 198, 209
Actium, 81, 88, 101, 160, 162, 164,
    170n.71, 231–32, 234, 283, 320–21,
    336, 347, 356, 376, 411, 422
Aedes Concordiae Augustae, 276–96
Aelius Gallus, 163, 425
Aelius Sejanus, L., 13, 166n.49, 442
Aemilius Lepidus, M., xi, 29, 85, 92, 95,
    136, 158, 160, 167, 173n.82, 380–
    83, 388, 390, 393, 418–19, 421, 422,
    432
Aemilius Lepidus, M. (son of preceding),
    168
Aemilius Paullus, L., 133–34, 422, 430–
    31
Aeneas, 174–211, 237, 280, 412
Aeolus, 203n.39
Aequi, 131
Africa, 106, 112, 412
Africa, North, 410, 415
Agrippa, M., 144
Agrippa Postumus, 47, 420, 422, 430–
    31, 433n.66
Ajax, 189, 196
Alba Longa, 126, 135
Albinius, L., 129n.19, 130, 130n.22,
    131–32, 137
Albius Tibullus, 266–67
Alexander, 2, 34, 147, 149n.36, 162,
    356, 413
Alexandria, 95, 99, 282, 336, 384, 385,
    390, 392, 411
Allecto, 182

Alps, 163, 321, 403–4, 410, 413, 415,
    416
Amata, 187, 192
Ampius Balbus, T., 438
Ampurias, 313–14, 325
Anchises, 178n.7, 179, 195, 197, 202,
    206, 207, 208, 210, 237
Annaeus Seneca, L., 34, 260, 262, 419
Annaeus Seneca, L., the elder, 145, 261,
    439–40
Antilochus, 222, 225
Antipater of Thessalonica, 265–66
Antistius Labeo, M., 443
Antistius Vetus, C., 356
Antium, 274
Antonius, M., xi, 13, 18, 28, 29–30, 32,
    37, 54, 63–65, 72, 78, 79, 88–89,
    92, 94–101, 116, 125, 143, 158, 160,
    161, 161n.20, 170n.71, 264, 265,
    277–78, 282, 308, 340–41, 344–46,
    350, 356, 396, 401, 411, 413, 415,
    422, 453
Aphrodisias, xiv
Apollo, 174, 175, 208, 238, 278, 280,
    281, 282, 285, 287–88, 290, 292,
    294–95, 348, 349–50
Apollonia, 385
Appian, 439
Aquillius Florus, L., 351–52
Arabia, 410, 415
Arabia Felix (Yemen), 163, 425
Araxes, 231–32
Archilochus, 216

Aristotle, 41, 43, 149, 243
Arles. *See* Colonia Julia Paterna Sextano-
   rum Arelate
Armenia, 95, 163n.34, 221, 231, 396–
   99, 410, 415, 416
Armenia Minor, 396
Arminius, 407
Arretium, 281
Arruntius, L., 144
Artavasdes, 95–96
Artemis, 206
Ascanius, 206, 207
Asclepius, 278–80
Asia, 102, 196, 345
Asia Minor, 312, 396, 414
Asinius Epicadus, 420
Asinius Pollio, C., xvi-xvii, 12n.42, 34–
   35, 96, 140, 143, 151n.47, 156n.2,
   214, 264, 436, 437, 438–39, 442,
   443, 446
Asterie, 218
Asturia, 399
Athenodoros, 33
Athens, 5
Atratinus, 112
Audasius, L., 420
Aufidius Bassus, 145, 156n.2
Augusta Emerita, 310–17, 322–25, 400
Augusta Raurica, 310
Augusta Treverum, 311
Augustodunum, 310
Aulestes, 188
Aurelius Opillus, 266n.16
Autun, 312, 318n.44
Aventine, 282, 314, 315

Baetica, 309
Balbus, 112
Balkans, 163, 172n.79, 401–03, 413
Barcelona, 312–16, 325
Barine, 228
Barium, 228
Baton, 278, 280, 281, 287, 293, 295
Bavaria, 403
Beziers. *See* Colonia Julia Baeterrae Sep-
   timanorum
Bohemia, 407
Bononia, 92
Britain, 163, 410–11
Brutus, M., xi, 29, 33, 34, 40, 109n.175,
   216, 438, 442

Caecilius Epirota, Q., 424
Caecilius Iucundus, L., 349
Caere, 130, 131–32, 137
Caesaraugusta, 310

Caesares, 126
Caesarion, 95
Caligula, 31
Callimachus, 270, 273
Calpurnius Bibulus, M., 11
Calpurnius Piso, Cn. (*cos. suff.* 23), 108,
   426
Calpurnius Piso Frugi, L., (*cos.* 15 B.C.),
   265–66
Camilla, 186–87
Campania, 17, 17n.66, 365, 377, 392
Cantabria, 320, 351, 399, 400, 410
Capena, 285
Capitoline, 276, 296, 411
Caracalla, 162, 164, 165, 166
Carpentras. *See* Colonia Julia Memino-
   rum Carpentorate
Carrhae, 396
Carthage, 149
Carthago Nova, 311
Cascellius, A., 103n.157
Cassandra, 279, 281
Cassius Dio, 74–75, 81, 102–3, 140,
   155–73, 251n.35, 261, 383, 401,
   407, 410, 420, 421
Cassius Hemina, L., 146n.24
Cassius Longinus, C., 29, 216, 438, 442
Cassius Parmensis, 202
Cassius Severus, 140, 169n.67, 439, 441,
   444, 445, 446
Castor and Pollux, 215, 282, 291, 342
Castricius, 426n.33
Cenomani, 130, 133
Ceres, 278–80, 282, 294–95
Chatti, 405
Cherusci, 406–7
Chloe, 218
Cilicia, 396
Cimbri, 58
Cimmerian Bosporus, 163
Circeii, 380, 381
Claudii Nerones, 390
Claudius, 173, 446n.121
Claudius Caecus, Ap., 127n.11, 129n.19,
   132–33, 137
Claudius Marcellus, M., 108, 121, 126,
   268–69
Claudius Nero, Tiberius, 251n.35
Claudius Pulcher, Ap., 49
Cleopatra, 64–65, 72, 90, 95, 98–101,
   158, 234, 278, 346, 356, 385, 411
Clodius Licinus, 144
Clodius Pulcher, P., 109n.178, 376
Coelius Antipater, L., 147
Cologne, 323, 406
Colonia Julia Augusta Paterna Faventia,
   310

Colonia Julia Baeterrae Septimanorum, 319
Colonia Julia Meminorum Carpentorate, 319
Colonia Julia Paterna Sextanorum Arelate, 312, 319, 323
Colonia Julia Urbs Triumphalis Tarraco, 37, 309, 323, 324, 399–400
Colonia Julia Vienna, 312, 316, 319
Commagene, 414
Commodus, 9n.31, 155, 157, 166
Conimbriga, 310
Cornelius Balbus, L., 29, 90n.88
Cornelius Cethegus, C., 130, 133
Cornelius Cinna, L., 73
Cornelius Cinna Magnus, Cn., 167n.56, 419, 422, 427, 429, 432
Cornelius Cossus, 128
Cornelius Gallus, C., 151, 169n.67, 259, 423–25, 437n.85
Cornelius Lentulus Maluginensis, Ser., 391n.27
Cornelius Merula, 392
Cornelius Scipio Aemilianus, P., 104n.159
Cornelius Scipio Africanus, P., 91, 147
Cornelius Scipio Asiaticus, L., 130n.23
Cornelius Sulla Felix, L., 12n.42, 18, 40, 64, 78n.40, 82, 93, 97, 106, 110, 114–15, 148, 167, 343, 344
Cornelius Tacitus, P., xi-xii, xvi, 28, 34, 35, 45–46, 74, 81, 110, 140, 150n.41, 153, 169n.67, 169n.68, 171, 172, 173, 251n.35, 260, 392–93, 408, 408n.61, 419, 429n.47, 432n.63, 437, 442, 444, 450, 453
Corvus, 445n.115
Craton, 443
Cremutius Cordus, 74n.19, 128, 140, 142n.8, 143, 144, 156n.2, 438, 439, 442, 446
Crete, 441
Cynthia, 272–73

Dahae, 231
Dalmatia, 163, 172, 321, 401, 402, 402n.28, 403, 410
Danube, 163, 403, 413, 415, 416
Dardanus, 174
Daunus, 195, 196, 202, 210
Decius Mus, P., 133, 137
Delius, Q., 143
Delphi, 282–83
Demetrios Poliorcetes, 347
Diana, 206, 238, 278, 280, 354–55, 356
Dido, 179, 192
Diomedes, 184, 187

Dionysius of Halicarnassus, 153, 443n.109
Dionysos, 282
Dirae (Furies), 194
Domitian, 421
Domitius Ahenobarbus, Cn., 96, 98, (cos. 32)
Domitius Ahenobarbus, L., 406–7
Donatus, Tiberius Claudius, 178n.7
Drances, 183–85, 196
Drusus Julius Caesar (son of Tiberius), 403
Drusus the elder, 124n.2, 134
Durmius, M., 352

Egnatius Rufus, M., 14n.51, 112, 237n.25, 418–19, 422, 427, 432
Egypt, 88, 101, 118n.210, 160, 162, 385, 387, 390, 394, 410, 414
Elbe, 323, 405–10, 413, 416
Ennius, Q., 37, 266n.16
Ephesus, 99
Ethiopia, 163, 410, 414
Etruria, 133
Etruscans, 131, 188
Eudemus Rhodius, 41
Euphranor, 278, 281
Euphrates, 223–24, 231, 396, 397, 398, 412
Euripides, 37, 206
Euryalus, 208
Eurydice, 230
Evander, 185, 199, 201, 203, 205, 206, 207, 208, 209, 210
Evora, 313–17

Fabii, 6
Fabius Ambusti f. Maximus, Q., 130n.23
Fabius Maximus, Paullus, 273
Fabius Maximus Verrucosus, Q., 133, 137
Fabius Pictor, Q., 147n.27
Fannius Caepio, 168, 418–19, 422, 425–26, 432, 435n.78
Flaminius, T., 91
Florus, 406, 408n.61
Fortuna, 235, 238; Fortuna Redux, 237n.25
Forum, 276, 277, 291, 314, 412
Fulvius Nobilior, M., 266n.16
Fulvius Plautianus, C., 166n.49
Furius Camillus, M., 131, 277

Gaius (grandson of Augustus), 121–22, 261, 322, 354, 398
Galatia, 414

Gallia, 60, 62, 106–7, 308, 309, 318, 320, 321, 374, 381, 383, 390, 391, 403, 404, 405, 410, 415
Gallia Aquitania, 309, 319n.45, 320
Gallia Belgica, 309, 318n.44
Gallia Lugdunensis, 309
Gallia Narbonensis, 92, 309, 310, 312, 316, 318, 319, 320
Garganus, 221
Gavius Apicius, 10
Gellius, A., 41
Geloni, 223, 226, 231
Germania, 8, 163n.33, 172, 320, 321, 404–9, 412, 413, 415, 416
Germanicus Julius Caesar, 286, 403, 408–9, 416
Giants, 215
Glanum, 312, 313, 316
Gracchi, 147
Greece, 7, 396
Gyges, 218

Hamilcar, 133
Haterius, 34
Hector, 193, 194, 200, 209
Heliopolis, 381, 384, 385, 394
Hephaistos, 257
Hercules, 205, 206, 208, 215, 400
Hermodorus, 314
Herod, 37, 153, 414
Herodotus, 150
Hirtius, A., 29
Homer, 37, 193, 200, 250
Horatius Cocles, 135, 136
Horatius Flaccus, Q., 40, 74, 137n.37, 151n.47, 211, 212–38, 243n.11, 249, 254, 262–63, 264, 266, 268–74, 292, 372, 381, 388–90, 393, 395, 400, 404, 411, 412, 446
Horus, 272–73
Hygieia, 278–80

Iberia. See Spain
Iccius, 218
Ilium, 317
Illyria, 96, 106, 160, 411, 415, 416
Illyricum, 163, 172n.80, 392, 401, 402, 404, 415
India, 284
Inn, 403
Insubres, 130, 133
Iullus Antonius, 271, 422, 428–30
Iulus, 128, 197, 202, 206, 207, 208
Iunius Silanus, D., 430

Juba, 285
Judaea, 410, 414
Julia (daughter of Augustus), 33, 121,

261, 262, 268, 354, 419, 420, 422, 428–30, 431, 432
Julia (granddaughter of Augustus), 430–31, 432, 433n.66
Julii, 126, 174–75, 177, 184, 189, 208, 211, 412
Julius Caesar, C., xi, xvii, 3, 11, 18, 23, 25, 28, 32, 39–40, 50, 54, 56, 58, 59–61, 63–67, 73, 79, 89–90, 92–93, 96, 104n.159, 106, 114, 125, 125n.6, 128, 153, 157n.7, 161n.20, 202, 208, 211, 214, 216, 234–36, 274, 284, 286, 308, 311, 319, 321n.54, 344–45, 352–53, 356, 374, 404, 434, 446, 452, 453
Julius Severus, 10
Junii, 6
Juno, 179, 182, 188, 193–94, 201, 206, 278, 280
Jupiter (Jove), 174, 179, 190, 193, 194, 205, 206, 207, 208, 214–16, 245, 278, 411
Juturna, 188, 190, 193

Kraton. See Craton

La Turbie, 321, 404
Labienus, T., 140, 144, 439–41, 446
Latinus, 174, 176, 182, 184, 185, 187, 188, 192, 196, 209
Latium, 194n.25, 207, 376
Lausus, 200, 203, 205
Lavinia, 176, 177, 187, 188
Lepidus, M., 444
Liber Pater, 279, 282–83
Licinius Crassus, M., 151, 172n.79, 422, 425
Licinius Crassus Dives, M., xi, 10, 11n.38, 92, 112, 125, 214–15
Licinius Lucullus, L., 107
Licinius Macer, 134
Licinius Varro Murena, L., 168, 237n.25, 259, 418–19, 422, 425–26, 432, 435n.78
Liguria, 133, 135n.30
Ligurinus, 220, 273
Lippe, 406
Livia (wife of Augustus), 167, 170n.70, 173, 251n.35, 278, 279, 287, 294, 345, 350, 384, 392, 402, 419, 421, 427
Livius, T., 34, 123–38, 139, 141, 143, 144, 145, 149, 151, 152, 153, 156n.2, 171, 172, 176, 395, 400, 437–38, 442, 446n.121
Lollius, M., 405
Lollius Urbicus, 10
Lucifer, 207

Lucius (grandson of Augustus), 121–22, 261, 322, 354
Lugdunum, 310, 323, 357, 405
Lugdunum Convenarum, 310, 320–21
Lusitania, 309, 316–17
Lutatius Catulus, Q., 349
Lycidas, 218
Lyon. *See* Lugdunum
Lysippos, 347

Macedonia, 106, 134, 422, 426
Maecenas, C., 11, 33, 96, 102, 144, 157n.7, 159n.13, 161, 164, 165, 166n.49, 170, 233–34, 258–75, 356, 369, 388, 421, 422, 426n.33, 434n.70, 436
Magii, 17n.66
Magus, 202, 205
Manilius, M., 279, 292–95, 386–87, 393
Manlius Torquatus, 388
Marcelli, 6
Marcomanni, 163, 405, 407, 416
Marcus Aurelius, 157
Marius, C., 90, 129, 148
Marius Tromentinus (or Trogus), C., 353
Marseilles. *See* Massilia
Marsyas, 278, 281
Massilia, 319, 321n.54
Mediolanum, 34
Medullini, 131
Melissus, C., 266n.16
Menenius Agrippa, 131, 137
Mercury, 214, 287–90, 348
Mérida. *See* Augusta Emerita
Messapus, 175, 188, 190, 191n.23
Metelli, 120
Metellus Pius Scipio, Q. Caecilius, 7n.25
Mezentius, 175, 200, 203
Minucius, M. 133
Mithridates, 58
Moesia, 402n.28
Mucius Scaevola, P., 135
Munatius Plancus, L., 99, 216
Murranus, 192
Mystes, 217n.5, 219–21, 223, 230
Mytilene, 259

Naples, 323
Narbo, 371–72
Narbo Martius, 319
Narbonne. *See* Narbo Martius
Naulochus, 164, 346, 347
Neaera, 216
Neptune, 341, 346, 347n.56
Nero, 31, 69, 260
Nero Claudius Drusus, 126, 127n.13, 163, 276, 277, 291, 323, 388, 391, 392, 403–6, 416

Nestor, 219, 222, 225
Niceratus, 278, 279, 280
Nicias (painter), 279, 282–83
Nicolaus of Damascus, 29, 153, 443n.109
Nicopolis, 347, 411
Nîmes, 312, 313, 317, 323
Niphates, 223, 226, 231
Nisus, 208
Noricum, 404, 410
Numicus, 174

Octavia (wife of M. Antonius), 95, 278, 345, 402
Octavia Minor (sister of Augustus), 354n.87
Octavius, C., 349
Octavius, Cn., 402
Opellius Macrinus, M., 166n.49
Opimius, L., 277
Opis, 187, 193
Oppius, C., 90n.88
Orange, 319, 321
Orpheus, 230
Ostia, 370
Ovidius Naso, P., 141–42, 239–57, 370, 383, 389, 412, 430, 445–46

Pacuvius Taurus, 38
Palatine, 282, 283
Pallanteum, 206
Pallas, 180, 182, 185, 198–210
Pannonia, 161, 163, 402, 402n.28, 403, 410, 412, 414, 445
Papirius Cursor, L., 130n.23
Paros, 294
Parthia, 61, 99, 112, 125, 143, 162, 163, 172n.80, 267, 321, 396–99, 410, 412, 415, 416
Patroclus, 200, 209
Pergamon, 354
Perseus, 134
Perugia, 85
Perusia, 344
Pescennius Niger, 9n.31
Petelia, 370
Petronius, C., 163
Petronius Turpilianus, P., 283, 355
Philip, 147
Philippi, 123, 125, 143, 159n.13, 160, 164, 216, 264, 343n.38, 343n.40
Phoebus, 271–72
Phraataces, 397–98
Phraates IV, 397
Piston, 278, 280, 287, 293
Plato, 149, 171
Plautius Rufus, 422, 430–31
Plinius Caecilius Secundus, C., 39

Plinius Secundus, C., 153n.53, 419
Plutarch, 28, 73
Polybius, 149, 150, 154
Polycrates of Samos, 279
"Pompeiani," 436
Pompeii, 281, 284, 349
Pompeius Magnus, Cn., xi, 2, 3, 23, 28, 34, 54, 58, 59–61, 64–65, 67, 79, 91–93, 98, 106–7, 111, 130n.20, 148, 149n.36, 284–85, 286, 341, 347n.56, 446
Pompeius Magnus, Sex., 72, 85, 94–97, 158, 160, 161, 162, 340–41, 346, 347, 347n.56
Pompeius Trogus, 144, 144n.17
Pomponius Atticus, T., 6
Pontus, 163
Porcius Cato Censorius, M., 30, 146n.25, 147–48, 266n.16
Porcius Cato Uticensis, M., 30
Porcius Latro, M. 261
Posidonius, 149n.36
Postumius Regillensis, A., 130–31
Priam, 206, 264
Priene, 315
Primus, M., 426
Proculeius, C., 426n.33
Propertius, Sex., 178, 181, 194n.25, 210, 263, 264, 265, 269, 272–73, 411, 412
Ptolemy, 347
Ptolemy Philopator, 284
Publius Rufus, 431, 433n.66
Publius Turullius, 202
Publius Venditius, 162
Puteoli, 117
Pyrrha, 218–19, 228
Pytheos, 315

Quinctilius Varus, P., 9, 172, 407–8, 414, 416
Quinctius Hirpinus, 228

Raeti, 403
Raetia, 163n.33, 404, 410, 412
Rhine, 163, 405–10, 415, 416
Rhodes, 47, 293, 294
Rhoemetalces, 37
Roma, 323
Romulus, 105, 116, 125, 127, 289–91, 387
Rutilius Rufus, 266n.16
Rutulians, 174, 182, 188, 190

Sabelli, 133
Sabini, 131, 133

Saepinum, 321n.56
Saint Rémy, 319
Saint-Bertrand-de-Comminges. See Lugdunum Convenarum
Salamis off Cyprus, 347
Sallustius Crispus, C., xvi, 12n.42, 145, 147–49, 437
Sallustius Crispus (adopted son of preceding), 260
Salvidienus Rufus, Q., 158n.8, 418n.4, 423
Samnium, 133, 137
Sanguinius, M., 352–53
Sarpedon, 205, 206, 208
Save, 401
Scribonia (wife of Augustus) 251n.35
Scythia, 219, 231
Sempronius Asellio, 148, 148n.32
Sempronius Gracchus, C., 277
Sempronius Gracchus, T. (moneyer), 346n.51
Sempronius Gracchus, Ti., 110n.179
Sempronius Tuditanus, C., 50
Sentius Saturninus, Cn., 124n.2
Septimius Severus, 160n.18, 162, 164, 165
Sergius Catilina, L., 78n.40, 277, 376
Seriphus, 441
Servius, 208, 210
Sestius, L, 109n.175
Sestus Quirinalis, L., 132n.25
Severi, 165n.43
Severus Alexander, 155, 161
Sibylla, 198, 209
Sicily, 160, 162, 340
Sinon, 264
Siscia, 401
Sol, 341, 351–52
Sosius, 98
Spain, 92, 106–7, 144, 160, 162, 267, 308, 309, 310, 313, 318, 325, 340, 350, 381, 383, 390, 399–401, 409, 410, 415, 416
Sthennis, 278
Strabo, 52, 402, 443n.109
Suetonius Tranquillus, C., 30, 36, 73, 118, 129n.19, 251n.35, 259, 262, 266n.16, 269–70, 385–87, 410n.74, 420, 427n.38, 444
Sugambri, 405
Sulpicius, P., 382
Switzerland, 403
Syria, 8, 106, 391, 396, 397, 414, 415

Tarentum, 94, 97
Tarquinius, Arruns, 131
Tarquinius, Sextus, 131

Tarquinius, Titus, 131
Tarquinius Superbus, L., 131
Tarraco. *See* Colonia Julia Urbs Triumphalis Tarraco
Tarragona. *See* Colonia Julia Urbs Triumphalis Tarraco
Tartarus, 196
Tarutius, 387
Tauromenium, 160
Telephus, 420
Tencteri, 405
Terentia (wife of Maecenas), 259
Terentius Varro, M., 49, 50, 134n.29, 135n.31, 387
Terentius Varro Murena, A., 426
Terminus, 349
Teutoburg Forest, 407
Teutones, 58
Theodotos, 35
Theogenes, 385
Theophanes of Mytilene, 149n.36
Theophrastus of Lesbos, 41
Theoros, 279, 281
Thracia, 412
Thrasyllus, 293, 294
Thucydides, 150, 158, 171, 178
Tiber, 117, 174, 203
Tiberius, 31, 34, 47, 69, 73, 89, 121–22, 143, 145, 156, 159n.14, 160n.15, 161n.20, 163, 164, 165, 166, 167, 169n.67, 170, 254, 276–78, 282, 287, 290–95, 319, 321n.54, 387, 388, 392, 396, 403, 404, 406–10, 416, 444, 446n.121, 447
Tigranes, 397
Timagenes of Alexandria, 35, 142n.8, 144n.17, 151n.47, 442–43
Titans, 215
Titius, M., 99
Tivoli, 315
Tolumnius, 188, 190
Trajan, 355n.93
Trebatius Testa, C., 94n.112
Trier. *See* Augusta Treverum
Troilus, 219, 222, 225
Tullius Cicero, M., 28, 32–33, 34, 39, 40, 58, 85, 90–91, 99–100, 115, 143, 148, 258n.3, 277, 349
Turnus, 174–211
Tyrol, 403

Ubii, 406
Usipetes, 405

Valerius Antias, 134
Valerius Catullus, C., 220, 253
Valerius Largus, 169n.67
Valerius Martialis, M., 253
Valerius Maximus, M', 131, 134; confusion of with M. Valerius, 136, 137
Valerius Messala Niger, M. 50
Valerius Messalla Corvinus, M., 130n.23, 143, 264, 264n.14, 266–67, 434, 442
Valgius Rufus, C., 212, 219–30, 232–34, 238, 382
Varius Rufus, 234, 264
Vedius Pollio, 38, 165n.45
Velitrae, 131
Velleius Paterculus, xii, xvii, 17, 73, 140, 141, 144–45, 400, 406, 407, 408, 416, 418, 438
Venus, 184, 189, 191, 198, 207, 273
Vergilius Maro, P., 34, 37, 74, 174–211, 230–35, 236–37, 264, 265, 269, 270, 280, 289, 386, 395, 411
Verona, 312
Verrius Flaccus, 134, 135, 136
Vesontio, 130n.20
Vespasian, 36
Vesta, 278, 279, 294–95
Vetii, 284
Vienne. *See* Colonia Julia Vienna
Vindelici, 403
Vinicius, 34
Vipsanius Agrippa, M., 9, 11, 33, 96, 98, 102–3, 107–8, 111, 121, 127n.13, 157n.7, 161, 161n.20, 162, 164, 170, 233, 258n.3, 259, 260, 261, 262, 266, 312, 324, 356, 382, 391, 392, 400, 420, 434, 440
Voconius Vitulus, Q., 346n.51
Volsci, 131
Volumnius, 137
Vulcan, 179, 185, 232

Weser, 407

Zaragoza. *See* Caesaraugusta
Zeuxis, 279, 281–82

Index of Scholars

Adcock, F., 67
Alföldy, G., 6, 44–45
Alvarez Martínez, J. M., 324
Anderson, M. L., 354n.87
Anderson, W. S., 217n.5

Badian, E., 107–8, 237n.25, 267n.19,
    417n.2, 428n.40
Bailey, D. R. Shackleton, xv n. 19,
    132n.25
Beloch, J., 21
Bengtson, H., 6
Béranger, J., xviii, 70
Bleicken, J., xviii, 51
Bloom, H., 255
Bollinger, T., xvii
Borghesi, B., 132
Bosworth, A. B., 438
Bouché-Leclercq, A., 386
Bowersock, G. W., xv n.24, xviii, 367
Bradley, K. R., 373n.34, 374–75
Braudel, F., 26
Braunert, H., 118
Bringmann, K., 92–93
Broughton, T. R. S., 132n.25
Brunt, P. A., xviii, 21, 35, 172
Buchheim, H., 83n.68
Buchner, E., 383–84
Büchner, K., 179
Burck, E., 179

Campbell, B., xviii
Carney, T. F., 6n.21

Christ, K., 405n.42
Classen, J.-M., 247
Clausen, W., 181, 199n.31
Collinge, N. E., 225n.15
Cornell, T., 147n.30
Crawford, M. H., 288n.62, 343n.39
Crook, J., xviii

Davreux, J., 281
Degrassi, A., 135
Dessau, H., 21

Eck, W., 6n.18, 367
Erikson, E. M., 25–26

Ferrero, G., 23
Finley, M. I., 23, 142
Focardi, G., 244, 247
Ford, B. B., 247
Fraenkel, E., 266, 269–70
Frank, T., 21
Frier, B. W., 135–36
Frisch, P., 127, 129
Furneaux, H., 140n.2

Gabba, E., 170
Galinsky, G. K., 198n.31, 453n.141,
    454n.148
Gamal, M. K., 239n.1
Gardthausen, V., xiii–xiv

Gelzer, M., 3, 10, 44–46
Gibbon, E., xii–xiii
Gilbert, R., xvii
Giua, M. A., 170
Goodyear, F. R. D., 140n.2
Goold, G., 386–87
Graham, A. J., 6n.18
Gramsci, A., 25
Grant, M., 311
Groag, E., 44
Gros, P., 314
Gruen, E. S., 213n.2, 321–22, 429n.48

Habicht, C., xviii
Haller, B., xvii
Hammond, M., xiv, 27
"Harvard School," 181, 197n.29,
     199n.31
Hennig, D., 440n.99
Hirschfeld, O., 132
Hölscher, T., 119
Hornsby, R. A., 196n.28
Housman, A. E., 386–87
Hubbard, M., 221n.11, 231

Jones, A. H. M., xviii, 23

Keppie, L., xviii
Kienast, D., xiii, 337n.7
Klingner, F., 209
Kloft, H., xvii
Kneissl, P., 365n.2, 371
Kraft, K., 405n.42
Kunkel, W., 52, 83n.67

Le Roy Ladurie, Emmanuel, 8, 25
Lange, L., 50
Last, H., 3, 23

MacMullen, R., 16
Malcovati, E., 31
Manuwald, B., 144n.20
Marache, R., 244, 247, 249, 254
Marg, W., 247, 248–49
Mazzarino, S., 18
Meier, C., xvii, 10, 23, 25, 48, 81–82
Meyer, E., xii–xv, 3, 23, 25, 28, 170
Meyer, P., 170n.69
Millar, F., xv n. 19, 19–20, 22, 170
Minadeo, R., 221n.11, 223n.12
Momigliano, A., xivn.13, xvin.26, 2n.3,
     2n.4, 20n.76, 21, 43n.5, 49
Mommsen, T., xiii, xv, 3, 5, 23, 25, 42–
     53, 77, 81, 93, 134, 135, 136

Montesquieu, xii
Münzer, F., 3, 10, 44–45
Murgatroyd, P., 234n.23

Namier, L. (Ludwig Bernstein Nami-
     erowsky), 4–5, 10, 26
Nicolet, C., 368–71, 379
Niebuhr, B. G., 23
Nisbet, R. G. M., 221n.11, 231
Nock, A. D., 338, 345
Nugent, S. G., 425n.28

Ogilvie, R. M., 136
Otis, R., 241
Owen, S. G., 245, 251

Parry, A., 181
Pflaum, H.-G., 6n.18, 9
Picard, C., 325
Pöschl, V., 180, 203, 204
Premerstein, A. von, 4, 24, 44, 77
Price, S. R. F., xviii, 377–78
Purcell, N., 372–73
Putnam, M., 180–81, 388, 390

Quinn, K., 180–81, 200, 204, 217n.5

Raaflaub, K., xviii
Ramage, E. S., xviii
Rolland, H., 312
Rostovtzeff, M., xv, 23

Sattler, P., xviii, 434n.70
Schmitthenner, W., 399n.11
Schurr, W., 27
Schwegler, A., 132
Scott, K., 246
Seager, R., 213n.2
Silverberg-Pierce, S., 319, 320
Simon, E., xviii–xix, 390
Stahl, H. -P., 236n.24
Stein, A., 44
Stier, H. E., 27
Sumner, G. V., 132n.25
Swan, P. M., 424n.21
Swoboda, E., 402n.28
Syme, R., xiii–xix, 1–53, 69, 76–80, 84,
     122, 238, 258, 262–63, 337, 381,
     402n.28, 407n.54, 428n.40, 429,
     431, 440n.99, 445, 446n.120, 450–
     51, 451n.136, 451n.138
Szramkiewicz, R., xviii

Tarn, W. W., 44
Thibault, J. C., 240
Torelli, M., 391

Vittinghoff, F., xviii

Wallace-Hadrill, A., xviii, 366–67
Weber, W., 3, 27, 43
Wells, C., xviii
Wiedemann, T., 244, 248–49

Williams, G., 246
Williams, R. D., 181
Wiseman, T. P., xviii
Woodman, A. J., xvii

Yavetz, Z., xvii

Zanker, P., xviii–xix, 74, 79–81, 125n.5,
   127, 334n.1
Ziegler, K., xviii

Index of Sources

LITERARY

Aelian
  Nat. anim. 2.11 . . . . 286n.54
    5.49 . . . . 286n.50
    6.61 . . . . 285n.49
    7.2 . . . . 286n.50
    7.15 . . . . 285n.49
    7.44 . . . . 284n.39, 284n.40
    9.8 . . . . 285n.49
    11.15 . . . . 286n.50
Ammianus Marcellinus
  17.4.5 . . . . 424n.22
Anthol. Palatina
  9.285 286–87
  10.25 265
Appian
  Bell. civ. 1.26 . . . . . 277, 373–74n.34,
                                        bis
    1.54 . . . . 374n.34 bis
    1.58 . . . . 374n.34 bis
    1.65 . . . . 374n.34 bis
    1.69 . . . . 374n.34
    1.74 . . . . 374n.34
    1.100 . . . . 374n.34
    2.148 . . . . 344n.41
    3.2–3 . . . . 90n.86
    3.7 . . . . 78n.40
    3.51 . . . . 343n.37
    4.7 . . . . 374n.34
    4.11 . . . . 374n.34
    4.13 . . . . 32n.30
    4.36 . . . . 374n.34
    4.38 . . . . 405n.40

    4.50 . . . . 422n.13
    4.73 . . . . 374n.34
    5.12–49 344
    5.92 . . . . 405n.40
    5.128 . . . . 95n.113
    5.130 . . . . .95n.113, 346
    5.132 . . . . .95n.113, 95n.114
    5.145 . . . . 401n.23
  III. 12–13 . . . . 401n.23
    15 . . . . 401n.23
    16 . . . . 401n.26
    16–17 . . . . 402n.28
    18 . . . . 401n.23
    18–28 . . . . 402n.27
    22 . . . . 402n.28
    27 . . . . 401n.25
    28 . . . . 402n.28
  Pun. 112 . . . . 104n.159
Aristotle
  Rhetoric 243
Aufidius Bassus
  Peter, *HRR* II 96 F 3 . . . . 407n.55
Augustus
  Res Gestae 1 . . . . . . .75n.25, 89n.83,
                                        175
    1.1 . . . . 94n.107
    2 . . . . 75n.28, 123, 175, 202
    3 . . . . 75n.30
    3.2 197
    4 . . . . 73n.11, 78n.4
    5 . . . . 75n.31, 111n.182,
                                111n.184, 434

Augustus *(continued)*
6 .... 73n.11, 111n.183,
                       114n.196
8 .... 82n.64, 103n.152,
                       113n.194
8.2 .... 433n.68
9 .... 75n.27
10 ....89n.81, 94n.112,
               95n.117, 109n.177
10.2 .... 167n.56, 382n.3
11 .... 237n.25
12.2 .... 400n.15
13 .... 102n.144, 400n.16,
                       414n.95
14 .... 121n.218
15 .... 102n.145, 107n.168,
                       121n.219
15–24 .... 14n.50
16 ....102n.146, 109n.176
19 .... 102n.147
20 .... 102n.147
21 202
22 ....102n.47, 121n.219
23 .... 102n.47
25 .... 72n.8, 75n.27, 100n.139,
                       101n.141
25.3 .... 265n.15
26.2 .... 409n.70
26.3 .... 404n.49
26.5 .... 163n.35
27.2 .... 397n.3
29 125
29.2 ..... 397n.5, 397n.6, 397n.7
30.1 .... 151n.45, 402n.29
30.2 .... 402n.30
31 284
32.1 .... 411n.77
34 ....52, 75n. 26, 75n.27,
             75n.32, 85n.72, 104
34.1 336
35 ..... 73n.12, 75n.32, 87n.78,
                       87n.79, 125
35.1 .... 412n.88

Malcovati, *ICAOF*⁵
Dicta 1 .... 32n.31
4 .... 35n.50
5 .... 35n.48
7 .... 33n.37
9 .... 36n.53
10 .... 38n.61
12 .... 37n.58
15 .... 38n.59
16 .... 35n.49
17 .... 33n.36
18 .... 34n.38
21 .... 33n.35
23 .... 34n.42

24 .... 34n.43
26 .... 34n.44
27 .... 33n.33
28 .... 33n.34
32 .... 34n.39, 34n.41
36 .... 39n.72
38 .... 39n.67
41 .... 30n.26
44 .... 35n.51
47 .... 32n.30
50 .... 38n.60
51 .... 38n.62
56 .... 37n.56
58 .... 37n.57
62 .... 30n.27
Epist. 8 .... 34n.45

Catullus
16 253
16.4 .... 223n.12
16.8 .... 223n.12
25.1 .... 223n.12
56.7 .... 223n.12
61.51–55 .... 228n.17
67.26 .... 223n.12
68.56 .... 220n.8
Cicero
Ad Att. 2.1–2 .... 149n.36
    6.1.17 ....7n.25
    8.11 .... 28n.19
    14.9.3 .... 90n.89
    14.10.3 .... 90n.89
    14.11.2 .... 90n.89
    16.8.1 .... 33n.32
    16.9.1 .... 33n.32
    16.11.6 .... 33n.32
    16.14.1 .... 90n.89
    16.15.3 .... 89n.84
Ad Brut. 24.7 .... 343n.37
Ad Fam. 5.12 .... 149n.36
    5.12.8 .... 149n.137
    7.1.3–4 285
    11.20.1 .... 32n.31
Ad Q. fr. 1.1.21 .... 39n.66
Cat. 3.21 277
De Div. 2.98 .... 295n.100
De Dom. 29.77 .... 109n.178
De Leg. 1.5–6 135
    3.3.10 .... 115n.202
De Leg. agrar. 2.17 .... 48n.26
De Or. 2.51–53 135
    2.52 135
De Prov. cons. 19.46 ..... 104n.159
De Rep. 2 .... 148n.33
    2.29.51 .... 91n.98

4.12 .... 441n.104
5.3.5 .... 91n.98
5.4.6 .... 91n.98
5.6.8 .... 91n.98
5.7.9 .... 91n.98
6.1.1 .... 91n.98
6.8.8 .... 91n.98
Har. resp. 3.5 .... 99n.135
11.22 .... 99n.135
Phil. 1.2.5 .... 90n.86
3.2.5 .... 90n.90
3.3.7 .... 90n.90
3.31 277
5.8.23 .... 91n.95
5.16.43 ....71n.1
5.16.45ff. 90n.91
5.17.48 .... 91n.95
5.18.51 .... 90n.92
5.19.53 .... 91n.95
5.20 277
13.11.24–25 ....90n.8
Pro Sest. 6 .... 132n.25
7.16 .... 109n.178
16.38 .... 99n.135
Cinna
F 6 (Morel) 230n.18
Consolatio ad Liviam 404
15–16 .... 403n.34, 404n.36
175 .... 403n.34, 404n.37
283 ....277, 291n.74
384–86 .... 404n.37
385–86 .... 403n.34
Cyprian
1 .... 291n.75

Dante
Div. Comm. Inf. 1.106–108 177
De Viris Illustribus
34 .... 133n.26
56 133
Dio Cassius
42.49.1–5 .... 160n.18
42.51.5 .... 114n.198
42.52.1–55.3 .... 161n.20
43.15.2–18.5 .... 157n.7
43.47.3 .... 114n.198
44.2.1–5 .... 160n.46
44.35.3 .... 156n.4
45.4.3 .... 158n.8
45.5–6 .... 158n.8
45.11.2 .... 158n.9
45.12.1–13.4 .... 160n.18
45.12.5 .... 158n.11
45.13.2–3 .... 161n.20
45.14.1–3 .... 158n.8

46.3 .... 158n.8
46.29.2 .... 343n.37
46.32 .... 158n.10
46.34.4 .... 158n.8, 158n.9
46.51.5–52.4 .... 158n.8
47.1.1 .... 158n.9
47.3.1–13.4 .... 158n.8
47.7.1–5 .... 158n.8
47.18.3–19.3 .... 344n.41
47.39.1–5 .... 158n.10
47.39.4–5 .... 159n.13
47.45.2 .... 160n.17
47.49.4 .... 167n.56
48.1.2 .... 158n.10
48.3.1–5 .... 343n.40
48.4–14 344
48.6.1–8.5 .... 160n.18
48.8.1–5 .... 165n.42
48.8.4 .... 160n.19
48.12.4–5 344
48.14.3–5 .... 158n.8
48.19.2 341
48.29.2–3 .... 158n.8
48.33.1–3 .... 158n.8
48.39 .... 345n.48
48.39–41 .... 162n.27
48.47.5–6 .... 160n.17
48.49–51 .... 162n.26
48.49.2–3 .... 405n.40
48.49.4 .... 160n.17
49.1–10 .... 162n.26
49.5.1–5 .... 160n.17
49.12.1 .... 158n.11
49.12.4 ....95n.116, 158n.8,
                                 167n.56
49.13.1–14.2 .... 161n.20
49.14.5 .... 164n.40
49.15.3 .... 95n.117, 167n.56
49.15.5 .... 94n.112
49.18.6 278
49.19.1–22.1 .... 162n.27
49.21.1 .... 162n.27
49.22.1 .... 162n.27
49.27.1 .... 161n.20
49.34.2 .... 401n.23
49.34.3–5 .... 161n.20
49.35.1–4 .... 163n.34
49.35.2 .... 401n.25
49.36.1 ....158n.11, 401n.24
49.36.1–37.6 .... 163n.35
49.37.1–38.4 .... 402n.27
49.37.6 .... 402n.28
49.38.1 .... 402n.28
49.38.2 ....163n.32, 410n.75
49.38.2–4 .... 163n.35
49.38.4 .... 161n.20
49.39.3ff. 95n.119

Dio Cassius *(continued)*

49.41.1–4 .... 95n.119
49.41.4–6 .... 97n.127
49.41.6 .... 158n.11
49.42.2–43.4 .... 162n.26
49.43.1–4 .... 96n.125
49.43.5 .... 75n.29, 142
49.43.8 .... 163n.35, 402n.27,
                               402n.28
50.1.1–2 .... 158n.9
50.1.2 .... 158n.10
50.1.4 .... 158n.11
50.2.2 .... 158n.9
50.2.4–6 .... 265n.15
50.2.6f. 99n.130
50.3.1 .... 99n.132
50.4.3 .... 100n.137
50.4.4 .... 100n.138
50.4.4–5 .... 158n.11
50.7.1–2 .... 158n.11
50.10 .... 282n.29
50.10.3–5 .... 165n.42
50.10.4–6 376
50.11.3 .... 162n.26
50.13.5 .... 162n.26
50.16–30 .... 170n.71
50.20.6 .... 265n.15
50.24.4 .... 163n.35
50.26.3 .... 100n.137
51.1.2–3 .... 411n.80
51.2.4 .... 75n.30
51.2.4–6 .... 167n.56
51.3.1–5 .... 161n.20
51.4 .... 78n.40
51.4.1–8 .... 161n.20
51.4.5–8 .... 164n.40
51.15.5–16.1 .... 167n.56
51.18.1 .... 411n.80
51.20.4–5 .... 102n.144
51.20.5 .... 405n.40
51.21.3 .... 165n.45
51.21.5–6 .... 405n.40
51.21.5–9 .... 411n.81
51.23.2–27.3 .... 172n.79
52.2–40 .... 102n.148
52.10.4 .... 421n.11
52.14.3–5 .... 159n.13
52.14.3–15.4 .... 166n.48
52.19.1–3 .... 166n.48, 166n.49,
                               434n.70
52.19.2 369
52.19.2–3 .... 159n.13
52.25.6–7 .... 166n.49
52.28.1 .... 164n.37
52.28.1–6 .... 165n.42
52.30.3–10 .... 165n.43
52.31.1–4 .... 166n.48

52.31.3–10 .... 167n.53
52.31.5–10 .... 421n.11
52.32.1–3 .... 166n.48
52.41.1 .... 102n.148
52.41.2 .... 161n.23
52.42 .... 433n.68
52.42.1 ....103n.151, 103n.155
52.42.8 .... 434n.70
53.1.1 .... 103n.150, 103n.158,
                               166n.50
53.2.1 .... 165n.45
53.2.3 .... 165n.45
53.2.4 .... 118n.210
53.2.5 ....103n.156, 160n.15
53.2.6–22.5 .... 170n.72
53.3–10 .... 170n.70
53.3.1–11.5 .... 166n.52
53.4.1–2 .... 173n.84
53.5.3 .... 173n.84
53.6.1 .... 173n.84
53.6.1–7.3 .... 173n.84
53.8.1 .... 173n.84
53.8.4–5 .... 166n.48
53.9.4 .... 173n.84
53.10.4–5 .... 410n.71
53.11.1–12.3 .... 167n.57
53.11.2 .... 168n.61
53.11.5 ....75n.24, 160n.16
53.12.3 ....75n.24, 160n.16
53.13.1 ....166n.50, 399n.11
53.13.2–15.1 .... 167n.53
53.15.2–3 .... 167n.53
53.16.1 .... 160n.16
53.16.7 .... 116n.204
53.16.7–8 .... 105n.163
53.17 .... 447n.122
53.19 421
53.19.1 ....167n.61, 168n.64
53.19.3–4 140
53.19.3–6 .... 168n.63
53.19.6 .... 173n.83
53.20.3 .... 108n.172
53.21.3 ....116n.203, 166n.51
53.21.3–6 .... 167n.53
53.21.4 .... 166n.50
53.21.5–7 .... 160n.16
53.21.6 .... 116n.203
53.21.6–7 .... 166n.50
53.22.1–2 .... 165n.45
53.22.5 .... 163n.32, 163n.35,
                          405n.40, 410n.75
53.23.1 .... 399n.12
53.23.5 .... 423n.19
53.23.5–24.3 .... 424n.21
53.23.6–7 .... 167n.53
53.23.7 .... 424n.21
53.24.1 .... 425n.25

53.24.1–3 . . . . 169n.67
53.24.4ff. 112n.191
53.24.4–6 . . . . 427n.36
53.24.6 . . . . 160n.16, 427n.37
53.25.1 . . . . 167n.53
53.25.2 . . . . 163n.32, 410n.75
53.25.5–8 . . . . 399n.12
53.25.6–7 . . . . 163n.34
53.26.1 . . . . 400n.20
53.26.4–5 . . . . 405n.40
53.26.5 . . . . 400n.16, 400n.17
53.28.3 . . . . 108n.173
53.29.1–2 . . . . 400n.13
53.29.3–8 . . . . 163n.32
53.29.4 . . . . 163n.35
53.29.7 . . . . 163n.35
53.30 . . . . 237n.25
53.30.1 . . . . 108n.171
53.30.2 . . . . 108n.173
53.31.1 . . . . 166n.50, 434n.74
53.31.2–3 . . . . 165n.45
53.32.3f. 107n.169
53.32.4 . . . . 109n.175
53.32.6 . . . . 109n.177
53.33.1 . . . . 167n.53, 167n.55
53.33.1–2 . . . . 166n.50
54.1.3 . . . . 111n.182
54.1.3–5 . . . . 166n.52
54.1.5 . . . . 160n.16
54.2.1 . . . . 112n.188
54.2.2 . . . . 112n.190
54.2.3–4 . . . . 165n.45
54.2.4 . . . . 427n.37
54.3.1 . . . . 160n.16
54.3.2–6 . . . . 426n.34
54.3.2–8 . . . . 169n.66
54.3.4 . . . . 436n.33
54.3.5 . . . . 161n.23
54.3.5–8 . . . . 426n.35
54.3.8 . . . . 160n.16
54.4.1 . . . . 112n.189
54.4.2–4 . . . . 171n.74
54.5.1–3 . . . . 400n.14
54.5.3 . . . . 123n.1
54.5.4–6 . . . . 163n.35
54.6 . . . . 237n.25
54.6.1 . . . . 111n.185, 166n.46
54.6.2f. 111n.186
54.6.3–4 . . . . 160n.16
54.6.5–6 . . . . 111n.185
54.6.6 . . . . 118n.210
54.7 . . . . 396n.2
54.7.6 . . . . 160n.16
54.8.1 . . . . 397n.7
54.8.1–2 . . . . 397n.5
54.8.1–3 . . . . 163n.33
54.8.3 125

54.9.1 . . . . 410n.71
54.9.1–2 . . . . 164n.35
54.9.1–3 . . . . 396n.2
54.9.4 . . . . 397n.3
54.10–11 . . . . 237n.25
54.10.1–2 . . . . 160n.16
54.10.5 . . . . 113n.194, 160n.16
54.11.2 . . . . 405n.40
54.11.2–6 . . . . . . 162n.26, 400n.14
54.11.3–5 . . . . 161n.20
54.11.4–5 . . . . 163n.34
54.11.6 . . . . 173n.83
54.12–15 . . . . 434n.71
54.12.2f. 421n.12
54.12.3 . . . . 115n.200, 420n.8,
                                     421n.12
54.12.4–5 . . . . 166n.50
54.13–14 . . . . . . 103n.154, 421n.12,
                                     433n.68
54.13.1 . . . . 160n.16
54.13.4 . . . . 160n.16
54.14.1 . . . . 115n.199
54.15.1 . . . . 169n.66, 422n.12,
                                     427n.38
54.15.1–3 . . . . 168n.65, 173n.83
54.15.1–4 420
54.15.4 . . . . 169n.66, 422n.13
54.15.4–8 . . . . . . 167n.56, 169n.68,
                                     434n.70
54.15.7 . . . . 166n.51
54.15.7–8 . . . . . . 160n.16, 444n.111
54.16.3–6 . . . . . . 160n.16, 166n.51,
                                     169n.68
54.18.1 . . . . 169n.66
54.18.1 . . . . 420n.8, 421n.12
54.18.1–3 . . . . 397n.7
54.19.1 . . . . 405n.42
54.19.3 . . . . 160n.16, 161n.23
54.19.6 . . . . 161n.23
54.20.4–5 . . . . 405n.41
54.20.6 . . . . 405n.42
54.22.1–4 . . . . 403n.34
54.23.2–3 . . . . 38n.63
54.23.2–6 . . . . 160n.16
54.23.6 . . . . 165n.45
54.23.7 . . . . 400n.15
54.24.5–6 . . . . 163n.35
54.25.1 . . . . 160n.16, 400n.15,
                                405n.43, 405n.44
54.25.5 . . . . 173n.83
54.25.5–6 . . . . . . 164n.41, 165n.42
54.25.6 . . . . 165n.45
54.26.3–9 . . . . 433n.68
54.26.8–27.1 . . . . 160n.16
54.27.2 . . . . 167n.56, 383
54.27.3 . . . . 391n.25
54.28.5 . . . . 127n.13

Dio Cassius *(continued)*

54.29 .... 162n.26
54.29.1–2 .... 161n.23
54.29.4 .... 165n.45
54.29.7–8 .... 171n.74
54.30.4 261
54.31.2–4 .... 402n.29
54.31.4 .... 160n.16
54.32.1 .... 405n.45
54.33.1 127
54.33.5 .... 160n.16
54.34.2–3 127
54.34.3–4 .... 402n.29
54.34.4 .... 160n.16
54.35.1 .... 433n.68
54.35.1–2 .... 278n.10
54.35.3–4 .... 171n.74
54.36.1 .... 392n.29
54.36.2 .... 402n.29, 402n.30
55.1.2–5 .... 405n.46
55.1.3 .... 406n.48
55.1.3–5 .... 163n.34
55.2.1–3 .... 406n.48
55.2.4 .... 402n.29
55.4.1–3 .... 420n.8
55.4.2–3 .... 167n.54
55.4.3 .... 116n.204, 166n.51,
                169n.66, 420n.8,
                427n.38, 433n.66,
                441n.102
55.5.4 .... 169n.67
55.6.1 .... 166n.52, 167n.58
55.6.2–3 .... 406n.49
55.6.3 .... 160n.16
55.7 261–62
55.7.1–6 .... 161n.23
55.7.3 .... 166n.51
55.7.4 .... 161n.24, 166n.49
55.7.5 .... 161n.23
55.8.1–2 278
55.9.5 .... 160n.16
55.9.5–8 .... 293n.85
55.9.6 .... 278n.11
55.10.1 .... 165n.45
55.10.2–3 .... 412n.87
55.10.3 .... 129n.19, 412n.89
55.10.6–7 .... 286n.53
55.10.7 .... 347n.59
55.10.9 323
55.10.12–16 .... 429n.46
55.10.14–15 .... 160n.16
55.10.18 .... 398n.8
55.10.18–19 .... 398n.9
55.10.20–21 .... 398n.10
55.10a 398n.9
55.10a.2 323
55.10a.2–3 .... 407n.54

55.10a.4 .... 398n.10
55.10a.6–9 .... 163n.34
55.10a.9 .... 173n.83
55.11.2–3 .... 293n.86
55.12.3 .... 166n.52, 167n.58
55.13.3 .... 433n.68
55.14–22 .... 428n.39
55.14–22.2 .... 167n.56
55.14.1f. 428n.41
55.14.1–22.1 .... 170n.70
55.14.2–3 .... 173n.84
55.14.2–21.4 .... 421n.11
55.15.2 .... 173n.84
55.15.4–7 .... 173n.84
55.22.1f. 428n.41
55.23.1 .... 165n.42
55.23.2 .... 165n.42
55.23.2–7 .... 170n.69
55.24.1–4 .... 165n.42
55.25.1–6 .... 165n.42
55.25.3 .... 165n.45
55.25.4 .... 168n.62
55.25.4–5 .... 168n.59
55.25.4–6 .... 435n.77
55.26–27.4 .... 440n.99
55.26.4f. 427n.37
55.26.4–5 .... 160n.16
55.27 ....445n.116
55.27.1–3 .... 431n.57, 433n.66,
                435n.79
55.27.3 .... 167n.67
55.27.4 .... 277n.7, 291n.75
55.28.5 .... 407n.56
55.28.6 .... 407n.57
55.29.1 .... 163n.35
55.29.3–31.4 .... 403n.31
55.31.1–4 .... 160n.16
55.32.1f. 431n.58
55.33.1–3 .... 403n.31
55.34.1 .... 166n.50, 166n.51,
                167n.53
55.34.2 .... 167n.53
55.34.3–7 .... 403n.31
56.2.4 .... 171n.74
56.2.4–5 .... 286n.51
56.11–16 .... 172n.78, 403n.32
56.12.3–5 .... 163n.34
56.13.1–2 .... 161n.20
56.16.4 .... 163n.34
56.17.1–3 .... 403n.33
56.18–22 .... 172n.81
56.18.1 .... 406n.52
56.18.1–2 .... 407n.58
56.18.1–24.5 .... 163n.34
56.18.3 .... 407n.60
56.18.4–22.2 .... 408n.61
56.23.2–4 .... 160n.16

56.24.1–5 .... 171n.74
56.24.6 .... 408n.64
56.25 ...... 276n.2, 277n.8, 278n.9
56.25.2–3 .... 408n.64
56.25.4 .... 114n.197
56.25.5 .... 295n.101
56.27 .... 441n.102
56.27.1 .... 169n.67, 445
56.27.1–3 .... 160n.16
56.28.1 .... 166n.52, 167n.58
56.28.4–6 .... 168n.60
                              435n.77
56.28.6 .... 168n.62
56.29.2 323
56.33.5–6 .... 164n.36, 410n.73
56.33.6 .... 410n.74
56.34.2–3 .... 125n.6, 130n.20
56.37.3 .... 160n.15
56.38.1–2 .... 167n.56
56.38.2 .... 161n.24
56.39.5 .... 166n.46
56.39.6 .... 166n.52
56.40.2 .... 165n.42
56.40.3 .... 166n.51, 167n.53
56.40.4 .... 165n.44
56.41.5 .... 165n.45
56.43 .... 453n.141
56.43.1 .... 166n.51
56.43.1–3 .... 116n.204
56.43.3 .... 400n.15
56.43.4 .... 159n.13
56.44.1–2 .... 160n.15
56.44.3f. 75n.23
57.9.2–3 .... 169n.67
57.19.1ᵇ–2 .... 169n.67
57.24 .... 439n.97, 442n.105
57.24.3 .... 142n.8
59.3.1 .... 167n.54
60.22.3 .... 339n.20
71.36.4 .... 157n.6
72.4.1–7.3 .... 166n.47
72.20.1–21.2 .... 166n.47
72.23.2–4 .... 171n.74
73.8.1–4 .... 161n.21
73.11.2–12.1 .... 161n.21
74.2.1–3 .... 166n.47
74.2.2–3 .... 164n.38
74.8.4–5 .... 164n.38
74.9.4 .... 164n.38
75.2.3–4 .... 162n.28
75.3.2–3 .... 162n.29
75.8.1–4 .... 166n.47
75.9.1–5 .... 162n.29
75.12.3–5 .... 161n.21
76.15.2 .... 164n.38
76.16.1–4 .... 164n.38
76.16.3 .... 165n.43

77.3.1–2 .... 164n.38
77.4.1–6.1 .... 166n.47
77.7–8 .... 162n.29
77.9.1–10.4 .... 164n.38
77.9.7 .... 165n.43
77.11.5 .... 162n.28
78.3.1 .... 162n.29
78.3.4–5 .... 161n.21
78.10.1–2 .... 171n.74
78.36.1–3 .... 164n.38
80.2.2–3 .... 161n.21
80.4.1–2 .... 161n.21
80.4.2–5.1 .... 161n.22
80.5.3 .... 171n.74
Diodorus Siculus
  15.51.1 .... 130n.22
  31.11.1 134
Dionysius of Halicarnassus
  Ant. Rom. 6.4.1 131
          6.5.4 131
          6.39.2 136
          6.57ff. 131
          6.96 131
          7.18.1–2 .... 153n.55
          7.26.4 .... 153n.55
Donatus, Tib. Claud. (ed. H. Georgii)
  Int. Verg. 2 .... 178n.7

Euripides
  Alc. 22 206
  Hipp. 1437f. 206
  Phoen. 559 .... 34n.40
Eutropius
  7.5 .... 405n.40
  7.9 .... 397n.6

Festus
  464L 134
  Brev. 7 .... 402n.29
Florus
  1.7 130
  2.22 .... 403n.34
  2.23 .... 401n.25
  2.24.8 .... 402n.29
  2.30.22 .... 406n.51
  2.30.23–27 .... 405n.46
  2.30.29–30 .... 406n.51
  2.30.31 .... 407n.60
  2.30.32–38 .... 408n.61
  2.30.39 .... 408n.63
  2.33.48–58 .... 399n.12
  2.33.53 .... 400n.17
  2.33.59 .... 400n.19
  2.34 .... 284n.43

Frontinus
   De aqued. 1.9 .... 96n.125
   Strat. 2.1.15 .... 402n.29

Gellius, Aulus
   Noctes Atticae 5.18.7ff. 148n.32
     9.11.10 .... 130n.23
    10.11.5 .... 34n.39
    10.24.1 .... 37n.56
    10.27.3 288
    13.5 .... 41n.82
    13.10.1–3 .... 444n.111
    15.7.3 .... 294n.92
Germanicus
   Phaen. 558–60 .... 385n.9

Herodotus
   7.206 .... 290n.72
Historia Augusta
   Alex. Sev. 28.6 .... 127, 412n.89
Homer
   Il. 18.98 .... 32n.30
Homeric Hymns
   33.10 .... 291n.79
   4.475ff. 288n.59
   4.523ff. 288
   4.525ff. 288n.59, 288n.61
Horace
   Ars poetica 263
    323 .... 40n.79, 263
   Carmen saeculare 262, 269
    49–52 237
    53–56 .... 214, 412n.83
    61–68 .... 281n.23
   Carmina 1.2 .... 214, 265
    1.2.41ff. 74n.22
    1.2.41–44 .... 287n.56
    1.2.44 211
    1.2.50 274
    1.4 218
    1.5 218–19
    1.6 233
    1.6.9–12 234
    1.10.9–12 .... 288n.58
    1.12 .... 214–15, 268–69
    1.12.57 215
    1.17.19 .... 221n.10
    1.21.3 .... 411n.76
    1.21.13–16 214
    1.23 218
    1.23.11 .... 219n.6
    1.29 218
    1.35.29 .... 411n.76
    1.35.29–40 235

    1.35.38–40 .... 214n.3
    1.37 234
    1.37.21 .... 76n.34
    2.1 .... 214, 264n.14
    2.1.2 .... 221n.11
    2.1.6ff. 151n.47
    2.8 228–29
    2.8.21 .... 228n.17
    2.8.21–24 .... 228n.17
    2.9 .... 214, 217–38
    2.9.10–12 .... 230n.18
    2.9.13–17 .... 217n.5
    2.9.17–18 219
    2.10 228–29
    2.11 .... 227n.16, 228
    2.12 233
    2.12.9–12 .... 144, 234
    3.3.9–12 .... 291n.76
    3.3.12 .... 215.4
    3.4 215
    3.4.34 .... 411n.76
    3.5.2 .... 215n.4
    3.5.2–4 .... 411n.76
    3.5.29 215
    3.6 215
    3.6.5 215
    3.7 218
    3.13 218
    3.14 .... 215–16, 400n.21
    3.14.27–28 216
    3.21 .... 264n.14
    3.24.25–29 216
    3.25 216–17
    3.30 272
    3.30.8–9 381–82
    4.1 273
    4.1.33–34 220
    4.2 271
    4.3 272
    4.5.1f. 117n.205
    4.5.5–8 .... 292n.84
    4.5.17–28 275
    4.6 272
    4.10 273
    4.10.4–5 220
    4.10.8 220
    4.11 .... 262, 273
    4.12 273
    4.13 273
    4.14.7–19 .... 404n.36
    4.14.41–52 .... 412n.83
    4.14.47 .... 411n.76
    4.14.50 .... 400n.21
    4.15 271–72
    4.15.1–16 271
    4.15.6–8 .... 412n.83
    4.15.13–16 .... 395n.1
    4.15.17–24 238

4.15.21–24 .... 412n.83
4.15.25–32 272
4.15.26 .... 282n.30
Epistles 1 ....262, 263
    1.1.14 .... 40n.78
    1.12.26–27 .... 397n.4
    1.12.27–28 .... 412n.83
    1.18.9 .... 40n.76
    1.18.56–57 .... 412n.83
    2 263
    2.1 .... 243n.11, 249, 263
    2.1.5–6 282
    2.1.7 282
    2.1.96 .... 284n.43
    2.1.226–28 269
    2.1.256 .... 412n.83
    2.2 263
    2.2.47–48 .... 224n.14
Epodes 1 265
    7.7 .... 411n.76
    7.17–20 .... 291n.73
    9 265
    12.16 .... 223n.12
    12.17 .... 223n.12
Satires 1.1.106 .... 40n.75
    1.2.28–30 .... 40n.76
    1.6.52–62 263–64
    2.1.10–20 .... 234n.22
    2.1.60ff. 40n.80
    2.2.53–69 .... 40n.76
    2.3.182–86 .... 96n.125
    2.6.1–4 .... 40n.81
Hyginus
Poet. astr. 2.7 289

Jerome
    Chron. 2048 ....439n.97, 441n.102
Josephus
    AJ 15.105 .... 397n.3
        19.162–273 .... 18n.67
Justin
    42.5.10–11 .... 397n.7
Juvenal
    6.158 .... 430n.53
    10.56–113 13
    12.102f. 286n.52
    Schol. on 6.157f. 430n.54,
                          431n.56

Livy
    Praef. 4 ....150, 152
        5 149–50
        9 25
        10 129

1.2.1 176
1.3.1–3 128
1.19.3 .... 124n.3, 128n.17
1.60.2 131
2.6.9 131
2.18.5–6 137
2.19.10 131
2.30.5 ....136n.33, 137
2.31.8–10 131
2.32–33 131
3.7.6 136
4.2.1 131
4.2.3 131
4.20.4–11 128
4.20.5–11 124
4.20.7 .... 128n.17, 423n.15
4.32.4 128
5.13.6 .... 288n.62
5.40.7 132
5.40.7–10 .... 132n.25
5.40.9 130
6.2.7–4.3 131
6.30.2 .... 130n.22
6.36.1ff. 131
6.42.4 131
7.20.4 .... 131n.25
8.30–36 .... 130n.23
9.18.9 129
10.17.1–10 133
10.17.11–12 ....133, 137
10.18 133
10.19.20 133
10.37.4 .... 147n.27
21.30.10 .... 395n.1
22.25.10 133
22.26.5–7 133
22.30 133
28.12.12 ...... 128n.17, 400n.19
29.22.10 144
30.41.4–5 .... 130n.21
31.21.18 133
31.49.7 .... 130n.21
31.50.7–10 .... 130n.21
32.7.14 .... 130n.21
32.28–31 130
32.30.11–12 133
33.22–23 130
33.23.5 133
34.44.4–5 .... 130n.21
34.45.3–5 134
34.58.8 .... 395n.1
35.9.1 .... 130n.21
42.61.5 .... 370n.20
44.17–18 134
45.41.5 134
Per. 59 .... 128n.17
    80 129
    116 .... 90n.86

Livy *(continued)*
    120 .... 93n.106, 94n.107
    121 ....124n.4, 151n.48,
                                      446n.121
    129 .... 95n.116
    133 .... 422n.13
    134 .... 405n.40
    138 .... 403n.34
    139 .... 323, 405n.45
    141 .... 405n.46
    142 .... 406n.48
Lucretius
    5.1302–5 .... 285n.47
    6.92–93 .... 224n.13

Macrobius
    Sat. 1.16.30 .... 292n.80
    1.19.16 289
    2.4.1 .... 37n.55
    2.4.4 .... 38n.60
    2.4.5 .... 38n.62
    2.4.9 .... 439n.97
    2.4.10 .... 37n.56
    2.4.11 .... 37n.56
    2.4.14 .... 37n.57
    2.4.18 .... 30n.27
    2.4.19 .... 36n.54
    2.4.21 .... 35n.47
    4.3 .... 284n.44
    7.1 .... 290n.71
Manilius
    Astron. 1.7–10 .... 279n.14
    1.13 .... 393n.31
    1.247–57 .... 279n.14
    1.247ff. 296n.102
    2.60–83 .... 279n.14
    2.164 291
    2.270ff. 294
    2.279–80 .... 295n.98
    2.281 .... 295n.96
    2.282 .... 295n.97, 295n.98
    2.439 .... 295n.98
    2.440 .... 279n.15, 291,
                          295n.97, 295n.98
    2.441 .... 295n.98
    2.442 .... 279n.15, 295n.96
    2.443 .... 295n.97
    2.444 .... 279n.15
    2.445 .... 279n.15, 295n.96
    2.446 .... 279n.15, 295n.98
    2.507–9 .... 386n.14
    2.509 .... 295, 387n.19
    2.608ff. 295n.99
    2.743–45 .... 292n.82
    2.945b 292n.82

    4.547f. 295
    4.548 293–94
    4.763ff. 294
    4.763–66 293
    4.773–74 295
    4.773–77 ..... 386n.14, 387n.18
    4.774 295
    5.726 .... 296n.102
Mark
    12.17 16
Martial
    1.4.8 253

Nepos
    Praef. 1 .... 149n.38
    Att. 18.1–4 .... 6n.16
    Cato 3.4 .... 147n.27
Nicolaus of Damascus
    FGrHist 90 F 27.106 .... 29n.25
    F 125 .... 154n.56
    F 130.59 .... 154n.56
    F 130.67 .... 154n.56
    F 130.81 .... 154n.56

Obsequens
    71 .... 405n.41
Orosius
    6.21.1 .... 399n.11
    6.21.3–10 .... 399n.12
    6.21.8 .... 399n.11
    6.21.11 .... 400n.6
    6.21.24 .... 397n.6
    6.21.27 .... 408n.62
    6.22.3 .... 453n.141
Ovid
    Amores 2.19.15 .... 221n.9
    3.9.63f. 425n.26
    Ars amat. 243, 244, 245, 251
    1.177–86 .... 398n.9
    1.201–12 .... 398n.9
    1.203 .... 280n.20
    Fasti 1.85–86 .... 412n.85
    1.318 .... 292n.80
    1.587ff. 292n.80
    1.607ff. 105n.163
    1.613–16 .... 291n.78
    1.640 ....276n.2, 277n.8,
                                278n.9
    1.641–44 277
    1.643–48 ......276n.2, 277n.8,
                                278n.9
    1.649 278
    1.704 279

1.707–8 .... 277n.7
1.717 .... 412n.85
2.631 .... 277n.4
2.684 .... 412n.85
3.415–28 383
3.420–22 .... 389n.22
3.421–22 279
3.881–82 .... 278n.10
4.809ff. 291n.73
4.857–62 .... 412n.85
4.951 .... 294n.91
5.550–52 .... 123n.1
5.550–62 .... 412n.87
5.563–66 .... 125n.7, 126,
                        412n.89
5.567–68 125
5.579–84 .... 397n.5
5.691–92 .... 288n.58
5.693ff. 291n.75
6.285–86 279
6.637f. 278
Metam. 240, 242, 252, 256–57
1.173–76 256–57
15.280–31 .... 412n.85
15.864 .... 294n.91
15.877 .... 412n.85
Pont. 2.9.71–80 .... 445n.118
  4.6.9–16 .... 445n.118
Trist. 1.7.15–30 .... 445n.118
2.27 253
2.27–52 253
2.37–38 252
2.54 246
2.55 246
2.61–62 252
2.61–66 252
2.63–66 252
2.77–80 252
2.125–38 253
2.135 252–53
2.135–36 253
2.147 253
2.161–64 .... 251n.35
2.169–78 .... 412n.86
2.188 253
2.211–12 251
2.211–14 252
2.213–44 251–52
2.219–24 252
2.225–32 .... 412n.86
2.239–44 252
2.271–72 250
2.275–76 252
2.345–61 .... 445n.118
2.353–58 253
2.445f. 424n.21
2.533–36 250

2.557–64 252
3.12.45–48 .... 412n.86
5.7.65–68 .... 445n.118

Paulus
  113L 136n.35
Pausanias
  2.3.4 .... 290n.72
  5.27.8 .... 290n.72
  9.22.1 .... 290n.72
  9.30.1 .... 288n.59
  9.34.3 .... 290n.72
  10.38.4 .... 411n.80
Phaedrus
  1.1.1–2 14
Pindar
  Pyth. 5.80 .... 290n.72
Plautus
  Aul. 422 .... 223n.12
  Mil. glor. 899 .... 264n.13
  Pseud. 695 .... 221n.10
  Truc. 207 .... 264n.13
    953 .... 264n.13
Pliny the Elder
  Nat. Hist. praef. 16 124,
                        152n.48
  Nat. Hist. praef. 20 ....148n.30,
                        153n.53
  3.20 321
  3.136–38 .... 404n.38
  4.5 .... 411n.80
  7.55 .... 439n.97
  7.148 .... 401n.25
  7.149 .... 259n.5, 429n.46
  7.149f. 419
  8.1–2 ....284n.39, 285n.48
  8.4–5 .... 286n.54
  8.11 ....147n.27, 285n.49
  8.13 .... 286n.50
  8.21 .... 285n.45
  8.28 286
  13.84 .... 146n.24
  21.9 .... 429n.46
  22.10 133
  22.13 .... 127n.14
  32.3 .... 348n.64
  34.30 .... 343n.38
  34.62 .... 278n.12
  34.73 .... 278n.12
  34.77 .... 278n.12
  34.80 .... 278n.12
  34.89 .... 278n.12
  34.90 ....278n.12, 295n.98
  35.27 .... 125n.8
  35.66 ....279n.13, 281

Pliny the Elder *(continued)*
    35.91 .... 250n.34
    35.93–4 .... 125n.8
    35.131 ....279n.13, 282
    35.144 ....279n.13, 281
    36.69 .... 384n.7
    36.101 .... 296n.103
    36.121 .... 96n.125
    36.196 ....279, 283n.36
    37.4....................... 279
    37.10 .... 163n.31
Pliny the Younger
    Epist. 2.3.8 124
    9.5 .... 39n.65
Plutarch
    Aem. 10 134
    Alex. 60.7 .... 283n.37
    Ant. 54.3–5 .... 95n.119
    56ff. 99n.131
    59 .... 143n.13
    60.1 .... 100n.138
    75.3 282
    75.4 .... 345n.48
    Apophth. Aug. 2 .... 38n.59
    7 .... 33n.36
    8 .... 34n.38
    12 .... 33n.35
    Caes. 28.5 .... 28n.21
    Cam. 21 130
    22.4 .... 132n.25
    41.6–42.1 131
    42 277
    Cic. 49.3 .... 34n.42
    Comp. Dion. et Brut. 5.2 .... 34n.43
    De E apud Delph. 9 .... 282n.31
    De Is. et Os. 35 .... 282n.31
    De soll. an. 17 .... 284n.40
    Fab. 13.3 133
    C. Gracch. 17 277
    Rom. 12 .... 387n.17
Pomponius
    Dig. 1.2.2.47 .... 444n.111
Porphyrion
    ad Hor. *Sat.* 1.3.82 .... 444n.111
Propertius
    1.6.23 .... 221n.10
    2.1....................... 265
    2.1.25–36 .... 412n.84
    2.1.42 ....178, 210
    2.10.13–18 .... 412n.84
    2.27.5 .... 411n.76
    2.34.61–62 .... 231n.19
    4 263
    4.1 272–73
    4.1.47 .... 194n.25
    4.1.87 .... 194n.25
    4.3.7 .... 411n.76

    4.4.11–12 .... 412n.84
    4.7 273
Prudentius
    Cont. Symm. 1.245–50 .... 291n.79

Quintilian
    Inst. 6.3.59 .... 284n.44
    6.3.63 .... 36n.53
    6.3.64 .... 38n.61
    6.3.77 ....37n.58, 323n.63
    10.1.75 .... 443n.108
    10.1.98 .... 445n.118
    10.1.104 .... 439n.97
    10.1.116 .....439n.97, 441n.101
    12.10.11 .....439n.97, 441n.101

Sallust
    Cat. 8 148
    9.2 277
    10 ....148n.35, 149n.40
    16.4 .... 78n.40
    38.3 ....23n.7
    53 148
    54 .... 148n.35
    Jug. 35 .... 148n.35
Seneca the Elder
    Controv. 2.2.12 .... 445n.118
    2.4.12–13 .... 261n.9
    2.4.13 440
    3 *praef.* 439n.97, 441n.101
    10 *praef.* 4–5 ....439, 440
    10 *praef.* 5 .... 436n.83
    10 *praef.* 7 .... 441n.100
    10 *praef.* 8 439–40,
                    441n.102
    10.5.22 ....433, 443n.108
    Suas. 1.7 .... 143n.13
    2.21 .... 445n.115
Seneca the Younger
    Ad Marc. 1.3 .... 439n.97
    22.4 .... 439n.97
    22.4–7 .... 442n.107
    26.1 .... 439n.97
    De Benef. 1.11.1 .... 39n.71
    2.2.1 .... 39n.71
    2.6.1 .... 39n.71
    2.20.2 .... 72n.10
    3.27 .... 34n.45
    3.27.1 .... 142n.8
    6.32.1f. 33n.37, 429n.46
    6.32.4 262
    De Brev. 4.5 .... 419, 427n.36,
                    429n.46

De Clem. 1.4.3 .... 72n.10
    1.9–11 .... 453n.141
    1.9.2–12 .... 428n.39
    1.9.6 ....419, 429n.46
    1.10.4 .... 33n.34
De Ira 3.23.3ff. 142n.8
    3.23.4 .... 34n.45, 35n.48
    3.23.4–8 .... 443n.108
Ep. mor. 91.13 .... 443n.108
Quaest. Nat. 5.12.4 128
Peter, *HRR* II 98 F 1 145
Servius
  ad Aen. 1.373 135
    3.93 .... 282n.31
    12.940 210
  ad Ecl. 5.66 .... 282n.31
    10.1 .... 424n.22
  ad Georg. 1.5 .... 282n.31
    2.162 .... 144n.16
    3.29 348
    4.1 .... 424n.22
Strabo
    3.4.17–18 .... 399n.11
    4.3.2 323
    4.5.3 .... 163n.35, 411n.77
    4.6.9 .... 403n.34
    5.4.7 323
    6.1.3 321
    6.4.2 .... 72n.10, 443n.109
    7.1.3 .... 405n.46
    7.1.4 .... 408n.65, 408n.66,
                408n.68, 410n.72
    7.3.11 .... 402n.30
    7.3.13 .... 402n.30
    7.5.3 .... 402n.28
    7.5.5 .... 402n.27
    7.7.5–6 .... 411n.80
    10.2.2 .... 411n.80
    11.13.3 .... 143n.13
    13.3.25 52
    16.1.28 .... 397n.6
    16.4.24 .... 163n.35
    17.1.10 .... 411n.80
    17.1.54 .... 397n.3
Suda
  s.v. "Polion" 143n.14
  s.v. "Timagenes" 443n.108
Suetonius
  Aug. 7 .... 291n.73
    7.2 .... 116n.204
    13.1 .... 33n.33
    15 .... 33n.34
    16.1 .... 374n.34
    16.2 .... 346–47, 412n.90
    17.2 ....99n.130, 100n.137
    18 .... 411n.80
    18.2 ....347, 348n.64

19.1 .... 169n.66, 419, 420,
        427n.36, 429n.45,
        431n.56, 432n.64
19.2 .... 431n.58, 433n.66
20 .... 401n.25
21 .... 403n.34, 406n.49
21.2 .... 410n.74
21.3 .... 397n.5, 397n.6
22 .... 411n.81
23 .... 405n.41, 405n.42,
        408n.61
23.2 .... 408n.62
25.4 .... 34n.39, 34n.41
26 .... 399n.12
28 .... 73n.15
28.1 .... 97n.127, 108n.172
28.2 274
28.3 .... 276n.1
29.1 123
29.2 .....123, 129n.19, 412n.87
31.1 .... 142, 445n.116
31.5 .... 103n.155, 115n.200,
       127, 129n.19, 274,
       347n.59, 412n.89,
       421n.12, 433n.68,
       434n.71
35 .... 144n.20
36 ....443n.110, 445n.115
40.2 .... 116n.203
40.3–5 .... 118n.209
42.1 .... 39n.72
42.3 .... 445n.116
43–45 .... 250n.34
44 .... 118n.209
44.1 .... 167n.53
50 ....27n.16, 163n.31, 347n.59
51 ....445n.114, 445n.115
51.2 .... 34n.45, 142n.8
51.3 447
53 .... 284n.44
53.1 .... 116n.204
54 ....34n.45, 39n.68,
       116n.204, 443n.110,
       444n.111
55 .... 142n.8, 442n.104,
       445n.114
56.1 ....126, 445n.114
56.2 .... 39n.67
56.4 .... 426n.33
58 274
59.3 323
65.1 .... 440n.99
65.1–5 .... 429n.45, 430n.54
65.2 .... 30n.26
65.4 .... 431n.58
66.2 ..... 424n.22, 423, 424n.21,
       425n.26

Suetonius(*continued*)
66.3 . . . . 161n.23, 259
69 . . . . 251n.35
70 345
72.3 . . . . 430n.54
74 . . . . 143n.12
75 347
81 . . . . 399n.12
81.1 . . . . 237n.25
85.1 . . . . 400n.18
85.2 . . . . 37n.55
89.2 . . . . 347n.59
94.4 350
94.5–9 349
94.12 . . . . . . 295n.101, 348n.60,
                             385n.9
98 . . . . 280n.21
98.2 . . . . 117n.206
98.4 . . . . 173n.85, 293n.87,
                            293n.89
99.1 . . . . 35n.51, 69
100.3 . . . . .72n.4
101.3 . . . . 429n.45, 430n.54
Calig. 16 441
19.1 . . . . 293n.87
Claud. 1.2 . . . . . . 405n.46, 406n.47,
                             406n.48
1.3–5 . . . . 406n.48
3.2–4.6 . . . . 173n.85
21.2 . . . . 289n.67
41.1 124
41.2 . . . . 447n.121
De Gramm. 6 . . . . 266n.16
16 . . . . 424n.21, 424n.22
21 . . . . 266n.16
Dom. 21 421
Jul. Caes. 20 . . . . 443n.110
76.3 . . . . 114n.198
78 . . . . 114n.198
80.2 . . . . 114n.198
83.2 . . . . 96n.120
Tib. 8.1 . . . . 426n.35
9 . . . .402n.29, 403n.34, 406n.49
9.1 . . . . 397n.5
10 . . . . 259n.5
10–13 . . . . 293n.85
11.4 . . . . 429n.45
14.4 . . . . 293n.86
16 . . . . 403n.31
17 . . . . 408n.61
18 . . . . 408n.64
20 . . . . 277n.7, 291n.75
59.1 . . . . 293n.85
61.3 . . . . 142n.8, 442n.105
62.3 . . . . 293n.87
Vesp. 23 . . . . 36n.52
Vita Horat. 262–63, 266, 270

Tacitus
Agric. 3.1 . . . . 451n.138
13 . . . . 411n.78
Ann. 1ff. 447n.122
1.1 . . . . xi, 81n.57, 437n.88
1.1.1 . . . . 73n.17, 74n.18
1.1.2 140
1.1.6 45
1.2 . . . . .xi, 40n.74, 419,
                            450n.130
1.2ff. 75n.23
1.2.1 . . . . 172n.76
1.3 . . . . 451n.137
1.3.4 . . . . 431n.58
1.3.6 . . . . 408n.65
1.3.7 46
1.6 47
1.7 . . . . 122n.20, 450n.31
1.9f. 419–20, 450n.130
1.9.2 . . . . 109n.177
1.9.3 . . . . 74n.18
1.9.3–5 . . . . 453n.141
1.10 . . . . .72n.9, 405n.41,
                        427n.36, 428n.45,
                            453n.141
1.11.4 . . . . 410n.73
1.37 . . . . 408n.64
1.39.1 . . . . .323, 406n.53
1.53 . . . . 428n.45
1.55.1 . . . . 408n.66
1.57–61 . . . . 408n.61
1.57.2 . . . . 406n.53
1.57.3 323
1.72 . . . . . . 34n.46, 439n.97, 441,
                            444n.113
1.72.1 . . . . 408n.66
1.72.3 . . . . 169n.67
1.72.4 . . . . 441n.102
2.3 . . . . 397n.3
2.4 . . . . 398n.9
2.7 . . . . 406n.48
2.26 . . . . . . 406n.49, 409n.67
2.30.3 . . . . 169n.67
2.41.2–4 . . . . 408n.66
2.43.2 . . . . 108n.171
2.49 . . . . 282n.29, 294n.94
2.88 . . . . 408n.61
3.5.1 . . . . 127n.13
3.18 . . . . 428n.45
3.24 . . . . 428n.45, 429n.47,
                        430n.54, 432n.63
3.28.2 . . . . 103n.156
3.30 260
3.55 . . . . 19n.71
3.56 . . . . 291n.77
3.56.1 . . . . 110n.80
3.58 . . . . 392n.30

3.75 . . . . 444n.111
4.21 . . . . .439n.97, 441
4.21.3 . . . . 169n.67
4.32.1–2 . . . . 153n.51
4.34 . . . . .436n.83, 442n.106
4.34f. 141n.6, 438n.92,
            439n.97, 442n.105
4.34ff. 143
4.34.1 . . . . 74n.19
4.34.3 . . . . .34n.44, 124, 128
4.34.4 143
4.44 . . . . 407n.54, 429n.45,
            429n.48
4.71 . . . . 430n.54
6.20–21 . . . . 294n.92
6.21 . . . . 293n.86
11.12–38 . . . . 429n.46
12.39 . . . . 406n.49
14.53.3 260
14.55.1–3 260–61
Dial. 19 . . . . 439n.97
26 . . . . 439n.97
Hist. 1.1 . . . . 140n.2, 437n.88
1.1.1 . . . . 73n.17
1.1.2–3 . . . . 150n.41
1.16.1 . . . . 166n.46
2.38 . . . . 28n.20
Terence
Adelph. 951 . . . . 264n.13
And. 719 . . . . 221n.10
Tibullus
1.7.3–12 . . . . 405n.40
2.1.31–36 . . . . 405n.40

Valerius Maximus
1.1.10 130
1.8.6 . . . . 289n.68
9.15.1 . . . . 90n.86
Varro
Ling. 3.12 . . . . 292n.80
Rust. 2.11–13 291
Velleius Paterculus
1.9.3 133
1.17 145
2.39.2 . . . . 126, 412n.88
2.47.1 . . . . 374n.35
2.57.1 62
2.61.3 . . . . 343n.37
2.69.5 . . . . 340n.22
2.73.2 . . . . 340n.22
2.78.2 . . . . 401n.22
2.79.1 266
2.86.2 . . . . 75n.30
2.88.1–3 . . . . 422n.13
2.88.2 . . . . 223n.12

2.89 . . . . .102n.149, 453n.141
2.89–90 418
2.89–93 144–45
2.89.1–4 . . . . 73n.14, 101n.142
2.89.3 . . . . 114n.197
2.89.4 . . . . 63, 433n.68
2.90.1 . . . . 402n.29
2.90.2–4 . . . . 400n.19
2.91.1 . . . . 397n.5
2.91.2 . . . . .418, 419, 426n.31,
            426n.33
2.91.3 . . . . 112n.191
2.91.3–4 . . . . .113n.193, 418
2.91.3–92.4 . . . . 427n.36
2.92.2–4 . . . . 112n.192
2.93.2 . . . . 259n.5
2.94.4 . . . . 397n.3, 397n.4
2.95.1–2 . . . . 403n.34
2.95.3 . . . . 112n.190
2.96.3 . . . . 402n.29
2.97.1 . . . . .405n.41, 405n.42
2.97.4 . . . . 406n.51
2.99.1–3 . . . . 293n.85
2.100.1 . . . . 397n.6, 398n.8
2.100.2–5 . . . . 428n.45
2.101.1 . . . . 398n.9
2.101.1–3 . . . . 398n.10
2.103.3–5 . . . . 287n.55
2.106.1–3 . . . . 407n.55
2.107.3 . . . . .407n.55, 407n.56
2.108.1–110.1 . . . . 163n.35
2.108.1 . . . . 407n.55
2.110.3–113.3 . . . . 403n.31
2.112.7 . . . . 431n.58
2.114.4 . . . . 403n.31
2.115.1–4 . . . . 403n.32
2.117.2 . . . . 407n.59
2.117.2–118.1 . . . . 407n.60
2.118.2–119.5 . . . . 408n.61
2.120.1–2 . . . . 408n.64
2.121.1 . . . . 408n.64
2.123.1 . . . . 408n.65
Vergil
Aeneid 1.6 194
1.78 . . . . 203n.39
1.95 201
1.206 . . . . 194n.25
1.261ff. 174
1.278–79 . . . . . . 395n.1, 412n.82
1.279 . . . . 162n.30
1.282 . . . . 118n.209
1.286 194
1.286ff. 174n.2
1.286–90 . . . . 412n.82
1.288 208
1.292 291
1.292–93 53

Vergil *(continued)*

1.658	340
2.149	264
2.293	194
2.431	199
3.167	174
3.182–87	281
3.714–18	412n.82
4.547	179
6.89	198
6.778–84	290–91
6.787	290
6.791–97	290
6.791–800	412n.82
6.792	231n.20
6.792–93	289
6.851	87n.80
6.853	197, 237
7.4	203n.39
7.37	176
7.96–101	177
7.98–101	174
7.104f.	177
7.206f.	174
7.240	174
7.241f.	174
7.406–66	182
7.583f.	182
7.595	175
7.596f.	182, 190
7.601–15	412n.82
8	231n.19
8.7	175
8.121	207
8.124f.	207
8.155f.	206–7
8.161–63	206
8.164	207
8.188	205
8.381	174
8.485	175
8.515	201
8.516	207
8.517	207
8.537	190
8.538	182
8.540	182
8.560–83	207
8.574	207
8.585–96	207
8.587	207
8.591	207
8.678	231n.20
8.721–22	232
8.722–23	231–32
8.725ff.	231n.19
8.725–28	230

9.44	198
9.133–39	183
9.138	183
9.224–313	208
9.257	208
9.481–97	205
9.641	208
9.642	208
9.643ff.	208
9.656	208
9.759	185
10.159–62	207
10.160	207
10.421	203
10.438	200
10.442	185, 200
10.443	201
10.446	200
10.449	200, 204
10.450	201
10.452	200
10.454	200
10.458	200
10.459f.	200
10.460	206
10.464–72	205
10.473	206
10.478	200
10.479–89	200
10.481	200
10.492	201
10.493	202
10.494	203, 204
10.494f.	201
10.497	203n.40
10.498	203n.40
10.500–505	202
10.501f.	203
10.503	204
10.503–5	203
10.507	204
10.507–9	205
10.508	185, 201–2
10.530ff.	204
10.531–34	205
10.532f.	202
10.534	202
10.791–93	205
10.827	203, 203n.39
11.5ff.	203
11.17	182–83
11.106	183
11.111	183
11.118	183, 196, 197
11.124ff.	183
11.132	183
11.178f.	199, 210

11.182–214 184
11.191 184
11.201 184
11.203 184
11.204 184
11.207 184
11.215–19 183
11.220f. 185
11.221 185
11.225ff. 184
11.258 184
11.276 184
11.283 184
11.305 184–85
11.347 185
11.361 185
11.362f. 185
11.364f. 185
11.369ff. 185
11.376 185
11.392ff. 185
11.396ff. 185
11.401–2 .... 231n.20
11.438–42 .... 185, 195–96
11.441 195
11.442 185
11.442f. 200n.34
11.445 185
11.460 186
11.486 186
11.492f. 186
11.493 186
11.506f. 186
11.515f. 186
11.522–25 186
11.530 186
11.531 186
11.585f. 187
11.593 206
11.825f. 186
11.841 187
11.841f. 190
11.872f. 186
12.2 187
12.3 187
12.6 .... 187, 190
12.9 187
12.11 .... 187, 192
12.12 187
12.13 196
12.14 196
12.15 187
12.16 .... 193, 200n.34
12.22 187
12.24 187
12.30f. 187
12.43f. 187, 196

12.45 187
12.49 .... 187, 196
12.70 187
12.74 187
12.79ff. 187, 196
12.80 196
12.82 188
12.95–97 187
12.97ff. 188
12.99f. 196
12.109 .... 188, 193
12.151 206
12.189 188
12.192 194
12.193 188
12.194f. 188
12.202 188
12.212 188
12.221 188
12.229f. 193
12.236 188
12.242f. 188
12.285f. 188
12.289–96 175
12.290 188
12.292 188
12.296 188
12.311 189
12.314 189
12.315 190
12.316f. 189
12.321 189
12.325 189
12.326 .... 189, 197
12.332 189
12.339f. 189
12.435ff. 189
12.447f. 189
12.452ff. 190
12.464 190
12.466f. 190, 200n.34
12.467 .... 200n.34
12.482f. 190
12.494 .... 191n.23
12.496 190
12.497 190
12.511f. 191
12.529–34 192
12.557 191
12.559 191
12.567 191
12.568 191
12.570f. 191
12.572f. 191–92
12.580–82 192
12.600 192
12.632f. 192

Vergil(*continued*)
12.641 192
12.646 192
12.648f. 192
12.667f. 192
12.679 192
12.694f. 192
12.697–790 193
12.700 193
12.765 196
12.791–842 193
12.797 189
12.820–40 280–81
12.836f. 194
12.839f. 194
12.850f. 194
12.857–952 194
12.863f. 194
12.867 194
12.868 194
12.881 .... 194n.26
12.889 194
12.895 194
12.913f. 195
12.914f. 195
12.916 ....194, 195
12.918 195
12.919 195
12.930 197
12.931 ....179, 195
12.932 195
12.936ff. 195
12.938–41 197
12.941 197
12.943 .... 197–98, 199, 201

12.945 ....198, 210
12.946 198
12.947 199
12.948f. 198, 199
12.949 210
12.952 ....196, 204
Ecl. 1 265
1.67 .... 411n.76
4 ....72n.4
4.43 .... 290n.71
5.65–80 .... 283n.35
8 264
Georg. 1 386
1.7 .... 282n.30
1.29 .... 411n.76
1.32–35 .... 386n.13
1.498ff. 74n.22
3 233
3.25 .... 411n.76
3.30ff. 231n.19
3.30–33 231
4 268
4.464–66 230
4.507 .... 230n.18
4.514 .... 230n.18
Vitruvius
3.2.5–6 314
3.2.6 315
4.4.1–2 314

Zonarus
9.16 133

INSCRIPTIONS

A Epigr.
1939.142 .... 366n.6
CIL
I²50 .... 405n.40
I²77 .... 405n.40
I²201 no. xxxviii 130n.20
I²240 .... 279n.18
I²285 no. 84 .... 132n.25
I²324 ....279n.18, 294n.23
I²341 .... 133n.28
III 6588 .... 384n.7
III 14147.5 (*ILS* 8995) 423n.19
VI 1.128 .... 355n.91
X 114 (*ILS* 6469) 371n.25
X 7501 .... 294n.93
XI 1829 134
XI 3083 (*ILS* 5373) 366n.6
XI 3135 .... 366n.6

XI 3200 (*ILS* 89) 366n.6
XI 3782 .... 366n.6
XII 4333 (*ILS* 112) 371n.27
XIII 1769 .... 287n.57
XIII 5381 .... 130n.20
XV 1445 .... 132n.25
Ehrenberg-Jones
100 .... 371n.27
Ephem. Epigr.
6.59 no. 64 .... 344n.42
ILLRP
173 .... 344n.41
409 .... 344n.41
1116 .... 344n.42
ILS
73 .... 344n.41
73a 344n.41
89 .... 360n.6

91 .... 384n.6, 384n.8
112 .... 371n.27
140 .... 414n.96
212 .... 405n.45
895 .... 405n.40
1792 ....9n.31
5373 .... 366n.6
6044 .... 13n.46
6469 .... 371n.25
8995 .... 423n.19

Inscr. Ital. 13.3
2 126
2–5 126
6 ....126, 133n.27, 135n.30
7 .... 126, 130n.20
8 126
9 .... 124n.2, 126
10 130–31
11 ....130, 131

12 ....127n.11, 132
14 133
15 .... 130n.23
60 ....131, 134, 136, 137
61 131
62 .... 130n.23
64 ....130, 133
78 ....131, 134, 136, 137
79 132
80 133
81 133–34

OGIS
656 .... 384n.7

PAPYRI

POxy
2820 .... 424n.23

COINS

Banti-Simonetti, *CNR*
I, p. 154 (nos. 7–8) 352n.80
I, pp. 232–34 (no. 1) 340n.24
I, pp. 232–34 (no. 4/3) 340n.24
I, pp. 232–34 (no. 5/1) 340n.24
I, pp. 232f. (no. 2/1) 340n.25
I, pp. 232f. (no. 4/2) 340n.25
I, pp. 250–53 (nos. 334–36)
    .... 340n.21
II, pp. 44f. (no. 115/1–3)
    ..... 341n.27, 341n.28
II, pp. 44f. (no. 115/4) 341n.28
II, pp. 105–6 (nos. 24–25)
    .... 344n.45
II, p. 109 (no. 33) 344n.45
II, pp. 111–12 (nos. 37–38)
    .... 344n.45
II, pp. 166 (nos. 21, 22, 22/1)
    .... 356n.95
II, p. 182 (no. 40) 352n.76
II, p. 183 (no. 44/1) 352n.76
II, pp. 183f. (nos. 44–45)
    .... 352n.75
II, p. 281 (no. 184/1) 352n.77
II, p. 281 (no. 185/4) 352n.77
II, p. 283 (nos. 187/9–10)
    .... 352n.78
III, p. 78 (no. 327) 355n.94
IV, pp. 82–84 (nos. 46–48)
    .... 342n.33
IV, pp. 162–64 (nos. 162–63)
    .... 350n.72

V, pp. 60–64 (nos. 399–401)
    .... 346n.53
V, pp. 64–69 (nos. 404–9)
    .... 348n.61
V, pp. 133–37 (nos. 508–14)
    .... 348n.66
V, pp. 142–44 (nos. 518–21)
    .... 348n.65
V, pp. 145–49 (nos. 522–25)
    .... 349n.70
V, pp. 162–66 (nos. 543–47)
    .... 348n.62
V, pp. 267f. (nos. 701–701/10)
    .... 342n.32
VII, pp. 142–45 (nos. 1369–72)
    .... 350n.73
VIII, pp. 177–80 (nos. 1–4)
    .... 354n.85
BMC Mysia
p. 139 (no. 248) 354n.90
BMCRE
I, p. 2 (no. 6) 355n.94
I, p. 5 (no. 22) 355n.94
I, p. 8 (no. 39) 352n.75
I, p. 11 (no. 58) 352n.78
I, p. 13 (nos. 69–73) 352n.80
I, pp. 18f. (nos. 95–99) 356n.95
I, p. 20 (no. 98) 356n.95
I, p. 21 (nos. 104–5) 353n.85
I, pp. 21f. (no. 106) 354n.88
I, pp. 21f. (nos. 108–9) 354n.88

BMCRE (continued)
  I, pp. 41–43 (nos. 217–19)
    .... 337n.10
  I, pp. 41–43 (nos. 224–25)
    .... 337n.10
  I, pp. 71–72 (nos. 410–23)
    .... 397n.7
  I, p. 75 (nos. 432–34) 337n.10
  I, p. 84 (nos. 489–91) 347n.55
  I, p. 91 (nos. 544–46) 350n.72
  I, p. 98 (nos. 594–95) 342n.33
  I, p. 98 (nos. 596–98) 348n.61
  I, p. 100 (no. 615) 346n.53
  I, p. 102 (nos. 628–30) 348n.66
  I, p. 103 (no. 633) 348n.62
  I, p. 104 (no. 637) 348n.65
  I, p. 104 (nos. 638–43) 349n.70
  I, p. 105 (nos. 644–46) 348n.64
  I, pp. 108–9 (nos. 671–78)
    .... 397n.4
  I, p. 110 (nos. 679–81) 397n.7
  I, p. 112 (nos. 691–93) 351n.74
  III, p. 136 (no. 688) 355n.93
BMCRR II
  p. 9 (nos. 4325–26) 342n.33
  p. 64 (no. 4524) 355n.94
  p. 65 (no. 4530) 355n.94
  pp. 78–79 (nos. 4583–87)
    .... 289n.66
  pp. 371–72 (nos. 95–103)
    .... 340n.21
  pp. 394f. (nos. 40–45) 340n.26
  pp. 399f. (nos. 63–64) 343n.38
  pp. 405f. (nos. 79–80) 342n.32
  p. 406 (nos. 81–82) 343n.38
  p. 409 (no. 95) 343n.38
  p. 463 (no. 16) 343n.39
  pp. 502f. (nos. 133–37) 345n.47
  p. 515 (no. 151) 344n.45
  p. 517 (nos. 152–53) 344n.45
  pp. 560f. (nos. 7–11) 341n.29
Brett, *Catalogue of Greek Coins*
  no. 2237 .... 283n.37
  nos. 2248–57 .... 283n.37
  nos. 2259–60 .... 283n.37
CRR
  no. 1104 .... 178n.7
De Guadán, *La moneda ibérica*
  nos. 323–26 .... 310n.9
  no. 328 .... 310n.9
  no. 975 .... 312n.16
  no. 976 .... 312n.16
  nos. 983–86 .... 312n.16
  nos. 987–89 .... 310n.9
  nos. 996–1000 .... 312n.16
  no. 997 .... 323n.63

  nos. 1001–3 .... 324n.68
  no. 1011 .... 324n.68
Giard, *Catalogue des monnaies de
  l'empire romain* I: *Auguste*
  p. 66 (nos. 13–18) 346n.53
  p. 68 (nos. 43–47) 348n.65
  p. 68 (nos. 49–51) 348n.66
  pp. 69f. (nos. 68–71) 348n.62
  p. 70 (nos. 73–77) 348n.61
  p. 71 (nos. 82–84) 342n.33
  p. 72 (nos. 92–96) 349n.70
  pp. 74–76 (no. 109) 355n.94
  pp. 74–76 (nos. 116–17)
    .... 355n.94
  pp. 74–76 (no. 136) 355n.94
  p. 79 (no. 173) 352n.76
  p. 79 (no. 174) 352n.75
  p. 81 (no. 203) 352n.77
  p. 88 (nos. 278–80) 352n.80
  p. 97 (no. 370) 356n.95
  p. 111 (nos. 522–25) 353n.85
  p. 111 (nos. 526–29) 354n.88
  p. 144 (nos. 908–10) 351n.74
  p. 160 (nos. 1023–27) 350n.73
Giard, *Le monnayage de l'atelier de Lyon*
  pp. 106f. (nos. 93–94) 350n.72
Kent, *Roman Coins*
  figs. 17–19 .... 342n.36
  fig. 22 .... 342n.36
  figs. 26–28 .... 342n.36
  fig. 102R 340n.23
Kraay, *Greek Coins*
  no. 573 .... 347n.57
Newell, *Coinage of Demetrius Poliorcetes*
  no. 115 .... 347n.57
RIC I
  no. 61 .... 385n.10
  no. 63 .... 385n.10
  no. 83 .... 385n.10
  no. 85 .... 385n.10
  no. 88 .... 385n.10
RIC[2] I
  no. 138 .... 289n.69
  nos. 140–41 .... 337n.10
  no. 144 .... 337n.10
  nos. 194–97 .... 347n.55
  no. 204 .... 347n.55
  no. 219 .... 350n.72
  no. 256 .... 346n.53
  no. 257 .... 348n.61
  no. 262 .... 342n.33
  no. 269a 348n.66
  no. 271 .... 348n.62, 349n.71
  no. 272 .... 349n.70, 349n.71
  no. 283 .... 283n.34
  no. 340 .... 289n.66

no. 352 .... 350n.72
no. 367 .... 356n.95
no. 403 .... 353n.85
no. 404 .... 354n.88
no. 423 .... 283n.33, 288n.64
no. 433 .... 337n.10
no. 476 .... 351n.74
nos. 513–20 .... 397n.4
nos. 521–26 .... 397n.7
no. 539 .... 292n.81
Robertson, *Roman Imperial Coins* I
p. 3 (no. 12) 352n.75
p. 4 (no. 15) 352n.77
p. 4 (no. 17) 352n.77
p. 5 (nos. 25–26) 352n.80
p. 9 (no. 46) 353n.85
p. 9 (no. 47) 354n.88
p. 48 (no. 248) 346n.53
p. 49 (no. 251) 348n.61
p. 50 (no. 258) 349n.70
p. 51 (no. 264) 348n.66
p. 52 (no. 267) 348n.62
p. 52 (no. 268) 348n.65
RRC
no. 11/1 .... 288n.62
no. 381/1a 343n.39
no. 450 .... 283n.32
no. 479 .... 340n.21

no. 480/24 .... 283n.32
nos. 483/1–2 .... 341n.31
no. 489/5 .... 340n.26
no. 490/1 .... 343n.38
no. 490/3 .... 343n.38
no. 491 .... 283n.32
no. 494/41 .... 288n.63
no. 497 .... 343n.38
no. 511/3a-c 341n.29
no. 518/2 .... 342n.32
nos. 525–26 .... 346n.51
no. 529/4 a-b 288n.63
Sutherland, *Roman Coins*
fig. 77 .... 343n.39
figs. 171–72 .... 345n.47
fig. 276 .... 340n.25
Sutherland-Kraay, *CCREAM*
no. 232 .... 349n.71
no. 233 .... 349n.71
nos. 284–85 .... 352n.80
nos. 1077–79 .... 350n.73
nos. 1229–34 .... 354n.90
Sutherland, *The Cistophori of Augustus*
nos. 40–44 .... 351n.74
nos. 88–90 .... 351n.74
Vives y Escudero, *La moneda hispánica*
pl. CXLVI nos. 6, 9, 10 .... 324n.68

Compositor: Graphic Composition, Inc.
Text: 10/13 Sabon
Display: Sabon